THOSE WHO CAN, TEACH

THOSE WHO CAN, TEACH

Sixth Edition

KEVIN RYAN
Boston University

JAMES M. COOPER
University of Virginia

HOUGHTON MIFFLIN COMPANY   BOSTON   TORONTO

DALLAS   GENEVA, ILLINOIS   PALO ALTO   PRINCETON, NEW JERSEY

This edition is dedicated to Marilyn and Shamim, for their substantive help, continuing support, and all around pluck.

Senior Sponsoring Editor: Loretta Wolozin
Senior Development Editor: Susan Granoff
Project Editor: Carla Tishler
Production Coordinator: Frances Sharperson
Manufacturing Coordinator: Priscilla Bailey
Marketing Manager: Diane McOscar

Cover: Photograph by Sam Haskins; U.S. Agency: Jackie Page, (212-772-0346)

Part Opening photo credits: Part I: Jim Kahnweiler; Part II: Denver Public Library Western History Department; Part III: Elizabeth Crews; Part IV: Mimi Forsyth/Monkmeyer Press Photo Service; Part V: Elizabeth Crews

Text credits:

Page 57: From John William Zehring, "How to Get Another Teaching Job and What to Do if You Can't." Reprinted with permission from the February issue of *Learning 78.* Copyright © 1978 Springhouse Corporation, 1111 Bethlehem Pike, Springhouse, PA 19477. All rights reserved.

Pages 56, 57, 58: From C. Emily Feistritzer, *Profile of Teachers in the U.S.— 1990,* (Washington, DC: National Center for Education Information, 1990) p. 11. Used by permission.

Page 125: From HANDBOOK FOR MIDDLE SCHOOL TEACHING by Paul George and Gordon Lawrence. A GoodYearBook. Copyright © 1982 by Scott, Foresman and Company. Reprinted by permission.

Text credits continue after Index

Printed in the U.S.A.

Library of Congress Catalog Card Number: 91-71962

ISBN: 0-395-47314-4

ABCDEFGHIJ-D-954321

CONTENTS

P A R T II FOUNDATIONS   69

V   TEACHERS   423

EDUCATION: A WORLD VIEW

PREFACE

O ur book, *Those Who Can, Teach,* is a book of questions. In fact, it was written in the first place to answer the question, "What are the things people beginning their formal study of education should know?" We have organized the chapters of our book around a series of questions that are likely to be of special concern to prospective teachers—and which we believe are keys to the central issues and concerns of education. We hope that these questions provide direction and focus to readers' study well beyond the time they spend with this book. For those who are contemplating careers in teaching, we believe that pursuing answers to these questions will help them clarify their career goals.

PURPOSE AND AUDIENCE

This is the Sixth Edition of *Those Who Can, Teach.* It is intended as a basic text for courses variously titled "Introduction to Education" or "Foundations of Education." We originally wrote this book because we couldn't find the kind of textbook our students and the students of many of our colleagues needed and wanted—a book that involves prospective teachers in the real issues of schooling and education and gives them a clear view of the skills and knowledge they will need to be successful professionals.

CONTENT OF THE SIXTH EDITION

Those Who Can, Teach, Sixth Edition, presents a frank and up-to-date examination of the field and foundations of education and, especially, the teaching profession. Although the text is firmly based in educational research and scholarship, it seeks to convey the important knowledge and issues in the field of education in a way that effectively bridges educational research and classroom practice.

Part I ("Self and Career") examines various motivations for teaching and provides timely information on salaries and employment opportunities. *Part II* ("Foundations") contains four chapters on topics that are "foundational" to the practice of teaching: the philosophy of education, the history of American education, the ethical and legal issues facing teachers, and the economic and political issues underlying the control and governance of schools. In *Part III*

("Schools: the Present"), the dynamics of school life are viewed from many different angles to give the prospective teacher a multilayered view of schools, from the nature of schooling to what is taught to the classroom environment. *Part IV* ("Students and Their Social Context") attempts to provide the reader with a vivid grasp of the diverse and changing nature of today's students and examines the critical social issues that affect American students and schools today. *Part V* ("Teachers") gives the reader a behind-the-scenes look at some of the common experiences of beginning teachers; examines the skills, attitudes, and knowledge essential to effective teaching; and evaluates the current status of teaching as a profession. The book concludes with an epilogue that offers a hopeful look at what our schools might become in the near future.

FEATURES OF THE REVISION

In the four years since we completed the last edition, education has been under intense national scrutiny. Seemingly, every month has brought a new report from a new blue-ribbon commission or a new plan for greater choice and quality in schools. Throughout the Sixth Edition, we discuss these *new reform proposals,* along with recent research on effective schools and recent national conferences such as the President's and Governors' Education Summit, and we try to evaluate their implications for schools and teachers today and in the near future.

Among the most significant changes in this edition is *increased coverage of multiculturalism and student diversity,* including a new chapter. Recent waves of immigration and new demographic patterns are changing quite dramatically the composition of our society and our schools. This greater multicultural diversity brings with it increased opportunities for our schools—and increased challenges. At the same time, schools are recognizing much greater diversity among all students in such areas as intelligence and various degrees of special needs and giftedness. To cover these important developments, we have added a new chapter (Chapter 10, "Who Are Today's Students?"). In addition, we focus greater attention throughout the text on the topics of multiculturalism and student diversity.

Another major change in this edition is the inclusion of an *international perspective.* Special inserts entitled "Education: A World View" appear periodically throughout the text to offer readers a comparative look at education and schools in other countries. Each insert is related to the theme of the particular chapter in which it appears (for example, "Life in Japanese Elementary Schools" in Chapter 9, "What Is Life in Schools Like?"), and each seeks to give the reader a larger window on education—a global perspective. (For a complete list of the text's "Education: A World View" inserts, see page xiii.) We have included these new inserts because we believe that prospective teachers for America's schools need to be aware of advances and developments in schools around the world, in part to gain a better understanding of what is truly unique about America's educational system and in part to be able to evaluate the many current reform suggestions based on international comparisons and critiques.

In addition, because education is such a changing and dynamic field, *every chapter has been changed and updated,* some quite substantially. For example, Chapter 2 contains new salary and job market data and a new section on the growing need for minority teachers; Chapter 3 presents new guidelines to help readers develop their own philosophy of education; Chapter 4 contains new coverage on the historical development of middle schools and expanded coverage of minority education; Chapter 5 contains new coverage of students' legal rights; Chapter 8 covers the most significant recent curriculum developments; Chapter 11 includes the latest data on social trends and issues, including timely new coverage of magnet schools, homeless students, and school dropouts; and Chapter 14 contains a new section on the Board for Professional Teaching Standards.

To enhance and assist student learning of text material, we have added a number of helpful new features to this edition: *marginal notes* throughout the text to reinforce key points; many *new graphs, tables, and summary charts* to clarify trends and data and to facilitate understanding of the book's core information; and an end-of-the-text *glossary of key terms* to reinforce learning of the book's key concepts.

Finally, the resource package accompanying this textbook has been expanded to include a set of *forty color overhead transparencies* and a *test bank data disk*, both free to instructors upon adoption of the text.

PEDAGOGICAL AND STYLISTIC FEATURES

Although there is much that is new in the Sixth Edition, there are also many features that have been retained. Chief among them is the book's *informal writing style*. We have tried to communicate the seriousness surrounding professional topics and at the same time weave in humor and create a sense of conversing directly with the reader. The text describes extensively the experiences of classroom teachers, often in their own words; this gives the text a greater sense of reality.

Many pedagogical features have been included to enhance the student's learning and the text's usefulness. *Dialogues* between the two authors appear periodically to highlight controversial points. *Special inserts* are included in each chapter to focus in depth on topics or research findings of particular interest to prospective teachers. *Education: A World View* inserts have been added to provide an international perspective to many important topics. *Biographies* of distinguished educators and teachers, such as John Dewey and Jaime Escalante, have been placed throughout the text. Further, the book is extensively illustrated with *cartoons, photographs, graphs, charts*, and *thought-provoking quotations*. In addition, *marginal notes* highlight the important points of every page, and each chapter begins with a *capsule overview* and a *list of key points* and concludes with a series of *discussion questions* and an annotated list of *suggested readings*.

ACCOMPANYING TEACHING AND LEARNING RESOURCES

The Sixth Edition of *Those Who Can, Teach*, is accompanied by an extensive package of instructor and student resources.

Kaleidoscope: Readings in Education, Sixth Edition, is a companion book of readings that can be used either in conjunction with the text or as a separate volume. This collection of more than seventy selections contains works by some of the most distinguished scholars in education along with the writings of practicing teachers. A mixture of topical and classical studies, the readings include diary entries, letters, teacher accounts, journal articles, and reports. There is also an easy-to-use chart that crossreferences topics discussed in *Those Who Can, Teach* with the readings in *Kaleidoscope.*

Accompanying the text is an *Instructor's Resource Manual with Test Items.* It contains over seven hundred multiple-choice test items and nearly one hundred short-answer and essay questions (with answer guides), developed according to sound principles and standards of test construction. New to this edition is a special section of easy-to-administer brief chapter quizzes. The instructional resource material in Part I of the manual has been thoroughly updated and revised to reflect new text content and offers for each chapter of the text a chapter overview, student objectives, supplementary lecture and discussion topics, student activities, selected references, and media suggestions.

The test items contained in the Instructor's Resource Manual are also available in computerized form in a *Test Bank Data Disk,* new to this edition, for use with IBM, Macintosh, or Apple microcomputers.

Finally, also new to this edition, a *set of forty overhead color transparencies* is available free to instructors upon adoption of the text. The transparencies include figures from the text as well as new material generated specifically for this set.

ACKNOWLEDG-
MENTS
Whenever any of us put pen to paper, we are indebted to many people. However, in the writing of this book, we are especially appreciative of the help given by the following individuals: Larry Laufman for his invaluable contribution to the research and writing of Chapter 4; William Geulcher for his aid in developing two of the cases in Chapter 1; Ernie Lundquist for sharing with us the secrets of the Cosmic Apple and for running out for coffee and sandwiches, and our colleagues and students for their many good ideas and continuing support. A number of reviewers also made key contributions to the organization and content of this edition, most notably:

Joseph A. Baust, Murray State University

Arnold Danzig, Northern Arizona University

Susan E. Dobbs, Kent State University

Jerry C. Long, University of Montana

Sue Marks, Elmira College

Susan L. Mintz, University of Virginia

Louise I. Sledz, Anne Arundel Community College

Sharon Thomas, Miami-Dade Community College

Neal K. Winkler, University of Wisconsin, Stevens Point

Jeffrey J. Zettel, National University, Sacramento

We would also like to thank Cathleen Kinsella Stutz for her work on the Instructor's Resource Manual; Sally Scott for her invaluable library research and

Preface

assistance in drafting Chapter 10 and a number of the international inserts; and Becky Burbach for working her magic on the word processor to produce clean copy of the chapters.

A very special acknowledgment is due to Marilyn Ryan for the substantial intellectual and psychological contributions she made to this book.

Writing and revising a book is a multifaceted process. Many people provide advice: some solicited and some not. We believe, however, that our best source of advice on this book and its companion *Kaleidoscope* has been the team we've worked with at Houghton Mifflin. Susan Granoff, who has worked with us now for three editions, is all we could ask for in an editor: smart, tough, detail-oriented, and most important, forgiving. She has been a real asset to this project. Loretta Wolozin, our sponsoring editor, has been with us for five editions and has been a continuing source of support, good ideas, and new directions. Carla Tishler, project editor, and newcomer with this edition, has helped us with the final stages of production, and we hope she is around for many more editions. Finally, we want to acknowledge our debt to the late William Mac-Donald. More than twenty years ago Bill convinced us that writing a different type of introduction to education would be fun and interesting. He was right and we thank him for launching *Those Who Can, Teach*.

A WORD ABOUT THE BOOK'S TITLE

The great Irish playwright, George Bernard Shaw, had a razor tongue to go along with his sharp wit. Shaw had many unpleasant things to say about schools and education, but one of his cruelest remarks was reserved for teachers: "He who can, does. He who cannot, teaches." It was an insulting comment when it was made some ninety years ago and it is an insulting comment today.

But the world has taken a number of turns since Shaw wrote the lines. There has been a worldwide explosion of educational activity. In Shaw's Great Britain, advanced education was only for the rich or very fortunate. Today most nations see the link between universal education and national prosperity quite clearly.

As a result, teaching is a much more demanding and crucial occupation than ever before. Developing a person's human potential and a nation's economic potential are serious endeavors.

Now we can truly say, "Those who can, teach!"

KEVIN RYAN
JAMES M. COOPER

THOSE WHO CAN, TEACH

I

SELF AND CAREER

Teaching is a profession in which self-knowledge plays a truly important part. To understand whether you want to get into teaching, you need to know your own desires, character, and motivation. These two chapters attempt to engage you in fitting knowledge of yourself with knowledge of the teaching career. Together they should serve as the beginning of an exploratory process that may continue for the rest of your life.

Why Teach?

CHAPTER PREVIEW

The purpose of this chapter is to help you answer a fundamental question: Why become a teacher? This chapter is first because of the underlying importance of the question. Because we believe it is important for you to discover your own motivation for choosing a career in education, we have designed this chapter to help you in the process of answering the question.

This chapter emphasizes that:

● There are a great variety of motivations why people select teaching as their occupation, and often the same individual has more than one reason for choosing teaching as a career.

● Teaching, like other occupations, often attracts people because of the rewards it offers them. The rewards of teaching can be divided into extrinsic and intrinsic rewards.

● To help you decide whether to become a teacher, you can draw on a number of sources of useful experiences, including actual encounters with teachers and children, vicarious classroom experiences, guidance from friends and acquaintances in the profession, and your own personal reflections.

● Different teachers have different motives for teaching. As you read the three cases of representative teachers we have presented, we hope you come to understand more fully your own motivations for teaching.

f you teach, it is likely that by the end of your second year of teaching you will have had both of the following experiences:

1. Someone at a party or some other social gathering will ask you what you do and how you like teaching. Soon, the person will tell you that he or she has always wanted to be a teacher and regrets having become a stockbroker/computer programmer/bookkeeper/sales rep/flight attendant/disc jockey. He or she may still give it all up and become a teacher.

2. You will get to know an experienced teacher who confides in you that he or she deeply regrets having become a teacher. In college the person felt definitely cut out for teaching, and actually enjoyed it in the beginning. But gradually he or she became fed up with the whole thing—bratty kids, pushy administrators, the same old faces in the teachers' lounge, the instant-expert parents, the boring curriculum. Now the person feels trapped in teaching and can't see any way to get out.

The purpose of this chapter, then, is to keep you from becoming "the other person" in either of these two scenes. It is to help you make a good decision about what to do with your life, particularly if you are undecided about becoming a teacher.

Centuries ago, Francis Bacon told us that "knowledge is power." Much earlier, Socrates recognized the special power of self-knowledge when he urged, "Know thyself." An understanding of one's motives in something as important as a career choice can help prevent faulty decision making.* A superficial motivation to teach can, and frequently does, lead to failure and disappointment. For instance, you may admire and want to emulate a former teacher. And you may, out of respect for this person, decide to teach without ever analyzing whether or not you have the capacity or drive. Or you may think it is admirable to like and help children. But in the process of actually working with, say, sixth-graders, you may discover that you can't stand sixth-graders or that you're not even particularly interested in children.

Clarifying your motives helps you to identify your strengths as a person and a prospective teacher as well as to cope with your shortcomings. Someone whose desire to teach grows out of a passion for art history has to know how to guard against hostility toward students who don't share that love of art. More

Understand your real motives (margin note)

---

* We ought to point out here a few idiosyncrasies in this book. For one thing, we sometimes speak to the reader in the third person, as in "One might argue . . ." or "The reader is warned. . . ." At other times, when we are especially interested in getting the reader's attention (your attention!), we use the second person, *you,* as in "You may not agree . . ." or "We would like you to. . . ."

In presenting opinions and observations, we sometimes use *we* and sometimes don't directly identify the author of the remarks. When we use *we,* it is usually when we are stating our views on a subject. The "non-we" statements are intended to be more factual, less debatable.

Finally, when referring to individual teachers, we sometimes use *he* and sometimes *she*. Our major reason for doing so is that both sexes represent a large percentage of the teaching profession's ranks. As a matter of fact, when you add up the percentage of men and the percentage of women in teaching, it makes up exactly 100 percent. Remember, you read it here first!

Real encounters with the young can help you decide if you genuinely want to teach.
(Elizabeth Crews)

than a few frustrated teachers have been heard to mutter, "Those ungrateful little whiners aren't worthy of Shakespeare" (or French infinitives, or the wonders of the protoplasmic process, or the niceties of quadratic equations). In any event, we have written this chapter—and, indeed, the entire book—in the hope that you will use it to gain a greater understanding of how you and a career in education might fit together.

EXAMINING YOUR MOTIVES FOR TEACHING

Make a list

We would like you to take a moment to write down what you feel are your motives for wanting to be a teacher. If you are unsure whether you want to be a teacher (this probably applies to the majority of readers), list your motives both for and against becoming a teacher. If you do not wish to use the space provided here, we suggest that you do write down your list in some permanent place. Although the purpose of this list is to help you think about yourself and analyze your career choice, you may wish to save it for future reference.

There is a reason why we use the plural, *motives*. Most of us have mixed motives, some altruistic and some selfish, about most of the things that are important to us. Our motives often conflict, and occasionally they are incompatible. In any event, one motive is rarely sufficient to explain a choice as complex as the career in which we plan to spend a large part of our lives.

WHY BECOME A TEACHER?

Motives for   *Motives against*

_____   _____

_____   _____

_____   _____

_____   _____

_____   _____

_____   _____

_____   _____

If you did not stop reading to think about your motives for wanting to be a teacher or to commit yourself in writing, you're probably like many other readers. What kept you from seriously engaging the question? Your answer to this question may tell you a good deal about yourself as a learner and, incidentally, about the educational system of which you are a product. Have you been trained to devour pages without really confronting the issues conveyed by the words? Have you learned to disregard your own views, even about issues quite central to you? Does it make you uneasy to probe your own motivation seriously? If your answers to these questions are "yes," you are like many other students.

However, we hope that this will be a different kind of book and a different kind of reading-questioning-thinking experience for you. We want it to be unlike so much else you read: things you pick up, spend time with, and put down again without having been moved or changed in any way. Because we are teachers, we want this book to have a very special impact on you and to help you make good decisions about whether you want to be a teacher and about what kind of teacher you want to become. For these reasons, you need to read this book in a different way. Take the book on fully. Encounter it. Participate in it. Fight with it. Laugh with it. Laugh at it. Improve it by adding yourself to it. You may be asked or nudged to do things that are not in keeping with your natural style of learning. Doing these things, however, should help you identify more clearly how you learn best and give you a sense of the various ways you can learn and know something.

We're asking you to invest something of yourself in this book. That old tired cliché "You get out of it what you put into it" applies here. So, again, if you didn't think about and write down your motives, go back and have a try at it.

There must be a nearly infinite number of answers to the question "What are my motives for wanting to become a teacher?" Here are a few examples you might check against your own list:

- I really like the idea of having an influence on 30 (or 150) kids every day.
- I would rather be a big fish in a little pond than a little fish in some big corporation out there.
- Teachers are my favorite people, and I want to stay among them.
- I can't think of anything else to do with my major.
- Teaching seems to be a fairly secure, low-risk occupation with many attractive benefits and lots of vacation time.
- I always loved history (mathematics, science, literature), and teaching seems to be a career that will allow me to work with what I love.
- The instruction I had in school was incredibly bad, and I want to correct that situation.
- I don't know what I want to do. So I'll teach for a while until I make up my mind.
- My parents would really be pleased if I were a teacher.
- Quite simply, I love children, especially the scruffy, unattractive ones everyone else ignores.

© 1981 United Feature Syndicate Inc.

- One of my students might become a famous painter, or the president of a major corporation, or who knows what. It would be nice to have a strong influence on just one significant life.
- I've never wanted to do anything else. As far back as I can remember, I've always wanted to teach.
- I really want to become a principal (or a coach, or a guidance counselor, or a college professor, or an educational researcher), and teaching seems to be the way one has to start.
- Education seems as if it's going to be the action field of the future, and I want to be part of it.
- I am happiest when I'm explaining something and helping people grow.
- Business is increasingly interested in training and educating its employees, and I want to be part of this emerging field.
- I don't like business and its grubby dog-eat-dog world, and teaching seems like a more humanistic option.
- I don't like what is happening to our society, and teaching seems to be a way to improve things.

THE REWARDS OF TEACHING

Someone's response to the question "Why teach?" can run the gamut from "What's in it for me?" to "How can I help others?" And at different times and in different moods our motivations may be quite different. The social psychologist Peter Drucker has quipped, "We know nothing about motivation. All we can do is write books about it." On the other hand, the motivational factors—those qualities that reside within teaching—are clearer and relatively constant. Researchers have identified a set of occupational rewards that can aid us in sorting out both the attractive and the unattractive qualities of a career in teaching.[1]

The two broad categories of rewards are extrinsic and intrinsic rewards. Extrinsic rewards are the public, external attractions of an occupation, such as money, prestige, and power. The intrinsic rewards of an occupation are the internal or psychic satisfactions one receives from one's work, such as a personal sense of accomplishment or an enjoyment of the work for itself. It will undoubtedly be no surprise to the reader that teaching is somewhat out of balance, receiving generally high marks on one set of rewards and low marks on the other.

Extrinsic Rewards

Teaching has rarely been cited for its abundance of extrinsic rewards. Although it offers more extrinsic rewards than occupations such as law enforcement and coal mining, when compared with other professions, teaching ranks low in extrinsic compensations.

SALARIES Salaries for teaching have improved substantially in recent years, and there are encouraging signs that more gains are ahead for teachers. Nevertheless, compared with salaries in occupational fields with similar educational requirements (for example, a college degree, specialized training), teachers'

Modest salaries

Figure 1.1 Average
Teacher Salary Compared
to Other Professions, 1989

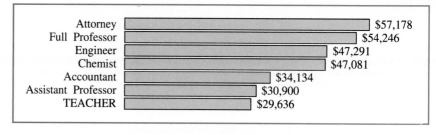

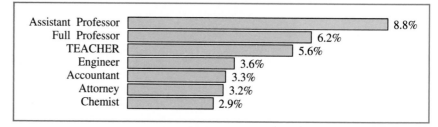

Source: F. Howard Nelson, *Survey & Analysis of Salary Trends 1990* (Washington, D.C.: The Research Department of the American Federation of Teachers), July 1990. Adapted by permission.

salaries do not fare well. Whereas some professional salaries begin low and then increase significantly, the salaries in teaching rise only modestly over the course of a teaching career. However, the importance of salary, like the whole issue of money, varies enormously from one individual to the next. And, as we shall see in the next chapter, the salaries paid teachers vary significantly from one geographical location to the next.

STATUS   *Status* refers to one's position in a group, where one stands relative to others. Whereas the status of a doctor or a beggar is rather clear, the status of a teacher is more difficult to discern. To young parents entrusting their child to the schools, the status of the teacher is quite high. To the same parents twelve or fifteen years later, on hearing that their child wants to become a teacher, the status may seem to have fallen. Although many acknowledge the vital nature of

Variable status   teaching, there are many others who treat teachers simply as social servants. One suspects, though, that the nation's current goals of reforming our educational system will increase the status of teaching.

POWER   Anyone who claims that teachers do not have power has forgotten what it was like to go to school without having done the assigned homework and to sit in fear of being called on by Mrs. Dorsey. Any individual who can make

Power over others' lives   another's day or ruin another's year has power. The power of the teacher is not a dollars-and-cents power, like that possessed by a captain of industry. It is the power of the big fish in the small pond. And although power is not usually seen as one of the rewards of teaching, it nevertheless is a quality that "resides in the

Flexibility and personal control over time

Intrinsic Rewards

The joy of helping others

Collegiality

office." Yet, as sociologist Dan Lortie has observed, "Teachers are not supposed to *enjoy* exercising power per se."[2]

WORK SCHEDULE   There is an old joke about a student in an education course being stumped on an exam by the question "What are the three best things about teaching?" Finally, in desperation, he writes "June, July, and August." Compared with other workers, teachers spend substantially fewer hours at their work sites. Ignoring what teachers do at home by way of preparing lessons and correcting papers, we can say they work six or seven hours a day for less than half the days of the year. Compared with those in the power and status occupations of corporate finance or medicine, teachers have much less demanding work schedules. Also, teachers have substantially more flexibility and personal control over how they use their time. The teachers' work schedule is one extrinsic reward that clearly is in their favor.

Extrinsic rewards tend to be tangible, like company stock options or high salaries. Intrinsic rewards are, by their very nature, in the eye of the beholder. What is one person's intrinsic reward, such as taking a busload of students on an overnight trip to the state capital, is another's living color nightmare. It is, however, the attraction to teaching's individual intrinsic rewards (or combinations of these rewards) that defines those who will be satisfied with the life of a teacher.

STUDENTS   The attraction of working with students has long been one of the strongest rewards perceived by teachers. The daily contacts, the conversations and exchanges, and even the struggles to motivate a student are a deep source of satisfaction for many teachers. Seeing children grow and develop—seeing them able to do things that they were unable to do at the beginning of the school year—is a genuinely fulfilling experience. Being important to others satisfies profound human needs, and teachers know they have this potential. Educational researchers Mihaly Csikszentmihalyi and Jane McCormick asked teenagers to tell who or what had influenced them to become the kinds of people they are, and 58 percent—almost three out of five—mentioned teachers.[3]

This reward is particularly meaningful to elementary school teachers, who spend so much time with the same group of fifteen to thirty children. Secondary school teachers, who are subject-matter specialists and see as many as 150 students in a day, identify working with students as an important attraction, but not to the same degree as their elementary counterparts.

STIMULATION AND SUPPORT FROM FELLOW TEACHERS   Even though teachers typically work in isolation from their colleagues, their contacts and interactions with colleagues are an important intrinsic reward. Teachers enjoy the shop-talk and camaraderie that is a part of school life. The way education is organized, teachers are not specifically rewarded for their individual job performance or for their expertise or that of their students. As a result, feelings of competition are not as prevalent as they are among occupational groups such as salespeople or

Contribution to society

lawyers, who must establish and hold a clientele. Teachers know they are working together and trying to make a school program a success. They know that they are part of a cooperative venture. And although there is a good deal of variation among teachers in the degree to which they value the stimulation and support of their colleagues, these aspects remain a strong attraction of the teaching life.

PERFORMANCE OF A SIGNIFICANT SOCIAL SERVICE   To many teachers, the greatest satisfaction from teaching is the sense that they are doing very important work for the good of society. This realization buoys them up and helps them make light of the less attractive aspects of teaching. Whereas other workers, government and otherwise, are aware in an abstract sense that they are contributing to the social good, teachers have flesh and blood reminders of the importance of their service directly in front of them in their classes. This particular reward is especially appealing to younger, under-thirty teachers, elementary teachers, and minority teachers. In the 1980s some policy analysts, such as Gary Sykes, suggested that, to many people entering the field, the service image of teaching was receding.[4] Activities in recent decades, such as collective bargaining and teacher strikes, might have taken some of the glow out of teaching as a service occupation. We, however, see a countertrend. As the 1990s began, a new spirit of social altruism became more apparent. A young Princeton graduate came up with the idea of recruiting liberal arts graduates to teach in some of

JAIME ESCALANTE (1930–   )

It is early in the fall term at Garfield High School in East Los Angeles, and the students in this calculus course are still nervous about being in the presence of a man who recently had a book written about him entitled *Escalante: The Best Teacher in America*. It is the morning after the second game of the World Series, and the teacher, known as "el professor," shouts out his first question: "Who won the game?" After a pause, the students begin enthusiastically to chant, "Dodgers! Dodgers!" Having captured their attention, Jaime Escalante smoothly segues to the math lesson. Slapping a baseball into his mitt, he probes, "As X approaches A, F of X is the trajectory. Could be a curve ball." And they are off—teacher and fifty-nine students—on a journey into the mysteries of calculus.

A teacher since he was in his late teens, Escalante, now in his sixties, has been teaching for almost all of his adult life. To the question "Why teach?" his response would bring together two of the most common reasons for

becoming a teacher: love of children and love of subject. When asked how a public high school teacher became the subject of an Academy Award–nominated motion picture, he replied,

I don't really know. I just helped my students reach the highest possible degree of personal development. I have knowledge, and I have a deep love for my students. When I came to this school in 1973–74, the students were not interested in education. The parents were not interested in education.

Although a modern American hero, Jaime Escalante was born in La Paz, Bolivia, the son of an elementary school teacher. Because of the social unrest in Bolivia in the late 1940s, he was able to earn an emergency teacher's certificate and began his career before he was twenty. While he was a high school math and physics teacher, his students began to accumulate prizes, and soon he gained national recognition. Still in his twenties, he organized the first Bolivian national symposium of physics and math

America's most problem-ridden schools, and she founded Teach for America. She has enlisted thousands of students. In our own classes, we see more and more students not only seriously considering teaching as a career, but also selecting teaching specifically because they see it as a way to pay back the country and to fulfill other service-related goals.

THE WORK OF TEACHING   The process of teaching is for many teachers a meaningful reward in itself. Whether it is lecturing, working with small groups, or designing instructional units, the actual work is gratifying. Like a pianist moving through a favorite sonata or a lawyer cross-examining a witness, teachers often draw their deepest satisfactions in and from the act of applying their craft. Of course, teachers vary in which activities they find rewarding. Some draw their rewards from the nurturing, cooperative environment they have been able to establish, some from unraveling complicated problems for students, and some from seeing students work and achieve independently. For these teachers, all else pales before their fulfillment in simply doing the work of the teacher.

Teaching as pleasurable activity

SOURCES OF USEFUL EXPERIENCE   One of the major educational insights to be applied to schooling in recent years concerns individual differences. There is a new appreciation for the unique learning styles and, often, the unique learning problems people have. As a result, the "one-true-way" approach to education is gradually slipping by the boards. The

teachers. In 1963, amid growing social strife in Bolivia, Escalante, now married and with two sons, decided to take his wife and young family to the United States.

The next ten years were years of adjustment and struggle for Escalante, years when he learned English, went back to college, and worked as a busboy and a cook. When he finally graduated, he took a job in the fast-growing computer industry and studied for the California Teaching Certificate in his free time. When the news came that he had passed the test and would be assigned to a run-down, troubled high school in the *barrio*, Jaime turned his back on a substantially larger paycheck and headed for Garfield High School.

Like many of the students in inner-city schools, Garfield's students were caught in a downward cycle of low expectations, low efforts, and low performance. When the school's accreditation was threatened, Escalante made his move. Supported by reform-minded administrators, he began setting high standards and making serious demands on students. They were not allowed into his class unless they proved that they had done their homework.

He skillfully used the time-honored carrot-and-stick approach. The carrot was college and the world of opportunities higher education opened up for them. The stick was his constant challenging of them: "You *burros* have math in your blood! Our Mayan ancestors were the first to develop the concept of zero!"

Jaime Escalante is not just an inspired teacher. And he is more than the man who has helped hundreds of Mexican-American children discover self-discipline and learning and the enormous self-pride that comes with those accomplishments. Escalante is a tide turner. He has set an idea in motion, the idea that the poor and immigrant children in our country are capable of great intellectual feats. He has shown how remedial, slowed-down education can be replaced by demanding, accelerated education. His key is making them believe, helping them realize, that they can be Somebody. "My skills are really to motivate these kids, to make them learn, to give them *ganas*—the desire to do something—to make them believe they can learn."

same insight about individual differences applies to making an intelligent career choice. Because people learn in such diverse ways and differ so much in what they already know and need to learn, we can give only sketchy guidelines here. We recognize four categories of experience that are potentially fruitful in the quest for an answer to "Should I teach?"

Real Encounters

Romantic images vs. real children

Ways for student teachers to get feet wet

People who plan to be teachers should test their commitment to teaching by putting themselves in actual school situations. As much as possible, students of teaching should observe in schools and participate in various activities that put them in contact with children and adolescents. Many teaching candidates avoid real contact with the young until they begin student teaching, only to find that young people are considerably different from the romantic images they had been manufacturing. "Those nasty little fifth-graders are so disgustingly . . . human!" one shocked student teacher said. Frequently, too, teaching candidates limit their encounters to normal elementary and secondary school students. They do not consider teaching children with mental or physical disabilities or even becoming a specialist such as a reading teacher. They have exposed themselves to only one segment of the opportunities and challenges of teaching.

Increasingly, school districts are using students as teacher aides and assistant teachers, both during the regular school year and in summer school. And a large number of teacher education programs have cooperative arrangements with schools whereby college students are given opportunities to play a variety of roles within the school, usually as part of their coursework in education. Schools, however, do not exhaust the opportunities. There is much to be said for nonschool contact with children, such as camp counseling, playground work, after-school recreation projects, work in orphanages and settlement houses, and youth-related church work. Other possibilities are coaching a team or sponsoring a club. The opportunities are many. The important thing, however, is to get your feet wet—to get the feel of working with children in a helping relationship.

LAST DAY

The last bell rang.
The building filled with shouts and cheers
And emptied soon. Yet one still sat.
He looked at me, and I could see in that thin face
An awful realization no other child had known:
The year was gone.
I knew, but I was older. I could bear
The lost and sickish feeling of farewell
From simple familiarity with it.
I went back to where he sat;
I said there would be other years.

I said that I would write him letters in the summer.
Somehow he knew, this child who had never had a letter in his life,
That warm words are always somehow cold on paper,
And never take the place of being close.
Slowly he gathered up his books.
Walking toward the door, he looked around the room.
What did he see? What had this been to him?
I knew, and yet I could not know.
It was the end
Of a year.

Reese Danley Kilgo, Phi Delta Kappan 51, no. 475 (May 1970). Reprinted by permission of the author and publisher.

Vicarious Experiences

The teacher in fiction

Not all learning has to take place in the school of hard knocks. In fact, civilization itself requires that we be able to capitalize on the experience of others. Artists and other talented people can make the experience of others accessible to us for enjoyment, edification, or both. There are great fictional classics about teachers and schools, such as *Goodbye, Mr. Chips* by James Hilton, *To Serve Them All My Days* by R. F. Delderfield, and *The Corn Is Green* by Emlyn Williams. And there are contemporary novels such as Bel Kaufman's *Up the Down Staircase* and Evan Hunter's *Blackboard Jungle*. (All five of these books have been made into films.) Recently there have been some fine nonfiction accounts of teaching. Among the best are Tracy Kidder's *Among Schoolchildren,* Garret Keizer's *No Place But Here,* and Samuel G. Freedman's *Small Victories* (all of which are cited in the For Further Reading section at the end of this chapter).

Films, such as *Dead Poets Society, Stand and Deliver, Pump Up the Volume,* and *The Breakfast Club,* and some television shows are other sources of vicarious experiences that help us relive our own experiences in school and also help us see school in a different light. These experiences can be a valuable source of learning and testing for prospective teachers, particularly if they approach the experiences somewhat more critically than does the ordinary television or movie viewer. We need to remember that books, films, and television portray school life as a much more intense and heightened set of human encounters than those which the normal teacher faces. Then, too, the flux and flow of life in a real school are not as easily seen. The drama of teaching is quiet, long term, and terribly real.

Guidance

Advice from others

Another aid is the advice and counsel of those who know you. Besides parents and friends (who sometimes are too close to you to be objective), you can consult former teachers, career placement counselors, and your college professors. The professors of education you are, and will be, working with can be particularly helpful, because they normally have a great deal of familiarity with the realities of teaching. You should exercise some caution here, however. First of all, choose people who know you well, rather than those who have just seen you at your better moments. Second, do not expect a comprehensive computer printout of hard data with a firm decision at the end. If you get a few glimpses of insight from the person whose advice you are seeking, be satisfied. Third, be cautious, since many people are compulsive advice givers. Frequently people generalize on the basis of too little knowledge, and they are often just plain wrong. Receive advice openly, but follow it cautiously.*

Reflection

Taking time out to think

The most important aspect of the real school encounters, guidance, and vicarious experiences you collect is that they provide you with data for reflection. By *reflection* we simply mean the process of trying to understand fully your experiences and their implications for you. People are often so busy experiencing things, or getting ready to experience them, that they fail to reflect on what they

---

* Although our good friend Ernie Lundquist has tried to claim credit for this thought, we believe that Shakespeare's Polonius beat him to it.

have done in a manner that will ensure that they get the most from the experience.

We cannot stress enough this point about reflection. It goes to the very heart of why we have written this book. Both of us are convinced that many people make very sloppy decisions about becoming teachers. Often they have not asked fundamental questions about themselves and about schools. This is precisely why we have organized this book around a series of questions such as "Why teach?" and "What is a school?" It is also why, as you have seen, we periodically ask you to stop and reflect on a particular question. Occasionally, we ask you to commit yourself in writing, since doing so can help you clarify exactly what you think. We have also included case studies, anecdotal material, and actual accounts by teachers. We hope that you will regard this material as vicarious experiences that will stimulate your own reflection. In effect, we are much less interested in telling you something than in presenting you with some tough questions. Although questions such as "What makes a teacher effective?" may sound simple, their answers—if there are any answers—are frequently quite complex. We hope that you will use these questions not only to guide your career

EDUCATION: A WORLD VIEW

WHY TEACH? A TURKISH EDUCATOR'S VIEW

Sezai Kaya

I have been a teacher educator and have been studying teacher education in the United States for a number of years. Regarding the motives to teach, I can see several differences between my home country and the U.S.

Status: The place of the teacher in Turkish society has traditionally been very important. Teaching is considered a "holy profession" in the public eye. The teacher has always been well-respected, and this tradition continues generation after generation. On the first day of the school year, parents bring their children to school and present them to the teachers because they will be entrusting their upbringing and education to these teachers. Socially and legally, the teachers exercise a great deal authority over the children's life. What is expected of a teacher is very ambitious and explicitly formulated. The teacher is required to be much more than a subject specialist and a qualified pedagogue. He or she must also be aware of the

forces (i.e., social, economic, and political) shaping the development of the country and must be aware of how education can contribute to coping with these forces.

Material Incentives: The basic salary of Turkish teachers is one of the highest among the public servants. Salaries are based on the years of service, education, and geographical region. Contrary to the situation in the U.S., the teachers in rural areas and less developed regions are paid considerably more. In addition to a fairly good salary, teachers can obtain cheaper goods and services at the government supported "Teacher's Markets"; they are provided with reasonably inexpensive vacations by the "Teacher's Holiday Villages"; and they can join "Teacher Housing Cooperatives." Teachers get a fifty percent discount at the theatre, cinema, ballet, and for public transportation. They also receive a fifty percent discount at the Ministry of Education's publication house. Teachers receive free health care at "Teacher's Health Care Centers" and free treatment at "Teacher's Hospitals." At retirement, they are also eligible to stay at Teacher's Retirement Centers," and they can use the facilities of the "Teacher's

choice, but also to help you reflect on the whole phenomenon of teaching and learning.

CASE STUDIES IN MOTIVATION TO TEACH

The rest of this chapter is composed of three case studies that illustrate some common motives for going into teaching. Each case study is followed by a set of questions and a comment. The cases are intended as examples of how particular abstract motives take shape in teachers' lives. We offer these case studies to you as vicarious experiences to use in examining your own motivations. You may also want to discuss the cases and the accompanying questions with other people. The shared experience of reading the cases and responding to the questions should help you probe and understand your own motivations. And, finally, the cases and accompanying comments raise important issues about the nature of teaching.

The three motives we have chosen are:

1. the desire to teach a particular subject
2. the desire to work out one's own problems
3. the desire to aid in the renewal of society

House," which is readily available in most towns and cities.

Recruitment: Prospective teachers enter the profession through two main avenues: an early recruitment program and the general University Entrance Examination. Turkey has a unique type of high school called a "Teacher's Lycee" which recruits candidates after middle school through a highly competitive examination. The recruits are expected to complete a full-time academic and professional preparation program in a boarding school for three years. Those students who are determined to be fit for teaching are given priority in the University Entrance Examination in order to be admitted to a Faculty of Education of a university. This leads to a Bachelor's degree after following a four-year program. The second source for recruiting teachers is the graduates of other high schools. One of the most exciting improvements in Turkish education is the initiation of scholarships and government subsidized housing for those students who choose teaching as a first choice in the UEE and enter into a Faculty of Education. This program seems to attract the best and the brightest candidates, particularly from low-income social groups.

Work Schedule: An advantageous work schedule attracts many candidates, particularly female students. Due to Turkey's high birth rate and an inadequate supply of teachers, most of the schools operate double or triple shifts. Consequently, teachers have either their mornings or afternoons free. Paid, two-month summer vacation is another feature that attracts many young people to teaching.

Job Security: Like other public employees, a teacher receives tenure at the *end of the first year of teaching.*

My personal experience is very similar to many teachers in Turkey. I entered the profession at the age of 15 by going into a boarding Teacher's Lycee where my moral, social, political, and professional convictions began to take shape. Inspired by my elementary school teacher and encouraged by my teachers at middle school, I consciously selected teaching as a career. Of course, all of the factors mentioned above played an important role in making that decision.

Source: Sezai Kaya, Ministry of National Education, Ankara, Turkey. Reprinted by permission.

Gregory was beginning to think that he should never have gone to his son Justin's open-house night. That's when it had all started. That's when he had decided to change careers and become a teacher. Now, as he sat across the desk from his new supervisor, Suzanne, for his first post-observation conference, he was filled with doubts. It wasn't simply that while he was plowing through his lesson on the greenhouse effect Suzanne was so busy taking notes. No, it was something deeper. There was something more fundamentally wrong.

Gregory was a forty-two-year-old, former chemical engineer with nineteen years of experience in industry. From the time he was eleven, about the age of his oldest students, he had loved science. As a college student, he had been proud and happy with his choice of chemical engineering as a major. He had been aggressively recruited in his senior year by a large firm, had accepted an excellent salary, and had been put on scientifically interesting projects. Within two years, he had met and married Barbara. Since Barbara also worked in his division, she was understanding when there was a big push on at the lab and he went weeks with long hours and no days off trying to complete a project. And, of course, since he was doing what he wanted to do, Gregory didn't mind either. Then three things happened. The first was Justin. The second was Melissa. And the third was a small, gnawing question that gradually got bigger and bigger: "Is this what I really want to do for the rest of my life?"

Gregory thought the uneasiness caused by the question was due to lack of exercise or "early-middle-age anxiety." He found himself increasingly frustrated by the fact that he was always doing the science that someone else was paying for and wasn't able to follow the questions that interested him. "Chasing the buck" was a lab joke, but it was more than that. He found himself frequently daydreaming about becoming a high school chemistry teacher, but kept putting it out of his mind. Then, at Justin's middle school one night, he saw and heard a fifty-five-year-old man bubbling over with enthusiasm over what he was teaching his sixth-graders. From that night on, Gregory's question became a roar. A few days later he made an appointment to talk to the teacher, and before he knew it, he was reading up on teaching and taking education courses at night. After a few courses, he was sure he wanted to switch careers. Even though it meant sacrifices for Barbara and the children, they were all for it. His co-workers at the lab and his parents were stunned.

A mid-life career switch

That was over a year ago. Since then, Gregory has taken more education courses, has done his student teaching in an excellent high school (teaching both chemistry and physics), and has gotten a job. Gregory's only disappointment has been that he had dreamed and planned on being a high school teacher, but the only available job (other than ones that would force him to move the family) was at the elementary level, as a fifth-grade teacher. The school superintendent realized that Gregory would be a real asset to his school district, but she did not have an opening in the high school until the next year, when the physics teacher was scheduled to retire. So she presented Gregory with a proposition: take some methods courses over the summer (at district expense), become a fifth-grade teacher for a year, help establish a new elementary science curriculum, and be the coordinator of the annual science fair. At

What drives many teachers is a desire to stay involved with a subject they love.
(Kathy Sloane/Photo Researchers, Inc.)

first, Gregory was quite wary about this possibility. He thought it would mean throwing away a good deal of his specialized knowledge and risking failure as an elementary school teacher, even though it would be for only a year. But after talking it over with Barbara and getting great support from his daughter, Melissa (herself a fifth grader), he agreed.

And then a funny thing happened. During the summer, as he took the methods courses and prepared himself for his fifth-graders, and especially as he tested ideas and plans with Melissa, he became more and more enthused about teaching children who he believed were "just becoming interested in the outer world." Once he started working with his fifth-grade students, he was hooked. They were so alive, so responsive, and so hungry to know about the world. What a challenge!

Now, though, in November, Gregory has misgivings. There is a flatness in his class that worries him. Much of the September curiosity has turned into an early case of the mid-winter blahs. But more than being just doubtful, now he is curious about what his supervisor thinks. "So, Suzanne. What did you find out? How did I do? You were writing up such a storm, I thought you would need another notebook!"

"Oh, I hope you didn't find that distracting. I probably should have warned you that I would be scribbling away."

"No, that's fine. I'm just curious to know how I did. Shoot!"

"Shoot? Okay, Greg, but I would much rather hear what you think. How did you think it went?"

"Well, I think pretty much as usual. Pretty much the way it has been going. They were a little quieter, perhaps because you were in there, but, in general, that was an average class."

"I did notice it being quiet, Greg. How do you feel about that?"

"As a matter of fact, I'm confused by it. Since September the decibel counter has been steadily falling in all my classes, but particularly when we are doing science. I couldn't get them to shut up in September. They ate up everything I presented, especially science. They just seem to have lost interest."

"From what I just saw, and from what I have observed passing by your door these weeks, I'd agree. Interest looks low."

"Suzanne, I can't understand this. I have really worked to find topics that will interest them. I built a whole unit on pollution last month with writing assignments and mathematics worked in. They said they were interested in heredity, so next month we're going to do family histories with interviews and collections of family facts and artifacts. They were all excited about this in September, but now I'm worried. The same with this current unit on the greenhouse effect. It was something they were wild about in September. What is the matter? Honestly, Suzanne, it feels like this ship is sinking!"

"Come on, Greg. Don't panic. I had a feeling that this would happen."

"What do you mean, 'You had a feeling'?"

"Well, when you came to interview last June, we were thrilled at the possibility of getting someone so knowledgeable and so experienced, and, particularly, someone who clearly loves science so much. But those same qualities made us hesitant, too."

"I'm not getting you, Suzanne. I know we were all concerned that I didn't have traditional preparation for elementary teaching. You're not saying I know too much and I like science too much, are you?"

"Yes and no. No, you don't know too much. And your love of science is a terrific asset. But, at the same time, they are keeping you from being the potentially fine teacher you can become. Greg, let me level with you. You are drowning these kids with information, even the interesting, relevant material you have been bringing in. And not just in science. It seems to me that you're doing all the work. What we are afraid of has happened. You were a great success in student teaching. I would kill for the recommendations you received!

But what works with high school juniors and seniors doesn't work with these elementary school wigglers."

"I'm not giving them high school material, really. This work is within their range. I don't mean to sound defensive, but, honestly, Suzanne, I feel stumped. I'm continually searching for interesting material."

"Greg, think 'romance.'"

"Romance? I thought you told me to do health and human sexuality in the spring!"

"No. No. Romance. Like in 'the romance of science' and 'the romance of writing.' Do you remember telling us during your interview how you fell in love—your words, Greg—fell in love with science in the fifth grade when you had to do a project for the science fair and you got all excited by the idea of a perpetual motion machine, which culminated in 'Gregory's Almost Perpetual Motion Machine,' a third-place award, and a lifelong love affair—your words, again—with science? Well, what I think you ought to do is a little time traveling and think about what caused *your* romance with science? Was it a fascinating question? An unsolved problem? The excitement of maybe solving a problem the adults couldn't? Or was it a teacher pumping facts and theories into you?"

"Oh-oh. I think the dawn is breaking. I've been so busy trying to teach them some basic information. . . ."

"I know. You have been so busy telling them about what you love that you forgot romance. You forgot that romance is a two-way street. It's a classic mistake of rookie teachers, even ancient ones like you. Sometimes you can get away with it in high schools, but not with the wigglers. Not with elementary schools."

"So what do I do now?"

"Well, let me put aside these notes and let's see if you and I can put a little romance into the rest of the week's lessons."

"A little pedagogical seduction! Suzanne, I think this is what I have been waiting for!"

Questions
1. How would you characterize Gregory's motivation to teach?
2. What sorts of things do you think his students were thinking and feeling about his classes?
3. Gregory is clearly an outstanding resource to the school. What, however, are his liabilities?
4. What clues should Gregory have been picking up?
5. What are some of the things Gregory might do to stimulate romance for science in his students?

Comment Love of a particular subject matter or content is an important and commendable motive for teaching. A major purpose of school is to pass on to the young the best of society's knowledge. Another important purpose is to develop in young people basic skills and, especially, a love for learning. A teacher who has a passion to convey subject matter is often quite effective at both of these goals.

We probably all have had certain teachers who seemed genuinely excited about their particular subject or discipline. Although such teachers often drive students very hard, they are the ones who usually make the greatest impact.

A balanced approach to subject matter

But carrying love for a particular subject to an extreme can cause trouble. Gregory's motive is not uncommon. Nor is the problem he worked himself into. Students have many needs. Students not only need to build a foundation in several different skills and content areas, but also need to develop an intrinsic interest in learning. This love for learning can be put on hold when the lover (the teacher) is too overpowering or too insistent. The great teacher, like the great lover, knows how to draw out another's interest and help students "fall in love."

Necessity of covering all subjects responsibly

The other side of a strong desire to teach a certain content or subject matter often is the motive of avoidance. Many of us feel uncomfortable with some of the elements or certain aspects of the curriculum that we are required to teach. For instance, it is not uncommon for some elementary school teachers to have a limited background in mathematics and, consequently, to be uncomfortable with presenting the subject. The result is that when time and energy are assigned to the various subjects, mathematics ends up being shortchanged. And the children are actually the ones who are most shortchanged. This same avoidance can be seen in many other subject areas. The physical education teacher who loves basketball finds it easy to extend the program for that sport at the expense of, say, gymnastics. The English teacher who loves interpreting literature finds it easy to avoid slugging it out with grammar, punctuation, and other essential writing skills. Although our tendency to avoid what we do not know or like is understandable, it is also irresponsible. Further, it is also unfair both to the students and to subsequent teachers, who will expect students to have a command over the avoided or neglected content.

Teachers who are strongly motivated by the desire to teach a particular subject matter need to be somewhat cross-eyed. Keeping one eye on what they want to teach, they need to keep the other eye on the students, on their day-to-day progress and needs. No one ever said that it is easy to be a good teacher.

Case Number Two: The Desire to Work Out One's Own Problems

Jean was a first-year teacher in a high school in Austin, Texas. As a result of desegregation efforts, her school was evenly balanced between Anglos and Hispanics. Jean was very pleased to be assigned to a school with such a heavy concentration of Mexican-American students because she was interested in social justice and in using the political process to obtain one's rights. Jean had been raised in a comfortable suburb adjacent to another city in the Southwest, so she thought she had some grasp of the issues faced by Mexican-American students. Also, her parents were politically involved and were usually on the side of the underdog.

Organizing students

Jean, like many new teachers, believed she had adequate mastery of the subject matter, but she worried about whether she would get along with the students. She was particularly concerned about her ability to relate to Hispanic students. Consequently, in the early weeks of school, she worked very hard to establish a rapport with the Mexican-American students in her classes. Some of them took Jean into their confidence, and they had long talks in her classroom after school. During one of these sessions, Miguel complained that the

It is noble to teach
oneself; it is still nobler
to teach others—and
less trouble.
— MARK TWAIN —

school by and large ignored the Hispanic students and that the Hispanic students were politically naive and unorganized. Jean suggested that they establish a student branch of La Raza, a political action group advancing the cause of Mexican-Americans.

The students became quite interested in this organization, and it began to take hold in the school. Although Jean received a good deal of satisfaction from this, she had a sense that all was not well. She had a regular monthly conference scheduled with the head of the English department, whom she both trusted and admired. At the beginning of the conference, the supervisor asked Jean what particular aspects of her teaching pleased her. Jean replied that she had good relationships with her Hispanic students. The supervisor asked how she had accomplished this, and Jean answered that she had spent a great deal of time talking with them as a group and that, under her sponsorship, the students had formed a group, *Estudianta por La Raza*. The supervisor, a woman with a great deal of experience in urban schools serving poor children, was not so pleased with Jean's apparent success as Jean was.

"Jean," she said, facing her, "what do you really want to do here? Is it your goal to organize the Hispanic students into a power coalition? Is that what you feel you're getting paid to do?"

"Well," Jean replied, "these kids just have to get organized. The only answer to the social oppression they've been living under is to organize and begin making their weight felt as a group."

"That may or may not be true," said the supervisor, "but that's not the point at issue. You have a mixed class of children, and you're here to help them acquire some understanding of each other, along with skills, knowledge, and outlooks that will help them survive and excel in society. But you wanted the Hispanic students to like you, so you identified with their feelings of separateness and their prejudices about Anglos. And, if you will, you have created two factions in your class and you treat each differently."

"*I* didn't do that!" Jean contested hotly. "Society did."

"No, Jean, you did," said the supervisor. "Instead of encouraging your students to confront and understand their prejudices and creating an atmosphere that would allow them to emerge as individuals capable of solving their own human problems, you encouraged them to value their prejudices and to think that they were right to maintain those prejudices. As an Anglo teacher teaching Hispanics and Anglos, you have a tremendous opportunity to help Hispanics understand the Anglo. You say you understand these kids, and that's important; but it's equally important that they understand you and other people like you. Is it your goal for Hispanic students to come to you whenever they have a problem with the Anglos and have you solve it for them? What happens when you are no longer around and those kids run into that problem? Do you think they're going to love and respect you for not teaching them how to work with Anglos? Not on your life. They're going to hate you for using them and failing to teach them what they need to know to get along."

"I honestly feel that I owe them something," Jean said. "And I just can't work it out that easily. What are you telling me to do? To ignore their problems and go back to 'business as usual' with the workbooks and all that?"

"You do owe them something, but 'them' means all those kids. You've got a rare opportunity here to help both the Hispanic kids and the Anglo kids learn how to master themselves and how to handle their prejudices so that they can settle the problems of living together without depending on you and the other Anglo liberals for help. You can get these kids to confront their fears, bring them out in the open, and deal honestly and rationally with them in class. You can deal with the issue through the subject matter, through composition, through general class discussion. These kids may discover that they are much more alike than different, regardless of their cultural backgrounds."

"I really don't think it will work," said Jean. "The Hispanic kids are angry, and they've heard too much discussion and too much bull to take more of it from an Anglo teacher."

"Look," the supervisor replied, "I taught psychology in a junior college thirty years ago while I was getting my master's degree. I had white kids from the ethnic neighborhoods of Chicago who weren't exactly thrilled at having an African-American teacher. But I knew that this class was okay when, in the middle of the unit on perception and prejudice, one of those white students said that he had thrown a stone at Martin Luther King, Jr., on his march into Cicero, and that he was amazed at his own ignorance in doing such a thing. Then an African-American student got up and said that he had actually attacked white people on the street for no good reason, and he, too, was amazed at his own prejudice. Here were some kids who were learning to see people as people. It can be done if the teacher has a clear sense of how the subject matter can help people understand themselves.

"When a student in the class began talking about 'whitey' or 'niggers,' as they did in the early meetings, we'd ask the class to stop and consider their feelings in view of the reading we'd done on fears and aggression. In that way each member of the class was forced to come face to face with his or her own doubts and fears. I'm a teacher, Jean, and I tried to use my subject matter and my objectivity to help students see themselves as the people they are. The more they understood themselves, the more they understood others in the class and saw them as people like themselves. That's why they could admit their failings in front of the whole class. I really feel, Jean, that teaching English gives you a good opportunity to do some of the same things. There seems to be one lesson that you have yet to learn about teaching, and that is. . ."

"Yes?"

"That teaching is a relationship to be ended, not to be continued."

"Would you explain what you mean by that?" Jean asked.

"Sure," said the supervisor. "Mature teachers prepare students for independence, not dependence. They try to get them to the point where they are able to fend for themselves. And I guess that's what I'm questioning about your relationship with your students. Are you really doing that for them?"

"I don't know," said Jean, softly. "I honestly don't know. I need to think about all this."

Questions   **1.** How would you characterize the personal problems Jean seems to be working out in her teaching?

2. Have you had experience with teachers who seemed to be working out personal problems in their classes? What kinds of problems? What was the effect on the class?

3. Have you ever known personal problems to be used effectively in a classroom? If not, can you imagine circumstances in which they might be used effectively?

4. How do you evaluate the advice Jean received from her supervisor?

5. What are some of the implications of the supervisor's statement that "mature teachers prepare students for independence, not dependence"? What are some ways that elementary and secondary school teachers can stimulate independence?

6. Did the supervisor think that organizing a student group of Hispanic students would have a bad effect on the school?

7. Was the supervisor simply telling Jean to teach the subject matter in which she had been trained and not to get involved in the lives of her students?

Comment   Insecurity is endemic in beginning teachers. They want assurance. As a result, some teachers seek to be popular with their students. There is a difference, however, between popularity and a genuine helping relationship. Popularity may

DIALOGUE*

Jim: I'm having a little trouble with this list.

Kevin: What's the matter? Can't you find your motive on it?

Jim: Seriously, it could be confusing to the reader. For instance, the desire to work out one's own problems. This seems much more likely to be an unconscious motive than the others.

Kevin: I agree, but some other motives can be hidden, too, like the desire for respect and prestige. On the other hand, some people go into teaching to relieve the anxiety and discomfort they feel about particular social wrongs. They are consciously seeking to work out something that is a problem to them.

Jim: All right, but I'm troubled about another thing. The way we've separated out these motives and the way we've written the cases make it appear that individuals are driven by a single, clearly visible motive. Life just isn't that way. We are driven by many motives, some of which may contradict each other.

Kevin: You're right. The way we've done it makes a very complex phenomenon seem too simple. But if we tried to portray the full range of human motivations in each case, we'd have two novels instead of three brief case

studies. But you bring up a good point, and I hope the reader is forewarned.

Jim: One final point. These pages read like THE list. We don't mean to give that impression.

Kevin: Right, we've left out all sorts of motives. For instance, some people go into teaching because they want to coach a state championship athletic team; some people use teaching as a second job so they can support themselves in what they really want to do, such as writing; and some people espouse a particular religious doctrine or economic system and are seeking converts. No, this list merely scratches the surface. We're just trying to get students to begin thinking (hard) about why they want to teach.

---

* Several times during the writing of this book, the authors had disagreements, misunderstandings, or minor conflicts in points of view. We had to talk these differences through and ended by illuminating each other and coming to some agreement. We want to share these discussions or dialogues with you not only to provide extra information on the topics in question but, more importantly, to show you that the questions that are at the center of our book cannot always be answered in black-and-white terms. We also hope you'll see that even if something can be stated in black and white, a good deal of gray may still be hidden beneath the surface.

Although the percentage of male elementary school teachers is low, most are very strongly motivated.

(Susan Lapides)

make a real helping relationship impossible. In a sense, this situation is what Jean got into with her Hispanic students. She achieved quick popularity by organizing their political aspirations, and that was why, as her supervisor pointed out, she thought she understood their needs. But she had not really given the students what they needed; she had given them only what she thought they needed. Had Jean understood better what she herself needed, as well as what she wanted, then her relationship with the students would have been more mature. Jean's experience illustrates the importance of examining one's own motives before attempting to motivate others. Perhaps if Jean had examined her own motives a bit more deeply, she would have realized that she had to overcome fear of rejection by her Hispanic students before she could teach effectively. The very fact that Jean spent much of her time worrying about relating to Hispanic students, rather than relating to Carlos, Juanita, Miguel, and Lucita as individuals, tells us that she had not grasped the importance of teaching at a personal level; she had, in truth, not yet acknowledged the individuality of her students.

One characteristic of maturity is the ability to work out one's own problems objectively. If Jean could have realized that her own fears of rejection and of confronting explosive feelings were detrimental to her, she would have seen that an important purpose of teaching is to help children discover that they can face and handle their own fears. Jean's supervisor tried to show her that she was forcing students to need her support rather than making them independent of her. She tried to tell Jean that her popularity may have been gained at the cost of her integrity as a teacher.

Case Number Three: The Desire to Aid in the Renewal of Society

Fred was in his late thirties. His disposition was so pleasant, and a smile came so readily to his face, that one of the other teachers in the large metropolitan high school referred to him as "everybody's father." Fred had a remarkable ability to remain relaxed when everyone else was tense, and he frequently broke up emotionally charged situations with an appropriate quip or humorous question.

Each year Fred asked to teach the Curriculum II freshman history class. Of course, his request was always granted because the Curriculum II classes were considered the dumping ground for slow students and students who had given up. Some of the other teachers regarded the Curriculum II classes as "punishment." Year after year, Fred worked happily with children nobody else really wanted.

Fred's freshman history class was one of the most active in the whole school. He took his students beyond the walls of the school on expeditions to day court, to the police station and jail, and through industrial plants in the area, and most years he sneaked in a baseball game. Yet his classes were not characterized by fun and games. The students worked very hard on long and involved homework assignments, intricate discussions of problems, and demanding tests.

At one point in a particular academic year, Fred invited another teacher to speak to the class on shipbuilding in the eighteenth century. The talk went well, and after the session the other teacher, James Power, commented to Fred that the temper of the discussion following his talk had been very different from what he had anticipated; the questions were thoughtful and displayed observation of detail that the guest speaker had not expected from a "bunch of Curriculum IIs."

Fred greeted Mr. Power's remarks with a chuckle. "You know, Jim," he said, "they really amaze me, too, sometimes. Most of these kids really have behavior problems, not intellectual ones. If you looked at their case histories, you'd find that the majority of them were 'dropped through the ranks'!"

"What do you mean?" asked Mr. Power.

"I mean that they were in regular classes a good bit of their scholastic lives. But when they became problems in class, their teachers decided that the cause of their poor behavior was that the work was too hard for them. So the majority of children in this class really represent the rebels, the nonconformists, the 'antisocials'! These are the kids who some teachers claim 'won't go along with the system.' They're the kids about whom teachers say, 'I don't care if they learn any history at all as long as they become good citizens.'"

"Yes, but you must admit that very few of them will go to college. Most Curriculum IIs just drop out," said Mr. Power.

"Maybe you're missing my point," said Fred. "I guess I'm saying that people can't be 'good citizens' unless they are contributing members of society, and that they should contribute something that they think is worth contributing. If they can't get the basic tools that make a person productive, how can they be good citizens? It's a lot more than getting jobs or making decent livings. As a matter of fact, I feel that these kids are much more capable than the kids we send to the university."

"In what sense?"

"In the sense that they are the least accepting of society as it exists now," replied Fred. "If you talked to some of them for an hour or so, you'd find that they really feel the school is hypocritical in many ways, and they aren't afraid to point out the hypocrisies. They'll tell you, for instance, that there are two sets of rules in the school, two sets of discipline procedures, two sets of privileges, and all the rest."

"But I hear the same thing from my 'honors' classes," protested Mr. Power. "Those kids know about the double standard, too. They often tell me that an honors student here can get away with anything from cutting class to smoking in the john. The 'double standard' isn't any secret in this school."

"You've got me wrong again, Jim. I know about that, but that wasn't what I was talking about. What these kids are saying is not that we expect too much of them, but too little. For instance, if a kid dropped from an A to a C in your honors history course, what would happen?"

"The kid would probably go in and see the counselor, by request."

Fred replied, "That's right. When a kid everyone believes is bound for college does poorly, people get concerned. They try to help the kid take a look at what's wrong. If one of these students goes from a C to an F, though, everyone says, 'Well, what more do you expect? The kid's only a Curriculum II and doesn't have the ability to sustain a C.' And they get all the inexperienced teachers and martinets in the school. Oh, they know that if they become real problems, they'll get counseling and possibly even better teaching. But that isn't their complaint. They know that the system isn't out to punish them. It just doesn't care enough about them to want to punish them. They know that the system would rather they just float along and not bother anyone. That's the double standard in this school—those that are cared about and those that aren't—that's what these kids will tell you. It's not injustice, it's no justice at all."

Double standards in
schools

"Is this why you request Curriculum II classes every year?" asked Mr. Power.

"That's part of it," said Fred. "But it's not the whole reason. I'm not quite that altruistic. No, I see in these kids something that frightens me. They have capability, but if it isn't developed, it can become capability for hate, a hate based on fear. They're a mark for anyone who comes along with a 'hate message'; I know it and it frightens me. They have to be taught to analyze critically, to think through problems and to care about other people. In my mind, that is what good citizens do. They have developed a capability for understanding, and that is what I am trying to do—develop that capability. I think

SELF AND CAREER

these kids need that capability developed even more than the kids in the honors classes do, because that attention the honors students get in the course of their day here will pull them through. Plenty of people challenge them, listen to them, and chastise them when they need it. But with these kids it's a different story."

"You know," said Mr. Power, "you're not just talking about the Curriculum II classes. I think the same thing is generally true of Curriculum I classes. It seems that a kid who's really bright gets a lot of attention, and so does the kid who is really slow, but it's that kid in the middle. . . ."

"You're right," said Fred. "The kids in this class are the bottom of that middle group in terms of the concern they arouse from the system. And they know it. Yet, as you saw today, they are capable. We owe them a decent set of expectations. I've maintained high expectations for the kids. I would prefer to slightly overmatch them intellectually than undermatch them, because no development is possible when you're being undermatched constantly."

"Don't they complain about being pushed too hard?" asked Mr. Power.

"Oh, sure! There's always a good deal of moaning, particularly in the early weeks, until they realize I don't dance to that tune. Pretty soon they settle in and decide to go along with the program. But then they realize that they are actually learning. At that point, they're hooked. They're mine and I wouldn't trade teaching them for anything!"

"Well, Fred, this has been most instructive. I came to teach and I ended up learning."

"Me, too. That's what keeps me going. And, Jim, please come back next semester."

Questions

1. How is Fred's commitment to social renewal specifically manifested in his classroom teaching?
2. According to Fred, what is the criterion for assignment to Curriculum II classes in his school? Was this true of your high school?
3. What is the double standard of which Jim Power spoke, and how do you explain it? What is the double standard of which Fred spoke, and how do you explain it? Did either of these double standards exist in your school?
4. How are Fred's expectations for his students different from those of the majority of teachers you have known? In what other ways is he different from most of the teachers you have known?
5. What do you think were Jim's major misconceptions as a teacher?
6. What does Fred see as the role of academic disciplines in education? If you had to, how would you argue against his position?

Comment

In addition to the serious injustice of underchallenging many of our students, Fred was reacting against the perversion of an important idea: teaching good citizenship. In Fred's school, as in many others, the idea of teaching good citizenship has been badly distorted.

During the 1930s, in a reform started by the American educator and philosopher John Dewey, many schools adopted the policy of awarding a grade for citizenship. Dewey and many of his followers envisioned training for citizenship as a process of working out in class actual problems that arise in a democracy. They valued informed dissent and wanted children to develop the intellectual wherewithal to make reasonable decisions based on the disciplined study of alternatives. They saw the schools as an appropriate place to teach students about the nature of such decisions and to give them low-risk but real practice in democratic decision making in a context where mistakes were not "for keeps."

As sometimes happens with reforms, educational and otherwise, the processes the reformers introduced to the classroom degenerated into empty forms. And, in time, the citizenship grade became more and more a judgment of docile *Misuse of citizenship* conduct. As long as the student "played the game" of democracy in the class-*grade* room, displaying a compliant attitude and voting for class officers (who usually were officers in name only), he or she was given a high grade in citizenship.

Citizenship became a code word among teachers. A teacher who was given a class of "low achievers" or "discipline problems" was sometimes told, "Don't worry about the academics with these children. Just make them 'good citizens.'" This meant that the teacher would not be expected to teach the students anything, for they were not considered to be capable of learning, but to keep them docile and out of everyone else's way. Parents were told that their child wasn't a very good student but "an excellent citizen." This meant that even though he or she didn't learn anything, the child did without question everything that students were supposed to do.

The use of a citizenship grade as a conduct mark is an absolute travesty of the system Dewey and the reformers designed, for in reality good citizens are not docile sheep who can be "conned" with impunity. Rather, they are men and women who can make the tough decisions that democracy needs in order to function as a system. And they thought that the grade would be a measure of the student's ability to use the processes of democracy in a profitable, efficient way.

The use of the word *citizenship* as a synonym for *docile conduct* was a perversion of its original intention.

The long-term effect of the misinterpretation of Dewey's ideas was to discredit citizenship as an appropriate goal for schooling. Citizenship became too closely associated with conformity and following orders. Yet in Fred's case, we see a person consciously attempting to develop educated citizens. Fred's visits to courthouses, legislative sessions, and factories, as well as the classroom study of major social problems, are very much in keeping with what Dewey and, indeed, Thomas Jefferson and James Madison had in mind when they spoke of educating for freedom.

SOME CONCLUDING THOUGHTS

Selecting a career involves answering many questions, questions such as "Will I be happy?" "Will this career provide me with a satisfying lifestyle?" "Will I be up to the challenge, and will I find the work satisfying?" and "Will I grow in the experience?" People considering teaching as a life's work should grapple with these questions that surround the motives for choice. But other, if you will, deeper motives also need to be scrutinized.

Working daily with students on a one-to-one basis can be stimulating, challenging, and deeply satisfying.

(*Carol Palmer*)

Teaching, like nursing, the ministry, and social work, is a service occupation. Built into teaching is the idea of contributing to the lives of others. For many people, the root of their decision to teach is deeper than a love of subject matter or an attraction to the life of a teacher. Many men and women select teaching for reasons that are, at heart, religious or humanitarian. We suspect that teachers who are truly satisfied are people whose choice has been grounded in this deeper motivation. And although such religiously based or humanistically motivated reasons for teaching are a private matter, it is a matter that each of us needs to explore very carefully. Of all the questions in this book, "Why teach?" is ultimately the most important one. How we answer determines not only whether or not we will teach, but what we will actually *accomplish* as teachers.

REASONS FOR TEACHING

In a 1985 survey, students planning to teach were asked to identify their motives for selecting teaching as a profession. They were also asked what factors would be important in their selection of a school district. Their responses are summarized in the following table.

- How would you rate each of the listed motives?
- What would be your criteria for the selection of a school in which to teach? Are your criteria the same as those of the majority of prospective teachers?

WANTED: Men and women with the wisdom of Solomon, the patience of Job, and the nerves of David before Goliath. Needed to prepare our young for productive life in the 21st century. Applicants must be willing to fill in gaps left by unfit, absent, or working parents, to satisfy demands of bureaucrats and politicians, and to teach the three Rs and moral values. Hours: 50 to 60 a week. Pay: only fair, but getting better. Reward: The luxury of always knowing you are doing something truly significant with your life.

1. People go into the teaching profession for many different reasons. Looking at the possible reasons listed below, could you tell us if, for you, they are (1) very important, (2) somewhat important, (3) not too important, or (4) not important at all?

| | PERCENT RESPONDING | | | | |
REASON	1	2	3	4	No response
Enjoy working with children	94	5	—	1	—
Important and honorable work	63	29	4	1	3
Chance to work with people who share my goals	55	35	8	2	—
Pleasant surroundings and working conditions	50	41	7	1	1
Doing something good for the community	46	42	9	2	1
Daily/yearly schedule that gives me time for myself	40	43	14	2	1
Job stability	38	43	15	3	1
Preferable to options in the business world	21	35	29	13	2
Good fringe benefits	20	48	25	6	1
Gives me geographic flexibility	19	37	28	14	2
Good salary	16	43	28	12	1

2. If you will be teaching in September, which of the following factors will be most important in your selection of a teaching position?

FACTOR	PERCENT CHOOSING THAT FACTOR
School system allows for professional growth	37
Sound, stimulating curriculum	31
Administration philosophy compatible with mine	30
Has discipline policy that supports me	24
Keeps me close to family or friends	21
Desirable new location	17
Best salary	17
Lets me teach the grade I want to teach	14
Best fringe benefits	9
Other	3
No response	2

Source: Reprinted from *Instructor,* September 1985. Copyright © 1985 by The Instructor Publications, Inc. Used by permission.

Discussion Questions

1. What questions about your own motivation has this chapter raised?
2. In your experience, did your teachers ever speak to you directly about their reasons for teaching? Did some teachers "tell" you by their actions what their motives for teaching were?
3. What, to you, is the most compelling reason to answer the question "Why teach?" What is the most compelling reason not to teach?
4. If you are currently planning to teach, what events in your life have helped you discover why you want to teach?
5. Which intrinsic and extrinsic occupational rewards have the most bearing on your current thoughts about a career?
6. Do you think of teaching as a calling? As a social service? If you do, why? If not, why not?

For Further Reading

Collins, Marva, and Civia Tamarkin. *Marva Collins' Way.* Los Angeles: Tarcher, 1982.
This book takes the reader inside the world of one of America's most inspiring and controversial teachers. Marva Collins describes her method of educating the children others forgot.

Freedman, Samuel G. *Small Victories.* New York: Harper and Row, 1990.
This book chronicles life in a New York City high school and its staff in the late 1980s. The highs and lows of teaching in urban schools are pictured, and the major problems affecting life in these schools are vividly presented.

Kaufman, Bel. *Up the Down Staircase.* Englewood Cliffs, N.J.: Prentice-Hall, 1964.
An easy-to-read, humorous, and poignant semifictionalized account of a beginning teacher's experience in a New York City high school. A thoroughly enjoyable book.

Keizer, Garret. *No Place But Here.* New York: Penguin, 1988.
This autobiographical account describes the life of a young English teacher's experiences coming to a small Vermont town. Rich in anecdotes of teaching in rural America and in wisdom about modern life, the book reports on essential truths of teaching.

Kidder, Tracy. *Among Schoolchildren.* Boston: Houghton Mifflin, 1989.
The author spent the entire school year observing a fifth-grade teacher and produced a rich and fascinating account of a teacher's year. The book shows how one teacher shaped and moved the lives of her students.

Mathews, Jay. *Escalante: The Best Teacher in America.* New York: Holt, 1990.
This is the biography of Jaime Escalante, who is profiled in this chapter and is the subject of the film *Stand By Me*. Escalante wins his students, largely urban Hispanics, with a combination of challenges to pride, demands of dedicated hard work, and demonstrated love.

Ryan, Kevin. *The Roller Coaster Year: Stories of First-Year Teachers.* New York: HarperCollins, 1991.

This book is a collection of twelve first-year teachers' accounts of their struggles and triumphs as they grappled with their new profession.

Notes   1. Sharon Feiman-Nemser and Robert E. Floden, "The Cultures of Teaching," in *Handbook of Research on Teaching,* 3d ed., ed. Merlin C. Wittrock (New York: Macmillan, 1986), pp. 510–511.

2. Dan Lortie, *Schoolteacher* (Chicago: University of Chicago Press, 1975), p. 102.

3. Mihaly Csikszentmihalyi and Jane McCormick, "The Influence of Teachers," *Phi Delta Kappan* (February 1986): V67, N6, 415–419. This article is reprinted in *Kaleidoscope.*

4. Gary Sykes, "Public Policy and the Problem of Teacher Quality: The Need for Screens and Magnets," in *Handbook of Teaching and Policy,* ed. L. S. Shulman and Gary Sykes (New York: Longman, 1983), pp. 111–112.

What Are Your Job Options in Education?

CHAPTER PREVIEW

The purpose of this chapter is to provide you with information regarding the availability of teaching positions in the elementary and secondary schools. The chapter also explores other career opportunities both within and outside the educational field. We feel that the material contained in the chapter is vital for you to make an enlightened career decision. Study the information carefully and discuss it with your instructors and your career planning and placement office. There may be more job options in your program of study than you have realized.

This chapter emphasizes that:

● Many factors influence the availability of teaching jobs (enrollments in teacher education programs, student enrollments in schools, ratios of students to teachers, geographical location, subject matter and grade level taught, and numbers of individuals entering teaching through alternative certification programs, for example). Although an oversupply of teachers exists in a few teaching fields, many other fields face a severe shortage of teachers.

● Teacher salaries have made some gains in recent years, with the average salary of classroom teachers in 1990–91 being just over $33,000. However, salaries vary tremendously from school district to school district.

● Certain job-hunting strategies will increase your chances of locating the right job for you. You may have to spend considerable time and energy preparing materials for your job search.

● Certification requirements differ from state to state for both general and specialized areas of teaching.

● A wide variety of careers are available to people trained as teachers. Should you be unable to secure a teaching position, or wish to change careers after you have taught, the skills you have acquired in teacher education can be transferred to related occupational areas.

● No matter what the job market may be at a particular moment, there has never been a surplus of good teachers. Better-prepared teachers will find it easier to gain employment and will improve the teaching profession and its public image.

"Pupil Enrollment Exceeds Estimates"

"State Grants Emergency Teaching Certificates to Scientists"

"School Bond Issue Defeated by Voters"

"National Survey Projects Teacher Shortages"

"College Enrollments in Teacher Education Up"

"Teachers Face Worst Layoffs in Decade"

Y ou have probably read newspaper headlines similar to these and may have wondered whether you will be able to obtain a teaching position when you graduate. Although we would like to answer this question for you personally, we obviously cannot. We can, however, provide you with information that may help you increase your chances of obtaining the kind of teaching position you are seeking. That is the purpose of this chapter.

WILL THERE BE JOB OPENINGS IN EDUCATION?

In the 1960s the United States went through a rare social experience. It became inundated with adolescents and young adults. The number of young people between the ages of fourteen and twenty-four increased during the decade by a staggering 52 percent. This great population bulge put a tremendous strain on the social agencies serving this age group. Welfare and recreational agencies, police departments (fourteen to twenty-four are the high crime years), and schools were unprepared to handle this large number of young customers. In education, it meant a grave teacher shortage throughout much of the decade. People became used to the idea of a high demand for teachers. Apparently, few noticed (1) that a high percentage of the students in this sixties population bulge were graduating from college and becoming teachers and (2) that the number of school-age children to be taught (and thus the number of career opportunities) was leveling off. As a result, in the early 1970s the teacher shortage was suddenly replaced by a teacher surplus. We went from feast to famine in our country in the space of a few short years.

Factors Influencing a Teacher Shortage

Students chose other careers

It seems, however, that the years of surplus are behind us. In fact, many educators expect a teacher shortage during the 1990s. Several things are happening. First, the number of college students going into education fell dramatically during the seventies. Probably as a direct response to the publicity about the very real job shortage in teaching and general uncertainty within the educational employment market, many young people chose other careers. In 1975 the number of newly qualified teachers was 261,000. By 1984 the number had fallen to 105,000, a decrease of 60 percent in just nine years. This declining trend had reversed itself by 1986, when the number of newly qualified teachers increased to 126,000.[1] Indications are that more and more college students and career switchers are choosing to become teachers. Despite this latest trend, the effects of the seventies and early eighties will be a teacher shortage for some time.

Second, the demand for additional teachers is expected to rise. Projections indicate that the yearly demand for new-hire teachers in public schools will increase from 187,000 in 1990 to 225,000 in 2001. The demand for elementary school new-hire teachers for the same time period will increase from 104,000 to 112,000, and the demand for secondary school new-hire teachers will increase from 83,000 to 113,000.[2]

Increase in secondary school enrollments

Third, enrollments in public schools are expected to increase through the year 2000, particularly at the secondary school level. Joining this growth is a continuing gradual decline in pupil-teacher ratios (at the elementary level from 18.6 in 1990 to 16.9 in 2000, and at the secondary level from 14.9 to 14.8). As a result, by 2000 the number of elementary and secondary classroom teachers should reach 1.53 and 1.24 million, respectively, an increase of 371,000 over the 1990 level (see Tables 2.1, 2.2, and 2.3).

Another factor that bodes well for the long-term job outlook for teachers is the fact that the teaching profession, like much of the rest of the American work force, is getting older, partly because teachers are remaining in teaching longer and partly because older people are becoming teachers. The average age

Aging of teacher work force

of new teachers hired between 1985 and 1990 was thirty-five years, and the average age of all public school teachers in 1990 was forty-two years. This national average of forty-two years varies greatly by geographic region: Northeast, thirty-four years; South, thirty-eight years; West, forty-nine years; and Midwest, fifty years.[3]

Table 2.1 Enrollment in Grades K–8 and 9–12 in Public and Private Schools (in millions)

	PUBLIC SCHOOLS			PRIVATE SCHOOLS		
	K–12	K–8	9–12	K–12	K–8*	9–12
1980	40.9	27.7	13.2	5.3	4.0	1.3
1985	39.4	27.0	12.4	5.6	4.2	1.4
1990+	40.8	29.5	11.3	5.4	4.2	1.2
1995+	43.7	31.1	12.6	5.7	4.4	1.3
2000+	44.2	30.8	13.4	5.8	4.4	1.4

* = includes nursery school enrollments
+ = projected
Note: Because of rounding, details may not add to total.

Source: Debra E. Gerald and William J. Hussar, *Projections of Education Statistics to 2001* (Washington, D.C.: National Center for Education Statistics, December 1990), p. 4.

Table 2.2 Pupil-Teacher Ratios in Public and Private Elementary and Secondary Schools (number of pupils per teacher)

	PUBLIC SCHOOLS		PRIVATE SCHOOLS	
	Elementary	Secondary	Elementary	Secondary
1980	20.4	16.8	18.8	15.0
1985	19.6	15.7	17.1	14.0
1990+	18.6	14.9	15.0	11.4
1995+	18.1	15.1	14.8	11.5
2000+	16.9	14.8	13.9	11.4
+ = projected				

Source: Debra E. Gerald and William J. Hussar, *Projections of Education Statistics to 2001* (Washington, D.C.: National Center for Education Statistics, December 1990), p. 57.

As a result of this trend, between the years 1991 and 2000, it is estimated that almost 1.95 million public school teachers will retire, averaging 177,000 retirements a year. In fact, retirements will account for 83 percent of the demand for new teachers during that time period.[4]

In spite of the positive long-term outlook for teaching positions, in times of economic hardship school districts may find it necessary to reduce the size of their teaching force to balance budgets. During the 1990–91 recession, for example, school districts in a number of states found it necessary to issue RIFs—reduction-in-force notices to teachers informing them that they were in danger of not being rehired for the following fall. In the spring of 1991, some ten thou-

Table 2.3 Classroom Teachers in Public and Private Elementary and Secondary Schools (in thousands)

	PUBLIC SCHOOLS			PRIVATE SCHOOLS		
	K–12	Elementary	Secondary	K–12	Elementary*	Secondary
1980	2,184	1,189	995	301	212	89
1985	2,207	1,237	970	343	246	97
1990+	2,401	1,361	1,039	384	281	103
1995+	2,602	1,451	1,151	414	300	114
2000+	2,772	1,532	1,241	439	316	123
* = includes nursery school teachers						
+ = projected						

Source: Debra E. Gerald and William J. Hussar, *Projections of Education Statistics to 2001* (Washington, D.C.: National Center for Education Statistics, December 1990), p. 56.

Table 2.4 Racial Distribution of Public School Teachers by Type of Community and Geographic Region, 1990

	American Indian, Alaskan Native	Asian, Pacific Islander	Black	White	Hispanic
	%	%	%	%	%
All public school teachers	—	1	5	92	2
By type of community					
Large inner city	—	7	21	67	5
Medium inner city	1	1	8	86	4
Small town	—	—	2	96	1
Suburban	—	1	3	94	2
Rural	1	0	4	97	—
By geographic region					
South	1	—	9	89	1
West	—	2	2	90	7
Midwest	—	—	2	98	—
Northeast	—	2	3	95	1

Source: C. Emily Feistritzer, *Profile of Teachers in the U.S.—1990* (Washington, D.C.: National Center for Education Information, 1990), p. 11.

sand California teachers, eight thousand New York teachers, and four to six thousand Florida teachers were warned of possible layoffs due to budgetary constraints. Although painful in the short run, such layoffs will probably be only temporary and will have little overall effect on the long-term demand for new teachers. The RIF notices do illustrate, however, that the demand for teachers is greatly influenced by school district budgets, which are, in turn, affected by the health of the state and local economies.

Severe Shortage of Minority Teachers

One of the greatest teacher supply-and-demand problems concerns minority teachers. At a time when the minority school-age population is increasing rapidly, the number of minority teachers is decreasing. The shortage is severe now and appears likely to become worse. Consider, for a moment, the following statistics. The total minority enrollment in elementary and secondary education rose from 24 percent in 1976 to almost 30 percent in 1986 and is projected to reach 38 to 40 percent by 2000.[5]

More minority students

Teaching, on the other hand, is becoming more and more white. Ninety-two percent of public school teachers are white, 5 percent are black, 2 percent are Hispanic, 1 percent are Asian or Pacific Islander, and less than 1 percent are Native American or Native Alaskan[6] (see Table 2.4). Graduation rates from teacher education programs closely mirror this distribution of minority teachers. Taking into account attrition rates and barring some extraordinary recruitment efforts, a further deterioration in these percentages is likely in the near future.

This shortage of minority teachers is problematic for several reasons. First, the growing population of minority children deserves to have positive minority role models who can help them develop self-esteem and guide them in a world still affected by racism. Second, the white children also need to have minority teachers as positive role models to help them overcome the effects of stereotyping and racism. And third, it is important for our country's well-being to have a teaching staff that reflects the diversity of racial and ethnic backgrounds in our country's population.

Fewer minority teachers

There are a number of reasons why this shortage of minority teachers exists. Before desegregation efforts, nearly one-half of the African-American professional workers were teachers. When schools desegregated in the 1960s, resulting in the consolidation of formerly all-black and all-white schools, thousands of African-American teachers were dismissed. Today other professions that pay more and have higher status are actively recruiting minority college students. Another causal factor has been the increasing use of competency tests, at either the beginning or the end of teacher education programs. Minority college students traditionally have not performed as well on standardized tests as white college students. As a consequence, many minority teaching candidates are either failing to pass these tests or are being discouraged from even considering teaching as a career.

What can be done to address this problem? Teaching salaries must continue to improve if teaching is to compete with other professions for well-qualified candidates. Assistance programs to help minority candidates to perform well on competency tests have demonstrated their effectiveness in a number of universities and need to be expanded to other colleges. Active recruitment programs for minority candidates must be developed and implemented, and they must reach down into the middle and high schools to encourage minority students to consider teaching as a career. Scholarship and forgiveness loan programs are needed for students who want to teach but who cannot afford college. And the American public must communicate, in a variety of ways, that it values teachers and the work they do.

Other Factors Affecting Teacher Supply and Demand

Will there be a shortage of teachers—elementary and secondary—in the 1990s? There is not a simple yes or no answer. Although little doubt exists that the demand for teachers will be greater, forecasters vary widely in their predictions about the available supply of teachers to meet the demand. Even the current situation is not clear. In 1991 some states reported shortages; others did not. To generalize about a nationwide teacher shortage ignores the differences that exist in available supplies of teachers who are trained in certain specialties or who are willing to teach in remote rural areas, the suburbs, or the inner city.

Estimates of shortages are based on rapidly changing situations influenced by unpredictable factors. No one can predict with certainty, for example, what percentage of those who are trained as teachers will choose to teach. Among other factors are the retirement rates of current teachers, anticipated enrollments in teacher education programs, re-entry of previously trained teachers into the profession, and changes in certification programs that may allow those not trained as teachers to teach. Traditionally, when shortages have existed, states and local districts have increased class sizes, hired less-than-qualified personnel, and issued emergency certificates to fill vacancies.

Responses to anticipated teacher shortages

In response to real and anticipated shortages, some states have already begun, through alternative certification programs, to certify individuals not trained as teachers; we'll discuss those programs later in this chapter. Other states have provided incentives for college students to enter teaching; forgiveness loans and scholarships are typical examples. For current staff, school districts have begun career-ladder and merit-pay programs to encourage teachers to continue teaching. Funds have been used to retrain teachers for new teaching fields or to enable nonteachers to receive the training needed to switch to teaching.

Teachers are not interchangeable units. They are prepared for different specialties (special education, primary grades, all-level art, or high school social studies, for example), and the job market in each one of these subfields is different. Even throughout the worst of the teacher surplus, serious shortages existed in some subfields; likewise, during times of teacher shortages there may be surpluses in some subfields. Finally, the job market for specific subfields may change frequently. It is unwise, therefore, to decide whether or not to become a special education teacher because you have heard that today there is, in general, either a surplus or a shortage of such teachers.

Teacher supply and demand, by subject area

Estimates of the demand for beginning teachers, by subject area, are listed in Table 2.5. The greatest estimated shortages of prospective teachers to fill jobs opening in 1990 were in special education, speech pathology/audiology, bilingual education, English as a second language (ESL), physics, and mathematics. Other areas in which demand was reported to be relatively high were computer science, Spanish, chemistry, and reading. Subjects or assignments in which the supply was estimated to most exceed the actual demand included social science, health education, art, and men's and women's physical education. However, an oversupply does not mean there are no jobs. It means, rather, that job seeking is more competitive and that the teacher graduate may have to relocate in a different community or commute a great distance to work.

Job availability by geographic area

Location, in fact, significantly influences the job market. Some communities have far more applications than available teaching positions. University towns, urban areas, and large cities usually have a great surplus of teachers. In contrast, rural America traditionally has had difficulty attracting and holding on to teachers. Generally speaking, teacher vacancies are greatest in the southeastern states (Kentucky, Tennessee, Alabama, Virginia, the Carolinas, and so on) and in the south central states (Texas, Oklahoma, Arkansas, and Louisiana). Hawaii and Alaska also report teacher shortages. There are fewer vacancies and/or more competition in the Great Lakes states (Michigan, Ohio, Indiana, Illinois, and Wisconsin) and the northeastern states (Maine, Vermont, New Hampshire, Massachusetts, Rhode Island, and Connecticut).[7] Even though differences in the overall job market from one locale to another may not be great, differences in demand for certain teaching fields can vary.

Table 2.5 Relative Demand by Teaching Area, 1990 Report

Teaching fields with considerable teacher shortages (5.00–4.25):	
Special education—LD	4.49
Special education—mentally handicapped	4.48
Special education—ED/BD	4.46
Speech pathology/audiology	4.41
Special education—multiple handicapped	4.39
Bilingual education	4.35
Special education—deaf	4.34
Teaching fields with some teacher shortage (4.24–3.45):	
English as a second language	4.00
Special education—other	3.98
Science—physics	3.93
Mathematics	3.91
Psychologist (school)	3.85
Computer science	3.84
Language, modern—Spanish	3.76
Library science	3.76
Special education—gifted	3.76
Counselor—elementary	3.67
Science—chemistry	3.62
Data processing	3.57
Counselor—secondary	3.56
Special education—reading	3.55

Overseas teaching opportunities

A large employer of teachers is the U.S. government. The Department of Defense operates approximately 271 schools in nineteen countries around the world. These schools enroll approximately 153,000 students and employ 16,000 educational personnel. Salaries are comparable to those in the United States, but preference is given to applicants who have at least one year of successful full-time employment as a professional educator.*

Private school teaching

Although most of the data presented in this chapter refer to public elementary and secondary schools, private education is a highly significant part of the American educational system. In the fall of 1990 there were over 27,000 private schools with an enrollment of 4.85 million elementary and secondary school students and a staff of 325,000 teachers. About 11 percent of the children attending elementary or secondary schools attended a private school in 1990–91.[8] Of these students, 86 percent attended private schools that were affiliated with

---

* For more information on applying for a job with the Department of Defense overseas schools, write U.S. Department of Defense, Office of Dependents Schools, Recruitment and Assignments Section, Hoffman Building #1, 2461 Eisenhower Avenue, Alexandria, VA 22331-1100.

Table 2.5 Relative Demand by Teaching Area, 1990 Report (*cont.*)

Teaching fields with balanced supply and demand (3.44–2.65):	
Language, modern—other	3.41
Science—other	3.36
English	3.28
Science—general	3.26
Industrial arts	3.23
Music—instrumental	3.23
Language, modern—French	3.22
Science—biology	3.17
Science—Earth	3.15
Language, modern—German	3.12
Music—vocal	3.12
Business	3.07
Agriculture	3.03
Social worker (school)	2.99
Elementary—primary	2.83
Elementary—intermediate	2.81
Speech	2.78
Home economics	2.69
Journalism	2.66
Teaching fields with some surplus of teachers (2.64–1.85):	
Driver education	2.57
Health education	2.02
Art	1.96
Social sciences	1.89
Teaching field with considerable surplus of teachers (1.84–1.00):	
Physical education	1.72

5 = greatest demand   1 = least demand
Based upon a survey of teacher placement officers—50 states
Source: The ASCUS Annual: A Job Search Handbook for Educators, (Addison, IL: Association for School, College, and University Staffing), 1991. p. 8. Reprinted by permission.

some religious group, whereas only 14 percent attended nonsectarian private schools. (See Figure 2.1.)

Since private schools employ almost 13 percent of all elementary and secondary teachers, they obviously offer an employment opportunity for new teachers. Many teachers who work in religion-affiliated schools do so because of religious motives. These teachers are often willing to work for less money than their public school counterparts, and, as a result, the average teacher salary in private schools is lower than that in public schools. But one study has reported

Salaries in private schools

Job opportunities for teachers in rural areas tend to be more plentiful than in many suburban and urban areas.

(Susan Lapides)

EDUCATION: A WORLD VIEW

STUDENT-TEACHER RATIOS

The ratio of students per teacher in a classroom is a variable that is often discussed as part of educational reform in the United States. It is often noted that if the number of students per teacher is decreased, particularly in the earlier grades of education, teachers have more opportunity to interact with and address the individual needs of each student. However, lower student-teacher ratios also require that more teachers be funded and available for teaching. Let's take a look at how these educational needs and economic realities are balanced in different countries.

Looking at student-teacher ratios in elementary grades by very broad categories of country income level, we see the direct impact of national economic standing on how many students a teacher is expected to work with. Low-income countries such as India and Nigeria report student–teacher ratios of more than 40 students to 1 teacher. Other third-world countries, such as Kenya and Mexico, report ratios over 30 to 1. In contrast, high-income countries, including the United States, report student-teacher ratios of less than 20 to 1 (see Figure 2.2).

Looking more closely at countries with high income levels, we see a much smaller though still significant range of variation in student-teacher ratios. The

Figure 2.1 Private Elementary and Secondary Schools and Their Enrollment, by Affiliation of School, U.S., 1987–88

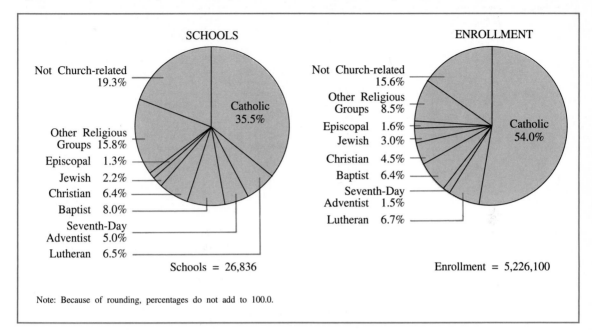

SCHOOLS

Not Church-related 19.3%

Other Religious Groups 15.8%

Episcopal 1.3%

Jewish 2.2%

Christian 6.4%

Baptist 8.0%

Seventh-Day Adventist 5.0%

Lutheran 6.5%

Catholic 35.5%

Schools = 26,836

ENROLLMENT

Not Church-related 15.6%

Other Religious Groups 8.5%

Episcopal 1.6%

Jewish 3.0%

Christian 4.5%

Baptist 6.4%

Seventh-Day Adventist 1.5%

Lutheran 6.7%

Catholic 54.0%

Enrollment = 5,226,100

Note: Because of rounding, percentages do not add to 100.0.

Note: Because of rounding, percentages do not add up to 100.0.
Source: Marilyn M. McMillen and Elizabeth Gerald, "Characteristics of Private Schools: 1987–88
(Washington D.C.: National Center for Education Statistics, 1990, pp. 2, 7).

United States has a higher student-teacher ratio—about 19 to 1—than most European countries. This is because the United States invests much more money in administrative positions than any other country. If some or all of the money spent on administrators, such as curriculum specialists, supervisors, counselors, and vice-principals went to hire more teachers, then the ratio would drop considerably.

Several factors besides income level affect student-teacher ratios, including the availability of teachers and particular cultural traditions. For example, although Japan and particularly Korea have high student-teacher ratios (23 and 36, respectively), their children are among the highest scorers on international tests of achievement (see Chapter 7). If low student-teacher ratios are desirable, how do we account for these high scores? Certainly Japanese and Korean families value education highly and provide a great deal of educational support to children outside of school. The teaching styles in these countries also emphasize teamwork and community ownership rather than individualism. Teaching larger groups of students, then, may not adversely affect learning in these countries.

How important a variable do you think student-teacher ratio is in providing quality instruction? How culturally bound is the concept?

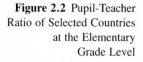

Figure 2.2 Pupil-Teacher Ratio of Selected Countries at the Elementary Grade Level

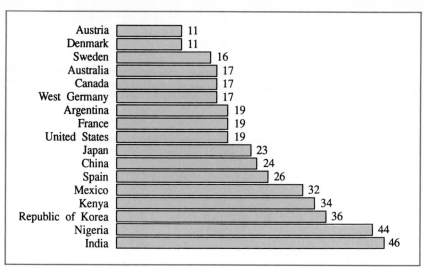

Source: Data from Table 3.4 of the UNESCO STATISTICAL YEARBOOK 1989. © UNESCO 1989. Used by permission.

that lower salaries tend to be offset by other, favorable working conditions. Compared with public schools, private schools have fewer disciplinary problems, stricter discipline, students who are less frequently absent, parents who are more supportive, more assigned homework, and more time spent in instruction in the central academic subjects.[9] Thus, for many individuals, teaching in a private school is an attractive alternative to teaching in the public schools.

There has been little experience in applying data on trends in population and teacher education enrollment to the educational job market. The information about employment prospects that you pick up here and elsewhere should be evaluated carefully and with some suspicion. For one thing, as we have noted, the educational job market may change rather rapidly. There is a great deal of movement in and out of the teaching profession, which of course affects the availability of jobs. Also, the employment figures are affected by the economy. For instance, when economic times are favorable, more money is available for schools, so more teachers are hired and the ratio of teachers to pupils goes down. When times are economically hard, the opposite is true, and teachers tend to hold on to their jobs more. Teachers' professional organizations have insisted for some time that we have had an undersupply of money rather than an oversupply of teachers. They argue that there would never be a surplus of teachers if we reduced class size and set lower pupil-teacher ratios.

Supply-and-demand forecasting difficult

As we have also suggested, demographic projections and supply-and-demand forecasting are not only hard to apply but also very inexact and short-lived. With difficulty, forecasters try to take into account factors such as retirement rates, supplies of former teachers re-entering the field, and programs that may attract individuals from nonteaching fields into the profession. What seems to be true for a particular geographic area, a particular teaching field, or a particular year may be out-of-date at the moment you are reading it.

Therefore, you ought to make every effort to get the most up-to-the-minute information possible about teacher supply and demand. You should consider such information carefully before making a choice about a career in education and, in particular, about a specific subfield within education. This is especially true for people who are unable to wait for openings in their area of teaching interest or unable to relocate. Sources of data with which to begin your search are your school's career counseling office, the department chairperson's or dean's office, the U.S. Department of Education, and the U.S. Department of Labor.

Never a surplus of good teachers

The bottom line, though, is that there has never been a surplus of good teachers in any field. Demand for teachers is expected to be high in the coming years. Regardless of the number of teachers available to fill the demand, if you are well prepared, you are likely to find a job.

WHAT ARE TEACHERS PAID?

We might answer the question by saying, "Not nearly enough." No one ever went into teaching because of the lure of big money. As we noted in Chapter 1, most of the rewards for teaching are personal rather than monetary. Most of teachers' satisfactions come from being of service to others and helping students learn. That does not mean, however, that you have to be a pauper to enjoy the satisfactions that come from teaching. Salaries are a legitimate concern for a prospective teacher; after all, everyone must have sufficient income to meet the costs of living. You will have to decide whether the salary you are likely to make as a classroom teacher will allow you to establish the type of lifestyle you want. Our purpose in this section is to give you some objective facts with which to make your decision.

Average teacher salaries

The 1990–91 average salary of classroom teachers in the fifty states and the District of Columbia stood at $33,015. This figure represented an increase of $23,747 (or 356 percent) over the 1970–71 average of $9,268, but taking inflation into consideration the increase is only $1,084, or 5.2 percent. The 1990–91 year marked the tenth year in a row that increases in the average salary surpassed inflation rates, but these recent gains were offset by previous periods of high inflation and minimal pay increases.[10] Table 2.6 lists average classroom teacher salaries from 1980–81 until 1990–91 and projected salaries through 1994–95. Figures 2.3 and 2.4 depict ranges of average teacher salaries by state in 1990–91 and the average teacher salary increases by state during the past decade. Keep in mind that these figures represent the average salary for *all* elementary and secondary school teachers. The average salary for first-year teachers in 1975–76 was $8,768; for 1980–81, it was $11,708; and for 1990–91, it was $21,542.[11]

Most public school salary schedules are usually determined by two factors:

Table 2.6 Average Public School Classroom Teacher Salaries, 1980–81 to 1990–91, and Projected Salaries, 1991–92 to 1994–95

School Year	Elementary	Secondary	Combined Average (Current Dollars)	Percentage Increase over Previous Year
1980–81	17,230	18,142	17,644	
1981–82	18,853	19,805	19,274	9.2
1982–83	20,227	21,291	20,695	7.4
1983–84	21,487	22,554	21,935	6.0
1984–85	23,200	24,187	23,600	7.6
1985–86	24,718	25,846	25,199	6.8
1986–87	26,051	27,247	26,567	5.4
1987–88	27,508	28,800	28,029	5.5
1988–89	29,011	30,233	29,563	5.5
1989–90	30,769	32,017	31,331	6.0
1990–91	32,448	33,701	33,015	5.4
1991–92 +			35,532	7.6
1992–93 +			38,195	7.5
1993–94 +			40,954	7.2
1994–95 +			43,838	7.0

+ = projected (with the middle high alternative projections)

Source: National Education Association, "Estimates of School Statistics 1990–91" (Washington, D.C.: NEA, 1991), p. 19. Projections for 1990–95 are from Debra E. Gerald and William J. Hussar, *Projections of Education Statistics to 2001*, (National Center for Education Statistics, December 1990, p. 66. Reprinted by permission.

Salary schedules

years of teaching experience and amount of training, usually expressed in terms of college credit-hours or advanced degrees. Thus the longer you teach and the more college education you receive, the more money you will make (see Table 2.7 for an example of a school district salary schedule).

As you can see from Table 2.8, salaries vary considerably from state to state. Each school district determines what it will pay its teachers, with many states setting a minimum base salary below which the school district cannot go. Generally, the large and middle-sized school districts pay better than the small ones. Many school districts offer extra pay for special duties such as directing the band or coaching athletic teams. Some also offer summer teaching or curriculum development jobs.

Fringe benefits

Most states and school districts provide public school teachers with a number of fringe benefits, including sick leave, health and life insurance programs, and retirement benefits. When applying for a teaching position, you should be sure to ask about these benefits.

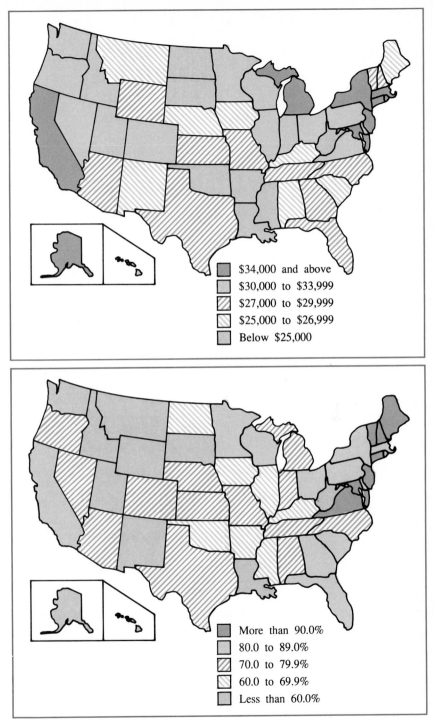

Figure 2.3 Average Teacher Salary, 1989–90

$34,000 and above
$30,000 to $33,999
$27,000 to $29,999
$25,000 to $26,999
Below $25,000

Figure 2.4 Average Teacher Salary Increase, 1980–81 to 1989–90

More than 90.0%
80.0 to 89.0%
70.0 to 79.9%
60.0 to 69.9%
Less than 60.0%

Source: F. Howard Nelson, "Survey and Analysis of Salary Trends 1990," (Washington D.C.: American Federation of Teachers, July 1990, p. 13). Used by permission.

Table 2.7 Teacher's Salary Schedule—200 Days—1991–92, Arlington, Virginia

Step	Bach	Bach + 15	Masters	Masters + 30	Doctorate
1	$26,272	$27,044	$27,816	$29,644	$31,937
2	27,044	27,816	28,588	30,798	33,075
3	27,816	28,588	29,644	31,937	34,233
4	28,588	29,361	31,206	33,779	36,071
5	29,361	30,266	33,000	35,388	37,683
6	30,811	31,827	34,402	36,995	39,291
7	32,374	33,386	35,812	38,370	40,660
8	33,857	34,795	37,209	39,757	42,051
9	35,263	36,199	38,618	41,130	43,428
10	36,667	37,683	40,020	42,502	44,801
11	—	39,165	41,427	43,877	46,190
12	—	40,567	42,828	45,267	47,557
13	—	41,971	44,236	46,641	48,939
14	—	43,379	45,643	48,015	50,326
15	—	45,452	47,827	50,180	52,542
16	—	47,269	49,742	52,189	54,643
17	—	48,865	51,387	53,910	56,432
18	—	50,390	53,069	55,644	58,270

The longevity amounts are added to the base pay after completion of the specified years of continuous service with the School Board.

Longevity Increments

1L—(after 20 years)—$ 543 3L—(after 30 years)—$1,629 5L—(after 40 years)—$2,715
2L—(after 25 years)—$1,086 4L—(after 35 years)—$2,172 6L—(after 45 years)—$3,258

Source: Arlington Public Schools, 1426 N. Quincy St., Arlington, VA 22207 (703-358-6110). Reprinted by permission.

Table 2.8 Average Annual Salaries of Classroom Teachers, 1990–91

STATE	Beginning Teachers Salary 1990–91	All Teachers Average Salary 1990–1991
1 Alabama	22,114	26,846
2 Alaska	29,850 b	43,406
3 Arizona	21,375 b	30,773
4 Arkansas	17,458 d	23,735 a
5 California	24,570 b	39,118 b
6 Colorado	19,786	31,819
7 Connecticut	25,312	43,398
8 Delaware	21,112	35,248
9 D.C.	23,327	39,362 b
10 Florida	21,368	30,555
11 Georgia	20,471	28,950 a
12 Hawaii	23,792	33,548
13 Idaho	15,685	25,510
14 Illinois	21,954 a	34,642 a

Table 2.8 Average Annual Salaries of Classroom Teachers, 1990–91 (*cont.*)

STATE	Beginning Teachers Salary 1990–91	All Teachers Average Salary 1990–1991
15 Indiana	20,247 a	32,931 a
16 Iowa	19,404	27,949
17 Kansas	16,954 f	28,188 f
18 Kentucky	19,311	29,115
19 Louisiana	17,486	26,170
20 Maine	18,878	28,531
21 Maryland	23,548	38,312 a
22 Massachusetts	21,800 b	36,090
23 Michigan	22,400 b	37,800 b
24 Minnesota	21,029	33,128
25 Mississippi	18,950 b	24,609 b
26 Missouri	20,293 b	27,636 b
27 Montana	18,400 b	26,696
28 Nebraska	18,344	26,592
29 Nevada	24,358 g	35,269 g
30 New Hampshire	20,635 b	31,273
31 New Jersey	24,500	38,411
32 New Mexico	19,124	25,800 a
33 New York	26,375 c	42,080 c
34 North Carolina	19,810	29,165
35 North Dakota	16,274	23,574
36 Ohio	18,452	31,964
37 Oklahoma	18,575 f	24,378 f
38 Oregon	20,357 g	32,295 g
39 Pennsylvania	23,250 b	36,057 a
40 Rhode Island	20,887	38,220 b
41 South Carolina	19,757 a	28,174 a
42 South Dakota	16,678	22,363
43 Tennessee	20,150	28,248
44 Texas	20,150 b	28,100 b
45 Utah	17,234	25,415 a
46 Vermont	18,509 b	29,714 b
47 Virginia	22,206 a	32,692 a
48 Washington	20,612 a	32,975 a
49 West Virginia	18,728	25,966
50 Wisconsin	20,689	33,077
51 Wyoming	19,238	28,996
U.S. Average	21,542	$32,880
Guam	19,217	25,842
Virgin Islands	19,081	28,000

a = estimate or preliminary; b = AFT estimate; c = median; d = excludes state-paid health insurance; e = includes extra duty and extracurricular pay; f = estimated to exclude fringes; g = includes 6% pension pick; h = based on total gross salary

Source: F. Howard Nelson, *Survey and Analysis of Salary Trends 1991* (Washington, D.C.: American Federation of Teachers, 1991). Used by permission.

The job market seems to be opening up for beginning teachers. During the late 1980s and early 1990s some school districts actively sought employees by visiting college campuses to interview and recruit prospective teachers. If this trend continues, you may have to spend considerable time and energy choosing rather than seeking a position. But no matter how great the demand for teachers is or

Figure 2.5 The Job Search: A Sequence of Planned Strategies

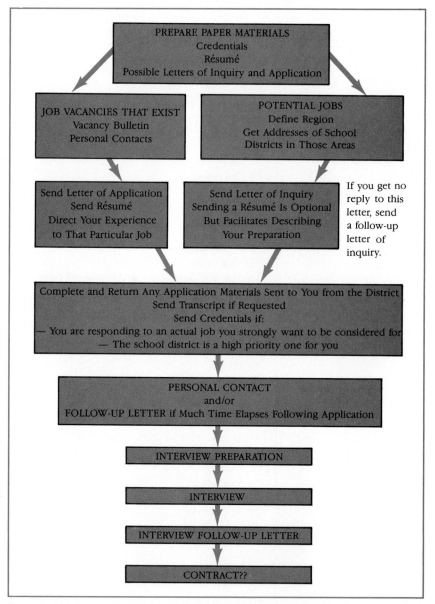

Source: Jan E. Kilby, "Job Search—A Sequence of Planned Strategies," *The ASCUS Annual: a Job Search Handbook for Educators, 1987* (Addison, IL.: Association for School, College and University Staffing, 1986), p. 9. Used by permission of Association for School, College and University Staffing, Inc. (ASCUS).

how effective you may be as a teacher, school district personnel are not likely to walk up to you and offer you a job unless you have taken a number of steps that we'll outline in this section. We will suggest several courses of action that will substantially increase your chances of finding the best teaching job for you.

First, you must be determined to campaign actively for a teaching position. Draw up a plan, in writing, of how you will proceed. Figure 2.5 provides you with a sample plan. Don't wait for happenstance. You might get lucky and land a job on your first try, but why take a passive attitude when you can do much to increase your chances of obtaining satisfying employment?

Job seekers frequently make two common mistakes.[12] One is to try one strategy, wait for results (positive or negative), then try something else. What you should do is pursue many avenues or strategies simultaneously. The second common error is to block oneself out at the wrong stage in the process. Some teachers only halfheartedly write for information or never complete the application form. Others withdraw their applications prematurely. Remember: You can always say "no" to a job that has been offered, but you can never say "yes" to one that has not been offered. Keep your options open.

Next, you need to get certain materials ready. These include your résumé, cover letter, credentials, transcripts, and interview skills. Your résumé allows you to present yourself the way you want to be presented to prospective employers. Its purpose is to help you get an interview with school district officials. You should have many copies of your résumé produced. A sample résumé appears in Figure 2.6.

Your cover letters, written to prospective school districts, should be addressed individually and not mass-produced. The content of the letters may be the same or similar, but the recipients of the letters should not feel that they are receiving a standard letter. And, incidentally, be sure to ask for an interview. That's why you are writing the letter.

Virtually all school districts require credentials, that is, the whole package from your college recommending you for certification. Be sure to check with the career planning and placement office about how to establish your credential file and what should go into it. Typically, this file will include letters of recommendation, a copy of your transcript, and a résumé. Career planning and placement office personnel will assist you in assembling this file, and they will send copies of your file to school districts upon your request. You should start on the file early in your program so you will have time to accumulate the required materials. Be familiar with the Family Educational Rights and Privacy Law, also known as the Buckley Amendment, which affords you certain kinds of legal protection regarding what goes into your file.* Your letters of recommendation should be recent and from people who can testify to your teaching ability.

Reproduce unofficial copies of your official transcript. Many applications require that transcripts accompany them. Since colleges charge several dollars

Job-search strategies

Develop a plan

Prepare materials

Establish your
credential file

---

* A copy of this law appears in the *Federal Register*, 53, no. 69 (Monday, April 11, 1988), pp. 11942–49. It can also be obtained by writing the U.S. Government Printing Office, Washington, DC 20402.

<u>Present Address</u>	<u>Permanent Address</u>
15 Underbrook Drive	110 Main Street
Columbus, Ohio 43214	Philadelphia, PA 19127
Phone: (614) 296-3201	Phone: (315) 436-2113
Until: June 11, 1992	

EDUCATION	Present highest degree data first and work backward. Identify: major, minor, course of study, institution granting degree and date of graduation.
CERTIFICATION	List all subjects, grade levels, and areas able to teach.
EXPERIENCE	Include those jobs that may relate to your ability to work with people; also include all jobs of significant duration and importance. Identify employer, your title, and brief description of the duties performed, including the percentage of college expenses earned. Start with most recent employment and record data in reverse chronological order.
	Include volunteer work without pay if it pertains to a strength you see in relation to teaching.
ACTIVITIES AND INTERESTS	Include clubs, organizations, Greek affiliations, honor societies, and sports. If an officer, specify which office.
MILITARY SERVICE	If applicable, include the branch of service, dates of service, rate or rank, and experience.
SPECIAL AWARDS AND GRANTS	If applicable, note name of award, when received, and brief award description. Work in reverse chronological order.
PERSONAL	This category is optional. It can include date of birth, height, weight, marital status, health, geographical preference, date available.
REFERENCES	State that credentials and references are available upon request.

per transcript, you can save money by reproducing the transcript yourself. Most school districts will accept unofficial transcripts (those sent from you rather than directly from the college) for the initial screening process. If you receive a job offer, you will then have to provide the school district with an official copy.

The success of your personal interview with the school district representative is one of the most important determinants of whether you get hired, so be

Prepare for interviews

prepared. Try to anticipate the kinds of questions that might be asked. (See page for some sample interview questions.) Try role-playing with a friend who plays the role of the interviewer while you play the candidate. Audiotape your "interview" so the two of you can criticize it. One survey indicated that the major factor school officials look for is whether the candidate has empathy for children. As one official stated,

> We take it for granted that a candidate who has successfully completed a teacher-training program and has been recommended for certification by the dean of the college has all the technical qualifications necessary, so we don't spend a lot of time worrying over grades and the like. What we do pay a lot of attention to and look for are the personality traits that tell us a person will work well with children, that tell us a person really cares about children.

You should ask those who write letters of recommendation for you to emphasize this aspect also.

Find out what jobs are available

Your next major task is to find out what jobs are available and where. Several strategies are possible. Your college's career planning and placement office not only can help you set up a placement file but also receives hundreds of notifications of position vacancies. Contact that office frequently to see if there are any vacancies that might interest you. Another source may be the teacher employment office operated by the state department of education. About one-third of the states run such offices, and you can register with them for free or for a slight charge. These offices send registered candidates a listing of openings in their specialty area for both state and out-of-state vacancies. There are private organizations that keep current nationwide teacher vacancy lists and that will attempt to match your qualifications with those vacancies for a nominal fee. Personal contacts are often very effective in securing a position. Don't hesitate to call friends and acquaintances who might be able to help you obtain interviews. They probably can't get you a job, but they may be aware of vacancies and whom you should contact. Contacting specific school districts directly is another way to determine what positions are available. Call, write, or visit the personnel office of the school districts in which you are interested. This will insure that you get current information directly from the school district.

Follow up your application

Regardless of which strategies you use, after sufficient time has elapsed remember to follow up your applications and interviews with phone calls and letters to inquire about the status of your application. The more personal the approach is, the more effective it will be. Phone calls are better than letters, and visits are more effective than phone calls. Many school districts don't know how many vacancies they will have until school opens in the fall, so don't give up too soon. This whole process sounds like hard work, and it is! Executing a campaign to find the teaching position you want takes effort, planning, and patience, but it also dramatically increases your chances of securing that position. It's worth your while.

All fifty states and the District of Columbia require public elementary and sec-ondary school teachers to be certified—that is, licensed to teach—by the de-partment of education in the state in which they work.* Traditionally, to qualify for certification, a teacher has had to complete an approved teacher education program. Besides conferring a bachelor's degree, which provides the necessary liberal arts background, teacher education programs also serve the state require-ment that prospective teachers take certain education courses. But in many states, the traditional route to certification—graduation from an approved teacher education program—is no longer the sole route to gaining a teaching certificate.

State license required to teach

Many states offer alternative routes; in 1990 thirty-three states were im-plementing some form of alternative certification procedure, with tremendous variation among these forms in the states.[13] For example, some states permit alternative certification routes only when there is a shortage of traditionally cer-tified teachers, whereas other states permit alternative routes only at the second-ary level. Still other states allow institutions of higher education to design alter-natives to their college-approved teacher education program. Very few states

Alternative certification routes

---

* Licensure and certification are terms often confused or misused. Licensure is a state respon-sibility, while certification is a professional designation. Frequently, however, the term certifi-cation, as in, "I'm going to get my certification to teach," is used when licensure is meant.

Rules for Effectively Updating Your Résumé

Résumés have one purpose: to get you an interview. The interview, not the résumé, leads to the job. Jobs come through people, not through paper. If you can get an in-terview any other way, skip the paperwork.

There is no right or wrong way to write a résumé, although some ways are more effective and sophisticated than others. All rules are broken in this business, some-times successfully. But each detail of the résumé-writing process should have your meticulous attention because people often are screened *out* on the basis of a poor letter and résumé. The following serve as guidelines and are based on books, articles, and the comments and prefer-ences of hundreds of employers.

1. Résumés should be copied, preferably by offset printing. This is important because it will make your résumé stand out as professional looking. It's not expensive—about $4 for 100 copies. The *copy*

of your résumé should always be accompanied by an *individually typed* cover letter.
2. Think of your résumé more as a piece of advertis-ing than as a comprehensive data sheet. Use wide margins and plenty of spacing to make it easy to skim.
3. A listing of coursework does not belong on the ré-sumé because it looks amateurish. If coursework is called for, send a transcript (or send a copy of your unofficial transcript).
4. Don't use a lot of dates or numbers that make the résumé hard to skim. Eliminate dates or place them at the end of a paragraph when describing experi-ence. Don't use them for headlines.
5. Use action verbs. Avoid using forms of "to be." Use verbs such as *initiated, created, instructed, de-veloped, supervised, managed, counseled, negoti-ated, maintained.*
6. Emphasize skills, especially those that transfer from one situation to another. The fact that you *co-ordinated* a fifth-grade field trip to Washington leads one to believe that you could coordinate other things as well.

have actually designed a certification path specifically for the growing number of adults who want to switch to teaching from other careers.

Generally, those certified through alternate means hold a bachelor's degree in the subject area they will teach and less than the normally required credit-hours in professional education courses. Often they are required to have at least a C+ college grade average and to have passed a basic skills test and often a test in a subject or specialty area. Alternative programs are a response to (1) teacher shortages and (2) the perception on the part of some lawmakers that courses in education contribute little and that subject-matter knowledge alone is necessary for beginning teachers.

The real differences among certification routes appear in what happens from the time one enters a program to the time one is granted a regular teaching certificate. The variations from state to state are enormous, ranging from granting full certification based on transcript and résumé analysis, to taking a few courses in professional education, to requiring a person to complete a traditional approved college teacher preparation program over time. For example, New Jersey's widely publicized program allows individuals with a baccalaureate degree to gain standard certification after a year of supervised practical experience in a classroom, successful performance on the NTE tests, and approximately two hundred hours of study in essential professional knowledge and skills. New

7. Forget your best prose. Use short, choppy phrases. Short is sweet.

8. Use positive words. Don't apologize for lack of experience or for weaknesses. This is not the place to hang out your dirty laundry. Be positive, capitalize on strengths, and leave out the negative or neutral words. If your health is "excellent," then don't say "not bad." Avoid negative prefixes or suffixes.

9. Résumés should be one or two pages. Never more. Anything longer is an autobiography, not a résumé.

10. Expound on your relevant experiences and condense descriptions of jobs or experiences that are not directly related to the work you're seeking. This means that you slant your résumé to the type of job you are seeking. Hence, you will need more than one résumé if you are applying for different types of jobs.

11. Make every word count. Use the K.I.S.S. system of writing: *Keep It Short and Simple.*

12. Omit "professional objective" or "job objective" unless you know exactly what it is and are closed to all other possibilities. Your job objective doesn't add that much to the résumé, but it can serve to screen you out. The cover letter is the best place to detail your objectives.

13. List your telephone number, including area code. Employers usually call to set up an interview.

14. At the bottom of your résumé, write: "Credentials and references available upon request." Have prospective employers request your credentials from you, not from your placement office. Don't list your references on your résumé.

15. Proofread your résumé. Then have a friend (or better, a professional proofreader) proofread your résumé. Even the pros have been known to send out résumés with humorous and embarrassing mistakes.

John William Zehring, "How to Get Another Teaching Job and What to Do If You Can't." Reprinted by special permission of *Learning*, The Magazine for Creative Teaching, February 1978. 1978 by Pitman Learning, Inc.

York, on the other hand, requires the individual to be enrolled in an approved college teacher education program leading toward certification, beginning the semester following employment.

How successful are these alternative certification programs? Although thirty-three states had some form of alternative certification option by 1990, only about twelve thousand teachers in the entire nation had been certified through alternative routes in the five years after 1985. That's about 0.5 percent of the 2.4 million teachers now working in public elementary and secondary schools, and only about 1 percent of new hires between 1985 and 1990.[14] Formal evaluation studies of alternative certification programs have been few and have sometimes been conducted by persons with vested interests in the outcomes. More objective evaluations are currently being conducted by reputable researchers, and the outcomes of these studies should be known in a few years. One positive feature of alternative certification programs is that they seem to attract minorities more than do traditional teacher preparation programs. Twenty-seven percent of all alternate-route teachers hired between 1985 and 1990 were from minorities.[15]

On the subject of alternative certification programs, a tension exists between those who want to break teacher education's monopoly in preparing new teachers and professional educators who believe that completion of an approved teacher education program is the public's best guarantee that a teacher is "safe

TYPICAL QUESTIONS ASKED DURING JOB INTERVIEWS

Most interviews follow a simple question-and-answer routine. Your ability to communicate effectively with a stranger in a stressful situation is of critical importance. Being prepared is the best way you can avoid a disorganized answer. Sometimes the interviewer plays "devil's advocate," disagreeing with a position you may articulate to see if you will back down from your position in order to be acceptable to an authority figure. You should be aware of this possibility; be prepared to assess your position straightforwardly, and then stand behind it. Avoid "waffling." Questions you may be asked include:

- Why have you chosen teaching as a career?

- Why do you want to work in this school district?

- What age level of children do you prefer? Why?

- What has your college preparation done to help you prepare for a teaching position?

- Do you have (multicultural, urban, learning problems) teaching experience?

- What do you remember most about your own education?

- What are your strengths and/or weaknesses as a potential teacher?

- What are some characteristics of a well-managed classroom?

- What are some examples of rules you would have in your classroom?

- What is your philosophy of education?

- How would you handle gifted/handicapped/disadvantaged students in your classroom?

- How do you motivate students to learn?

- Tell me about your student-teaching experience.

- What would you do for the first day of class?

- What do you see yourself doing over the course of the next several years to improve your abilities as a professional?

- Do you have any questions for me? (Have some!)

to practice.'' The variety of alternative certification programs that exists across the various states is testimony to the differing views on how teachers should be prepared.

Increased requirements for certification

Since the mid-1980s many states have increased the requirements for certification, adding test requirements such as the NTE or, in some cases, state-developed minimum competency tests of basic skills. Sometimes prospective teachers are examined on their content-area knowledge. Increasingly, competency testing is used to screen candidates for certification. In addition, some states require U.S. citizenship, some an oath of allegiance, and several a health certificate. And some local school districts may require teacher applicants to take written examinations or meet other requirements to be hired.

Differences among states. . .

Because the requirements for certification do differ from state to state, you should become aware of the requirements for the state in which you will seek employment. Someone in your placement office or in your school of education most likely will be able to acquaint you with certification requirements. Your education library will probably contain books that list the certification requirements for all the states. Should you not be successful there, you can call or write directly to the teacher certification office in the states in which you are interested. A directory of state teacher certification offices in the United States is listed in the Appendix at the end of this book. A number of states have reciprocal

---

During a job interview you will answer many questions. But to gain the information that will help you choose among the jobs offered to you, you will also need to ask questions. Remember, you are interviewing the prospective employer, too. Before you accept a position, you will need to know about:

The school district—

- What are the characteristics of the student population?
- What is the size of the district?

The curriculum—

- What courses are offered in your discipline?
- What classroom resources (texts, AV materials) are available?

The students—

- What is the typical class size?
- What are the characteristics of the students you would teach?

The instructional assignment—

- Why is this position available? What other assignments are included with the job? How are teachers evaluated?

The faculty—

- How many new teachers are hired each year?
- How many faculty are there in your department? In your building?

Salary and fringe benefits—

- What is the district salary schedule?
- Is medical insurance provided?
- Is graduate study reimbursed?

These are just a few suggestions. For a more complete list, see Jan E. Kilby, ''Critical Information to Know about School Districts,'' *The ASCUS Annual: A Job Search Handbook for Educators, 1987* (Addison, Ill.: Association for School, College and University Staffing, 1986), p. 7; and C. Bruce Johnston, ''Practice Makes Perfect: Sample Interview Questions,'' *The ASCUS Annual: A Job Search Handbook for Educators, 1991* (Evanston, Ill.: Association for School, College and University Staffing, 1990, p. 18. The above questions were also taken from these sources.

There is always a demand for good teachers even in areas such as art education in which jobs are relatively scarce.

(*Michael Siluk/The Image Works*)

agreements to accept one another's certificates as valid. If you move from one state to another, you may want to check whether your teaching certificate is accepted by the state to which you are moving.

Besides the basic certificates for teaching at the elementary and secondary levels, many states require different certificates, or endorsements, for such specialization areas as special education, bilingual education, and kindergarten. If, as you gain experience, you want to move out of teaching into a supervisory, administrative, or counseling position, you will probably need a special certificate.

. . . and specialization areas

If it is at all possible for you to be certified or endorsed in more than one teaching area, you would be wise to do so. Adding a second field of certification will make you more attractive to prospective employers, particularly in smaller school districts, where less flexibility exists in hiring specialists who teach in only one area. If you are going to be an elementary school teacher, having an additional certification in reading, special education, early childhood education, or bilingual education would be very worthwhile. Another way of increasing your appeal to prospective employers would be to take a major or minor in mathematics, one of the sciences, or instructional technology. Elementary school teachers with expertise in these areas are in short supply. If you are going to

Pursue more than one certification area

teach at the secondary level, you can broaden your appeal b̶ by
to teach in two or more subject fields. For example, if you are a S̶p̶
minor in French; if you are a chemistry major, minor in physics or ma̶
Any doubling up of teaching fields will work to your advantage.

In summary, individual states use certification requirements to assure
public that the teachers teaching the youth of our society have been adequate̶ly
prepared. Certification requirements should present you with little difficulty as
long as the teacher education institution you attend meets the general regulations
of the state department of education and as long as you maintain contact with
the college official responsible for coordinating the education program with the
state certification requirements.

IF YOU DON'T TEACH, WHAT THEN?

Suppose that despite all your job-seeking efforts you are unsuccessful in
finding the position you want. Or suppose that after teaching a few years you
decide that teaching is not for you. What will you be prepared to do after receiving training as a teacher? Has your training equipped you with skills that are
in demand in fields outside education? For many different reasons, a substantial number of teachers each year find themselves looking for jobs outside
education.

Teaching skills
transferable to other jobs

What generic or transferable skills are you likely to have developed in your
preparation as a teacher that are needed in most businesses and professions?
Since teachers are constantly making lesson plans based on certain objectives
and activities, you have undoubtedly developed certain planning and decision-
making skills, along with the ability to organize and implement these plans on
a daily and long-term basis. You have learned to work under pressure and

DIALOGUE

Kevin: I'm a little disturbed by these alternative certification programs.

Jim: Me too. There is more to good teaching than knowing your subject matter. Now is the wrong time to
abandon courses in professional education.

Kevin: You're absolutely right. Now, more than ever before, we have a base of knowledge about what constitutes effective teaching. Teachers should learn that.

Jim: Not only that. They should learn it before they start
teaching. Arts and sciences classes, as important as
they are, don't prepare people to manage classrooms,
to use technology for instruction, to assist exceptional

children, to assess learning, to learn how children develop intellectually and emotionally . . . .

Kevin: I agree. Even if you could learn some of those
skills on the job, how many students should have to
suffer through your apprenticeship?

Jim: And that list doesn't include the ethics of the profession and principles of effective practice in teaching
reading, writing, math, science, and so on.

Kevin: If teaching is ever going to gain professional status, teachers will have to be prepared as professionals.
We don't assume that people with degrees in biology
or chemistry are qualified to be doctors.

Jim: And I don't think we should assume they're qualified to be teachers, either.

meet deadlines. You have learned to keep accurate and usable records. By keeping track of each student's work and tests in order to evaluate his or her performance, you have developed a capability of record keeping. You are familiar with libraries and audio-visual resources and have knowledge of research skills.

Teachers are also required to develop human relations skills, to relate to both children and adults. One of the major reasons why many people choose to enter teacher education programs is that they enjoy being around and working with people. In this regard you have probably developed and will continue to develop further sensitivity and empathy for other people. Communication skills are developed and refined in teacher education programs and are essential in almost any job that requires human interaction. Being able to manage groups of people in a flexible manner is a skill needed in many types of jobs. In short, many of the skills required by teachers are also required for other types of work. Naturally, additional training may be necessary, depending on the exact type of work. Now let's examine some alternative careers.

Other educational jobs

In addition to teaching, a number of educational occupations exist, including librarian, counselor, supervisor, administrator, and school psychologist. Although those roles don't involve full-time teaching of children, they usually require a minimum of two or three years of teaching experience and additional certification. All these roles are important in the educational enterprise, should you decide that you are still interested in education but that elementary or secondary school teaching is not for you. You could also investigate employment in early childhood education and day care centers. Because early childhood education is a growing field, numerous new occupations are developing within it, such as reading specialists to help diagnose learning abilities and curriculum specialists to help plan the studies. State, local, and federal government agencies need researchers, planners, evaluators, and many others to administer the growing number of early childhood projects they fund. Government agencies, such as the U.S. Department of Education, hire many former teachers to help administer projects that are funded by the federal government.

Training and development in corporations

Many large businesses conduct extensive training programs for their employees and require the services of people who can design and implement training programs. Many people who have been trained as teachers find their way into such jobs. During 1985 some 300,000 people were employed (full- and part-time) in training and development in the United States.*

Recreation and leisure jobs

The field of recreation and leisure activities attracts many people trained as teachers. Workers in this field plan, organize, and direct individual and group activities that help people enjoy their leisure hours. They work with people of various ages and socioeconomic groups, the sick and the well, and the emotionally and physically handicapped. Employment settings range from wilderness to

---

* The American Society for Training and Development, 600 Maryland Ave., S.W., Washington, DC 20024, can provide more information about corporate career opportunities for teachers.

Being a librarian is one of the many educational careers available besides classroom teaching.

(*Elizabeth Crews/The Image Works*)

rural to suburban and urban, including the inner city. Example of recreation program jobs include playground leaders; program specialists in dance, drama, karate, tennis, the arts, and other physical activities; recreation center directors; therapeutic recreation specialists; camp counselors and wilderness leaders; senior citizen program leaders; civilian special services directors in the armed forces; and industrial recreation directors. Recreation workers held about 186,000 jobs in 1988, not including summer workers. The majority worked in local, public tax-supported agencies such as municipal and county park and recreation departments.[16]

Jobs in publishing

The publishing industry affords numerous job opportunities for education-oriented writers, editors, and salespeople. If you have good writing and analytic skills, you might be interested in helping develop or edit textbooks for use in elementary and secondary schools and in colleges. If you enjoy meeting people and traveling, being a textbook sales representative might appeal to you. Another growing area is the development of computer software related to education. The need for good computer programs that students and teachers can use for instructional purposes means that jobs in developing these programs are available for persons with educational and computer programming backgrounds.

Training as a teacher is also important for work related to professional organizations such as the National Education Association and the American Federation of Teachers, Phi Delta Kappa and Kappa Delta Pi, and the National Association of Mathematics Teachers and the National Council for the Social Studies. These organizations, and others like them, hire people for field work, writing, research, and other staff positions.

A FINAL WORD

This chapter has introduced you to the uncertainty surrounding the question "Will teachers be in short supply during the 1990s?" Those who make projections do not agree. As we have seen, the relative supply and demand of teachers varies by field and geographic area. And alternative certification programs could partially offset the predicted shortages resulting from insufficient enrollments in teacher education programs.

Many indicators, however, point to a great demand for teachers in the coming years. Impending retirements in the current teaching force and increased school enrollments resulting from a "baby boomlet" are already creating a demand that teacher education programs cannot meet. No longer are women's career choices skewed toward teaching, nursing, or secretarial work. As a result, a smaller percentage of women choose to teach. And even the recent modest enrollment gains at teacher education institutions can't keep pace with the increasing needs in the schools. The National Center for Education Statistics makes these predictions about the need for new teachers in public elementary and secondary schools: In 1988, 155,000 new teachers were hired; in 1992, 190,000 will be needed; and between 1993 and [2001], an average of 217,000 new teachers will be needed each year.[17]

However, numbers are not the only issue. Does the teaching profession attract the brightest and the best among college graduates? Many critics, citing trends in SAT scores and the academic backgrounds of teacher education graduates, answer "no." But we repeat: there has never been a surplus of good teachers. If you and your credentials are good, you will be in demand, no matter what the job market may be at a particular moment. Preparing yourself well for school districts' needs, especially gaining expertise in more than one teaching field, can expand your job options and make you more attractive to prospective employers.

America has become an education-oriented society. We are realizing that reaching our individual and national goals depends on achieving high levels of education. This means we are committed to more and better education, to lifelong learning in and out of schools. Over sixty years ago, President Calvin Coolidge said, "The business of America is business." Today and into the future, the business of America is education.

Teaching is where the action is and will continue to be!

Discussion Questions

1. What is the present and projected teacher supply in the field that currently interests you most? In the geographic area? How do you expect that to affect your ability to find a position you want?

2. Are you prepared to leave your current location to find a teaching position? Are you willing to teach in an urban school? A rural school? A private school?

3. Is the average beginning teacher's salary about what you expected? Is it sufficient money for you to maintain a lifestyle that is comfortable for you?

4. What ways can you think of to increase your chances of being hired when you are ready to teach?

5. What are some effective job-hunting strategies?

6. Do you have any opinions about the alternative certification programs currently offered in some states?

7. Are there any education-related occupations other than teaching that might be of interest to you?

For Further Reading

The ASCUS Annual: A Job Search Handbook for Educators. Evanston, IL.: Association for School, College and University Staffing.

> An annual publication designed to assist both new and experienced educators in their job searches, and the single most important reference on this topic. The *Annual* is usually distributed through career planning and placement offices in colleges and universities, but it may also be obtained from the ASCUS office, 1600 Dodge Ave., S-330, Evanston, IL 60201-3451, 708-864-1999.

Bastress, Frances. *Teachers in New Careers: Stories of Successful Transitions.* Cranston, R.I.: Carroll Press, 1984.

> Accounts by twenty-one former teachers, providing details about their experiences as teachers and the strategies they used to make successful career changes.

Beard, Marna. *Alternative Careers for Teachers.* 2d ed. New York: Arco Publishing, 1985.

> A very useful book for teachers considering a career switch.

Bolles, Richard Nelson. *What Color Is Your Parachute?* Berkeley, Calif.: Ten Speed Press, 1991.

> A practical manual for job hunters and career changers. Updated yearly.

Fine, Janet. *Opportunities in Teaching Careers.* Lincolnwood, Ill.: National Textbook Company, 1989.

> A paperback that explores job opportunities in education.

Zehring, John William. "How to Get Another Teaching Job and What to Do If You Can't." *Learning* 6 (February 1978): 44, 46–51.

> An excellent, brief article about how to find a teaching job and, if you don't, what other options are open to you.

References for Locating Sources of Job Vacancies

- *Academic Journal: The Educators' Employment Magazine.* The Academic Journal, Box 392, Newtown, CT 06470. Published biweekly.

- *Affirmative Action Register.* 8356 Olive Boulevard, St. Louis, MO 63132. Published monthly.

- *Boarding Schools.* National Association of Independent Schools and Colleges and Secondary School Admissions Test Board, 75 Federal Street, Boston, MA 03220. Published annually.

- *Career Guide to Professional Associations: A Directory of Organizations by Occupational Field.* Cranston, R.I.: Carroll Press, 1980. A detailed alphabetical directory of more than 2,500 professional organizations by occupational field.

- *Chronicle of Higher Education.* 1255 Twenty-third Street, N.W., Washington, DC 20037. An independent newspaper published weekly, except during the last two weeks in August and the last two weeks in December.

- Colgate, Craig, Jr., and Patricia Broida, (eds.). *National Trade and Professional Associations of the United States and Canada and Labor Unions.* Washington, D.C.: Columbia Books. Published annually and contains descriptions of 6,300 associations, 550 of which are education-related.

- *Directory of Public School Systems in the U.S.* Association for School, College and University Staffing, 1600 Dodge Avenue, S-330, Evanston, IL 60201–3451. Published annually.

- *Education Week.* 4301 Connecticut Avenue, N.W., Suite 250, Washington, DC 20008. An independent newspaper published forty times per year.

- Elliott, Norman F. (ed.). *Patterson's American Education.* Educational Directories, Inc., Box 199, Mount Prospect, IL 60056.

- *Encyclopedia of Associations.* Detroit: Gale Research. Published annually and contains over 14,000 associations, 930 of which are education related.

- *Handbook of Private Schools.* Boston: Porter Sargent. Published annually.

- *NEA Today.* National Education Association, 1201 Sixteenth Street, N.W., Washington, DC 20036. Published nine times a year.

Notes

1. Martin Frankel and Peter Stone, *New Teachers in the Job Market, 1987 Update,* (Washington, D.C.: U.S. Department of Education, National Center for Education Statistics, OERI, July 1990), p. 3.

2. Debra E. Gerald and William J. Hussar, *Projections of Education Statistics to 2001* (Washington, D.C.: U.S. Department of Education, National Center for Education Statistics, OERI, December 1990), pp. 58–60.

3. C. Emily Feistritzer, *Profiles of Teachers in the U.S.—1990* (Washington, D.C.: National Center for Education Information, 1990), p. 11.

4. Debra C. Gerald and William J. Hussar. *Projections of Education Statistics to 2001,* p. 58.

5. Laurence T. Ogle (Ed.), *The Condition of Education 1990, vol. 1* (Washington, D.C.: National Center for Education Statistics, 1990), p. 62.

6. C. Emily Feistritzer, *Profile of Teachers in the U.S.—1990,* p. 9.

7. *The ASCUS Annual: A Job Search Handbook for Educators, 1991* (Evanston, Ill.: Association for School, College and University Staffing, 1990), pp. 6–7.

8. Sharon A. Babbit and Frank H. Johnson, *Key Statistics for Public and Private Elementary and Secondary Education: School Year 1990-91, Early Estimates* (Washington, D.C.: U.S. Department of Education, National Center for Education Statistics, December 1990), pp. 4–5.

9. James Coleman, T. Hoffer, and S. Kilgore, *Public and Private Schools,* Report to the National Center for Education Statistics, 1981.

10. National Education Association, "Estimates of School Statistics, 1990–91" (Washington, D.C.: NEA, 1991), p. 17.

11. *Survey and Analysis of Salary Trends 1987 and 1991* (Washington, D.C.: American Federation of Teachers, July 1987 and 1991); 1987 figures reported by telephone conversation, and 1990 figures appear on page   of the 1991 edition.

12. Most of the ideas in this section are taken from John William Zehring, "How to Get Another Teaching Job and What to Do If You Can't," *Learning* 6 (February 1978): 44, 46–51.

13. C. Emily Feistritzer, *Alternative Teacher Certification: A State-by-State Analysis, 1990* (Washington, D.C.: National Center for Education Information, 1990), p. 44.

14. C. Emily Feistritzer, "Breaking the Teaching Monopoly," *The Wall Street Journal*, June 29, 1990, p. A12.

15. C. Emily Feistritzer, *Profile of Teachers in the U.S.—1990*, p. 10.

16. *Occupation Outlook Handbook, 1990–91 Edition* (Washington, D.C.: U.S. Department of Labor, 1990), p. 119. Information about careers in parks, recreation, and leisure services is available from National Recreation and Park Association, Division of Professional Services, 3101 Park Center Drive, Alexandria, VA 22302.

17. Debra E. Gerald and William J. Hussar, *Projections of Education Statistics to 2001*, p. 58.

FOUN

J ust as the subjects of anatomy and chemistry are essential to the practice of medicine, so there are areas of organized knowledge that are essential to the practice of education. These areas, called the foundations of education, provide the intellectual underpinnings of professional practice.

This section covers several of these key areas: philosophy, history, the law, politics, and finance. These, in addition to the subjects of psychology and sociology, make up what is known as the foundations of education. Truly professional teachers ground their daily practice in the wisdom and knowledge gleaned from these foundational areas.

3

What Are the Philosophical Foundations of American Education?

CHAPTER PREVIEW

This chapter is about the role of philosophy, a key foundational discipline in the work of the teacher. Philosophy is described, four different philosophies are outlined, and their applications to the classroom are discussed.

This chapter emphasizes that:

● Philosophical knowledge has a fundamental role in clarifying questions of education.

● Philosophical thought has distinct characteristics. Four branches of philosophy—metaphysics,

epistemology, axiology, and logic—relate rather directly to the work of the teacher.

● Four philosophies of education—perennialism, progressivism, essentialism, and existentialism—not only are abstract systems of thought but also have practical implications for the classroom teacher.

● Teachers need to have a philosophy to guide their practice.

A medical student who wants intensely to be a surgeon, has marvelous hands, and displays a high level of technical skill, but who does not know how the body functions or what constitutes health, can hardly be called a doctor.

An aspirant to the ministry who loves to work with people and possesses a marvelous gift of speaking, but who has no opinion about humanity's relationship to God or about the purpose of religion, can hardly be said to be suited for religious ministry.

And a person who has a great desire to be with young people, wants to live the life of a teacher, and possesses great technical skill, but who lacks purpose and direction, is hardly a teacher.

These three individuals are like wind-up toys, moving along blindly without a plan or an intellectual compass. And although this image may be somewhat dramatic, there *are* people who prepare for professions without getting to the core meaning of what those professions are all about. Such thoughtless and robot-like behavior can cause problems in any occupation or profession, but particularly in teaching. What kind of a teacher can someone be who does not have a view of what people are and a vision of what they can become? Who cannot clearly define right and wrong in human behavior? Who doesn't recognize what is important and what is unimportant or can't distinguish clear thinking from sloppy thinking? The person who would take on the responsibility for educating the young without having seriously wrestled with these questions is, to say the least, dangerous, for he or she is going against the very grain of what it means to be a teacher. In fact, it is safe to say that such a person is not a teacher, but a technician.

Philosophy as foundation

This chapter introduces you to philosophy, one of the foundational subjects in education, which, along with history and psychology and, to some degree, economics, political science, sociology, anthropology, and the law, forms the intellectual underpinning upon which the practice of education rests. The image of two houses, one built on sand and the other on a sturdy foundation, may help here. The teacher who grounds his or her teaching in a well-thought-out philosophy will be able to withstand shifting pressures and strong controversies. However, the teacher who has based his or her practice on intellectual sand will be buffeted about.

Philosophy and the educator

Many people use the word *philosophy* casually. We have all heard people talk in vague language about heady issues and then say offhandedly, "Well, I'm just philosophizing," as if that were another term for simply thinking out loud. In addition, some people debase the meaning of the term *philosophy* by speaking of their "philosophy of education" when they are merely giving their ill-considered opinions on whether children should have recess in the morning or in the afternoon. This trivialization of the concept of philosophy is unfortunate, because a philosophy of education should be very precious to the teacher. Schools attempt to do many things for children, from teaching them to get along with others to helping them develop their physical skills. But, at heart, schools are teaching the process of thinking and are attempting to put children in touch with the best ideas that humankind has produced. The study of philosophy, therefore, aids the teacher in systematic and careful reflection on issues and questions that are central to education. It also assists the teacher in considering what is known about such basic concepts as *learning, teaching, being educated, knowledge,* and *the good life*.

WHAT IS PHILOSOPHY?

Love of wisdom

The word *philosophy* is made up of two root words, one being "love (*philo*)" and the other "wisdom (*sophos*)." Philosophy, then, is the *love of wisdom*. Although all people do not love wisdom in the same way or to the same degree, we humans are all questioning beings—seekers of answers. As children we are preoccupied with such lofty questions as "How do I get less veggies and more dessert?" We progress to such questions as "How does the teacher always know

Philosophical issues and questions affect the everyday life of students.
(*Elizabeth Crews*)

Fundamental questions

Sources of our philosophy

Concern with meaning of words

to call on me when I don't have the answers?" and "What do I need to do to get a decent grade in geometry?" and "Which is the best college for me?" Ultimately, we may move to more advanced levels of questioning: "Who am I?" "What is the purpose of life and what am I doing here?" "What really does it mean to be a good person?"

Until relatively recently—about one hundred years ago (prior to the growth of the social sciences)—most people relied on religion and philosophy for answers to these questions. Whereas religion is said to represent the revealed word of God, philosophy represents a human attempt to sort out by reason the fundamental questions of existence. Many of the great thinkers of Western civilization—Plato, Aristotle, St. Thomas Aquinas, René Descartes, Jean-Jacques Rousseau, Immanuel Kant, John Locke, John Stuart Mill, William James, and John Dewey—have been philosophers. Because education has always been a central human concern, philosophers have thought and written a great deal about education and the questions surrounding it.

Only a few people in our society are professional philosophers, who earn their daily bread (usually a rather meager fare) by pursuing answers to the fundamental questions of life. However, all of us who wrestle with such questions as "Who am I?" and "What am I doing with my life?" are engaged in philosophical activity. Although there is a distinction between the few professional philosophers and the great number of us who are amateurs, the questions we ask and the answers we glean are of great importance and usually have a major impact on the practical affairs of our lives and on how we choose to spend our life force.

The very practical decision of whether to become a teacher or a real estate broker, or whatever, almost always has its roots in a person's philosophy of life. In developing a philosophy, we draw on many influences: our experiences in life, our religious views, and our reading of literature and history and current events. A major difference between professionals and amateurs, however, lies in the precision of their methods.

Philosophy is an extremely pure and abstract science. Philosophers do not work with test tubes or white rats. They do not use telescopes or microscopes. They do not fly off to remote societies to observe the natives. The method or process of philosophers is questioning and reasoning; their product is thought— often very wise thought. Basically, philosophers are concerned with the interpretation of meaning. They want to understand the real meaning of words.

We have said that "humans are all questioning beings." A philosopher, to understand more fully the meaning of our statement and thus to be able to judge its value, would want to determine what we mean by *questioning*. Do we mean that to be a human one must put questions to others? Or that humans must question themselves? Are the questions simple questions ("Am I hungry now?") or lofty ones ("What is the most significant way I can spend my life?"). A philosopher would ask a similar set of questions about what we mean by the word *being*. The philosopher's method, then, is to ask questions to get at the real meaning of things, believing that the answer is often less important than the question, because the question often brings accepted practice under new scrutiny.

Although some philosophical discussion and writing involves technical language, it generally uses "plain language," the ordinary language of people. However, philosophers try to be extremely clear and careful about their use of terms. They do not want their ultimate prey—meaning—to be lost in a thicket of fuzzy language. Also, philosophers engage in a dialectical process: they proceed from raising questions to proposing answers to examining carefully the implications of those answers. This process usually leads to more questions, which are probed in turn. The philosopher Robert Zend could have been speaking for the majority of his colleagues, and at the same time kidding them, when he said, "Being a philosopher, I have a problem for every solution."

Because philosophers deal with the abstract and use pure reason as a tool, one might think that philosophy is a dull and quiet subject and that a philosopher is a peaceful scholar who sits in a field and gazes abstractedly into the distance. Perhaps it would be more accurate to envision the philosopher as sitting in a mine field or a briar patch. People occasionally turn against and challenge the philosopher. As the great ancient Greek philosopher Socrates learned, question asking is not always well received: it is seen by some people as "rocking the boat." In Socrates' case, his fellow citizens were made so uncomfortable by his questioning that they forced him either to capitulate intellectually or, as he ultimately chose, to take his own life.

Although it seems that philosophy deals with simple issues in simple language, behind the philosopher's questions are raging debates about profound issues that can have far-reaching implications: for example, the question "What is a human?" hides other questions, such as "When can a fetus be aborted, if it should be at all?" and "What rights do severely disabled persons have?" and on and on.

In the first century A.D., the philosopher Epictetus went to the heart of the discipline when he wrote, "Here is the beginning of philosophy: a recognition of the conflicts between men, a search for their cause, a condemnation of mere opinion . . . and the discovery of a standard of judgment." The American philosopher William James said, "There is only one thing a philosopher can be relied on to do, and that is to contradict other philosophers." Nevertheless, it is from these intellectual conflicts and contradictions that much of humanity's wisdom has emerged.

THE TERRAIN OF PHILOSOPHY

Philosophy covers a large range of intellectual turf. The terrain of philosophy is divided into several areas, including four that are particularly important to the teacher: metaphysics, epistemology, axiology, and logic. These terms may be foreign to you, but we assure you that these four branches of philosophy are central to the educative process and, in fact, speak directly to the work of the teacher.

Metaphysics

Metaphysics involves the attempt to explain the nature of the real world, the nature of existence. Metaphysics tries to answer the question "What is real?" It tries to answer this question without appealing to the authority of religion or revelation. Further, metaphysics is more akin to a theoretical than to an empirical science. The metaphysician characteristically believes that to answer questions regarding such matters as the nature of humanity and the universe, simply collecting data and attempting to formulate statistically significant generalizations is not adequate. From most metaphysical perspectives, the nature of humanity cannot be captured by measuring or counting. A person is more than the sum of his or her height and weight, IQ and SAT scores, and other "vital" statistics.

In probing the nature of reality the metaphysician asks a whole array of questions: "Does life have meaning?" "Are human beings free or totally determined?" "Is there a purpose to life?" "Is there a set of enduring principles that guide the operation of the universe?" "Can these principles be known?" "Is there no such thing as stability but, rather, an ever-changing world?"

These abstract questions are ones that the educator cannot dismiss. Ultimately, the purpose of education is to explain reality to the young. The curriculum and how we teach it represents one statement of what that reality is. Although teachers may not actually be metaphysicians, they do take a stand on metaphysical questions. If a teacher decides to teach because he or she believes the most important thing in the universe is a human mind, that very real career decision is driven by a metaphysical view: the importance of an individual person. The people on school boards also take stands on metaphysical issues. Such questions are woven into the fabric of schooling. Whether or not a particular school system emphasizes vocational education depends very much on someone's decision about the nature and purpose of humanity.

Epistemology

What is truth?

Epistemology deals with questions regarding knowledge and knowing. The epistemologist seeks the true nature of knowing and asks such questions as "What is truth?" and "Is truth elusive, always changing and always dependent on the truth seeker's particulars of time, place, and angle of vision?" Some people, whom we call *agnostics,* are convinced that knowledge of ultimate realities is an empty hope. Some, whom we call *skeptics,* reject this position and hold instead to a questioning attitude toward our capacity to really know the truths of existence.

How do we acquire knowledge?

Epistemology deals not only with the nature of truth, but also with the way in which we know reality, and the way in which knowledge is acquired. There are a variety of ways by which we can know, and each of these ways has its advocates and detractors. Among the ways of knowing are: by divine revelation, by authority, through personal intuition, from our own senses, from our own powers of reasoning, and through experimentation.

Questions concerning knowledge and knowing are, almost by definition, of great concern to the teacher. The epistological question "How do you know this or that?" goes to the heart of teaching methodology. If a teacher wants her students to have a concept of democracy, how does she proceed? Does she explain the characteristics of different forms of government, such as monarchy and oligarchy, and then the characteristics of democracy? Or does she take a more

Philosophy is systematic reflection upon the common experience of mankind.
— ROBERT MAYNARD HUTCHINS —

Creationist controversy

hands-on approach and have the students do a role-playing exercise during which one student is appointed class dictator and, in order to prepare them to see the value of democracy, the rest must obey the student-dictator's orders.

Besides there being different ways of teaching knowledge, there are different ways of knowing. The student who has only read about the virtues of democracy "knows" it in an epistomologically different way than the student who has been bullied and harassed for several days by the teacher-appointed dictator.

Even if the teacher is not particularly interested in these issues, other people are interested, and sometimes they are also interested in knowing the teacher's viewpoints. Of paramount concern to many people is the question of the true origin of humankind and how one knows it. This issue is sometimes called the *creationist controversy*. One faction insists that the public schools should present the evidence of our origin that is given in the Book of Genesis, which we know by divine revelation. Another viewpoint insists that the way to know the truth of the origin of the human race is through the scientific theory of evolution. So behind this ongoing educational and social conflict is a fundamental question of epistemology.

Because there are many different things for people to know, and because these things differ so greatly in fundamental character, it seems unlikely that there is one, and only one, method of knowing. In fact, it is becoming increasingly clear that individuals differ in their degree of comfort with different methods of learning. Much of the teacher's work is helping the student find the most effective way of knowing for a particular question.

Axiology

Axiology focuses on the nature of values, inquiring about the various kinds of values and which of those values are most worth pursuing. As human beings, we search for the correct and most effective way to live. In doing so, we are engaging questions of values. Of course, different people look at life and come up with very different sets of values. For instance, hedonists believe in seeking pleasure and living for the moment. On the other hand, stoics have an austere

What is a value? way of looking at life and seek to be unaffected by pleasure or pain. Many people answer the question, "What is a value?" from a religious perspective, asserting that God gives value to life, and thus makes existence meaningful.

Most people would agree that schools have a dual responsibility: to make people smart and to make them good. To the degree that teachers accept the second function, they are grappling with an axiological issue. In fact, teachers are intimately involved with questions of values. Young people are seeking ways to live lives that are worthwhile. Also, society expects a teacher to help children establish values that will help them both as individuals and as contributing members of society. Values such as honesty, respect for other people, and fairness are necessary if we are to live together in harmony. But although there is a large core of values that a majority of people agree on, such as respecting others and avoiding violence in the settling of disputes, there are other value issues that will always be controversial. Sexual behavior, capital punishment, and abortion are examples of contemporary social issues that involve a wide range of viewpoints about what is right.

Ethics and aesthetics Axiology has two subtopics: ethics and aesthetics. *Ethics* takes us into the realm of values that relate to "good" and "bad" behavior, examining morality and rules of conduct. Once teaching children how to deal with issues of good and bad and right and wrong was the primary purpose of schooling. In recent decades the pendulum has swung the other way and schools have been much more concerned with factual knowledge and skills than with ethical knowledge. There are, however, many signs that schools are being called back to help children deal with ethical issues.[1]

Not only does the subject of ethics teach us how we can intellectually ascertain the "right" thing to do, but it often is used to help us establish a particular set of standards, such as a code of ethics. In Chapter 5, "What Are the Ethical and Legal Issues Facing Teachers?" we will give particular attention to these issues.

Aesthetics deals with questions of values regarding beauty and art. Many discussions about the value of a particular film or book or work of art are attempts to come to some aesthetic judgment on the value of the work.

Logic *Logic* is the branch of philosophy that deals with reasoning. One of the fundamental qualities that distinguishes human beings from brutes is that humans can *think*. The great technological progress that we have made in the last few thou- **The human ability to think** sand years is largely attributable to our progress in thinking. We have learned not only how to think clearly but how to communicate effectively with one another. Logic focuses on reasoning and modes of arguing that bring us to valid conclusions. The pursuit of logic is an attempt to think clearly and avoid vagueness and contradictions. Certain rules of logic have been identified, and they constitute the core of this branch of philosophy.

A primary task of the schools is to help children think clearly and communicate logically. There are two types of reasoning that are commonly taught in schools: deductive and inductive. In the first, *deductive reasoning,* the teacher **Deductive reasoning** presents a general proposition and then illustrates it with a series of particulars.

The most highly developed form of this is the classic method of the syllogism. In a syllogism, one makes two statements, and a third statement, a conclusion, is *deduced* or drawn from them. For instance:

> All human beings are mortal.
> I am a human being.
> Therefore, I am mortal.

Again, in deductive reasoning, such as in this example, the general proposition, an abstract concept, is followed by a factual statement, which in turn leads to a new factual statement and the creation of new knowledge. Or, in October a 5th grade teacher writes on the board:

> All trees which shed their leaves at the end of a growing season are deciduous trees.

As a two week project, Mrs. Wells asks her class to observe and record data about the trees that surround their school. For two weeks, the students observe the three dozen maple trees shed their leaves during the fall at the end of the trees' growing season. The teacher then rewrites her earlier sentence on the board:

> All trees which shed their leaves at the end of a growing season are deciduous trees.

And, using their observational data (and a little intellectual nudging from Mrs. Wells), the students complete the syllogism:

> Maple tree shed their leaves at the end of the growing season.
> Therefore, maple trees are deciduous.

The students over the next week try to identify types of trees which fit the deciduous classification.

Much of what a teacher does in school is helping children both acquire the intellectual habits of deductive thinking and expand their storehouse of knowledge through this process.

Inductive reasoning works in the opposite fashion. The teacher sets forth particulars, from which a general proposition is derived or "induced." For instance, after presenting a series of specific examples of people engaging in reasoning activities, the teacher may claim that these are evidence for the general proposition that "people are reasoning beings." Or, the teacher may wish to lead the students to the discovery that water is essential to plant growth. Then she might give each child two similar plants (a different type of flora, from weeds to flowers, for each child) and then have each student daily feed one plant with water and leave the other plant without water. After ten days the teacher might have the students report the condition of their plants, and from all of these individual reports she might lead the students to generalize about the necessity of water to plant life.

Another example of deductive and inductive approaches to learning occurs each September in classrooms around the world. Each fall teachers go through

Inductive reasoning

the process of forming a new community, of transforming a group of individuals into a "class." One of the first things teachers do with this new community is work to establish a set of rules. This code of behavior and procedures is usually established in one or other of two ways. Take, for example, Mrs. Stutz and Mr. Kaya. On the first day of school, using the deductive method, Mrs. Stutz writes on the board several rules she has found effective over the years (e.g., "Everyone must be considerate of others."). Then she asks her third-graders for examples of being considerate and inconsiderate, and writes their answers on the board (e.g., "people yelling out instead of raising their hands" and "hogging all the construction paper" and "some kids not letting others play with the guinea pig"). Then Mrs. Stutz shows the students which examples are and are not able to be deduced from her rule.

Mr. Kaya, on the other hand, asks his sophomore mathematics class each September what kind of a classroom they think is most effective and satisfying. He then writes their suggestions on the board (e.g., "one where the smart kids do not get all the teacher's attention" and "one where yelling out answers isn't allowed"). If he doesn't find all the particulars he thinks are important, Mr. Kaya adds a few (e.g., "You have to do your own homework and you can't just copy someone else's homework assignments"). Then he asks the students to induce or reach some general rules from these particular suggestions (e.g., "Students must raise their hands before answering" and "Everyone does his or her own work").

One of the ongoing debates among educators is between advocates of deductive and inductive teaching. As is true for most controversial issues, good cases can be made for both sides of the argument. Both forms of reasoning are

Need for both needed. Both have different strengths and weaknesses. For instance, in the plant example, using induction to teach the simple concept "Living plants need water" means a good deal of work for the teacher. But the rewards can be great: the student who has closely observed his pet petunia shrivel up and die will hold that concept in a special way.

Logic, however, is not confined to inductive and deductive reasoning. To use logic means to think clearly, in many different ways. Teachers need logic in many aspects of their work, from trying to understand the behavior of a child who seems to have an erratic learning pattern to developing tests that accurately measure what has been taught in a course. Most of all, teachers need to model this clear, logical thinking to students.

These four branches of philosophy—metaphysics, epistemology, axiology, and logic—address some of the major concerns of the teacher. The answers they suggest to the teacher and the implications they have for actual classroom practice are areas to which we now turn.

SCHOOLS OF PHILOSOPHY

Answers to the philosophical questions that pepper the preceding section have almost infinite variety. Over the years, however, certain answers by certain philosophers have been given more attention and allegiance than others. These more enduring sets of answers or world views represent schools of philosophy. Some started with the early Greek philosophers and have grown and developed through the centuries. Other schools of thought are more recent and offer fresh, new formulations to ultimate questions.

Why four philosophies

We have chosen to present four of Western culture's philosophies. We have selected these not because they are our pick of the "Top Four on the Philosophical Hit Parade," but because each viewpoint is currently influential in educational thought and practice. In the case of each of these philosophies, we present you first with a brief statement of the core ideas and then with a statement by a teacher (fictitious) who is committed to that particular philosophy. We have attempted to demonstrate that these positions are not just windy abstractions or the preoccupations of ivory-tower thinkers. Rather, these positions shape what people teach and how they teach it.

Perennialism

Nature is unchanging

Perennialism views nature and, in particular, human nature as constant, as undergoing little change. Beneath the superficial differences from one century or decade to the next, the rules that govern the world and the characteristics that make up human nature stay the same. The perennialist, too, is quite comfortable with Aristotle's definition of human beings as rational animals. Education is of crucial importance to perennialists because it develops a person's rationality and thus saves the person from being dominated by the instinctual or animal-like side of life. It is the intellect, not the body or emotions or instincts, that sets a person apart from the beasts. To develop intellect means to learn how to dominate and direct instinctual and emotional energies toward higher, more rational purposes. Therefore, the nourishment of the intellect is believed to be the essential role of the school.

For the perennialist, the intellect does not develop merely by contact with that which is relevant or satisfying. The intellect is nourished only by truth. Truth, since it resides in the nature of things, is constant and changeless. Although our grasp of it is incomplete, truth is best revealed in the enduring classics of Western culture. Classical thought, then, is emphasized as a subject matter of schools. Perennialists believe that instead of focusing on current events or students' interests, the curriculum of the schools should consist of the teaching of disciplined knowledge, the traditional subjects of history, language, mathematics, science, and the arts. Perennialists place particular emphasis on literature and the humanities because these subjects provide the greatest insight into the

"Great Books approach"

human condition. Although this view of the curriculum is evident in many places in education, in its most complete form it is known as the "Great Books approach," developed by Robert Maynard Hutchins and Mortimer Adler. The Great Books, which constitute a shelf of volumes stretching from Homer's *Iliad* to Albert Einstein's *On the Electrodynamics of Moving Bodies,* are a perennialist's ideal curriculum.

As the 1990s began, on many campuses across the nation and in the press a controversy arose over the content of literature, history, and philosophy courses. Scholars and students criticized colleges and high schools for promoting a "Eurocentric" view of knowledge and culture, one that ignored the contribu-

In some philosophies of education, such as perennialism, the authority and centrality of the teacher are key elements.

(*Mimi Forsyth/Monkmeyer Press Photo Service*)

tion of all but "dead, white, male writers and thinkers." They urged a more inclusive curriculum, one that gave greater attention to women, minorities, and Eastern, African, and Hispanic cultures. Whereas some took this movement as a direct attack on the perennialist's curriculum, others saw it as a natural and useful extension of the perennialist's search for the best of the world's wisdom. One perennialist friend of ours, who is cautiously open to this new opening, suggested, "Sure, students should know about Islamic literature and Eastern philosophy, but they should first get to know their own neighborhood, Western culture."

For the perennialist, then, immersion in these great works aids students in reaching the perennialist's goal, which is a state of human excellence that the ancients called *paideia*. This is a state not only of enlightenment, but also of goodness. And, as such, it is a goal that perennialists believe all humans should seek.

The Paideia Proposal   A decade ago, Mortimer Adler and a group of educators breathed new life into perennialism with the publication of *The Paideia Proposal* and then a series of supporting books.[2] *The Paideia Proposal* presents this educational philosophy not as an austere, joyless curriculum, but as an exciting, involving, intellectual and aesthetic journey. Several of the Paideia Group who worked with Adler in formulating this plan are both minority-group members and superintendents of big-city school districts serving a large population of poor and minority students. Much of the appeal of *The Paideia Proposal* is that it asserts that all children, not just the gifted or the privileged children of the rich, should have this classical education. Members of the Paideia Group see it as providing both quality and equality in education.

Education, then, is of great importance to the perennialists; but it is an education that is rigorous and demanding. They hold that education should not attempt to imitate life or be lifelike. Rather, education is a preparation for life. Students should submit themselves to a disciplined search for the classical wisdom rather than try to search for what might seem to be personally meaningful.

Disciplined book learning prepares for life

In summary, the perennialists' view is that one learns by encountering the great works and ideas of the past. It is a view that leans heavily on the authority of the collected wisdom of the past and looks to traditional thought to guide us in the present. Further, it sees education as protecting and conserving the best thought from the past. In this sense, the perennialist favors a very traditional or conservative ("conservative" as in *conserving* the best of the past) view of education.

THE PERENNIALIST TEACHER   I came into education twelve years ago for two reasons. First, I was bothered by what I thought was all the nonsense in the curriculum and by all the time I, and other students, wasted in school. There was so much time given over to elective courses, many of which seemed to be little more than the teacher's hobby. There were so many discussions, discussions that seemed to go nowhere and seemed only vaguely to touch on the supposed content of the course. I often felt as if we were simply sharing our ignorance. My second reason for becoming a teacher is a more positive one. I am convinced that our society, our culture, has great ideas—ideas that have been behind our progress in the last 2,500 years. We need to share these ideas—no, teach these ideas to the young.

Humans not inherently good

Essentially, I see my job as a teacher as passing on to the next generation, as effectively and forcefully as I can, the important truths: for instance, about human dignity and the capacity of people to do evil. That has always been the teacher's role, until recent times, when we seem to have lost our way. I am convinced that a society that doesn't make the great ideas and the great thoughts the foundation of education is bound to fail. Nations and societies do falter and fall. The last fifty years have seen several formerly prominent nations slip to the wayside while other younger, more vigorous countries, like Japan and Korea, have risen. I am convinced that most of those failed countries fell because of the inadequate education they provided. I am dedicated to the goal of not letting that happen here.

I think kids are just great. In fact, I've given my life to working with them. But I just don't think it is fair to them or to me or to our country to allow them to set the rules, decide what they want to learn, or tell me how to teach it. Sure, I listen to them and try to find out where they are, but I make the decisions. My job is to teach; theirs is to learn. And in my classroom those functions are quite clear. Really, students are too young to know what are the really important things to learn. They simply don't know what they need to know. As a teacher, as a representative of the large culture and of society, that's my responsibility. Turning that responsibility over to students or giving them a huge say in what is taught just strikes me as wrong.

Self-discipline needed

I have another currently unpopular idea: I believe that students should be pushed. School should be very demanding, because life is very demanding. All of us, when we are young, are lazy. We would much rather play than work. All of this trying to make school like play is just making it more difficult for students to really acquire the self-discipline needed to take control of their lives. What schools are turning out right now—and it pains me to say this—is a lot of self-important, self-indulgent kids. And it's not their fault. It's our fault as teachers and parents.

And the answer is so simple! We just need to go back to the great ideas and achievements of the past and make them the focal point of education. Also, when we achieve this goal, the students don't mind working. The kids and the other teachers tease me about being a slave driver. I don't really pay attention to that. But I do pay attention to the large number of students, both college bound and not college bound, who come back two or three years out of high school and tell me how much they value having been pushed, how glad they are that I put them in contact with the very best!

Progressivism

Progressivism is a relatively young philosophy of education. It came to prominence in the 1920s through the work of John Dewey. That this philosophy rather quickly had a major impact on American education almost guaranteed that it would become controversial.

Nature is always changing

Progressivism views nature as being in flux, as ever-changing. Therefore, knowledge must continually be redefined and rediscovered. Whereas other philosophies see the mind as a jug to be filled with truth, or as a muscle that needs to be exercised and conditioned, the progressive views the mind as a problem solver. People are naturally exploring, enquiring entities. When faced with an obstacle, they will try to get around it. When faced with a question, they will try to find an answer.

Emphasis on problem solving

For the progressive, education aims at developing this problem-solving ability. The student should start with simple study projects and gradually learn more systematic ways to investigate until he or she has finally mastered the scientific method. Method is of great importance to the progressive. On the other hand, knowledge—formal, traditional knowledge—is not given the same honored place. For the progressive, there is really no special, sacrosanct knowledge. The value of knowledge resides in its ability to solve human problems. Regarding the school curriculum, progressives believe that a student can learn problem-solving skills from electronics just as easily as from Latin, from agronomy just as well as from geometry. Progressive teachers often use traditional subject matter, but they use it differently from the way it is used in a traditional classroom. The problems that the students are trying to solve are of paramount importance.

The subjects contribute primarily through providing methodologies to help solve the problems, but they also provide information that leads to solutions. The focus is on *how* to think rather than on what to think.

Progressive educators believe that the place to begin an education is with the student, rather than with the subject matter. The teacher tries to identify what the student's concerns are and tries to shape those concerns into problem statements. The student's motivation to solve the problem is the key. The teacher helps students shape the problem, to move from hunches about the solution to a development of hypotheses, and then on to methods of testing those hypotheses. Rather than being a presenter of knowledge or a taskmaster, the teacher is an intellectual guide, a facilitator in the problem-solving process. Students are encouraged to be imaginative and resourceful in solving problems. They are directed to a variety of methods, from reading books and studying the traditional disciplines to performing experiments and analyzing data.

The progressive school has a unique atmosphere. It is not the storehouse of wisdom or a place with clearly defined roles and authority structures. Rather, the school is a small, democratic society, a place where students are not only preparing for life but are also living it.

Progressive educators believe that the school should be democratic in structure so that children can learn to live well in a democracy. Group activity and group problem solving are emphasized. This is one reason why many teachers who describe themselves as progressive educators are enthusiastic about cooperative education, a new approach to classroom instruction that will be described in Chapter 8.

Implicit in the progressive approach is the belief that children not only must learn to solve their own problems, but also must develop the view that they can and should be involved in the problems of their neighbors. Often, then, the problem-solving activities of the progressive school spill out into the community, dealing with issues like ecology and poverty. In this way, students learn an important principle of progressive education: knowledge should be used to redesign the world.

Progressive education is seen by many persons as a new philosophy of education for a new people. As opposed to most other philosophies, it is very American. It has no undue reverence for the past or authority; rather, it is future-oriented and practical.

THE PROGRESSIVE EDUCATOR   I'm a progressive educator and proud of it. I'm not ducking that label just because it is unpopular in many quarters these days, usually by people who don't really understand what it is. Quite honestly, for the life of me, I cannot understand how a teacher can be anything *but* a progressive educator.

I'm dedicated to a few simple and, I believe, obvious principles. For one thing, children are, by their very nature, "good." And, as such, we should treat them that way rather than try to dominate them. Instead of rejecting their curiosities, I believe we should build on them. Schools should be exciting, involving places where students are caught up in interesting activities.

Margin notes:

Student's concerns most important

Involvement in community

Humans inherently good

Group problem solving and learning by doing play important roles in the progressive educator's classroom.

(*Harriet Gans/The Image Works*)

I really think that I'm a progressive educator because I have looked at my own experiences. I know I learn best when I'm trying to solve a problem that really interests me. And somehow I've always been able to get much more interested in how we're going to solve the problems of our own society than in the affairs of the Athenians and Spartans. I can get much more involved in a research problem about which stereo system gives the best value for the dollar than about some dry economic problem presented to me by a teacher. And I really don't think I'm different from the overwhelming majority of students.

I see many of my fellow teachers spending all their energy damming up student curiosity and busily imposing work on students. And then the teachers wonder why they're so tired or why they're burnt out. I'm sure it's quite tiring to try to convert children into file cabinets and to stuff facts into their heads all day.

It's not that I think that ideas and content and the traditional subjects are worthless. Far from it. I teach much of the same material as the other teachers. However, I get there by a different route. I let the issues and problems emerge and then give the students a chance to get answers and to solve problems. And, as they quickly learn, they have to know a great deal to solve some of the problems. Often they get themselves involved with some very advanced material. The only difference is that now they want to. Now they have the energy. And, boy, once they get going, do they have energy! No, it doesn't always work. I

Group problem solving

have students that coast, and I've had projects that have failed. But I'd put my track record against those of my more traditional colleagues any day.

One of the things that sets me apart from others is that I'm not so hung up as others are on what I call the "talky" curriculum. I am convinced that students learn most effectively by *doing,* by experiencing events and then reflecting on and making meaning out of what they have experienced. I think more science is learned on a nature walk than from the same time spent reading a textbook or hearing teacher explanations. I think students learn more abstract principles, such as democracy, from trying to set up and maintain a democratic society in their classroom than from a lot of learned lectures and dusty prose on the subject. I'm trying to get to their hearts and their heads. The traditional approach gets neither place.

Learning through direct experience

To me life is a matter of solving problems. New times have new problems and demand new knowledge. I don't want my students to be ready for life in the eighteenth century, or even the twentieth century. I want them to be effective, functioning, curious citizens of the twenty-first century. They are going to need to be able to develop solutions to fit new and unique problems. Although much knowledge is important, they need to realize that knowledge is only today's tentative explanation of how things work. Much of what we know now is incor-

JOHN DEWEY
(1859–1952)

John Dewey, the father of progressivism, is widely considered the single most influential figure in the history of American educational thought.

No prodigy as a child, Dewey attended public schools and the University of Vermont. As a graduate student in philosophy at Johns Hopkins University, he was deeply influenced by the thought of William James, the philosophical pragmatist. Dewey recognized the implications for education of James's argument that ideas are valuable only insofar as they help solve human problems. Calling his own philosophy *instrumentalism,* to emphasize the principle that ideas are instruments, Dewey argued that philosophy and education are identical, both involving the practical, experimental attempt to improve the human condition.

The public school curriculum in the nineteenth century was scholarly and classical, designed to improve the mind by filling it with large doses of approved culture. Dewey denounced this curriculum as the invention of a parasitical leisure class totally unsuited to the demands of industrialized society. He claimed that the schools were divorced from life and that they failed to teach children how to *use* knowledge. The schools, he said, should teach children not what to think but how to think through a "continuous reconstruction of experience." In *Democracy and Education,* published in 1916, Dewey pointed out that Americans were being called on to make crucial political decisions unprecedented in history, and that the schools offered no preparation for the responsibility of citizenship in a democracy. Dewey called for concentrated study of democratic processes as they are manifested in the units of political organization with which the child is familiar—the school, the local community, and the state government—in ascending order of complexity. But his most radical suggestion was that students be given the power to make decisions affecting life in the school in a democratic way. Participation in life, rather than preparation for it, he considered the watchword of an effective education.

In 1893 Dewey established an elementary school at the University of Chicago. It was experimental in two senses: in its use of experiment and inquiry as the method by which the children learned, and in its role as a laboratory

rect and will have to be replaced. We should share that "truth" with students. But, more important, we must help them to be problem solvers.

Essentialism

Essentialism is another uniquely American philosophy of education, but it has had more impact and meets with more favor outside the United States than does progressive educational thought. Essentialism, in fact, began in the 1930s and 1940s as a reaction to what were seen as the excesses of progressive education.

Two origins—idealism and realism

Essentialism has its philosophical origins in two older philosophies and draws something from each. From *idealism,* it takes the view of the mind as the central element of reality: the mind is our tool for learning the essential ideas and knowledge that we need to live well. From *realism,* it takes the tenet that the mind learns through contact with the physical world: therefore, to be able to observe and measure the physical world accurately is essential if a person is going to know reality.

Essential skills and knowledge to be learned

The essentialists believe that there exists a core of information and skill that an educated person must have. Further, essentialists are convinced that the overwhelming number of children can and should learn this core of essential material. The school, then, should be organized to transmit this knowledge and skill as effectively as possible.

for the transformation of the schools. The activities and occupations of adult life served as the core of the curriculum and the model teaching method. Children began by studying and imitating simple domestic and industrial tasks; in subsequent years they studied the historical development of industry, invention, group living, and nature. This curriculum was in keeping with Dewey's argument, espoused in *The School and Society,* that we must "make each one of our schools an embryonic community life, active with types of occupations that reflect the life of the larger society and permeated with the spirit of art, history, and science." Dewey also believed it was the absence of cooperative intellectual relations among teachers that caused young children's learning to be directed by a single teacher and older children's learning to be compartmentalized.

The late 1920s to the early 1940s—the era of progressive education—saw a massive attempt to implement Dewey's ideas, but the rigid manner in which they were interpreted led to remarkable extravagances in some progressive schools. Some considered it useless to teach geography because maps changed so rapidly. Some would encourage students who, when asked why they were not studying for an exam, replied that they wanted to come to

it fresh! The role of subject matter was gradually played down in progressive schools; the method and process were regarded as more important. The rationale was that it was more important to produce a "good citizen" than a person who was "educated" in the classical sense. Well into his nineties, Dewey fought vehemently against these corruptions of his views.

Throughout his long life, Dewey was a social activist, marching for women's right to vote, heading a commission to investigate the assassination of Trotsky, organizing a protest against the dismissal of a colleague at the City College of New York, and the like. Though he had enormous influence on the schools and on American intellectual life, his advocacy of a socialist economy and welfare state caused him to be characterized by some as an archfoe of the American way of life.

The centrality of John Dewey's thought to American education has waxed and waned over the years. Traditionally more popular in universities than in actual classroom practice, Dewey is often invoked by people attempting to make the schools more humanistic and the curriculum more relevant to the current world. Whether in favor or out, John Dewey represents the United States's most distinctive contribution to educational thought.

Essentialism begins to sound a good deal like perennialism. Although these two views have much in common, there are some important differences between them. For one thing, the essentialists do not focus so intently on "truths" as do the perennialists. They are not so concerned with the classics as being the repository of all worthwhile knowledge. They search for what will help a person live a productive life today, and if the current realities strongly suggest that students need to graduate from high school with computer literacy, the essentialist will find a place for this training in the curriculum. In this regard, the essentialists are very practical and pragmatic. Whereas the perennialist will hold fast to the Great Books, the essentialist will make more room for scientific, technical, and even vocational emphases in the curriculum. Essentialists see themselves as valuing the past, but not being captured by it.

Beyond the classics

For essentialists, the aim of education is to teach the young the essentials that they need in order to live well in the modern world. To realize this goal, the school should teach the child the essentials of organized knowledge. Since the established disciplines are the "containers" of organized knowledge, these disciplines are what should be taught in schools. The elementary years, however, should concentrate on the basics—the "three Rs" and the other foundational tools needed to gain access to disciplined knowledge that one begins to come in contact with in high school.

Although there is some debate about what is "essential" in the curriculum, essentialists believe that this is not a debate to which children can contribute fruitfully. Therefore, the role of the student is simply that of learner. His or her interests and motivations or psychological states are not given much attention. Nor are the essentialists much captured by what they would call a "romantic" view of children as naturally good. They do not see the students as evil, but rather as deficient and needing discipline and pressure to keep learning. School is viewed as a place where children come to learn what they need to know. Teachers are not guides, but authorities. The student's job is to listen and learn. Given the imperfect state of the students, the teacher must be ingenious in finding ways to engage their imaginations and minds.

Student as learner, teacher as authority

Progressive and essentialist educators each claim that their particular approach is the true American philosophy of education. A case can be made that they both are, but that each reflects different aspects of the American personality. Progressivism represents the antiauthoritarian, experimental, and visionary side; essentialism speaks to our more conservative, structured side. Many of the tensions in education today are between these two philosophical strains.

THE ESSENTIALIST TEACHER   In my view, the world is filled with real problems, and the young people who leave school have to be ready to take up the challenge of life and solve those problems. So for me the watchword in education is *usefulness*. I think everything that is taught has to pass the test of whether or not it is useful. My job as a teacher is to find out what is useful and then to make sure the students learn it.

Usefulness and relevance important

I believe that school should be relevant to the young. However, my view of what is relevant is very different from the views of lots of other people. For me relevance is not what is personally "meaningful" or a "do-your-own-thing" approach. What is relevant is what helps the individual live well and what benefits humanity. For that we need to look very carefully at the past and sort out the most valuable learning. That is what should be taught and what should be learned. I find the back-to-the-classics approach quite valuable. However, most advocates go too far. They also stress the humanities and the arts a little too much and tend to underplay science and technology. If children are going to function in today's world, and if our world is going to solve all the problems it's confronted with, we have to give more attention to these subjects than we have in the past. But, clearly, the past is the place to begin our search for the relevant curriculum.

It's not the most pleasing or satisfying image, but I think the concept of the student as an empty jug is the most accurate one. Certainly kids come to school with lots of knowledge and lots of interests. However, the job of school is to teach them what they don't know and teach them in a systematic and organized way. It's not to fill their minds with isolated fragments of information, but to fill them with systematic knowledge. They need tools to learn, and, as they get older, they need human insights and skills that come from the disciplines. Given that there is so much to learn, this emphasis on student interest and projects and problem solving is quite wasteful. There is plenty of time for that outside of school or when school is over. Inside the school, the teachers are the authorities, and the students are there to learn what they don't know. The

Task-orientation and accomplishment

environment should be task-oriented and disciplined. It doesn't have to be oppressive or unjust or any of that. I tell my students that learning is not necessarily going to be fun, but that at the end of the year they will have a great sense of accomplishment. I'd take accomplishment over fun anytime. By and large, most students do, too.

Existentialism

Modern existentialism was born amidst the pain and disillusionment of World War II and the period immediately following it. Existentialism's founder, Jean-Paul Sartre, broke with previous philosophers and asserted that existence comes before essence. His approach differed from that of most philosophers, who defined the nature of humans as rational animals or problem solvers or what-have-you, and then spoke about existence. To Sartre, our existence comes first; then we define ourselves in some sort of relationship to that existence. In other words, the existentialist believes that we should not accept any predetermined creed or philosophical system and from that try to define who we are. We've got to take the responsibility of making that decision of who we are. The process of answering the question "Who are we?" has a start but really no ending. It begins at a very crucial event in the lives of young people. Sartre calls that event the

Jean-Paul Sartre's "existential moment"

existential moment—that point somewhere toward the end of youth when we realize for the first time that we exist as an independent agent. We are suddenly struck with the fact that *I am!* With that realization come the existential questions, "Okay, I exist, but who am I and what should I do?"

The European brand of existentialism tends to be a very austere philosophy. Its practitioners tend to reject all other philosophies. Although there is a vital school of existentialism, called Christian Existentialism, with roots in the work of the Danish minister-philosopher Søren Kierkegaard, "mainline" existentialists reject God and the concept of a benevolent universe. They believe that we live an alien, meaningless existence on a small planet in an unimportant galaxy in an indifferent universe. Whatever meaning a person can make of life has to be his or her own meaning. There is no ultimate meaning. Whereas some people might be paralyzed by this view, existentialists find the definition of their lives in the quest for meaning. The very meaninglessness of life compels them to instill life with meaning.

The only certainty for the existentialist is that we are free. This freedom, however, is wrapped up in a search for meaning. To the existentialist we define ourselves—that is, we make meaning in our world—by the choices we make. In effect, we are what we choose. No more. No less. No God will throw us a life preserver. No circumstance will shade our responsibility. We are responsible for what we do and what we are.

The one thing the individual can be sure of is death—the complete ending of any kind of existence. Existing in a meaningless world with no afterlife provides the ongoing tension in the existentialist's life. "Why struggle, why continue, if there is no hope?" It is in accepting this question and the "death dread" buried in it, that the existentialist can gain some dignity.

Existentialism has affected American education in a somewhat softer view. The *meaningless universe* aspect is downplayed, and the *quest for personal meaning* is emphasized. Existentialism has entered American education not under the flag of existentialism, but under several different flags: the "Human Potential Movement" of the 1960s and 1970s, which stressed the development of all aspects of the person, and an approach to moral education called "Values Clarification" in which each individual discovers his or her own values. Existentialism's influence in the schools has been strong but somewhat subtle.

Given the fact that by law our schools must be theologically neutral (they cannot advocate any religious world view), there is, by default, an unanswered question about the meaning of existence. In a way, though, the existentialists' approach of finding meaning through a quest for self has filled this gap. Children are warned not to accept anyone else's answers or values, but to search for their own. They learn that they should make their own choices and their own commitments in life, rather than being told what they should choose and to what they should commit themselves.

As it exists in the classroom, existentialism is not a set of curricular materials. Rather, it is a point of view that influences all that the teacher teaches and how he or she teaches. It tries to engage the child in central questions of defining life. It tries to help the child acknowledge his or her own freedom and accept the responsibility for that freedom. It aims to help the child realize that the answers imposed from the outside may not be real answers. The only real answers are the ones that come from inside each person, that are authentically his or her own.

For this reason, the existentialist is against not only the heavy hand of authority, but also the group emphasis in education. Homogeneous grouping and

Existentialism in American education sometimes takes the form of an ongoing quest for personal meaning.

(*Paul Conklin/Monkmeyer Press Photo Service*)

group projects and social adjustment are always keeping from the child the ultimate truths: you are alone and you must make your own meaning. The group, or social emphasis in the form and content of education, is a drug or anesthetic that prevents perception of the ultimate nature of the way things are. On the other hand, movements and activities that help the child confront his or her own freedom go to the essence of what school should be all about.

Individualized, not group, learning

THE EXISTENTIALIST TEACHER When I was in college the last thing I thought I'd become was a teacher. I was really turned off by education—all of that fact cramming and mind bending. I still am quite negative about most of the education that is going on around me. I get along with most of my fellow teachers and

I guess I look like them on the surface, but I look at the world in a very different way, and that makes some of them uneasy. They are busy trying to give the kids this dogma, that dogma—whether it's democracy or the scientific method. And nothing makes them quite so uptight as students seriously questioning what they have to say. Students who question to see if they have it right so they can get it right on the test are fine. But, probing or challenging questions are signs that the students reject what they're getting, and that really makes teachers nervous.

What drives me is getting the kids to listen to their own rhythms. So much of their lives are programmed from home, from television, from the crazy peer-group fads and the press of group-think in the school. I'm trying to get them to break through all that. I want them to begin to find out who *they* are and what *they* feel and what *they* think. I want them to have authentic reactions to things and realize that those are the ones that are important, not what the world's authorities tell them is important. It sounds quite simple, but it is very difficult. They find great security in not thinking. I guess we all do. It's so much easier to take someone else's answers and pretend that they are ours. But that is just another form of slavery.

People sometimes call what I do a radical approach, and I think that's more bunkum. The aim of education has always been the examined life. Socrates said it long ago: "Know thyself." That's what I'm aiming at. This may sound like I

© Jules Feiffer

have them look off into space and ask the question "Who am I?" Far from it. I try to get my students passionately involved in life. I try to get them to have peak experiences, whether from watching a sunrise or hearing a Mozart sonata. This often leads to their own insight. Also, they have a lot to learn about the way the world works, and they have lots of skills they have to learn. And I'm busy getting them ready to take on that task.

What I don't do is spend a lot of time on all these grouping—or what I call leveling—activities. I let them know that they are individuals, and I have a very individualized instructional approach. My students spend a great deal of time on individual tasks, and they always go at their own rate. If there is anything that I emphasize, it's managing their own freedom. The major message of school for me is that you've got lots of choices, but you are responsible for what you do with them. This is the reason I stress *values clarification*. This approach makes them discover their own values and take the whole issue of values quite seriously.

The other thing I stress is *freedom*. They need to know that freedom is at the core of being a human being. I'm not talking about a "do-your-own-thing," pleasure-oriented freedom. I mean a freedom that fully embraces one's responsibility. It is this kind of freedom that allows a person to become heroic. This may sound silly, but I found my educational philosophy at the back end of a car. A couple of years ago I was driving home from school and at a red light read the motto on a New Hampshire license plate ahead of me: "Live free or die." That's it. That's the whole ball game.

YOUR PHILOSOPHY OF EDUCATION

At this point you may very well be confused, and possibly discouraged. To expect to be able to understand and evaluate critically every aspect of each philosophy is to expect of yourself what few professional philosophers are able to do. What you have just finished reading is a précis of some of the major ideas of Western civilization (see Table 3.1 for a summary). Some of these ideas have been around for centuries, and some are the fruits of great twentieth-century thinkers. Selecting the philosophy by which you will live and by which you will guide your professional activities takes much more investment of time and thought and energy than reading our short chapter.

Some teachers, like the teacher-philosophers in this chapter, settle on one philosophical view, and that view structures all of their work. While few teachers are pure and consistent models of philosophical approaches, most teachers lean strongly to a particular philosophical view, even if they may not be fully conscious of their position or be able to give it a label. Typically, they have a particular view of the learner, of how the learner should be approached, and of what is most worth knowing. However, few teachers are philosophical purists.

Some teachers label themselves eclectics. Eclecticism embodies the idea that truth can be found anywhere and that therefore people should select from various doctrines, systems, and sources. The eclectic teacher selects what he or she believes to be the most attractive features of several philosophies. He or she

Table 3.1 Four Philosophies and Their Applications to Education

	Perennialism	Progressivism	Essentialism	Existentialism
Metaphysics What is real? Does it have meaning?	Life has meaning in the context of the collective wisdom of Western culture.	Meaning is in the context of the individual, who is a "problem solver."	What is relevant is what helps an individual live well and benefits humanity.	"Existence before Essence." Reality is always in terms of our relationship to existence—no meaning outside ourselves.
Epistemology Knowledge & knowing— what is truth?	Truth is changeless, revealed in classics of Western culture.	Must be known in the context of individual experience: Nature is ever-changing—a flux. Learn how to learn.	Truth exists in the classics *and* modern science. Student must learn process and content.	No eternal truths. We are free to make our own meaning.
Axiology Values Ethics Aesthetics	Changeless. Determined by culture.	Determined by each individual in interaction with his or her culture.	Determined by the natural order of things. Values exist in the best of culture.	Determined by the individual. Stresses values clarification.
Logic How we think Deductive and inductive	Rationality is developed by studying classics.	Emphasis is on inductive thinking and problem solving.	Western culture learned through hard work and regular exposure to essential knowledge.	The only real answers come from within.

might take from existentialism a search for the authentic self, and from essentialism a curricular viewpoint dominated by the criterion of usefulness.*

Eclecticism is quite popular, but often for the wrong reasons. It sometimes appears as the easy way out of philosophical uncertainty. Why not simply take what you please from the philosophical cafeteria of ideas? One problem with this approach is the possibility of inconsistency. To take one's view of society from the existentialist, which gives primacy to individual freedom, and one's teaching methodology from the progressivist, who stresses group membership and democratic process, is liable to make everyone confused. Selecting eclecticism cannot be an excuse for lazy thinking.

Eclecticism as sloppy thinking

* In the process of writing this chapter, we discovered that we are really traditional, but progressive, essentialists who are searching around for a Great Books Club to join.

Table 3.1 Four Philosophies and Their Applications to Education (*cont.*)

	Perennialism	*Progressivism*	*Essentialism*	*Existentialism*
The Teacher	Passes on to next generation the accumulated wisdom of the past.	Develops problem-solving abilities. School is a small democracy. Helps children do what they want to do.	Teaches essential knowledge. School is where children come to learn what they need to know. Task-oriented.	Helps the child confront his or her freedom. Stresses freedom and the responsibility to choose.
Teaching Strategies	Cultivates rational powers through contact with the culture's best and through imitation.	Stimulates students to plan and carry out activities and research projects using group processes and democratic procedures. Teacher is facilitator and resource.	Avoids methodological frills and soft pedagogy and concentrates on sound, proven instructional methods. Teacher is expert.	Promotes freedom and responsibility. Teacher attempts to create a learning environment for students' self-definition.
The Child	Is there to learn what is taught.	Is naturally good. Learns by doing by discovering.	Is there to listen and learn.	Is alone and must make own meaning.
Curriculum	Based on materials reflecting universal and recurring themes that cultivate rationality.	Centered on students' interest in real problems and interdisciplinary solution seeking.	Strong emphasis on basic skills in elementary schools and on disciplined knowledge and scholastic achievement in secondary schools.	Subject matter, particularly liberal education, is a foundation for gaining personal freedom. Emphasizes humanities and the arts while de-emphasizing science.

Source: Adapted from a table by James Hotchkiss. Used by permission.

On the other hand, most teachers feel quite free and justified in borrowing teaching methodologies and strategies that are associated with various philosophies of education. The ardent perennialist teacher may choose to involve his sixth-grade students in a "hands-on" project constructing a large topographical map of Odysseus's ten years' journey to his home after the fall of Troy. Conversely, the free-spirited existentialist teacher may insist that each student

*Sixty years ago I knew
everything: now I know
nothing: education is a
progressive discovery of
our own ignorance.*
— WILL DURANT —

Eclecticism as a real
teaching strategy

memorize and be able to recite fifty lines of *The Odyssey*. Although this type of eclecticism may, in a narrow sense, seem philosophically inconsistent, at its root is the recognition that no philosophy of education is able to dictate the ideal methodology or learning strategies for all situations or all students. Related to this is the growing realization (to be discussed further in Chapter 10) that different students possess a great range of learning styles, and that what works with one student may flop with another.

So, whereas eclecticism, when thought out, can be a serious philosophical position and whereas eclecticism in the selection of teaching strategies is quite justified, choosing to be "eclectic" should not be a substitute for thought. Selecting one's philosophy of education is no weekend chore. Still, an eclectic philosophy of education may provide a way station or temporary stopping place for the individual who is working toward a unified philosophy of education.

Coming to fully understand questions about the true nature of reality or the purpose of existence is a life's work. The great majority of this book's readers are in the college years, and we are not suggesting that readers sit themselves down, think through all these issues, and come up with a tight set of philosophical answers that will last a lifetime. Rather, we hope that we have focused—or refocused—your attention on some of life's essential questions and on some

KEVIN AND JIM'S GUIDE TO DEVELOPING YOUR OWN PHILOSOPHY OF EDUCATION

For many readers of this text, developing one's own philosophy of education must seem a daunting task. It is made even more demanding when one realizes that before one has a philosophy of education one needs to do the groundwork of forming or adopting a particular philosophy: that is, one must have a general theory of how the world is put together, what laws regulate the universe and underlie all knowledge and reality. For younger readers, in particular, who lack a great storehouse of experience and are relatively new to the world of ideas, the prospect of having to form a philosophy of education is unsettling. But that is as it should be. Something as fundamentally important as a person's basic understanding of reality should not come easily, like buying shoes or going for a walk.

Everyone, at some level, has a philosophy of life. It may be as crude as "Whatever makes me happy is therefore good" or as elaborate as a professional philos-

opher's own version of enlightened self-interest as the basis for improving the human species. But all philosophies of life ought to be something that individuals have worked out in their own minds and that they use to guide their interpretations of life and their decisions. Their philosophy is the lens through which they observe and interpret reality. As already mentioned, developing a philosophy of education is then a subset of having a guiding philosophy. It is the playing out of the educational implications of one's basic philosophy. But how does one develop a philosophy of education? What follows are some suggestions you might consider.

1. Read this chapter carefully, trying to understand what the terms mean and how they relate to the different schools of philosophy described. Realize, too, that this chapter is meant only as a door opener, a beginning.

2. As you read, "try on" the ideas. Look at the world through the lens or angles of vision of each philosophy, searching for the one or ones that best "fit" you. Once you have made a tentative decision, start integrating the chosen philosophy into your everyday life. "Well, if I really think 'Man is alone in a

issues that are at the very core of teaching. In fact, the college years have always been considered a time of questioning and a time of testing the ideas that have, up to this point, been largely imposed on people by their education and cultural milieu. The undergraduate years should be a time of searching for answers to the basic questions of human identity. The uncertainty that goes along with this searching process is often an important step in self-growth.

The college curriculum is designed to aid this frequently unsettling process. A major purpose of that curriculum is to present the student with a spectrum of society's best thinkers and their attempts to understand their own existence. The reason for the general education component of teacher education programs (that is, the courses in the arts and sciences that are required of the prospective teacher) is to provide a chance for future teachers to think through these fundamental issues of human existence. Often, however, this obvious purpose gets lost, and students go through the courses in a mechanical way, untouched by the philosophical content of the curriculum. On the other hand, the infamous college bull sessions may be where the real philosophical inquiry goes on; they are frequently thinly veiled discussions of what really counts in life and what one should try to do with one's life. In effect, then, both the formal apparatus of college and the curriculum and the informal opportunities to meet, talk, and test

hostile universe,' I ought to do X, Y and Z." Discuss your views with your classmates and your teachers. (Be careful, though, how you talk to your parents. From firsthand experience as parents, we can tell you that this topic can panic them!)

3. Take a philosophy course or two as part of your general or liberal education. This will give you a systematic exposure to philosophical thought. Also, it will give you a structured opportunity to explore your own thinking more carefully.

4. Think about how you would want your own child educated. Depending on whether you are an inductive or deductive thinker (see pp. 77–78), start with the child and decide what and how you would want him or her to be taught, or start with your philosophical principles (e.g., man is a rational being) and deduce educational principles from them (e.g., the aim of schooling should be to develop a student's capacity for reasoning). What would a school for your child be like? What would it emphasize? What would it de-emphasize?

5. As you take education courses and read education texts, ask yourself, "What is the teacher's or author's philosophy of education? What does he or

she hold as most important? What is the underlying idea that is driving the point being made here?" (We acknowledge that this is difficult, but with practice, this ability develops.)

6. As you observe in classrooms during your teacher education program (and even on your own campus), try to figure out what the teachers' philosophy of education is. If you can do it in a way that won't upset or ruffle them, ask them questions, such as "What do you hope your students become?" and "What would be an ideal outcome of your teaching?" and "What is the most important thing students should be getting from their education?"

7. Try to have a quiet and private conversation with your favorite teacher from elementary or secondary school (or a teacher you have met during teacher education) and ask about his or her philosophy of education. ("I've wondered about something. Do you have a reason for never directly answering children's questions and instead urging them to find the answers for themselves?")

8. Think. (That's what philosophy is all about.)

your ideas with a variety of people should help you discover where you stand on some of these essential human questions.

As we said at the very beginning of this chapter, the teacher who is going to be more than a technician has a special obligation to take philosophical issues and questions seriously. Teachers owe it to themselves and to their students to understand where they are going and why they are going there.

Discussion Questions

1. At the present time, where are you in your own evolution or development of a philosophy of education? At the beginning of the quest? Just tying up some loose details?
2. What role, if any, does religion play in your philosophy of education?
3. Why do superintendents and principals often ask teaching candidates about their philosophy of education?
4. First, think back on the characteristics of your favorite teacher. Are you able to match up his or her views with those of any of the teacher-spokespersons or schools of philosophy mentioned in this chapter?
5. Which of the four branches of philosophy mentioned in this chapter (metaphysics, epistemology, axiology, or logic) is the one with which you feel most at home? What do you believe are the implications of this for your own teaching?
6. At this point, which of the philosophies of education (perennialism, progressivism, essentialism, or existentialism) appeals to you most? Why? What do you see as the most telling argument against this philosophy of education?
7. Which of these philosophies of education appeal to you least? Why? Are there any aspects of these philosophies or their application to the schools that you like and could endorse?

For Further Reading

Duck, Lloyd. *Teaching with Charisma*. Boston: Allyn and Bacon, 1981.
A textbook that summarizes the major philosophical positions and the key questions of schooling to which each of these philosophies is addressed and that does so in a readable and lively style.

Fenstermacher, Gary D., and Jonas f. Soltis. *Approaches to Teaching*. New York: Teachers College Press, 1986.
This slim volume demonstrates how two philosophers can unpack the term *teaching* and explain what is behind several different approaches to instruction.

Gutek, Gerald L. *Philosophical and Ideological Perspectives on Education*. Englewood Cliffs, N.J.: Prentice-Hall, 1988.
This textbook is a comprehensive and up-to-date account of the competing schools of educational philosophy and their application to schooling. In addition, Gutek provides thumbnail sketches of key figures.

Morris, V.C., and Y. Pai. *Philosophy and the American School*. 2d ed. Boston: Houghton Mifflin, 1976.
An excellent textbook that summarizes the major philosophical positions and addresses how they bear on schooling in our current society.

Phenix, Phillip H. *Realms of Meaning: A Philosophy of the Curriculum for General Education.* New York: McGraw-Hill, 1964.

>A superb book that describes the several ways men and women come to know the world. The author distills the essence of several disciplines and shows how they contribute to our sense of meaning. Highly recommended.

Notes   1. Association of Supervision and Curriculum Development, *Moral Education in the Life of the School* (Alexandria, Va.:ASCD, 1989).

2. Mortimer J. Adler, *The Paideia Proposal: An Educational Manifesto* (New York: Macmillan, 1982); *Paideia Problems and Possibilities* (New York: Macmillan, 1983); *Paideia Program and Educational Syllabus* (New York: Macmillan, 1984).

CHAPTER 4

What Is the History of American Education?

CHAPTER PREVIEW

American schooling and education did not develop overnight into our current system. The system as we know it has its roots in the social, economic, political, and religious history of the nation. To understand our present educational system, its successes and failures, and the problems it still faces, we must look to our past. There we can identify the forces that have affected and continue to affect the development of American education. This chapter reviews the history of schooling and education in the United States, pointing out six important forces that have influenced their development and examining the contributions that significant men and women have made.

This chapter emphasizes that:

● Education in colonial America was originally religious in orientation but differed in form according to the geographical areas of the colonies. Schooling in colonial America was not universal; it was primarily for white males.

● During the nineteenth century, influenced by the ideas of Thomas Jefferson and Benjamin Franklin and led by such reformers as Horace Mann, free public education became a reality. Common schools at the elementary level were tax-supported and open to all children in an attempt to cultivate a sense of American identity and loyalty.

● The nineteenth century also saw the development of public high schools that were designed to prepare young people, within a single institution, for either vocations or college; this goal of providing comprehensive educational opportunities was unique to American education.

● Private education has always played an important role in America, particularly in our nation's early days. Even today, almost 11 percent of the children of elementary and secondary school age attend private schools. Many private schools have a religious affiliation, offering alternatives to the public schools' secular emphasis.

● Equal educational opportunities for minorities and women have not always existed in America. Ethnic groups such as African-Americans, Hispanic-Americans, Native Americans, and Asian-Americans, as well as women, have had to fight uphill battles to attain educational rights and treatment equal to those afforded white males.

It is a rare college student who feels a burning urgency to answer the question "What is the history of American education?" Unless you are a history buff, you will probably ask yourself, "Why do I need to know this stuff? How will it help me do a better job in the classroom?" In truth, knowing something about the history of American education probably will not directly affect your classroom practices. So why should you study this aspect of education? There are, we think, some very good reasons.

First, understanding American educational history will give you a sense of perspective. Educators are occasionally accused of being faddist, which implies that we blindly follow each new approach or idea, thinking it is the greatest thing since sliced bread. On the other hand, we are sometimes accused of reinventing the wheel, spending a great deal of energy discovering something that has been in the educational literature for years or was a significant part of the education program of a different culture.

Second, although studying the history of American education will not give you answers to the immediate problems you are likely to face in your classes, it will enable you to better understand the culture and context in which you will be working. It will help you obtain the "big picture" of why things operate as they do in today's schools.

Finally, studying the history of education will help you appreciate its truly noble heritage. Schools have been a progressive instrument in the lives of the majority of the people who have attended them. They have freed people from superstition and false information, and have given them new skills, positive values, and world-expanding visions of what each individual can become and what we as a people can become. Some of the greatest people who have walked the earth—Socrates, Jesus, Gandhi—saw themselves essentially as teachers. Teachers, then, are part of an old, progressive, and indeed, inspirational human endeavor. Knowing our educational history and acquiring a historical perspective will help you live up to and extend this tradition.

THEMES IN AMERICAN EDUCATION

Reading this book, surrounded by college classmates and friends, may seem a natural step in your educational career. Kindergarten or nursery school led to elementary school, then to middle school or junior high school, which was followed by high school and now college. You may have taken this progression for granted, assuming that's the way things have always been.

Not so. You are sitting at a level of education that was attained only by the elite of earlier generations. You are already close to the top of an educational pyramid for which the foundation was laid almost 350 years ago. The growth of the pyramid has been shaped and energized by six major forces in American educational history:

1. *Local control* Originating in New England during colonial times, the concept of local control of schools spread during the nineteenth century with the common school district system. Because of a fear of a strong federal government, the framers of the United States Constitution made no reference to education. As a result, state governments assumed the role of educational authorities and then in turn delegated substantial powers to local school boards. Not until the mid-twentieth century did the federal government become substantially involved in educational matters.

2. *Universal education* In the colonial period, education was reserved for a small minority. Slowly, often in one-room rural schools, universal elementary education was achieved by the end of the nineteenth century; universal secondary education was attained by the early twentieth century; and today a college education is generally available to all who actively seek it.

3. *Public education* In the colonial period, education was generally private and primarily for the middle and upper classes. Nationhood brought not only the spread of publicly supported education but, by the early twentieth century, compulsory education as well. Nevertheless, private education still remains a small but important part of the whole educational system.

4. *Comprehensive education* The basic abilities to read, write, and do arithmetic were once sufficient to prepare most children for their adult roles in society. However, the growth of urban, industrial life in America during the nineteenth and early twentieth centuries also demanded that people be educated for work. The result was the comprehensive public high school, which includes both training for trades and preparation for college.

5. *Secular education* In earliest colonial times, the purpose of education was religious training. Beginning in the eighteenth century and then progressing through the twentieth, the function of American education has become increasingly secular, concerned with producing socially responsible citizens. Religious study has remained primarily in the private sector.

6. *Changing ideas of the basics* Literacy and classical learning were the main goals of colonial education, whereas practical skills for a pragmatic, democratic society were the aims of the nineteenth-century schools. Technical and scientific literacy have become the basics in the computer- and space-aged late twentieth century.

Contemporary issues

And these six forces continue to shape the character of American schooling and education. Many contemporary educational issues have their roots in these six themes. Consider these as examples:

- *Local control* Should a national curriculum for elementary and secondary schools be implemented?

- *Universal education* How can the quality of education that students receive be insured regardless of whether they live in wealthy or poor school districts?

- *Public education* Should private schools receive public tax support and, if so, for what purposes?

- *Comprehensive education* Should the schools require all students, vocational and college prep, to follow a common curriculum?

- *Secular education* Should public schools be required to teach both creationism and evolution?

- *Changing ideas of the basics* Is computer literacy a new "basic" of education and, if so, how will schools finance new programs that train students to use computers?

These are just a few of the issues facing policy makers in the 1990s. As you read the rest of this chapter, try to keep in mind the key themes in the history of American education and see if you can make the connections between these historical forces and the topics that educators debate today. In this chapter we'll give you the background to understand today's debates about the nature of education and schooling. Throughout the rest of the book you'll find treatments of many of these topics: equality of educational opportunity, what should be taught in the schools, the relationship of private and public education, and the role of the federal government in supporting public education, to name a few. Enjoy this chapter's tour through history, but don't think of it as a dead-end journey into the past. What happened in colonial America has had a great impact on the schooling you received and the system you will enter as a teacher.

ELEMENTARY EDUCATION

Colonial Origins

Dame schools and apprenticeships

In the 1600s, some girls received elementary instruction, but formal colonial education was primarily for boys, particularly those of the middle and upper classes. Both girls and boys might have received some preliminary training in the *four Rs*—reading, writing, arithmetic, and religion—at home. Occasionally, for a small fee, a housewife offered to take in children, to whom she would teach a little reading and writing, basic prayers, and religious beliefs. In these *dame schools,* girls also learned some basic household skills, such as cooking and sewing. The dame schools often provided all the formal education some children, especially girls, ever received.

Throughout the colonies, poor children were often apprenticed or indentured to local tradesmen or housewives. Apprenticeships lasted three to ten years, generally ending around age twenty-one for boys and eighteen for girls. During that time, an apprentice would learn the basic skills of a trade and might also be taught basic reading and writing, and perhaps arithmetic, as part of the contractual agreement.

Although the lines were not drawn hard and fast, the three geographic regions of the colonies developed different types of educational systems, which were shaped by each region's particular settlement patterns. New England colonists emphasized community-controlled, religiously oriented schools. Settlers in the South tended toward private education and tutors, with community schools seldom getting much support. The Middle Colonies saw the development of private venture and denominational schools.

NEW ENGLAND TOWN AND DISTRICT SCHOOLS   In New England, the Puritans believed it was important that everyone be able to read the Bible and interpret its teachings. As early as 1642, Massachusetts passed a law requiring parents to educate their children. That law was strengthened in 1647 by the famous *Old Deluder Satan Act.* Because Satan assuredly would try to keep people from understanding the Scriptures properly, it was important for all children to be

Old Deluder Satan Act

government but not protected or financed by it, flourished, and the use of public funds to educate everyone's children did not become customary.

In these private schools, parents paid the teacher directly on a contractual basis. The instructor managed the school and curriculum, accepting or rejecting students as desired. The denominational schools in the Middle Colonies shared the New England concern for proper religious training as a primary goal, but they also began early to offer, in addition to the basics, practical subjects such as bookkeeping or navigation.

The Common School

Prior to the American Revolution, the term *common school* referred to schools that provided education for the average person, but it was not necessarily at public expense or available to all. The Revolution brought with it a new ideal of the common school that, like the Revolution itself, was nevertheless rooted in the colonial period. The early New England laws had already set the precedent that all children should be taught how to read and that the civil government had authority over education. This implied a communal obligation to provide *universal education*—that is, schooling for everyone. However, even in colonial New England, it was the students' parents who had to pay for the schooling.

In the first blush of the new republic, however, conditions began to favor the idea that some sort of elementary education should be provided free, at public expense and under public control, for everyone who could not afford or did not want private schooling. Even though the Constitution had relegated control of education to the states, the impetus for such public schooling came from the

Northwest Land Ordinances

federal government, in particular as a result of the enactment of the Northwest Ordinances of 1785 and 1787. Concerning the sale of public lands in the Northwest Territory (from present-day Ohio to Minnesota), Congress passed the Northwest Ordinance of 1785. Every township was divided into thirty-six sections, of which one was set aside for the maintenance of public schools. Congress reaffirmed, in the Ordinance of 1787, that "religion, morality, and knowl-

CLASSROOM DISCIPLINE IN EARLY AMERICAN CLASSROOMS

In her study of classroom behavior in nineteenth-century schools, Barbara Joan Finkelstein writes that teachers were so committed to discipline that they believed that "the acquisition of knowledge represented a triumph of the will as well as the intellect. Consistently, in every kind of teaching situation, we find that teachers treated academic failure, not as a reflection of their own inabilities as instructors, but as evidence of the students' personal and moral recalcitrance; and this tendency was institutionalized on a grand scale in the village and city schools of the 1850's, 1860's, and 1870's. Indeed, the evidence suggests that teachers in every setting only rarely distinguished between the intellectual and the social aspects of student behavior as they meted out rewards and punishment." To many teachers, corporal punishment or humiliation seemed appropriate treatment for children who did not learn their lessons, for academic incompetence was considered a sign of moral laxity.

Reprinted from David B. Tyack, *The One Best System;* (Cambridge, Mass.: Harvard University Press, 1974), p. 55.

edge, being necessary to good government and the happiness of mankind, schools and the means of education shall forever be encouraged."[2]

ARGUMENTS FOR THE COMMON SCHOOL   The common school was the ideal of educational reform in the first half of the 1800s because liberal thinkers began to view education in a new light. They emphasized, first, the political significance of universal education. Following the American Revolution, it was recognized that a democratic government would be only as strong as the people's ability to make intelligent choices, which in turn depended on a basic education for all. It was also argued that education was a natural right, just like the very rights for which the Revolution had been fought. Benjamin Franklin and Thomas Jefferson suggested educational plans, as did other leaders of the Revolution.

Necessary for democracy

The early period of independence saw an increased concern with citizenship and nationhood. The War of 1812, coming so soon after the Revolution, impressed upon Americans the idea that their separate regional backgrounds had to be put aside if the new nation was to remain united and free. A system of common schooling would strengthen unity. Similarly, an influx of immigrants in the 1840s and 1850s, following a period of upheaval in Europe, further stimulated demand for an educational system that would serve to "Americanize" the waves of foreigners and keep society stable.

Many supporters of the common school also focused on its economic and social effects. Unlike that in the European social structure, class membership in America was rather fluid: wealth and social status in this country did not depend so much on the social class into which a person was born. Since there was no inherited class of nobility, one's own initiative and talent became the criteria for success, and it was believed that a common education would fuel everyone's upward mobility. Universal education was thus seen by the newly evolving working class as a means of equalizing economic and social opportunities. As a result, another reason given for spreading educational opportunity was that better-educated people would increase productivity and enhance everyone's prosperity while diminishing crime and reducing poverty.

Necessary for equal opportunity

Whereas the *New England Primer* reflected the religious orientation of much colonial education, the textbooks of the nineteenth century emphasized morality and Americanism. No other book was more popular than the six-volume series of *McGuffey Readers,* which sold more than 100 million copies between 1836 and 1906. Besides training students in (American) English language and grammar, these texts introduced poetry and the writings of statesmen, politicians, moralists, and religious leaders. "They assumed the Fatherhood of God, the brotherhood of man, the wickedness of war, crime, and inhumanity, and above all, they buttressed the concept of the sacredness of property and bulwarked the position of the middle class in society."[3]

McGuffey Readers

Although universal education at this time was meant only for whites, the same arguments advanced by its advocates were used later to extend universal education to include racial and ethnic minorities and exceptional children, to name just a few groups that have been denied equal educational opportunities. The desegregation efforts of the 1950s and 1960s were based on these very arguments. (For further discussion of the issue of equal educational opportunity, see pages 131–143 of this chapter and pages 393–402 of Chapter 11.)

ARGUMENTS AGAINST THE COMMON SCHOOL   As proper as these thoughts may sound to the modern ear, they often encountered opposition. The arguments against the common school were based on economics as much as on educational or political principles. The question concerned who would have to pay for this universal education: Why should one family pay for the education of another's children? The same question had been asked in the colonial period, and many people still felt that schooling, especially for the poor, should be the responsibility of religious groups. Still others felt that a free public school would gradually weaken or dilute the particular culture or religion that they had sought to establish in America. If ethnic groups commingled, what would be the fate of each one's native culture and language?

Who pays for universal education?

NOAH WEBSTER

(1758–1843)

Although best remembered today for his *American Dictionary of the English Language,* first published in 1828, Noah Webster was best known in the nineteenth century for his *American Spelling Book* (also known as the *Blue-Backed Speller*). This small, blue-backed booklet appeared in 1783 and became the most widely used schoolbook during the early nineteenth century.

A native of Connecticut, Webster attended and graduated from Yale University. During his lifetime he was a lawyer, schoolmaster, politician, and writer. Although Thomas Jefferson, expressing his opinion of Webster in 1801, wrote, "I view Webster as a mere pedagogue, of a very limited understanding," Webster's intellectual interests were of an astounding breadth. He wrote a paper on epidemic and pestilential diseases, edited John Wingate's historical journal, wrote several scientific treatises, discoursed on banking and insurance, and, along the way, mastered twenty-six different languages, including Sanskrit!

Webster was an intensely patriotic individual who believed that America had to shed itself of its British influence and develop its own sense of American cultural identity and unity. The best way to do this, he believed, was to reshape the English language and literature so that they would reflect the unique American culture and create a national language that was free of localism. The creation of an American language would bind the people together and help produce a strong sense of nationalism. In his dictionary there appeared for the first time ever such American words as *plantation, hickory, presidential,* and *pecan.*

Webster knew that if Americans were to develop this sense of national identity and pride, the process would best be started at an early age. Accordingly, he wrote his blue-backed speller, one of the most successful books ever written. Roughly 100 million copies were printed, and it is estimated that more than a billion readers used the book—a record surpassed only by the Bible. Oftentimes, the *American Spelling Book* was the only book schoolchildren had, since it served as a combination primer, reader, and speller. The book abounded in moral stories and lessons, as well as word lists and guides to pronunciation. Webster must be credited with the fact that Americans differ from the British in writing *color* instead of *colour* and *center* instead of *centre.* Not only did he set the style for American spelling, but he made it the liveliest subject in the classroom. Spelling bees and other spelling games brightened up what otherwise was typically dull instruction.

Known as the "schoolmaster of the republic," Noah Webster campaigned for free schools for both boys and girls, where children could learn the virtues of liberty, just laws, patriotism, hard work, and morality. He was an educational statesman whose work, more than anyone else's, helped to create a sense of American language and national culture.

> *If a nation expects to be ignorant and free, in a state of civilization, it expects what never was and will never be.*
>
> — THOMAS JEFFERSON —

The availability of women teachers at low salaries during the late nineteenth century helped keep education costs down but, at the same time, contributed to the low salary problem that is still with us today.

(*Historical Pictures Service*)

What about religious study?

And what was to be done about religious study? The ability of different religious groups to exist together in one school, as in democracy itself, demanded that no one religious group be favored over another. Although there were many competing proposals, the common schools ultimately settled on the teaching of basic moral values, such as honesty and sincerity, as substitutions for direct religious instruction. However, falling back on this least common denominator did not satisfy many religious groups.

The debate over what role the schools should play in developing values, morals, and ethics continues today. We'll return to the subject of moral or character education in Chapters 5 and 10 and we'll give more attention to the controversies surrounding the role of religion in the public schools and multicultural and bilingual education—issues that relate very closely to the arguments for and against the common school.

VICTORY OF THE COMMON SCHOOL Many seeds of the common school movement were sown in the form of one-room schools, mandated in the early New England school laws and in the Northwest Ordinances of 1785 and 1787. Between 1820 and 1920, the establishment of common schools made steady progress around the country. By the middle of the nineteenth century and certainly by the end of the Civil War, thanks in large part to the efforts of Horace

Mann and other common school advocates, the ideal of universal elementary education was generally acknowledged, if not universally practiced. By 1867, two states (Massachusetts and Vermont) and the District of Columbia had passed compulsory attendance laws in addition to making common schools generally available. By 1900, thirty-two states had such laws, and all states did by 1930. In the North and West, states gradually passed laws for school systems to be supported by tax money and controlled by the state.

Public school enrollment burgeons

As a result, between the Civil War and World War I the number of students in schools grew enormously. In 1870, 57 percent of children between five and eighteen years old were enrolled in some form of schooling. By 1918, more than 75 percent of that age range were enrolled.[4] In 1870, average attendance was forty-five days a year; in 1918, more than ninety days. Thus, the hundred years between 1820 and 1920 witnessed extraordinary growth in the commitment to free, publicly supported, universal education.

Other Developments in Elementary Education

EUROPEAN INFLUENCES   From Europe came new ideas about proper education. One of the most far-reaching experiments was the *kindergarten,* a "children's garden," where pleasant children's activities, such as songs and stories, were used to lay a foundation before formal education began. Friedrich Froebel of Germany developed the first kindergarten in 1837. The curriculum of Froebel's school expressed his emphasis on children's individual differences. Each child was encouraged to explore activities in art, science, music, and language,

Froebel's kindergartens

HORACE MANN

(1796–1859)

Horace Mann was the radical educational reformer of his day. Though trained as a lawyer, he became eminently successful as an educator and politician. Asked why he had exchanged the practice of law for education, he answered that "the interests of a client are small compared with the interests of the next generation."

Born in Franklin, Massachusetts, not long after the Revolutionary War, Mann received only the most rudimentary schooling until he was fifteen. Most of his education was self-acquired, a circumstance that profoundly influenced his philosophy of education. He studied diligently in order to be admitted to Brown University, where he became a brilliant student. In 1827, Mann was elected to the Massachusetts House of Representatives, and a luminous political career lay ahead of him, but he became committed, instead, to education and to the use of political methods to bring about educational reform.

Mann made it his aim to abolish the cruel floggings that were then routine in the public schools. Schoolmasters believed it their duty to drive the devil out of their students, and many schools administered from ten to twenty floggings a day. Most schoolkeepers believed flogging to be an aid to learning. Not only were students treated cruelly; attendance at school was itself a punishment. Schools were often little better than hovels: the lighting was poor and many buildings were unsanitary and unsafe. Mann criticized corporal punishment and inadequate facilities in public speeches, lectures, and letters, and lobbied for reform in the state legislature and in Congress.

Horace Mann strongly believed in the ideals of the common school and championed its cause throughout his career. He saw education as a tool of liberation by which the poor could raise themselves, African-Americans could become emancipated, and handicapped children could adjust to their disabilities. After all, Mann reasoned, education had brought him fame and position. It was over 150 years ago, then, that the idea of social mobility through education was born in America.

For education to be as powerful a force as he en-for example, in a spirit of cooperation and play. In the kindergarten, play helped children express themselves to develop their unique physical, spiritual, emotional, and intellectual selves. The first American experiments were actually made before the Civil War, but in 1873 a public school kindergarten was established in St. Louis, and the idea spread rapidly.

European influence also resulted in greater emphasis on the interests of the child in elementary education. Johann Pestalozzi modeled his educational doctrines in a Swiss experimental school at the beginning of the nineteenth century. Pestalozzi attempted to educate the heads, hearts, and hands of his pupils, relying on attitudes of acceptance and love of the individual student to reach large numbers of poor and handicapped children. Among his instructional techniques were *object lessons,* lessons that focused on actual objects and pictures. He also emphasized learning through sense perceptions and sequencing of learning experiences from the known to the unknown.

Pestalozzi and Herbart

German educator Johann Freidrich Herbart, influenced by Pestalozzi's thinking, also contributed to a science of education. For Herbart, the goal of education was to develop cultured human beings guided by the highest ethical principles. Education, then, was primarily a moral enterprise.

European thinkers, and American educators influenced by them, believed that students could learn best by direct experience, by using their senses and relating new learning to their previous knowledge. As a result, some schools incorporated a lot of physical activity and manual training in their curriculum.

visioned it, Mann thought it imperative to lengthen the school term and to raise teachers' salaries. To make learning more relevant and enjoyable, he helped introduce new textbooks designed to illustrate the relationship between knowledge and the practical problems of society. Mann organized libraries in many schools, making books readily available to students. He believed less in the formal curriculum than in individual learning—undoubtedly because of his own self-education.

Mann was responsible for the establishment of the Massachusetts Board of Education and for the founding in 1839 of the first public normal school (a two-year school chiefly for the training of elementary teachers) in Lexington, Massachusetts. Although the normal school opened with only three students, the concept spread and was widely imitated throughout the country. Mann was intensely interested in teacher training, and he believed that teachers should be intellectual, moral, and cultural models for their communities.

Many of Mann's ideas were controversial, but he was most violently denounced for his position on religion in the schools. Though a religious man, he believed that

religious training belonged outside the schools, which should be run by the state. As a result of his views, Mann was attacked from many Boston pulpits.

Mann did not limit his reformist zeal to educational issues. When he was elected to Congress in 1849, he denounced slavery and attacked the industrial system, urging that workers be better paid, child labor be abolished, factories be made safer, and slums be eliminated. No educator, he said, could remain neutral about social injustice. Theories and ideals must be put into practice in society; otherwise, he argued, education is mere empty words.

Mann was regarded as a dreamer and a visionary by many of his colleagues. When he took over the presidency of Antioch College in 1852, opened its doors to all races and religious sects, and admitted women on an equal basis with men, some educators predicted that these measures would promote the collapse of higher education. Mann aroused further annoyance by remarking that many Antioch students were more brilliant than their professors. Were he alive today, Mann might still be fighting for ideas he espoused more than a century ago. Many people have not accepted these ideas yet.

This innovation was not designed to train technical workers but rather to complement and round out traditional intellectual instruction. Maria Montessori, whose major contributions appear on page 115, was particularly influential in developing a curriculum that emphasized learning through the senses for young children. Followers of Johann Herbart, in particular, advocated instructional methods to help learners make connections between what is known and what is to be learned.

The thoughts of Froebel, Pestalozzi, Herbart, and Montessori, among others, entered American education through their influence on issues of curriculum and instruction. The emphasis on the child's interest and experience, advocated by the progressive educators (described in this chapter and in Chapter 3) and still strong in American elementary education, owes much to these European thinkers.

CURRICULUM CHANGES   During the colonial period, it was hardly necessary for one to know anything beyond the three Rs unless one was wealthy and wanted to go on to college. In the early and mid-nineteenth century, the common school curriculum simply expanded on the traditional curriculum. The primary concern was less with religious training and more with obtaining functional knowledge for life after school. Subjects such as spelling, geography, history, and government were added because they were considered important for good

JOHANN PESTALOZZI

(1746–1827)

For many people, the choice of teaching as a life's work is clear and simple. For others, the path is hidden and their journey unclear. The famed Swiss educator Johann Pestalozzi was one of those who took a less direct route. Well into middle age, Pestalozzi gave every sign of being a bungling failure. As a youth in Zurich he hated school, and afterward he pursued a long series of abortive occupational ventures. Nor was he a success as a personality. Raised by his widowed mother and a maid, he developed great sensitivity but remained overly dependent on women. In later life, the fame he achieved reportedly went to his head. But despite all his personal failings, Pestalozzi is both a hero and a model for educators.

After attending the University of Switzerland, where he finally learned to enjoy studying and became active in social and political reform, Pestalozzi established an orphanage in his own home, where he taught neglected children the rudiments of agriculture and simple trades. But the orphanage failed in 1780, and Pestalozzi, in despair, went into seclusion to write *The Evening Hour of*

a Hermit, a moving compendium of aphorisms and reflections.

Much later, at the age of fifty-two, he began a new career. When Napoleon's armies massacred the citizens of the town of Stans, he collected several dozen destitute children and cared for them under extremely difficult conditions. Pestalozzi made the Institute for the Poor an educational experiment, teaching the children to spin, weave, and do farm work, as well as to study. But because he had accepted more students, including retarded children, than he could accommodate, he was forced to close the school for lack of funds. This was one more failure in an uninterrupted series, but Pestalozzi was undaunted. He had found his vocation in teaching and his happiness among children.

In 1805 Pestalozzi founded a boarding school in an abandoned castle at Yverdon, which flourished for twenty years. It quickly became famous and attracted students from all over Europe. Its curriculum, which emphasized drawing, writing, singing, physical exercise, group recitations, map making, and field trips, was based on the principle of "sense impression"—the idea that we understand only what we observe clearly, and that words and ideas have meaning only when they are related to concrete

citizenship. Natural science, physical training, and mechanical drawing were also included to provide a complete, well-rounded education.

In 1893 the Committee of Fifteen was appointed by the National Education Association to study the issue of curriculum, and the committee's report highlighted the needs and structure of a subject-centered curriculum. The eight-year elementary curriculum was to concentrate on the study of grammar, literature, arithmetic, geography, and history. Around this core, subjects such as drawing, natural science, hygiene, music, physical education, algebra, and morals would be intertwined. The eight-year sequence of the curriculum not only reflected the considerable expansion since the early days of the common school but also showed a clear commitment to a traditional, subject-centered orientation.

Committee of Fifteen

APPLICATION OF PSYCHOLOGY TO EDUCATION　Among various new developments in the early 1900s was the growth of psychology and its application, in theories of learning and behavior, to education. These theories challenged traditional educational wisdom and did so on scientific grounds. Statistical methods and standardized testing were increasingly used to evaluate intelligence and educational achievement. Although far from perfect, these methods began to provide a basis by which educational standards and the effectiveness of different methods of instruction could be measured objectively around the nation.

Scientific methods

objects. Pestalozzi thus made great contributions to our understanding of teaching methods, putting considerable stress on the importance of concrete situations in the child's learning. The study of geography involved field trips and the construction of elaborate models of whole territories. Pestalozzi anticipated modern methods of math instruction by using concrete objects to develop number competence. Four students or four chairs, for instance, illustrated the concept *four*. Students learned to read and write with slates, pencils, and alphabet cards. Pestalozzi also emphasized the importance of art in the curriculum, not only to provide an emotional outlet for the children but also to encourage creativity and develop intellectual discipline.

Pestalozzi's educational theory was built on the assumption that human beings are motivated by three drives: primitive impulses, social needs, and ethical yearnings. He conceived of education as the process by which ethics triumph over animal impulses. His model of learning was the family, with the teacher acting like a parent and serving as a model to be imitated. The ideal of love governed Pestalozzi's philosophy of education—love that should not be modified or withdrawn even if the student misbehaves. The teacher, he was convinced, should never pun-

ish or show disapproval, a very novel attitude in the early nineteenth century. The Yverdon curriculum offered carefully graded instruction, allowance for individual differences, and ability grouping; in general, Pestalozzi was less concerned with "meeting standards" than with the integrity of the students and their work.

Misunderstood by his contemporaries, who considered him too radical and emotional and accused him of taking children too seriously, Pestalozzi nevertheless achieved fame and international influence within his lifetime. He came to be called the Christopher Columbus of elementary education because he opened up so much new territory in that field. Several foreign governments sent teachers to Yverdon for instruction—Pestalozzi's teacher-training department was unique at the time—and he was made an honorary citizen of the French Republic and knighted by the czar of Russia.

When he died in 1827, he was buried in a school yard. Later, the citizens of the Swiss town at Aaragon erected a statue for him, an honor usually reserved for politicians and soldiers.

Advocates of love and acceptance in the educational process owe and acknowledge a heavy debt to Johann Pestalozzi.

Table 4.1 Major European Educational Thinkers

Name	Dates	Nationality	Major contributions
Johann Comenius	1592–1670	Czech	Emphasized sensory experience in learning
			Materials and instruction should be based on developmental stages of child growth
			Developed textbooks that were among the first to contain illustrations
			Stressed that schools should be joyful and pleasant places
John Locke	1632–1704	English	Believed that at birth the mind is a blank slate, *tabula rasa*
			Believed we acquire knowledge of world through our senses
			Pioneer of the inductive, or scientific, method
			Recommended utilitarian and practical learning in a slow, gradual process
Jean Jacques Rousseau	1712–1778	Swiss born/ French citizen	Like Comenius, recognized different stages of human growth
			Believed nature, not school, was the best teacher; wrote the novel *Emile,* which expressed these ideas
			Preferred the primitive, emotional person to the rational, scientific individual
			Wanted to liberate the child and adult from restrictions of social institutions, including schools
Johann Pestalozzi	1747–1827	Swiss	Stressed the importance of children learning through their senses and concrete situations
			Believed humans are motivated by three drives: primitive impulses, social needs, and ethical yearnings
			Education is the process by which ethics triumphs over animal impulses
			Advocated love and unconditional acceptance of children; schools should be like warm and loving homes

Table 4.1 Major European Educational Thinkers (*cont.*)

Name	Dates	Nationality	Major contributions
Johann Herbart	1776–1841	German	Believed the chief aim of education was moral development
			Developed the concepts of curriculum correlation—each subject should be taught so it relates to other subjects
			Believed history, geography, and literature were core subjects
			Developed Herbartian method of instruction: (1) preparation; (2) presentation; (3) association; (4) systematization; and (5) application
Friedrich Froebel	1782–1852	German	Introduced the kindergarten, or "child's garden," whose goal was the cultivation of the child's self-development, self-activity, and socialization
			Believed the teacher should be a model of human dignity and cultural values
			Songs, stories, and games stimulated the child's imagination and transmitted the culture
Maria Montessori	1870–1952	Italian	Established preschools run on the principle of allowing children freedom within a carefully designed environment
			Curriculum focused on three types of experiences: practical, sensory, and formal studies
			Developed learning materials designed to develop sensory and muscular coordination
			Required considerable training of teachers to implement the structured curriculum

CONSOLIDATION   The growth of school enrollments, especially outside the cities, would not have been possible without the consolidation of smaller school districts into larger, unified systems. Although the one-room school had served well in the days of the frontier, as areas developed it became clear that the smaller, poorer districts could not provide the educational opportunities available in larger, wealthier ones. As early as 1869, Massachusetts allowed two districts to merge. In 1910, more than half the states allowed such unification. By the 1920s, the growth of industry and the invention of the automobile (and the school bus) helped consolidate the large number of one-room schools around the country into centrally located, modern facilities that could serve larger areas better than the old district schools.

THE PROGRESSIVE EDUCATION ASSOCIATION John Dewey (who is discussed more fully in Chapter 3) and other educators tried to create new, experimental, child-centered schools in the early 1900s. In 1919, the establishment of the Progressive Education Association was a formalized attempt to reform education according to the following principles:

1. The child should have freedom to develop naturally.
2. Natural interest is the best motive for work.
3. The teacher is a guide, not a taskmaster.
4. A student's development must be measured scientifically, and not just by grades.
5. Students' general health and physical development require attention.
6. The school and the home must work together to meet children's needs.
7. The progressive school should be a leader in trying new educational ideas.[5]

The progressive school movement eventually went in several different directions. Some educators argued for letting children be free to do whatever they wanted; others tried to make the school into a community center for recreation, adult education, and even social reform. Critics ranged from traditionalist advocates of the subject-centered curriculum to some progressives, like Dewey himself, who argued that the ties between society and the child would be broken if children were granted total freedom to do whatever they wanted.

The 1940s brought a rather conservative reaction to the progressivism of the previous generation. However, it is good to remember that many ideas we take for granted now—such as teaching through student projects, field trips, and nonlecture methods of instruction—were hotly debated innovations that were

Influence of progressives

introduced by progressive educators. Many "new" ideas were in fact first tried by progressives: inquiry-based discovery learning; mastery learning, in which students move at their own pace through sequenced problem solving; performance contracting for individualized learning; differentiated staffing, in which staff are trained for different skills so as to create an educational team; flexible scheduling, in which school time is not necessarily bound to calendar time or specific hours; open classrooms, in which students can move about freely among a variety of activities and learning centers; team teaching; and nongraded schools, in which students can move at their own pace with variable requirements.[6]

SINCE WORLD WAR II Soon after the atomic bomb fell on Hiroshima in August 1945, people began to realize that we had entered a new age. The role of the United States in world affairs increased tremendously, thus broadening the scope of educational objectives. Studying problems of the world community and the availability of air-age maps and polar projections are just a couple of examples. The use of the single textbook was supplemented by a great variety of learning resources. Other major developments in elementary education included an emphasis on providing special educational programs for exceptional children and the rapid increase in kindergartens. Between 1948 and 1953, the number of schools offering special education services increased by 83 percent, and enrollments in kindergartens in public schools increased from 595,000 in 1939–40 to 1,474,000 in 1953–54.[7]

Special education receives attention

During the 1950s and 1960s, with the stimulus of the Soviet launching of the space satellite Sputnik, a number of national curriculum projects were developed and implemented in the elementary schools, particularly in mathematics, science, and social studies. These curricula stirred up controversy because many individuals believed that they were too theoretical and not practical enough.

New curriculum projects

Also during the 1950s and 1960s, two types of students received major attention from elementary school educators: the gifted and the disadvantaged. The gifted students received attention because of our nation's concern over the Cold War with the Soviet Union and our perceived need to produce scientific breakthroughs to insure our military superiority over the Soviets. As the movement for civil and human rights gained momentum, more and more curriculum reform movements also focused on the "culturally disadvantaged" child. In response to judicial decisions and to protests by minority groups, the federal government advanced significant financial aid to change schools to better address the needs of these children. Compensatory education programs such as Head Start and Title I of the Elementary and Secondary Education Act were implemented to improve the learning of disadvantaged children. (See Chapter 11 for more details on compensatory education programs.)

Education of gifted and disadvantaged

As achievement test and SAT test scores declined during the 1970s, many parents, politicians, and educators argued that the schools had tried to accomplish too much and had lost sight of their basic purposes. A return to the basics seemed to be the cry of the late 1970s and the early 1980s. Whether elementary schools in the 1990s will tend to emphasize academic rigor alone or shift again toward practices more compatible with a progressive philosophy remains to be seen. However, at the beginning of the 1990s standardized test scores show little improvement. Academic rigor continues to be emphasized, but more programs are being developed to meet the needs of students who are at risk of dropping out.

Back to the basics

Although a public elementary school education is now available universally, the issues of what constitutes a proper education—how comprehensive it should be, how secular it should remain, and how basic learning should be defined—are far from resolved. (Chapters 8, 9, 11, and the epilogue describe in more detail the current elementary school curriculum, life in present-day schools, social issues affecting the elementary schools today, and the authors' visions of schools of the future.)

SECONDARY EDUCATION

In the history of American secondary education, there have been four major institutions. The first type of secondary school, prevalent in the early colonial period, was the *Latin grammar school,* whose main purpose was to prepare

Table 4.2 Types of Elementary Schooling

Type of school	Location	Time period	Purpose
Dame schools	Most of the colonies	Seventeenth century	Private school held in housewife's home; taught basic reading, spelling, and religious doctrines
Town schools	New England	Seventeenth and part of eighteenth century	Locally controlled institution, public but not free; simple curriculum of reading, writing, catechism, and arithmetic
Moving schools	New England	Eighteenth century	Provided schooling for communities spread out over wide areas; an itinerant teacher moved from village to village
District schools	New England, primarily	Mid-eighteenth to mid-nineteenth century	Replaced town and moving schools; public but not free; each district hired its own schoolmaster, again with emphasis on basic skills
Private tutoring	The South, primarily	Seventeenth to early nineteenth century	For children of wealthy
Private venture schools	Primarily Middle Colonies, but widespread	Eighteenth–nineteenth century	Private schools, offering whatever subjects the schoolmaster chose and parents wanted for their children
Common schools	New England, Middle Colonies, and the South at first; now universal	1830 to present	Provided free, public, locally controlled elementary schooling; curriculum emphasized basic skills, moral education, and citizenship
Kindergartens	Widespread	1855 to present	Emphasized play and constructive activities as preparation for elementary schools

students for college. The *English grammar school,* established in the latter half of the colonial period, was intended to provide a practical alternative education for students who were not interested in college. The third type of school, which flowered in the early national period, was the *academy.* Although its major purpose was to combine the best of both types of grammar schools, the academy gradually took on a college-oriented direction in the nineteenth century. Finally, evolving naturally from the elementary common school, the *public comprehensive high school* became the predominant form of secondary education in America in the twentieth century. A uniquely American institution, the comprehensive high school provides, within a single institution, both a preparation for college and a vocational education for students not going on to college.

Four types

LATIN GRAMMAR SCHOOLS   In the colonial period, all secondary education (that is, all education beyond the elementary level) served the sole purpose of training for entrance to college. The earliest secondary institution was the Latin grammar school, whose name gradually came to mean "college preparatory school." The term *prep school* still carries that classical connotation today.

Early Forms

A boy entered a Latin grammar school around age seven or eight and spent the next seven years learning Latin texts written either by ancient Romans or medieval scholars. Much work was memorized, and over three or four years the student learned composition and writing of Latin verses. Following this, the student studied Greek, moving in the final year to classical Greek writers and the New Testament. He also might have given some attention to the study of the Hebrew language.

Emphasis on classical education

The first Latin grammar school in the colonies is generally considered to have been established in 1635 in Boston. It was public, open to boys of all social classes. The Old Deluder Satan Act of 1647, which required communities of fifty or more families to establish elementary schools, also required communities of one hundred or more families to establish Latin schools. By 1700, there were twenty-six such secondary schools throughout New England; however, enrollment was generally small and was limited primarily to the upper class. Only 202 students were enrolled in the two existing Boston Latin schools in 1769.[8] At first, Latin grammar schools were found primarily in New England; a bit later they were instituted in the Middle Colonies. Wealthy families in the South generally either hired tutors or sent their sons back to England for college preparation.

ALTERNATIVE FORMS OF COLLEGE PREPARATION   During the colonial period, many students (especially in the South) received their secondary education from tutors or at private venture schools, which were more common in the Middle Colonies. Instruction provided by a single schoolmaster obviously lacked variability and dependability. Gradually, corporate schools were developed; these institutions were governed by a board of trustees or directors and were able to continue as a corporate endeavor beyond the tenure of any particular teacher.

ENGLISH GRAMMAR SCHOOLS   The growth of middle-class businesses in the 1700s led to the demand for a secondary education that would provide practical instruction in everything from navigation and engineering to bookkeeping and foreign languages. Thus there arose private English grammar schools, which catered to the growing number of students who needed more than elementary instruction but were not interested in preparing for college. Classes were offered at various times and places, sometimes to girls as well as to boys. Commercial subjects, rather than religious ones, were taught. Some subjects, such as music, art, and dancing, were actually not practical but were meant to train students for socializing in polite company.

Commercial subjects

SECONDARY EDUCATION OF FEMALES   In the 1700s, private venture English grammar schools were more flexible than the Latin grammar schools and, as a result, were the first secondary institutions to accept female students. Depending on the sophistication of the particular school and the preferences of its clientele, girls typically studied the three Rs, geography, and French, but they also sometimes learned English grammar, history, and Latin. Some practical vocational subjects such as bookkeeping were occasionally taught along with such traditional and socially accepted skills as art and instrumental music.

English grammar schools

Because of the somewhat larger number of private venture schools in the Middle Colonies, girls who lived there probably had greater educational opportunity than girls who lived elsewhere. Quaker leaders, including William Penn and French-born Anthony Benezet, were concerned with and supported the education of several deprived groups, such as African-Americans and Native Americans—and women.

In the South, the daughters of wealthy landowners could receive traditional instruction in the various arts and letters, such as music, dancing, and French, which would give them the social skills appropriate for the lady of a household. By the end of the colonial period, there was a double-track education that was as clearly set for middle- or upper-class girls as it was for boys in the English or Latin grammar schools.

Two tracks in South

The Academy   A new type of secondary school grew up during the second half of the eighteenth century. The academy was an attempt to combine Latin and English grammar schools through separate Latin and English departments within one school. Academies were unlike the Latin grammar schools in that the primary language of the academy was English; they were unlike the English grammar schools in that classical subjects were also included in the curriculum. Gradually, the academy took the place of both other types of school.

BENJAMIN FRANKLIN'S ACADEMY   In 1751, Benjamin Franklin established an academy in Philadelphia. Its curriculum was typical of that offered at most academies. It differed from Latin grammar schools in that it focused on practical, useful studies rather than on college preparatory courses. It was an English school, emphasizing the reading and writing of English grammar, rhetoric, and literature to facilitate the communication that one would need in business and trade. Arithmetic, geometry, and astronomy were the forms of mathematics studied. History, in English translations, geography, political science, religion, and morality were also taught. Both classical and modern languages were offered,

Emphasis on practical studies

and students chose languages appropriate for the type of occupation they eventually would enter.

Although Franklin's academy offered all these courses when it was first established, over the years the emphasis shifted back to the classical languages and curriculum. This gradual change was not uncommon in academies, but the ideal of a utilitarian curriculum remained.

GROWTH OF ACADEMIES   The number of private academies grew rapidly following the American Revolution, in response to the growing need for practical business training. As many as one thousand academies existed by 1830, but the highest point was around 1850, when about six thousand academies were in operation.[9] Compared with the Latin grammar schools, the academies included instruction for a larger age range, which on the low end overlapped the curriculum of the common schools, and on the upper end sometimes provided instruction that was as extensive as that of colleges. Because they were private institutions, the academies were also at greater liberty to accept girls.

FEMALE ACADEMIES   The real surge of development in education for girls and young women came in the first half of the 1800s with the growth of academies and seminaries that were established especially for young women. Female academies were established by Emma Willard in Troy, New York (1821); by Catharine Beecher in Hartford, Connecticut (1828); and by Mary Lyon in South Hadley, Massachusetts (1837). A secondary education acquired at one of these institutions was often the highest level of education women would ever receive. Eventually, some of these academies themselves became colleges.

The female academies had to buck the established tradition against formal education for women, who in many quarters were still considered intellectually inferior to men. The schools compromised somewhat by offering courses related to home economics in addition to more classical subjects.

In practical terms, the leaders of the women's education movement were committed to two goals. One was to produce women who could handle the domestic chores and challenges of wives and mothers intelligently and wisely so as to "become companions rather than satellites of their husbands."[10] The curriculum of female academies, therefore, was designed to include subjects similar, but not identical, to those at men's institutions. Domestic skills were presented as practical applications of the more abstract traditional subjects. The other goal of women's education was to train women as teachers.

Practical skills and teacher training

The Public High School

Although the private academies reflected the democratic independence of the middle class, their tuition and fees effectively cut out participation by the poorer working class. In the years following the American Revolution, the growing demand for free public elementary education understandably provided a basis on which to argue for free secondary education. Such schooling at public expense was the educational system most appropriate for democracy, it was argued, and the only system that could maintain democracy.

At the beginning of the 1800s, the appeal of the academies had been to provide training in studies that prepared students for a practical livelihood and not necessarily for college. By the 1840s, the same goal was being demanded of public high schools. Seen in retrospect, the academies were really a link between the earlier grammar school and the later high school.

In 1821, Boston created the first public English high school; a second one, for girls, was established in 1826. The number of public high schools throughout the states increased slowly but steadily as an extension of the common school system. Unlike the academies, high schools were governed by the public rather than by private school boards. Although by no means universally accepted, the argument for free public high schools was a logical one, being based simply on the inherent inequality of providing elementary schools for all and secondary schools only for those who could afford tuition.

A luxury or a right?

Opponents of the idea of public high schools did not dispute the need for common elementary schools. They did argue, however, that secondary school was a luxury and was not within the domain of the taxing authorities. In 1874, however, in the famous *Kalamazoo* case, the Michigan courts ruled that the school district could tax the public to support high schools as well as elementary schools.

Debate over the Secondary Curriculum

In the late nineteenth century, debate shifted from whether public secondary schools should be supported to what the content of the curriculum should be. Guidelines for the curriculum were derived largely from the goals that were expressed for the schools. One goal was to reduce social tensions and strengthen the democratic form of government by bringing together all social classes and ethnic groups. Another goal was to provide better preparation for Americans to participate, upon graduation, in the full range of industrial occupations. In addition, the high schools were to offer specialized vocational and technical training. Finally, the high schools were supposed to provide both a terminal educational experience for most students and a bridge to higher education for those who were capable and chose to pursue further studies.

THE ARTICULATED CURRICULUM   The question of how to achieve these goals generated much debate between 1880 and 1920. The issue was one of *articulation*, referring to the smooth joining of different parts in the educational pyramid.

© 1962 United Feature Syndicate Inc.

In the case of public high schools, several types of articulation were debated. Outside the pyramid, the concern was to provide a curriculum that matched the objectives of different sectors of society. Inside, the concern was how to link the high school curriculum with that of the elementary school, on the bottom, and with college entrance and occupational requirements, on the top.

Linking curricula with college and work

Industry and organized labor made it clear that they wanted high schools to give sound training in technical, commercial, and vocational fields. On the other hand, like a recurring echo, other voices made the case for teaching a basic set of cultural subjects, which they argued had practical application in that students would be trained how to think well, whatever the specific topic.

THE NEA COMMITTEES In the 1890s, the National Educational Association commissioned several committees to investigate these matters: the Committee of Fifteen on Elementary Studies (1893), the Committee of Ten on Secondary Studies (1892), and the Committee of Thirteen on College Entrance Requirements (1895). The Committee of Ten was probably the one that had the most far-reaching impact. However, to put it mildly, one senses a bias in the composition of the committee: there were five college presidents, one professor, two headmasters, and one high school administrator—and no high school teachers![11]

Subject-matter orientation

All three committees tended to be oriented toward subject matter. They subscribed to the now-discarded theory of mental discipline, which holds that a subject, in and of itself, can train the mind to reason better, in the way that exercise affects the body. Essentially, the committees sought to standardize elementary and secondary education as a pre-university experience. The Committee of Thirteen developed the idea that standardized numbers of high school course units, similar to credit hours, in foreign language, mathematics, English, and so forth, should be required for college admission. So although lip service was given to the terminal and vocational aspects of secondary education, courses for the traditional curriculum still guided educational decision making.

THE COMPREHENSIVE HIGH SCHOOL Between the Civil War and World War I, the secondary curriculum shifted considerably. The basic mathematics courses in arithmetic, geometry, and algebra tended to be taught in a more commercial and practical context. American literature began to compete with English literature, and commercial English was added to the study of literary English. The classical languages continued to give way to the modern foreign languages. In the sciences, physiology, chemistry, physics, botany, and astronomy were joined by meteorology, zoology, forestry, agriculture, and geology. Physical education was added to the curriculum. In the social studies, the number of courses in American history grew, although European history continued to be central. Civics and citizenship were added to history. Moral philosophy fell away completely and was replaced by purely commercial courses such as typing, stenography, commercial law, domestic science and home economics, industrial arts, and manual training. Significantly, an increasing number of parallel curricula—such as English, college preparatory, manual training, science, and so forth—might be offered in a single high school.[12]

A more diverse curriculum

GROWTH OF JUNIOR HIGH AND MIDDLE SCHOOLS   Despite the NEA Committee recommendations, how to divide grade levels for elementary and secondary training was an issue that was debated for some time. The main question was when to stop teaching basic skills and start teaching content: Should there be eight elementary grades and four of secondary school, or six elementary and six secondary? The pattern of ending elementary school after sixth grade, with six grades of secondary school, gradually gained acceptance, but this division came under fire for several reasons. Educators wanted to introduce new studies to the curriculum. They sought to give greater attention to the pupils as individuals and to gain greater understanding of adolescent development in general. There was also growing concern about keeping pupils in school past the elementary level.

In an attempt to resolve these issues, educators began to experiment with various ways to reorganize the grades. Finally, in the school year of 1909–10, in both Columbus, Ohio, and Berkeley, California, a separate program was established for the intermediate grades 7, 8, and 9. The new grouping was called *junior high school*. By 1916, 184 urban school systems had some form of intermediate school, with grades divided in patterns of six elementary–two intermediate–four secondary, or six elementary–three intermediate–three secondary. By 1926, over 800 systems had a six–three–three organization, and that pattern has predominated ever since.[13]

Since the 1960s, however, the system of five elementary–three intermediate–four secondary grades has become increasingly popular, with a middle school for grades 6, 7, and 8 rather than a junior high school. Advocates argue that middle schools have significant advantages over junior high schools; for one thing, they offer a unique environment where ten to thirteen-year-olds are free to grow up at their own rates and where attention is focused on the needs of this age group rather than on mimicking the high school's emphasis on academic and sports competition, as is often the case with junior high schools. Because of the earlier onset of puberty in today's children, sixth-graders may be better served in a school designed for early adolescents in grades 6, 7, and 8 than in an elementary school. And giving the ninth grade, which is still considered the first year in the college entrance sequence, to the high school frees middle schools to try new programs and new approaches without having to make them specifically applicable to college preparation.

Since the middle 1980s there has been a deepening national commitment to the improvement of the education of early adolescents, with a strong emphasis on personal growth and development. In 1989 the Carnegie Corporation issued a report, *Turning Points: Preparing American Youth for the 21st Century*, that outlined many of the problems that confront these youngsters and that offered recommendations to build support for and educate young adolescents through new relationships between schools, families, and health and community institutions. As this report states, "There is a crucial need to help adolescents at this early age to acquire durable self-esteem, flexible and inquiring habits of mind, reliable and relatively close human relationships, a sense of belonging in a valued group, and a sense of usefulness in some way beyond the self. They need to find constructive expression of their inherent curiosity and exploratory energy; and they need a basis for making informed, deliberate decisions—especially on matters that have large consequences, such as educational futures and drug use."[14]

Middle school characteristics

Elements that encourage this kind of support and that are desired characteristics of effective middle schools include:

1. a home base and teacher-advisor for each student
2. flexibly scheduled school days, often with some form of block schedule
3. interdisciplinary team teaching
4. multiage student grouping
5. a curriculum that focuses on student personal development, skills for continued learning, and introduction to the areas of organized knowledge
6. personalized instruction with students progressing at their own rates
7. a wide range of exploratory activities[15]

A recent report indicated that middle school growth is on the increase. In the 1980s at least 35 percent of the new schools established were of the middle school type, compared with just 4 percent of the junior high school type.[16]

VICTORY OF THE COMPREHENSIVE HIGH SCHOOL   In the twentieth century, public high schools continued to spread. The process of consolidating school districts, which we discussed earlier in the context of combining the one-room schools, also made the comprehensive high school available to many students who otherwise would not have had access to it. In 1890, students in public high schools were only 1.6 percent of all students enrolled. By 1920, they represented 10.2 percent of all students; by 1950, 22.7 percent; and by 1980, 32.9 percent of America's school enrollment was in public high schools. In actual numbers, over 2 million students attended public high schools in 1920; by 1950, 5.7 million were attending; and by 1980, the number had risen to 13.2 million. Because of declining birthrates, the estimated number of high school students had fallen to 11.3 million by 1990. This decline in public high school enrollment is expected to reverse itself, however, during the 1990s, and projected enrollments by the year 2000 are expected to be back up to 13.4 million.[17] (See Table 4.3.)

Enrollment soars

SECONDARY EDUCATION TODAY   The most remarkable observation that can be made about secondary education today is how little it has changed over the last one hundred years. There have been changes, of course, but they have been small relative to the changes that have occurred in American living patterns, values, technologies, and careers. The curriculum revolves around subjects that are taught by specialists and that are not very different from the subjects that were offered in schools during World War I. As we will point out in Chapter 9, Larry Cuban's study of schooling in the secondary schools reveals that instructional practices there have changed very little from 1890 until the present day.

Table 4.3 Historic Summary of Public Elementary and Secondary School Enrollments (in thousands)

	Total	Elementary	Secondary
1870	6,872	6,792	80
1880	9,867	9,757	110
1890	12,723	12,520	203
1900	15,503	14,984	519
1910	17,814	16,899	915
1920	21,578	19,378	2,200
1930	25,678	21,279	4,399
1940	25,434	18,833	6,601
1950	25,112	19,387	5,725
1960	36,087	27,602	8,485
1970	45,619	32,597	13,022
1980	40,918	27,677	13,242
1990*	40,801	29,546	11,255
2000*	44,186	30,754	13,432

* = projected

Sources: Thomas D. Snyder, *Digest of Education Statistics 1990* (Washington, D.C.: U. S. Department of Education, National Center for Education Statistics, 1989), p. 45; and Debra E. Gerald and William J. Husser, *Projections of Education Statistics to 2001* (Washington, D.C.: U. S. Department of Education, National Center for Education Statistics, 1990), p. 4.

High school structure resists change

The reason lies in the basic structure of the high school. Its organizing framework, developed in the nineteenth century, persists today across all regions of the country. High schools are complicated organizations, requiring considerable orchestration to work efficiently. A change in one part of the system means that other parts must also change in reaction to the first change. As a result, relatively little change occurs.

Yet the 1980s and 1990s have witnessed strong efforts to revise some aspects of the secondary school curriculum. In response to numerous reports on the condition of secondary education, legislators have enacted reforms designed to make the curriculum more academically rigorous, to insure minimum competency levels of high school graduates, and to prepare students for the demands of an increasingly technological society. In Chapters 8 and 9 we will detail what some of these reports discovered about what is taught in the high schools and what life there is like; we'll also discuss reforms enacted in the late 1980s. Chapter 11 will give you a better idea of some of the problems facing secondary education, and in the epilogue you can read our recommendations for the future.

PRIVATE EDUCATION

Private schools have always been part of American education. Historically, they have served three major purposes, providing (1) instruction for various religious denominations, (2) an exclusive education for the wealthy, and (3) an alternative

Table 4.4 Types of Secondary Schooling

Type of school	Location	Time period	Purpose
Latin grammar schools	New England, Middle Colonies; a few in the South	Seventeenth and eighteenth centuries	Emphasized Latin and classical studies; designed to prepare young men for college
English grammar schools	Middle Colonies and New England; a few in the South	Eighteenth century	Private secondary schools designed to provide practical rather than college preparatory studies
Academies	Middle Colonies, New England; a few in the South	Eighteenth and nineteenth centuries	Private secondary schools designed to prepare young people for business and life; emphasized a practical curriculum, but gradually shifted back to college preparation
High schools	New England, Middle Colonies at first; now universal	1821 to present	Provided public secondary schooling; combined functions of Latin grammar schools and academies (college preparation and preparation for life and business)
Junior high schools	First in California; now universal	1909 to present	Designed to provide students in grades 7–9 with better preparation for high school
Middle schools	Universal	1950 to present	Designed to meet the unique needs of preadolescents, usually grades 6–8; an alternative to junior high schools

for any group that finds the available forms of education unsatisfactory. For more than 150 years, until the growth of the common school movement in the early 1800s, *most* education in America was private.

Since the middle of the nineteenth century, by far the largest private school enrollments have been in schools run by the Roman Catholic church. The earliest Catholic schools existed primarily in the Spanish-speaking Southwest and in French-speaking Louisiana. However, Irish and Italian immigration, after 1840, increased the support of Catholic institutions in the North and East. The total number of Catholic schools grew from about one hundred in 1840 to about three thousand in the 1880s, to eight thousand in 1920, and up to over thirteen thousand in the early 1960s. Many Catholic schools have closed since the mid-1960s; by 1989, the number of Catholic schools had declined to just under nine thousand.[18]

EDUCATION: A WORLD VIEW

CONTROL OF SCHOOLS

As is mentioned in this chapter, local control of schools has been an important theme of American education. In the United States the legal responsibility for the operation and administration of public schools is delegated to each state. Typically, statewide goals and priorities are established, curricular offerings are selected and refined, rules and regulations are delineated, and accomplishments and needs within the state are reported. In addition to these policy-making activities, states facilitate the actual operation of school systems through such activities as administering state and federal funds, certifying teachers, and providing educational data and analysis.

The federal government, on the other hand, is not directly involved in the administration of public schooling. However, our federal government has widespread involvement in the schools through more indirect means, such as by supporting school lunch programs, administering education for Native Americans, and underwriting college student loans.

Many policy decisions and administrative activities in American education occur at the local level. Although legal responsibility lies with the state, local educators usually deal with the many practical responsibilities of running schools, such as hiring school personnel, deciding how funds will be used, and determining what programs

will be offered to students. Many current efforts in school reform are focusing on increasing the control of schools at the local level; these efforts include movements for parental choice of schools, site-based management of schools, and teacher empowerment in decision making. As familiar as this description may seem, other countries balance state and local control quite differently than the United States. Let's take a look at local control of schools from a French and British perspective.

In France, public education has been highly nationalized since Napoleon's time. At the federal level, the Ministry of National Education is quite powerful, overseeing education from a preprimary level (beginning at age two) through higher education. This federal ministry approves a program of study and curriculum at all levels. Teachers are expected to follow national guidelines for teaching, detailed plans of study, and specific timelines in completing curriculum. Though teachers in preprimary classrooms are given some flexibility in how they choose to teach, teacher conformity is strongly encouraged at higher levels of education. State inspectors enter classrooms regularly to observe teachers and class sessions. On each teacher, reports are made evaluating the extent to which he or she is meeting national guidelines for education. These reports are then entered in teacher files and subsequently influence teacher promotion. After the federal government establishes a national program of study, it selects the textbooks that are to be used in the schools.

Despite the growth in Catholic schools, by 1890 only about 11 percent of all elementary and secondary students were enrolled in private schools. The number continued to decline to a low of 7.3 percent in 1920 but then gradually increased to a high of 13.6 percent in 1960. It is currently almost 11 percent and is expected to remain about the same during the rest of the twentieth century.[19] The largest number of private school students are enrolled in Catholic schools, with a total student membership of about 2.6 million, compared with an estimate of 1.6 million students in other religious schools and an estimate of 693,000 students in nonsectarian schools.[20]

Discrimination against private schools

The steady reduction in the percentage of private school students in the nineteenth and early twentieth centuries was not only a sign of public school strength; it also reflected outright discrimination and pressure against those who wanted to be "different." An extreme case followed World War I, when Ne-

There are also lists of forbidden texts that are binding on all schools. Few schools have libraries of large enough size to provide reading materials other than those approved by the government. National examinations and certificates play a large role in measuring student achievement of national education objectives. Private schools do exist in France, but the overarching necessity to prepare their students for the same national examinations and certificates as public schools provides the federal government with an indirect means of influencing private education as well.

In contrast, public education in England is largely governed at the local level. Local education authorities (LEAs) have primary control of the governance of public education and are typically composed of members of the city or county council. Each LEA has its own budget and provides guidelines for individual schools in the area. LEAs themselves are typically involved with broad questions of resources for the schools, such as staffing, buildings, and equipment. They provide some guidance to individual schools in the choice and use of curriculum, but only in a very general sense. Individual schools within LEAs are given a great deal of autonomy. They are commonly treated as separate units that can decide their own policies and balance their own budgets. Specific decisions about the curriculum and the use of particular teaching styles are left to the discretion of teachers. With this localized approach to educational decision making, different schools even within the same neighborhood may vary widely. In keeping with this community-based control of education, parents are given the right to choose the type of school they consider appropriate for their children.

Traditionally, the national government has had few direct powers over the LEAs. However, in 1988, the Education Reform Act established a national curriculum for schools for the first time. Over a period of several years, the curriculum will be defined and implemented in each of ten required subject areas. Of particular interest will be the coordination of the national curriculum with the traditional system of national exit exams. Similar in some ways to the national exams required in France, the British General Certificate of Education, Advanced Level, is a formal examination that determines whether the candidate is qualified to graduate from high school. Little or no consideration is given for grades earned in previous years of study. Success on this exam is typically required for entry into college. It remains to be seen how the national curriculum will influence educational practice and governance in England.

George Thomas Kurian (ed.), *World Education Encyclopedia,* vol. 1 & 2, (New York: Facts on File Publication, 1988), pp. 406–426; 1321–1339; Martin R. Davies, "The English National Curriculum: A Landmark in Educational Reform," *Educational Leadership,* 48(5), 28–29.

braska passed a law prohibiting the teaching of German in either public or private schools. However, in 1922, the Supreme Court ruled that a state could not interfere with the prerogative of parents to educate their children as they see fit—in this case at a private school that taught the German language—simply on the grounds of desiring to "foster a more homogeneous people with American ideals. . . ."[21] When, in 1925, an Oregon law required all children to attend public school, a Roman Catholic school and another private school successfully challenged the law on the grounds that their Fourteenth Amendment rights were being abridged.

Still an important alternative

It is significant not only that over the past one hundred years public schools have clearly become the principal mode of education in America, but also that private education has remained an important alternative to the public schools for about 10 to 15 percent of the population. These figures reflect a paradox. On the one hand, from early days, private schools have represented the freedom of immigrant groups to pursue life in America and to educate their children as they choose. That privilege was essential to the young democracy and still represents a basic freedom of choice in America. On the other hand, some argue that private education supports a caste system that is, in principle, not democratic. In addition, they argue, private education casts the quality of public education in a harsh light. The very existence of private forms of education can be viewed as an implied criticism either of the quality of public education or of its availability on equal terms to all comers, irrespective of class, religion, or race.

Should taxes aid private schools?

The major breakthrough for private and religious schools was the passage of the Elementary-Secondary Education Act of 1965, which funneled millions of dollars into private schools through federal programs. In addition, private schools in many states have been receiving assistance ranging from pupil transportation, textbooks, health services, and general auxiliary services to salary supplements for teachers. In general, state assistance in areas other than transportation, milk, school lunch programs, and textbooks has been attacked in the courts. People oppose the use of tax money to support private schools for reasons ranging from outright prejudice to fear that such assistance will undermine the public school system. The National Educational Association and the American Federation of Teachers have consistently opposed the allocation of public money to private schools, on the grounds that the public schools are not adequately funded now and that the situation will worsen if tax money goes to private schools.

The other side of the argument is that the private schools, which provide education for millions of students a year, are lightening the burden of the public schools. If, for example, the Catholic school system should collapse, 2.6 million new students would enroll in the public schools, creating a massive shortage of space, teachers, and money. Advocates of private school aid argue that by partially subsidizing private schools to keep them in operation, the public schools can avoid a deluge of students whom they would be unable to assimilate readily. Estimates of total expenditures for the 1988–89 school year indicate that private elementary and secondary schools spent $15.7 billion.[22] If these schools were to shut down, the public schools would incur a substantial portion of these costs.

Although strict separationists and opponents to public aid to private education have had the support of the courts in recent decades, the controversy over public and private schooling is hardly over. Tensions between private and public education continue to exist, rising in one area, abating in the next. Sometimes the tension is creative, sometimes destructive. The issue is far from being resolved.

EDUCATION OF MINORITIES

The picture of American education drawn up till now has been quite rosy, because the educational achievements of this country over the past 350 years are indeed impressive. There is, however, a less pleasant side to the picture. The history of education provides insight into people's values in general, and the educational experience of minorities tends to reflect how a society relates to them. The somewhat idealized image of the melting pot begins to break down when we look at the experience of nonwhite groups.

Minorities excluded from equal educational opportunities

Ethnic minorities such as African-Americans, Hispanic-Americans, Native Americans, and Asian-Americans traditionally have not been afforded equal educational opportunity in America. It was not until the late nineteenth century, for example, that the federal government made any serious effort to provide education for Native Americans. Prior to that time what formal education they received usually came from missionary groups. American society is still suffering today from the effects of educational neglect of various minority groups.

Education of African-Americans

BEFORE THE CIVIL WAR   As is true of colonial education generally, the earliest motivation to educate African-Americans was religious. In New England, as early as 1717, the Reverend Cotton Mather started an evening school for slaves. In the South, the first attempts to educate African-Americans were carried out by clergymen, particularly English representatives of the Society for the Propagation of the Gospel in Foreign Parts. To dubious slave owners, ministers defended the education of slaves not only as a religious duty to save their benighted souls, but also because conversion to Christianity, it was believed, would make them more docile.[23]

Schools for free African-Americans in North

In the North, schools were established for free African-Americans. In 1731, Anthony Benezet, a French-born Quaker, started a school for slave and free African-American children in Philadelphia. Another school was begun by Benjamin Franklin, as president of the Abolitionist Society, in 1774. In 1787 an African Free School was established in New York City with an enrollment of forty students, which grew to over five hundred by 1820. The city provided funds in 1824 and took over the school in 1834, thus providing education for African-Americans before many white children were receiving it.

Yet conditions were not all bright in the North. In 1833, Prudence Crandall, a white schoolmistress in Canterbury, Connecticut, began to take in African-American girls. The villagers boycotted the school, threw manure into its well, and attempted to burn it down. Finally, a mob broke the windows, and the school ultimately was closed.[24]

In the South, following slave rebellions in the early 1800s, states gradually prohibited altogether the teaching of African-American children, whether slave or free. Some slaves were taught to read by favorably disposed masters. However, slave owners generally reasoned, probably correctly, that reading would lead to thinking, and thinking would lead to the desire for freedom. As the Civil War approached, abolitionist agitation often came from the few liberal colleges, such as Oberlin, in Ohio, and Bowdoin, in Maine, that allowed the enrollment of African-American students.

SINCE THE CIVIL WAR In the period following the Civil War, the seeds for the education of African-Americans that had been sown before the war slowly began to sprout. During the period of Reconstruction, from 1865 into the 1870s, the federal government, through the Freedmen's Bureau and the occupying army, attempted to promote African-American voting registration and schooling. Help also came from private and religious philanthropies in the North. Because it was hoped that whites also would benefit from these endeavors, schooling was advocated for the general public as well. As we pointed out earlier, the common school movement was weakest in the South, and at first most whites refused to participate not only in integrated schools but also in segregated schools, both of which they felt the northern carpetbaggers were forcing on them.

The Tuskegee Normal School was established in 1881 by Booker T. Washington.
(Brown Brothers)

By the end of Reconstruction, southern whites began to allow the existence of separate schools for African-Americans. African-American enrollment in the schools, which had been only 2 percent of the school-age children in 1850, was 10 percent by 1870 and 35 percent by 1890, though it dropped somewhat after that during a period of severe repression by the new white state governments.[25] During this period "Jim Crow" laws were passed separating African-Americans from whites in all areas of life. The vote was effectively taken away from the newly enfranchised African-Americans by poll taxes and "grandfather rules," which allowed the vote only to those African-Americans whose families could vote before the Emancipation, thereby excluding all the freed slaves.

Into these conditions, a young African-American teacher named Booker T. Washington (1856–1915) was called to start an African-American normal school in Alabama, at the Tuskegee Institute, in 1881. What he found there were only a few students, no physical plant, and a hostile white community. Washington, who had been born a slave, realized that the traditional curriculum of the classics would neither prepare his students to help other African-Americans learn nor help to ameliorate the tensions with the white community. Believing strongly in the idea of learning by doing, Washington instructed his students to build the school themselves. In this process, they learned practical skills, grew produce that could be sold to the white community, and in general showed the whites that African-American people could be productive members of society. Booker T. Washington gradually came to be considered the outstanding African-American leader of the time by the white establishment.

But there were a growing number of young African-Americans who, unlike Washington, had not been born into slavery and who felt that Washington's policy of conciliatory training for menial positions in white society would not profit African-American people in the long run. They believed that practical training is necessary, but that there must also be an intellectually sound and academically rich program of study for the "talented tenth" who would form the African-American intellectual leadership. This was the view of W. E. B. DuBois (1868–1963), an African-American intellectual and scholar who held a doctorate from Harvard.

In 1862 the U.S. Congress passed the Morrill Act. This legislation granted each state a minimum of thirty thousand acres of federal land with the proviso that the income from the rent or sale of these lands must be used to establish colleges for the study of agriculture and mechanical arts. A total of 6 million acres of federal land was donated to the states. These land-grant institutions (such as the University of Illinois, Texas A & M, and Michigan State University) became the great multipurpose state universities that now enroll hundreds of thousands of students from all segments of society.

In 1890 Congress enacted a second Morrill Act that increased the endowment of land to the original land-grant colleges but forbade money being given to a college with an admission policy that discriminated against nonwhites *unless* a separate facility for African-Americans existed nearby. This second Morrill Act thus provided federal support to states to create "separate but equal" colleges for African-Americans. As a result of this legislation, a number of "1890 institutions" were created for the higher education of African-Americans. Many of these historically African-American colleges (Florida A & M and North Carolina A & T, for example) still exist today as integrated institutions.

In 1896, in the case of *Plessy* v. *Ferguson,* the Supreme Court upheld the constitutionality of *separate but equal* accommodations for African-Americans. Originally in reference to seating in a railroad car, the ruling was quickly extended to the schools. The practical significance of this ruling was to add federal sanction to the legal separation of African-American schoolchildren from white children, most notably in the South, for almost the next sixty years.

That the southern schools for African-Americans were not equal to those for whites is woefully clear from looking at financial expenditures alone. In 1912, the southern states as a group paid white teachers $10.32 per white child in school but paid African-American teachers only $2.89 per African-American child. In the 1930s, in ten southern states, African-American children made up 34 percent of the school population but received only 3 percent of the funds available for school transportation. As a result, the percentage of southern African-American children attending school ranged from 13 to 17 percent less than white children enrolled; African-American children also attended school an average of twenty-one fewer days a year than did white children. Consequently, it took African-American children from one to four and one-half additional years to complete the eight years of elementary education. During this same period, 55 percent of southern African-American schools were still housed in one-room buildings, and an additional 19 percent were in two-room buildings. Discrimination existed also in the distribution of federal funds, particularly in vocational education, the largest and most important educational program subsidized by the federal government.[26]

Most northern states did not have legal segregation of schools, but the crowding of African-Americans into isolated neighborhoods often resulted in segregation. Furthermore, the large numbers of southern African-American children who migrated with their parents to northern cities often had to be demoted because they had not mastered the same amount of material as their northern agemates. Generally, even in the North, African-American teachers taught African-American children.

Although these conditions continued in varying degrees through the 1940s, some gains were nevertheless achieved. The average daily attendance of African-American children increased and approached that of white students. The salaries of African-American teachers also increased, reducing the gap between the salaries of African-American and white teachers with equal training. After African-Americans had served in two world wars to "save democracy," the National Association for the Advancement of Colored People (NAACP), founded in 1909, began taking their cases to the courts. Beginning with universities rather than elementary schools, the NAACP succeeded in getting the courts to rule various law school facilities to be separate yet clearly unequal.

The stage was finally set for the precedent-shattering case of *Brown* v. *Board of Education of Topeka* (1954), in which the Supreme Court ruled that separate educational facilities are inherently unequal. At the time, the case seemed a climax to one hundred years of struggle to gain educational equality

"Separate but equal"

Southern African-American schools impoverished

De facto segregation in North

However, some gains

Brown v. *Board of Education*

together with so-called emancipation. As the events of the last four decades have shown, the task has not yet been achieved. Debate still exists about what constitutes an equal educational opportunity. Does providing educational equality merely require that equal resources are provided, or should schools be held accountable for educational outcomes such as standardized test scores, dropout rates, and public school achievement? Current approaches to fostering equal educational opportunity include the use of compensatory education programs, desegregation and integration strategies, and magnet schools. Each of these strategies and the parameters and responsibilities of providing an equal educational opportunity will be discussed in more detail in Chapter 11, "What Are the Tension Points in American Education?"

Education of Native Americans

As early as 1622, in an ominous forecast of future policies, one colonist wrote back to England that it was easier to conquer the Indians than to civilize them.[27] The education of Native Americans received less public attention than that of African-Americans because Native Americans were considered an impediment to westward expansion, they were far from major population centers, and their dealings were largely with the federal government.

Initially, the education of Native Americans, like that of African-Americans, had a religious purpose. Once they had been put on reservations, the Native Americans received schooling from missionaries, who attempted to "civilize" them through the three Rs and, of course, the fourth R—religion. These missionary schools were gradually replaced in the 1890s by government boarding schools, which tried to assimilate Native Americans by prohibiting them from speaking their native language and teaching them skills associated with white society, such as farming and mechanical skills for boys and domestic chores for girls. Little emphasis was placed on academics.

The people who had been Native Americans for twenty thousand years finally became American citizens in 1924; however, that did not mean they controlled their own education. The federal government, through the Bureau of Indian Affairs, directed the education of Native Americans until the mid-1970s. During this time Native American participation was virtually ignored, as was acknowledgement of their culture in their educational programs. The elimination of Native American languages and culture was an important strategy in the efforts to assimilate Native Americans.

By 1965 Native Americans began to demand control of their schools, and a few demonstration sites for such schools were funded. These schools were able to include much of the native culture in their curricula, but they were still financially dependent upon the federal government, which meant limited instructional materials and lower-paid teachers than many public schools.

Between 1972 and 1975 Congress enacted three bills that affected Native American education and self-determination. These bills encouraged the establishment of community-run schools, offered grants to develop culturally relevant and bilingual curriculum materials, placed the Office of Indian Education under the U.S. Office of Education (now the Department of Education), and established an advisory council made up of all Native Americans. The Bureau of

* * * * * * * * * * * *

My son, Wind Wolf, is not an empty glass coming into your class to be filled. He is a full basket coming into a different environment and society with something special to share. Please let him share his knowledge, heritage, and culture with you and his peers.

— ROBERT LAKE —

Education of Native Americans began in the eighteenth century with schools run by missionaries.

(Denver Public Library Western History Department)

Indian Affairs is still actively involved in educational matters, but now in a supportive rather than directive capacity.

Today the education of the Native American population in the United States is still plagued by a prevalence of poverty, underachievement, absenteeism, overage students, and a high dropout rate—almost 50 percent between grades 8 and 12. A culturally appropriate curriculum is a necessity to overcome these deficiencies. As is the case with all minority populations, the failure of society as a whole to acknowledge their contributions as a people can result in a loss of their self-worth. This, in turn, can prevent members of that population from succeeding in society, limit their future contributions, and deprive all Americans of a rich contribution to the world.

Education of Hispanic-Americans

Discrimination against Hispanics

As with Native Americans, the first contact Spanish-speaking people had with the United States was often a result of annexation and warfare. Although they had lived in the continental United States for over four hundred years, Hispanic people came into contact with Anglo-Americans only about 150 years ago, and almost from the beginning, there was a cultural clash. Hispanic children first attended religious mission schools, which were gradually replaced by secular public schools. In the process, Spanish language and Hispanic culture were subjected to a type of discrimination that was perhaps less blatant than that against

African-Americans but just as pervasive. The common school of the nineteenth and twentieth centuries, although it opened educational and social opportunities in Anglo-America, often sealed off those opportunities for Hispanic-Americans. Hispanic children tended to receive lower scores than Anglo children on English-language IQ tests, which not only were written in a language that was not their own but which also reflected Anglo middle-class values. Thus, an image of Hispanic children's intellectual inferiority was reinforced.

Since the 1940s, the courts have acknowledged that de facto segregation exists between Anglo and Hispanic schoolchildren and have required corrective integration plans. The 1965 Elementary and Secondary Education Act provided new support to the education of many Hispanics, as it did to the education of

Bilingual education

Native Americans. Another response has been the establishment of bilingual education programs to provide general instruction in the native tongue at the same time that students learn English. As a result, students can enter the English-language curriculum at the appropriate age level for their grade. Bilingual education is just one facet of a general effort toward multicultural education that removes ethnic stereotypes and tries to give a more adequate representation of the Hispanic-American experience. (See Chapter 10 for further discussion of multicultural and bilingual education.)

There is much concern about the education of Hispanics in the United States, although significant progress has been made. For example, between 1970

High dropout rates

and 1988 the proportion of Hispanics that completed four years of high school climbed from 32 percent to 51 percent and those that completed four years of college rose from 5 percent to 10 percent.[28] Although these figures show encouraging progress, they also indicate that almost one-half of Hispanics don't complete high school and 90 percent don't complete college. Furthermore, reading and mathematics proficiencies are significantly lower for the Hispanic population in comparison with the white population. The public schools have not served these students well, and the cost in human and economic terms is enormous. As demographers project higher and higher percentages of Hispanic students enrolled in public schools during the 1990s, the schools' response to their needs will have important consequences for society.

Education of Asian-Americans

Asian-Americans are often discussed as though they were a homogeneous subgroup of Americans. However, the term *Asian-Americans* actually encompasses many ethnic, national, and linguistic groups. This diversity is evident

Diversity among Asian-Americans

from the historical beginnings of different groups of Asian-Americans in the United States and persists into educational issues today.

The three largest groups represented within Asian-Americans are the Chinese, the Japanese, and the Filipinos. Chinese immigrants began arriving in the United States in the 1840s. Most of them were poor and largely uneducated. They helped fulfill a great need for cheap, unskilled laborers in the railroad and other industries in the American West. Intense discrimination was present, however, in part because of competition with white workers for employment. By 1882, an exclusionary act was passed by Congress halting Chinese immigration. Japanese immigrants began arriving in the United States in 1890–1920. Many supplied labor for agricultural industries in Hawaii, until another exclusionary act was passed in 1924 limiting Japanese immigration. Filipinos began immigrating to the United States in the early 1900s. By 1930, their entry into the United States was also limited by a congressional exclusionary act.

Discrimination against Asian-Americans

Discrimination against early Asian-Americans was rampant, especially in the West, where most Asian-Americans settled. School segregation of Chinese-American children in California lasted until at least 1946. Japanese-American children in California were forced to attend segregated schools up until World War II. With the outbreak of World War II, anti-Asian hostility subsided somewhat for immigrants of Chinese, Filipino, and Korean descent. However, the "yellow peril," perceived as emanating from Japanese-Americans, resulted in the imprisonment in detention camps of over 110,000 Japanese-Americans, most of whom were American-born citizens.

Recent Asian immigration

With the end of World War II, discrimination against Asian-Americans began to subside. Naturalization rights were extended to resident Asian aliens. With the postwar expansion of the American economy, many Asian-Americans benefited from greater job opportunities. Previous immigration restrictions were lifted in 1965, and the influx of Asian immigrants greatly increased. Since the U.S. withdrawal from Vietnam in 1975, enormous numbers of Indochinese immigrants have come to the United States and entered our school systems. Adaptation of more recent Asian immigrants has varied because of a range of educational levels and previous socioeconomic circumstances. Results of the 1990 census estimated that Asian and Pacific Islanders numbered roughly 7 million, or slightly more than 3 percent of the United States population. It is projected that by the year 2000 this group will constitute 4 percent of the population.[29]

Stereotypes camouflage problems

With the higher educational achievement and income levels of some Asian-Americans, this group has often been touted as a "model minority" that has overcome discrimination through hard work, perseverance, and industriousness. However, this rosy stereotype is misleading, and has at times contributed to misconceptions and complacency in meeting the educational needs and concerns of Asian-American students.

Language difficulties

Many recent Asian-American immigrants to the United States have little or no knowledge of the English language. This creates formidable language and cultural barriers for students entering the U.S. education system. It may lead to serious family-school discontinuities, alienation from school, and dropout problems. The U.S. Supreme Court established in *Lau* v. *Nichols* (1974) that schools must offer students sufficient special instruction to be afforded equal educational opportunity. There is a pressing need for adequate language instruction for this subgroup of Asian-Americans, and as immigration continues to increase, it is likely this need will grow in our school systems. Educators are still researching the most appropriate and effective means of providing these students an education. (See Chapter 10, "Who Are Today's Students?" for a more complete discussion of bilingual education.)

Need for multicultural education

Another need of Asian-Americans in our current educational system is for increased multicultural education. Curricula in many U.S. schools have been criticized as having an Anglo-centric orientation that pays little attention to the contributions of minority groups in our history. Teachers, when conforming to

Table 4.5 Significant Dates in the History of Minority Education in the United States

1862	The Morrill Act provides for land-grant institutions that now enroll hundreds of thousands of students from all segments of society.
1865	After the Civil War several African-American institutions of higher education are established, including Virginia Union (1865) and Howard University (1867).
1890	The new Morrill Act requires that federal funds be available only to colleges with nondiscriminatory admission policies unless separate facilities for African-Americans exist nearby. As a result, a number of "separate but equal" institutions are established.
1896	In *Plessy* v. *Ferguson*, the U.S. Supreme Court declares the constitutionality of the "separate but equal" doctrine.
1910	Native American children are integrated with white children in local school districts, and a public school curriculum is established in Native American government schools.
1944	The GI Bill of Rights is enacted, serving to break down class barriers and to increase the presence of minority students on college campuses.
1950	The U.S. Supreme Court rules in *Sweatt* v. *Painter* that the University of Texas must admit African-Americans to its law school. In *McLaurin* v. *Oklahoma State Regents for Higher Education*, the U.S. Supreme Court rules that segregation of African-Americans within an integrated institution is illegal.
1954	In *Brown* v. *Board of Education of Topeka*, the U.S. Supreme Court rules that segregation in the public schools is unconstitutional. One year later the Court orders school desegregation.
1964	President Lyndon B. Johnson signs the Civil Rights Act of 1964 prohibiting discrimination on the basis of color, race, religion, or national origin.
1965	The Elementary and Secondary School Education Act provides funds for promoting racial integration in U.S. public schools.
1968	The Bilingual Education Act provides federal funds to help schools develop bilingual education programs. *(table continues next page)*

Table 4.5 Significant Dates in the History of Minority Education in the
United States (*cont.*)

1971	The U.S. Supreme Court rules unanimously in *Swann* v. *Charlotte-Mecklenburg Board of Education* that busing may be ordered to achieve racial desegregation.
1972	The Indian Education Act is passed providing for programs for parental participation in education and for attention to culturally related education needs of Native Americans.
1974	In *Lau* v. *Nichols,* the U.S. Supreme Court establishes that students who do not understand English are being denied a meaningful education. The Court directs the San Francisco board of education to offer Chinese-speaking students sufficient special instruction to enable them to benefit from education. In years to come, prime beneficiaries of this decision will be Spanish-speaking Americans.
1975	The Indian Self-Determination and Education Assistance Act is passed allowing tribes to contract educational services through the Bureau of Indian Affairs rather than through state education agencies.
1978	In the *Regents of the University of California* v. *Bakke,* the U.S. Supreme Court bars quota systems in college admissions but affirms the constitutionality of programs giving advantage to minorities.
1981	The beginning of the Reagan presidential term of office coincides with limited enforcement of civil rights laws.
1986	In *Riddick* v. *School Board of Norfolk,* the U.S. Supreme Court permits the first school district in the United States to end Court-ordered busing of elementary school students.
1988	Overriding President Reagan's veto, Congress passes the Civil Rights Restoration Act of 1987, strengthening the effectiveness of civil rights statutes prohibiting discrimination in federally funded programs.

stereotypes of Asian-Americans as industrious and talented in math and science, may impose unrealistic expectations on Asian-American students, thereby hindering their academic and social development.

Impediments to parental involvement

Parental and community involvement of Asian-Americans in the education process also needs to be fostered. Parents of Asian-American students are frequently noted as being concerned with their children's education. However, because of the respect traditionally afforded educators, they are hesitant to intervene when they are dissatisfied with their children's educational progress. Another deterrent to parental participation is the fact that a much higher proportion of Asian-American families have two parents employed, a situation that

Table 4.6 Significant Dates in the History of American Education

1635	Establishment of the Boston Latin grammar school
1636	Founding of Harvard College, first English-speaking college in the Western Hemisphere
1642	Massachusetts first education law
1647	Massachusetts Old Deluder Satan Act: towns of fifty families or more must provide instruction in reading and writing; towns of one hundred families or more must establish grammar schools
1687–1690	First edition of the *New England Primer*
1701	Episcopal Society for the Propagation of the Gospel in Foreign Parts is founded to begin educational activities in the colonies
1751	Opening of Benjamin Franklin's Philadelphia Academy
1783	Noah Webster published the *American Spelling Book*
1785, 1787	Northwest Ordinance Acts, requiring new states in that territory to set aside land for educational purposes
1821	First public high school in the United States opened in Boston; Emma Willard established first school for women's higher education
1823	First private normal school in the United States opened in Concord, Vermont
1827	Massachusetts law requiring public high schools
1837	Horace Mann made secretary of Massachusetts state board of education
1839	First public normal school in the United States established in Lexington, Massachusetts
1855	First German-language kindergarten established in the United States
1860	First English-language kindergarten established in the United States
1862	Morrill Land Grant College Act established college of agriculture, engineering, and military science in each state
1872	*Kalamazoo* case, court decision legalizing general taxes for high schools
1896	*Plessy* v. *Ferguson,* Supreme Court decision used to support constitutionality of separate schools for whites and blacks
	(table continues next page)

Table 4.6 Significant Dates in the History of American Education (*cont.*)

1909	First junior high school established in Berkeley, California
1910	First junior college established in Fresno, California
1919	Progressive Education Association established
1925	Oregon court decision against making private education illegal
1932	New Deal programs during the Great Depression provided federal funds for education of the poor
1944	GI Bill of Rights provided federal funding for the continued education of veterans of World War II (later extended to veterans of the Korean and Vietnam Wars)
1954	*Brown* v. *Board of Education of Topeka* decision of the Supreme Court requiring desegregation of public schools
1957	Soviet Union launched Sputnik, leading to criticism and re-evaluation of American public education
1958	National Defense Education Act provided funds to improve science, math, and modern foreign language instruction, as well as guidance services
1962	Supreme Court decision against Bible reading and prayer in public schools
1964	Economic Opportunity Act provided funds for Job Corps and Head Start
1965	Elementary-Secondary Education Act provided more federal aid to public schools
1972	Title IX Education Amendment passed outlawing sex discrimination in educational institutions receiving federal financial assistance
1975	Education for All Handicapped Children (Public Law 94–142) passed
1979	Department of Education established in federal government with cabinet status
1981	Education Consolidation and Improvement Act increased block grant funding for education, signaled declining federal role in education
1983	Publication of *A Nation at Risk,* which was the first major document in the current reform movement
1984	Carl D. Perkins Vocational Education Act continued federal aid for vocational education until 1989
1986	Public Law 94–142 extended to include preschoolers

makes attendance at traditional teacher conferences or PTA meetings difficult. Efforts are being made, such as by the Vietnamese Parents Association in the Washington, D.C., metropolitan area, to organize and voice the needs of Asian-American students. Increasing numbers of Asian-Americans are also being elected and appointed to offices and positions that play a role in educational policy making.[30]

As the numbers of Asian-American students continue to grow, it will become increasingly important for teachers and administrators to be knowledgeable of and sensitive to the special problems and needs of Asian-American students and their families. To serve these students adequately in our schools, it is particularly important to keep in mind that Asian-Americans are a changing and complex group whose achievement, aspirations, and learning styles should not be stereotyped.

A FINAL WORD

At the beginning of this chapter we identified six major forces that have shaped the history of American education and schooling. You will encounter these forces again and again in the rest of the text as we deal with contemporary issues in education. The universal and public nature of the educational system strikes, for example, at the issue of equal educational opportunity and questions of school finance and governance. Current controversies over the content of education—questions about the secular or sacred nature of the curriculum, debate about the need for standards of cultural literacy, and efforts to provide excellence in education without sacrificing equality of opportunity—arise from origins in America's colonial times. Throughout this book you will find treatments of modern-day educational concerns like the ones mentioned, since these six themes continue to play themselves out in an evolving educational system.

Discussion Questions

1. Why is it important for teachers to know the history of American education? How might you use such knowledge?
2. How did the moral lessons you were taught in school compare with those taught in earlier American schools?
3. Why did the educational development of colonial America differ among the New England, Middle, and Southern colonies? In what ways were the educational systems different?
4. What factors contributed to the development of the common school movement? Who were some of the leading advocates of this movement toward universal, free education?
5. What made the development of the American secondary school so unique in the history of the world?
6. What has been the role of private education in American history?
7. In what ways were the histories of the education of minority groups and women similar?

For Further Reading

Best, John Hardin, and Robert T. Sidewell (Eds.). *The American Legacy of Learning: Readings in the History of Education*. Philadelphia: Lippincott, 1967.
An excellent book of readings that pursues the major themes of public education.

Butts, R. Freeman. *Public Education in the United States: From Revolution to Reform.* New York: Holt, 1978.

> An interpretative history of public education viewed in the context of the social, political, economic, religious, and intellectual development of American civilization from 1776 to 1976.

Cremin, Lawrence A. *The Transformation of the School: Progressivism in American Education, 1876–1957.* New York: Knopf, 1961.

> A Pulitzer Prize–winning book on progressive education.

Meyer, Adolphe E. *An Educational History of the American People.* 2d ed. New York: McGraw-Hill, 1967.

> A lively, flamboyantly written history of American education. Readers will be delighted with the author's "nontextbook" use of language.

Pulliam, John D. *History of Education in America.* 4th ed. Columbus, Ohio: Merrill, 1987.

> A clearly written history of the major events in American education.

Spring, Joel. *The American School, 1642–1985.* New York: Longman, 1986.

> This book focuses on the social, political, and ideological forces that have shaped the evolution of schooling in America from colonial times to the present.

Turning Points: Preparing American Youth for the 21st Century. Report of the Task Force on Education of Young Adolescents, Carnegie Council on Adolescent Development. New York: Carnegie Corporation of New York, 1989.

> This report examines the various problems that today's young adolescents face and offers comprehensive recommendations for improving the educational experiences of all middle-grade students, but especially for those at risk of being left behind.

Tyack, David B. *The One Best System: A History of American Urban Education.* Cambridge, Mass.: Harvard University Press, 1974.

> A moderate yet critical view of American urban education.

Tyack, David, Robert Lowe, and Elisabeth Hausot. *Public Schools in Hard Times: The Great Depression and Recent Years.* Cambridge, Mass.: Harvard University Press, 1984.

> An analysis of public schools during and after the Great Depression of the 1930s, with a focus on how educational values were affected by financial scarcity.

Notes

1. Willystine Goodsell (Ed.), *Pioneers of Women's Education in the United States* (New York: AMS Press, 1970/1931), p. 5.
2. R. Freeman Butts and Lawrence A. Cremin, *A History of Education in American Culture* (New York: Holt, 1953), p. 245.
3. Charles W. Coulter and Richard S. Rimanoczy, *A Layman's Guide to Educational Theory* (New York: Van Nostrand, 1955), p. 130.
4. Butts and Cremin, *A History of Education in American Culture,* p. 408.
5. John D. Pulliam, *History of Education in America,* 3d ed. (Columbus, Ohio: Merrill, 1982), pp. 157–159.

6. Pulliam, *History of Education,* pp. 178–180.

7. Gene D. Shepherd and William B. Ragan, *Modern Elementary Curriculum,* 6th ed. (New York: Holt, 1982), p. 440.

8. Edward A. King, *Salient Dates in American Education, 1635–1964* (New York: Harper and Row, 1966), p. 3.

9. Butts and Cremin, *A History of Education in American Culture,* p. 260.

10. Merle Curti, *The Social Ideas of American Educators,* 2d ed. (Totowa, N.J.: Littlefield, Adams, 1959), p. 183.

11. Pulliam, *History of Education,* p. 101.

12. Butts and Cremin, *A History of Education in American Culture,* p. 443.

13. William T. Gruhn and Harl R. Douglass, *The Modern Junior High School,* 3d ed. (New York: Ronald Press, 1971), pp. 46–53.

14. *Turning Points: Preparing American Youth for the 21st Century*, Report of the Task Force on Education of Young Adolescents, Carnegie Council on Adolescent Development (New York: Carnegie Corporation of New York, 1989), p. 12.

15. Paul George and Gordon Lawrence, *Handbook for Middle School Teaching* (Glenview, Ill.: Scott, Foresman, 1982), p. 102.

16. William M. Alexander and C. Kenneth McEwin, *Schools in the Middle: Status and Progress* (Columbus, Ohio: National Middle School Association, 1989), p. 50.

17. Debra E. Gerald and William J. Hussar, *Projections of Education Statistics to 2001* (Washington, D.C.: U.S. Department of Education, National Center for Education Statistics, December 1990), p. 4.

18. Thomas D. Snyder, *Digest of Education Statistics 1989* (Washington, D.C.: U.S. Department of Education, National Center for Education Statistics, 1989), p. 70.

19. Ibid., p. 5.

20. Sharon A. Bobbitt and Frank H. Johnson, *Key Statistics for Public and Private Elementary and Secondary Education: School Year 1990–91, Early Estimates.* (Washington, D.C.: U.S. Department of Education, National Center for Education Statistics, December 1990), p. 4.

21. Herbert M. Kliebard (Ed.), *Religion and Education in America: A Documentary History* (Scranton, Pa.: International Textbook, 1969), p. 119.

22. Snyder, *Digest of Education Statistics 1989,* p. 30.

23. Earle H. West (Ed.), *The Black American and Education* (Columbus, Ohio: Merrill, 1972), pp. 7–8.

24. Eric Lincoln and Milton Meltzer, *A Pictorial History of the Negro in America,* 3d ed. (New York: Crown, 1968), pp. 108–109.

25. *Historical Statistics of the United States, Colonial times to 1970.* Vol. I. (Washington, D.C.: U.S. Govt. Printing Office, 1975), p. 370, Table Series H 433–441.

26. Franklin Frazier, *The Negro in the United States,* rev. ed. (New York: Macmillan, 1957), pp. 427, 432–436, 438.

27. R. Freeman Butts, *The Education of the West: A Formative Chapter in the History of Civilization* (New York: McGraw-Hill, 1973), p. 279.

28. *Education That Works: An Action Plan for the Education of Minorities*, Quality Education for Minorities Project (Cambridge, Mass.: Massachusetts Institute of Technology, 1990), p. 31.

29. Peter Schmidt, "After Slow Start, Asian-Americans Beginning to Exert Power on Education on Policy Issues," *Education Week,* February 27, 1991, p. 19.

30. Ibid.

5

What Are the Ethical and Legal Issues Facing Teachers?

CHAPTER PREVIEW

The intention of this chapter is to sharpen your sense of the ethical dimension of being a teacher and your understanding of the legal underpinnings for many aspects of school life. The chapter describes many common ethical problems faced by teachers, along with legal issues and recent court rulings that have affected them.

This chapter emphasizes that:

● Ethics and the law are closely related, but they also differ.

● Ethical teaching has six specific characteristics.

● In addition to teaching's everyday ethical dimensions, teachers confront certain other, more complex ethical problems.

● Teachers need to understand fully how two basic legal terms, *due process* and *liability,* relate to their work.

● Broad areas of the law—from contracts to copyright, from self-defense to religion in the classroom—permeate school life.

● Students have rights under the law, such as the rights to due process and privacy, and teachers need to understand these rights and respect them.

I f each of us were the only person on the face of the earth, we could behave exactly as we chose. We would not have to worry about the rights or feelings of anyone else. We would be free of the constraints and demands imposed by others as we went about doing our own will. Quite obviously, though, this is simply not the case. Each of us exists within a group within a group within a group: a family, a local community, a nation-state, a world community. The English poet John Donne said it most succinctly: "No man is an island." Everyone who walks the earth is bound by real, if unseen, connections with his or her fellow humans.

Our systems of ethics and laws are a major part of these invisible connecting fibers. Together they make coexistence in a neighborhood and on a planet possible. Together they make civilized society possible. Ethics, as we said in Chapter 3, brings us into the arena of values, the realm of what is "good" and "bad" behavior. *Ethics* refers to a system or a code of morality embraced by a particular person or group. Law is related to, but still different from, ethics. *A law* is a rule that members of a given community must follow. *The law* is a system of such rules that governs the general conduct of a particular community's citizens.

Whereas ethics may be invisible obligations that we feel, laws typically are statements that have been hammered out by legitimate authority and used in court as standards by which to judge, and often penalize, the actual behavior of individuals. As a matter of fact, what someone might refer to as an unstated law is not a law at all, but rather an ethical statement. The intertwined ethical and legal roots of Western culture stretch far back in human history, to ancient Greece and beyond. And the importance of the relationship between the ethical and the legal was well captured by the Greek statesman and orator Pericles, who said, "We are a free democracy, but we obey the laws, more especially those which protect the oppressed and the unwritten laws the transgression of which brings shame."[1]

Laws, then, are concrete, made by people and usually written down for the public to see; ethics, on the other hand, are ideas, less tangible and much less observable. Most of our laws, however, are simply the codification of what we see as our moral or ethical obligations to one another. Ethically we ought not steal one another's property, and this ethical obligation has been codified into the laws of our nation and states. Ethically we ought to speak the truth to others, and there are laws that flow from the ethical obligation governing different types of lies, which have different types of consequences. It needs to be noted, however, that sometimes laws are unethical (such as the racial segregation laws that existed in this country only three decades ago), and there are ethical obligations that are not always written into law (such as the ethical obligation to require one's child to wear a helmet when riding his or her bike through busy streets).

But what does all this have to do with teachers? (We thought you would never ask!) First, it is the responsibility of teachers to convey to the young the moral message that each person is linked to the rest of us, that as a species and as family, community, and national groups, we are ethically and legally bound

Ethics and the law

Law as codified ethics

Teachers' responsibility

Teachers' unique power

up in the affairs of others. Second, teachers have a unique set of ethical relationships and legal obligations that are embedded in their work, and, therefore, teachers carry a special ethical and legal burden. This second issue is the subject of this chapter.

At the heart of the teacher's unique ethical and legal relationship with students is power. Compared with a corporate executive or a military officer, it may not appear that a teacher has a great deal of power. But the teacher has a special type of power. Henry Adams caught the sense of the teacher's *long-term* power in the words "A teacher affects eternity: no one can tell where his influence stops." The teacher's powerful influence arises from the fact that he or she has an impact on people when they are still at a very malleable and impressionable stage. The poem on the opposite page makes this point. Teachers take "a piece of living clay and gently form it, day by day." Many careers are open to you, but few offer such truly inspiring power.

Even if the idea of possessing this power may have no immediate appeal to you, it nevertheless is a career fact of life. It resides in the "office" of teacher. The teacher is in command of the classroom insofar as he or she has the responsibility for what goes on. Teachers evaluate their students. They not only "mark" them with tangible symbols that become part of students' official records; they also mark their minds and hearts.

As our erstwhile friend Ernie Lundquist once put it, "Show me the guy who claims he was never afraid of a teacher, and I'll show you a damned liar." Strong words from the normally mild-mannered Ernie, but right on target. The teacher's work, then, has a powerful effect on children. Because of the potential for abuse of this power, there are codes of ethics to guide the teacher and a body of laws governing the work of teaching. Since ignorance of the law (and ethics) is no excuse, we urge you to take the material in this chapter quite seriously.

THE TEACHER

I took a piece of plastic clay,
And idly fashioned it one day.
And as my fingers pressed it,
Still, it moved and yielded to my will.
I came again when days were past,
The bit of clay was hard at last.
The form I gave it, still it bore,
And I could change that form no more.

I took a piece of living clay,
And gently formed it, day by day;
And molded it with power and art—
A young child's soft and yielding heart.

I came again when years were gone,
It was a man I looked upon,
He still that early impress bore,
And I could change that form no more.

Unknown

THE ETHICS OF TEACHING	In a sense, individuals lose "their freedom" when they get married. And, in a similar sense, people lose their freedom when they become teachers. In both situations, commitments are made, and ethical constraints come with these commitments. Constrained by ethics, the teacher is not always able to act in a manner that he or she finds most satisfying. The teacher cannot respond with sarcasm to a student's foolish or rude remark. Even though a child—sometimes even a very small child—can fill a teacher with a rush of anger, the teacher cannot act on that anger. A student may come to school with a new and outrageous hairdo or an embarrassingly absurd outfit, but the teacher is not free to laugh uproariously or even comment wryly, as he or she might do with friends.

The Characteristics of Ethical Teaching

Being an ethical teacher means having a rather special relationship with one's students and also with the other people with whom one works. Consider the following situation, as told to educator Kenneth Howe by a practicing teacher:

> Marilyn Henderson is a 5th grade language arts teacher at Willoughby Elementary in South Lake, a medium sized city with a population of roughly 150,000. Marilyn is troubled to learn that Connie Severns, a 5th grade social studies teacher, whom Marilyn worked with previously in another school in the South Lake system, will be transferred to Willoughby. Marilyn believes Connie to be incompetent and is uncomfortable with this knowledge, especially in light of the fact that her students will be moving through Connie's class. As Marilyn recalls, "Connie didn't teach anything: she *couldn't* teach anything." Others in the district share Marilyn's assessment of Connie as a teacher and apparently with good reason. Connie seems totally to lack control. Children cry and complain about the chaos, some steal things from her purse, and on one occasion another teacher discovered a child chasing Connie around the room.
>
> Marilyn had previously tried to do something about Connie's incompetence, but met with little success. The teachers' union advised her that they would have to stand behind a tenured teacher, and the school administration claimed to have to follow procedures (which could take years according to Marilyn). At this point in time (prior to Connie's transfer), the principal of Willoughby called the affected teachers together. He, too, was concerned about Connie's transfer and proposed that they discreetly and surreptitiously "write things down" to build a case which they could use to have Connie fired. Marilyn is asked to be a part of this. What should she do?[2]

This story provides just a peek at the teacher's ethically complex world. Howe suggests that in dealing with issues involving ethical judgment, each of us as a teacher needs to exhibit six characteristics: appreciation for moral deliberation; empathy; interpersonal skills; knowledge; reasoning; and courage.[3]

APPRECIATION FOR MORAL DELIBERATION We need, first of all, to see an ethical dilemma, such as Marilyn's, as a situation in which there are conflicting

Teachers are people of great power in the lives of students, and with that power comes ethical responsibilities.

(*David Pratt/Positive Images*)

"Seeing" competing interests

and competing moral interests (Connie's need for a job, the students' need for a competent teacher, and the other teachers' need to be fair in what they say to and about Connie). We need to see the complex moral dimensions of the problem and appreciate that care must be taken to protect the rights of all parties.

EMPATHY   *Empathy* is the ability to mentally "get inside the skin of another." We need to feel what the others in an ethically troublesome situation are thinking *and* feeling. In the case described, we would need to empathize with the principal who is inheriting a questionable teacher, with the students and their parents, with Connie, and with Marilyn and the other teachers.

Feeling what others feel

INTERPERSONAL SKILLS   Ethical behavior must extend outside our own heads. When ethically questionable issues arise in our lives as teachers, we cannot simply mull the matter over. We have to act—in the world of real people. Therefore, teachers need the communications skills to deal sensitively with issues that demand great tact. They need to be able to call up the right words, with the right feeling and tone, and to address the issue at hand openly and honestly.

Acting with sensitivity

KNOWLEDGE   One of the tools of a teacher who is able to deal effectively with ethical issues is raw knowledge. We need to remember the facts that will enable us to put an issue in context. What does Connie actually do in the classroom? What formal procedures are in place to deal with ineffective or incompetent

Knowing all the facts

teachers? We need to be able to formulate reasonable approaches to the problem and then, from experience, to anticipate the consequences of each approach. In Marilyn's case, she needs to be able to think clearly about the alternatives—such as participating in the principal's questionable plan or, perhaps, directly confronting Connie—and she must think through, with some degree of accuracy, what the likely consequences of such action would be.

REASONING   To reason is to reflect systematically on an issue. When we reason about an issue, we move step by step through it and draw conclusions. Or we may compare a particular event or action with some moral principle and come to some conclusion. For instance, Marilyn may hold as a moral principle that people should not deceive others, and, further, that spying is deception. Through reasoning, she may come to the conclusion that what the principal has asked her to do is spying. Of course, this leaves Marilyn with another problem: how to tell her principal that his plan is unethical.

Thinking systematically

COURAGE   To feel, to know, to reason: these are not enough. To *be* ethical, we must act; and action can take courage. To be ethically correct often requires the will power to act in what we perceive to be the right way, rather than in the comfortable way. Frequently, when confronted with a seemingly no-win dilemma like Marilyn's, our tendency is to ignore it in the hope that it will simply go away. However, as the theologian Harvey Cox sees it, "Not to decide is to decide." Among other things, Marilyn is going to have to find a way to tell her principal that she simply cannot be a part of his secret reporting network. Besides courage, this will take tact!

Confronting, not evading, problems

Ethical Dilemmas in Teaching

Although teachers spend most of their professional lives working with students in an instructional manner, sometimes other concerns break in and demand their attention. Some of these concerns involve ethical problems. Recently, as teacher education students interviewed practicing teachers they asked them to describe an ethical situation they had encountered in the last few years. The four cases that follow are based on those interviews.

As you read each case, take time to reflect carefully on it. Is it really a situation involving ethics? Does it involve unfairness or a breach of ethical standards? Are there complexities that cause ethical conflicts? What are they? What are the consequences of various courses of action? Who needs to be considered as you try to decide on a course of action? What, specifically, would you say or do? As you work through these situations, keep in mind the six characteristics described by Kenneth Howe. Also, discuss these cases with other people. Frequently, we see much more in a situation involving ethics and recognize many other possible courses of action once we have talked to others about it.

Case Number One: To Strike or Not to Strike

You are a tenured, first-grade teacher who has been teaching in an urban area for five years. Like many of the other teachers, you are frustrated and angry at the city's and the school board's treatment of teachers. You have seen oceans of the taxpayers' money going toward civic projects (a domed athletic stadium, a newly renovated city hall and downtown area), while teacher's salaries and the conditions in the schools have deteriorated. Like your colleagues, you are desperate to get the attention of the citizens, so you support your professional association's decision to strike.

Strike hurts poor students

The teachers walked out three days ago, and gradually you are realizing that the real losers in this strike are your twenty-eight first-graders, many of whom come from disorganized, poverty-ridden homes. You believe that whereas many children in other parts of the city can probably afford to lose the time in school, yours cannot. They are at a critical point in their basic skills development. Also, they have just learned to settle down and really become engaged in their work. You are sure that prolonging the strike will mean disaster for the students. Then, on the strike's fourth day, several of your students' parents approach you, saying that they have secured a church basement and, if you will only come and teach, classes can go on there. However, such action may undermine the strike and will appear to be a betrayal of your co-workers. What do you do?

Case Number Two: A Big Deal or a Little Fudge?

Your community has recently been plagued by drugs, and increasingly they are coming into the schools. You are a sixth-grade teacher and there has only been sporadic evidence of drugs in your building. On the other hand, your principal has been making what seems to you a big deal out of very little in his crusade to stamp out drugs in "his elementary school." He has threatened the student body, first-graders through sixth-graders, in a special assembly about what will happen to them if they are caught with drugs of any kind. Most of your inservice training time this year has been taken up with the subject of drugs. You are concerned about the misuse of drugs in our society. However, you, like most of the other teachers, find the principal's preoccupation with drugs overzealous and slightly laughable, and you are afraid of what will happen to the first offender he catches.

Overzealous principal

Coming from lunch, you see Alan, one of your sixth-graders, showing two of his friends a plastic bag containing what appear to be three or four marijuana joints. Startled, but unsure that you have actually seen what he has, Alan shoves the bag into his pants pocket. You act as if nothing had happened and usher the boys into class. To gain time to think, you set the students to work on a composition.

Alan is a kid with a spotty record in the school. His family life is rumored to be rather chaotic, but he has behaved himself well in your class. You have never seen the slightest evidence that he has been high in school. Knowing Alan, you guess he got the dope from one of his brothers and brought it to school to impress his friends. On the other hand, you could be wrong, and the situation could be much more serious. One thing you are sure of is that if you report what you saw to the principal, as you are expected to, he will move in on Alan like a SWAT team. As you are mulling all this over, Alan and his friends are nervously watching you and anxiously looking back and forth at one another. Then, suddenly, Alan gets up, comes to your desk, and asks if he can go to the boys' room. What do you do?

You enjoy teaching, but not testing. You are proctoring the final exam for your freshman algebra class. You like your students and know they have worked hard, but now they are struggling with and being stumped by your test questions, which you were sure were going to seem easy. It is a little hard, too, to see the students who have coasted all year gliding right through your exam as if it were so much whipped cream. In the midst of your musing, you glance across the room and see Floyd stuffing what looks like a crib sheet up his sleeve. He has been trouble all year. You are certain he copied 90 percent of his homework assignments on the bus; he was mouthy and disruptive in class, and you are fairly sure he cheated on two of the other major tests. Now, finally, you've got the drop on him.

Good student cheating

As you move quickly across the room toward Floyd, you see that Judith is copying formulas from a ribbon-like spool of paper. You cannot believe it! Judith is your favorite student, and she recently was elected secretary of next year's sophomore class. She is a very conscientious, diligent girl who gets good grades, but not out of natural brilliance. She gets them the old-fashioned way—through hard work. She has very high standards and puts a good deal of pressure on herself. Although you cannot imagine what has led her to cheat, you suspect that the pressure for good grades she puts on herself is the root cause. You are standing in the middle of the room, trying to decide what to do.

Case Number Four:
Righting Wrongs

You expected to encounter a sour apple or two in the teaching profession, but Kingsley is authentically rotten. He is lazy, way out of touch with his field, hostile to students, and totally uncooperative toward his colleagues and the high school's administrators. He has been tenured for twelve years and has been acting this way for about eleven. He flaunts his behavior, occasionally referring to himself as "the Untouchable One." In addition to being mean, he is also smart.

For reasons you can only guess at, Kingsley is carrying on some kind of personal vendetta against one of the best students in the senior class. Ken's father has been out of work for three years, yet Ken has overcome a great deal in that time. This year, as editor of the school newspaper, he took a dull, sports and soft-gossip paper and made it genuinely interesting, addressing issues of real concern to the entire high school population and doing it in a mature, evenhanded way. In the process, Ken seems to have gotten on Kingsley's wrong side, and Kingsley, his senior-year English teacher, is making him pay. Ken has told you, as his social studies teacher and friend, about what is going

A mean teacher

on in English. Besides regular ridicule and baiting, Kingsley has given him very low marks on writing assignments and term papers that you frankly think are across-the-board A work. As a result, Ken is running a low C in English, which has been his best subject, and this could mean that he will get no honors at graduation. Worse, it will probably bring his average down just enough so that he will lose the state scholarship he needs to go to college next year.

You have tried to talk with Kingsley about the situation, but after smugly telling you about "a teacher's right and responsibility to give the grade he sees fit," he in effect told you to "butt out." In as professional a manner as possible, you have discussed the matter with the principal, but he has told you that although he sympathizes, his hands are tied. Finally, it dawns on you that there is something you can do. Ken is running a solid B-plus/A-minus in social studies as you enter the last weeks of the school year. If you were to change a few grades upward so he will receive an A-plus, it could compensate for the unjust grade he is receiving from Kingsley. It would also assure Ken of getting the state scholarship. You would love to see Kingsley's face at graduation, too. What will you do?

The Everyday Ethics of Teaching

Although being able to think and feel your way through situations like those just described is important, there are other, less weighty ethical dimensions to the teacher's role that also demand attention. We are referring to the "everyday" ethics of teaching. These obligations cover a large area of the teacher's professional life, but since they are so commonplace, we will make only nodding reference to them. By *everyday ethics of teaching* we mean the regular decisions the teacher has to make, such as using "sick days" only for true illness and not

NEA CODE OF ETHICS
Preamble

The educator, believing in the worth and dignity of each human being, recognizes the supreme importance of the pursuit of truth, devotion to excellence, and the nurture of democratic principles. Essential to these goals is the protection of freedom to learn and to teach and the guarantee of equal educational opportunity for all. The educator accepts the responsibility to adhere to the highest ethical standards.

The educator recognizes the magnitude of the responsibility inherent in the teaching process. The desire for the respect and confidence of one's colleagues, of students, of parents, and of the members of the community provides the incentive to attain and maintain the highest possible degree of ethical conduct. The Code of Ethics of the Education Profession indicates the aspiration of all educators and provides standards by which to judge conduct.

The remedies specified by the NEA and/or its affiliates for the violation of any provision of this Code shall be exclusive and no such provision shall be enforceable in any form other than one specifically designated by the NEA or its affiliates.

Principle I—Commitment to the Student

The educator strives to help each student realize his or her potential as a worthy and effective member of society. The educator therefore works to stimulate the spirit of inquiry, the acquisition of knowledge and understanding, and the thoughtful formulation of worthy goals.

In fulfillment of the obligation to the student, the educator—

1. Shall not unreasonably restrain the student from independent action in the pursuit of learning.
2. Shall not unreasonably deny the student access to varying points of view.
3. Shall not deliberately suppress or distort subject matter relevant to the student's progress.
4. Shall make reasonable effort to protect the student from conditions harmful to learning or to health and safety.
5. Shall not intentionally expose the student to embarrassment or disparagement.
6. Shall not on the basis of race, color, creed, sex, national origin, marital status, political or religious beliefs, family, social or cultural background, or sexual orientation, unfairly:
   a. Exclude any student from participation in any program;

for minor matters or for personal vacations; preparing classes conscientiously; being on time; not playing favorites; and not gossiping about students or their family situations, fellow teachers, or (most difficult!) administrators. We mean fully correcting the papers that students turn in and taking grading as seriously as you want them to take it. We mean realizing how precious are the minutes and hours that students have put in your hands and making sure that they do not waste their time with you. The everyday ethics of teaching, then, means *doing the job as it ought to be done.*

Codes of Professional Ethics   Teachers do not struggle alone when they face ethical issues. Besides their own understanding, reasoning, courage, and other qualities, they have the support of a professional group.* Recently, educational philosopher Jonas Soltis wrote,

---

* Whether or not teaching really *is* a profession is an important question and is the subject of Chapter 14.

---

   b.   Deny benefits to any student;
   c.   Grant any advantage to any student.

7. Shall not use professional relationships with students for private advantage.
8. Shall not disclose information about students obtained in the course of professional service, unless disclosure serves a compelling professional purpose or is required by law.

Principle II—Commitment to the Profession

The education profession is vested by the public with a trust and responsibility requiring the highest ideals of professional service.

In the belief that the quality of the services of the education profession directly influences the nation and its citizens, the educator shall exert every effort to raise professional standards, to promote a climate that encourages the exercise of professional judgment, to achieve conditions which attract persons worthy of the trust to careers in education, and to assist in preventing the practice of the profession by unqualified persons.

In fulfillment of the obligation to the profession, the educator—

1. Shall not in an application for a professional position deliberately make a false statement or fail to disclose a material fact related to competency and qualifications.

2. Shall not misrepresent his/her professional qualifications.

3. Shall not assist entry into the profession of a person known to be unqualified in respect to character, education, or other relevant attribute.

4. Shall not knowingly make a false statement concerning the qualifications of a candidate for a professional position.

5. Shall not assist a noneducator in the unauthorized practice of teaching.

6. Shall not disclose information about colleagues obtained in the course of professional service unless disclosure serves a compelling professional purpose or is required by law.

7. Shall not knowingly make false or malicious statements about a colleague.

8. Shall not accept any gratuity, gift, or favor that might impair or appear to influence professional decisions or actions.

National Education Association, *Code of Ethics of the Education Profession,* adopted by the NEA Representative Assembly, 1975. Reprinted by permission of the Association.

When a person becomes a member of a profession, he or she joins a historical community of practice with a telos, a general purpose, that one must be committed to in order to be a professional. In medicine the general purpose is to promote health, and in education it is to promote learning. The clients put their trust in the professional's honest commitment to the purpose. There is thus built into the form of the practice itself a moral obligation on the part of the practitioners. To breach that obligation is to act unprofessionally. Likewise, in the tradition of a practice like teaching, certain standards of conduct and of manner develop in support of the telos and become recognized as a desirable part of the moral climate of the practice. In the treatment of students, of subject matter, and of colleagues, honesty, truth, and justice become central virtues of the practice.[4]

Ethical essence of teaching

The way teachers do their work is regulated, then, by their own ethical standards and those of the teaching profession. Ethics is a code of behavior or standards of conduct that are, by their nature, general and that refer to how teachers *ought* to behave.

Three codes

Whereas some professions have formulated their own universal code of ethics (like the Hippocratic oath taken by all medical doctors), there are several codes of ethics for teachers. The best known is the National Education Association's (NEA) code, which includes such statements as "The educator strives to help each student realize his or her potential as a worthy and effective member

THE EDUCATOR'S OATH

I hereby affirm my dedication to the profession of education. With this affirmation I embrace the obligations of professional educators to improve the general welfare, to advance human understanding and competence, and to bring honor to the endeavors of teaching and learning. I accept these obligations for myself and will be vigilant and responsible in supporting their acceptance by my colleagues.

I will be always mindful of my responsibility to increase the intelligence of students through the disciplined pursuit of knowledge. I will be steadfast in this commitment, even when weary and tempted to abdicate such responsibility or blame failure on obstacles that make the task difficult. I will be persistent in my commitment to foster respect for a life of learning and respect for all students.

To perform faithfully these professional duties, I promise to work always to better understand my content,

my instructional practice, and the students who come under my tutelage. I promise to seek and support policies that promote quality in teaching and learning and to provide all engaged in education the opportunity to achieve excellence. I promise to emulate personally the qualities I wish to foster, and to hold and forever honor a democratic way of life that cannot exist without disciplined, cultivated, and free minds.

I recognize that at times my endeavors will offend privilege and status, that I will be opposed by bias and defenders of inequality, and that I will have to confront arguments that seek to discourage my efforts and diminish my hope. But I will remain faithful to the belief that these endeavors and the pursuit of these goals make me worthy of my profession, and my profession worthy of a free people.

In the presence of this gathering, I bind myself to this oath.

Judith Lanier and Philip Cusick, "The Educator's Oath," *Phi Delta Kappan* (June 1985): 711–712. Used by permission.

of society." The American Federation of Teachers has a "Bill of Rights," which speaks to the issue of the ethical treatment teachers should *receive*. It contains what it refers to as self-evident truths, for example: "The right of teachers to be secure in their jobs, free from political influence or public clamor, shall be established by law. The right to teach is a property right, based upon the inalienable rights to life, liberty, and the pursuit of happiness."[5] A third example, *The Educator's Oath,* is newer[6] and is the closest in form to the Hippocratic oath. These codes of ethics, particularly the NEA's and *The Educator's Oath* (both reproduced in this chapter), provide the teacher with a general set of ethical guidelines.

THE TEACHER AND THE LAW

Once upon a time, teachers were like the kings and queens of small kingdoms. Their authority was wide and their decisions were rarely questioned. Students who would not or could not do the work were "held back" or told not to come back. Students who did not conform to the teacher's standards of behavior were expelled. Students and their parents tended to view education as a special opportunity that put definite responsibilities on their shoulders. (We older teachers refer to this period as Camelot.) In the last few decades, the attitude toward schooling in our country has changed. The authority of the teacher has eroded noticeably, and more and more students are fixated on their rights as students rather than on their responsibilities as students. There are many reasons for this change, but suffice it to say that we have become a very litigious society. Our country has more lawyers per capita than any nation in the world. And our recent increased use of the courts to settle differences and conflicts has had its impact on the work of the teacher.

Rise in litigation

On the other hand, it can be argued that the new consciousness of the teacher's legal responsibilities and our heightened sense of students' rights has helped rid the school of dictatorial practices by teachers and administrators, the systematic denial of rights to students, such as freedom of speech and prayerful assembly (under certain conditions), and the abusive use of corporal punishment. The new presence of the law in educational matters is, like many changes, a mixed bag.

Law = collective judgment

Woodrow Wilson once said, "The law that will work is merely the summing up in legislative form of the moral judgement that the community has already reached." Our laws, then, are our collective social judgments and decisions about what is fair. Laws differ from ethics, though, because they apply to all the people, not a particular group like doctors or teachers. They are public, whereas ethics can be someone's private standards. And they have judicial teeth, whereas ethics do not. Rarely is a teacher suspended or expelled or even sanctioned by the teaching profession for violations of the NEA's Code of Ethics.[7] However, teachers are regularly affected by the law, and occasionally even feel its lash in a courtroom.

The Teacher and Due Process

A young junior high teacher, on a lark, changes his "image." He comes to school one Monday morning sporting a shaved head and a silver earring. He is fired on Tuesday.

A woman teacher gives a speech at a meeting of the local Gay and Lesbian Alliance. The newspaper runs a story on the event, and the superintendent asks her to resign quietly.

A business education teacher has been teaching for three years and has only been visited by administrators twice during that period. He loves teaching, but has only just recently begun to feel competent. Instead of getting the expected letter from the superintendent outlining the upcoming tenure review process, he receives a dismissal notice claiming that his teaching is not up to the district's standards.

The league-winning coach of a school's womens' soccer team is tired of battling with her principal over field time, transportation, and "every penny I need to spend on adhesive tape." In July, she quits and takes a job coaching at the school's archrival. In August, she discovers she is being sued for breach of contract.

A young new teacher discovers that she has been given the heaviest teaching load in her middle school, the most-difficult-to-manage students, and the heaviest assignment of "extracurricular duties" (daily lunchroom duty, after-school bus-departure monitoring, and seven weekend assignments, from chaperoning dances to supervising a service club's "Community Clean-Up Day"). None of this was stipulated in her contract. Her colleagues tell her that it is a tradition to "load it on rookie teachers," so she doesn't say anything. The next year she is given the same assignments, plus morning bus duty, and the principal wants her to start a photography club.

All of these examples represent violations of the teachers' rights to due process. *Due process* is one of the most important principles embedded in our nation's laws. The essential meaning of due process is that fairness should be

Due process = fairness

rendered and that our rights as individuals should not be violated. Teachers cannot be treated in a willful or arbitrary way. Due process protections come directly from two amendments to our Constitution. The Fifth Amendment states that "no person shall . . . be deprived of life, liberty, or property, without due process of law," and the Fourteenth Amendment specifies that "nor shall any State deprive any person of life, liberty, or property, without due process of law."

When judging the fairness of an action, there are two due process con-

Two concerns

cerns. One, *substantive due process,* has to do with the issue itself. The other, *procedural due process,* is concerned with the fairness of the process followed. For example, if a teacher is fired because he wears a nose ring, this is an issue of substantive due process. Is this matter substantive enough in this particular circumstance to deny a teacher employment? What is a fair decision in this matter? There is also the matter of how the case is handled. Suppose the teacher, after hearing several rumors that the nose ring is irking the superintendent, gets a curt letter saying his "services are no longer needed"? Is this process fair? Has the teacher had a fair chance to defend himself? Due process, then, has two aspects, substantive and procedural, both of which must be dealt with fairly.

The precise meaning of procedural due process changes from state to state, but the Supreme Court decision in *Goldberg* v. *Kelly* (1970) indicated that "the minimum procedural safeguards . . . demanded by rudimentary due process" would include:

The opportunity to be heard at a reasonable time and place.

Timely and adequate notice giving details of the reasons for the proposed suspension or dismissal.

An effective opportunity to defend oneself, including oral presentation of evidence and arguments.

An opportunity to confront and cross-examine witnesses.

The right to retain an attorney.

A decision resting solely on the legal rules and evidence adduced at the hearing.

A statement of the reasons for the determination and the evidence relied on.

An impartial decision maker.[8]

Minimal procedural safeguards

A TEACHER'S CONTRACT FROM THE 1920S

We stated at the start of this section that through the first half of the twentieth century teachers often could act like a form of royalty, having enormous power over the lives of children. At the same time, however, teachers were often treated like second-class citizens. The following is taken from a contract young women teachers had to sign if they wished to teach in a particular community. Such contracts were not uncommon in this country in the 1920s.

I promise to take a vital interest in all phases of Sunday-school work, donating of my time, service, and money without stint for the uplift and benefit of the community.

I promise to abstain from all dancing, immodest dressing, and all other conduct unbecoming a teacher and a lady.

I promise not to go out with any young men except in so far as it may be necessary to stimulate Sunday-school work.

I promise not to fall in love, to become engaged, or secretly married.

I promise not to encourage or tolerate the least familiarity on the part of any of my boy pupils.

I promise to sleep at least eight hours a night, to eat carefully, and to take every precaution to keep in the best of health and spirits, in order that I may be better able to render efficient service to my pupils.

I promise to remember that I owe a duty to the townspeople who are paying me my wages, that I owe respect to the school board and the superintendent that hired me, and that I shall consider myself at all times the willing servant of the school board and the townspeople.*

Contracts or no, teachers could be dismissed for divorcing, for gambling, for being seen in public with a person of the opposite sex or a different race, or for even the rumor of sexual immorality. The organizations a teacher belonged to might be a term of employment. In some communities teachers could be dismissed for joining the Ku Klux Klan and in others for not joining the Klan. Nowadays, fortunately for us, the law and the courts have come to define more clearly the use of power by and against the teacher.

*The contract terms are from T. Mineham, "The Teacher Goes Job-Hunting," *The Nation* 124 (1927): 606. Facts in the last paragraph are from Louis Fischer and David Schimmel, *The Rights of Students and Teachers* (New York: Harper & Row, 1982), pp. 4–5. Used by permission.

The principle of due process and these guidelines reach into many corners of the teacher's life, as we shall see in the next section.

Contracts, Tenure, and Dismissal

Teaching is, of course, a vocation and a career. It represents an individual's choice of what to do with his or her life. But few teachers are "independent operators," like painters or novelists or even some lawyers. Teachers in public and private schools are not employed by the principal or the superintendent, but are employees of the local board of education, or in the case of private schools, usually of a board of trustees. And, as such, they have a legal set of relationships with the board.

CONTRACTS TO TEACH A teacher, new or old, signs a contract with his or her board of education (or trustees), which outlines the rights and responsibilities of each party to the agreement. Typically, the contract will deal with salary, the area or areas of instruction, class size, length of teaching day, and the procedure teachers should follow if they have a grievance (that is, a formal complaint against the employer or concern about some aspect of their work). Also, if the teachers in a district are represented by a particular teachers' association or union, the contract will acknowledge it as the teacher's bargaining agent.

Elements of legal contracts

For a *contract* to be considered a legally enforceable document, it must:

1. have a lawful subject matter
2. represent a meeting of the minds of both parties
3. include an exchange of something of value (called a *consideration*)
4. be entered into by parties who are competent to do so
5. be written in proper form (instead of in vague terms, such as "pay the teacher what he or she is worth")

In addition, the school board must act officially to ratify a teacher's contract.[9] Contracts are for a set period of time. Most new teachers work on a contract that has to be renewed annually if the teacher is to stay on. Even teachers on tenure (which will be discussed shortly) sign a yearly contract stipulating the terms of employment. Occasionally, teachers work under a *continuing contract,* which states that its terms will remain in force until the teacher is given notice that termination will occur on a particular date.

Sometimes a teacher is dismissed (or less euphemistically, fired). And sometimes a teacher leaves a position for a different job in or out of education. If either party, the teacher or the board of education, violates any of the terms of a contract, such actions are called a *breach of contract* and can lead to lawsuits. When an injured party successfully sues the other party for breach of contract, the court may order that the contract be fulfilled, or that the injured party receive monetary damages, or both. The district may have to rehire the teacher and pay damages. The teacher who walks away from a job may have to pay the district's cost of finding a replacement. Since a contract governs many important details of a teacher's life, study it carefully before putting your signature in the space provided.

Breach of contract

TENURE   The word *tenure* comes from the Latin root "to hold," as in "hold that job." New teachers begin their careers as probationary employees. They are full-fledged teachers, but they are on trial in their school district. States differ, but typically teachers can remain in this temporary status for three years. At that time, they are eligible for tenure. Tenure represents permanence of position, and the teacher who has tenure has, in effect, a long-term right to a contract with the

Long-term rights   school district. Once granted tenure, a teacher can only be dismissed "for cause"—that is, for a good reason that will stand the scrutiny of the courts, such as sexually molesting a student, gross negligence, or gross incompetence.

Tenure laws, like most of the laws governing schools, are developed by the individual states. The Supreme Court of Pennsylvania in 1957 nicely stated the value and purpose of tenure:

> Time and time again our courts have stated that the purpose of the tenure provisions of the School Code (state law) is the maintenance of an adequate and competent teaching staff, free from political or arbitrary interference, whereby capable and competent teachers might feel secure, and more efficiently perform their duty of instruction.[10]

Special conditions   Bear in mind two additional points about tenure laws. First, a teacher is granted tenure not as a third-grade teacher or as a vocational education teacher, but simply as a teacher. School boards have the right to transfer and reassign teachers within the district. Second, states differ on their tenuring procedures. In some states tenure comes automatically with the fourth year's contract. In others, teachers must first pass the formal tenure review process, which examines performance and assesses their professional competence.

DISMISSAL   Occasionally teachers fail; they simply cannot handle the job. Or they make a big mistake, such as striking a child in anger. Occasionally, too, teachers have "philosophical differences" with administrators, sometimes further complicated by mild or severe cases of "personality conflict." These situations, and many more, may result in an attempt to dismiss a teacher and are covered by the laws in each state.

DIALOGUE

Jim: Pretty cool treatment of a hot issue.

Kevin: What do you mean?

Jim: **Tenure** is not just another topic. It is quite controversial and may become even more controversial in the future.

Kevin: You are right. It seems the world is split down the middle between those who think tenure is a necessary

protection for teachers against whimsical or even unjust actions of school officials, and . . .

Jim: And those who think it is permanent job security for the incompetent. An insurance policy for the weak and inept.

Kevin: My guess is that if tenure is going to stay with us and not be thrown out by an angry public, it will have to be redefined so as not to be a cover for the ineffective or lazy teacher.

Jim: Yes, we need it; but we need to consider, too, the children who are supposed to be served by the schools.

Circumstances differ somewhat between probationary and tenured teachers. If a school district decides in the middle of a school year (and therefore in the middle of a contract) to dismiss an untenured teacher, the teacher always has a right to a full hearing and due process. On the other hand, if the district decides not to extend a second- or third-year contract to a new teacher, the situation is not as clear. Although there are some states, such as Illinois, in which an untenured teacher who is not being rehired can demand a hearing on why, in most states the school district does not have to justify its reasons for not rehiring.

The legal situation for tenured teachers is different from that of probationary teachers. Tenure is protected under the Fourteenth Amendment and is considered part of the teacher's property. In a sense, the tenured teacher has "earned" and "owns" the job, and he or she can be separated from it only under very special circumstances. Here the teacher can call upon the full protection of the law, as he or she would if someone were trying to take away a home or a car. To justify dismissal, the school district must prove that the tenured teacher has violated some provision of the tenure law. Again, states vary concerning what they consider due cause for dismissal. However, the most common reasons include immorality, insubordination, incompetence, and unprofessional behavior. It is the responsibility of the courts to weigh the individual situation, to review the law on the subject, and to determine whether or not the case justifies dismissal.

There is, however, one category of dismissal where the teacher's standing and conduct do not seem to play much of a part. It is called *reduction in force* and happens when there are more teachers than are needed and a school district, for economic reasons, must let some of the teachers go. The jargon term for reduction in force is *riffing*. During the last two decades, many school districts around the nation were forced to reduce in force because of a decline in the student population combined with severe budget constraints.

Sometimes the courts allow schools to dismiss teachers as a result of curricular reorganization; for example, a school board might decide to drop its classical language department. Normally, though, riffing occurs in a climate of economic crisis. Although those selecting which teachers to rif typically respect the seniority principle (bad news for beginning teachers), states vary. In some states the law is relatively silent about whom the school district can let go and how it can do so, leaving the decisions up to the individual boards.

The Teacher and Liability

When you were in elementary or secondary school, did you ever wonder (as we did) why teachers seemed to get so upset with students who ran in the halls, bounded down the stairways, or went in for a little friendly wrestling? The probable reason behind their concern may be well expressed in one word: *liability*. It means blame, as in "The teacher can be held liable for the student's separated shoulder." That is, the teacher behaved negligently or intentionally in a way that allowed the injury to happen.

Teachers are responsible for ensuring the safety and well-being of their students in their own classrooms and work spaces and in the activities they oversee. This includes field trips and after-school clubs and activities, such as band, sports, and play rehearsals. Teachers are also liable if they observe students in

Probationary teachers

Tenure as "property"

Reduction in force

Arenas of liability

The school and the teacher share liability for the safety of students.
(*Paul Conklin/Monkmeyer Press Photo Service*)

some potentially dangerous act that eventually turns out to be harmful and they do nothing. Turning one's back on misbehavior in no way lessens this responsibility. Teachers can be held liable for acts of omission.

Absence from classroom

A major potential source of liability is the teacher's absence from the classroom. For a variety of reasons, teachers sometimes leave their classrooms unattended and, thus, their students unsupervised. If an injury occurs during an absence and a suit is brought, the court is quite concerned, first, with whether the teacher's absence contributed to the possibility of the injury (Would it have happened if the teacher had been there?) and, second, with what special circumstances surrounded the absence. If some of the students had a history of fighting or if clear evidence suggested that the class might behave irresponsibly, then the court will lean toward finding the teacher liable. If the teacher had a good reason to be away from the class or if whatever happened was a freak event, then the teacher will have little to worry about from the courts.

There will always be injuries and accidents in schools. With all of the students and all of the activity of a school program, it is to be expected that something unplanned and hurtful will happen. From the standpoint of liability, teachers need to be able to show that they have been "reasonably prudent." They need to be able to demonstrate, for example, that:

- They made a reasonable attempt to anticipate dangerous situations.
- They provided proper supervision.
- They took precautions.
- They established rules.
- They gave a warning to minimize the chances of students getting hurt.

Liability insurance

Since teachers are vulnerable to legal suit, it is important that they be covered by some form of liability insurance. However, in recent years, many teachers have been scared into buying more insurance than they need or, more commonly, into buying insurance when they are already covered by school district insurance policies. Before beginning to teach, therefore, the new teacher ought to check on-the-job coverage with the district's personnel director.

One area in which experts claim teachers are particularly at risk is automobile liability.[11] Often, teachers volunteer to take students in their own cars to a game or a debate or on a field trip. Even though teachers may have personal insurance, they often do not have enough to cover liability claims if a serious accident happens. Before taking students in a private car, the teacher needs to be sure that the district's insurance policy covers such cases or that his or her own policy is adequate.

Automobile liability

In all these issues of liability, it is important for the teacher to use good judgment. In life, accidents happen and there may be no liability. If a school injury results in a legal suit, the courts, as noted, will attempt to determine if the teacher was providing *reasonable* care and, in general, acting in a *prudent*, or wise and careful, manner.

Self-Defense

With so many people normally crammed into a school, it is to be expected that conflict will occasionally occur and that some sort of hostile behavior may befall teachers. For instance, a teacher may have to break up a playground fight or stop some students from vandalizing another student's locker. Or a student may strike a teacher.

Self-defense is defined broadly here to take in all these situations. In the case of the first two, fighting and vandalism, the teacher is expected to intercede in the interest of safety. In the case of a fight, for instance, the teacher must act to stop the students from hurting one another. Strong words usually are effective, but sometimes the teacher must become physically involved. The operating principle here is "reasonable force." If a teacher uses reasonable force, and if, in the process of stopping the fighting and separating the students, a student suffers an injury (say, a strained wrist or dislocated arm), the courts will typically find that the teacher is not liable. If the same injuries resulted from a fight the teacher did not act to stop, he or she may be held liable.

"Reasonable force"

In more obvious cases of self-defense, a student threatens or actually strikes a teacher, and the principle of reasonable force applies here too. What constitutes reasonable force is generally a matter of common sense, but the heat of the moment can make good judgment difficult. In one case, for example, a male seventh-grader who weighed all of 110 pounds struck a 220-pound coach. The coach grabbed the boy, lifted him off the ground, and threw him against a wall, breaking the child's back. When brought to court, the teacher-coach claimed self-defense. He lost—and big. In the court's view, it is usually the teacher's responsibility to keep a level head.

Assault and battery

A teacher's recourse against an abusive student is governed by assault and battery laws. *Assault* has come in the law to mean a threat to do harm. Threats should always be taken seriously and reported to the principal, but their legal status depends very much on the student's ability to carry through on the threat. An angry fourth-grader's threat to "do something terrible to you" does not have the same status as a high school junior's threat to put sugar in your car's gas tank.

Battery means a willful attack on another resulting in harm. Being unintentionally knocked to the hall floor by a rushing student is not battery. (It may, however, call for some disciplinary action by the school.) Being intentionally pushed by a student or a parent is an entirely different matter and makes the pusher immediately liable.

Incidents of assault or battery should be promptly reported and disciplinary action demanded or legal charges filed. Often teachers, particularly new teachers, are hesitant about making a fuss or turning offending students into the proper school authorities. But verbal abuse and physical violence have no place in our elementary and secondary schools.

Freedom of Expression

If an employee of a business "sounds off" in a very public manner about his or her boss, the law provides the employee no protection against being fired. For much of our history, this was the case for public school teachers also. Even throughout most of this century, teachers who publicly criticized administrators' decisions or school board policies received little sympathy from judges. The attitude of the courts was that judges had no business interfering in the legitimate affairs of the schools. Things changed, though, as a result of Marvin Pickering.

Pickering's free speech case

Pickering, a high school English teacher, wrote a long and sarcastic letter in the local newspaper about his superintendent and school board. He accused them of, among other things, taking the local taxpayers "to the cleaners," making excessive expenditures on athletics, and forcing teachers to live in an atmosphere of totalitarianism. Pickering was fired; he sued for his job and the original court verdicts upheld the firing. Although his letter contained factual errors and exaggerations, when the case was appealed before the Supreme Court in 1968, the Court ruled in Pickering's favor, ordering that he be reinstated and compensated.[12] In effect, the Court said that society needs to balance the interests of a teacher, as a citizen commenting on issues of public concern, and the interests of the state, as the teacher's employer trying to promote smoothly running schools. So although the Court affirmed the teacher's right to free expression, it pointed out that this First Amendment protection is not an absolute right. Many situations are possible, such as when teachers become disruptive forces in a school or are irresponsible in their statements, in which the courts will fail to support them. For instance, in 1981 the courts ruled against a teacher who had claimed that the racially derogatory comments he made to his principal and assistant principal were constitutionally protected.[13]

Expression is not limited to spoken and written words. Dress styles, arm bands, and buttons have been used in recent years to "make a statement." Typically, the courts support teachers (and students) in these cases of free *symbolic* expression. A key issue here involves the potential of this type of expression to lead to "substantial disruption" within the school. For instance, if a teacher wears a Ku Klux Klan button in a high school with black students, or if two groups of students are feuding and their wearing their "colors" or jacket insignia has been known to provoke fighting, then the symbols can be forbidden. On the other hand, these judgments cannot be the matter of a teacher's or administrator's "taste." Bans on symbolic expression of one's views or preferences must be based on clear indications that the efficiency or safety of the school is endangered. As with many legal issues discussed in this section, the courts apply a "balancing test," reviewing each case individually and attempting to weigh the rights of the teacher or students to free expression against the legitimate interests of the particular community. As the court stated in the 1970s *Scoville* v. *Board of Education* case, "Freedom of speech includes the right to criticize and protest school policies in a nondisruptive manner, but it does not include the use of 'fighting' words or the abuse of superiors with profane and vulgar speech."[14]

ACADEMIC FREEDOM   Academic freedom is a subcategory of freedom of expression. Academic freedom deals largely with issues in the classroom and the teachers' (and students') rights to discuss ideas and read material of their choosing.

Conflict often arises from discussions of controversial issues, such as sexual mores or abortion. If such issues are a part of the school's curriculum, there is rarely a problem. But when they are "added" to the curriculum by the teacher, he or she needs to be able to make a reasonable case that they are relevant to the curriculum. Dismissal for teaching controversial issues may or may not be upheld by the courts. Teaching volatile issues, such as homosexuality or the alleged characteristics of different races, that might potentially disrupt a particular school are frowned on by the courts. So, too, is teaching controversial material considered unsuitable for the age of the students.

Political issues, both local and national, are also a point of tension. While in the classroom, teachers clearly may treat current political controversies, but they must deal with them neutrally and in a balanced way. Away from work, advocating a particular cause is fine, as long as the teacher does not behave as a partisan supporter in the classroom.

Particular essays and books that contain sexually explicit material or even words that are offensive to certain members of a community have been a great source of legal controversy in schools. In one important case, *Keefe* v. *Geanakos* (1969), a Massachusetts English teacher, Robert Keefe, assigned his students an article from the well-respected *Atlantic Monthly*. The article contained a particular offensive word. (Hint: The word was *not* "mother beater.") Mr. Keefe's assignment caused a storm, and he was eventually fired for refusing to agree that

Symbolic expression *(margin note)*

Boundaries of freedom *(margin note)*

The Keefe case *(margin note)*

he would not assign the article again. Subsequently, he was reinstated by a 1969 circuit court decision because the offending word existed in a number of books already in the school library; because the school board had not notified him that such material was prohibited; and, finally, because that court believed that the

Censorship in Schools: Protection or Suppression?

The headlines of newspapers and weekly magazines regularly report challenges to certain instructional and library materials. Those who would censor the texts used in classrooms and the books shelved in school libraries are a diverse group: religious fundamentalists, racial minorities, and members of some women's organizations, to name a few. During the 1989–90 school year, there were 244 challenges, an increase of 40 percent over the previous year. In 33 percent of those incidents, materials were removed or access to them was restricted. "The censorship movement in America is flourishing," says Arthur Knopp, president of People for the American Way, an organization that monitors censorship efforts.

Among the most frequent grounds for challenges are "the Three S's": swear words, Satanism, and sex. In Monroeville, New Jersey, for example, a parent objected to a school copy of Webster's Dictionary because it contains sexually explicit definitions. It was removed. In Texas, schools have banned certain jewelry, clothing and symbols—including the peace sign and Star of David—that some believe are associated with Satanism.

Organizations like the American Library Association and the Association for Supervision and Curriculum Development have fought against efforts to censor educational materials, arguing that such restrictions infringe on the climate of intellectual freedom in the nation's schools. Recently, such groups have been joined by the Commission on Academic Freedom and Pre-College Education, an arm of the American Association of University Professors. Commission Chair, and (former) President of the University of Virginia, Robert M. O'Neil, expresses the central premise of the commission's report: "that resistance to censorship in the schools cannot be left only to those who are its victims. Restrictions on free inquiry and learning must be of concern to educators at all levels." In their 1986 report, *Liberty and Learning in the Schools,*

members of the commission argue for more freedom in classrooms and libraries, not less, to enable students to function in a democratic society. In the members' words, "removing a book from the school library because a passage in it offends members of the community increases in some measure the probability that the student will see suppression as an acceptable way of responding to controversial ideas."

Of course, not all members of a community will agree that educators must be allowed to use their professional judgement in selecting the materials for teaching and learning. Decisions about what students should read and learn inevitably provoke controversy in a society as diverse as ours. Albert Shanker, president of the American Federation of Teachers, describes the tensions underlying the censorship controversy:

> There is a tension between a teacher's academic freedom and a community's right to prescribe an appropriate curriculum for its students, between a teacher's academic freedom and his responsibility not to indoctrinate his students, between the school board's right to set a curriculum and a parent's right to determine what is appropriate for his child, . . . between a student's right to learn whatever he wants and the parent's right to shield his child from potentially harmful ideas.

As a student and a teacher and possibly a parent, you may find yourself pulled in several directions by these tensions. Scattered evidence indicates that fear of litigation and community disfavor causes self-censorship on the part of teachers and librarians. Are restrictions on instructional and library materials a form of protection or suppression? Chances are you will be faced with the need to answer this question many times as you teach.

Source: "Schools fend off more attempts at censorship," *U.S.A. Today* (Thursday, August 30, 1990), p. 1D. Commission on Academic Freedom and Pre-College Education, *Liberty and Learning in the Schools* (Washington, D.C.: American Association of University Professors, 1986). Quotations are from the preface and p. 9. The Shanker statement is from p. 3 of this report.

word was not all that shocking to the students. As the decision stated, "With the greatest respect to such parents, their sensibilities are not the full measure of what is proper education."[15]

Issues of academic freedom often generate a great deal of heat. When they reach the courts, a number of considerations are brought to bear, among them,

1. the teacher's purpose
2. the educational relevance of a controversial publication
3. the age of the students involved
4. the quality of disputed teaching material and its effects on the class[16]

Perhaps the most important point to remember is that academic freedom is limited: it cannot be used to protect the incompetent teacher or the indoctrinating zealot.

Lifestyle and the Teacher

Teachers and community values

Teachers bring into their classrooms more than their minds and their lesson plans. They bring their attitudes and values and, as discussed in Chapter 13, these teach, too. In fact, elementary and secondary teachers have traditionally been considered extensions of the family in passing on to the young the community's positive values. In past generations, teachers who behaved in ways counter to the community's values were dismissed. Teachers were summarily fired for homosexuality, being pregnant and single, living with someone of the opposite sex, using illegal drugs, being drunk, or committing a crime. However, the late sixties saw a reconsideration of the community's right to require certain standards of behavior and individuals' rights to their own lifestyle and values. And although some areas are still legally quite uncertain, on many questions judicial opinion (the way judges are tending to rule) is clear.

PERSONAL APPEARANCE: HAIR, CLOTHES, AND WEIGHT In the late sixties and early seventies, long hair, beards, and mustaches were in style and were sometimes considered to be a "value statement." In fact, one of the great "counterculture" events of the era was the play, and later movie, *Hair*. During this period, the courts tended to rule in favor of teachers' rights to do what they wished with their hair, as a matter of free expression. Since that period, however, the courts seem to have reversed themselves. Increasingly, they are siding with school districts' rights to impose reasonable grooming codes for teachers and asserting that teachers do not have a *constitutional* right concerning their "style of plumage."[17]

Less lenience today

The situation is similar for clothing. Courts are upholding districts' judgments on skirts that are considered too short or the requirement (in some districts) that male teachers wear neckties. Courts are asserting that the First Amendment does not extend to "sartorial choice."

In an age of fitness, obesity may be its own punishment. However, does a school district have a right to fire a teacher because it decides that the teacher is too fat? A California school district released a forty-two-year-old female physical education teacher because, at 5 feet 7 inches and 225 pounds, the district felt that she was "unfit for service." Her principal argued that she "did not serve as a model of health and vigor" and was restricted in her ability to perform on the trampoline, in gymnastics and modern dance, and in other aspects of the program.[18] Here, though, the court sided with the teacher, claiming that the district had not (actually) proved that her girth had impaired her performance.

PRIVATE SEXUAL BEHAVIOR   In the past, sexual behavior was considered an area where a community had a complete right to impose its standards on those people selected to teach its children. Currently, however, the courts are increasingly viewing teachers' private sexual habits or preferences as separate from their public, professional lives as teachers. A landmark case involved Marc Morrison, who was fired after his former lover, another male teacher, reported their brief relationship to the superintendent. Believing that the state's law requiring teachers to be models of good conduct applied to the case, that teachers are required to impress on their charges "principles of morality," and, further, that homosexual behavior is contrary to the moral standards of the people of California, the school district felt it was on solid ground in dismissing Morrison.

The Morrison case

However, in 1969 the California Supreme Court ruled in Morrison's favor. It acknowledged that homosexuality is, for many people, an uncertain or controversial area of morality. But, in addition, it made an important distinction between a teacher's private life and his or her professional performance. Since there was no evidence that Morrison's sexual preference had ever been part of his relationship with his students or in any way affected the performance of his teaching duties or, in fact, affected his relationship with his fellow teachers, he was reinstated.[19]

Similarly, cases involving pregnancy out of wedlock and unmarried couples living together are being settled in favor of the individual teacher. However, the conditions cited above are required. The behavior must not intrude into the classroom or seriously affect the teacher's professional performance. Flaunting one's deviation from the community's standard tends to increase the chances of dismissal being upheld in the courts. In all these cases, though, circumstances play a crucial role in the court's final opinion.

CONDUCT AND STUDENTS   Whereas the courts have become increasingly lenient on issues of private sexual behavior, the line is being held firm with regard to socially unaccepted behavior that spills over into the classroom. There are few surer ways to lose one's teaching position than to make a sexual advance to a student. Usually, one event is enough to sustain a dismissal. The same goes for smoking marijuana, taking other drugs, drinking to the point of drunkenness, or even using excessively obscene language in the presence of students. Here, the teacher bears the full weight of the responsibility to be a role model.

Teacher held accountable

In general, then, except in matters of personal appearance, the courts are allowing teachers a good degree of freedom in their private and personal lifestyle, as long as their choices and their behavior do not adversely affect their performance as teachers.

Copyright Laws   Good teachers are always on the hunt for effective teaching materials: stories that carry a special message, a poem that captures an idea with beauty and economy, an article that contains that latest information about an issue students are studying. Having once found the "perfect" piece, it is difficult to resist the temptation simply to copy it and share it with the class. And the wide availability of photocopying equipment makes this practice all too easy.

Justification for laws

Printed matter is the product of someone's labor, the same way a painting or a piece of furniture is. The creator or author has a legal right to receive a reward for his or her labor. Without such payment, few could afford to write books and plays and essays. For this reason, first in 1909, and more recently in 1976, the U.S. Congress passed copyright laws to protect writers and publishers from the unauthorized use of their material.

For teachers, the heart of the new copyright law is its *fair use* guidelines, which help specify what printed materials teachers may photocopy and under what conditions they may do so. The general principle behind fair use is "not to impair the value of the owner's copyright by diminishing the demand for that

Fair use guidelines

work, thereby reducing potential income for the owner."[20] In other words, if people simply copy printed materials whenever they want, they will not buy the books, and publishers and authors will suffer. Some copying is allowed, of course, and it is important for teachers to know what they may and may not do. *Teachers may:*

- make a single copy for class preparation of a chapter from a book; a newspaper or magazine article, short story, essay or poem; or a diagram, chart, picture, or cartoon from a book or magazine
- make a copy for each of their students of a poem, if it is fewer than 250 words and printed on not more than two pages; and one copy for each student of an article or short story if it is fewer than 2,500 words

Teachers may not

- make copies of the same author's work more than *once* a semester, or make copies from the same anthology or text or periodical issue more than *three times* a semester
- make copies of a work for their class if another teacher in the same building already has copied that same material for his or her class
- create a class anthology by copying material from several sources (a favorite trick of many teachers!)
- make multiple copies of weekly newspapers or magazines specifically designed for classrooms, or of consumable materials, such as copyrighted games, exercises, and particularly worksheets from workbooks
- Charge more for legally permissible copies than it cost to copy them

These guidelines may seem overly restrictive and technical, but in fact, teachers have more liberal guidelines for copying than the average citizen.

VIDEOTAPES   As more and more households and schools acquire VCRs, the temptation to tape material "off the air" becomes greater and greater. Teachers want to build tape libraries of material to use in instruction. Although this may be effective pedagogy, it may not be legal. Video is also covered by our copy-

Special rules right laws. Copyrighted television programs (and most of them are copyrighted) can only be kept for forty-five days, after which they must be erased or taped over. Also, during the first ten days after the taping, the teacher may show the tape only twice: once for initial presentation and once when "instructional reinforcement" is called for. Finally, schools cannot routinely record material on the possibility of later use by a teacher. It can only be done at a teacher's request.

Reporting Child Abuse

The abuse of children by their parents and other adults is an old and heinous crime. It can consist of the neglect or, worse, the physical or mental violation of a child. In recent years, there has been a major effort in the United States to bring this problem out into the open and make moves to curtail it. Teachers can *and are now required* to make a major contribution to this effort.

Child abuse includes beating and scarring children. It also includes failure to provide a child with enough food, adequate clothing, or even dental care. High on the list, too, is incest, a frequently secret form of abuse that poisons the lives of many children. As a result of recent efforts in this area, all fifty states now require the reporting of *suspected* child abuse. Teachers have been a major target of this legislation, since they are often the only ones close enough to see or sense the violation an abused child has undergone.

Teachers must report suspicions

The laws vary somewhat from state to state, but they are quite specific about the teacher's role. The law does not say that teachers *may report*, but that they *must report* suspected incidents. The teacher conveys any suspicions to the principal or to the social agency that deals with child abuse. To protect teachers

Table 5.1 Selected U.S. Court Cases Dealing with Teachers' Rights and Responsibilities

Case	
Pickering v. *Board of Education* (1968)	A teacher can criticize the operations of a school as long as this does not interfere with the normal running of the school.
Morrison v. *State Board of Education* (Cal. 1969)	A teacher's sexual orientation is not grounds for revocation of certification, particularly when it in no way affects the performance of professional tasks.
Keefe v. *Geanakos* (1969)	Assigning reading material with offensive words is not, in itself, grounds for dismissal.
Scoville v. *Board of Education* (1970)	A teacher's free speech is protected, but abusive or profane or "fighting" words are not.

from the reaction to an incorrect report or from the anger of an offending parent, the reporting is kept confidential. Further, teachers are granted immunity from accusations of slander or any possible libel suit. Without such protection, many teachers would hesitate before reporting their suspicions. Child abuse is clearly one of those areas where it is better to act and be wrong than to play it safe. (For a more detailed discussion of the problem of child abuse, see Chapter 10, "Who Are Today's Students?")

Law, Religion, and the School

- May public tax money be spent for support of parochial schools?
- What religious observances, if any, are permitted in public school classrooms?
- May religious holidays be observed in public schools, and if so, which ones?
- From what public school activities can an individual be excused for religious reasons?
- Are extracurricular religion clubs allowed in public schools?
- May parents insist that schools provide alternative textbooks consistent with their religious beliefs?

"Congress shall make no law respecting an establishment of religion, or prohibiting the free exercise thereof. . . ." During the past two centuries the American judicial system has interpreted the First Amendment to the Constitution inconsistently with respect to religion and the public schools. The controversy surrounding this issue is not new: it has been a bone of contention since the beginning of public education in the United States. Where do we stand today?

Until the middle of the twentieth century, religious observances, including Bible reading and prayers, were common in the public schools. In fact, Bible reading and the recitation of the Lord's Prayer were required by the constitution or by statutes in a number of states. In *Abington School District* v. *Schempp* (1963), however, the Supreme Court ruled both to be unconstitutional.

Rulings against prayer

In a 1962 decision (*Engle* v. *Vitale*), the Court had already ruled against the recitation of a nondenominational prayer, holding that Bible reading and prayer violate both clauses of the First Amendment. The Court recognized that the schools involved did not compel a child to join in religious activities if his or her parents objected but held that the social pressures exerted on pupils to participate were excessive. In essence, no distinction was felt to exist between voluntary and compulsory participation in religious activities.

Objective use of Bible

In its 1963 decision, the Court did note that the study of comparative religion, the history of religion, and the relationship of religion to civilization were not prohibited by this decision. It would also appear that, although the Bible may not be used to teach religion, it may, if objectively presented, be used in such areas of study as history, civics, and literature. Indeed, most thoughtful people would agree that failure to be conversant with the Old and New Testaments makes the understanding of Western history and literature impossible. In the same way, if a student set out to learn about Chinese culture and was not

Reprinted by permission: Tribune Media Services

permitted to read Confucius, he or she would be doomed to a very limited understanding.

In a more recent case, the Supreme Court approved the right of public school pupils who so desire to say prayers and read scriptures of their choice in the morning before school starts or after the regular school day has ended. If prayers are said during lunch period, they must be silent. In a related instance, the Court ruled unconstitutional an Alabama law providing for silent prayer time during the school day; the majority of the justices indicated, however, that time for silent "meditation" would be permissible.[21]

Released time ruling

An associated issue is "released time." In a series of decisions, the Court ruled that a state could not allow teachers employed by specific denominations to conduct religion classes in public school buildings during the regular school day. However, the Court did rule constitutional a New York City program that permitted students to leave the school grounds during the day to receive religious instruction elsewhere. Its reasoning was that the state must be neutral in regard to religion, and, since no public funds were involved, the school should cooperate with religious institutions by adjusting students' schedules.

Are extracurricular religious clubs legal in public schools? Court decisions provide no clear guidelines here. In at least one case, a district judge ruled in favor of such clubs based on students' right to free speech. Yet a U.S. circuit court of appeals overturned the decision, maintaining that such clubs violated the First Amendment's "establishment of religion" clause. The Supreme Court did not clear the waters: the five-justice majority upheld the district court opinion on a technical point but declined to comment on the constitutional issues raised.[22]

Religious extracurricular clubs

The *Abington* case, mentioned earlier, provided a test for the appropriateness of religious practices in public schools: Does the proposed practice inhibit or promote religion? In the case of direct religious instruction, posting religious materials, or distributing religious pamphlets, the answer has been straightforward. None of these activities are permitted because they promote religion. But growing numbers of parents have begun to challenge public school practices on the grounds that they inhibit a religion. These people, too, are concerned about the religious neutrality of the public schools.[23]

That fundamental questions such as "What is a person's true nature?" can be dealt with in public schools from every perspective but the religious one strikes many people as unfair and simply wrong. They think that, by ignoring the religious dimension of life, the public schools create a distorted, and ultimately dangerous, view of humankind—a view labeled *secular humanism*. Secular humanism asserts the dignity of human beings but ignores the idea of God and the spiritual. Speaking to this issue, Stephen Arons has written, "When government imposes the content of school, it becomes the same deadening agent of repression from which the framers of the Constitution sought to free themselves."[24] Many parents are voting not only with their pocketbooks, by turning down school budgets and tax requests for public schooling, but also with their feet, by walking away from the public school system. The increase in private schools in the 1980s (to almost 27,000 by 1987–88), with 21,660 being sectarian)[25] was in part a sign of parental concern about religious content in their children's education. Many of the newly opened schools were related to a Protestant church and maintained a Christian curriculum. But while private education is expanding, other parents are demanding a public school curriculum more compatible with their religious beliefs. Two examples of religiously based disagreements with the public schools can be seen in the controversies over certain textbooks and over the teaching of the origins of the human race.

Secular humanism issue

THE CREATIONISM VERSUS EVOLUTION CONTROVERSY   Major concern over the teaching of evolution versus creationism dates to the 1925 *Scopes* trial in Tennessee. Precedent was established then for teaching the theory of evolution in the public schools. But what about equal time for the biblical account of creation? In 1982, the Louisiana Legislature passed the Balanced Treatment for Creation-Science and Evolution-Science Act, which quickly came to be known as the Balanced Treatment Act. The act defined scientific creationism as "the belief that the origins of the elements, the galaxy, the solar system, of life, of all the species of plants and animals, the origin of man, and the origin of all things and their processes and relationships were created ex nihilo (from nothing)

Balanced Treatment Act

and fixed by God.''[26] The act, in addition to requiring that scientific creationism be taught whenever evolution was taught, also required the development of curriculum guides for teaching creationism, along with research service for those teaching creationism, and additionally prohibited school boards from discriminating against anyone who taught scientific creationism. On the other hand, the act provided none of these resources or protections for those teaching evolution. Again, after several challenges and lower court rulings, the case, *Edwards* v. *Aguillard,* reached the U.S.'s highest court, and in 1987 the Supreme Court ruled seven to two against the Balanced Treatment Act. The Court's prevailing opinion stated that the Balanced Treatment Act was not balanced in that its provisions favored the teaching of creationism over evolution. Further, the Court asserted that the Balanced Treatment Act was motivated by the legislature's desire to promote a particular religious viewpoint, and thereby violated the Constitution's provision against the establishment of a state-sponsored religion. Although the issue of a balanced treatment of these two views of how life began seems to be over, the tensions between secular and religious views of human beings' origins and nature are not over.

THE TEXTBOOK CONTROVERSY   Recent court cases have been launched by fundamentalist Christian parents who argue that texts used in their children's public school classes are anti-Christian and consequently a violation of their children's constitutional rights. In a 1986 Tennessee case, a U.S. district judge agreed that students' constitutional rights were violated when they were expelled after they refused to read certain texts. However, the following year the U.S. Court of Appeals for the Eleventh Circuit reversed the decision of the lower court and ruled that the texts in question did not promote or require a person to accept any other religion.[27]

Tennessee case

Alabama case

Shortly after, another challenge to the public schools' choice of textbooks was made in Alabama by fundamentalist parents, students, and teachers. Forty-four different textbooks used in history, social studies, and home economics courses were cited as advancing *secular humanism.* Some religious parents and teachers see this as a necessary compromise in the schools of a pluralistic nation such as the United States, but others see the schools as subtly separating children from their religious traditions and making secular humanists of them. In this Alabama textbook case (*Smith* v. *Board of School Commissioners for Mobile County*), the courts followed a similar pattern as in the Tennessee case just described. Initially, the district court ruled that secular humanism is a religion and that some of the textbooks in question did discriminate against theistic religion. On appeal, this decision was reversed and the court ruled that the textbooks promoted neither secularism nor any other religion.[28]

RELIGIOUS NEUTRALITY   Religion is a central force in the lives of many Americans. There are many different religions represented in the United States, and over 90 percent of Americans are affiliated with some formal religion. A 1991 poll of 113,000 Americans reported that only 7.5 percent said they had "no religion."[29] But although Americans are religious, we are also committed

> *Teaching about religion is not the same as teaching someone to be religious. In our multicultural, multiethnic society, understanding another person's faith will foster tolerance and harmony, a goal common to all religions.*
>
> — MARGARET BARTLEY —

Case	Decision
Scopes v. *State of Tennessee* 154 Tenn 105; 289 S.W. 363 (1925)	The court upheld the state law prohibiting the teaching of evolution as an explanation of the origins of the universe.
Engle v. *Vitale* (1962)	Bible reading and prayer in schools are in violation of the First Amendment; because of the social pressures involved, there is no difference between voluntary and compulsory prayer in school.
Schempp v. *School District of Abington Township* (1963)	Reading the Bible and reciting the Lord's Prayer in schools are in violation of the First and Fourteenth amendments; however, the Bible may be studied for educational purposes.
Edwards v. *Aguillard* (1987)	Schools teaching the biblical explanation of creation without giving equal time to evolution violate the Constitution's provision against the establishment of a state-sponsored religion.
Smith v. *Board of School Commissioners for Mobile County* (1987)	Textbooks that do not teach theistic religion are not by that fact alone trying to promote secular humanism.

to religious tolerance (including the belief in atheism or agnosticism) and to the separation of church and state. Nevertheless, there are bound to be tensions over religious issues in our schools. Thomas McDaniel offers the following four guidelines for following what he calls *a religious neutrality principle* in the classroom:

Suggested guidelines

1. Students may not be required to salute the flag nor to stand for the flag salute if this conflicts with their religious beliefs.
2. Bible reading, even without comment, may not be practiced in a public school when the intent is to promote worship.
3. Prayer is an act of worship and as such cannot be a regular part of opening exercises or other aspects of the regular school day.

4. Worship service (e.g., prayer and Bible reading) are not constitutional even if voluntary rather than compulsory. Not consensus, nor majority vote, nor excusing objectors from class or participation makes these practices legal.[30]

This principle of religious neutrality does not mean, however, that the public school must ignore religion. On the contrary, public schools are free to study the history and contributions (pro and con) of individual religions, to read the Bible as literature, and, in general, to expose students to our culture's religious heritage. When teachers cross the line into advocating a particular religion or involving students in prayer, then they become vulnerable to court suit.

STUDENTS AND THE LAW

Of the legal issues that affect the life of the teacher, many of the most important issues relate quite directly to students and their rights. Students have a special status under the law, particularly public school students. Since they are *compelled* to attend *state* schools, students can become involved in a number of different legal issues. In this final section we will touch on a few of the more significant and current student-related issues that can affect the teacher.

In Loco Parentis: Due Process and the Student

For years, the courts used the legal principle of *in loco parentis* in cases involving students. The phrase means that the teacher or teachers stand "in the place of the parents." Parental concern and guidance are suggested by this term. The teacher is expected to treat the student in a caring and informal manner, instead of in the formal and legalistic manner that governs relationships "out in the world." By the same reasoning, since we do not require due process in the home, for a long time it was not valued in the schools.

Gradually, though, in court cases such as *Tinker*[31] and others, the *in loco parentis* principle has eroded, and the courts have come to appreciate that students often need to be protected from the arbitrary use of authority. As a direct result, many schools have developed clear statements governing procedures for expulsion, suspension, student privacy, freedom of speech and publication, and various breaches of discipline. Informing students of the rules, procedures, and consequences of violations in these areas is a major step toward providing due process rights. Still, the most important aspect of due process is the spirit of fair and evenhanded justice with which teachers respond to the daily events of the classroom.

More explicit rules today

Suspension and Expulsion

Schools are crowded, busy places, filled with growing minds and bodies, throbbing with restless energy. In order to keep things on track and moving forward, schools have rules and procedures to guide the behavior of students. Amid all the activity and stress of school life and society as a whole, it is surprising that students' conduct breaks down so infrequently. Nevertheless, on occasion it does. Ever since schools began, individual students have had difficulty keeping the rules and staying out of trouble. In recent decades, as schools have tried harder to keep older youth from dropping out and as drugs and violence have

Rising discipline problems

increased in society as a whole, problems have increased. Some students, having been persuaded to stay in school, find little to capture their imaginations and to motivate them. For these students, school continues to be a place of failure and frustration. Trouble is often close behind.

Some of the more common forms of school infractions today are stealing; vandalizing school property or someone's private property; bringing a weapon to school; possessing, using, or selling drugs or alcohol; fighting (or encouraging others to fight); and repeatedly disobeying the reasonable directives of teachers and other school personnel.[32]

School districts, of course, are not powerless in the face of these kinds of disciplinary breaches. For the good of maintaining a safe and effective academic environment, schools can suspend students for a period of time or expel them completely. This power must be wielded in a manner that ensures that the students' constitutional rights to due process are protected. And it is here, in the administration of suspension and expulsion, that school administrators in particular have become tangled in the courts.

Lopez suspension case

One of the most important cases was the 1975 suspension case, *Goss* v. *Lopez*,[33] involving Dwight Lopez, a high school sophomore from Columbus, Ohio. Lopez was suspended for ten days for allegedly becoming involved in a cafeteria disturbance. This suspension occurred without a hearing and without any prior notification. Although a suspension of this length and without a hearing or prior notice was in accord with the Ohio statutes, a suit was filed stating that Dwight Lopez's constitutional rights had been violated. The basis for this suit was that because there was no notice or hearing, the student's due process protection had been breached. The case rather quickly went to the Supreme Court, which ruled in favor of Lopez on the grounds that suspension from school is a loss of liberty and that precautions need to be exercised to protect students in

THE TEACHER'S TEN COMMANDMENTS: SCHOOL LAW IN THE CLASSROOM

Thomas R. McDaniel, a professor of education at Converse College in Spartanburg, South Carolina, has written on the law and the classroom teacher for a number of years. His Teacher's Ten Commandments are taken from his article of the same name. The article, which we highly recommend, was first published in *Phi Delta Kappan* (June 1979, pages 703–708), and has been since reprinted in *Kaleidoscope: Readings in Education*, the volume put together by your authors to accompany this text.

Commandment I: Thou shalt not worship in the classroom
Commandment II: Thou shalt not abuse academic freedom

Commandment III: Thou shalt not engage in private activities that impair teaching effectiveness
Commandment IV: Thou shalt not deny students due process
Commandment V: Thou shalt not punish behavior through academic penalties
Commandment VI: Thou shalt not misuse corporal punishment
Commandment VII: Thou shalt not neglect students' safety
Commandment VIII: Thou shalt not slander or libel your students
Commandment IX: Thou shalt not photocopy in violation of copyright law
Commandment X: Thou shalt not be ignorant of the law

similar cases. In addition, the Court stated that "longer suspensions (longer than ten days) or expulsions for the remainder of the school term, or permanently, may require more formal procedures."

In a 1988 case with some similar elements, *Honig* v. *Doe,* the Supreme Court ruled against California school officials.[34] A school district had suspended indefinitely two emotionally disturbed students on the grounds that they were dangerous, and the court ruled that this suspension was a violation of the Education for All Handicapped Children Act, PL 94-142. This law allows school authorities to suspend dangerous handicapped students for a maximum of ten days. Longer suspensions require either the permission of parents or the consent of a federal judge.

Violation of PL 94-142

In another 1988 case, *Newsome* v. *Batavia Local School District,* the issue was the procedure used in suspending a student.[35] In this case, a student was accused by two fellow students of offering to sell them marijuana on school property. The principal followed procedures that had been established since the Lopez case. He informed the student, Arthur Newsome, of the allegations (without revealing the names of the accusers). In addition, he gave the boy an opportunity to respond to the charges, and Newsome denied the accusations. The principal then told Newsome and his mother that he planned to go ahead with suspension hearings, but apprised them of their opportunity to have an informal meeting on the matter and also the possibility of an appeal to the Board of Education. The Newsomes obtained a lawyer's services, and after the board hearing a suit was filed claiming that Arthur Newsome's rights had been violated in that, first, he had not been allowed to cross-examine his accusers (the two students); second, he had not been allowed to cross-examine the administrators who had handled his case and recommended the suspension; third, the administrators had violated his rights by taking part in the board's closed deliberations; and, fourth, new evidence had been introduced during the closed-door sessions, thus violating his rights further. The court, the Sixth Circuit Court, dismissed the first three complaints but agreed with the fourth. They viewed the introduction of new evidence without benefit of the accused's presence a violation of rights.

Newsome drug-selling case

The Newsome case suggests that there is a trend away from an emphasis on student rights, as in the 1975 case of Lopez, toward the collective rights of the school. Newsome won only on one point; on all the other points, the court backed the school. But, although the pendulum of judicial decisions seems to be moving back in favor of the authority of the schools, the implications for teachers and administrators dealing with matters potentially leading to suspension or expulsion are clear.

Guidelines for schools

- First, documentation. Before suspension and expulsion can take place, students must be notified (either in writing or orally) of the nature of their offense and what the intended punishment is.

- Second, the school must give the students a clear explanation of the evidence upon which the disciplinary charges rest.

- Third, the school must give the students an opportunity to refute the charges before a fair and impartial individual with decision-making authority.

Corporal Punishment

Extent of use

Although there is hardly an educational theorist living who advocates it, corporal, or physical, punishment is alive and well in the American schools. Currently, thirty-eight states expressly permit its use, and twelve expressly prohibit it. Many states, however, currently have legislation pending that would abolish corporal punishment, but many states are silent on the matter, and it is left up to local school districts to decide. Approximately 50 percent of students attend school in districts that do not allow corporal punishment.[36] In 1977 the Supreme Court had an opportunity to disqualify corporal punishment but refused to rule.

Limits on use

What does this situation mean for teachers, from a legal point of view? First, they must know the rules of their state and school district. Second, they must be aware that the courts have ruled that corporal punishment can be administered only under certain conditions. Thus, teachers must be sure that they are using only "moderate" and "reasonable" corporal punishment and using it only to establish discipline. A teacher who severely punishes a child, especially if there is any permanent disability or disfigurement, is quite liable to suit. Further, the punishment must be in scale with the crime—no paddling for whispering. Also, punishment cannot be administered out of spite or revenge or anger. In ruling on cases of excessive corporal punishment, the courts scrutinize the teacher's state of mind and motivation. The instruments of corporal punishment and where it can be administered are also matters of concern to the courts. Fists are totally inappropriate; so are switches and canes. Blows must not strike parts of the body where the risk of injury is high.

These are the legal rulings surrounding the use of corporal punishment. However, from an ethical standpoint, corporal punishment is usually inappropriate. Many other ways of dealing with students who have misbehaved do not carry the negative effects of corporal punishment. Other forms of punishment, such as temporary or prolonged isolation from other students, may cause distress, but none rely on the autocratic use of pain (and fear) that is at the heart of corporal punishment.

Search and Seizure

As we write this, the nation is in the grip of a major cycle of drug use. Many students, even young students of junior high and elementary ages, possess and sell illegal drugs. Schools have these problems because American youth spend so much of their time with drugs. And drugs are only one problem relating to search and seizure. Students also bring alcohol, pornography, and even dangerous weapons to school.

Locker search rules

A student's locker may be searched by an appropriate school official, usually an administrator, *if there are reasonable grounds* to suspect that the locker contains something illegal or dangerous. The New York State courts have gone further in stating that "not only have the school authorities the right to inspect but the right becomes a duty when suspicion arises that something of an illegal nature may be secreted there."[37] On the other hand, courts have found that it violates students' rights under the Fourth Amendment, and is therefore illegal, for school personnel systematically to spot-check lockers in hunts for drugs, weapons, or other illicit materials. Students' rights are still more closely protected when it comes to searches of clothing and body searches.

School personnel may not randomly search students' lockers, but they may search a student's locker if there are reasonable grounds for suspicion.

(*Mimi Forsyth/Monkmeyer Press Photo Service*)

The most important criterion, in cases of search and seizure, is "reasonableness," as is shown in the 1985 Supreme Court case *New Jersey* v. *T.L.O.*[38] A teacher found two high school girls smoking in the bathroom and immediately brought them to the assistant vice principal's office. One girl admitted to smoking, but the other denied not only smoking on this occasion, but even being a smoker. The administrator then asked this young woman to come into his private office, where he opened her purse and discovered a pack of cigarettes. He also glimpsed cigarette-rolling papers. Deciding to look further, he found more than cigarettes. He found marijuana, a pipe, empty plastic bags, a wad of bills, and a list of "people who owe me money." Enter the police. The girl was turned over to the juvenile court, where she was judged to be delinquent. She appealed on the basis that the search of her purse had violated her constitutional rights and that therefore the evidence against her had been obtained illegally.

The case went to the U.S. Supreme Court, and the girl lost. The Court stated, "The legality of a search of a student should depend simply on the reasonableness, under all the circumstances, of the search." Reasonableness appears to be determined, first, by whether or not the search has been initiated by a "reasonable" suspicion. Having seen rolling papers, it was reasonable to look

Criterion of "reasonableness"

for marijuana, since the two are so often intimately related. The second criterion of reasonableness is that its scope and conduct must be "reasonably" related to the circumstances that gave rise to the search. Further, school officials must take into consideration the age and sex of the students and the nature of the offense.

Another way of saying this is that school authorities must have "probable cause" for such strong action, which means that they must have reliable information—not just suspicion—that the individual is hiding dangerous or illegal material. Mistakes here, particularly in the case of unwarranted strip searches, can be not only painfully embarrassing to the students but also very expensive for the school district.

Probable cause

Finally, the police do not have the same *custodial relationship*—the same kind of responsibility toward students—as school officials. Therefore, police, as a general rule, need a warrant and the consent of school officials to search individual students or their lockers.

Freedom of Speech

The right to say what we want, where we want, is near and dear to Americans. It is the mother's milk of a free society. Justice William O. Douglas stated, "Restriction of free thought and free speech is the most dangerous of all subversions. It is the one un-American act that could most easily defeat us." But although our courts vigilantly protect this right, it is not an absolute right. The great Supreme Court justice Oliver Wendell Holmes wrote that freedom of speech does not give a person the right to yell "Fire!" in a crowded theater or to knowingly and maliciously say or write lies that damage the reputation of another. It is hardly surprising, therefore, that the right to free expression frequently clashes with the school's responsibility to maintain a safe and orderly environment and one in which people's feelings and reputation are protected.

Importance and limits

During the 1960s and early 1970s, many of the social protests and antiwar demonstrations spilled over into the schools, particularly the high schools. In one school, students who had been suspended for wearing an antiwar arm band took the issue to court, claiming that the school was interfering with their right to freedom of expression. The Supreme Court ruled in favor of the students, stating that their black arm bands were a form of symbolic speech in protest to the Vietnam War and should not be prohibited. A key point in this affirmation of students' First Amendment rights was the passive and nondisruptive nature of the students' protest. The Court's ruling stated that there was no evidence that the wearing of arm bands "materially and substantially interfere with the requirements of appropriate discipline in the operation of the schools."[39]

Tinker case—symbolic protest

This case, *Tinker* v. *Des Moines Independent Community School District* (1969), was highly influential and set the tone for other court decisions regarding students' rights. One justice, Hugo Black, dissented, and his argument foretold the growing concern of the Court that protest and dissent within schools jeopardized the primary mission of the school:

> I think the record overwhelmingly shows that the armbands did exactly what the elected school officials and principals foresaw they would, that is, took the students' mind off their classwork and diverted them to thoughts about the highly emotional subject of the Vietnam War.

And I repeat that if the time has come when pupils of state-supported schools, kindergartens, grammar schools, or high schools, can defy and flout orders of the school officials to keep their minds on their own schoolwork, it is the beginning of a new revolutionary era of permissiveness in this country fostered by the judiciary.[40]

The tide of court opinion in favor of student rights to free speech clearly could be seen to be receding in the 1968 case of *Bethel School District No. 403 v. Fraser.*[41] Matthew Fraser, a high school student in Bethel, Washington, nominated a fellow student for vice president of the student government in a formal speech at an assembly before six hundred of his fellow students. Despite the warning of two teachers, Fraser built his speech on an elaborate, graphic, and explicit sexual metaphor comparing the nominee to a sexual organ. The court records of this case fail to tell us the outcome of the election, but Matthew Fraser got the axe. He was suspended for three days and removed from the list of candidates to speak at graduation. Fraser sued, won initially, but when the case went to the Supreme Court, lost by a seven-to-two decision. The Court affirmed the school's right to "establish standards of civic and mature conduct" and to enforce them.

Fraser's case—lewd speech

School newspapers have long been the arena for struggles over freedom of speech and freedom of the press. Often the very best efforts to make the paper "vital" and "relevant" draw the newspaper staff into controversies. And this is what happened at Hazelwood East High School in the spring of 1983.[42] Attempting to make their paper, *The Spectrum,* speak more directly to the real issues confronting their fellow students, the staff submitted two controversial articles, one dealing with the personal accounts of three Hazelwood students who had become pregnant and the other focusing on divorce and its effect on students.

Kuhlmeier case—school newspapers

In line with standard practice, the advisor and teacher of the journalism class that produced the paper passed the issue on to the principal for his approval. The principal eliminated the two pages containing the offending stories and sent the other four pages to the printers. Although the identities of the students were protected and, in the case of the pregnant girls, there were no graphic accounts of sexual activity, the principal believed that, given the small size of the school, the anonymity of the pregnant girls was violated. He was also concerned about the effect of the articles' frank sexual comments on young readers. Finally, he raised the issue of the one-sidedness of the divorce article, in which an inattentive father was portrayed as the villain in the piece. In response, Kathy Kuhlmeier and the six other journalism students sued, contending that their freedom of speech rights had been violated.

During the next five years, the *Spectrum* case was first decided in the federal court in favor of the school district, then overturned in favor of the students by the Seventh Circuit Court of Appeals, and finally in 1988 the *Spectrum* case was brought before the Supreme Court. By a vote of five to three, the Court ruled in favor of the school district. Although dissenting justices complained about the potential for "thought control" and the "denuding of high school students of much of the First Amendment protection that Tinker in itself pre-

Students' rights lose ground

scribed," the majority supported the principal's actions as legal and responsible. As stated in the majority opinion,

> A school may in its capacity as publisher of a school newspaper or producer of a school newspaper or producer of a school play disassociate itself not only from speech that would substantially interfere with its work or impinge on the rights of other students but also from speech that is, for example, ungrammatical, poorly written, inadequately researched, biased, prejudiced, vulgar or profane, or unsuitable for immature audiences. . . . A school need not tolerate student speech that is inconsistent with its basic educational mission even though the government could not censor similar speech outside the school.[43]

Taken together, these three cases, all involving various forms of speech and expression, suggest that in schools freedom of speech and expression is hardly absolute. Students may be punished for offensive or disruptive speech or publications. Schools, then, are something like Justice Holmes's crowded theaters, and the students' freedom of speech is somewhat limited. Students can and should express themselves, but in an orderly and nonviolent way. And the school has the right and responsibility to be certain that language is not used to hurt or scandalize the students in their charge.

Students with AIDS

Crack, Uzis, and AIDS: these are but the latest indicators of a harsh outside world spilling into the schools, schools that should be safe havens that protect and nourish our children. In fact, schools have always been menaced by the outside world, whether in the form of drugs and alcohol, of knives and guns, or of diseases such as tuberculosis and polio. Still, the AIDS menace took the schools by surprise. AIDS, or acquired immune deficiency syndrome, burst on the scene in the United States in the early 1980s as a deadly plague among, first, sexually active gay men and, second, drug users who shared infected hypodermic needles. This new epidemic did not significantly affect the schools until AIDS-contaminated blood brought the disease to children who had received blood transfusions. One of these children was seven-year-old Randy Ray of St. Petersburg, Florida.[44]

Case of Randy Ray

Randy, a hemophiliac, was discovered to have been exposed to the virus through the transmission of blood in a hospital, apparently a few short months before blood products were screened for the AIDS virus. Doctors soon discovered that Randy's two brothers, Richard and Robert, also tested positive. When the Ray parents enrolled their children in the DeSoto County schools for the 1986–87 year, they informed the schools of their sons' condition. School officials refused to allow the boys to attend schools, presumably out of fear that they would infect other students, and made some arrangements for home instruction. The family moved to another community and met a similar fate. They moved back to DeSoto County and decided to sue to have their sons returned to regular classroom instruction. National consciousness about AIDS was growing, and the entire subject was laced with misinformation and frightening tales. The fact that the Ray boys were hemophiliacs and prone to bleeding added to the controversy. It was a classic case of conflict between the good of the many (protection against the possibility of being infected with a strange and deadly disease) and the rights of the individual (three innocent young boys).

This highly charged case went to the U.S. district court and was handled with great wisdom and compassion by Judge Elizabeth Kovachevich. After reviewing the available research on the topic, she ruled as follows:

> The court finds that the actual, on going injury to (the boys) in this case clearly outweighs the potential harm to others, and that the public interest in this case weighs in favor of returning these children to an integrated classroom setting. . . . *Unless and until* it can be established that these boys pose a real and valid threat to the school population of DeSoto County, they shall be admitted to the normal and regular classroom setting, to which they are, respectively, educationally entitled.[45]

The judge, however, stipulated a number of conditions to ensure that the good of the larger community was protected. Among these were a watchdog community of public health personnel, school officials, and parents; and special rules for the boys about covering sores and lesions, following "elevated standards of hygiene" and avoiding contact sports and all incidents that might result in blood spills or the transmission of the AIDS virus.

Issue not over   But although this particular case appears to have been resolved in a humane and sensible manner, the AIDS epidemic is still raging and more and more children with AIDS, now largely the result of being born of AIDS-infected mothers, are entering our schools. Ignorance, fear, and prejudice are at war with the rights of these children, the need to protect the larger community, and our growing research-based knowledge of AIDS. And, in all likelihood, our schools will be the legal battleground where much of this will be worked out.

*Records and
the Student's Right
to Privacy*

We live in what has been called an Information Age, where each of us has a history tucked away on computer disks. For students, this history may be composed of school records, various psychological tests, and ratings by teachers on everything from citizenship to punctuality. Teachers and other staff members judge a student's character and potential, and those judgments are used by other people to decide whether or not the student should go to this school or get that job. Certainly it would seem that we need some system of exchanging information about one another. Otherwise, we would only hire our friends or only go to schools where enough people knew us to vouch for us. However, the kind of information in school records may be very imperfect, and there is a serious danger of its being misinterpreted or falling into the wrong hands and being misused.

Abuse has been more than potential. A series of situations came to light in the early seventies in which information was poorly used or in which parents and students were denied access to records (for example, when a diagnosis was used to justify sending a child to a class for the mentally retarded). In response, *The Buckley amendment*   Congress in 1974 passed the Buckley amendment. Its full and formal name is the Family Educational Rights and Privacy Act, and it outlines who may and may not see a student's record and under what conditions. A clear winner from this legislation is parents, who previously were kept from many of the officially recorded judgments that affected their children's futures. The amendment states that no school will receive federal funds if it prevents parents from exercising the right to inspect and review their children's educational records. Parents must receive an explanation or interpretation of the records if they so request.

However, the Buckley amendment does not give parents the right to see a teacher's or administrator's unofficial records. For instance, a teacher's private diary of a class's progress or private notes about a particular child may not be inspected without the teacher's consent.

The downside of Buckley

Although the Buckley amendment has undoubtedly reduced the potential for abuse of information, it has had a somewhat chilling effect on teachers' and others' willingness to be candid in their judgments when writing student recommendations for jobs or colleges. Because students may elect to see a teacher's letter of recommendation, some teachers choose to play it safe and write a vague, very general letter that lacks discriminating judgments, pro or con, about the student. In effect, some faculty members and other recommenders have adopted the attitude "Well, if a student doesn't trust me enough to let me write a confidential recommendation, I'll simply write an adequate, safe recommendation."

Still, the Buckley amendment's impact, in our view, has been positive. In the past, many students lost opportunities for higher education and desirable jobs because of inaccurate statements in recommendations or in their school records. One professor reported to us an incident that occurred in his school in 1975, when the Buckley amendment came into being: "Our counselors at the junior high school where I taught were 'purging' the records of subjective comments with black markers. In one student's permanent record folder a *Playboy* magazine fell out. It seems a grade school teacher took it from Carl, and included it in his permanent record because she wanted future teachers to know 'what kind of kid Carl really was.'"

A FINAL WORD

This chapter has been the beginning of what we hope will be your ongoing probe of the important role that two related issues, ethics and law, play in the life of the teacher. Together, they surround and permeate the school environment. Whereas ethical issues may raise timeless questions, some laws continually change, and even now, the courts may have given a different complexion to some of what we have said in this chapter. Also, the chapter has touched on many issues only lightly, and has omitted others owing to lack of space. We urge you to move on from this introduction to investigate further the work of the teacher in its larger ethical and legal framework.

1. Can you remember examples of the "everyday ethics" of teaching shown by the teachers you had in elementary and secondary schools? Can you remember examples in which your teachers' ethical behavior was questionable?
2. Review the four ethical situations described in the first part of this chapter.

Table 5.3 Selected U.S. Court Cases Related to Students' Rights

Case	Decision
Tinker v. *Des Moines Independent Community School District* (1969)	Students are allowed to protest symbolically (as with arm bands) if this protest does not interfere with schooling.
Goss v. *Lopez* (1975)	Suspending a student without a hearing (due process) is in violation of the student's constitutional rights; students' liberties must be protected.
New Jersey v. *T.L.O.* (1985)	Schools can search students' lockers and personal effects if there is reasonable cause to do so.
Bethel School District No. 403 v. *Fraser* (1986)	Schools have the right to establish standards of speech and to enforce them.
Kuhlmeier v. *Hazelwood School District* (1986)	Schools have the right not to print student articles that they feel may violate the sensibilities of other students; schools are not public forums.
Ray v. *School District of DeSoto County* (1987)	Children with AIDS are no threat to other children in school if certain precautions are followed, and denying them entrance violates their rights.
Newsome v. *Batavia Local School District* (1988)	Schools cannot suspend students on the basis of evidence that has been introduced outside the accused's presence; however, students must prove all due process procedural violations.

Which one do you believe represents the "easiest" dilemma for you to solve? Why? Which appears to you to be the most difficult? Why?

3. Do you believe that tenure practices are justified and lead to better schools?
4. How do you feel about the current controversies over the place of religion in public schools? Of prayer? Of the Bible and other religious works?
5. Do you understand the concept of due process, and can you recall from your school experience situations in which a student's or teacher's due process rights were violated?

6. Teachers are expected to be people of good character and role models to students. What are the limits of this expectation? What are some points at which the rights of the school district end and the rights of the teacher begin?

For Further Reading   *Deskbook Encyclopedia of American School Law.* Rosemount, Minn.: Data Research, 1991.

> This excellent annual reference book is an easily accessible source of the current law on the legal issues surrounding all phases of public and private education.

Fischer, Louis, and David Schimmel. *The Rights of Students and Teachers.* 2d ed. New York: Harper and Row, 1987.

> This book, written by men who are both lawyers and professors of education, bridges the worlds of the courts and the classroom with great detail and clarity.

Fischer, Louis, David Schimmel, and Cynthia Kelly. *Teachers and the Law.* New York: Longman, 1981.

> Another comprehensive, highly readable book on the major legal issues confronting teachers. This book is organized around common legal questions, such as "How secure is my tenure?" and "When am I liable?"

Goodlad, John I., Roger Soder, and Kenneth Sirotnik. *The Moral Dimension of Teaching.* San Francisco: Jossey-Bass, 1990.

> This book of readings explores the moral and ethical aspects of teaching from many angles and from the vantage point of several different disciplines.

McDaniel, Thomas R. "The Teacher's Ten Commandments: School Law in the Classroom." *Phi Delta Kappan* (June 1979): V. 60, No. 10, 703–708.

> Summarizes in a small space the major issues faced by teachers and provides the legal findings for each. This excellent essay has been reprinted in the companion reader to this text, *Kaleidoscope: Readings in Education,* 6th ed. (Boston: Houghton Mifflin, 1992), edited by your not-so-humble servants.

Monk, Robert L., and Ernest I. Proulx. "Legal Basics for Teachers." *Fastback 235.* Bloomington, Ind.: Phi Delta Kappa, 1986.

> This pamphlet provides legal guidelines in such areas as field trips, corporal punishment, negligence, and student locker and body searches.

Strike, Kenneth, and Jonas Soltis. *The Ethics of Teaching.* New York: Teachers College Press, 1986.

> This short book is an excellent source of ways to approach the topic of ethics in teaching and contains a number of practice cases.

Notes   1. Quoted in Carleton W. Washburne and Sidney P. Marland, Jr., *Winnetka* (Englewood Cliffs, N.J.: Prentice-Hall, 1963), p. 358.
2. Kenneth R. Howe, "A Conceptual Basis for Ethics in Teacher Education," *Journal of Teacher Education* 37 (May–June 1986): 6. Used by permission of the publisher.
3. Ibid., p. 6.

4. Jonas F. Soltis, "Teaching Professional Ethics," *Journal of Teacher Education* 37 (May–June 1986): 2. Used by permission of the publisher.

5. "Bill of Rights," The American Federation of Teachers. Washington, D.C.: American Federation of Teachers.

6. Judith Lanier and Philip Cusick, *Phi Delta Kappan* (June 1985): V. 66, No. 10, 711–712.

7. John Martin Rich, "The Role of Professional Ethics in Teacher Education," *Journal of the Association of Teacher Educators* 7 (Fall 1985): 22.

8. *U.S.L. Week 4223*, March 24, 1970, quoted in Louis Fischer and David Schimmel, *The Rights of Students and Teachers* (New York: Harper and Row, 1982), p. 323. Much of this chapter is drawn from the material presented in this excellent and highly readable book and also from Louis Fischer, David Schimmel, and Cynthia Kelly, *Teachers and the Law* (New York: Longman, 1981).

9. Fischer, Schimmel, and Kelly, *Teachers and the Law*, p. 13.

10. *Smith v. School District of the Township of Darby*, quoted in ibid., p. 29.

11. Robert L. Monk and Ernest I. Proulx, "Legal Basics for Teachers," *Fastback 235* (Bloomington, Ind.: Phi Delta Kappa, 1986), p. 35.

12. *Pickering v. Board of Education*, 225 N.E.2d 1 (1967); 391 U.S. 563 (1968).

13. *Anderson v. Evans*, 660 F.2d 153 (6th Cir. 1981).

14. *Scoville v. Board of Education*, 425 F.2d 10 (7th Cir. 1970).

15. Fischer, Schimmel, and Kelly, *Teachers and the Law*, p. 139.

16. Ibid., p. 139.

17. Ibid., p. 187.

18. Ibid., p. 238.

19. Ibid., p. 216.

20. Thomas R. McDaniel, "The Teacher's Ten Commandments: School Law in the Classroom," *Phi Delta Kappan* (June 1979): V. 60, No. 10, 707.

21. Thomas L. Reddick and Larry Peach, "Guidelines for Teachers Using Religious Materials," *Clearing House for the Contemporary Educator in Middle and Secondary Schools* 60 (October 1986): 86.

22. Benjamin Senor, "Even After the Supreme Court Ruling, We're Still in the Dark About Religion Clubs at School," *American School Board Journal* 173 (August 1986): 17.

23. *Abington School District v. Schempp* 83 S.Ct. 1560, 374 U.S.203, 10 L.Ed 2d 844 (1962).

24. Stephen Arons, "Separation of School and State," *Education Week*, November 17, 1984, p. 24.

25. Marilyn McMillian and Elizabeth Gerald, "Characteristics of Private Schools: 1987–88" (Washington, D.C.: National Center for Education Statistics, April 1990), p. 2.

26. Thomas J. Flygare, "Supreme Court Strikes Down Louisiana Creationism Act," *Phi Delta Kappan* (September 1987): V. 69, N. 1, 77–79.

27. *A. Mozert v. Hawkins County Board of Education* U.S. Dist. Ct. (E.D. Tenn.) 647 F Supp. 1194 (1987).

28. *Smith v. Board of School Commissioners of Mobile County* No. 87-7216 (11th Cir. September 26, 1987).

29. Ari L. Goldman, "Portrait of Religion in U.S. Holds Dozens of Surprises," *New York Times*, April 10, 1991, p. 1.

30. Thomas R. McDaniel, "The Teacher's Ten Commandments: School Law in the Classroom," *Phi Delta Kappan* (June 1979): 703. Used by permission.

31. *Tinker v. Des Moines Independent Community School District*, 393 U.S. 503 (1969).

32. McCarthy, M. M., and N. H. Cambron-McCabe, *Public School Law: Teacher's and Students' Rights*, 2d ed. (Boston: Allyn and Bacon, 1987).

33. *Goss v. Lopez*, 95 S.Ct. 729 (1975).

34. *Honig v. Doe* 108 S.Ct. 592, 605 (1988).

35. *Newsome v. Batavia Local School District*, 842 F.2d 920 (6th Cir. 1988).

36. Temple University Center for the Study of Corporal Punishment and Alternatives in the School, cited in *American Education* (John Johansen, Harold W. Collins, James A. Johnson) Edition Sixth Dubuque: Wm. Brown, 1990, p. 71.

37. Fischer, Schimmel, and Kelly, *Teachers and the Law*, p. 207.

38. *New Jersey* v. *T.L.O.,* 105 S.Ct. 733 (1985).

39. *Tinker* v. *Des Moines Independent Community School District,* 383 U.S. 503 (1969).

40. Quoted in D. Cecil Clark and Beverly Romney Cutler, *Teaching: An Introduction* (San Diego: Harcourt Brace Jovanovich, 1990), p. 185.

41. *Bethel School District No. 403* v. *Fraser,* 106 S.Ct. 3159 (1986).

42. *Kuhlmeier* v. *Hazelwood School District,* 56 U.S.L.W. 4079, 4082 (12 January 1988).

43. op. cit.

44. *Ray* v. *School District of DeSoto County,* 666 F. Supp. 1524 (M.D. Fla. 1987).

45. Quoted in Thomas J. Flygare, "Judge Orders Children with AIDS Virus Back into the Classroom," *Phi Delta Kappan* (January 1988): V. 69, No. 5, 381–382.

6

How Are Schools Governed, Controlled, and Financed?

CHAPTER PREVIEW

Very few beginning teachers are concerned about issues related to school governance and control. The topic seems remote to them; it is something administrators and representatives of teacher organizations care about, but it does not seem particularly vital for beginning teachers concerned with learning how to survive. We feel differently; we believe that beginning teachers must have some understanding of the way schools and school systems operate since they will be affected personally by control, governance, and financial decisions. Not understanding how these decisions are made and how they might affect you as a teacher will reduce your effectiveness as a professional.

This chapter emphasizes that:

● Although the right to govern schools is delegated legally, control and influence over school operations are often exercised by people without legal authority.

● Legal responsibility for school governance belongs to the state. Traditionally, policy decisions and administration have been delegated to local boards of education. The school district superintendent is the educational leader and chief administrator of the school district.

● In the first wave of the mid-1980s educational reform movement, states led the way in legislating new policies and locating new funding sources. In the second wave, teacher empowerment and site-based management became the focus. The third wave is urging greater coordination of health, education, social, and transportation services for children at risk and their families.

● Professional educators, state governments, local school boards, parents, teachers, the business community, standardized testing, the federal government, and the courts all exert influence and some measure of control over educational decisions in the United States.

● Court rulings have also shifted the responsibility for public school financing from dependence on local property taxes to greater reliance on state support.

● During the Reagan administration, the federal government's role in education decreased significantly. President Bush's desire to become the "education president" may lead to a greater role for the federal government, but not to the level it played during the 1960s and 1970s.

Although the sources of influence on public education are never static, the 1980s and the early 1990s have been a time of growing interest in reforming the schools. As a result, the number of groups who wish to influence public education policy has been increasing. In the first wave of the reform movement that followed the publication of *A Nation at Risk* in 1983, state governors and legislatures showed strong leadership. Many states reasserted their policy-making role in public education by prescribing curriculum offerings, mandating new academic calendars, and demanding greater use of standardized testing to measure student outcomes. In this first wave of reform the school was seen as the object of change. Throughout this chapter you'll see examples of the growing state role in school governance issues.

In the subsequent waves of reform, attention has turned to schools and their teachers as the agents of change rather than as the objects of legislated reform. As the Carnegie Forum on Education and the Economy asserts, "Without a profession possessed of high skills, capabilities, and aspirations, any reforms will be short-lived."[1] As efforts grow to empower teachers as true professionals, to build collegial relationships among administrators and teachers, and to involve local communities in the work of their schools, implications arise for current patterns of governance and control.

We have tried in this chapter to draw from literature and experience to describe how things really are, not how they're supposed to be. The result will, we hope, give you insight into school control that will help you be a better, more professional teacher.

How Governance Differs from Control

How is *governing* different from *controlling?* The right to govern is delegated legally, but domination or command that results in "control" of people or a situation is not necessarily officially sanctioned. Often, however, the governing person or group also exercises control, as in the case of a strong president or a monarch whose powers are not constitutionally restricted. In other instances, those who govern exercise little real control, as in the case of a figurehead monarch who is manipulated by someone behind the scenes. Such situations have occurred from time to time in monarchies when young children have succeeded to the throne and the real power and control have been wielded by advisors and guardians. Between these two extremes is the situation in which those who legally govern share power with persons or groups possessing no legal authority. This state of affairs prevails in public education. Considerable control over the operation of our schools is often exercised by persons without legal authority, largely through personal connections and the exertion of pressure on legal officeholders.

Who Legally Governs Public Education?

In most countries, the public schools are a branch of the central government, federally financed and administered, and highly uniform in curricula and procedures. In the United States, however, responsibility for the public schools has evolved as a state function as a result of the Tenth Amendment to the U.S.

Constitution. Each of the fifty states has legal responsibility for the operation and administration of public schools within its own boundaries. In most aspects of public education (we will discuss certain exceptions later), the authority of federal, county, and city education agencies is subject to the will of the state authorities.

Education a state function

Although legal responsibility for school governance belongs to the states, policy decisions and administration have ordinarily been delegated to local boards of education, which exist because Americans have come to insist on control of schools at the local level. Recently, states have been reasserting their policy-making prerogatives. Will increased regulation by state governments bring more uniformity to the often widely diverse levels of efficiency and achievement of school systems across the nation, and even within individual states? Many educators, legislators, parents, and businesspeople are interested in this question.

State vs. local control

The State Authorities

THE STATE BOARD OF EDUCATION   The state's legal responsibility for public education requires it to establish an organizational framework within which the local units can function. The result is the establishment of state boards of education to exercise general control and supervision of schools within the state. The state board of education is the state's policy-making body. It typically establishes goals and priorities for education in the state, formulates education policy and curricular offerings, establishes and enforces rules and regulations for the operation of educational programs, represents the public in matters regarding the governance of education, reports to the public on accomplishments and needs, and makes recommendations to the governor and/or state legislature for the improvement of education. The state board of education establishes and enforces minimum standards for the operation of all phases of elementary and secondary education from the state to the local school system level.

Policy-making function

The procedure for selecting state board members varies from state to state. In most states, members are appointed by the governor, but in about one-third of the states members are elected by the people or by representatives of the people. Two states have ex officio members who serve on the state board because of the positions or offices they already hold. The number of members on a state board of education varies from state to state, but nine to fifteen members is quite typical.

Selection of members

THE CHIEF STATE SCHOOL OFFICER   The executive officer of the state board of education—whose title may be, depending on the state, chief state school officer, superintendent of education, commissioner of education, secretary of the state board of education, or something else—usually is responsible to the state board of education for the administration of public education. Responsibilities normally involve teacher and administrator licensure, organization of the program of studies, curriculum revision, application of the state finance law, approval of school sites and buildings, collection of statistical data, and direct supervision of elementary and secondary educational programs. This officer exercises little direct administrative authority over local educational officers, but

Duties

his or her indirect influence is widely felt on the local level. In some states the officer is elected by the voters, whereas in others he or she is appointed by the state board of education or the governor.

THE STATE DEPARTMENT OF EDUCATION The chief state school officer, as well as being the executive officer of the state board of education, also serves as the administrative head of the state department of education (sometimes called the state department of public instruction). Whereas the state board of education is involved with policy making, the state department of education is responsible for the *operation* of school systems at the state level and consists of a large bureaucracy of officials, often numbering in the hundreds.

Originally organized to provide statistical reports, state departments of education have grown in size, power, and influence. (See Figure 6.1) Their primary responsibilities usually include administering and distributing state and federal funds, licensing teachers and other educational personnel, providing schools with technical assistance in improving curriculum and teaching, providing educational data and analyses, providing administration for special programs, and accrediting college and university educational licensure programs. Most schools, school districts, and colleges of education are strongly affected by the policies and actions of these state departments. School and college personnel, including public school teachers, actively serve on advisory committees and task forces to assist the chief state school officer and the state department of education in their decision-making processes.

Operational responsibilities

The Local School District To facilitate local control of education, the state creates local school districts for the purpose of carrying out the educational program in conformity with state educational policy. The school district is thus a unit of the state government and is usually distinct from the local municipal government.

THE SCHOOL BOARD The policy-making body of the school district is the local school board of education, which represents the citizens of the district in setting up a school program, hiring school personnel to operate the schools, determining organizational and administrative policy, and evaluating the results of the program and the performance of personnel. Although school board members are usually elected by the citizens of the local district, they are officially state officers and not, as many people think, simply local representatives. Since local school boards are agencies of the state, board members must operate the schools in conformity with the guidelines and policies established by the legislature, the state board of education, and the state department of education. The tension between states' efforts to regulate educational policy and local districts' desires to determine their own policies has increased as states have taken the initiative in the recent educational reform movement. In the next section of this chapter, we'll look at who controls the schools.

Figure 6.1 Organizational Structure of a Typical State School System

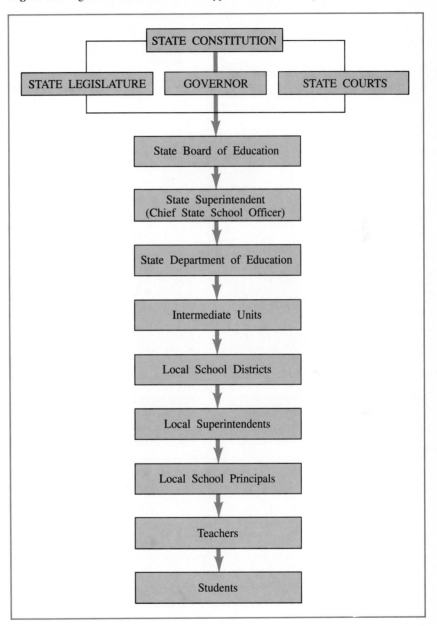

Figure 6.2 Organizational Structure of a Hypothetical School District

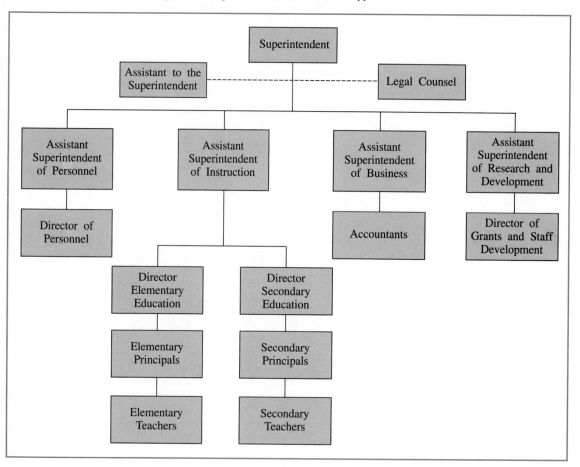

Source: From *Educational Administration; Concepts and Practices* by Fred C. Lunenburg and Allan C. Ornstein © 1991 by Wadsworth, Inc., p. 28. Reprinted by permission of the publisher.

Importance

The responsibilities of the more than fifteen thousand local school boards in the United States are of critical importance since these boards direct the public school systems. School boards represent the community in establishing the school district's educational program, and their policy decisions directly affect the students, teachers, and taxpayers in the community. The success of America's program of public education depends on the selection of board members who are able men and women. Serving voluntarily, usually without pay, school board members help determine the broad policies under which the schools operate. Even in times of increasing state regulation, local school boards retain decisions about how funds will be used, what staff will be provided, and the particular nature of the programs offered to students.

Methods of selecting school board members are usually prescribed by state law; approximately 85 percent of the school boards are elected by popular vote, and the remainder are appointed. When board members are appointed, the responsibility for making appointments falls most frequently to the mayor or city council.

What does the composite profile of school board members look like?[2] From 1972 to 1985 the proportion of women serving on boards increased from 12.0 to 36.1 percent, but by 1990 it had fallen somewhat to 33.7 percent (see Table 6.1). Whites constitute the overwhelming majority of school board membership—93.5 percent. The South easily has the highest percentage of African-American school board members (16.7 percent), and the Pacific states have the highest percentage of Hispanic and Native American school board members (5.3 and 2.9 percent, respectively).

Most school board members are middle-aged (almost 45 percent are between forty-one and fifty years old, and 77 percent are over the age of forty). Although school board members tend not to be rich, they certainly must be considered affluent: 72 percent of them have annual family incomes over $40,000, as compared with the less than $35,000 average income for a family of four in the United States. School board members are also well educated, with one-third of them having bachelor's degrees and another third having graduate degrees of some sort. Only 10 percent stopped their education with a high school degree or less. Over 62 percent are in professional or managerial occupations.[3] These fig-

Table 6.1 Profile of School Board Members, 1990

Characteristic	Percentage	Characteristic	Percentage
Sex		*Ethnic Background*	
Male	61	Black	2.9
Female	39	White	93.5
		Hispanic	1.3
		American Indian	.9
		Oriental	.2
		Other	.2
Age		*Family Income*	
Under 25	.2	Under $20,000	1.9
26–35	6.1	$20,000–39,999	22.5
36–40	15.9	$40,000–59,999	27.7
41–50	44.7	$60,000–79,999	19.6
51–60	19.9	$80,000–99,999	10.9
Over 60	12.5	More than $100,000	14.2

*Due to rounding, some totals may not add up to 100 percent.

Source: Jessee L. Freeman, Kenneth E. Underwood, and Jim C. Fortune, "What Boards Value," *American School Board Journal* (January 1991) 178: 34. Adapted by permission.

ures indicate that in many ways school board members are not typical of the public they serve. Whether or how this atypicality influences their values and decisions is not known. Can you think of any ways in which it might?

THE SUPERINTENDENT OF SCHOOLS The superintendent, a professional educator selected by the local school board to act as its executive officer and as the educational leader and administrator of the school district, is undeniably the most powerful officer in the local school organization. A superintendent's duties are

Duties many. The superintendent must recruit, select, place, and promote personnel. In addition, the superintendent has responsibility for providing and maintaining funds and facilities. Planning the budget and supervising the maintenance, construction, and renovation of buildings also are not uncommon tasks for a superintendent. Decisions about how to improve educational opportunities, including all aspects of curriculum and instruction and the organization of schooling to accomplish district goals, may originate with the superintendent. And the superintendent generally has responsibility for maintaining harmonious relations with the community by communicating the mission of the schools to the public and marshaling support for district programs.[4]

EDUCATION: A WORLD VIEW

EDUCATION REFORM IN CHINA

In contrast to the United States's system of governing public education predominantly at the state level, education in China is highly centralized and controlled by the Communist party. The Ministry of Education is the central unit responsible for administering and managing the national education system. It conducts such functions as controlling the content of national exams given to students in all grades twice a year, monitoring textbooks, promoting teacher training, and determining class time allocation and length of holidays. Individual primary and secondary schools are administered in large part by education departments at the provincial, municipal, and autonomous regional levels but are also affected by offices of education at the city or county level.

In recent years, China has been undergoing rapid economic change and modernization. In order to promote economic expansion and meet new needs for a skilled

work force, the Chinese are increasingly realizing the importance of educational development. After years of stagnation during the Cultural Revolution (1966–1976), some major changes are taking place to provide the intellectual and vocational preparation needed for the Chinese people to participate in modern society.

At the foundation of these changes are some basic shifts in how the Communist party views education. Li Shenzhi, the vice chairman of the Chinese Academy of Social Sciences, describes some of these changes in ideology. He explains that during the Cultural Revolution the well-educated were treated with suspicion and contempt. Colleges and universities were closed, and faculty members were told to go out to the countryside to "learn from the people." Knowledge was viewed as foreign and of little practical value. Today, however, the party stresses the importance of knowledge and education in economic advancement and in maintaining a "wholesome, spiritual" society.

To foster educational reform, the party has established a National Education Commission. This committee

Theoretically, the superintendent's role is administrative and executive—he or she (only 5 percent of the nation's superintendents are female!) keeps the schools functioning—whereas the local school board of education retains legislative and policy-making responsibilities. In practice, however, the superintendent has become the major policy maker in the school district. Since the turn of the twentieth century, the powers associated with operating a school have gradually shifted from school boards to superintendents.

The superintendent's acquired powers come with a price. Arthur Blumberg observes that, in the process of becoming more powerful, superintendents have "opened up their work lives and their personal lives to the costs of having to continually live with conflict."[5] When Blumberg asked them to describe their jobs, superintendents compared themselves to directors, producers, conductors, and coaches. Most saw themselves as leaders and change agents within their systems.[6] As nontenured employees of school boards, superintendents have no formal constituency to support their policy initiatives other than the supporters they cultivate. And losing that constituency can mean the loss of a job.[7]

Political nature of the job

The political nature of the superintendent's job is magnified by the comparative influence exerted by teachers' unions, citizens' groups, members of

is charged with helping to implement and govern changes in the educational system. Simultaneously, the management and financing of schools are being decentralized to give more power to local levels of government. A major purpose of this decentralization is to make it easier to finance educational innovations at a local level that cannot be supported on a larger, national scale.

One of the major goals for improving education in China is to increase school attendance and/or availability. Current goals for the year 2000 include one-quarter of the population receiving an education through the senior middle level (twelve years), one-half through the junior middle level (nine years), and one-quarter through basic elementary education (five or six years). Heavy emphasis is being placed on vocational and technical training at the senior middle school level to help address acute shortages of skilled workers.

Because of the lack of human and economic resources in education since the Cultural Revolution, the national government established a system of "key schools" in which the best teachers, facilities, equipment, and instructional supplies were channeled to roughly 10 percent of the schools. Only students receiving high scores on educational exams are admitted to these "key schools." Now, as attention turns increasingly to improving the quality of education in China, this system of allocating resources is being criticized as elitist. The exam system of determining educational eligibility to attend key schools or to progress to the next level of education is also coming under scrutiny. Critics claim that the exams overemphasize book learning, test only a narrow range of abilities (Chinese and mathematics), and ignore other indicators of academic success. Currently, other means of evaluating student achievement and ability, such as personal recommendation by the school principal, are being tried.

Attention is also being given to the important issue of improving the skills and abilities of teachers. Extensive inservice training programs are being provided, and teachers colleges are being expanded in size and number.

Austin Swanson and Zhang Zhian, "Education Reform in China," Phi Delta Kappan 68 (January 1987): 373–378. Adapted by permission.

school boards, federal and state legislatures,[8] and business. The powers of this position may diminish as teachers' unions become stronger, as the community expresses concern about costs and school effectiveness, and as standardized testing programs come to control the curriculum. Later, we will look at what roles the groups mentioned play in controlling American public education. But first, let's examine the role of an individual whose leadership greatly determines how successful a school is in educating children—the school principal.

THE SCHOOL PRINCIPAL   For the schools within a school district, the superintendent and the local school board of education select professional educators to serve as principals. High schools and middle schools may have a staff of administrators, including assistant or vice principals with specific responsibilities for discipline or curriculum and instruction. At the elementary level, principals may be responsible for more than one school building or may serve part-time as teachers. Whatever the pattern of administrative assignments, those who act as principals are generally considered to be a part of the administrative organization, directly accountable to the superintendent and the local school board of education.

Responsibilities   As administrators, principals usually interview prospective faculty members and make faculty assignments, supervise and evaluate staff members, schedule students and classes, manage school budgets, administer district discipline policies, procure and dispense supplies, and hold parent-teacher confer-

A principal's leadership style and values set the tone for the way a school functions.
(*Richard Hutchings/Photo Researchers, Inc.*)

ences. The tasks are many; to list them all would be impossible. Historically, the role of the principal has included management, supervision, and inspection duties.

Importance of leadership

Principals also play a leadership role that can have a significant effect on the academic success of their schools. Researchers have labeled schools that produce measurable improvements in students' achievement as "effective" schools. Among the characteristics common to effective schools is strong leadership by the principal. (We shall talk at more length about these characteristics in Chapter 7.) Effective principals foster a productive working and learning environment. They do so by understanding the mission of the school, communicating it to the staff and students, and rewarding excellent performance. They also represent the school to parents and the community. Involving parents and community members in the school's activities and securing their support for these activities is an important function of the principal.

Effective school principals demonstrate several qualities of leadership, according to a survey of Texas elementary and secondary administrators. Interviews of staff, students, and administrators, combined with observations in the principals' schools, reveal these five leadership qualities: clear visions that focus on students and their needs, an ability to translate those visions into goals and expectations, an ability to provide an environment to support those goals and expectations, skill at monitoring progress, and skill at intervening to support and correct behavior when necessary. In schools led by effective principals, teachers and students stress their perceptions that the school pulls together, values learning, and is a supportive place to be. Effective principals establish a feeling of community and work to accomplish the goals they establish, constantly gathering information about the progress toward the goals and assisting teachers and students in their efforts.[9] Thus, the principal can play a key role in establishing relationships among faculty and students and in setting standards for the accomplishment of student and teacher objectives.

WHO CONTROLS AMERICAN PUBLIC EDUCATION?

Multiple sources of control

There is no easy answer to the question "Who controls American education?" It is like asking who controls America. The president does, but so does Congress. The Supreme Court does, but so do the local police. Multinational corporations do, but so does a small but influential group of community activists. Similarly, formal, legally constituted bodies control or influence certain aspects of public education as a consequence of the authority invested in them. Federal and state legislatures exert influence on public education through the passage and enforcement of legislation. Professional educators—including superintendents, principals, and leaders of professional organizations—possess a major portion of the control and decision-making power over public education by virtue of the offices they hold and the organizations to which they belong (for example, the National Education Association or the American Association of School Administrators). These professional organizations, although they lack legal authority, have considerable influence.

In recent years, business and industry have also begun to form partnerships with schools to better influence the education of their future employees. The widespread attention to school reform has mobilized the nation's governors to voice their opinions about governance and control issues. And the use of standardized tests to measure the effects of reform initiatives represents another controlling factor in American public education.

It is not the intention of this chapter to examine in detail the authority and power that enable each of these groups to control certain aspects of public education. However, a brief look at the interplay of control exercised by professional educators (particularly school superintendents), local school boards, state governments, parents, business, standardized testing, the courts, and the federal government yields some fascinating insights into how decisions about public education are actually made.

Professional Educators

Among the most influential forces in controlling the schools are groups of *professional educators*. By this term, we mean the organizations to which many teachers belong: the National Education Association, already mentioned, and the

Many teachers' organizations participate in making policy on teacher salaries, curriculum, textbook selection, and other issues important to the smooth functioning of a school system.

(Mike Boroff/TexaStock)

American Federation of Teachers. We also mean state departments of education, departments and schools of education in colleges and universities, educational accrediting agencies, and other groups, such as superintendents and other school administrators.

One observer of American education, James D. Koerner, argued in 1968 that the people most directly involved with schooling—classroom teachers, parents and other laypersons, and academic specialists in departments other than education—have for too long been dominated by the professional education "fraternity."[10] For instance, at the state level, the state board of education is entitled to do nearly anything it chooses, within the limits of the law, with respect to education in the state. However, Koerner asserted that it rarely governs in any but the most general way. The state board of education usually allows the state department of education (staffed by professional educators) to make policy, or yields its power to local school authorities.

In recent years the role of teachers' organizations in determining educational policy has greatly increased. The state affiliates of the two major national teachers' organizations, the National Education Association and the American Federation of Teachers, are among the most effective lobbying groups in their states. (See Chapter 14, "Is Teaching a Profession?" for more on these two teacher organizations.) They have well-articulated positions on particular issues, represent thousands of teachers who can be mobilized to vote for or against particular legislators, and spend considerable amounts of money to make their positions known. State politicians pay considerable attention to these teachers' organizations because of their power and influence. At the local level, largely as a result of collective bargaining techniques, including work stoppages or the threat of them, teachers' organizations have won more and more power over educational policy.

Today, many teachers' organizations have won recognition as the official bargaining representatives of their members, whereas in the past, school boards insisted on dealing with teachers as individuals. Teachers' organizations are also demanding that issues previously considered the prerogatives of local school boards and superintendents be subject to collective bargaining. Among these issues are teacher and paraprofessional salaries, clerical and secretarial assistance, curriculum development, fringe benefits, inservice training, class size determination, textbook selection, and even the appointment of department heads and other school administrators. Yet teachers' efforts to negotiate their teaching role and its conditions have not always been welcomed by local school boards and superintendents.

At the local level, who is in control? Does power rest with the local school board, or do the professional educators staffing the schools exert the greatest influence? Let's look at some recent studies to consider the current relationship of the superintendent with local authorities.

Superintendents Versus Local School Boards

Theoretically, the local school board makes policy, and the superintendent, as the board's chief executive officer, executes board-mandated policy. From the board the superintendent receives legal authority and responsibility for designated governance decisions. But how a school board and superintendent actually operate to control a school may depend on their relationship.

Conflict

Two independent observers, Larry Cuban and Arthur Blumberg, have characterized this relationship as one of conflict. Cuban asserts that "conflict is—and always has been—the essence of the superintendency."[11] He goes on to write that conflict is inevitable when individuals have incompatible goals, resources are scarce, and misperceptions occur among those influencing policy decisions. Cuban also describes the conflict between superintendent and board and local groups as one of seeming competitors seeking to achieve their goals at the expense of the other participants.

High turnover rate

Although the turnover rate for superintendents (a measure of conflict between board and chief officer) has not reached the highs of the 1870s and the early 1900s, 53 percent of all superintendents have had their current jobs for five or fewer years.[12] (See Figure 6.3.) The percentage is even higher for superintendents in our nation's one hundred largest school districts: 71 percent.[13] Cuban maintains that the issues over which boards and administrators disagree may change as a result of shifting political concerns, changes in school funding or demographics, or constantly changing coalitions of teachers or local constituencies. But the relationship remains one of conflict regardless of particular issues.

School boards and superintendents search constantly for local constituencies to provide the funding and support for school programs. And with every school board election, new points of view may be brought to the governance of the district. Superintendents must weather these changes in points of view and the emerging coalitions resulting from board member turnover. Sympathies with the school's mission may be in a constant state of flux. Cuban summarizes this situation: "In any public institution in which governance is shared between a lay board and a hired professional, the making of policy requires some level of political activity."[14]

Political nature of job

For his book *The School Superintendent: Living With Conflict,* Arthur Blumberg interviewed twenty-five superintendents. He found references to the political nature of the superintendent's role to be common. One superintendent reported, "I see the superintendency, more than ever before, as just totally immersed in politics. It is very, very political. And what I'm really talking about is the entire political arena, not just the politics of education."[15] That political

Figure 6.3 Superintendents' Years of Experience in Current Job

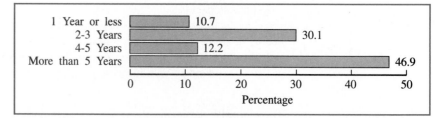

FOUNDATIONS

sensitivity and skills may be required for a successful career as a superintendent is distasteful to some people, including some superintendents. But regardless of superintendents' level of comfort with the political nature of manipulating and exercising organizational power, their survival as nonelected public officials rests on their ability to mobilize support and manage conflict.

In the words of another of Blumberg's superintendents, "Being political means having a real sense of the workings of groups—power groups, pressure groups, decision-making processes."[16] Superintendents have to balance pressures that come from a range of sources—groups mobilized to defeat the school budget, a group organizing to protest a book used in a high school literature class, individuals attempting to influence the football coach's game strategy, or an organization trying to institute a program for gifted children. Superintendents who lack awareness of the relationships among such groups will seem constantly distracted by competing demands for their attention and interest.

Within the past century the balance of power has gradually shifted from local school boards to their superintendents.[17] At the turn of the century, reaction against corrupt practices removed educational policy making from local political parties. The increasing complexity of school systems and the growing tendency to view educational administration as a profession also enhanced the power of the superintendent's position. Today, in many school districts, for example, the school board agenda is prepared by the superintendent with occasional suggestions from the board members. Matters relevant to the educational program are often conspicuously absent from the agenda. Because local school boards often lack adequate staff to do their own research, they must rely on professional educators (primarily the superintendent and his or her staff) for such services. As a result, the superintendent has become the major policy maker in the schools.

Will the position of superintendent continue to dominate local policy making? The high turnover rate among superintendents may indicate that local boards are more powerful than we have imagined. And superintendents are often the direct recipients of pressure exerted by local groups and state and federal regulations. Blumberg notes that since the mid-1960s the power of the superintendency has diminished.[18] Teachers' organizations have grown, communities are more concerned about costs and school effectiveness, and parents and students assert their legal rights with more vigor. In a time of competition for control of the schools, superintendents find themselves trying to balance the competing interests to maintain the stability of the school organization. Again, one of Blumberg's respondents reports, "It's always a balancing act because there are so many pressure groups. . . . now I have so many different constituencies out there with so many different interests that my problem is to try to keep them appeased."[19]

Superintendents' powers diminishing

Is the relationship between superintendent and local school board, representing many interested lay people, necessarily one of conflict? Blumberg describes the relationship from the superintendent's perspective:

> Regardless of one's personal feelings of competence, there are basic insecurities connected with the job, and they revolve around the superintendent's relationship with the school board, both in its interpersonal process dimension and in its political structure, fact-of-life dimension. School boards are not by definition mean or capricious, though they are subject to influence attempts from the political and vested-interest breezes that blow in a community—as they properly should be. The superintendent's relationship with the school board seems to reflect the continuing conflict concerning how schools should be run in American society.[20]

Boards rate superintendents

We should note, however, that a national survey of school board members indicated a high level of satisfaction with their superintendent's performance. Over half of the respondents said that their school board was very satisfied with the job their superintendent was doing, and nearly a third more said the board was satisfied. Only 7 percent expressed dissatisfaction.[21] Key factors in an effective superintendent–school board relationship were good communication; providing board members with constant, reliable information; and mutual trust and respect. The major reasons for dismissing a superintendent other than those stipulated in state law and regulations were a loss of confidence in the superintendent's integrity, a loss of faith in the superintendent's leadership, and evidence of mismanagement of school finances. In terms of board members' expectations for superintendents, the top priorities were program improvement, solving personnel problems, meeting facility needs, and improving evaluation procedures.[22]

Findings like these bode well for superintendents and board members who desire a productive working relationship. Perhaps the struggle for control of the schools naturally produces conflict among competing interests; the extent to which the superintendent and the school board are adversaries in this conflict seems to be subject to control by their mutual trust, sharing of information, and the ability of the superintendent to provide needed leadership.

State Government

Reform wave 1

The 1980s witnessed what one educational analyst has described as three waves of reform: wave 1 (1982–1985); wave 2 (1986–1989); and wave 3 (1988–the present).[23] Wave 1 was primarily concerned with trying to fix the existing educational system by raising standards for students and teachers alike and by in-

SUPERINTENDENTS SPEAK OUT

The superintendent is under considerable pressure from individuals and groups to make decisions in their favor. Arthur Blumberg has compiled from many superintendents personal descriptions of those pressures and conflicts. We have included a few of the statements to bring you a better sense of the problems and frustrations associated with the job of superintendent.

One superintendent describes dealing with an array of groups and individuals:

> Well, you always have superintendent-board conflict, particularly when there are factions on the board. The superintendent's in the middle trying to balance these. Then there is the administrative staff, whether it be principals, assistants or whatever. Obviously there's the union. Community groups all over the place. Sometimes student interest groups. . . . The news media is constant. TV, the local paper vs. the city paper. And there are support groups, booster clubs, for athletics, the bank, even art. And special interest groups. For the handicapped, for example. They're coming right off the walls of late. There are the federal and state mandates. All the titles and categorical aid programs. The PTA's, the businessmen, the clergy, real estate interests. Parents with kids with specific problems. I'm going 100 miles an hour all the time. You always have another mountain to climb.

Another superintendent describes the many different kinds of pressures he has experienced:

> I'm talking, for example, about problems with the

community and with the kids. I'm talking about being involved with parents or being involved in a lawsuit because of an insurance recovery. I'm talking about having to go to the state capital and speaking with legislators because bills under construction are very poor for education. I'm talking about dealing with curriculum matters—sex education, for example—and knowing all the ramifications of how the churches feel about it. Or knowing whether or not it's important to have the same reading series in a building for all grade levels. Or dealing with intricacies of budgeting or the overwhelming number of personnel issues we deal with. This is a human enterprise. All aspects of it. There are no material products that we deal with. They're all human. And this intensifies and magnifies the number of problems.

Because the superintendent interacts with so many different constituencies and has to make so many decisions, conflict is an inevitable part of the job. A third superintendent states,

> It's all an indication, I guess, of the fact that no matter what you do, you immediately begin to infringe upon people's territory. It is really an unbelievable job. The whole job is conflict-ridden. And sometimes the central character in the conflict—the superintendent—ends up being a casualty of it, no matter how rational and reasonable he thinks he's being. Eventually, I think it gets to everyone.

Arthur Blumberg with Phyllis Blumberg, *The School Superintendent: Living with Conflict* (New York: Teachers College Press, 1985), pp. 188–189, 197.

creasing testing and accountability measures. Hundreds of millions of dollars were invested by the states in an effort to shore up their educational systems. As with past major periods of educational reform, that of the 1980s was initiated by forces external to the public schools. The leadership for many of these programs came from governors and state legislatures as the states replaced the federal government as the unit of reform action. Professional educators and local school boards found themselves responding to, rather than initiating, reform measures. As Michael Kirst described, "Now state government officials create education policies, and local interest groups react to them. Educators lost control of the state agenda quite a while ago."[24]

Over seven hundred pieces of top-down legislation constituted wave 1 reform. These actions were hardly complete when they began to be attacked. Instead of reforming the existing system by simply increasing standards, the critics asserted that the country needed to start a major overhaul—a restructuring—of **Reform wave 2** the current educational system. The major philosophical foundation of wave 2 reformers was that educational improvement is contingent on empowering teachers to work more effectively with children. The individual school, with increased parental involvement, was the focus of the second wave of reform. The three areas most often stressed in reports were: (1) the professionalization of teaching, (2) the development of decentralized school management systems, and (3) the enactment of specific reform topics that had been overlooked in wave 1, for example, programs for at-risk students.

As with wave 1, the governors of the various states were in the forefront of wave 2 reforms. In 1986, the nation's governors issued a report, *Time for Results: The Governors' 1991 Report on Education*. Lamar Alexander, then governor of Tennessee, explained the common thread in the governors' proposals: "To sum it up: the Governors are ready for some old-fashioned horse-trading. We'll regulate less, if schools and school districts will produce better results."[25] Governor Alexander expressed the belief that excellent schools will result if local districts have the authority to determine their own means for accomplishing the goals that state legislatures will help determine. But the states will also hold their schools accountable for achieving the hoped-for results.

Reform wave 3 Wave 3, which is still occurring, calls for reform measures to go beyond schooling to embrace a comprehensive system for the delivery of services to children. "Children's policy," rather than school policy, is the call. These reformers envision an integrated interorganizational, interprofessional service model that results in a major redesign of programs for children, with both the family and the school at the service hub. Health, social, educational, and transportation services need to be redesigned for cooperative delivery. If wave 3 reforms are to be successful, state governments, which regulate these services, will need to play active parts in the process.

Let's now turn our attention to a key factor in the improvement of schools—the parents.

Parents The local parent-teacher organization (PTO) serves as a communications link between parents and the formal school organization, with teachers usually acting as representatives of the schools. Formally, the school system ordinarily operates by means of *down-the-line communications,* from the superintendent to the principal to the teacher, and then to the parents. When the formal hierarchy does not respond to *up-the-line communications* from parents or teachers in a satisfactory manner, parents can resort to an informal communications system in an attempt to get a more favorable response.

An instance of informal communications occurred when the energetic principal of a New Haven, Connecticut, school in a low-income neighborhood organized the PTO in an attempt to improve the school's facilities. He began by going to an important neighborhood leader and persuading her that the children in the school needed help. Convinced, the woman and the principal went to work on the PTO. To arouse parent involvement, they convinced the PTO to endorse a hot lunch program; this required the PTO to raise funds and hire kitchen help.

CHOICE: A CONTROVERSIAL ISSUE

When, over thirty years ago, the economist Milton Friedman introduced the notion of providing parents with school vouchers that they could "cash in" to pay for the school of their choice for their children, most Americans considered it a crazy idea. Today the issue of public school choice is one of the major educational reform issues in the United States.

Proponents of public school choice argue that choice is necessary to improve schools' performances. Public schools, they argue, are monopolistic in nature, and currently suffer from poor student achievement and a lack of responsiveness to the concerns of parents and students. Parents need to be able to choose which school they want their children to attend, regardless of where they live, because:

- There is no one best school for everyone.
- It is necessary to provide diversity in schools.
- Students will perform better and accomplish more in schools they have chosen.
- Parents will be more supportive of and satisfied with schools they have chosen.
- Schools of choice create shared values and expectations that result in the accomplishment of common goals.

Opponents of public school choice express concern

Opponents of public school choice express concern over: the possible creation of elitist schools that skims off a district's brightest students; what will happen to schools and their staffs that substantially lose, or gain, enrollment; the possibility of resegregating schools; and the apathy of many parents and their unreadiness to make informed choices about their children's education.

By 1990, Minnesota, Arkansas, Iowa, and Nebraska had adopted statewide plans that allow students the choice of transferring to virtually any school district in their state, and many school districts in other states were permitting intradistrict transfers. In his AMERICA 2000 education plan (see page 227) President Bush has also endorsed choice strategies that include private schools. Although many educators have long opposed school choice, the National Education Association and the American Federation of Teachers appear to be warming to the concept. These teachers' organizations, however, play down the notion of competition among public schools, and now speak of choice as a way of empowering teachers in restructuring schools to meet the needs of specific groups of students. The 1990 Gallup poll of the public's attitudes toward the public schools indicates that the public favors, by a two-to-one margin, allowing students and their parents to choose which public schools in their communities the students will attend. However, the verdict is still out as to whether or not public school choice will improve the quality of the education students receive.

Public Schools of Choice (Washington, D.C.: Association for Supervision and Curriculum Development, 1990), p. 10.

As the PTO became more active, the principal began a campaign for a new school to replace the old one. When the city administration raised obstacles, the principal called together the PTO members and other neighborhood leaders to ask their support for the construction of a new school. Within twenty-four hours they were exerting pressure on the city school board and the administration. Needless to say, the school was built.

However, most PTOs are comparatively impotent in achieving educational aims. Educators interested in implementing educational reform at the local level question whether reforms will last if parents are not actively involved in the work of their schools. These reformers realize that leadership of local teachers and citizens is essential to put new policies into effect. But how might an effective partnership of parents and teachers be accomplished?

In their 1986 report,[26] the governors strongly endorse partnerships between parents and their schools. Among their recommendations is the call for a school

Call for partnerships

Family support and emphasis on the value of education are extremely important influences on a child's success in school.
(© Eugene Richards/Magnum Photos)

system more responsive to what students and their parents say they need. Specifically, the governors suggest that parents should have choices among the available public schools in their states. They also recommend that states help school districts develop techniques to involve parents. By 1990, twenty states had enacted parent involvement legislation.[27] Examples of effective techniques include forming task forces of parents and citizens to monitor school improvements, offering parenting classes for the public, encouraging regular parent-teacher conferences, and giving awards for outstanding citizen involvement programs and individual citizen efforts. Public service announcements have also been used to encourage parents to help their children with their homework, to provide a place to study, or to volunteer at their children's schools. Not all educators will welcome increased parent involvement in the work of the schools, because they fear a loss of their influence in governance and control. But without parental support, efforts to improve students' achievement are likely to fail.

How to involve parents in influencing school policies and practices is a particularly vexing problem in the large cities. One experiment that bears watching is occurring in Chicago. In 1988, the Illinois state legislature enacted an educational reform law designed to give Chicago parents more power in how their schools were run. Labeled as the worst school system in the nation by then Secretary of Education William Bennett, Chicago was plagued by bureaucratic policies and inefficiencies. The Illinois state legislature responded by creating councils at each of the 570 Chicago city schools. Each school council has eleven members: two teachers, two community representatives, the principal, and six parents; this council makes decisions about curriculum, budgets, and the hiring and firing of principals. This is a bold effort to transfer power and authority to school sites, away from centralized authority, and to make schools more accountable to parents and the local community. The coming years should provide insights regarding how much training parents need to be effective decision makers, and whether parent-dominated school councils can focus on academic concerns and not become mired in politics. Initial results are mixed. Some school councils have hired or fired administrators on the basis of ethnic and racial preferences, but others are making excellence their standard and are achieving impressive results.

Business

Historical influence

Business influencing education is not a new phenomenon. Whether it was to educate immigrants, gear up for the Industrial Revolution, or catch up with the Soviets after the launch of Sputnik in 1957, American business has sought to shape public schools to meet its needs. It also influenced the way educators thought about schooling. When the United States experienced tremendous industrial growth in the early years of this century, many of the principles of efficiency and standardization that produced success in industry were also applied in the schools. Schools were compared to factories whose products were students; newly developed tests measured the quality of the school's products; in the name of efficiency, the class sizes and teacher loads were increased; the public demanded a profitable return on the money "invested" in schools. That many educators continue to speak of the schools, a child-oriented social institution, in these business terms indicates the appeal of standardizing and controlling the schools' outcomes.

But the relationship between business and education is changing, going beyond imitation of business practices to cooperative partnerships. Concern about the country's economic condition and its standing in international trade markets and concern about the quality of U.S. public education have prompted partnerships between educators and business executives. A mutual interest in helping students develop as educated and employable citizens guides these collaborations; gone is the trend to blindly mimic industrial practices as educational policy.

Recent restructuring efforts

During the 1980s and continuing into the 1990s the business community has been at the forefront of the efforts to restructure public education. Business leaders have been substantially involved in virtually every educational reform report. As a result, they have become both the strongest critics and the staunchest advocates for public education. The chief executive officers of such major corporations as Procter & Gamble, Xerox, Apple Computer, Eastman Kodak, Coca-Cola, IBM, RJR Nabisco, Exxon, and many others have demanded and pushed for educational reforms in state capitals, the halls of Congress, and the White House.

Committee for Economic Development

In its 1985 publication, *Investing in Our Children: Business and the Public Schools*,[28] the Committee for Economic Development, a respected group of business leaders, suggests that businesses can help improve the counseling services in junior high and high school guidance departments. Some corporations have "adopted" schools or disadvantaged students in schools, providing technical, managerial, and financial aid or exposure to successful adult role models. The committee suggests that schools should be informed about the performance of their graduates in the work place. And businesses can also encourage employees to participate in local school activities by providing flexibility in their working hours. The committee's report especially emphasizes the need to redirect vocational training by providing students with *both* strong academic instruction and the kind of on-the-job training available in the best cooperative education programs.

Investments in school reform

Of the $2.1 billion that business donated to educational causes in 1988, only about 10 percent went to the public schools; the rest was allocated to universities and vocational schools.[29] But since then this figure has gone up dramatically and will continue to increase sharply. For example, in 1989, Coca-Cola and RJR Nabisco announced multiyear budgets for public school programs of $50 million and $30 million, respectively. When one also considers the dollar value attached to the personnel time invested in the more than one hundred thousand business-school partnerships formed since 1983, the amount is considerable by any measure.[30]

Why should the business community show such interest? The initiatives to improve the quality of American education go beyond altruistic impulses. Like the nation's governors, many business leaders are convinced that education reform is essential to the health of the American economy. When the Committee for Economic Development completed a major study of American productivity, it indicated that "economic productivity and the quality of education cannot be separated. Particularly in the modern world, education and economic performance are indivisible."[31]

Competition from Asian and European manufacturers in world markets, a growing U.S. trade deficit, and industry's perception that entry-level workers lack proper job skills have focused attention on educating the American work force. In fact, U.S. companies spend more than $50 billion annually on remedial education for their workers.[32] Businesses would prefer that beginning employees have the skills associated with a broadly based education; their training could then focus on upgrading the skills needed because of the shift from a production company to high-technology and service economies.

What kind of education will best prepare tomorrow's workers? According to the Committee for Economic Development, a general education would include "schooling that teaches students to think critically and analytically, to cooperate and communicate as well as compete, to assume responsibility for themselves, to solve problems, and to continue to learn."[33] The co-directors of the committee's study assert, "The business community does not need students who are narrowly trained; on the contrary, it needs students who are broadly educated and able to assume a wide variety of roles in tomorrow's workplace."[34] Increasingly, employers believe that the economic future of the country depends on the competence of their employees. As a result of these beliefs, businesspeople are exerting pressure and influence in an attempt to get the schools to do a better job in preparing students to be members of a productive work force.

The influential Hudson Institute report, *Workforce 2000*, predicts that just as agriculture lost its central role in the American economy at the beginning of the century, so will manufacturing lose economic importance as the twentieth century draws to a close. Instead, a shift to services is occurring: jobs tend to have more high and low earners, and fewer in the middle. The fastest-growing jobs will be in professional, technical, and sales fields requiring the highest education and skill levels. Of the fastest-growing job categories, all but one, service occupations, require more than an average level of education. The report predicts that only 27 percent of all new jobs will fall into the lowest two skill categories in mathematics, language, and reasoning skills (compared with 40 percent of current jobs). By contrast, 41 percent of new jobs will be in the three highest skill groups (compared with only 24 percent of current jobs).[35] The implications of these projections are that greater numbers of well-educated people will be needed for our economy, while the poorly educated will be competing for a shrinking pool of low-paying, dead-end jobs in the service sector. For example, in language development, a job rated 6 (high) might require an individual to read literature or scientific and technical publications, and to write journals or speeches. A level 2 might require only the ability to read stories and simple sentences, write compound and complex sentences, and speak using all tenses. In math, the top skill group would be expected to use advanced calculus, econometrics, or statistical probabilities. A level 2 group would be expected only to add, subtract, multiply, compute ratios and percents, and interpret bar graphs.

Everyone does not see business involvement in education as being totally

Workforce 2000

on the plus side. Some express concern that business intrusion will follow its financial support—that schools may be unduly shaped to meet business needs. Another concern centers around business's provision of free curriculum and instructional materials for teachers. Critics argue that corporate handouts are not just supplementary gifts but sophisticated marketing tools that contain subtle and not-so-subtle messages that promote the corporation's biases and that are designed to promote brand identification and product loyalty. Among the most controversial proposals is that of Whittle Communications to create "Channel One," a commercial program that promises to deliver ten minutes of high-quality news programming directly to public school classrooms in exchange for two minutes of advertising. While Whittle Communications is busy signing up schools to participate, many educators are attacking the plan as gross commercialism and a dangerous precedent. As Bill Honig, California's superintendent of public instruction, states, "The problem is, they want us to sell access to our kids' minds, and we have no right, morally or ethically, to do that."[36]

"Channel One" controversy

There is no question that the role of the business community in educational affairs has greatly expanded since the mid-1980s, and most people see this as positive. Businesses and corporations, with a vested stake in the outcomes of public education, will undoubtedly continue to be major players in the reformation of our educational system. The challenge for educators will be to walk the line between partnerships and cooperation, and exploitation for commercial purposes.

Cooperation or exploitation?

Standardized Testing: Another Controlling Factor

As programs for school improvement proliferated in the 1980s, the trend to assess the quality of schools and teachers by using standardized tests also grew in influence. In 1984 the U.S. Department of Education issued the first of several wall charts with state-by-state comparisons of students' scores on college entrance examinations. In 1986 the St. Louis Board of Education used student test scores as one factor in evaluating teachers' performance and making decisions about their promotions and salary increases.[37] As of 1990, twenty states had required high school students to perform well on tests of general academic competence as a prerequisite for graduation, and forty-seven states had required local public school districts to test students at some point(s) between grades 1 and 12. Thirty-nine states required aspiring teachers to pass a state-prescribed, standardized test before entering a teacher education program and/or before being licensed to teach.[38] During the 1980s students' and teachers' scores on standardized tests became the report card for the schools.

Increase during 1980s

Many educators express grave concerns over what they perceive to be an overemphasis on testing. Measuring school excellence by standardized tests poses a danger arising from the limited and simplistic nature of the tests. Evaluation expert George F. Madaus warns that tests external to the schools can be limiting if schools pattern their curricula to conform to the content of the tests.[39] School may fail to teach what is difficult to test. In some instances, the content and actual form of a test have become the curriculum itself, as weeks of classroom drill have centered on previous versions of tests.

Overemphasis on testing?

Others worry that standardized tests overemphasize technical information and underemphasize educators' professional judgments about the worthiness of a school's programs. With a national call to emphasize more problem solving, critical thinking, and writing skills, educators see a contradiction in stressing standardized tests that don't measure these outcomes. They are calling for more "authentic assessment," that is, using such things as actual specimens or examples of students' work to determine educational achievement.

Authentic assessment

Currently, there is a strong movement in the United States to create national standards for student achievement linked to some form of national assessment. More and more policy makers believe that student achievement will not increase markedly until high standards are set and quality work by all students is expected and rewarded. Current standardized tests are seen as only reflecting minimum standards and as being insufficient to measure high learning outcomes. Many educators and local school officials worry that such a movement to national standards will erode local control of the curriculum and limit teacher autonomy. They also worry that the state of the art in assessing high standards of learning is insufficiently developed to warrant moving quickly to national standards and assessment measures.

National standards

Although standardized tests played a dominant role during the 1980s in controlling many aspects of education, educators and policy makers alike are dissatisfied with their current uses. The 1990s will see a search for better and more authentic ways of measuring high standards, both for students and for teachers. The new NTE, for example, will incorporate both paper-and-pencil and performance measures to assess teacher competency. One thing seems certain, however: assessment, in whatever forms it takes, will continue to be a controlling influence on public education.

Control by the Federal Government

THE FEDERAL COURTS   It could be argued that the most powerful educational policy-making group in the United States is the judicial branch. Many groups, frustrated by school policies, have turned to state and federal courts for relief. The history of education has been shaped by important court decisions on the duties and responsibilities of school officials in such areas as school desegregation, religion in the schools, student rights, and, particularly at the state level, school finance. The U.S. Supreme Court has played a particularly important role in changing educational policy in this country. Because its rulings have altered or reduced the power of state and local educational authorities, some of the Court's decisions have generated deep resentment among those who abhor this "federal intrusion" into state rights. Other people applaud the Court's decisions as steps to make American education more responsive to broad democratic principles.

Important influence

The courts alone, as powerful as they are, however, cannot do everything. Often federal administrative action needs to be joined with more detailed judicial rulings and pressures. In the famous 1954 case of *Brown* v. *Board of Education of Topeka,* the U.S. Supreme Court ruled that the doctrine of "separate but equal" had no place in public education. But how was this momentous judgment

Enforcement necessary

to be implemented? The Court decided only that "all deliberate speed" should be employed to abolish the dual school system for African-Americans and whites, but no judicial guidelines were developed to steer the process. As a result, for a decade, almost no changes occurred.

The stalemate was broken in the 1960s by a combination of new congressional laws on civil rights and education and the strong enforcement of desegregation by President Lyndon Johnson's administration. The Supreme Court also eventually upheld the use of busing as a specific way to bring about desegregation. In many local desegregation cases, however, many lower-level federal judges found themselves involved in monitoring, resolving disputes, and enforcing their rulings, including the details of school administration—boundary changes, personnel replacements, and so on—because the local school system ignored or resisted the original order to desegregate. The degree of involvement on the part of the district federal judges in overseeing court rulings depends, then, on whether other branches of the government choose to enforce these rulings. (See Chapter 5 for a more detailed discussion of the impact of Supreme Court decisions on American education.)

THE U.S. DEPARTMENT OF EDUCATION   Educational interests are primarily represented in the federal government through the Department of Education, which became a separate cabinet-level department in 1979. Some thought it would not last beyond 1983, when President Reagan proposed to dismantle it.

Figure 6.4 Federal Funds for Education, by Agency, Fiscal Year 1990

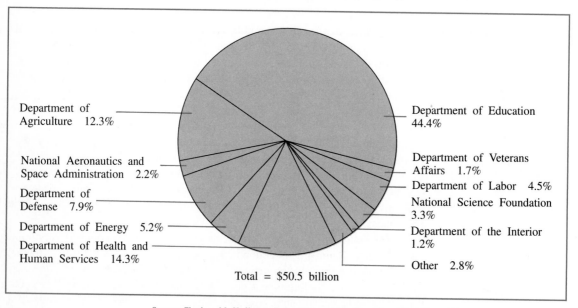

Department of Agriculture   12.3%

National Aeronautics and Space Administration   2.2%

Department of Defense   7.9%

Department of Energy   5.2%

Department of Health and Human Services   14.3%

Department of Education 44.4%

Department of Veterans Affairs   1.7%

Department of Labor   4.5%

National Science Foundation 3.3%

Department of the Interior 1.2%

Other   2.8%

Total = $50.5 billion

Source: Charlene M. Hoffman, *Federal Support for Education: Fiscal Years 1980 to 1990,* Washington, D.C.: National Center for Education Statistics, May 1991), p. 3.

Significant role today	But today the Department of Education is a significant part of the federal government and still retains its cabinet-level status. (See Figure 6.4) In 1990, for example, of the $50.5 billion spent by the federal government on education, 44 percent ($22.4 billion) came from the Department of Education's budget.[40] The department administers a variety of programs, including ones concerned with elementary and secondary education, postsecondary education, educational research and development, vocational and adult education, special education, and civil rights.

Although education is not specifically mentioned in the federal constitution, there has always been some degree of federal involvement in education. The level of involvement often fluctuates depending on whether Republicans or Democrats control the White House and Congress, and the particular ideology professed by the party in power. After a period of downsizing under President Reagan, the Bush administration and Congress seem disposed to increase somewhat the federal government's role in helping the United States solve its educational problems. That role in financing public schools will be discussed in the next section.

HOW ARE SCHOOLS FINANCED?

The total amount of money available to a school district for education is the sum of locally raised revenues, state aid, federal aid, and miscellaneous revenues. Historically, most of the money used to support public elementary and secondary schools has come from local revenue sources, primarily the property tax. In the 1970s, for the first time in American history, the state's share of support for public education exceeded the local share (see Table 6.2). Increased state revenues have helped to offset the decreases in local and federal funding of the schools.

The percentage of revenue received from federal, state, and local sources varies considerably from state to state (see Table 6.3). Federal contributions to state revenues for public education range from a high of 15.5 percent for Mississippi to a low of 2.7 percent for New Hampshire. Local contributions to revenues range from a high of 89.6 percent for New Hampshire to a low of 0.1 percent for Hawaii, which has a statewide school district. Let's look in more detail at state and local funding patterns.

State and Local Funding

Sources of revenue

How is money raised to pay for educational expenditures, and by what systems of taxation? State revenue systems are as diverse as school finance plans and reflect the socioeconomic make-up, the political climate, and the educational needs of each state. State systems rely on a wide variety of revenue sources. Whereas local governments rely primarily on the property tax for income, state governments use a combination of sales, personal income, corporate income, and excise taxes to generate revenues. Some states fund their schools partly with income from state-run lotteries. As of 1989, ten states, including California, Florida, Michigan, and New York, assigned all or part of their lottery proceeds to education. In Florida, lottery proceeds accounted for approximately 3 percent of the 1988–89 education budget. Though this may sound like a lot of money,

Table 6.2 Percentage of Revenue Received from Federal, State, and Local Sources for Public Elementary and Secondary Schools

SCHOOL YEAR	PERCENTAGE OF REVENUE			
	Federal	State	Local	Total
1919–20	0.3	16.5	83.2	100
1929–30	0.4	16.9	82.7	100
1939–40	1.8	30.3	68.0	100
1949–50	2.9	39.8	57.3	100
1959–60	4.4	39.1	56.5	100
1969–70	8.0	39.9	52.1	100
1979–80	9.8	46.8	43.4	100
1981–82	7.4	47.6	45.0	100
1982–83	7.1	47.9	45.0	100
1984–85	6.6	48.9	44.4	100
1986–87	6.4	49.8	43.9	100
1988–89	6.3	50.2	43.5	100
1989–90	6.3	49.4	44.3	100

Source: Thomas D. Snyder, *Digest of Education Statistics 1990* (Washington, D.C.: National Center for Education Statistics), p. 148; and "Education Vital Signs," *American School Board Journal* 177 (December 1990): A27. Reprinted with permission from *The American School Board Journal*, December 1990. Copyright 1990, the National School Boards Association. All rights reserved.

Table 6.3 Percentage of Revenue by Government Source for Public Elementary and Secondary Schools, for Selected States, 1989–90

SCHOOL YEAR	PERCENTAGE OF REVENUE		
	State	Local	Federal
California	66.8	25.1	8.0
Hawaii	92.0	.1	7.9
Michigan	36.3	59.0	4.7
Mississippi	56.7	27.8	15.5
Nebraska	24.3	70.8	4.8
New Hampshire	7.8	89.6	2.7
New Mexico	76.4	11.6	12.0
New York	43.4	51.7	5.0
Texas	43.1	48.9	7.9
Virginia	34.7	60.6	4.7
Wisconsin	39.1	56.8	4.1

Source: Education Vital Signs, *The American School Board Journal* 177 (December 1990): A22–A27. Reprinted with permission from *The American School Board Journal*, December 1990. Copyright 1990, the National School Boards Association. All rights reserved.

Bill Honig, state superintendent of education in California, explains that often lottery funds designated for education merely supplant regular tax dollars rather than actually provide additional education income.[41]

A majority of the states require the citizens in a school district to vote on either the property tax rate to support education or the school budget itself. In the early 1980s the prospects for passing school budgets and school tax referendums were bleak. Taxpayers, rejecting proposals to increase funds for education, were repudiating the prevailing method of raising local school revenue: the heavy reliance upon local property taxes. Efforts such as California's Proposition 13 and Massachusetts's Proposition 2½ lowered local property taxes sharply. In some places, this tax revolt resulted in shortened school years, reduced curricular offerings, teacher layoffs, and the curtailment of extracurricular activities.

Rising expenditures per pupil

But starting in 1983, national commission reports on the condition of education in the country began to appear and spurred interest in funding educational reform. In most states, educational reform became a high priority. During the 1980s, per-pupil expenditures rose by over 39 percent after inflation. The average expenditure per pupil in daily attendance was $4,896 for 1989–90.[42] Most of this new money came from the states, as their share of the financing of education increased from 47.8 percent in 1983–84 to 49.4 percent in 1989–90.[43] Although somewhat offset by inflation, growing enrollments, and changes in local and federal spending, funding from state sources has increased dramatically as a result of the reform emphasis. However, because of the effects of the economic recession that hit different regions of the country during 1989–1991, this trend has stalled or even been reversed in certain states.

ARE AMERICANS WILLING TO PAY FOR EDUCATION?

The 1989 Gallup poll on the public's attitudes toward the public schools provides information to help answer this question. When asked if they would be willing to pay more taxes to improve the quality of public schools in poorer states and communities, 62 percent of those polled responded positively. Thirty percent of respondents indicated they were not willing to pay more taxes. An even higher percentage of respondents were willing to pay higher taxes to fund programs in the early grades to reduce class size to as few as fifteen pupils: 68 percent indicated "yes" and 25 percent opposed higher taxes.

People were deeply concerned about what they perceive to be the declining quality of the nation's inner-city schools, and substantial majorities would be willing to pay more taxes to expand Head Start programs, to screen young children for health problems, and to provide day care for the children of working parents.

Are Americans willing to pay for education? In spite of the large amounts of money that have already been expended in educational reform efforts, the answer is "yes" for programs that address areas of considerable concern to the American public.

Stanley M. Elam and Alec M. Gallup, "The 21st Annual Gallup Poll of the Public's Attitudes Toward the Public Schools," *Phi Delta Kappan* 71 (September 1989): 41–54.

From state to state, the expenditures for education vary widely (see Table 6.4), ranging from over $8,000 per pupil each year to less than $3,000 per pupil per year. The reason for these differences is primarily economic. A state's ability to pay for education depends on the personal income level of its residents. In general, the southern states fund education at lower levels than the northern states.[44] Are students who reside in some of the sunbelt states deprived of a

Table 6.4 State Expenditures per Student, 1989–90 (reported in ascending order). (U.S. average is $4,896.)

$2,500–2,999	North Carolina ($4,164)	Michigan ($5,073)
	New Mexico ($4,180)	Oregon ($5,085)
	Missouri ($4,226)	Wyoming ($5,391)
Utah ($2,733)	Montana ($4,254)	Vermont ($5,418)
	Nevada ($4,260)	
	Ohio ($4,394)	
$3,000–3,499	Georgia ($4,456)	$5,500–5,999
Idaho ($3,016)	$4,500–4,999	Maine ($5,577)
Mississippi ($3,220)		Pennsylvania ($5,728)
Arkansas ($3,272)		Wisconsin ($5,763)
South Dakota ($3,312)	Hawaii ($4,504)	Delaware ($5,848)
Louisiana ($3,313)	Iowa ($4,590)	Maryland ($5,887)
Alabama ($3,319)	California ($4,620)	
Oklahoma ($3,484)	Washington ($4,639)	
	Kansas ($4,706)	$6,500–6,999
	New Hampshire ($4,833)	
$3,500–3,999	Illinois ($4,853)	
	Colorado ($4,878)	Rhode Island ($6,523)
	Minnesota ($4,935)	Massachusetts ($6,740)
Tennessee ($3,503)	Virginia ($4,986)	
North Dakota ($3,581)		
South Carolina ($3,692)		$7,000–7,999
Kentucky ($3,824)	$5,000–5,499	
Arizona ($3,858)		
Nebraska ($3,874)		Alaska ($7,252)
	Florida ($5,051)	District of Columbia ($7,407)
		Connecticut ($7,930)
$4,000–4,499		
		$8,000–8,999
Texas ($4,011)		
West Virginia ($4,094)		New York ($8,165)
Indiana ($4,126)		New Jersey ($8,439)

Source: "Education Vital Signs," *American School Board Journal* 177 (December 1990): A22–A27. Reprinted with permission from *The American School Board Journal,* December 1990. Copyright 1990, the National School Boards Association. All rights reserved.

FOUNDATIONS

quality education? The connection between funding and excellence of education is often disputed, but two sociologists have found that states spending more money on education also have students with higher average SAT scores, adjusting for the population of those taking the test in that state.[45]

School Finance Reform and the Courts

Unequal funding

Many knowledgeable educators and politicians argue that one of the greatest causes of unequal educational opportunity is the method used to finance school systems. School districts whose property values are high generate much more money to finance their schools than districts whose property values are low. Within the same state, for example, the average amount of money spent per child in one district may be more than twice the amount spent in a nearby district. Such spending differentials result in great educational disparities, as measured by pupil-teacher ratios, training and experience of staff, and availability of facilities, equipment, and counseling services. These spending differentials also result in considerably restricted curricula for some schools. For example, in one school there may be only two years of Spanish and no physics offered, while in another school there is a full program of French, Spanish, German, Chinese, and mathematics through calculus available to students. Many large cities and rural areas whose deteriorating tax bases suffer unusually heavy demands for other municipal services, and whose problems of raising sufficient revenues are therefore substantial, are particularly disadvantaged. In addition, these areas have high proportions of pupils with costly educational needs that require added spending. Low-achieving students, non-English-speaking students, and children with handicaps are among the pupils who impose high costs.

Serrano v. Priest

As a result of several court decisions, efforts to equalize the disparities in funding within states have succeeded in shifting some of the responsibility for funding from local school districts to the state level. In 1971 a class action suit, *Serrano* v. *Priest*, was filed by pupils and their parents against California state and county officials concerned with financing public schools. The suit charged that the school financing scheme was unconstitutional. The Supreme Court of California supported the parents' claim that the quality of a child's education may not be a function of wealth other than the wealth of the state as a whole. The court also held that the California system of financing schools on the basis of local property taxes violates the Fourteenth Amendment to the U.S. Constitution.

In 1973 the Supreme Court of the United States, by a five-to-four vote, reversed a similar decision (known as the *Rodriguez* case) involving the school finance system of the state of Texas. The Court found that the Constitution was not violated because the right to an education is not guaranteed explicitly or implicitly by the Constitution. Although federal law had not been violated, the Court did indicate that the finding should not be interpreted as a victory for the status quo. In effect, issues of inequity in school finance were returned to the province of the state courts and legislatures.

Equality, a state concern

Since the *Rodriguez* case, other state courts have ruled that their school financing systems violate their state constitutions. Many state constitutions, unlike the U.S. Constitution, contain equal protection clauses that can be interpreted to include education as a protected right. More than twenty states have reformed their school finance laws since 1973. In a reaffirmation of their earlier decision, the California Supreme Court asserted in the *Serrano II* case that "there is a direct relationship between cost and the quality of educational opportunities afforded."

Between June 1989 and June 1990, three significant court rulings on school finance occurred in Kentucky, Texas, and New Jersey. The Kentucky Supreme Court handed down a decision that was much broader than traditional school finance rulings: it declared all aspects of the state's school system inadequate and charged the governor and legislature to design and implement an entirely new educational system. Within one year the Kentucky legislature approved a massive education package that includes such innovations as altering the role of the state education system, mandating site-based management, creating a statewide system of rewards and sanctions for schools, and focusing on early childhood education through prekindergarten programs and ungraded primary schools.

Kentucky, Texas, New Jersey rulings

EDUCATION: A WORLD VIEW

ARE WE SPENDING ENOUGH?

Many politicians, arguing against the need for increased spending on education, assert that the United States already spends more on public education than most comparable countries but gets worse results. "Money is not the answer," they claim.

A recent study of international comparisons of public spending on education refutes the assertion that the United States spends more than other countries. Comparing public spending as a percent of gross domestic product (GDP) (the total value of a country's output, income or expenditure) for fifteen industrial countries, the study concluded that the United States ranked eleventh, spending 3.7 percent of its GDP on elementary and secondary education. (See Figure 6.5) As the figure indicates, the Scandinavian countries of Denmark, Sweden, and Norway topped the rankings by spending 5.5, 5.4, and 5.0 percent, respectively, on elementary and secondary education. Surprisingly, Germany, Australia, Japan, and Switzerland ranked below the United States. When only higher education expenditures are compared, the United States ranked ninth with a 1.0 percent expenditure.

These figures indicate that the United States devotes fewer resources to elementary and secondary education than do most industrialized nations. Claims that the United States spends more than other countries on education are misleading. Of course, simply spending more money is not the only answer to our educational woes. But the data presented here suggest, at least in part, that we may "get what we pay for." Particularly since the United States might be expected to spend proportionally *more* than other countries because of certain characteristics of our school system and society. Our decentralized school system is more expensive than a single, centrally administered system that characterizes many of the other industrialized nations. Our population is more diverse than most countries, thus presenting unique challenges. And the very high number of U.S. children living in poverty creates additional demands for schools. Given these factors and the relatively low level of investment in our elementary and secondary schools, our low rankings in comparative measures of performance perhaps should not be surprising.

F. Howard Nelson, *International Comparison of Public Spending on Education* Research Report, (Washington, D.C.: American Federation of Teachers, 1991): pp. 13 and 31.

Figure 6.5 Public Spending on Education as a Percent of Gross Domestic Product, 1987

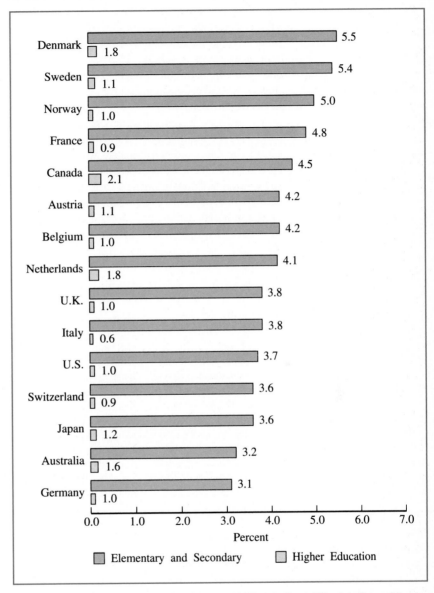

Source: F. Howard Nelson, *International Comparisons of Public Spending on Education,* (Research Report, Washington, D.C.: American Federation of Teachers, 1991), p. 13. Used by permission.

In the Texas case, *Edgewood* v. *Kirby,* the state supreme court declared the state's school-funding formula unconstitutional. The court noted that the three hundred thousand students in the poorest schools have less than 3 percent of the state's property wealth to support their education, whereas the three hundred thousand students in the state's richest schools have more than 25 percent of its property wealth. Thus the rich districts, the court said, can tax low and spend high, but the property-poor districts "must tax high merely to spend low."[46] The decision marked over twenty years of debate and legal action in Texas on this issue.

The New Jersey Supreme Court, in a unanimous decision, declared the state's school-funding system unconstitutional as applied to poorer urban districts. The court ordered the state to bring spending in its poorest city school systems up to the level of its wealthiest districts, thus setting an important precedent never previously ordered in a school finance case. The court found that because the state does not provide these poor districts with enough money for even a basic education, the state's current system denies students in these dis-

Year-round Schools

One innovative way that some school districts are trying to cut costs is to implement year-round schooling to maximize the use of school facilities throughout the year. By 1990, more than 733,000 students participated in year-round programs at 859 public schools, and by 1991 education officials expect attendance to increase another 50 percent, to 1.1 million (*Boston Globe,* March 19, 1991, p. 1). The major push for year-round schools has occurred in fast-growing states, such as California, Utah, and Florida, but by 1990, twenty-two states had at least one school operating all year.

Year-round schools began in 1968 in Hayward, California, where school was held in session for nine weeks, followed by a three-week break. This pattern was repeated four times a year. Other schools have developed different patterns of attendance, but all keep their facilities open all year and stagger schedules so some students are always in attendance. That lets schools house 25 to 50 percent more students without increasing class sizes. In Los Angeles County, the nation's second largest school district, all the public schools went to a "90/30" calendar by mid-1991; two eighteen-week (90-day) semesters, with six weeks (30 days) off in between.

Although the primary impetus for moving to year-round schools seems to be tighter budgets and overcrowded schools, some educators say the main benefits will come from increased student learning, particularly with at-risk students. Some researchers have documented what they call a "summer slippage" among these children. Because these children often lack home and community resources for reinforcing what they have learned in school, they lose much of the year's learning over the long summer break. Going to school year-round and taking shorter vacation periods cuts down on student forgetting and seems to reduce student absenteeism.

Many teachers are highly enthusiastic about year-round schools. As one elementary school principal put it, "The teachers here love it. . . . They get their breaks just when they are most needed" (*Teacher Magazine* (April 1990): 20). Not everyone is wild about the concept, however. Some parents and teachers object because many schools lack air conditioning for summertime instruction. Some parents whose children attend several different schools do not want them on different schedules. And many parents find it difficult to schedule vacation periods convenient to the whole family. It is too early to tell how widespread year-round schooling will become, but indications are that they have considerable appeal for a variety of reasons. Would you enjoy teaching in such an arrangement? What are the pluses and minuses of such a system, in your opinion?

tricts "the right to the same educational opportunity that money buys for others."[47] Rejecting the argument of the state's administration that better management, not more money, is what is needed to improve urban schools, the court declared that evidence in the case "shows beyond doubt that money alone has not worked," but it "does not show that money makes no difference." To the contrary, the court argued, "the entire state aid program itself is based on the assumption that money makes a difference in the quality of education."[48]

State governments continue to wrestle with the problems of equalizing educational opportunity and financial responsibility, as other court cases involving school financing are under consideration in Alaska, Connecticut, Indiana, Michigan, Minnesota, North Dakota, Oregon, and Tennessee.[49]

Pressures for equality

Educators, parents, and public officials are greatly concerned that the quality of a child's education not depend on whether the child lives in a school district with high property values. Many of these concerned citizens are urging that state governments become responsible for raising educational revenue and for distributing the full costs of local schools to the school districts. The school districts would continue to be in charge of the operation of the local schools but would no longer carry the burden of raising needed money.

The different states will probably try many different schemes for financing public schools. And no doubt the issue will continue to be complex and the problems difficult to solve. Generally, the courts have interpreted education to be a function of the state and local school districts as agents of the state. State legislative bodies will need to develop school finance systems that can be expected to produce equal educational opportunities without unnecessarily undermining local control of the schools.

Federal Funding

Although the federal government may provide less money for public schools than do state or local governments, federal funds are strategically important and have a far greater impact than their proportion of school funding would suggest.

FUNDING IN THE PAST   Much of federal aid to education has traditionally been *categorical:* that is, the money must be spent for designated purposes that are stated generally in the legislation and more precisely by the federal agency administering the funds. As a result, the federal government has been able to exert influence on school districts and institutions that have accepted or sought its aid. For example, to qualify for federal funds to improve its reading program, a school district would have to conform to the guidelines and restrictions accompanying the money. Many financially stricken school districts have been grateful for additional funds, regardless of the regulations they carry.

Categorical aid

Strong funding, 1960–1980

During the period from 1960 to 1980 federal education programs thrived. A large number of categorical aid programs designed to reach particular groups of students and teachers or to promote particular activities were enacted. During these years, federal aid to public elementary and secondary schools increased more than 1,400 percent, and the federal government's share of elementary and secondary school revenues increased from 4.4 to 9.8 percent.[50] Congressional acts apportioning federal funds for education provided money to colleges, cities, states, and agencies to finance a wide variety of projects, including construction of buildings and other educational facilities; improvement of instruction or administration; development of educational personnel, including teachers and paraprofessionals, particularly for high-poverty areas; provision of loans for prospective teachers; and funding for educational research.

During the Reagan administration (1981–1989) a significant change in federal aid to education occurred: a reduction of categorical grant programs and their replacement by block grants to state and local education agencies. *Block grants* are sums of money for general purposes that may be spent in ways determined by state and local governments with only minimal federal restrictions. In 1981 Congress passed the Education Consolidation and Improvement Act, which in part consolidated twenty-eight individual categorical programs into one block grant program. Some categorical funding has remained, however, including funds for children with handicaps, vocational education, and bilingual education.

Providing states and local districts with unrestricted funding carries its own danger.[51] Will the state educational agencies distribute funds equitably, directing the majority of aid to the districts where children show the greatest need for high-cost programs? And when the money gets to the districts, will they use it to serve the children who need the funded programs most? Will states discontinue needed programs once funded by categorical aid but no longer required by the federal government? Controversy centers on the comparative lack of impetus that block grants give to implementing desegregation efforts, in contrast to earlier federal funding programs. Moreover, not all public school educators agree with current block grant provisions that require sharing of funds with children in private schools.

On the other hand, local administrators have welcomed the reduced paperwork associated with block grant funding. Those who agree with the spirit of President Reagan's *"new federalism"*—meaning less intrusion by the federal government into state and local affairs and, in education, a return to local autonomy in guiding school policies—have also welcomed these block funding programs.

Although the Reagan administration consistently submitted budget requests for the Department of Education that were lower than congressional appropriations for the previous year, Congress consistently appropriated more money than the administration requested. Between fiscal years 1980 and 1988 congressional appropriations increased from $14.5 to $20.3 billion.[52] Adjusted for inflation, however, federal expenditures from 1980 to 1988 were essentially level. Thus, the Reagan administration was successful in holding the line on federal expenditures for education. Moreover, the federal government's share of support for public education fell from 9.8 percent in 1980 to 6.3 percent in 1990 (See Table 6.2). This decrease reflected President Reagan's intent to reduce the role of the federal government in educational matters and to return educational policy making to state and local authorities.

WHAT LIES AHEAD?   In his campaign for the presidency and during his first years of office, George Bush stated that he would like to be known as the "ed-

States remain key actors

ucation president." In addition to convening in the fall of 1989 an education summit with the nation's governors at the University of Virginia to start the process of identifying national education goals (see Chapter 8) in 1991, President Bush proposed the AMERICA 2000 Education Strategy to create "a new generation of American schools." Highlights of the AMERICA 2000 strategy include creating 535 New American Schools that would address the six national goals and receive both public and private support, establishing alternative teacher and principal certification, establishing three to seven research and development centers (using private funds raised by business leaders) to design the new schools, creating new incentives for states and localities to adopt comprehensive choice policies, and developing new standards, tests, and accountability measures to monitor results. President Bush requested $690 million for the education strategy in the 1992 budget, not including $150–200 million from the business community to "jump-start the New American Schools R & D Teams. . . ."[53] At the same time that President Bush initiated his AMERICA 2000 education strategy, many Democratic members of Congress began putting forth some of their own initiatives, including financial aid for urban education, reinstitution of a type of Teacher Corps program, and funding for preschool programs. These members of Congress want to see a much greater federal role in educational reform.

Regardless of whether the Democratic or Republican education agendas carry the day, the gigantic federal deficit and the cost of servicing the federal debt will severely curtail new initiatives that require large expenditures of funds. The main action for education reform will continue to be in the states' arenas. The federal government's role in education, at least until the federal debt is greatly reduced, is likely to be that of a vocal, but minor, partner. With the political changes occurring in the Soviet Union and Eastern Europe and the end of the Persian Gulf War, perhaps the United States will eventually reap a "peace dividend" that can be applied to its educational problems, but don't expect it anytime soon.

Discussion Questions

1. Can you offer any examples, from your own experience, of the distinction between governance and control? How do you suppose the persons in control in your examples obtained their power? What were the advantages and disadvantages of this state of affairs in the situations involved?

2. In light of what you have learned from this chapter, what do you think of Paul Woodring's statement that "education is too important to be left to the educators"?

3. From what you have read about the role of the superintendent, what impressions have you formed about the power of the superintendent and the constraints on that power?

4. Did the schools you attended work in partnership with business and industry? Did your education prepare you for further education and entry into the work force? What, in your opinion, is an appropriate relationship between business and schools?

Rob Rogers, The Pittsburgh Press. United Features Syndicate
Reprinted by permission of UFS, Inc.

5. The National Education Association and the National Association of Secondary School Principals make this statement about successful secondary schools: "In good secondary schools, the principal and teachers develop and maintain a variety of cooperative links with the community. Family and community involvement and support complement the efforts of the school." Describe some of the cooperative links you would suggest at either the elementary or secondary level.

6. How involved should the states' governors and legislatures be in public education? What are the advantages and dangers of increased involvement by state governments in public education?

7. Of the methods of school financing discussed in this chapter (local property taxes, state financing through statewide taxes, and state-run lotteries), which do you believe is most equitable? Why?

8. If, as Ernest Boyer suggests, Americans want local control of schools but national results, what suggestions could you make to the federal government for balancing those two desires?

For Further Reading

Blumberg, Arthur, with Phyllis Blumberg. *The School Superintendent: Living with Conflict.* New York: Teachers College Press, 1985.

> Based on interviews with twenty-five superintendents of schools, this book offers rich descriptions of the experience of being a superintendent.

Burrup, Percy E., Vern Brimley, Jr., and Rulon R. Garfield. *Financing Education in a Climate of Change.* 4th ed. Boston: Allyn and Bacon, 1988.

> A comprehensive text on how schools are financed in this country, the role of the federal government, and significant court cases affecting school finance.

Campbell, Roald, et al. *The Organization and Control of American Schools.* 6th ed. Columbus, Ohio: Merrill, 1990.

> A good overview of the American educational system, including both governance and control issues.

Chubb, John, and Terry Moe. *Politics, Markets, and America's Schools.* Washington, D.C.: The Brookings Institute, 1990.

> Written by two respected scholars who assert that the school reform movement hasn't worked and is destined to fail because a massive, deadening bureaucracy is ruining American education. The answer, they say, is an entirely new system based on parental choice.

Kimbrough, Ralph B., and Michael Y. Nunnery. *Educational Administration: An Introduction. 3rd ed.* New York: Macmillan, 1988.

> A good survey of the principles of educational administration and the organization of schools in the United States. The role of the superintendent as an instructional leader in nicely explained.

Kirst, Michael W. *Who Controls Our Schools? American Values in Conflict.* New York: Freeman, 1984.

> Drawing on his background as a former president of the California State Board of Education, a consultant, and an academic researcher, Kirst provides historical and political perspective on issues of finance and governance.

Wirt, Frederick M., and Michael W. Kirst. *Schools in Conflict. 2nd ed.* Berkeley, Calif.: McCutchan, 1989.

> An analysis of the politics of education by two leaders in the field.

Notes

1. Task Force on Teaching as a Profession, *A Nation Prepared: Teachers for the 21st Century* (Washington, D.C.: Carnegie Corporation, 1986), p. 2.
2. Jessee L. Freeman, Kenneth E. Underwood, and Jim C. Fortune, "What Boards Value," *American School Board Journal* 178 (January 1991): 34.
3. Carla Yock, Katherine E. Keough, Kenneth E. Underwood, and Jim C. Fortune, "Happily Ever After," *The American School Board Journal,* 177 (January 1990): 34.
4. Arthur Blumberg with Phyllis Blumberg, *The School Superintendent: Living with Conflict* (New York: Teachers College Press, 1985), p. 32.
5. Ibid., p. 27.
6. Ibid., pp. 34–40.

7. Ibid., pp. 7–8.

8. Ibid., p. 60.

9. William L. Rutherford, "School Principals as Effective Leaders," *Phi Delta Kappan* 67 (September 1985): 31–34.

10. James D. Koerner, *Who Controls American Education?* (Boston: Beacon Press, 1968), p. 155.

11. Larry Cuban, "Conflict and Leadership in the Superintendency," *Phi Delta Kappan* 67 (September 1985): 28.

12. "Education Vital Signs," *American School Board Journal* 177 (December 1990): A13.

13. *Education Week,* November 14, 1990, p. 3.

14. Cuban, "Conflict and Leadership," p. 29.

15. Blumberg and Blumberg, *School Superintendent,* p. 45.

16. Ibid., p. 54.

17. Ibid., p. 77.

18. Ibid., p. 60.

19. Ibid., p. 67.

20. Ibid., p. 83.

21. Carla Yock, Katherine E. Keough, Kenneth E. Underwood, and Jim C. Fortune, "Happily Ever After," *The American School Board Journal,* 177 (January 1990): 30.

22. Ibid., pp. 31–32.

23. Joseph Murphy, "The Educational Reform Movement of the 1980s: A Comprehensive Analysis," in *The Educational Reform Movement of the 1980s,* ed. Joseph Murphy (Berkeley, Calif.: McCutchan 1990), pp. 3–55.

24. Deborah Burnett Strother, "An Interview with Michael Kirst," *Phi Delta Kappan* 69 (October, 1987), p. 161.

25. Lamar Alexander, "Summary of 'Time for Results,' Report on Education by Governors' Group," *Chronicle of Higher Education,* September 3, 1986, p. 78.

26. *Time for Results, The Governors' 1991 Report on Education* (Washington, D.C.: National Governors' Association, 1986), pp. 12–13, 78–82.

27. Frank E. Nardine and Robert D. Morris, "Parent Involvement in the States," *Phi Delta Kappan* 72 (January 1991), p. 365.

28. *Investing in Our Children: Business and the Public Schools* (New York: Research and Policy Committee of the Committee for Economic Development, 1985).

29. Brian Dumaine, "Making Education Work," *Fortune,* Special Issue: Saving Our Schools (Spring 1990): 12.

30. Ibid.

31. Denis P. Doyle and Marsha Levine, "Business and the Public Schools: Observations on the Policy Statement of the Committee for Economic Development," *Phi Delta Kappan* 67 (October 1985): 114.

32. Reagan Walker, "The Education of Business," *Teacher Magazine* (January 1990): 67.

33. Doyle and Levine, "Business and the Public Schools," p. 118.

34. Ibid., p. 118.

35. *Workforce 2000: Executive Summary* (Indianapolis, Ind.: Hudson Institute, June 1987), p. xxi.

36. Thomas Moore with Nancy Linon, "The Selling of Our Schools," *U.S. News & World Report,* November 6, 1989, p. 40.

37. Blake Rodman, "Rating Teachers on Students' Test Scores Sparks Furor, Legal Action in St. Louis," *Education Week,* September 17, 1986, pp. 1, 18.

38. Richard J. Coley and Margaret E. Goertz, *Education Standards in the 50 States: 1990* (Princeton, N.J.: Educational Testing Services, August 1990), pp. 3, 6, 10.

39. George F. Madaus, "Test Scores as Administrative Mechanisms in Educational Policy," *Phi Delta Kappan* 66 (May 1985): 609–610.

40. Charlene M. Hoffman, *Federal Support for Education: Fiscal Years 1980 to 1990,* (Washington, D.C.: National Center for Education Statistics, May 1991), p. iii.

41. Chris Pipho, "Education and the State Budget Squeeze," *Phi Delta Kappan* 70 (April 1989): 582–583.
42. "Education Vital Signs," p. A21.
43. Snyder, *Digest of Education Statistics 1990,* p. 147; and "Education Vital Signs," p. A27.
44. "Education Vital Signs," pp. A22–A27.
45. Lala Carr Steelman and Brian Powell, "Appraising the Implications of the SAT for Educational Policy," *Phi Delta Kappan* 66 (May 1985): 606.
46. "Rich Schools, Poor Schools," *Teacher Magazine* (December 1989): 15.
47. Michael Newman, "Finance System for N.J. Schools Is Struck Down," *Education Week,* June 13, 1990, p. 18.
48. Ibid.
49. "Rich Schools, Poor Schools," p. 15.
50. Richard A. Rossmiller, "Federal Funds: A Shifting Balance?" in *The Impacts of Litigation and Legislation on Public School Finance,* ed. Julie K. Underwood and Deborah A. Verstegen (New York: Harper and Row, 1990), p. 8.
51. Anne T. Henderson, "Chapter 2: For Better or Worse?" *Phi Delta Kappan* 67 (April 1986): 597–602.
52. Rossmiller, "Federal Funds: A Shifting Balance?" p. 20.
53. Ibid., p. 22.

PART

III

SCHOOLS:
THE PRESENT

T he 1980s was a time of many proposed reforms and changes in how schools should
operate. The 1990s are beginning where the 1980s
left off, by re-examining what schools' functions
should be, what curriculum should exist, how to
take advantage of new technologies, and how to
make schools more responsive to the intellectual and
emotional needs of both students and staff.

This section examines these issues, particularly by looking at what researchers and observers
have discovered about the purposes of schools, what
constitutes effective schools, what they teach, and
what life is like in schools in contemporary United
States.

7 *What Is a School?*

CHAPTER PREVIEW

The purpose of this chapter is to help you examine the nature of schools and schooling in our society today. We mention a number of different avenues for you to take to reach an understanding of schools. In addition, you will be confronted with different views of a school and models of schooling. At the end of the chapter, we touch on your role in school reform.

This chapter emphasizes that:

● Education is a large, all-encompassing endeavor, whereas schooling is simply one aspect of education.

● The purpose of school determines much of what happens in school. Among the ways to determine the aims of school are to read formal state-

ments of purpose and to rely on one's own experiences in and observations of schools.

● Schools can be defined by comparing them with models, or abstract representations of reality.

● Schools play a critical part in passing on a society's values to the young.

● Schools in our culture are both similar and different in many ways. The teacher's role varies a great deal depending on the type of school.

● Recent research has given us interesting answers to the old question "What is a good school?"

● Because there is much unfinished work in our schools, there is a place for committed and energetic young men and women in the teaching profession.

W hat is a school? This may not strike you as a particularly profound question. In fact, it probably seems rather tame. School is an everyday thing. We have spent vast stretches of our time there. Much of what we are—intellectually, socially, and emotionally—can be traced to our experiences in school. School is just . . . school. However, behind the familiar words and images lie thorny issues that have baffled theoreticians and practitioners of education for years. Quiet communities have been split into warring camps because of their inability to agree on an answer to this question. Let us see if you can answer the question "What is a school?" In the space below, jot down a definition or two of *school*.

_____

_____

_____

_____

_____

Your answer to the question reflects who you are and what your experience with school has been. Perhaps you responded in one of the following ways:

- A school is an agency that weans children from the protective warmth of the family and trains them for what society has decided is useful work.

- A school is a bunch of bricks and mortar, chalkboards and water fountains (usually with wadded gum in them) all put together in a standardized and predictable way.

- A school is a place where they fix your mind so you think like everyone else.

- A school is where children fall in love with learning.

- A school is a tax-supported babysitting agency.

- A school is a place where young savages become civilized citizens.

- A school is where we are taught to compare ourselves with other children our age and, thus, discover our *true* worth.

- A school is a place where we explore who we are and how we can become full, creative human beings.

- A school is where children learn to be virtuous.

- A school is a place where the children of one generation come together to unite against the generation in power.

- A school is a fun palace.

- A school is a perverse cafeteria, catering to our appetite to know but leaving us permanently hungry.

- A school is a fact factory.

- A school is a tax-supported institution where the dead wisdom and worn-out skills of the past are force-fed to the young.
- A school is where education takes place.

Each of these descriptions says a great deal about the school experience of the person who formulated it. Our conviction is that your definition of *school* is a cognitive map that greatly affects how you think about schools. What does your definition say about you and your experience?

EDUCATION AND SCHOOLING

Definition of education

It is commonly believed that school is where people go to get an education. Nevertheless, it has been quipped that today children interrupt their educations to go to school. The distinction between *schooling* and *education* implied by this remark is important. Like *school, education* has myriad definitions. We have sprinkled a few such definitions here and there throughout the book for you to sample. For the moment, however, let us say that *education* is a process of human growth by which one gains greater understanding and control over oneself and one's world. It involves our minds, our bodies, and our relations with the people and the world around us. Whereas education takes many institutional forms, strictly speaking it is a process, an activity characterized by continuous

The classroom is the arena where a certain type of structured and organized education takes place.
(Carol Palmer)

development and change. The end product of the process of education is learning.

Education is much more open-ended and all-inclusive than schooling. Education knows few bounds. It can take place anywhere, whether in a jacuzzi or on the job, whether in a kitchen or on a tractor. It includes both the formal learning that takes place in schools and the whole universe of informal learning, from hooking a worm on a line to burping a baby. The agents of education can range from a revered grandparent to the guests on a late-night television talk show, from a child with mental retardation to a distinguished scientist. Whereas schooling has a certain predictability, education quite often takes us by surprise. We go to the movies to relax and come home with a vivid sense of poverty's corrupting influence on the human spirit. We get into a casual conversation with a stranger and discover how little we know about other religions. People are engaged in education from the cradle to the grave. Infants learn how to satisfy themselves by sucking their thumbs. A widowed grandmother reads about life on a Sioux reservation and goes on to become passionately involved in helping Native Americans. *Education,* then, is a very broad, inclusive term. It is a lifelong process, a process that starts long before we begin school and that should be an integral part of our entire lives.

Schooling, however, is a specific, formalized process, whose general pattern varies little from one setting to the next. Throughout the country, children arrive at school at approximately the same time, take assigned seats, are taught by an adult, use the same or similar textbooks, do homework, take exams, and so on. The slices of reality that are to be learned, whether they are the alphabet or an understanding of our governmental system of checks and balances, have usually been specified in advance. What is learned as a result of schooling is also limited by the boundaries of the subject being taught: if a little boy wants to learn what a girl *really* looks like, he just knows that school is not the place to make his investigations. In the same way, high school students know they are not likely to find out in their classes how practical politics in their community really operates or what avant-garde filmmakers are up to. Finally, schooling tends to be limited to the young. There are, then, definite conditions surrounding the formalized process of schooling.

The Role of the School

Schools are created for the express purpose of providing a certain type of educational experience, which we call the *curriculum*. The curriculum, which will be discussed more fully in Chapter 8, "What Is Taught?" represents what a community believes young people need to know in order to develop into good and productive adults. Or, at least, the curriculum includes what the school policy makers in a particular community believe young people need to know. In effect, the curriculum represents a social bet. It is what the older generation thinks the young will need to live well in the twenty-first century. That's why curriculum decisions are so important. If the curriculum turns out to be a losing bet, the social consequences are severe.

Teachers are trained and hired to fulfill the purposes of the curriculum. In simpler societies, when a boy could learn to be a man by following his father

Takes place everywhere (margin)

Definition of schooling (margin)

Curriculum as social wager (margin)

Schooling as planned education

around and imitating the men of the village and a girl could learn to be a woman by doing the same with her mother and the women, schools were not necessary. Formal schooling became a social necessity when the home and the community were no longer effective or competent at training the young, through informal contacts, for adulthood. Societies have realized that education is too important to be left to chance. Whereas important things are sometimes learned on street corners, and grandparents often are excellent teachers, the formal educative process is simply more reliable. There is an excellent possibility that if education is acquired randomly, the young will grow up with a lopsided understanding of the world and poor preparation for adult life. The chance schooling of the street has educated many in such skills as how to exploit one's fellow humans, and it has produced many a street hustler who can't read. Occasionally we see families with the intellectual resources, skills, and time to educate their young themselves, but this is all too rare amid the complexities and demands of modern life. Also, for each individual set of parents to educate their children—even with the help of older children, grandparents, and neighbors—is wasteful and socially inefficient. So schools have been established to do the job. There may very well come a time, however, when herding children into school buildings five days a week is no longer the best method our society can think of.

The distinction between education and schooling is often blurred because the two concepts are undifferentiated in most people's minds. Keeping the differences between these two concepts clearly in mind is often particularly difficult for the people who should be most sensitive to them, that is, teachers who "do" education "in" schools. People enter teaching because they wish to educate. However, the everyday experiences of working in a school cause their allegiances to shift from abstract educational ideals to the network of personalities and ideas surrounding the particular schools where they teach. They become invested in schooling, in the way things are—the routines of homework and quizzes and detention—and, to varying degrees, they forget education. For this reason alone it is important for the teacher to keep alive the questions "What is a school for?" and "What is my contribution to this child's or this class's education?"

DISCOVERING THE PURPOSES OF SCHOOL

By distinguishing between education and schooling we may have clarified the question "What is a school?" but we have not yet answered it. We need to think further about the goals of a school. The following sections describe some ways to search out a school's purposes and functions.

Formal Statements

High-level statements . . .

The most direct method is to read official statements of purpose. Like most institutions, our schools have occasioned many official attempts to explain what they are all about. A couple of illustrations may suffice. In 1986, a report sponsored by the Carnegie Foundation, *A Nation Prepared: Teachers for the 21st Century,* reasserted an old theme in writings about American education, the link between education and the common good:

> From the first days of the Republic, education has been recognized as the foundation of a democratic society for the nation and the individual alike. . . . School must provide a deeper understanding necessary for a self-governing citizenry. It must provide access to a shared cultural and intellectual heritage if it is to bind its citizens together in the common will. It certainly must enable the citizens of this Republic to make informed judgements about the complex issues and events that characterize life in advanced economies at the end of the twentieth century. The cost of not doing so might well be the gradual erosion of our democratic birthright.[1]

Four years later, in his 1990 *State of the Union Address,* President George Bush pledged his administration and the nation's governors to the achievement of six educational goals by the year 2000. Among them were "U.S. students must be the first in the world in math and science" and "Every school will be free of drugs and violence and will offer a disciplined environment conducive to learning."[2]

. . . versus reality

Both the goal statements by a prestigious foundation and those by our national leadership are representative of public and formal views of the purposes of the schools. They are eloquent and important, but they are also quite remote from the daily life in schools. They may point teachers in the right general direction, but such statements have little value in the fast-moving world of the classroom. When a teacher is struggling to come up with an approach to a map-reading lesson, purposes such as providing "a deeper understanding necessary for a self-governing citizenry" and "access to a shared cultural and intellectual heritage" are rarely specific enough to be helpful.

A teaching instinct?

Another factor limiting the value of statements of purpose is their after-the-fact quality. Purposes and goals are determined for public consumption, not as guides to moment-by-moment behavior. They are not intellectual cornerstones for real curricular decisions about what should be taught and how it should be taught. They do not affect a school's decision to teach the children to read or not to push other children or not to talk while the teacher is talking. These lessons will be taught in schools that have opposing goals and in schools that have no written statements of purpose at all. In other words, schools do not come into existence to fulfill stated purposes. Some years ago the noted educational psychologist J. M. Stephens speculated that "the very existence of schooling may stem not from a deliberate decision of groups or societies, but from blind, spontaneous tendencies which are developed by evolutionary demand and which are found to be prevalent in human beings, although more pronounced in some people than in others."[3]

A final point about statements of purpose is that they may mask completely contradictory practices. What we say and what we do is not always the same. One needs, therefore, to look beyond the formal statements on paper to see the true, operational purposes of schools. Take, for example, the contradictory messages a teacher receives about what to do to help his or her students. In her recent book, *Teachers at Work*, Susan Johnson reports the frustrations of teachers who are caught between their desire to teach what they feel the children need and the drive by school boards and school administrators to have tangible evidence that students are making appropriate progress in areas such as mathematics and reading. One method of stimulating teachers to give great attention to these areas is to make the results of standardized tests publicly available. Johnson quotes one teacher, Richard Sand, who was angered by recent comparisons of achievement scores in local newspapers.

> We just had all the state testing at grades three, seven, and eleven. A year ago, when all this was introduced, it was: "This is to help you better understand what you're doing for the kids. It is not designed for comparison." Yet in the last three weeks . . . all they did was compare. It is extremely depressing to pick up the newspapers and read about schools being weighted by their CAT scores, their SAT scores, when at the same time, we're being told by so-called experts . . . that we have to do more hands-on work with the kids, get out of the schools more. It's the same people saying these things. "Scores have to go up. Get them out in the world." Yet, if I don't have them here and can't sit down and work with them, I can't help them with their skill problems.[4]

Personal Experience

If formal statements by commissions and individuals can be misleading, why can't we simply rely on our own experience? We have all spent a large portion of our lives in schools, and each of us has a rich store of ideas and impressions to draw on. Personal experience is undeniably a very important source of data to help us come to know what a school is. Understanding the school from personal experience has, however, two limitations. One is the angle from which we have seen our own schools; the other is the narrowness of that angle. The position from which the student observes, experiences, and comes to know the school is just one of several vantage points. Teachers have another very different point of view; administrators another; parents another; students actively involved in school affairs another; and foreign visitors to our schools another. For instance, the students in a seventh-grade American history class finish the year confused and upset because their teacher has raised serious and unanswered questions about the structural poverty in our country. But the teacher feels that unsettling the students and goading them to ask new questions is exactly what should be accomplished. The principal, on the other hand, is worried about all the calls from the children's parents, some claiming the teacher is turning their

Angle of vision

children into malcontents and threatening to withdra_____
school. Many of the parents think their children are too___
plex social issues. One community group has conde_____
American, unprofessional, and a troublemaker. Anot_____
to the teacher's defense for making education social_____
fying American idealism. A foreign visitor may be_____
shocked by the lack of respect afforded the teacher,_____
told the students so little and asked them so many questio__
which we perceive, then, affects what we see of a school and the judgm__
make about it. We have to make up somehow for the limitations of our angle of
vision if we are really to know what a school is.

The angle of perception or vision is not the only limitation of personal experience; the narrowness of the slice of experience we observe is also a factor. You have just composed a word picture of a school you have attended. Contrast your word picture with these two:

- strong smell of disinfectant and human sweat in the air / gritty sound of chalk scraping blackboard / fear of getting beat up on the way home / drab, greenish paint everywhere / asphalt playground with basketball backboards, but broken hoops

- bright colors and sunny rooms / same alphabet cards as grade school on top of board / knowing everyone—all 105—in the school / bonfire pep rally for whole community before regional football championships / rows of computers in each classroom

Certainly, the two word pictures differ immensely. It is quite doubtful that their authors went to the same school. The first description suggests a rather rundown school in an urban slum. The second could be a relatively new school in a rural area. The point is that the same word, *school*, conjures up very different images in two minds. This is because schools, and the experience of going to school, vary radically within this country. The public school in a small citrus-growing town along the Rio Grande River, serving mainly Mexican-American children, is worlds away from the private preparatory school for boys on the outskirts of New Haven, Connecticut. The racially mixed elementary school in a tense working-class neighborhood can be profoundly different from the busy, innovative elementary school in a quiet suburb just fifteen freeway minutes away. When we call on our own experience to answer the question "What is a school?" we must remember that each of us has had quite limited experience. A great variety of people, motives, activities, and outcomes are covered by the simple word *school*. Nevertheless, there *are* many points of commonality in the school experiences of people in this country, and we will explore these points later in this chapter and throughout this volume.

MODELS OF SCHOOLS

A *model* is a representation of reality. All of us create mental models to help us sort out the hundreds of thousands of sounds and sights we encounter daily and to organize them into sensible patterns. Scientists, in particular, use theoretical models in their efforts to predict events and to explain why certain things have occurred. Models can be similarly useful to us as we attempt to answer the question "What is a school?" A number of descriptive models have been developed to explain the purposes and functions of a school. A few such models are briefly described in the following paragraphs. As you read, think about how well each model describes the schools you know.

The School as Factory The school prepares children for industrial work. The modern school, which was in fact designed during the Industrial Revolution, preadapts children to the world of work by immersing them in a crowded, noisy environment ruled by a time clock and dominated by the production mentality. Large numbers of students (raw material) are brought together to be processed by teachers (workers), who are overseen, in turn, by administrators (supervisors). As in a factory, regimentation, lack of individualization, and systemization (seating, grouping, grading) are the major operating principles. The final product of the school is "a good worker."

The School as Preparer for College The school prepares the student for more schooling. The goal of the school is to ready the boy or girl for admission to college. As a result, the here and now is not nearly so important as the future. Using this model, the curriculum of the

The school as factory is a powerful metaphor that is often all too obvious from its external appearance.

(*Lew Merrim/Monkmeyer Press Photo Service*)

secondary school is justified to the degree to which it prepares students to do college-level work. Likewise, the elementary school curriculum is justified to the degree to which it prepares students for success in secondary school. Students' needs and interests are given slight attention because the focus is on the demands of the curriculum at the "next level up."

The School as Bureaucracy

The school is a training ground for life in a modern, bureaucratized society. According to this model, the school is a set of experiences that wean the child from the protective and highly personalized care of the family so that he or she can deal with the impersonal governmental and economic bureaucracies to be encountered in later life. School teaches us how to cooperate and interact easily with large numbers of people we do not know well. We learn how to live by rules in whose formulation we had little or no voice. According to this model, the school helps modify individuals so that they will not oppose the bureaucracy, thus ensuring the safety of the system.

The School as Babysitter

The school relieves the parents of full-time responsibility for their children. The school is valued as a repository or "dumping ground" that enables parents, particularly mothers, to pursue new alternatives. In an industrial state such as ours, releasing women from extended childrearing frees them for other work. A variant of this is the mean babysitter model: the parents are free to be continually loving and permissive to the child, while the school dispenses discipline and sometimes punishment.

The School as Shopping Mall

The school, particularly the high school, is a large structure made up of different customer-oriented enterprises, all competing for the student's "business." Students going to college frequent the academic boutiques. Students interested in particular occupational opportunities frequent the vocation-oriented specialty shops. Other students just drift around, casually shopping and socializing.[5]

WHAT THE SCHOOL IS

The school is an entry into the life of the mind. It is, to be sure, life itself and not merely a preparation for living. But it is a special form of living, one carefully devised for making the most of those plastic years that characterize the development of *homo sapiens* and distinguish our species from all others. School should provide more than a continuity with the broader community or with everyday experience. It is primarily the special community where one experiences discovery by the use of intelligence, where one leaps into new and unimagined realms of ex-

perience, experience that is discontinuous with what went before. A child recognizes this when he first understands what a poem is, or what beauty and simplicity inhere in the idea of the conversation theorems, or that measure is universally applicable. If there is one continuity to be singled out, it is the slow converting of the child's artistic sense of the omnipotence of thought into the realistic confidence in the use of thought that characterizes the effective man.

(Reprinted from Jerome Bruner, *On Knowledge: Essays for the Left Hand* (Cambridge: Belknap Press, Harvard University Press, 1964), p. 118.

The School as Social Escalator

The school is seen as the vehicle by which one rises in society. School is the royal road to economic well-being and social prominence. Success in school is the ticket to the upper rungs of the community. Although athletic and artistic success in school escalates some students to prominence, academic achievement provides the boost for most. Failure and poor performance in school acts as a "de-escalator" for many students.

The School as Social Panacea

The school here becomes the society's problem solver. If poverty exists or parents are neglecting their responsibilities, the school is seen as a panacea and assumes this responsibility. Whereas schools once were limited to passing on the moral and intellectual heritage to students, in this model schools "do what is needed." Driver's education, multicultural education, sex education, drug education, and AIDS education are all examples of the school attempting to solve new social problems.

The School as Developer of Human Potential

The school attempts to insure that each individual develops her or his capacities—intellectual, social, and physical—to the fullest possible measure. The teachers are specialists in identifying students' strengths and needs and in matching the instructional program to these strengths and needs. The cornerstone of the school is the uniqueness of each child, and the school is designed to be flexible and have a positive impact on the child. By focusing on the individual child, the school runs the risk of preparing self-oriented, highly individualistic students.

The School as Acculturator

The school brings together people of divergent backgrounds to accommodate themselves to and share one culture. The school's role in the United States, therefore, is to teach "the American way of life" and to pass on the customs, values, and social patterns of the dominant group to immigrants and others who have been excluded from full participation in this society. According to this view, the school is a melting pot whose function is to minimize the influence of minority ethnic, racial, and religious influences.

A cautionary note: A phenomenon as varied and widespread as a school cannot be explained by a single model. A model is only as good as its ability to explain reality to us. Therefore, a model of a school has value only to the degree that it helps us understand what we already know about schools and to make sense of the new information we receive.

SCHOOLS AS TRANSMITTERS OR RE-CREATORS OF CULTURE

Hidden behind these various models of school are different purposes for schools, different ways of interpreting the mission of schools, and, therefore, different curricular emphases. Two perspectives are especially prominent: first, the school is the social institution where the young receive from the older generation the very best of their culture; second, the school is the social institution where the young learn skills and become agents of social change.

Transmitting Culture　In the model of the school as acculturator, schools exist in order to advance society by insuring that the young know and appreciate the dominant values of their society's culture. Here the very reason for schools is to advance the society by insuring that the young know and appreciate their culture, or what the French sociologist Émile Durkheim called the "social facts." Instead of stressing personal growth or individuality, Durkheim saw the school as developing the "so-

Social emphasis　cial being," which he described as

> a system of ideas, sentiments, and practices which express in us, not our personality, but the group or different groups of which we are part; these are religious beliefs, moral beliefs, and practices, national or occupational traditions, collective opinions, of every kind. Their totality forms the social being. To constitute this being in each of us is the end of education.[6]

This mission of transmitting the culture is often misunderstood as simply filling up the minds of students with everything that the older generation knows. This is incorrect on a number of points.

First, and obviously, the world in all its variety—people, anteaters, hurricanes, eggplants, computers, ballets—is simply too much to deal with. Schools

Selected knowledge　have to be selective. They must choose fragments from the universe of knowledge. The goal, of course, is to select those bits and pieces that truly will be of value. Prime candidates for selection are, for instance, the harnessing of energy and the checks and balances of democratic government.

Second, transmitting the culture does not mean simply filling up students as so many empty jugs. The aim is to make them lively, active, and creative

Cultured individuals　participants in the community. Nevertheless, although students' individuality is important, that individuality is viewed in relation to what they know about and possess from the culture. The question is, "Are they *cultured* individuals?" And

Smith Family by Mr. and Mrs. George Smith. © 1971 Washington Star Syndicate. Reprinted with permission of Universal Press Syndicate. All rights reserved.

further, successful students participate in this "jug filling" through self-discipline and study.

Preference for one's own culture

The third error is more subtle. Although educators may think they are passing on the world's best and most vital knowledge to the young, what they are usually doing is transmitting their own particular culture and its values. However, this is perfectly consistent with Durkheim's view of schools transmitting their culture.

By *culture* we mean the system of norms and standards that a society develops over the course of many generations and that profoundly influences the everyday behavior of people in that society. More simply, culture is as people do. The implication, clearly, is that American public schools teach the American way of looking at the world and the American way of doing things. By and large, this is not a conscious process. It was not consciously introduced into the curriculum. If we ask educators what, broadly speaking, they are trying to do, they are likely to reply that they are teaching what the real world is and how to deal with it. But, again, our schools teach our version of reality and our way of handling the real world. And so, too, do the schools of other countries. Schools in northern India differ markedly from those in Ghana, and both have sharp

Students Talk About Schools and Teachers

All things considered, like lack of money and big classes, I think schools do a good job. I mean, you can't always do what you want to do. Somebody always has to get you to move your butt.
RURAL INDIANA SENIOR

Schools should teach us all the different alternatives that are open to society, but they should also show that there's a basic foundation to life.
NORTHEAST STATE STUDENT COUNCIL PRESIDENT

Schools usually have one thing in common—they are institutions of today run on the principles of yesterday.
FIFTEEN-YEAR-OLD STUDENT

In my view, the sooner we all get out of the stuffy classroom, the better it will be for everybody. Life is much more interesting if you can go out and see something instead of just sitting in a desk and being loaded with information about it.
LYNNE, AGE FIFTEEN

The best teacher I ever had . . . she didn't give you busy-work, like read then answer questions. She let you

speak and listened to your opinions. She helped us think about ourselves. In her classroom, the class was run by the class.
CHICAGO JUNIOR

A teacher can be very rude and cruel to a child, but any objection on his part is treated as impertinence. Education is a search after the truth, and to find the truth one must be humble. This is impossible if teachers are too proud to admit when they are wrong.
JANET AGE SIXTEEN

Schools should give us guidance to understand the nature of life and existence. I find myself in a vacuum groping for the meaning of life.
SCOTTISH SENIOR

We've got great teachers. They're like family. They respect us and joke with us and we work together.
DROP-IN STUDENT, CHICAGO INDUSTRIAL ARTS CENTER

Third, fourth, and sixth quotation from Edward Blishen (Ed.), *The School That I'd Like* (Harmondsworth, England: Penguin Books, 1969). Other quotations from Catherine McKenzie Shane, "Coping, Caring, Communicating: Youth Looks at the Future," *Phi Delta Kappan* Vol 58, N. 1 (September 1976): 120. Reprinted by permission.

Must understand other
cultures

Must communicate with
immigrants

differences with their counterparts in the United States. However, the schools of each country are attempting to perform a similar function: to transmit the unique culture of the country to its newest members, the young.

This desire to insure that the young share the common culture may explain why in many school systems we teach American history in the third grade, the seventh grade, and again in the eleventh grade, and why, for instance, we give little attention to the history of China. China is, however, the most populous nation in the world, and it has one of the oldest and richest cultural heritages. Most scholars and foreign policy experts are sure that China will loom large in the future of this country. Nevertheless, until recently the American people had developed the habit of ignoring China, and as a result its existence is hardly acknowledged in some schools.

There is danger inherent in this tendency of schools to concentrate on transmitting the dominant culture. If schools offer the young an understanding of only the prevailing culture, the result may be an attitude of smug cultural superiority, a phenomenon that frequently leads nations and individuals to foolish actions. In cultural terms, what we do not know we frequently do not respect. Without mutual respect people easily become enemies. In recent decades, instantaneous electronic communications, rocket-delivered nuclear weapons, and interdependent national economic structures have increasingly made the world a global village, and our students must learn how to function in this new world.

During the 1980s and 1990s, the United States has experienced an enormous immigration from Southeast Asia, the Middle East, Central America, and elsewhere. These new Americans tend to be young. They and their children are hungry for education. Although they are eager to learn American ways and American culture, teachers and students need to be respectful of the culture these students bring with them. Indeed, the presence of new Americans can be a valuable resource in the effort to increase multicultural understanding and appreciation. Therefore, although American schools need to transmit American culture, we must realize that what we call "American culture" has always embraced many cultures.

Reconstructing Society

Schooling as social
leaven

Some of the issues just mentioned—the threat of nuclear weapons, a highly interdependent world economy, large numbers of immigrants—plus the hunger, suffering, and injustice that is a present reality in our world, lead some educators to the view that schools must become the tool of social reconstruction. Their vision is of a school that acts as a leaven to the society. Instead of seeing schools as places where the collective wisdom of the past dribbles down to those who have the capacity and the interest to make use of it, these educators assume a much more active, even assertive role for the school. Thirty years ago, the educator George S. Counts wrote:

> We must abandon completely the naive faith, that school automatically liberates the mind and serves the cause of human progress; in fact, we know that it may serve any cause. [It] may serve tyranny as well as freedom, ignorance as well as enlightenment, falsehood as well as truth, war as well as peace, death as well as life. It may lead men and women

to think they are free even as it rivets them in chains of bondage. Education is indeed a force of great power, particularly when the word is made to embrace all the agencies and organized processes for molding the mind, but whether it is good or evil depends, not on laws of learning, but on the conception of life and civilization that gives it substance and direction. In the course of history, education has served every purpose and doctrine contrived by man. If it is *to serve the cause of human freedom, it must be explicitly designed for that purpose* (emphasis added).[7]

Social reconstructionists, then, see the school forming the young into agents of change, but also participating in the decision about how society needs to change.

Whereas educators who lean toward cultural transmission tend to be philosophically attracted to perennialism and essentialism, social reconstructionists incline toward progressivism. (See Chapter 3 for a description of these philosophies.) They have little reverence for the accumulated wisdom of the past and more concern for the world's problems and the necessity to create a new order. They see the successful student not so much as a *cultivated* person as an autonomous citizen ready to join with others to tackle the world's ills and help in the reconstruction of the society.

But even among social reconstructionists, there is a wild range of emphases and views. Today there are two dominant kinds of social reconstructionists: one we will call *democractic reconstructionists* and the other *economic reconstructionists. Democratic reconstructionists* such as James Shaver see the solution to certain trends and to certain current issues, such as racism, poverty, and the destruction of the ecosystem, in an aroused and skilled citizenry.[8] The school's mission, then, is to prepare students for vigorous participation in their government. The focus of schooling is on developing knowledge of democratic processes, critical thinking skills, and group process skills so the student can fruitfully work with others for social improvement. Other democratic reconstructionists, such as Fred Newmann, want to develop these same skills but advocate a more activist position.[9] Newmann has developed a *social action* curriculum, which has students not simply acquiring skills and knowledge about social conditions but actually attempting to change conditions through social action. For instance, in teaching environmental competence, Newmann has students select, study, and actively work on a community environmental problem, such as the polluting of landfills with unrecycled garbage.

Economic reconstructionists tend to take a harsher view of the dominant culture and see schools as the pliant servants of those in power. Instead of humanistic institutions attempting to free individuals from their own and life's limitations, schools are institutions operating for the economic powers-that-be. Schooling, then, is "a function of dominant socio-economic values," and in the United States today, those are the values of corporate America.[10] These theorists and critics, because of their deep suspicions of, and sometimes outright disgust with, capitalism are often called neo-Marxists.

One noted economic reconstructionist is the Brazilian educator Paulo Freire. Freire's first book, *The Pedagogy of the Oppressed*, describes his work with poverty-stricken, illiterate peasants in his native Brazil.[11] As Freire tried to

Progressive orientation

Democratic reconstructionists

Economic reconstructionists

teach these adults to read, he saw that they were trapped in an economic and social web over which they had little control. He saw, too, that the normal mechanisms of education—such as grading and control by the teacher—imposed on the peasants passivity and subservience to authority. For Freire, the typical methods and routines of schooling are a form of oppression in that they keep people from becoming fully human. To counter this, Freire taught literacy by helping the peasants, first, to name their problem (such as a polluted water supply); second, to analyze the problem (sewage contamination of the springs); and, third, to collectively take action (design and build a new sewage system) to solve the problem. In this manner, education becomes a tool both to develop the human potential of people (such as the ability to read) and to free them from oppressive conditions (lives of poverty and disease).

Although both types of reconstructionists, democratic and economic, focus on social problems and attempt to foster in students the attitudes and skills necessary to solve them, the economic reconstructionists question more deeply the fundamental economic and social arrangements in a society. They see education as a necessary means to fundamentally restructuring the power structures in a society. Money, power, and control of education are tightly bound together.

WHAT ARE SCHOOLS LIKE TODAY?

Similarities

Procedural commonalities

Schools in the United States are remarkably similar to one another. Or, said another way, the culture that is transmitted by the school varies very little from one system to another. A primary reason for this similarity is the general uniformity of schooling procedures. For instance, the number of hours of instruction and days in the school year is practically the same throughout the United States. Other similarities in schooling procedures include the length of classes, the time between classes, the use of bells, the number of pupils in each class, the awarding of credits (Carnegie units) for the completion of courses, the requirement of a fixed number of Carnegie units for graduation, the types of extracurricular activities, the bureaucratic structure within the school systems, and the sources of educational funding. Also similar are the school rituals, such as book fairs, pep rallies, and graduation ceremonies.

Legislated sameness in curriculum

Curricular offerings are also similar in American schools today. Not only has the education of youth been mandated by state legislation, but certain types of educational programs or competencies are being adopted by state legislatures across the country. For instance, as of 1990, twenty states had passed legislation requiring students from schools throughout the state to pass a minimum competency test before they received their high school diplomas.[12] This, plus the fact that an additional twenty-seven states (for a total of forty-seven) have some form of minimum competency testing, creates strong pressure for curricular uniformity.[13] Course content also is similar because expressed societal goals are quite uniform throughout the United States. In addition, much of what is taught in schools is influenced by the books and materials that are used. Because the large textbook companies sell the same books and series of books from state to state and from coast to coast, commonalities are further emphasized. You can rest assured that ninth-grade math courses are just about the same whether you are in Portland, Poughkeepsie, or Punxsutawney.

Similar books

In addition to schooling procedures and curricular offerings, actual teaching methods provide another element of uniformity in schools today. Verbal explanations, presentations and questioning, and assigning of seatwork and drill on new material are among the main tools of the teaching trade.

Differences

Different school emphases

But although there are many similarities and commonalities from school to school, at another level there are great differences. All American schools today are *not* alike, and the actual experience of teaching in one school may be profoundly different from that in another school. Some schools stress certain types of goals and focus on certain specialties. These specialties may be in the form of a vocational trade, a college preparatory program, a certain type of learning style, such as extensive hands-on activities, and even specific sports programs. Then, of course, we need to consider the intensity with which a set of procedures is being followed. Some schools have more rigid structures than others, with more rules and regulations for both teachers and students. Also, the model, as discussed earlier, to which the school tries to adhere is determined by the community, and thus schools have different goals and curricular emphases.

Funding and socioeconomic differences

Funding for schools is another source of difference. Whereas one district may have enough money to support numerous extracurricular activities, special workshops and enrichment programs for its teachers, and material support for its curricular offerings, another district may have to struggle simply to keep a supply of relatively up-to-date textbooks. The working conditions and morale of the faculty would certainly be affected in those two districts. Also connected with the funding issue is the socioeconomic status of the community and the attitudes of students coming to the school. A community composed of families who are struggling to put food on the table may not have a large revenue base to support its schools, and this affects the quality of the material support in the school. Furthermore, the child coming from a home with a constantly blaring television set, no books, and little money even for "extras" will enter the school with a set of experiences, expectations, and even skills entirely different from those of the child whose family has the means to subscribe to five magazines, allows only moderate television watching, and spends a good deal of time reading to the child. In some communities, many educated parents are ready and willing to help teachers with enrichment units and transportation and chaperoning for field trips. In such communities, parents rarely fuss when students bring home requests for ten dollars to get a special enrichment book or fifteen dollars for some special field trip. Thus, the school's socioeconomic setting will affect curricular offerings, instructional activities, schooling procedures, teacher morale, and a host of other interconnected factors.

Geographic differences

Further, there are vast differences in schools depending upon their geographical setting. Whether a school is set in a city, a suburban community, or a rural community greatly affects the nature of the schooling and the relationships between the school and the community. The situation is seen most dramatically in the case of rural schools. Rural schools tend to serve a rather homogeneous population, but one that is spread out over a physically large area. One result is that many of the students are bused in from homes that are a great distance from the school. This makes participation in sports and other extracurricular activities difficult.

On the other hand, rural schools are often the focal point of their community, with the school facilities being used for a variety of civic activities. In addition, rural schools have unique problems and unique opportunities. One problem, particularly acute in high schools, is trying to provide a rich academic and vocational program for a relatively small student population. In such circumstances, three or four years of two modern languages, a full series of science and mathematics courses, plus a number of vocational training options, can become extremely expensive. On the positive side, however, the smallness of rural schools makes for a closer community. Student-faculty relationships tend to be closer. Students tend to be involved in a greater range of activities. For instance, for a small rural school to have a football team, a yearly play, a chorus, a debate team, a science club, and other common extracurricular activities, a typical student may have to be involved in two, three, or four different activities. The result is that the student tends to be "stretched" by this range of activities. In many urban schools these activities (including gym and sports) are either not offered or have been severely cut back. On the other hand, in many suburban schools there are even more activities, but each activity may engage a much smaller percentage of students than in rural schools.

Finally, there are the differences between the nation's public and private schools. Besides the public schools, there is the vast network of private religious schools in the United States. In addition, there is the much smaller but prestigious network of private secular and religiously nondenominational schools. The different purposes and different clienteles of these schools often make for quite distinctive variations. In 1990-91, approximately 5,200,000 students attended parochial or private (K-12) schools.[14] This figure represents 13 percent of the country's elementary and secondary school children, and the percentage is growing because many parents appear to want their children to have a different type of education from that being provided by their public schools.

Four Categories of Schools

So, amid the similarities are some very real differences. After studying the elementary schools in a major American city, Russell C. Doll came up with four categories into which, more or less comfortably, all the schools he examined would fit: type A is highly academically oriented; type B is average academically oriented; type C is low academic–semi-problem-oriented; and type D is highly problem-oriented.[15] What does this mean for teachers? Teacher activities will be quite different in each of the four types of schools. For instance, in the highly academically oriented school, teachers generally operate in an atmosphere supportive of quality teaching, academic planning, and program review and improvement. Parents and students normally perceive little need for sweeping changes, since the schooling process is working well in these settings.

Type A schools tend to resist educational fads and stick to the fundamentals. Parents do not expect the teachers to be innovative, but they do expect teachers to insure that the children can read well, compute, and write with sufficient skill to edge out close competition in the upper grades. In these schools,

Rural schools

Public and private schools

Type A: fundamentals

teachers feel the pressures from parents and students to "turn out the work." Teachers in type A schools often find the schools academically challenging, and there is little need for the teachers to be disciplinarians, but they frequently feel the strain of continually having to perform with excellence.

Type B: innovation

In type B schools (the average academically oriented schools), there is often a strong climate of acceptance and encouragement for educational change. The school situation for the most part is stable; the majority of students are academically talented, but some are academically slow. Teachers are comfortable and generally feel accepted. However, the school is very open to innovation, and change causes the teachers to be involved in a turmoil of shifting programs and priorities. Administrators, parent groups, or groups of teachers are continually pushing the latest educational fads. The brunt of implementing these fads and ill-conceived innovations falls on the classroom teacher. Doll compares the staffs of these schools to "well-conditioned marathon runners who, at each quarter mile, were given two ounces of lead to carry. Little by little teachers are worn down by mundane and trivial things that add up to drains in time and energy."[16]

Type C: struggle

In type C (low academic–semi-problem-oriented) schools, teachers try to maintain an academic program and climate like those in the type B schools. However, they continually deal with extraneous concerns: discipline problems, truancy, student transferrals in and out, special government or district aid programs, and interminable record keeping. Most stressful for the teacher is the continual strain of trying to teach content while maintaining good classroom management, a major preoccupation in these schools. In other words, the teacher needs to combine the qualities of a good teacher and a good classroom manager. The amount of physical and emotional energy demanded merely to cope leaves many teachers with little to devote to the teaching programs.

Type D: survival

The name of the game in type D (highly problem-oriented) schools is "to keep order and to survive." Multiple forces keep teachers from devoting their time and energy to the instructional program. The teachers focus on ways to improve classroom management rather than on the teaching of content. Teacher absenteeism is high as a consequence of the stress inherent in this type of school. Indeed, these schools can sometimes be physically dangerous to both the students and the teachers.

The reader should keep two things in mind here. First, stress, tension, and difficulty are part of existence. Few people, whether they are stockbrokers or truck drivers or social workers, don't experience some setbacks or strain. Teaching is no exception. Second, Doll's description is based on one study of one city's elementary schools at one rather turbulent moment in history. The picture of teaching that emerges strikes us as being overly harsh, but we do believe the study points out the falsity of the view that a school is a school is a school. The physical, emotional, and learning climates can be distinctly different in each type of school and thus can affect each teacher's performance. But it must be kept in

Each type has attractions

mind that teachers are different, too. Many teachers find deeply satisfying human and professional rewards from teaching in a trouble-ridden, type D school, and they would be unhappy in a type A school. So, too, for each of the types. The point is that teachers should look at the circumstances and qualities of the school district and the school when considering a teaching position. They should assess their own abilities and preferences before deciding to teach in a particular type or category of school. Armed with an understanding of the differences in schools and an understanding of their own abilities, teachers should be equipped to identify the setting in which they will be most effective and find the greatest satisfactions.

WHAT IS A GOOD SCHOOL?

Schools as human "product"

It should be clear, then, that the simple label *school* often hides vast differences. Also, from the preceding chapters, particularly from Chapters 3 and 4 on different philosophies of education and the history of our schools, it should be evident that a school is a *made* institution. By this we mean that a school is the product of people's intellectual and physical energies and that, at any particular moment, the way a school happens to be reflects efforts that have gone into creating and maintaining it. Like towns and civilizations, schools also rise and fall. They are human creations—dynamic and continually on the move.

A second point is that no school—at least in the authors' experience—is "right" or "good" for all students. But although we believe this is true, we also believe that some schools are better than others. That is, some schools provide a significantly better education for a much larger percentage of their students than do others. And it is these schools—referred to in the educational literature as *effective schools*—to which we will turn in this section.

How can you tell whether a school is effective? What are the signs or qualities of an effective school? As you have done earlier in this chapter, stop for a moment and jot down your thoughts. What do *you* believe are the characteristics of an effective school?

_____

_____

_____

_____

_____

_____

Definition of "effective schools"

One major problem associated with this question is the criterion to be applied. Effective or good in what dimension? In happy students? In a teaching staff with high morale? In the percentage of students that get promoted or graduate? That go on to colleges? What kinds of colleges? In numbers that succeed in business or professional life? In athletics? Socially? Ethically? *Effective*, as currently defined in most of the educational research literature, refers to students' achievement test scores in basic skills (for example, reading and mathematics). Although such tests measure skills that are hardly the only objectives of education, achievement of these academic areas is an important and widely acclaimed outcome of schooling. Also, achievement in reading and mathematics is easier to measure than good citizenship or interest in ideas.

Characteristics of an Effective School

In recent years, a number of large studies have looked for the qualities of effective schools.[17] Among the most significant characteristics they found to be correlated with high achievement in the basic skills are the following: high expectations for student performance, communication among teachers, a task orientation among the staff, the ability to keep students on task, the expenditure of little time on behavior management, the principal's instructional leadership, the participation of parents, and the school environment.

THE TEACHER'S EXPECTATIONS   Through their attitude and their regular encouragement, teachers in effective schools communicate to students their belief that the students will achieve the goals of instruction. Students receive a strong impression that they can perform. In effect, the teachers get across to students a "can-do" attitude about learning.

High, "can-do" expectations

"I'm *not* an underachiever. You're an overexpecter."

Courtesy Randy Hall.

COMMUNICATION AMONG TEACHERS   Teachers do not operate in a vacuum, each in his or her isolated classroom. Instead, teachers in effective schools talk among themselves about their work. They know about each other's curriculum. They converse about one another's students. They know the materials and activities that go on in one another's classrooms. And, they are helpful to each other. In short, effective schools have teachers who are good colleagues.

High degree of colleagueship

TASK ORIENTATION   The faculties of effective schools appear highly task-oriented. They begin instruction early in the class period and end instruction late in the period. The staff approach their teaching responsibilities with a serious air and waste little time in class. Whether the classes are formal or informal, underneath the surface of events lies a seriousness of purpose that is understood by the students.

Serious attitude

TIME ON TASK   *Time on task* refers to the teacher's ability to keep the students engaged in academic work. For some time, the research of Bloom,[18] Madaus,[19] and others has demonstrated the tight link between the amount of time spent on academic learning tasks and students' achievement. This characteristic addresses the ability of a teacher to get students engaged in an academic task (such as reading or solving math problems) and to keep them working. As a variable in the formula for achievement, *time on task,* or *academic engaged time,* is turning out to be one of the most powerful and promising in the educational literature.

Keep students working

Research indicates that time on task—the teacher's ability to keep students engaged in academic work—significantly contributes to students' achievement.

(*Susan Lapides 1991*)

BEHAVIOR MANAGEMENT   We have all been in classrooms with teachers who spent huge chunks of time trying to quiet students to get them "on task," or who, in the course of correcting one student, disturbed all the rest, causing a ripple of distraction to flow through the room. Teachers in effective schools have learned techniques to keep to a minimum the time devoted to managing students, both to handle discipline problems and to simply implement the learning activities. In addition, in effective schools teachers do *not* routinely resort to corporal punishment.

Maintain classroom order

THE PRINCIPAL   Research in the last several years has demonstrated the importance of the principal's influence. From this research has emerged a new appreciation of the principal. Instead of being simply a faceless bureaucrat meaninglessly shuffling papers in his office, the principal of an effective school is an instructional leader. He or she has strong views and is vitally concerned about the quality of teaching and learning in the school. However, the principal is perceived as democratic in approach and cooperative in relationships with faculty. The effective principal gains teachers' confidence and clearly communi-

Instructional leader

EDUCATION: A WORLD VIEW

· ·

THE JAPANESE EDUCATIONAL SYSTEM

As we have stressed in this chapter, schools are a social construct. They are a "made" institution. They reflect the values, the biases, and the priorities of their society. As a consequence, different societies with different cultures and different ambitions have very different schools. In recent years, as Japan has become more and more of an economic competitor, analysts in the United States have credited much of the Japanese' success to their schools. But what are their schools like?

- Kindergartens exist in Japan, but they are not compulsory. Half of the kindergartens are supported with private tuition and half with public funds. The same pattern holds for day care centers.
- The school pattern is six years of elementary school, three years of lower high school, and three years of upper high school. School is compulsory from age six to age fifteen, from first year through lower high school.

- During the elementary year and somewhat into lower high schools, the schools avoid making a distinction between students on the basis of achievement or academic ability. There are no tracks, levels, or remedial programs. Cooperation, rather than competition, is stressed. Also, students almost never skip a grade or are held back. Promotion is all but automatic.

- Japanese students, however, must pass rigorous exams to enroll in upper high school, and schools are ranked in prestige according to difficulty. Ninety-three percent enroll in some form of upper school, and 33 percent go on to higher education. The competitive nature of this exam system has helped spawn a huge system of private, after-school cram schools. High school students spend as many as twenty to thirty hours a week cramming (at an equivalent cost of up to 15,000 dollars per year!)—in addition to serving their regular school time and doing homework.

- Japanese schools are divided into three terms: two sixteen- to seventeen-week terms and one nine- to

cates to the faculty a vision of what the school should accomplish and how each can contribute to its achievement.

Support from the home

PARENTS   An effective school reaches out and draws in parents, instead of ignoring them or keeping them at arm's length. Parents are treated as key members of the learning team, as partners with the professional staff in helping their children achieve academic success. In addition to aiding in intellectual achievement, the involvement of parents can help improve students' self-concepts and work habits.

Conducive to learning

THE SCHOOL ENVIRONMENT   A school that is noisy, unsafe, hostile, and generally unruly is rarely a place of learning—academic learning, at least. On the other hand, an environment that is quiet, safe, pleasant, and orderly is conducive to learning.

Although these seven characteristics of effective schools show a certain "masterful grasp of the obvious," it was not too long ago that the research

ten-week term. This leaves them five or six weeks annually for vacation.

- The curriculum at all levels is the same, since the Japanese have a highly centralized system. School authorities have attempted to provide similar school facilities, books, teaching methods, and standards.

- Compared with U.S. students, who attend school approximately 180 days a year, Japanese students attend 243 days a year. However, approximately thirty of these days are given over to field trips, sports days, cultural festivals and graduation ceremonies. Since Japanese students go to school six days a week, but one of those days, Saturday, is a half day, the total classroom instruction time is closer to 195 days per year.

- Japanese schools place a great emphasis on homework. The average number of hours per week for primary students is 8.3 hours; for lower high school, it is 16.2 hours; and for upper high school, it is 19 hours (American students' averages are 1.8 hours, 3.2 hours, and 3.8 hours, respectively).

- Teachers in Japan are given high status and relatively good salaries, but they are also subject to close public scrutiny. Besides being skilled teachers, they are expected to be moral models for the young. Teaching is a competitive and desirable occupation and has many more applicants than there are teaching positions. All teachers must pass a standard national examination in order to be certified.

- Japanese schools reflect Japanese culture. Education is esteemed in Japan—this is clearly reflected in the status of teachers. The Japanese place high value on hard work and self-discipline. Whereas Americans prize the individual and value what is current and new, Japanese prize the group (such as the family, the corporation, and the nation) and value tradition. When making schools and educational systems, culture is certainly a real, but hidden, designer.

Source: *Japanese Education Today* (A Report from the U.S. Study of Education in Japan). Washington, D.C.; U.S. Office of Education, 1987.

community had very little to tell us about what makes a good school. In fact, many interpreted the then influential Coleman Report of the mid-sixties[20] to mean that schools—no matter what their characteristics—did not make a difference. All you had to know was the socioeconomic level of the children and you had a very good indicator of what kind of academic achievement was taking place. Now, at least, we have clarified some of the qualities that faculties should strive for, particularly if their aim is academic achievement in the basic skills.

Characteristics of an
Effective School:
Another View

In a ten-year study of 140 schools, Ed Wynne identified a number of characteristics that distinguished successful schools from unsuccessful ones.[21] Here, however, the measure of success was not scores on achievement tests but rather a more holistic view of the outcomes of schooling. Among the characteristics that Wynne's research found to be associated with successful schools were coherence, good communications within the school community, vital subgroups of teachers, a wide range of student incentives, a clear student discipline policy, and an extracurricular program stressing service to others.

Wide understanding of
objectives

COHERENCE   Coherence was the characteristic most commonly associated with successful schools in Wynne's study. By *coherence*, he means that positive elements in the school were pervasive. In contrast, schools lacking coherence were never all bad, but displays of effectiveness or caring seemed mixed with negative elements. Different teachers had very different expectations of children. The discipline policy was inconsistent. One hall would be dirty and the next sparkling. Schools with coherence exhibited not only a similarity of standards, but also a meshing of many elements.

Staff conduct is one such element. In the effective schools, each staff member worked hard at his or her job while at the same time striving to relate that work to the aims of the whole school. A school's staff includes not only teachers and administrators but also counselors, lunchroom attendants, security guards, custodians, and other school employees. In effective schools, the staff and even the students and parents knew what constituted good performance. For example, they all knew that a good teacher "cares" and that caring is displayed by overt conduct, such as regular and timely attendance, well-organized lesson plans, reasonably orderly classes, routinely assigned and appropriately graded homework, friendly but authoritative relations with students, purposeful use of class time, and supportive relations with colleagues. Teachers also set performance goals for students and translated these goals into precise objectives.

Many strategies used

GOOD COMMUNICATIONS   Good coherence was not maintained unless most members of the school community were kept well informed. In the typical school, there are many barriers to adequate information flow, but in the better schools, a variety of strategies were used to overcome the problems. For example, numerous methods or techniques were used for communicating between the school and the home: report cards and notification of quiz and examination results, periodic newsletters to parents, notes from teachers, regular parent-teacher meetings, and diverse activities to encourage parents to visit the school often.

TEACHER SUBGROUPS Good schools tended to create vital subgroups of teachers. These subgroups were assigned relatively clear, plausible goals: to plan and evaluate criteria, to shape homework policies, to redesign report cards, and the like. These tasks gave subgroup members the reward of their own sense of accomplishment in working collectively toward important and valuable ends. Members of the subgroups who failed to perform these tasks received strong group disapproval. Erring staff members tended to change or to seek work somewhere else.

Task-oriented groups

STUDENT INCENTIVES Effective schools were very good at creating a wide variety of schoolwide incentives, such as honor societies and public recognition of achievement, to foster and encourage learning. The weaker schools used some of the same tactics, but with fewer resources and less energy.

Variety of rewards

STUDENT DISCIPLINE Rules for student discipline were precisely and clearly stated and consistently enforced. Punishment for rule infraction was incremental; that is, repeat offenders received harsher punishments. All staff members enforced the rules equally, considering such enforcement to be a professional responsibility. The rules were reviewed periodically, and obsolete and unenforceable provisions were removed.

Clear and consistent rules

One characteristic of an effective school is its ability to offer and promote extracurricular activities like this chess club.

(Elizabeth Crews)

EXTRACURRICULAR ACTIVITIES Extracurricular and student service activities were important in good schools. Most of these activities were socially constructive in that they promoted conduct that was helpful to others. Pro-social behavior (that is, behavior that contributes to the common good in some way) was recognized and rewarded in numerous ways, such as by issuing certificates. In addition, school spirit in good schools was valued by teachers, supervisors, and students.

It would appear, then, that whether or not one is measuring *school effectiveness* by test scores on math and reading tests or by the more holistic measures used by Wynne, certain features stand out in the schools that are most successful in socializing students to behave in ways that the school values. The principal and staff in such schools agree on what they are doing, communicate their expectations to students, consistently enforce rules, and provide an environment conducive to accomplishing the learning tasks and regularly monitoring students' academic progress.

The Good School and You

Other possible qualities

Attempts to answer the question "What is a good school?" are still incomplete. The characteristics just cited are those that have been identified in rather extensive research projects. And studies continue. We have a strong suspicion that there are a number of qualities, not mentioned here, that dramatically contribute to the making of a good school. Among these characteristics are a pervasive sense of curiosity, a passion for excellence, a strong belief in students' capacity to grow, and an environment of kindness and support. Perhaps the reason that the research does not demonstrate these as characteristics of effective schools is that there are not enough schools where these qualities prevail.

Most readers have been, are, or will be observing and working in schools as part of their teacher-training program. We urge you to look for the characteristics and qualities we have discussed as you visit schools. In particular, we urge you to keep these qualities in mind when you are seeking your first teaching position. Often, prospective teachers are so concerned with making a good personal showing that they fail to notice or ask questions about the school in which they want to work. Since one's first teaching assignment is so formative, we urge you to review these qualities when you make that all-important choice.

THE UNFINISHED WORK OF THE SCHOOLS

Understand your school

It is probably clear by now that there is no single satisfactory answer to our question, "What is a school?" This and many other questions that we ask in this book are too large and elaborate to be adequately answered here. We pose them and talk about them anyway to aid you in your investigations into the issues behind the questions. People contemplating careers in education must commit themselves to working out answers to these questions. It seems unlikely that you can make a good career choice if you lack an understanding of the institution you are considering entering. And if you hope to survive and be happy within an institution, you will need to know how it works. You need to know what the institution says it is doing ("We are training future workers" or "We are educating well-rounded citizens prepared to excel in college") and what it actually

The 23rd century scholars made another exceptionally interesting observation. They pointed out that 20th century institutions were caught in a savage cross-fire between uncritical lovers and unloving critics. On the one side, those who loved their institutions tended to smother them in an embrace of death, loving their rigidities more than their promise, shielding them from life-giving criticism. On the other side, there arose a breed of critics without love, skilled in demolition but untutored in the arts by which human institutions are nurtured and strengthened and made to flourish. Between the two, the institutions perished.

— JOHN W. GARDNER —

Today's challenges

does. You need to know what a particular school's expectations of you, as teacher, will be so that you can decide how to respond or if you wish to respond at all. Finally, if you hope to improve the schools, that is, make them better because of your involvement with them, you need a realistic view of what is now going on in the schools and a vision of what the schools can become.

We cannot stress enough that schools are human inventions. As we established earlier, people bring schools into being for particular social purposes. The overall purposes of school are to advance the common good and to help people live happy and successful lives. However, if schools are to serve a society, they must at least keep pace with that society. Many people who are concerned about our schools feel that they are moving very slowly while the rest of society experiences dynamic change. In effect, the schools are out of phase with the society, always being either too far ahead (which is the rarity) or lagging behind (the more normal situation!) the needs of the people they exist to serve.

As happens frequently in times of tension, views polarize in the manner suggested by John Gardner's statement on this page. Nevertheless, the purposes for which schools are brought into being are still vital. People still desire good schools for their children. And, as you will see later in this book, many excellent ideas are being generated and movements are under way for the renewal of our schools.

Some readers may be uncomfortable with the idea that it is their job to renew the schools. Many may feel that becoming a good classroom teacher is enough. Teachers, however, are more than technicians in charge of their classrooms. As professional people, they and their colleagues *must* have a strong and clear voice in deciding how their services are rendered. It follows that the teacher is not responsible simply for his or her own performance, but bears responsibility for the total educational enterprise. To live up to this responsibility requires a deep understanding of the schools and much hard work, but it is the very critical nature of the problems confronting the schools that makes teaching such an exciting occupation today.

In recent decades, schools have become increasingly important in the life of each individual and to the well-being of society. Strong pressures for reforms and the restructuring of schooling are being exerted at this time. Two ideas are coming into sharp focus for Americans: first, our individual and national survival depends on the quality of our educational system; and, second, the majority of our schools are inadequate to the demands of the modern world. What these two issues strongly indicate is that, in the immediate future, education is where the action will be. You have a chance to complete this unfinished work of the schools.

Discussion Questions

1. Can you think of some pieces of information you picked up on the street that you later "unlearned" in school? Can you think of some things you learned in school that your experience later taught you were untrue? Which has happened more often? What is your reaction?
2. To what extent did the schools you attended serve the purposes suggested by the various models we described? Can you suggest any models we have overlooked?

3. Which of the models of schools we have discussed is illustrated by the cartoon on page 245? Is it inappropriate to any of the models we have discussed? Does it seem to you an apt comment on your own education?
4. How do you feel about the school as transmitting the culture rather than "the truth" or "just the facts"? What are some of the problems with the school being a transmitter of cultures? What happens if the state takes a very strong hand in this? Are there any examples in history in which the state used schools to promote a particularly dangerous culture?
5. What are some commonalities of schools that have not been mentioned in the text? What are some of the dissimilarities or unique features from one school to the other that you have observed?
6. Did your elementary school fit into one of Russell C. Doll's categories? Where did it fit and why? If not, how was your school unique? And, perhaps more importantly, why do you think it was unique?
7. This chapter cites several factors or variables that are associated with good schools. Which five are, in your opinion, the most important, and why do you think so?

For Further Reading Freedman, Samuel G. *Small Victories: The Real World of a Teacher, Her Students and Their High School*. New York: Harper and Row, 1990.

> A newspaper reporter spent a year in a high school on New York's Lower East Side, a school struggling to serve the children of the poor. It is a moving, but not particular hopeful, account of life in a school.

Goodlad, John. *A Place Called School: Prospects for the Future*. New York: McGraw-Hill, 1983.

> The author reports on a major study of American schools. Although what Goodlad finds going on in schools will disturb many people, he offers many stimulating suggestions for change.

Grant, Gerald. *The World We Created at Hamilton High*. Cambridge: Harvard University Press, 1988.

> The product of a large research study, this highly readable book describes the evolution of a high school from its birth in 1953 through the mid-eighties. As such, it is a chronicle of where education in this country has been and how our schools became as they are today.

Hampel, Robert. *The Last Little Citadel: American High Schools Since 1940*. Boston: Houghton Mifflin, 1986.

> This book describes the paramount changes that have been made in American high schools in the last half-century. The term *high school* has remained the same, but what goes on inside high schools is radically different.

Johnson, Susan Moore. *Teachers at Work: Achieving Success in Our Schools*. New York: Basic Books, 1990.

> An analysis of the school as workplace. Based on interviews with teachers, this study explores the question of why the best teachers are leaving the classroom.

Lightfoot, Sara Lawrence. *The Good High School: Portraits of Character and Culture.* New York: Basic Books, 1983.

> This book is a highly readable account of life in several high schools. The author provides us with an insight into the minds of a variety of teachers, administrators, and students.

Powell, Arthur G., Eleanor Farrar, and David K. Cohen. *The Shopping Mall High School.* Boston: Houghton Mifflin, 1985.

> This book attempts to answer the question of why high schools are so purposeless and so unable to achieve their goals. The authors' answer is that our high schools have modeled themselves after our shopping malls, trying to be all things to all educational consumers.

Rutter, Michael, et al. *Fifteen Thousand Hours.* Cambridge: Harvard University Press, 1979.

> Based on an extensive study of British schools, this book details the effects of fifteen thousand hours of classroom time. It proves that schools do make a difference.

Schlechty, Phillip C. *Schools for the Twenty-First Century.* San Francisco, CA: Jossey-Bass, Inc., Publishers, 1990.

> This book provides an innovative framework to help leaders identify where changes are needed in curricula; understanding the roles of teachers, students, and principals; grading systems; and classroom schedules in an effort to make schools more responsive to children and society.

Wynne, E. A. *Looking at Schools: Good, Bad, and Indifferent.* Lexington, Mass.: Heath, 1980.

> This book, different from many other reports on effective schools, deals with the qualities of six schools that foster good character among students.

Notes

1. Task Force on Teaching as a Profession, *A Nation Prepared: Teachers for the 21st Century* (New York: Carnegie Corporation, 1986), pp. 14–15.
2. George Bush, *The State of the Union,* The White House, Washington, D.C., January 1990.
3. J. M. Stephens, *The Process of Schooling: A Psychological Examination* (New York: Holt, 1967), p. 8.
4. Susan Moore Johnson, *Teachers at Work* (New York: Basic Books, 1990), p. 142.
5. Arthur Powell, Eleanor Farrar, and David K. Cohen, *The Shopping Mall High School* (Boston: Houghton Mifflin, 1985).
6. Émile Durkheim, *Education and Society* (Glencoe, Ill.: Free Press, 1956), p. 124.
7. George S. Counts, *Education and the Foundations of Freedom* (Pittsburgh: University of Pittsburgh Press, 1962).
8. James Shaver and William Strong, *Facing Value Decisions: Rationale Building for Teachers* (Belmont, Calif.: Wadsworth, 1976.)
9. F. M. Newmann, "Student Engagement and High School Reform," *Educational Leadership* 46 (1989): 34–36.
10. Henry Giroux. "Critical Pedagogy: Cultural Politics and the Discourse of Experience," *Journal of Education* 67, no. 2 (1987): 23–41.
11. Paulo Freire, *The Pedagogy of the Oppressed* (New York: Herder and Herder, 1970).
12. Richard J. Coley and Margaret E. Goertz, *Educational Standards in the 50 States: 1990—A Research Report* (Princeton, N.J.: Educational Testing Service, June 1990), pp. 26–27.

13. Ibid., p. 3.

14. Sharon A. Bobbitt and Frank H. Johnson, *Early Estimates Key Statistics for Public and Private Elementary and Secondary Education: School Year 1990–91* (Washington, D.C.: U.S. Department of Education OERI, December 1990), p. 4.

15. Russell C. Doll, "The Defining and Limits of Educational Innovation and Change," in *Innovative Practices in Teacher Education: Preservice Through Inservice*, ed. Barry L. Klein et al. (Atlanta: Georgia State University, 1977), pp. 374–406.

16. Ibid., p. 384.

17. In preparing this section, we have drawn on the following studies: W. B. Brookover, *Effective Secondary Schools.* (Philadelphia: Research for Better Schools, 1981); R. Edmonds, "Effective Schools for the Urban Poor," *Educational Leadership* 32 (1979): 15–17; M. Rutter et al., *Fifteen Thousand Hours* (Cambridge: Harvard University Press, 1979); J. Stallings and G. Mohlman, *School Policy, Leadership Style, Teacher Change and Student Behavior in Eight Secondary Schools* (prepared for the National Institute of Education, Mountain View, Calif.: Stalling Teaching and Learning Institute, 1981); R. Blum, *Effective Schooling Practices: A Research Synthesis* (Portland, Ore.: Northwest Regional Education Laboratory, April 1984); J. E. Chubb, "Why the Current Wave of School Reform Will Fail," *The Public Interest* 90 Winter, 1988: 28–49; and H. J. Walberg, "Productive Teaching and Instruction: Assessing the Knowledge Base," *Phi Delta Kappan* 71 February 1990: 470–478.

18. B. S. Bloom, *Human Characteristics and School Learning* (New York: McGraw-Hill, 1976.)

19. G. Madaus et al., *School Effectiveness: A Reassessment of the Evidence* (New York: McGraw-Hill, 1980).

20. J. Coleman et al., *Equality of Educational Opportunity* (Washington, D.C.: U.S. Government Printing Office, 1966).

21. Edward A. Wynne, "Looking at Good Schools," *Phi Delta Kappan* 62 (January 1981): 377–381.

CHAPTER PREVIEW

The curriculum of the schools is examined constantly by teachers, school boards, education professors, textbook publishers, and parents. Recently the formal curriculum has come under the scrutiny of national foundations, state and local task forces, and departments of education. What knowledge is most worth knowing? What should be taught in the schools? The 1960s was a decade of much new curriculum development. In the 1970s, many educators questioned the impact and relevance of these curricula for the needs of individual students and society. During the 1980s, the many commission-report recommendations for the most appropriate curriculum for American students and schools brought curricular issues to national attention. The 1990s will likely seek to balance the need for common curricular emphases throughout the country with the cherished belief that curriculum is a responsibility best left to the individual states and school districts.

This chapter emphasizes that:

• The school curriculum, which has evolved over time as a result of shifting purposes, consists of all the organized and intended experiences of the student for which the school accepts responsibility.

• The 1980s marked a time of renewed public attention to the purpose of schooling. Among the issues addressed by commission reports and national studies has been the shape of the formal or explicit curriculum. Reformers often call for a core curriculum to accomplish excellence in education for all students by means of more rigorous academic requirements. Educators ponder what learning should be common for all.

• Major curriculum reforms began to occur in the 1950s and 1960s in science, mathematics, social studies, reading and language arts, and foreign languages. The impact of these reforms has diminished considerably since their heyday in the 1960s and early 1970s. The present curriculum in most subject areas is in a state of flux as the implications of the 1980s reform movement are being assessed.

• Textbooks have such a strong impact on what is taught in the classrooms that some people argue that texts represent a national curriculum.

• Major innovative instructional approaches used across the curriculum include: mastery learning, cooperative learning, critical thinking and problem solving, writing across the curriculum, and microcomputing.

• The relevance of the schools' curricula to individual and societal problems is a continually debated issue.

B aseball, debating, reading, biology . . . Yes, along with love, tolerance, and independence, frustration as well as mathematics and dramatics, values and ceramics, woodshop and poise, history and boredom, auto mechanics and leadership—all are learned in school, some intentionally, and others incidentally or in spite of the teachers' intentions.

Definition of curriculum

We define the *curriculum* as all the organized and intended experiences of the student for which the school accepts responsibility. In other words, the curriculum is not just the intellectual content of the subjects taught, but also the methods used to teach them, the interactions that occur between people, and the school-sponsored activities that contribute to the "life experience."

During your high school years, many daily activities organized under the auspices of the school were probably considered "extracurricular." The formal courses of study—history, science, mathematics, English—were curricular, whereas participation in the football team, cheerleading, Future Teachers Club, or the band belonged to another, lesser category. But, we ask, shouldn't all activities that are school-sponsored and contribute to the growth and development of the students be considered part of the curriculum? We strongly suspect that informal learning experiences are at least as important to intellectual and social development as are the formal courses of study. Consider, for example,

Formal or informal?

the following list of educational goals.* Choose the three or four you consider most important and decide whether each is best achieved in a context of formal courses, informal school experiences, or a combination of the two:

1. develop skills in reading, writing, speaking, and listening
2. develop pride in work and a feeling of self-worth
3. develop good character and self-respect
4. develop a desire for learning now and in the future
5. learn to respect and get along with people with whom we work and live
6. learn how to examine and use information
7. gain a general education
8. learn how to be a good citizen
9. learn about and try to understand the changes that take place in the world
10. understand and practice democratic ideas and ideals
11. learn how to respect and get along with people who think, dress, and act differently
12. understand and practice the skills of family living
13. gain information needed to make job selections
14. learn how to be a good manager of money, property, and resources
15. practice and understand the ideas of health and safety
16. develop skills to enter a specific field of work
17. learn how to use leisure time
18. appreciate culture and beauty in the world

* These eighteen goals were part of a questionnaire given to a sample of Phi Delta Kappans. The results of the questionnaire can be found in the September 1973 issue of *Phi Delta Kappan*, pp. 29–32.

A strong argument could be made that each of these goals is best attained through a combination of formal and informal learning experiences. Some, certainly, cannot be achieved through formal educational channels alone. This chapter examines the formal curriculum, those subjects that are taught in schools and some of the forces and instructional approaches that influence how they are taught. The next chapter, Chapter 9, will examine the informal curriculum, the school and classroom environments that shape the students' experience of life in school.

We begin by studying the formal curriculum because the typical elementary or high school is organized according to subject-matter divisions and most of the efforts that go into curriculum development are still concentrated around traditional subject matter. Some historical background may help explain the current strong emphasis on traditional subject-matter areas.

WHERE DOES THE EXISTING CURRICULUM COME FROM?

Throughout their history, American schools have changed in structure and curriculum to reflect various visions of what children should learn. Michael W. Kirst describes the American public as insisting that "the schools be and do everything for everyone." As a result of generations of organized political action by many groups within our society, the schools have become subject to a series of demands, expectations, and hopes too numerous and overwhelming to be fulfilled with any degree of success. Kirst describes our educational system as "a mixture of successes and performance problems, viewed through a cloud of unrealistic expectations."[1] The eighteen goals you just read will give you an idea of what schools have been expected to accomplish, often with little additional time or resources as new goals have been added to the list. The public's perception of the schools' missions has undergone changes since the early years of schooling in this country. Let's take a look at how the question "What is most worth knowing?" has been answered over the years.

What follows is not a thorough history of American curriculum but a brief overview of the country's changing educational goals that have promoted major curriculum changes. This overview should help you better understand the purposes that influence today's curriculum.

Shifting Purposes: From Colonial Times Through the 1970s

During the colonial period of our history (from approximately 1620 until the 1770s), knowledge of the community's concepts of right conduct and religious belief was considered the most important thing children should learn. During the 1770s, the time of the Revolutionary War, the schools began to focus on political ends. Although not universally available, education was seen as essential to produce a populace literate enough to continue the democratic form of government. Schools extended their curricula beyond the Bible teachings of earlier years to include knowledge necessary for trade and commerce or a university education.

As the common school developed in the mid-1800s (as described in Chapter 4), it was influenced by the purposes of producing a literate and moral citizenry. The curriculum emphasized conservative republican virtues and moral values molded by teachers and the *McGuffey Readers*.

As American society experienced rapid changes in the twentieth century—massive immigration, depression, world wars—the definitions of the formal curriculum reflected equally rapid changes. Those who thought that the schools should prepare students for places in the world of work attempted to shape the curriculum for that purpose. Others, with a progressive philosophy, thought that the schools' curriculum should help children gain knowledge of themselves, develop as individuals, and acquire democratic social competence to reform society. During the so-called progressive education era of the twenties, thirties, and forties, the schools emphasized citizenship and self-adjustment and the curriculum was primarily child-centered or society-centered. By the 1950s, the curriculum of the schools had become broad and diverse in response to these competing demands for vocational preparation, reconstruction of society, and personal development.

Critics of American education in the 1950s used the 1957 launching of Sputnik by the Soviet Union as evidence that American schools were deficient. The American public—which had complacently believed American schools to be far superior to any other country's—reacted against what they considered the "softness" of the curriculum and demanded a return to the "meat and potatoes" of learning—the academic disciplines, with particular emphasis on science and mathematics. As a result, curriculum development during the fifties and sixties became largely discipline-centered.

Prosperity was a major factor in the extensive curricular changes of the fifties and sixties. The middle class saw education as the path to a good life for their children. The more education one received, the more likely one was to earn a good income and enjoy the comforts of life. As a result, more students were competing for college entrance, and middle-class parents wanted to be certain their children were prepared for the growing competition. Because the public was willing to spend increasing amounts of money for education and because of concern for national defense and worldwide prestige, the federal government poured huge amounts of money into curriculum development projects, teacher-training workshops, and research. The influence of the federal government on the development of new curricula during this period cannot be overestimated.

Another contributing factor was the tremendous postwar knowledge explosion, which was forcing new approaches to curriculum planning by making many areas of existing curricula, such as geography, obsolete. In addition, a combination of social and political factors encouraged a new approach to the educational needs of the country, including new emphases on multicultural and bilingual education.

These curriculum trends continued throughout the 1960s and 1970s, but the focus on teaching specific disciplines underwent significant changes during this period. Instrumental in leading these changes was the publication of Jerome Bruner's book, *The Process of Education*.[2] Bruner's ideas were the most profound and elegant expression of the spirit and convictions behind the movement for curriculum change. Bruner's basic thesis was that any discipline could and should be studied, at any level of complexity, in terms of its "structure." Bruner defined the structure of a discipline as the concepts and methods of inquiry that

Progressive education

Massive federal support

Bruner—structure of disciplines

are its most basic components. Instead of studying random facts or incidental phenomena, students should learn the principles that constitute the heart of a discipline; in this way they will *learn how to learn*. Teachers were encouraged

Discovery (inquiry) method — to let students discover meanings for themselves using a *discovery* (or *inquiry*) *method*. The concepts fundamental to the discipline's structure would be studied over and over throughout the school years, but each time from an increasingly complex point of view. The curriculum of the discipline would resemble a spiral; as students moved along the spiral, they would re-encounter familiar concepts in more complex forms.

Bruner's concepts were implemented in numerous curriculum projects that had considerable impact on the public schools' curricula, particularly in the areas of mathematics, biology, chemistry, physics, and foreign languages. These new projects had less impact at the elementary level than at the secondary level, except, notably, in mathematics and possibly science. Elementary school educators objected to planning from the top down, feeling that such an approach

Table 8.1 Curriculum Trends in American Education

Time period	Key events and trends	Curriculum characteristics and emphases	Dominant educational philosophies
1620–Revolutionary War	Education limited by sex and socioeconomic class Northwest Ordinance, first national education law	Religious training Moral development Reading, writing, arithmetic basics Bible teaching	Perennialism
1770–1820s	Revolutionary War (1775–1783) U.S. Constitution ratified (1788) War of 1812 (1812–1815)	Moral development Knowledge necessary for either trade/commerce or university education Literacy to continue democratic form of government	Perennialism
1820s–1880s	Establishment of common schooling Civil War (1861–1865) Morrill Land Grant Act (1862)	Basic tools of literacy for practical education Conservative republican virtues and moral values (*McGuffey Reader*) Cultivation of American identity and loyalty Melting pot theme	Perennialism

(table continues next page)

Table 8.1 Curriculum Trends in American Education (*cont.*)

Time period	Key events and trends	Curriculum characteristics and emphases	Dominant educational philosophies
1880s–1950s	World War I (1914–1918) World War II (1939–1945) Great Depression (1930s)	Child-centered, not subject-centered, curriculum Activities and experiences rather than verbal and literacy skills Cooperative rather than individual learning activities Citizenship and self-adjustment	Progressivism
1950s–1970s	Launching of Soviet satellite Sputnik (1957) Cold War *Brown* v. *Board of Education* (1954) Elementary and Secondary Education Act (1965) Vietnam War and protests Education for All Handicapped Children Act (PL 94-142) (1975)	*1950s–1960s* Structure of the discipline Discovery method of teaching *1970s* Career education Mainstreaming Multicultural education Flexible curriculum—many electives	Existentialism Essentialism
1980s–early 1990s	America's preeminence in world economy declines Educational reform reports End of Cold War War in Persian Gulf	Back-to-basics movement Core curriculum Strengthening of academic requirements Academic excellence Mainstreaming Multicultural education	Essentialism Perennialism

failed to take sufficient account of the developmental processes of young children and that it separated rather than integrated the disciplines.

By the 1970s, reaction against the structure of the disciplines approach became more vocal. As youth made demands for freedom of choice in the educational system, secondary schools responded with a more flexible curriculum and a proliferation of electives. The curriculum of the 1970s was described as a smorgasbord, a "do your own thing" collection of courses with little focus or balance. In the 1970s it seemed that no particular knowledge was considered any better than any other knowledge.

Curriculum Reform in the 1980s

A Nation at Risk

The 1980s came to be characterized as the decade of educational reform prompted by nationwide commission reports. In 1983, such a report, *A Nation at Risk: The Imperative for Educational Reform,*[3] grabbed the nation's attention, calling for (1) more academic course requirements for all high school students, (2) more stringent college entrance requirements, (3) upgraded and updated textbooks, (4) longer school days and years, and (5) a career-ladder plan for teachers, including higher salaries and peer evaluation. This publication spurred the states to engage in extensive educational reform. It was probably the most influential educational report of the last half of the twentieth century. It was followed closely by John Goodlad's *A Place Called School: Prospects for the Future,* Ernest L. Boyer's *High School: A Report on Secondary Education in America,* and the National Science Foundation's *Educating Americans for the 21st Century,* to name just a few of the many subsequent reports. Within months of the first reports, over 175 state task forces formed to address issues such as career ladders for teachers, merit pay, professional development, evaluation and testing of teachers, and higher academic standards for students. This last issue especially has influenced the curriculum now offered at elementary and secondary schools.

BACK-TO-BASICS MOVEMENT During the late 1970s and early 1980s, a perceived decline in the quality of education, as evidenced by declining scores on standardized tests, led to a *back-to-basics movement.* To the degree that this movement had spokespersons, they were among both the very best and the least educated people in the country. Although what they were striving to achieve was not always clear, their disenchantment with the public schools and their desire to return to a more rigorous, more traditional curriculum was evident and often

Rigorous, traditional curriculum

stated quite sharply. Proponents urged more emphasis on basic subjects, particularly reading, writing, and arithmetic, but also science, history, geography, and grammar. Rather than believing schools should provide more electives for students to choose from, back-to-basics supporters wanted students to take more traditional academic courses, such as history and foreign languages, and more courses with rigorous demands and standards. They wanted the schools not only to teach content, but also to help children acquire the capacity to work hard. They believed that to foster a society made up of strong citizens, our schools must turn out individuals able to take on difficult tasks that they can see through

The back-to-basics curriculum of the 1970s and early 1980s emphasized the teaching of reading, writing, and mathematics.

(Richard S. Orton/The Picture Cube)

to completion. Back-to-basics proponents saw the schools as catering to the students' desire for entertainment and escapism. They wanted the schools to demand more orderly and disciplined student behavior. They wanted the authority and centrality of the teacher to be reasserted, and they desired a more structured teaching style. Finally, back-to-basics advocates frequently wanted the schools to return to the teaching of basic morality and, in particular, the virtue of patriotism.

Excellence in education

Although the term *back-to-basics* is seldom heard now, many more educators than were involved in that movement have called for similar kinds of school reforms in the name of "excellence in education." The recommendations for greater academic rigor in public school education have been adopted by many state legislatures. The early advocates of the back-to-basics movement offended many educators with their pressure tactics, hostile language, and the deep strain of idealistic nostalgia in their desire to return to a simpler society; but behind much of their rhetoric were ideas and aspirations that most educators believe in. For years, the schools have been asked to expand the curriculum with more and more subjects. Each time a social priority or social ill has surfaced, the schools have been expected to add a new entry to the curriculum and thus solve the problem. Many people inside and outside education believe that the schools have attempted to be "all things to all people," and that it shows. If nothing else, then, the back-to-basics movement, as subsumed in the more recent excellence-in-education movement, has refocused the public and educators on the primary mission of the schools: to help children develop the necessary skills to live good and productive lives and contribute to the well-being of society.

CURRICULAR ISSUES AND REFORM REPORTS IN THE 1980S On the heels of the back-to-basics movement, the pendulum of curricular opinion began to swing toward a core curriculum providing a similar education for all students. Shunning the 1970s concept of any knowledge being as worthy as any other knowledge, prominent educators in the 1980s believed that a core of knowledge representing the best human thought and invention can be identified and taught to every student. Although agreement on what constitutes this core varies, some general notions are common to this essentialist perspective of the curriculum.

Core curriculum

In response to the realization that the schools have been asked to do too much, curriculum reformers of the 1980s attempted to define some unifying major purposes for the schools. The reports written by these reformers strongly supported the development of students' academic competencies. The College Board identified five basic academic competencies expected for college entrants:

EDUCATION SUMMIT

In September 1989, President George Bush convened an historic education summit in Charlottesville, Virginia, home of the University of Virginia. The meeting was historic because it was only the third time in history that a president of the United States had called together all of the states' governors to address an issue of national importance, and it was the first time that education had been the focus of such a gathering. With all of the cabinet members and all but one of the nation's governors present, a "Jeffersonian compact" was forged by the administration and the governors. This compact was essentially an agreement that the time had come, for the first time in U.S. history, to establish clear national performance goals that will make the country internationally competitive.

By February 1990, the Bush administration and the governors had established six national education goals to be achieved by the year 2000:

1. All children in America will start school ready to learn.

2. The high school graduation rate will increase to at least 90 percent.
3. American students will leave grades four, eight and twelve having demonstrated competency in challenging subject matter, including English, mathematics, science, history, and geography; and every school in America will insure that all students learn to use their minds well so that they may be prepared for responsible citizenship, further learning, and productive employment in our modern economy.
4. U.S. students will be first in the world in science and mathematics achievement.
5. Every adult American will be literate and will possess the knowledge and skills necessary to compete in a global economy and to exercise the rights and responsibilities of citizenship.
6. Every school will be free of drugs and violence and will offer a disciplined environment conducive to learning.

How realistic do you think these goals are? Which do you believe will be the most difficult to achieve? What policies or strategies need to be enacted if these goals are to be achieved?

reading, writing, mathematics, reasoning, and studying.[4] A comparative list developed for those entering the world of work after high school reveals similar expectations. John Goodlad in *A Place Called School* (1984) rejected university and state requirements for specific courses as curricular guidelines but still argued for better balance and overlap among the fields of study.[5] He recommended that each student complete a combination of common courses and electives within five domains: mathematics and science, literature and language, society and social studies, the arts, and the vocations. Goodlad also recommended that the core comprise not a common set of topics but a common set of concepts, principles, skills, and ways of knowing.

CULTURAL LITERACY

The American schools have traditionally played a central role in instilling the ideas and attitudes that maintain our pluralistic society as "one nation." Thomas Jefferson, who quite consciously thought of himself as a teacher, believed that the American experiment would fail without a universal educational system to develop in individuals their notions of self and their relationships to one another. Speaking of education, Jefferson said, "No other sure foundation can be derived for the preservation of freedom and happiness." The schools were, and continue to be, seen as part of our national fabric. They have helped to weave the many ethnic and religious strains together to make a seamless national garment. Or at least that's the theory.

Questions are being raised now about whether the schools today are providing a shared understanding of our culture, history, and traditions. Does the current curriculum of our schools reflect our national diversity to the exclusion of our national unity? Critics argue that the schools have focused on celebrating national diversity and pluralism but have failed to help students develop a shared national identity and common cultural framework. In effect, the schools concentrate on teaching verbal and numerical literacy but neglect cultural literacy. The advocates of cultural literacy hope to reform the school curriculum to rescue what they call "cultural illiterates."

A *cultural illiterate* is someone who is unaware of the central ideas, stories, scientific knowledge, events, and personalities of a culture. For instance, in our culture people could be considered culturally illiterate if they did not know who Benedict Arnold, Nathaniel Hawthorne, and F. Scott Fitzgerald were; if they had never heard of Henry the Eighth, Attila, Cleopatra, or Alexander the Great; if they had no awareness of supply and demand, of gravity, of ecological balance; if they did not understand literary references to Cain and Abel, David and Goliath, Cinderella, Pinocchio, Sodom and Gomorrah, Robin Hood, and Hamlet; if they had never heard of and did not know the significance of Troy, Jerusalem, Mecca, Little Bighorn, Bull Run, and Selma; or if they did not recognize such patriotic songs as the "Battle Hymn of the Republic," "America the Beautiful," and "This Land Is Your Land."

Influential in the call for greater attention to cultural literacy is University of Virginia English professor E. D. Hirsch, Jr. He defines such literacy as not just a technical proficiency with an endless list of factual knowledge, but an acquaintance with the background knowledge that authors assume general readers have. Although much cultural literacy is gained at home, a great deal of it, according to Hirsch, "comes from the first ten or eleven years of schooling. Further, since many poor and minority and immigrant children do not receive cultural literacy at home, it is especially important that they receive it in school. Otherwise, they will be permanently 'out of it.' "

What does this mean for the school curriculum? All of the specific implications are not obvious. But the debate over the meaning of cultural literacy again raises the question of schooling's purposes as expressed in the formal curriculum.

Other reports, like *Educating Americans for the 21st Century* (1983) and *Science for All Americans* (1989),[6] emphasized the need for greater scientific and technological literacy. The National Science Foundation, sponsors of the first report named, recommended that all secondary students should be required to take at least three years of mathematics and of science and technology. The foundation emphasized that all students need knowledge of science and technology to inform them about issues such as the role of nuclear energy and the threat of acid rain. A fundamental educational problem is, in Stephen Graubard's opinion, "that scientific knowledge and understanding by any reasonable standard, is so uncommon among Americans of all ages and races today that it is no exaggeration to speak of mass illiteracy in the sciences."[7] The authors of the National Science Foundation study maintained that the "new" basics of reading, writing, arithmetic, communication, problem solving, and scientific and technological literacy are needed by all students.

Greater scientific literacy

Ernest L. Boyer's *High School* (1983)[8] focused attention on mastery of language as a first priority for the school curriculum. Boyer believes that the three-track vocational, academic, and general system should be abolished. A core curriculum would include literature, arts, foreign languages, history, civics, science, mathematics, and technology. According to Boyer's report, four goals appropriate for the schools are developing students' capacity to think critically and communicate effectively, helping students learn about themselves and their heritage, preparing students for work and further education, and helping students fulfill their social and civic obligations.

Boyer—emphasis on language

Mortimer Adler, author of *The Paideia Proposal* (1982) and *The Paideia Program,* (1984),[9] also speaks for a group of educators recommending a common course of study for all students. Like Boyer, the Paideia Group based its

Paideia Proposal

DIALOGUE

Kevin: I have mixed feelings about the cultural literacy movement.

Jim: How so?

Kevin: I agree that the country and its people need a common identity, a sense of who we are as Americans. But don't you remember how narrow the curriculum was before the seventies, when minority history and literature started appearing in textbooks? I don't want to go back to those days.

Jim: I think I see what you mean. Before the seventies, students weren't able to read about African-American scientists, or Hispanic authors, or women athletes, for that matter. But maybe we've gone too far. It's hard to communicate with somebody who isn't acquainted with the basics of America's history, literature, music, inventions, sports—what makes America America.

Kevin: O.K., O.K., I love my mom and eat apple pie too. But isn't part of "what makes America America" its interweaving of diverse cultures? After all, wouldn't life in America be different without tacos and Crispus Attucks and LeRoi Jones and Kate Chopin and . . .

Jim: We agreed, though, that the schools can't teach everything.

Kevin: Good point! Why don't we work this out later, in the book's epilogue?

recommendations on the assumptions that education is a lifelong activity, that every child can learn, and that each child deserves the best education, which is currently available only to those on a high track. Arguing against a differentiated curriculum and for a general education, Adler and his colleagues believe that all students should be prepared to continue learning. They believe the schools should help students with self-development, citizenship, and the basic skills common to all work. Basic schooling should be general and liberal, nonspecial-

Table 8.2 Summary of Major Educational Reform Report Recommendations

Author/name of report	Major recommendations
National Commission on Excellence in Education, *A Nation at Risk* (1983)	More academic course requirements for all high school students More stringent college entrance requirements Upgraded and updated textbooks Longer school days and years Career-ladder plan for teachers, including higher salaries and peer evaluation
John Goodlad, *A Place Called School* (1984)	All students should complete common courses in five domains: mathematics and science; literature and language; society and social studies; the arts; and the vocations The core should contain a common set of concepts, principles, skills, and ways of knowing
Ernest Boyer, *High School* (1983)	Mastery of language should be the first priority for the school curriculum Abolish the three-track system: vocational, academic, and general Institute a core curriculum that would include literature, arts, foreign languages, history, civics, science, mathematics, and technology
Mortimer Adler, *The Paideia Proposal* (1982) and *The Paideia Program* (1984)	Recommends a common core of courses Schools should help students with self-development, citizenship, and the basic skills common to all work Basic schooling should be general and liberal, nonspecialized, and nonvocational
National Science Foundation, *Educating Americans for the 21st Century* (1983)	Emphasizes need for greater scientific and technological literacy All students be required to take at least 3 years of mathematics and of science and technology Declares the new "basics" to be reading, writing, arithmetic, communication, problem solving, and scientific and technological literacy

ized, and nonvocational, in the Paideia Group's view. Courses within the group's proposed program would be required of all students; in the course of the program all students would acquire organized knowledge, develop intellectual skills, and enlarge their understanding, insight, and aesthetic appreciation.

We see, then, that during the 1980s educators wrestled with traditionally troublesome curricular questions. What knowledge is best for all? Should a core curriculum consist of specified subjects? Or can the core be considered a list of competencies, skills, or concepts? Who should decide the content of a core? Difficult decisions face schools in the 1990s as they try to provide a curriculum that answers these questions without again attempting to do too much with little hope of success.

WHAT IS THE PRESENT CURRICULUM?

Looking at the courses of study prescribed by the fifty states, one discovers that the similarities far outweigh the differences. Parts of this chapter discuss some reasons for this phenomenon, such as the influence of national reform movements and the uniformity of available textbooks. But for now, let's examine what is presently taught in elementary and secondary schools across the country. At both levels the curriculum is organized into subject-matter areas, which ordinarily are reading, language arts and English, mathematics, science, social studies, foreign languages, the fine arts, physical education and recreation, and electives and vocational education.

Reading

Reports of millions of illiterate or functionally illiterate American adults have generated renewed interest in the teaching of reading. Illiterates over age eighteen number at least 27 million, approximately one out of six U.S. adults. Their ranks increase by 2 million each year.[10] The economic impact of illiteracy in this country has been estimated at $6 billion annually, in the form of illiteracy-related welfare costs and unemployment compensation. This figure does not include the cost to society of crime, much of which may be related to the functional illiteracy of many criminals.[11] The Commission on Reading, a group of educators responsible for the 1985 report *Becoming a Nation of Readers*,[12] notes our society's need for increasingly high levels of literacy among its citizens, a need challenging the schools to surpass literacy goals arrived at by comparisons to past generations or foreign countries. The Commission on Reading offers hope, however, that America's need can be met by increased attention to reading instruction and a greater reliance upon research-tested techniques.

Current Issues

Several issues emerge in discussions of reading education. The debate over two word-recognition techniques—*phonics* (instruction in the relationships between letters and speech sounds) and the *whole-word method* (which emphasizes the identification of whole words at a glance)—has given way to a more eclectic approach with the emphasis on the teaching of reading in context. Regarding reading comprehension, many reading experts emphasize that comprehension is a matter of construction. To comprehend a text requires readers to coordinate information from the text, from the context in which they read, and from their background information relevant to the text. Reading lessons, then, should prepare students for a reading selection, assist their reading, and conclude with discussions that help them construct meaning.

Recent studies have also criticized basal readers, narrow interpretations of a child's readiness to read, and wasted class time consumed with worksheets. Instead, parents and teachers are encouraged to read aloud to children[13] and to use language-experience approaches that encourage children to talk about what is important to them and, with the aid of adults or older students, to write, read, illustrate, and dramatize their own stories.[14] This approach to reading instruction is called the *whole-language* curriculum. Whole-language proponents see reading as part of general language development, not as a skill isolated from listening, speaking, and writing. The whole-language approach "(1) provides a literate environment that stimulates and supports the use of language; (2) integrates language arts skills and knowledge by requiring their use in real situations; (3) emphasizes the pupil's own oral language; (4) uses children's literature to develop an interest in reading and broaden reading horizons; and (5) stresses the

Whole-language curriculum

EDUCATION: A WORLD VIEW

• •

NEW ZEALAND'S APPROACH TO READING AND LANGUAGE

New Zealand has one of the world's highest literacy rates. How has this island nation with a diverse student body been so successful? Barbara Mabbett, of the Ministry of Education in New Zealand, explains that schools are typically small, with over half serving under 120 students. With such small numbers, mixed-level teaching is common.

Parental involvement is also emphasized. Parents are encouraged to participate in home-school associations, to help with class outings, to raise funds, and to assist in reading, language, and art classes. A 1989 reform established that parents should form the majority on every school governing body.

New Zealand has a national curriculum consisting of syllabi that describe aims and objectives for each subject, various teaching approaches, and suggestions for evaluation and assessment. No basals are used in teaching reading. Teachers are given extensive control in choosing their own resources and materials. The Department of Ed-

ucation provides exemplary materials, including the "Ready to Read" books. These approximately sixty-five books are the result of a nationwide invitation for original scripts of "real books." These scripts have been trialled, edited, and illustrated to form much of the framework for early reading programs. Teachers then augment these books with other books from around the world.

A handbook, *Reading in Junior Classes,* describes some key principles in learning to read and serves as a reference to teachers. Some of these principles include the importance of integrating reading, writing, and talking; reading for meaning; using natural idiomatic language in learning to read; and using a combination of teaching approaches to address the many ways that people learn. However, this handbook serves only as a reference: the exchange of ideas among teachers is considered the most important element in improving instruction. Inservices, workshops, and conferences are all seen as vital to promoting good teaching.

Barbara Mabbett, "The New Zealand Story," *Educational Leadership,* 47, 6: 59–61. Reprinted with permission of the Association for Supervision and Curriculum Development and the author. Copyright © 1990 by ASCD. All rights reserved.

functional uses of language."[15] In reaction to the criticism against basal readers, many textbook publishers are now publishing literature-based reading programs, as alternatives to basal readers, that use real literature and do not teach skills in isolation.

Variety of method seems the key to reading instruction; no one method teaches all children. Without doubt, the success of the reading curriculum is central to students' success in all other curricular areas. In Ernest Boyer's words, "Language is not just another subject. It is the means by which all other subjects are pursued."[16]

Language Arts and English

The *language arts* program seeks to develop in children the skills of reading,* writing, speaking, and listening, as well as a knowledge of culture as represented in literature. The importance of language arts cannot be overemphasized since no subject can be successfully studied without adequate language skills. Most elementary language arts programs share the common goal of developing in the student the following abilities:

1. to communicate clearly in oral and written forms
2. to understand and use oral and written language in both receptive and expressive forms
3. to use comprehension and problem-solving strategies
4. to decode new words and encode or spell words in a variety of reading and written situations
5. to use research and study skills to interpret content in subject-matter areas
6. to express, interpret, and enjoy creative thoughts
7. to appreciate language and literature in a variety of life situations[17]

Language arts curricula must be organized to foster continuous growth and increasing sophistication in the four major skill areas during the elementary years, and graded elementary schools ordinarily employ sequential curricula. Along with other curriculum areas, language arts and English underwent revision in the 1960s. One thrust of this revision was to make English more relevant and meaningful to culturally diverse students by using more examples of contemporary writing, including selections by African-American authors. Standard English and traditional grammar gave way to exploring acceptable alternative grammatical structures without prescribing proper and improper usage. English classes offered improvised drama, imaginative writing, personal response to literature, and informal classroom discussion.

Shifting emphases

Education in language arts and English has drawn considerable criticism in recent years because many graduating students have found they do not possess the basic reading and writing skills needed for employment. College entrance

---

* Although reading is considered a language arts topic, we have chosen to treat it separately in this chapter.

exam scores in the 1970s and early 1980s declined in verbal skills, then rose slightly during the mid-1980s, and have since stabilized, but they are still well below the national averages of the 1960s and early 1970s.

Discontent with student verbal skills helped lead to the back-to-basics movement of the late 1970s. The ensuing emphasis on a return to the teaching of fundamental skills in more traditional ways had considerable impact on the language arts curriculum in many school districts. The result was more reading of classical literature, more learning of traditional grammar, and more emphasis on formal rather than personal writing. English educators who advocate teaching writing as a process, reading young adult novels in the classroom, using linguistic-based exercises to improve writing, and communicating as an expression of ideas and feelings often find themselves in opposition to those calling for a return to hard-cover anthologies and traditional grammar workbooks. In addition, many reactionary religious and political groups have objected to the reading material taught in schools. Books written for adolescent audiences are often subject to criticism by these groups, sometimes on grounds of sexual explicitness, and

Book banning

book banning has risen in America over the past ten to fifteen years, with such classics as J. D. Salinger's *The Catcher in the Rye* and *The Diary of Anne Frank* being removed from both school libraries and reading lists in a number of school districts.

Among the issues concerning language arts teachers today are selecting literature relevant to student interests yet representative of an accepted literary tradition; instructing critical thinking; encouraging writing across the curriculum (discussed later in this chapter); integrating the various language arts by, for example, linking reading and writing or speaking, listening, and reading; and maintaining a balance between composition and literature in the curriculum.

Concern still exists regarding American students' abilities to read and write well. A 1988 assessment from the National Assessment of Educational Progress indicates that at all grade levels students spend little time reading or writing, whether in or out of school.[18] According to the report, half of the students in all grades reported reading ten or fewer pages each day for schoolwork. Only half of the twelfth-graders reported writing more than two papers in the previous six weeks, and most said their writing consisted of only a few paragraphs.

Recent techniques

Helping students become better writers has been a vexing problem for teachers for many years. The recent impact of the National Writing Project, teaching teachers to join their students in "writing process" methods, has been significant. Another breakthrough appears to be occurring as students learn to use microcomputers as word processors. The microcomputers allow students to receive feedback from the teacher and other students, to make multiple revisions, and even to check their spelling before printing their papers. Teachers using this procedure with their students report excellent results and increased enthusiasm for writing among their students.

Mathematics

"New math"

Before the 1950s, schools emphasized student mastery of basic computational skills. In the 1960s, a new type of mathematics curriculum—known as the *new math*—was developed. It viewed mathematics as a language that both communicates ideas about numbers and describes the quantitative aspects of ideas and objects. As a result, the new math stressed *structure* rather than drill and computational skills. The new math tended to be abstract, and for the average student its conceptual theories were of little practical use.

Although some die-hard traditionalists advocate returning to the teaching of good old 'rithmetic, doing so seems both unwise and unlikely. If a renewed emphasis on computational skills is needed, the emphasis should occur within the new curricular emphases of the past thirty years, not by a return to an outmoded content.

Both traditional and new math are found in today's secondary schools. Traditional math courses featuring drill and practice, computation, and memorization are taken by non-college-bound students. College-bound students still take modern mathematics, algebra, geometry, and optional fourth-year courses that place strong emphasis on structure, learning by discovery, definitions, properties, sets, rigor, statistics, calculus, trigonometry, and other abstract concepts.

In 1989 two national reports on mathematics education called for dramatic changes in both the curriculum and the instructional practices in our schools. Among the recommended changes are:

National report recommendations

- coming to see mathematics as a helping discipline, not as a subject that sorts and rejects students on their inabilities to perform

- moving away from students' passively receiving instruction to their active involvement, supported by technologies such as computers and calculators, in investigating numerical, spatial, and data-related situations

- involving students in constructing their conceptions of mathematics through the use of manipulatives, discussing the results of their investigations, and writing the results of their experiences

EDUCATION: A WORLD VIEW

. . . .

MATHEMATICS PROFICIENCY: CAN THE UNITED STATES BE NUMBER ONE?

The Bush administration, supported by the nation's governors, set a national goal for American students to be first in the world in mathematics by the year 2000. Take a look at Table 8.3. Do you think being first in mathematics is a feasible goal? What would it take for the United States to achieve this goal?

After taking international standardized tests in mathematics, students were asked to respond "yes" or "no" to the statement "I am good at mathematics." What nationality of students do you think indicated the highest

percentage of positive responses? Which students do you think reported the lowest percentage of positive responses? You may be surprised. Sixty-eight percent of students in the United States indicated they were good at mathematics—the highest percentage of any nationality of students. Korean students came in last in the percentage of students who felt they were good at mathematics. What are some implications of these findings for improving the mathematics proficiency of American students?

Thomas Ellinger and Deborah Carlson, "Education in Korea: Doing Well and Feeling Bad," *Network News and Views* 9 (October 1990): 91–92. Reprinted from *Foreign Service Journal,* June 1990.

Table 8.3 Percentages of 13-year-old Students in Six Countries Performing At or Above Each Level of the Mathematics Proficiency Scale: 1988

Country/province	300 (Add and subtract)	400 (Simple problems)	500 (Two-step problems)	600 (Complex concepts)	700 (Advanced concepts)
Korea	100	95	78	40	5
Quebec (French)	100	97	73	22	2
British Columbia	100	95	69	24	2
Quebec (English)	100	97	67	20	1
New Brunswick (English)	100	95	65	18	1
Ontario (English)	99	92	58	16	1
New Brunswick (French)	100	95	58	12	<1
Spain	99	91	57	14	1
United Kingdom	98	87	55	18	2
Ireland	98	86	55	14	<1
Ontario (French)	99	85	40	7	0
United States	97	78	40	9	1

Source: International Assessment of Educational Progress, *A World of Differences, International Assessment of Mathematics and Science,* 1989. Educational Testing Service. Reprinted by permission of Educational Testing Service, the copyright owner.

- using a variety of instructional formats (small groups, individual explorations, peer instruction, whole-class discussions, project work, and cooperative learning strategies)
- exploring alternative reasoning strategies and methods for reaching solutions rather than rushing to the "one right way"[19]

Use of microcomputers

The use of calculators and computers will certainly increase in the future as mathematics education focuses less on computational skills and more on developing concepts, relationships, structures, and problem-solving skills. Moreover, the use of microcomputers and computer programming in mathematics classes adds a great deal of practical utility for many students. Not only do the computers create interest in the curriculum, but students are receiving valuable experience that may prove useful as they seek jobs. Business leaders polled by the College Board agree that secondary students should receive keyboard experience, gain exposure to various kinds of equipment and programming languages, and study a broad range of computer applications.[20]

Integration of skills

In addition to using technology and emphasizing problem solving, mathematics programs have been moving away from the traditional compartmentalization of arithmetic, algebra, geometry, calculus, and so on. As newer topics—probability, statistics, computer science—are emphasized, course designers have begun to integrate a variety of mathematics skills and topics in one course or

Mathematics curriculum can teach students to construct their own conceptions of mathematics, as shown here through the use of compasses in an elementary math class.
(Susan Lapides 1991)

across several courses. The blending of mathematics with other subject areas, including consumer economics and personal finance, will continue as a trend toward broadening students' applications of their mathematical understandings and skills.

Science

There's good news and bad news concerning science education in the United States. The bad news is that American youth don't know much science; the good news is that the country is reaching consensus on how to remedy the problem.

Achievement very low

According to a synthesis report of the National Assessment of Educational Progress (1989), science achievement for nine-, thirteen-, and seventeen-year-olds is dismally low. For example:

- Science achievement of seventeen-year-olds in 1986 was well below that in 1969, and that of thirteen-year-olds was below that in 1970.

- Only 7 percent of seventeen-year-olds had the knowledge and skills needed to do well in college-level science courses.

- More than half the nation's seventeen-year-olds were inadequately prepared either for jobs that require technical skills or to benefit substantially from specialized on-the-job training.

- U.S. students rank near the bottom in science achievement among seventeen developed nations.[21]

Numerous reports have concluded that science education has become a passive learning experience, dominated by teacher lectures based on textbooks and measured by standardized tests that demonstrate how well students have memorized facts rather than how well they can apply concepts. As a result of such instruction, student interest in science typically drops off before high school.

Two major questions drive the science education reform: Where will the next generation of scientists come from? and How can all students be prepared to make informed judgments about such critical and science-based issues as environmental pollution, energy sources, and biotechnology? The school reform of the mid-1980s that required students to take more science did not address what the goals and purposes of science education are and how we can achieve a high scientific literacy for the greatest number of students.

PROJECT 2061   In 1985 the American Association for the Advancement of Science initiated Project 2061 (named for the year that Halley's Comet is expected to return) with the goal of reforming science, mathematics, and technology education. The first report of a three-phase project, *Science for All Americans* (1989), mentioned earlier in this chapter, defines scientific literacy and presents recommendations on the scientific knowledge, skills, and attitudes that all students should acquire in their education from kindergarten through high school. Even though some of the content is already covered in today's curriculum, the report calls for fundamentally different coverage than current practice.

Call for major reform

First, boundaries between academic disciplines, such as biology, chemistry, and geology, should be reduced and linkages among them emphasized. Second, students need to memorize fewer facts than in today's science, mathematics, and technology courses. Ideas and thinking skills are emphasized over specialized vocabulary and memorized procedures. Third, the curriculum should help students develop a set of cogent views of the world by including such concepts and principles as the structure and evolution of the universe; basic concepts related to matter, energy, force, and motion; the human life cycle; physical and mental health; medical techniques; social change and conflict; and the mathematics of symbols.

Phase II of Project 2061 will lay out the blueprint for action by creating a national K–12 science curriculum with choices that can be made at the local level. During Phase III, which is expected to take ten to fifteen years, school districts will create strategies to implement the curricula and other science education reforms.

A greater consensus exists about science instruction at the elementary school level than at the secondary school level. Unlike the science curriculum reforms of the 1960s, recent efforts have started at the primary rather than at the secondary grades. These efforts are aimed at getting children to become scientists by defining problems, asking questions, developing hypotheses, observing phenomena, recording data, and checking findings through repeated trials.

Teaching fewer concepts more thoroughly and encouraging critical thinking skills are other characteristics of these efforts.

S/T/S approach

One popular approach uses the term *science/technology/society (S/T/S)* to describe its programs. Students start by investigating problems that affect their communities or by exploring technology. Thus the approach draws on students' natural curiosity and interest. The National Science Foundation has funded several projects in the past few years to promote S/T/S approaches.

Less consensus exists at the secondary school level, where science tends to be split up into specific and somewhat isolated disciplines. Some of the secondary-level issues that science educators have identified are updating the biology curriculum, linking the separate disciplines (biology, chemistry, physics) to each other and with mathematics, and changing scheduling of the high school day to allow longer lab sessions. It also appears likely that the goals of Project 2061 will have a strong effect on what and how science is taught in the secondary school.

Social Studies

Definition

Social studies—the study of people, their ideas, actions, and relationships—is not a discipline in the same sense as mathematics or science, although it draws on the various social science disciplines (history, geography, political science, economics, psychology, sociology, and anthropology), as well as on religion, literature, and the arts for its content and methods of inquiry. (A *discipline* has been defined as an area of inquiry containing a distinctive body of concepts and principles, with techniques for exploring the area and for correcting and expanding the body of knowledge.[22]) Unlike in the sciences and mathematics, fundamental concepts and processes in social studies have not been identified and agreed on by curriculum builders. History has traditionally been the leading discipline of the social studies at both the elementary and secondary levels, and although some inroads have been made by other disciplines, it still remains dominant.

For the past forty or fifty years the pattern of social studies courses taken in high school has remained relatively standard. Civics and world history are traditionally offered to ninth- and tenth-graders. American history is usually taken in the eleventh grade. Elective courses like American government, economics, and sociology are available for twelfth-graders. A trend in secondary social studies education is the addition of more required courses. Although U.S. history remains a pervasive course of study in middle and secondary programs, courses in citizenship, world or global studies, and geography are gaining prominence.[23]

Curriculum boring, incoherent

In the elementary schools, social studies receives little attention, serving primarily as another opportunity to teach reading and writing skills. Where social studies is taught, history and geography are the dominant disciplines. The approach at all levels is a textbook-centered curriculum, and many of these textbooks are bland, boring, and banal.

Today the social studies curriculum at both the elementary and secondary levels is a hodgepodge of different approaches and lacks coherence. Recognizing this problem, the National Commission on Social Studies in the Schools issued in 1989 a report describing a sequential social studies curriculum spanning the elementary and secondary grades. This report stated the goals of the social studies curriculum as enabling students to develop:

1. civic responsibility and active civic participation
2. perspectives on their own life experiences so they see themselves as part of the larger human adventure in time and place
3. a critical understanding of the history, geography, economic, political, and social institutions, traditions, and values of the United States as expressed in both their unity and diversity
4. an understanding of other peoples and the unity and diversity of world history, geography, institutions, traditions, and values
5. critical attitudes and an analytical perspective appropriate to the analysis of the human condition[24]

American students ignorant

Although national assessment data reveal that American high school students are woefully ignorant of both history and geography, social studies does not seem to have the same pressure and momentum for reform as does science and mathematics. Whether the report from the National Commission on Social Studies in the Schools helps to reverse this trend remains to be seen.

Lack of momentum, however, does not mean there is no debate over what needs to be done. Some social studies educators emphasize the multidisciplinary nature of social studies; others lament the loss of a required program of history courses. Some groups favoring more history in the curriculum encourage teachers and students to make creative and critical inquiries into history, avoiding the rote memorization that has so often characterized history learning.*

Current issues

Currently a major debate rages over whether the social studies curriculum overemphasizes European history and culture at the expense of Asian, African, and Latin American history and culture. Some large urban school districts, such as Detroit and Washington, D.C., are planning to implement an Afrocentric curriculum in an attempt to engage the predominantly African-American student body in the study of their cultural heritage. Critics of this approach argue that if these students are denied access to the European history and culture, they will be disadvantaged in participating in mainstream American culture, which derives much of its cultural heritage from Europe. This debate is likely to continue during the 1990s.

Civic learning or *civic intelligence* is another issue gaining the attention of social studies educators. Advocates of this new focus call for courses to acquaint a racially and culturally diverse student population with the heritage common to the American democratic tradition.[25] These new courses would extend the basic study of American law and government to include trends in history, issues in contemporary society, and questions of character and values. Through critical study of case histories and current news reports, students would learn to apply principles of democracy to everyday concerns they will face as citizens.

---

* For more information, see "What's Become of History?" and "Bringing Back History," *The Harvard Education Letter* 2 (July 1986): 4–6.

The "new civics" courses may help unify educators calling for issues-centered, traditional historical, critical-thought, and character-education approaches to the teaching of social studies.

Foreign Languages

Audiolingual approach

The foreign language programs of our public schools have changed considerably over the last forty to fifty years. Prior to World War II, most foreign language instruction stressed reading and writing, to the virtual exclusion of listening and speaking. Furthermore, foreign language instruction was almost exclusively the domain of the secondary schools. The 1950s introduced a new kind of foreign language instruction to elementary as well as high schools. This new *audiolingual* approach was designed to develop competence in speaking and listening to others speak a foreign language. As evidence of this dramatic change, the number of language laboratories—rooms equipped with listening tapes, headsets, and machines that can monitor the pace of each student and allow each to respond to the tapes—grew nationwide from several dozen in public schools in 1957 to eight thousand by 1966.

However, the use of language labs has declined dramatically. By the 1970s, many foreign language instructors had concluded that the audiolingual approach of the early 1960s was not very successful.[26] Enrollments in college foreign language classes declined nearly 10 percent between 1965 and 1975. Budgets for foreign language instruction were cut as it was placed lower and lower on the scale of school priorities. Since many colleges dropped foreign language requirements, a corresponding decline in enrollments occurred in the elementary and secondary schools. By 1980, only 15 percent of high school students were enrolled in foreign language courses.[27] Since the mid-1980s this trend has been reversed. College enrollments in subjects like Chinese, Russian, Japanese, Latin, and Spanish have increased dramatically. Many universities have implemented core curriculum requirements and increased admission standards for incoming freshmen by requiring two years of foreign language study in high school.

Increasing enrollments

By numerous measures the study of foreign languages in the schools is booming. The American Council on the Teaching of Foreign Languages reports that the number of students in grades 7–12 enrolled in foreign language classes jumped by more than 1 million between 1982 and 1985. States such as Texas, Florida, New York, and Oklahoma have experienced 50 percent increases in student enrollment since 1983. And a study of high school transcripts by the U.S. Department of Education shows that whereas only one of two students in 1982 had received any foreign language credit, two of three students had received credit in a comparable survey taken in 1987.[28]

Foreign language departments in the public schools are trying to make the study of foreign languages more attractive by expanding their course offerings and integrating language study with concerns for international and multicultural education. Leaders in the field emphasize the cultural foundations of language, asserting that language study increases linguistic competence and cultural sensitivity.[29] Attention to techniques used in elementary bilingual education—immersion, partial immersion, or the Foreign Language in the Elementary Schools

Program—has focused instruction on developing fluency in speaking, writing, and comprehension. Proficiency-oriented instruction that focuses on what the learner *can do with language* rather than what the learner *knows about language* marks modern-day language teaching. Early introduction of foreign language continues to gain support; alternative secondary schools, such as international schools, schools-within-schools, and magnet schools, have begun to integrate international studies and foreign language study. Concern about the United States's competitiveness in a global economy has led many business leaders and politicians to urge greater emphasis on foreign language instruction in our schools. More and more states are responding to these urgings, and it appears that the 1990s will see an increased emphasis on learning foreign languages.

The Arts

Teachers of the fine and applied arts have been fighting an uphill battle to maintain a secure position in the regular school curriculum. During the 1960s, budgetary cutbacks were made in the arts to finance enriched programs in mathematics and the sciences. During the 1970s, however, many public school art programs became sources of pride. In the 1980s, educators debated the role of the arts in relation to various versions of core curricula. And in the 1990s, these debates are continuing.

What is taught, when

Art and music in the elementary school are ordinarily taught by regular classroom teachers, although some schools hire specialist teachers in one or both areas. Dance and drama are largely ignored in the elementary school, although children of this age are less inhibited and seem to enjoy these activities more than do students in the secondary schools. The small amount of instruction provided in the arts for elementary students is contrasted in high school by drama clubs, orchestras, bands, and dance groups. In most instances, instruction in music or dance during a child's elementary school years takes the form of private instruction outside the public school.

Artistic learning has three essential elements: (1) the development of abilities to create art forms, (2) the development of powers of aesthetic perception, and (3) the development of the ability to understand art as a cultural phenomenon. Programs in the arts have tended to emphasize the creation of an art object or the development of a performance; newer programs center on aesthetic education and art as a way of knowing and perceiving the world. For most students, this trend will be useful.

Curriculum specialists have suggested integrating the arts with other subject matter to show the usefulness of the arts. There is little doubt that the arts play a crucial role in the development of cultured, educated individuals and that they respond to a deep instinct in humanity. Whereas the 1983 College Board study places the arts among the list of six basic academic subjects, other national studies have de-emphasized the arts in their attention to mathematics, science, and language arts as basics. Arts educators disagree about the future shape of their programs: Should the arts be considered for basic courses or as an enrichment program, and should arts courses follow rigorous academic models or blend a combination of affective experiences with cognitive learning? The lack of agreement about a rationale for arts education in the public schools reflects

A basic or a frill?

Musical instruction and performances, such as this practice for a band concert, are rare in elementary schools.

(*Larry Kolvoord/Texastock*)

its uncertain future in the push for rigor and academic excellence in other core subjects.

Physical Education, Health, and Recreation

Physical education is education of, by, and through human movement. It contributes to several broad areas of personal development: (1) physical fitness, (2) skill and knowledge development, and (3) social and psychological development.

Physical fitness is often confused with physical education, but it represents only a part of physical education programs. The physical education curriculum also tries to meet various biological, psychological, social, and mental needs of students. For example, the acquisition of values such as cooperation, teamwork, and respect for the rights of others also counts as a desired outcome. By concentrating on such long-range goals, particularly those that can be practiced on a lifelong basis, the individual student receives more than training or conditioning.

Emphasis on lifelong sports

In the early 1960s, physical education curricula stressed highly skilled, competitive activities to the detriment of other legitimate physical education activities. As a result, many children felt frustrated and humiliated when they did not excel. During the 1970s and early 1980s, however, the programs began to emphasize lifelong sports such as golf, tennis, swimming, and other individual sports. Elementary programs are often designed around types of games ranging from cooperative to competitive, individual to social, and group to team, all designed to develop children's skillful movement. Secondary programs have broadened their offerings to include self-defense, modern dance, yoga, and soccer. There is currently greater emphasis on recreation and less on competition. In addition, less rigid sex roles and federal legislation (Title IX) have opened up more opportunities for girls to participate in a wider variety of recreational and sports activities.

Physical education curricula are currently responding to four needs: (1) to develop aerobic capacity to maintain acceptable cardiorespiratory efficiency, (2) to achieve appropriate levels of body fat, (3) to acquire strength to perform expected tasks of living, and (4) to achieve flexibility and abdominal strength to avoid lower back injuries. To address these needs, sports skills are alternated with fitness development through such activities as swimming, jogging, bicycling, and cross-country skiing. Information on exercise and nutrition are provided students so they can understand how to balance caloric intake and maintain an appropriate body fat level.

Health education

The health curriculum addresses such topics as injury prevention and safety, prevention and control of disease (including AIDs), substance abuse, nutrition, family life (sexuality), consumer health, and mental and emotional health. More than most academic subjects, health education strives to change students' attitudes and behaviors, to get them to take fewer risks and to take preventive measures. Much more emphasis is now placed on instructional practices such as peer counseling than on stern lectures or horror stories designed to frighten youth. Programs designed to teach youngsters how to resist peer pressure and to feel good about themselves have shown success in reducing substance abuse.[30]

Sex education controversial

Programs of sex education often suffer from conservative political opposition. In spite of these pressures, some states, such as Virginia, have implemented statewide "family life" programs that educate youngsters in the basics of human sexuality. Because of the seriousness of the problem, much effort is going into AIDS education efforts and programs. It remains a fact, however, that youth in the United States have an appallingly poor knowledge of the various aspects of sexuality. The United States, without a systematic program of sex education, has one of the highest national rates of teen-age marriage, unwanted pregnancies, abortion, and venereal disease, whereas Sweden, for example, with a compulsory sex education program, has the lowest incidence of such problems.

Elective Courses

Most high schools today offer their students a number of options regarding the courses they take. Whereas the average high school student graduates with eighteen to twenty units—a year-long course representing one unit—large high schools may offer as many as one hundred courses. The average student, then, will probably choose among optional courses according to individual interests and academic or career ambitions.

Non-college-bound students

Although college preparation has been the major goal of many high schools, increased effort has been made recently to provide comprehensive programs for students not planning to attend college. This trend is especially evident in rural areas, where small local high schools are being replaced by comprehensive regional high schools. Some of the courses involved, such as technology education, distributive education, home economics, business education, and agriculture, are specifically vocational. Others, such as driver education and consumer education, have been added to the curriculum because of an obvious societal need or in response to student interest.

More graduation requirements

A trend disturbing those who teach elective courses is the increase in requirements for graduation from high schools, which leaves less time for elective courses. Some argue that a common general education provides the best foundation for future work or academic study; others hope to maintain a large percentage of the curriculum as electives. Issues raised by teachers of elective courses focus attention on the purpose of comprehensive schooling and on what is "basic."[31]

Vocational Courses

Recent criticism

Vocational education has come under fire from those who note its inadequacy in preparing students for careers in high-technology fields or in the country's now-dominant service economy. Two surveys of business and industry leaders conducted by the College Board and the Committee for Economic Development find that employers value applicants with high levels of literacy, positive attitudes toward work, and the ability to learn.[32] More important for job applicants than specific job skills, which may be outmoded before the students even graduate, are general competencies in reading, writing, speaking and listening, mathematics, and reasoning. Employers are willing to train students in specific skills on the job. Moreover, vocational education has been criticized for too often tracking male and minority students, thus limiting their access to an academic curriculum. It is important to consider what sort of education is most likely to improve employment opportunities for disadvantaged or minority students.

More apprenticeship programs?

Some educators and labor officials urge that the lines between academic and vocational education be blurred and that all youngsters be provided with more applied learning experiences. Further, they argue that the general education track in high school should be eliminated. Although 42 percent of all high school students are enrolled in a general education track, nearly two out of three high school dropouts come from that track. In addition, "apprenticeship" programs such as exist in West Germany are being praised. Under such a program students receive on-the-job training with a company for four days a week and participate in classroom instruction on the fifth day. Such programs are designed to assist youth in the school-to-work transition.[33]

ADDITIONAL INFLUENCES ON CURRICULUM

Although we can examine what is taught in the schools independently in terms of the subjects offered, the curriculum as experienced by the students is affected by a number of other factors. The individual teacher, of course, is a major variable in what students actually learn. The classroom and school context also affect the delivery of the curriculum. We have chosen to focus on two other major influences on the curriculum that is actually delivered to students, textbooks and emerging instructional approaches.

Textbooks

Provide a national curriculum

Education in the United States is constitutionally the domain of the various individual states; that is, the states are empowered to establish curricula and to organize and finance school systems. Unlike many countries in the world, we have no national curriculum that is established by the federal government and implemented throughout the country. Some educational observers assert, however, that we do possess a national curriculum of sorts, called textbooks. Several recent studies have concluded that most of what students do in classrooms is textbook-related. For many teachers, content ideas are derived solely from the text, and the materials used most frequently in their lessons are the textbook, workbook, teacher's guide ideas for boardwork, and accompanying dittos and tests. The objectives and goals for student learning are defined by the textbook (even the text you are now reading), learning activities and materials are provided to teachers as part of the textbook package, and tests, geared to the textbook's objectives, are usually prepared for the teacher's use.

Twenty-two states have a textbook adoption process. Most of these states have open hearings, where citizens have the opportunity to examine textbooks that are being considered for statewide adoption and to express their objections to particular books. Because textbook adoption is a multimillion-dollar business, publishing companies must be careful not to include material that might be found

EDUCATION: A WORLD VIEW

SUCCESS IN SCHOOL AND WORK OPPORTUNITY

The United States has traditionally valued higher education. Much of our secondary education is geared to developing academic skills needed for college entry. We are widely known for our extensive system of colleges and universities. However, only about 50 percent of our youth go on to college. The other 50 percent are non-college-bound students who intend to directly enter the work force. In the United States, preparation of noncollege youth has evolved with no coherent strategy. There is no institutional bridge to help noncollege youth seek employment because it is generally not seen as the school's responsibility to help the student make the transition from school to work. Therefore, little emphasis is placed on the relevance of school and secondary education to the world of work. The federal government does sponsor some brief skill training and job placement assistance under the Job Training Partnership Act, but this program is geared primarily to the economically disadvantaged. Some occupational training is available from other sources, including vocational skills programs, apprenticeship training programs (typically conducted by employers and unions), the military services, and public community colleges.

As many jobs become more complex and require greater skill even at entry levels, it is becoming increasingly important to attend to the needs of our noncollege youth. Strategies for developing skills, finding jobs, and facilitating the transition to work are needed. The U.S. General Accounting Office has examined the national policies of countries that have tried to address the needs of their noncollege youth work force, including England, Germany, Japan, and Sweden, to see how they approach preparing noncollege youth for employment. This is what they found.

In 1983, England introduced an initiative to improve how English youth are prepared for employment. The curriculum was revised to more directly relate to the world of work and to provide such work place skills as teamwork and problem solving, as well as to allow direct

SCHOOLS: THE PRESENT

offensive by influential groups and factions. One can certainly question whether there is an inherent conflict between the notion of a pluralistic nation and the conservative forces that influence the textbook industry and, therefore, the curriculum of our nation.

Waves of educational reform movements in the 1980s addressed issues of student achievement and teacher competence. A third reform movement is directing attention to the quality of the textbooks that determine the curriculum. Criticism of texts is varied. Some critics claim they are "dumbed down" to meet readability requirements; the writing style, designed to meet arbitrary criteria for lengths of words and sentences, can be awkward, stiff, and difficult to read. Others believe textbooks attempt to include too much material and so lack depth of coverage. Michael Kirst describes many texts as "dull, drained of excitement, and diluted in content."[34] Insightful description, memorable detail, and necessary explanation may be sacrificed to the textbook's need to cover all topics demanded by multiple audiences. And critics focus on typical textbook emphases on skill development instead of the stimulation of students' interest and intellect; these emphases, they say, create texts that are dry, barren of ideas, devoid of concepts, and lacking in the vigorous style that stirs students to comprehend and retain what they read.

Call for better textbooks

work experiences. Special teachers work with representatives of employment services to inform students of jobs and to facilitate placement. Funding is provided for school-employer linkages in which students who achieve certain academic and behavioral goals are offered training and employment. National standards of vocational qualifications exist to guide training content and to measure the competencies that guide and motivate young people entering employment.

Germany has an extensive apprenticeship program for non-college-bound youth. Students typically take vocational and academic classes one or two days a week and receive on-the-job training with employers for the remainder of the week. Training may last three years and is intended to prepare students for eventual jobs in higher-skill middle management. National apprenticeship curricula, examination, and certification procedures are used to insure quality of training and to measure apprentice competency.

In Japan, high schools are ranked academically. Students must take entrance exams to attend their school of choice. In turn, high schools have direct ties with employers in the world of work. More prestigious employers, who have better jobs to offer, typically recruit students from higher-ranked schools. Japanese high schools also nominate and rank their students for job offers on the basis of academic and behavioral performance. Using these direct indicators of school performance, employers then interview and hire graduates.

Swedish schools offer occupational training for noncollege students. This training may take place in school or with an employer. Job placement assistance is offered by schoolteachers, school counselors, and special employment staff who work with youth up to age twenty-five. Employment and training services are guaranteed to all unemployed teenagers. Although programs vary by age group, they typically consist of an individualized plan for education, training, and employment.

Training Strategies: Preparing Noncollege Youth for Employment in the U.S. and Foreign Countries, (Washington, D.C.: United States General Accounting Office, May 1990).

At least one state is addressing these concerns. California has made a concerted effort to improve the quality of textbooks to accompany its extensive statewide curriculum reforms. In recent years the state demanded—and got—major improvements in textbooks for mathematics, science, reading, and history. Publishers howled at having to develop new textbooks just for California, even though it is the biggest textbook market in the country, spending $400 million each year for 11 percent of the nation's public school children.[35] However, the publishers complied. Many concerned educators and parents hope that California's efforts to improve textbooks will influence the standards set by other states' textbook adoption procedures.

Kirst and others have noted the shortcomings of many adoption systems that allow too little time and money to support the selection of excellent texts by qualified personnel. Whereas some curriculum personnel call for schools to spend more money on textbooks, many others claim that teachers and curriculum developers rely too much on textbooks. What are appropriate criteria by which to judge the texts to be purchased? For example, how meaningful is a recent copyright? One thing appears certain: textbooks are one of the major determinants of our nation's elementary and secondary school curricula, and that situation does not appear likely to change in the near future.

Innovative Instructional Approaches

The instructional approaches used by teachers also shape the delivery of the curriculum. Although these approaches have remained amazingly constant since the 1890s, especially at the secondary level, some alterations to traditional, teacher-centered instruction have taken hold.[36] Potential for further change exists. All of the trends discussed here can be used in a variety of subject areas with students of many age and ability levels. Several of the trends we will consider have been empirically tested to determine their effect on student achievement, self-concept, and cooperation among students. Some approaches borrow an instructional technique once associated with a single subject area—writing—and now applied across the curriculum. We will examine five nontraditional instructional influences on the curriculum: mastery learning, cooperative learning, critical thinking, writing across the curriculum, and microcomputing.

MASTERY LEARNING   One approach to individualizing instruction and improving learning, called *mastery learning,* has been developed by Benjamin Bloom, a noted educational psychologist, and his associates. The problem has been, Bloom asserts, that most students are provided with the same instruction in terms of amount, quality, and time available for learning. When this occurs, students who possess more aptitude for given subjects will outperform students possessing less aptitude. But if one accepts that students are normally distributed according to aptitude, one can match the kind and quality of instruction and the amount of time available for learning to the characteristics and needs of *each* student. Then the majority of students may be expected to achieve mastery of the subject, and hence the name *mastery learning.*

Implementing mastery learning is not easy, but successful techniques have been identified and can be summarized as follows:

1. Define instructional objectives behaviorally so the teacher and learner know exactly where they are and what must be accomplished.
2. Teach the behavior or attitude sought in the objective directly rather than building to or around it.
3. Provide immediate feedback to all learner responses.
4. Set the level of instruction so that students are maximally successful.
5. Divide instruction into small, self-contained modules.
6. Control the stimulus so the teacher knows exactly what the learner is responding to.
7. Provide positive feedback to reinforce the learner's "critical" response, that is, the response that corresponds to the desired behavior identified in the instructional objective.[37]

Bloom's basic message is that even though differences in intelligence and aptitude do exist in every classroom, teachers can adjust the nature of instruction and the time allowed for each student so that more students can succeed. It should be noted that mastery learning strategies are especially critical during the early grades of school, because if students do not acquire certain basic skills, catching up in the later grades becomes exceedingly difficult.

Results seem favorable

The effects of mastery learning strategies generally seem favorable. In a 1986 review of the studies on mastery learning strategies, Guskey and Gates concluded that "group-based applications of mastery learning have consistently positive effects on a broad range of student outcomes, including student achievement, retention of learned material, involvement in learning activities, and student affect."[38] The achievement results show variations across age levels and subject areas, but the results are "overwhelmingly positive." In recent years this review has come under attack, as has other research on the effects of other instructional approaches, because several of the studies cited were less than four weeks in duration.[39] However, even these critics support the use of mastery learning, particularly in connection with other instructional approaches.

Tutoring even better

Research comparing achievement outcomes of students in classes using conventional instruction, mastery learning strategies, and one-to-one tutoring indicates the superiority of tutoring over mastery learning and of both methods over conventional instruction.[40] A comparison of time spent on tasks and student attitudes and interests also indicates the benefits of tutoring over mastery learning methods. In recent years Bloom, his associates, and other educational researchers have been developing ways of using mastery learning strategies in conjunction with other instructional strategies such as cooperative learning and critical thinking.[41] The integration of these methods is still under study, but the emphasis on the complementary nature of the models is expected to enhance learning for all students.

Bloom and his associates also have been working to discover sets of teaching and learning conditions that can help students in classrooms achieve as they would if individually tutored. Their work has led them to focus on five factors that can improve teaching and learning in schools: (1) mastery learning; (2) care with initial prerequisites, that is, taking the time at the beginning of each school year to review course prerequisites taught in the previous school year to insure the mastery of those prerequisites; (3) a supportive home environment; (4) reading automaticity, that is, promoting independent reading ability by encouraging uninterrupted pleasure reading both at school and at home; and (5) the use of higher mental processes, that is, regularly using instructional materials and methods that rise above the simple acquisition of knowledge.[42]

COOPERATIVE LEARNING Cooperative learning in classrooms is another trend influencing what is taught in the schools. Those who have analyzed the "hidden" curriculum, or the implicit teachings that schools communicate to their students, have observed that American schools tend to reward competitive or individual accomplishment more than cooperative effort.[43] Arguing for cooperative learning techniques, some educators maintain that such techniques can change the ways students learn, their attitudes toward what they are taught, and their perceptions of themselves and others. Many of the methods depending upon student-student interaction have been empirically tested to determine their effects on student achievement, motivation, and perceptions of fellow students. Although estimates indicate that teachers use variations of small group learning only 7 to 20 percent of the time,[44] cooperative learning techniques offer promise for those who wish to enhance the teaching of subject matter with the teaching of cooperation.

Cooperation is encouraged as students work in small groups, receiving rewards for doing well as a group. Jigsaw II, a modification of a technique first developed by Elliot Aranson and his associates, provides an example of how cooperative learning techniques work.[45] First, heterogeneous groups of students read material in narrative form (a textbook chapter, story, or biography) to learn concepts. Within a group or team, individual members are assigned an aspect of the material with which they are to become "expert." After everyone has read the assigned material, the experts from the various teams regroup to talk about their assigned topic with their counterparts on the other teams. Next, the experts return to their original teams, teaching their topic to team members. Finally, the team members are quizzed on all topics in the narrative material. On the basis of a team score compiled from an individual-improvement scoring system, high-scoring teams are recognized by the teacher in bulletin board notices or class newsletters. Designers of Jigsaw II describe the students in teams as motivated to work hard because each student depends upon teammates to get the information necessary to perform well on quizzes.[46]

Robert Slavin, a prominent researcher of cooperative learning, concludes that "there is wide agreement among reviewers of the cooperative learning literature that cooperative methods can and usually do have a positive effect on student achievement."[47] He goes on to emphasize that two conditions are essen-

Successful use of cooperative learning strategies depends on the appropriate use of group, not individual, rewards.

(*Spencer Grant/The Picture Cube*)

tial if the achievement effects of cooperative learning are to be realized. First, the cooperating groups must have a group goal that is important to them. Second, the success of the group must depend on the individual learning of all group members: that is, there must be individual accountability as well as group accountability. Slavin is philosophically opposed to having individual grades largely determined by team performance.

Cooperative learning has been found to be a particularly effective instructional tool in teaching at-risk students who require immediate feedback to their learning attempts. It works well because it gives students power. As schools become aware of the need to do away with tracking and to encourage heterogeneous grouping, cooperative learning provides a means by which all students can feel essential to the classroom learning process. It enables students to recognize that they all, when given a chance, have something to contribute to everyone's learning. Cooperative learning has quickly become a major instructional method in the United States, particularly in middle schools.[48]

Helps at-risk students

CRITICAL THINKING AND PROBLEM SOLVING A growing interest in helping students become better thinkers and problem solvers is evidenced by the sudden flurry of publications, workshops, curriculum study institutes, journal articles, and course requirements addressing the topics of thinking and problem solving. Most states provide school programs in critical thinking. The programs are no doubt diverse, since educators disagree about the nature of critical thought and how best to teach it or its components. Although many people favor teaching critical thinking, there is a diversity of definitions for what critical thinking is.

Definition At the heart of these definitions, however, is the intent to help students evaluate the worth of ideas, opinions, or evidence before making a decision or judgment.

Some educators favor approaches that help students detect bias; others help students identify a wide range of propaganda strategies. The teaching of philosophy is also proposed as a way to provide criteria by which students can judge others' thinking. Still other approaches identify component skills (making inferences, testing hypotheses, identifying assumptions, for example) within the realm of critical thinking and advocate direct instruction in each skill. Socratic questioning, too, is suggested as a way to teach the art of thinking.

Problem solving is a component of critical thinking that has received increasing attention and use. Though the term is used in a number of ways by educators, *problem solving* generally refers to the process of either presenting students with a problem or helping them identify a problem and then observing and helping them become aware of the conditions, procedures, or steps taken to solve the problem. The problem to be solved may range from putting puzzles together, to solving simple science or math problems, to solving more complex mental, logical, or social dilemmas. Problem solving has been found beneficial across subject areas (such as reading, writing, math, and social skills), across ability groupings (from mildly handicapped to gifted students, for example), and across age groups (from preschool to medical school). It may be presented as an individual activity, as when independently predicting outcomes in a reading passage, or be used with a group, as when simulating "survival" activities in a wilderness setting that require group cooperation. In the many diverse ways of teaching problem solving, the emphasis is on the *process* of reaching a solution. Proponents of problem-solving instruction point out that if students become more aware of their mental processes, they will be able to exercise greater control over their own learning and thinking in future situations, both in and outside of the classroom. In group problem-solving activities, students may also benefit from interacting with each other and being exposed to the variety and range of different approaches used by peers in solving the same dilemma.

Integration with subject areas What is the role of critical thought in the curriculum? At one time educators debated whether students can best learn effective thinking through separate courses and units of study or as an integrated part of every course. Greater agreement now exists that although students do benefit from stand-alone courses in critical thinking, they must also learn to think within the context of each discipline. The integration of critical thinking into subject areas appears to be the direction of the future, especially since the curricula of the schools are already so crowded.

Classroom environment important Closely related to the problems of defining critical thinking and relating it to the existing curriculum is the need to create classroom environments conducive to critical thought. If, as Barry Beyer suggests,[49] critical thought consists

> *Research on cooperative learning and peer tutoring has shown that programs in which students help each other to learn can enhance their achievement. Further, the social benefits and increased self-esteem of students working together are considerable. . . . In a time of increasing expectations . . . we cannot ignore a powerful, free instructional resource available in any school: The students themselves!*
>
> — ROBERT SLAVIN —

"Certainly, children should be taught to think critically—but not too critically!"

© Glen Dines

not only of specific mental operations but also of a frame of mind, how can teachers nurture a critical frame of mind? A review of the research on critical thinking[50] indicates that a critical spirit is as important as critical thought: students should apply critical thinking broadly, inspect their own thinking, and act in a way consistent with their thinking. When students learn to solve problems in the classroom—not by rote but by identifying the problems, thinking through the possible solutions, and determining the best possible solutions themselves— then perhaps, when they leave school, they will be better able to identify daily problems in their lives and work toward solutions.[51] The crucial task is to make it possible for them to learn to set goals and identify strategies for themselves. As Bruce Joyce has observed, "By teaching students how to reason independently we increase their power to teach themselves. . . .[52]

Given the competition from other important goals, whether critical thinking and problem-solving skills survive as a part of the curriculum depends on at least three factors: the availability of good instructional materials; appropriate training for teachers; and the degree to which critical thinking and

Aids subject-matter learning

problem-solving skills can be integrated into, as opposed to being added onto, the curriculum.

WRITING ACROSS THE CURRICULUM   The *writing across the curriculum* movement has been a center of curricular interest for a growing number of English educators since the 1960s. Also called *writing to learn* or *writing to learn in the content areas,* the idea emphasizes writing as a tool for students' learning, not only in English classes but in all subject areas. Answering the question "Why write?" Donald Murray explains, "Writing begins with all that we have known since we were born, and perhaps with a lot of knowledge that was born in us. We write, first of all, to discover what we know and then what we need to know."[53] As a result of a process of writing and thinking, Murray concludes, "The more you write the more you will discover about your subject, your world, and your self. . . . We do not write what we know as much as *to* know. Writing is exploration. We use language to combine experience and feelings and thoughts into a meaning which we may share with a reader. Why write? I write, above all, to learn."[54]

How can teachers use the act of writing as the medium through which subject-matter learning takes place? Stephen Tchudi and Joanne Yates have recommended procedures for developing content-area writing lessons that create situations that motivate students to write, using their subject-matter knowledge in the process.[55] These lessons help students make new connections, play with new ideas and concepts, and ultimately reach a better understanding of the content of their study of history, the mathematics, science, computers, and art, for example. Teachers who implement writing across the curriculum emphasize writing as a tool that enables students to continue learning, not as evidence of knowledge already acquired.[56]

Writing as thinking tool

The interest in critical thinking and problem-solving skills goes hand in hand with deep and widespread concern over writing skills.[57] At a time when processing and manipulating information, rather than amassing and regurgitating it, are seen as essential to our economic survival, clearly, we must consider thinking and writing as inextricably connected. Students in social studies classes may be asked to take a written stand on school issues, moral questions, or political problems. Music students may write their own ballads. Science classes may work together to predict the future in story form or to write futuristic headlines and news features. Children in math classes can create their own word problems and keep records of what they have learned, their questions, and their observations. Art classes can write scripts for slide shows and cartoon strips or create illustrated guides and storybooks. Teachers at many grade levels and in many subject areas can ask students to keep informal journals or "learning logs." In these journals students record their responses to what they have read and studied, and so can interact with text material and with the teacher's responses to students' queries and remarks. These samples are just a few examples of the many ways that teachers use writing as a thinking tool for students to use and apply their knowledge in the content areas. When teachers also use writing to enhance their learning in their own specific disciplines, they model for students the benefits of developing this important skill.

MICROCOMPUTERS IN EDUCATION   Heralded by some as being as revolutionary as Gutenberg's movable type, computers have been used in education since the 1960s, but the first commercially feasible microcomputer became available in 1975. The use of microcomputers at the elementary and secondary school levels dramatically increased during the 1980s. By 1990 there were over 2 million computers in U.S. schools. Over 95 percent of all elementary and secondary schools had at least one computer intended for instructional use, compared with 18 percent of schools in 1981. These figures indicate that there is an average of one computer for every twenty-two students enrolled in U.S. public schools.[58] Improved technology and lower costs are the primary reasons that computer usage in the schools has risen so precipitously and is projected to continue at a similar pace.

Dramatic increase

School administrators are using computers for various managerial and organizational purposes, such as class scheduling, payroll accounting, personnel reporting, and student attendance record keeping. These uses in school systems are very similar to the uses in business. Of unusual significance, however, is the use of computers for instruction.

The two major functions of *computer-based instruction (CBI)* are *computer-assisted instruction (CAI)* and *computer-managed instruction (CMI)*. In CAI the student receives instructional help from the computer. Because of their data storage capacity, patience, and branching capability, microcomputers lend themselves to individualized instruction. CMI helps the teacher plan for and monitor student learning experiences. Individual learning plans can be stored in the microcomputer and retrieved as needed. Student testing and assessment can be programmed and the results filed. Additional CMI applications include record keeping, scheduling of student activities, and time and resource management.

CAI and CMI

Software designers have only begun to explore the computer's potential as an instructional tool for all grade levels and subject areas of the curriculum.[59] In the language arts area, students can bridge the processes of reading and writing by using word processing and composition materials that help them generate ideas for writing, create text on the screen, read it, and revise it. Drill and practice programs are also available to help students with topics like spelling, punctuation, capitalization, and grammar rules. Social studies teachers may want students to study computers as a subject: What does the computer revolution imply for the country's society, economy, and morals, for example? Or social studies teachers may use computers to immerse their students in environments (called *simulations*) in which they are required to solve complex problems and immediately learn the consequences of their decisions. An example is the program called the Oregon Trail, in which students embark on a trip on the Oregon Trail during the nineteenth century and have to make decisions about how to spend their money in outfitting their wagon train with provisions, ammunition, and equipment. As events occur on the trail, students receive immediate feedback regarding the adequacy of their decisions. Computers also may allow students to tap data banks that will assist their research of social studies and language arts topics.

Use in subject areas

Simulated environments can also be used by science teachers to encourage students to solve problems in a real-world context. If these problems are chosen to span the disciplines, teachers can help their students see science knowledge as a useful tool for living. In addition, software materials can simulate lab work, allowing students to practice gathering, analyzing, and displaying data. Again, data bases offer nearly limitless sources of information.

In mathematics computers can help students compare formula versus approximation techniques for speed, accuracy, and utility in various applications. For drill and practice sessions, computers can be programmed to provide students with immediate feedback regarding the correctness of their responses to problems and exercises. On a more sophisticated level, computers can be programmed to allow students to manipulate symbols and components within formulas and then to verify the relative effects of their manipulations. Students who learn better through pictures or images can be helped by the graphic display capabilities of the computer.

Electronic networks Electronic networks, using microcomputers, now allow students and teachers to share information and experience across cities, states, or even continents, thus ending some of the isolation of the classroom. For example, one elementary school classroom in Charlottesville, Virginia, has been communicating electronically with an Alaskan Eskimo village. The Virginia children sent a message stating that they knew the Alaskan youngsters liked to eat fish, but they wanted to know what kind of fish they preferred. The Eskimo children responded that they did indeed eat fish, but they would rather order pizza. So much for stereotypes!

Use in special education Some of the most impressive applications of computer-based technologies are in the field of special education. Word processors allow students who cannot hold a pencil to write. Speech synthesizers provide some students with the means to communicate orally for the first time. A beam of light used with a computer and television monitor enables severely and profoundly handicapped persons to direct their eye gaze at the monitor to turn on radios, close doors, and do many other physical activities they otherwise would be unable to accomplish.

Many teachers are enthusiastic about introducing their students to the world of technology—word processing, computer graphics, programming, simulated problem solving, interactive videodiscs, to name just a few activities associated with the proliferation of microcomputers. Teachers report that students seem motivated to use the equipment. Often, students quickly master computer-related skills and surpass their teachers' knowledge. Many teachers see this as positive. Researchers comparing groups of children using computers with groups not using them find the users to show greater enthusiasm for school, greater intrinsic motivation, and greater student-to-student interactive learning.

Questions and issues But problems exist. Are there enough microcomputers in the schools for all students to have access? Will computers increase the disparities that already exist between poor children and those from middle- or upper-class families, since the latter groups of students have many more opportunities at home and at school to use computers? Are teachers trained to use computer techniques in conjunction with the current curriculum? How can schools effectively select software to suit their needs? Is quality software available? Will schools overemphasize the use of machines, forgetting that students also need to spend time with people? Before

"Roger, it won't kill you to help your own father with his computer."

Drawing by Modell; © 1984 The New Yorker Magazine, Inc.

microcomputing can achieve its potential in the schools, these and other similar issues must be explored.[60]

Some educators note that students seldom use computers to work with information sources, more often using their machines for drill and practice exercises or to learn keyboarding procedures. For teachers to make effective use of applications like word processing and data base management, students must have extended computer access. Providing one computer per classroom may be like asking thirty children to share one pencil. Also, teachers' efforts to use computers should be supported by training; up to this point the burden of integrating computers into the curriculum has been placed on teachers. Critics also describe the shortcomings of currently available software. When computers are not properly programmed to keep records of students' work, teachers cannot monitor students' progress effectively. Or computers can fail to reach their potential for individualized instruction by failing to provide feedback to students that helps them correct their errors or by failing to provide opportunities for advanced students to branch out to more challenging material.

Will microcomputers find a permanent place in the curriculum? We ought to keep in mind that one of the major goals of schools is to prepare students for

Importance in work place

the world of work. The new information technologies—computers, microprocessors, video devices, and inexpensive means of storing and transmitting information—are creating a revolution comparable to the invention of printing. Already this revolution is causing profound changes in the way business and industry are conducted. "Smart machines" now perform jobs formerly done by humans. The field of robotics, pioneered by Japanese industry and made possible by the microprocessor, is becoming a major element in industry. As the computer has changed the work place and society at large, schools find themselves under pressure to modify vocational education programs and to include opportunities for all students to become comfortable with the tools of an age of high technology. Business, industry, and institutions of higher education will place new demands on schools to produce graduates with greater knowledge of science and technology and with the thinking skills to make the best use of constantly developing information techniques.

What do we see as the future of microcomputers and schooling? The next five years will witness continued expansion of microcomputer use in the schools, but it is unlikely that it will result in any radical or startling changes in schooling. Budgetary and fiscal problems will impede really major investments in computers. Even if schools could make the hardware available, software producers still would have a long way to go to develop programs of sufficient quality and variety to satisfy teachers.

Teacher anxiety

Another problem that must be overcome before computers will be used commonly in classrooms is teachers' fears: fear of the unknown; fear of obsolescence or replacement; and a fear best called "math anxiety," based on the erroneous assumption that computer work is primarily mathematics. Colleges of education and school districts have a tremendous task ahead of them if one of their goals is computer literacy among teachers. If prospective teachers graduate from college with little or no experience in using microcomputers, they are likely to resist using them in their classrooms. On the other hand, if new teachers have had extensive experience with microcomputers as part of their teacher preparation, they will more likely demand access to computers as part of their instructional activities.

IS THE EXISTING CURRICULUM RELEVANT TO TODAY'S SOCIETY?

Before one can determine whether a particular curriculum is relevant, some difficult questions must be asked: Relevant to what? To life in society as it is now, as it probably will be in the future, or as it ideally should be? Relevant for whom? For the intellectual elite or for everyone? For the individual learner, or for society and its needs? And who determines social needs—the adults who represent the "establishment," or some other group? The question of curriculum relevance is very complicated, for it draws on one's entire philosophy of education. Is education's primary purpose to help students develop their minds by exploring ideas of the past that have proved to have enduring meaning? Or is education's primary purpose to help students experience growth through interaction with their environment? Is there a particular body of knowledge or repertoire of skills that all members of our society should possess? Or should students be free to explore many different areas in accordance with their own needs, curiosities, and interests? Should education give priority to the study of immediate problems and to developing the processes, understandings, and skills necessary for their solution? Or should education concentrate on guiding behavior according to agreed-upon standards and on study of the past as a way of preparing for the future?

In a society as large and pluralistic as the United States, all these philosophical positions, and more, have committed supporters. How can the schools incorporate in their curricula such diverse philosophies? If a certain philosophy is dominant within a given community, the curriculum of the community's schools is likely to reflect that set of beliefs, and those who don't agree will remain dissatisfied. On the other hand, some communities are responding to these diverse philosophical conceptions of the curriculum by providing alternative schools, each with a different curriculum emphasis, from which parents may choose.

Two basic philosophies Mortimer Smith argues that all educational philosophies, however diverse, fall into two basic categories, and he characterizes them as follows:

> On this matter of priorities in education, the picture seems clear: One group believes that the school must maintain its historic role as the chief institution in charge of intellectual training; another group—and perhaps the dominant one in public education—maintains that intellectual training is only a part of the school's total program, and not necessarily the most important part.[61]

If one considers the school's primary objective to be the intellectual training of students, any curriculum that does not emphasize scholarship will be judged irrelevant. Conversely, if one believes that the school should emphasize the development of the "whole child"—the child's emotional and social, as well as intellectual, growth—a curriculum devoted exclusively to English, history, the sciences, mathematics, and foreign languages will be considered inappropriate for many students and thus irrelevant. What one considers to be a relevant curriculum, then, depends on the philosophical position one takes. At the present time there are conflicting trends in the academic curriculum, each representative of a different philosophy of what the school's academic emphasis should be.

The Curriculum in a Changing World Our society and our environment are presently undergoing change at a rate unprecedented in human history. The population of the world, now numbering over 5 billion, is expanding at a tremendous pace and exerting severe pressure on the environment. We are consuming natural resources at an alarming rate; agricultural surpluses fail to reach the most needy, and many starve. Acid rain from industrialization threatens vegetation and wildlife; pollutants contaminate the air we breathe and the water we drink. At the same time, we are destroying huge tracts of vegetation that provide us with oxygen. Racial, ethnic, and gender prejudices, which had gone unchallenged for decades, are no longer being endured by their victims. Nations possess the power to annihilate one another at the push of a button. Bands of terrorists can alter tenuous balances of power among countries. In short, we have reached a point at which *all* human beings must work together to survive another century on this planet.

What are the best survival strategies for a society influenced by such rapid external changes? Perhaps the most basic function of all education is to increase the survival chances of the group. As long as the environment remains stable or changes very slowly, the skills necessary for survival seem to remain constant. In such times, when a culture is proved able to insure the survival of the group, education can be content to transmit that culture. In times of change, however, educators are faced with questions about which concepts and skills remain useful for survival and which should be discarded in favor of new ideas. Just because the environment is changing, should the curriculum change, too? Are there essentials that students of every time and situation should learn?

THE SABER-TOOTH CURRICULUM

In his classic satire on curriculum irrelevance, Harold Benjamin—using the pseudonym J. Abner Peddiwell—describes how the first school curriculum was developed in the Stone Age. The earliest educational theorist, according to Benjamin's book, was a man named New Fist, who hit on the idea of deliberate, systematic education.

Watching children at play, New Fist wondered how he could get them to do the things that would gain them more and better food, shelter, clothing, and security. He analyzed the activities that adults engaged in to maintain life and came up with three subjects for his curriculum: (1) fish-grabbing-with-the-bare-hands, (2) woolly-horse-clubbing, and (3) saber-tooth-tiger-scaring-with-fire. Although the children trained in these subjects enjoyed obvious material benefits as a result, some conservative members of the tribe resisted the introduction of these new subjects on religious grounds. But, in due time, many people began to train their children in New Fist's curriculum and the tribe grew increasingly prosperous and secure.

Then conditions changed. An ice age began, and a glacier crept down over the land. The glacier brought with it dirt and gravel that muddied the creeks, and the waters became so dirty that no one could see the fish well enough to grab them. The melting waters from the approaching ice sheet also made the country wetter, and the little woolly horses migrated to drier land. They were replaced by antelopes, who were so shy and speedy that no one could get close enough to club them. Finally, the new dampness in the air caused the saber-tooth tigers to catch pneumonia and die. And the ferocious glacial bears who came down with the advancing ice sheet were not afraid of fire.

The thinkers of the tribe, descendants of New Fist, found a way out of the dilemma. One figured out how to catch fish with a net made from vines. Another invented traps for the antelopes, and a third discovered how to dig pits to catch the bears.

Some thoughtful people began to wonder why these new activities couldn't be taught in the schools. But the elders who controlled the schools claimed that the new skills did not qualify as *education*—they were merely a matter of *training*. Besides, the curriculum was too full of the standard cultural subjects, fish-grabbing, horse-clubbing, and tiger-scaring, to admit new ones. When some radicals argued that the traditional subjects were foolish, the elders said that they taught fish-grabbing not to catch fish but to develop agility, horse-clubbing to develop strength, and tiger-scaring to develop courage. "The essence of true education is timelessness," they announced. "It is something that endures through changing conditions like a solid rock standing squarely and firmly in the middle of a raging torrent. You must know that there are some eternal verities and the saber-tooth curriculum is one of them!"(pp. 43–44)

The Saber-Tooth Curriculum was written in 1939, but its continuing applicability seems to be one of the "eternal verities."

J. Abner Peddiwell [Harold Benjamin], *The Saber-Tooth Curriculum* (New York: McGraw-Hill, 1939). One chapter of this book is reproduced in *Kaleidoscope: Readings in Education*, the companion volume to this text.

In the 1960s and 1970s, a time of great social change, the schools reflected the spirit of change. The curriculum expanded to include all manner of courses considered relevant to society's needs. In the eighties we heard a call for more stability in the curriculum. Those with a more conservative philosophy of education believe that in the seventies we gave up a unity and common culture that bound us together. The essentialists and perennialists among them would like to see a return to traditional academic content, usually in the form of core curricula described earlier in this chapter.

To which new values and ideas should the curriculum adapt? How can the schools preserve a common culture in times of increasing technological and social change? Educators debate the need to completely overhaul the curriculum and what adaptations to make, if any, to new environmental characteristics. We must continually examine the relevance of the school's curriculum. This is the challenge to curriculum developers: how best to increase our chances of survival. How can the curriculum sustain things of enduring value yet make the necessary adaptations to insure that we survive?

Discussion Questions

1. In your opinion, should the curriculum emphasize cultural learning common to all Americans or should the pluralistic nature of our diverse cultural backgrounds receive emphasis? Is it possible to do both?
2. With which of the curriculum reforms advocated by Goodlad, Boyer, and Adler do you agree? Disagree?
3. What is your view of the recent developments in your favorite subject field?
4. In your opinion, is the prevalent use of textbooks in the schools a positive or negative influence on teaching and learning? Can you see both the benefits and the dangers? If so, what are they?
5. Which of the instructional approaches described in the chapter appeal to you, and why?
6. What would you do to improve the curriculum of the public schools?
7. Are there aspects of our current curriculum that you would equate with the Saber-Tooth curriculum?

For Further Reading

Anderson, Richard C., et al. *Becoming a Nation of Readers: The Report of the Commission on Reading.* Champaign, Ill.: Center for the Study of Reading, 1985.

A book that makes reading research available to teachers and parents.

Block, James H., et al. *Building Effective Mastery Learning Schools.* New York: Longman, 1989.

A comprehensive, functional treatment of mastery learning and how it fits within the context of current educational public policy debates on issues of student learning.

Eisner, Elliot W. *The Educational Imagination.* 2d ed. New York: Macmillan, 1985.

A stimulating, controversial book regarding forces influencing today's curriculum.

Hirsch, E. D., Jr. *Cultural Literacy: What Every American Needs to Know.* Boston: Houghton Mifflin, 1987.

> A provocative treatise asserting that literacy requires the early and continued transmission of specific information, the common knowledge that enables students to make sense of what they read.

McNeil, John D. *Curriculum: A Comprehensive Introduction.* 4th ed. Glenview, Ill.: Scott, Foresman/Little, Brown Higher Education, 1990.

> A comprehensive overview of major curriculum issues, including brief descriptions of new directions in the various subject fields.

Peddiwell, J. Abner [Harold Benjamin]. *The Saber-Tooth Curriculum.* New York: McGraw-Hill, 1939.

> A satirical spoof on the origins of schools, the inadequacies of the curriculum, and the reluctance of educators to keep the curriculum relevant to societal needs. Humorous and entertaining reading.

Slavin, Robert E. *Student Team Learning: An Overview and Practical Guide.* Washington, D.C.: National Education Association, 1986.

> A brief but outstanding and useful text for teachers about one of the most effective cooperative learning strategies.

Tyler, Ralph W. *Basic Principles of Curriculum and Instruction.* Chicago: University of Chicago Press, 1950.

> A little booklet that is the classic rationale for curriculum development. Tyler stresses the need to use several data sources, including the learners' needs, to develop an adequate curriculum. Although developed in the fifties, Tyler's principles for curriculum development are still held to be valid.

The following journals contain many interesting and helpful articles for teachers in the respective subject-matter fields.

- *science*—The Science Teacher; School Science and Mathematics
- *mathematics*—The Mathematics Teacher; School Science and Mathematics
- *social studies*—The Social Studies; Social Education
- *reading and language arts*—Language Arts; The Reading Teacher
- *English*—English Journal
- *foreign languages*—Modern Language Journal
- *physical education*—Journal of Health, Physical Education and Recreation
- *music*—Music Educators' Journal
- *art*—Art Education; Arts and Activities; School Arts
- *vocational education*—Industrial Education; Journal of Home Economics; Business Education Forum; Business Education Review

Notes   1. Michael W. Kirst, *Who Controls Our Schools? American Values in Conflict* (New York: Freeman, 1984), pp. 3, 4.

2. Jerome S. Bruner, *The Process of Education* (New York: Random House, 1960).

3. National Commission on Excellence in Education, *A Nation at Risk: The Imperative for Educational Reform* (Washington, D.C.: U.S. Government Printing Office, 1983).

4. College Board, *Academic Preparation for College* (New York: College Board, 1983).

5. John I. Goodlad, *A Place Called School: Prospects for the Future* (New York: McGraw-Hill, 1984), pp. 286–287.

6. National Science Board Commission on Precollege Education in Mathematics, Science and Technology, *Educating Americans for the 21st Century* (Washington, D.C.: National Science Foundation, 1983); and *Science for All Americans*, A Project 2061 Report on Literacy Goals in Science, Mathematics, and Technology (Washington, D.C.: American Association for the Advancement of Science, 1989).

7. Stephen R. Graubard, "Nothing to Fear, Much to Do," *Daedalus* 112 (Spring 1983): 236–237.

8. Ernest L. Boyer, *High School: A Report on Secondary Education in America* (New York: Harper & Row, 1983).

9. Mortimer Adler, *The Paideia Proposal: An Educational Manifesto* (New York: Macmillan, 1982); *The Paideia Program: An Educational Syllabus* (New York: Macmillan, 1984).

10. Martha L. Brown, "Fighting Illiteracy: Let's Not Slight 'School Literacy'." *Network News and Views* 8, no. 10 (October 1989): 61. Reprinted from *Chicago Tribune*, Tuesday, August 22, 1989.

11. "Facts on Illiteracy in America" (Syracuse, N.Y.: Literacy Volunteers of America).

12. Richard C. Anderson et al., *Becoming a Nation of Readers: The Report of the Commission on Reading* (Champaign, Ill.: Center for the Study of Reading, 1985).

13. Elizabeth L. Fontaine, *Reading Aloud to Your Child* (Saratoga, Calif.: R & E, 1985).

14. Patricia M. Cunningham, "They Can All Learn to Read and Write," *Educational Leadership* 43 (February 1986): 82–83.

15. Allan A. Glatthorn, "What Schools Should Teach in the English Language Arts," *Educational Leadership* 46 (September 1988): 46.

16. Ernest Boyer, cited in "Boyer Sees Symbol System Mastery as Top Priority," *ASCD Update* 27 (May 1985): 1.

17. Adapted from a list appearing in Gene D. Shepherd and William B. Ragan, *Modern Elementary Curriculum*, 6th ed. (New York: Holt, Rinehart and Winston, 1982), pp. 204–205.

18. Robert Rothman, "Students Spend Little Time Reading or Writing in School, NAEP Finds," *Education Week*, June 13, 1990, pp. 1, 9.

19. National Research Council *Everybody Counts: A Report to the Nation on the Future of Mathematics Education* (Washington, D.C.: National Academy Press, 1989); and *Curriculum and Evaluation Standards for School Mathematics* (Reston, Va.: National Council of Teachers of Mathematics, 1989).

20. College Board, *Academic Preparation for the World of Work* (New York: College Board, 1984), p. 4.

21. Kathleen McCormick, "Battling Scientific Illiteracy: Educators Seek Consensus, Action on Needed Reforms," *Curriculum Update* (Alexandria, Va.: Association for Supervision and Curriculum Development, 1989), pp. 1–2.

22. Arthur W. Foshay, "Knowledge and the Structure of the Disciplines," in *The Nature of Knowledge: Implications for the Education of Teachers*, ed. William A. Jenkins (Milwaukee: University of Wisconsin, 1961).

23. Irving Morrissett, "Status of Social Studies: The Mid-1980s," *Social Education* 50 (April–May 1986): 303–310.

24. *Charting a Course: Social Studies for the 21st Century*, A Report of the Curriculum Task Force of the National Commission on Social Studies in the Schools (Washington, D.C.: National Commission on Social Studies in the Schools, 1989), p. 6.

25. Robert Marquand, "Needed: A Good Civics Course," *Christian Science Monitor*, July 3, 1986, pp. 1, 29–30.

26. Gerald A. Hayn, "High School Language Instruction in the 1970s," *Hispania* 56 (March 1973): 98.

27. John D. McNeil, *Curriculum: A Comprehensive Introduction,* 4th ed., (Glenview, Ill.: Scott, Foresman/Little, Brown Higher Education, 1990), p. 354.

28. John O'Neil, "Foreign Languages: As Enrollments Climb, A New Focus on 'Proficiency'," *Curriculum Update* (Alexandria, Va.: Association for Supervision and Curriculum Development, January 1990), p. 2.

29. "Language Competence and Cultural Awareness in the United States: A Statement of the Position of the Joint National Committee for Languages and the Council for Language and International Studies," *Modern Language Journal* 68 (Spring 1984): 44.

30. McNeil, *Curriculum: A Comprehensive Introduction,* 4th ed., p. 340.

31. Linda S. Lotto, "The Unfinished Agenda: Report from the National Commission on Secondary Vocational Education," *Phi Delta Kappan* 66 (April 1985): 568–573.

32. College Board, *Academic Preparation for the World of Work; Investing in Our Children: Business and the Public Schools* (New York: Committee for Economic Development, 1985).

33. Lynn Olson, "Federal Agencies Sound the Alarm over the 'School-to-Work Transition,'" *Education Week* May 23, 1990, pp. 1, 19.

34. Michael Kirst, "Choosing Textbooks: Reflections of a State Board President," *American Educator* 9 (Summer 1984): 21.

35. Diane Ravitch, "When the Lobbyists Throw a Learning Curve," *Network News and Views* 8 (August 1989): 70. Reprinted from the *Los Angeles Times,* Sunday, July 16, 1989.

36. Larry Cuban, *How Teachers Taught: Constancy and Change in American Classrooms 1890–1980* (New York: Longman, 1984).

37. Joan S. Hyman and S. Alan Cohen, "Learning for Mastery: Ten Conclusions After 15 Years and 3,000 Schools," *Educational Leadership* 37 (November 1979): 104–109.

38. Thomas R. Guskey and Sally L. Gates, "Synthesis of Research on the Effects of Mastery Learning in Elementary and Secondary Classrooms," *Educational Leadership* 43 (May 1986): 78.

39. Robert E. Slavin, "On Mastery Learning and Mastery Teaching," *Educational Leadership* 46 (April 1989): 77–79.

40. Benjamin S. Bloom, "The Search for Methods of Group Instruction as Effective as One-to-One Tutoring," *Educational Leadership* 41 (May 1984): 4–17.

41. See Slavin, "On Mastery Learning"; and Daisy E. Arredondo and James H. Block, "Recognizing the Connections Between Thinking and Mastery Learning," *Educational Leadership* 47 (February 1990): 4–10.

42. Benjamin S. Bloom, "Helping All Children Learn in Elementary School—and Beyond," *Principal* 67 (March 1988): 12–17.

43. Nancy B. Graves and Theodore D. Graves, "Creating a Cooperative Learning Environment: An Ecological Approach," in *Learning to Cooperate, Cooperating to Learn,* ed. Robert E. Slavin et al. (New York: Plenum, 1985), pp. 406–409.

44. Roger T. Johnson and David W. Johnson, "Student-Student Interaction: Ignored but Powerful," *Journal of Teacher Education* 36 (July–August 1985): 22–26.

45. Robert E. Slavin, *Using Student Team Learning,* rev. ed. (Baltimore, Md.: Johns Hopkins Press, 1980), p. 34.

46. Robert E. Slavin, "Students Motivating Students to Excel: Cooperative Incentives, Cooperative Tasks, and Student Achievement," *Elementary School Journal* 85 (September 1984): 53–63.

47. Robert E. Slavin, "Research on Cooperative Learning: Consensus and Controversy," *Educational Leadership* 47 (December 1989–January 1990): 52.

48. Joyce L. Epstein, "What Matters in the Middle Grades—Grade Span or Practices?" *Phi Delta Kappan* 71 (February 1990): 438–444.

49. Barry K. Beyer, "Critical Thinking: What Is It?" *Social Education* 49 (April 1985): 271.

50. Stephen P. Norris, "Synthesis of Research on Critical Thinking," *Educational Leadership* 42 (May 1985): 44.

51. John Barell, Rosemarie Liebmann, and Irving Sigel, "Fostering Thoughtful Self-Direction in Students," *Educational Leadership* 45 (April 1988): 14–17.

52. Bruce Joyce, "Models for Teaching Thinking," *Educational Leadership* 42 (May 1985): 7.

53. Donald Murray, *Write to Learn* (New York: Holt, 1984), pp. 3–4.

54. Ibid., p. 228.

55. Stephen N. Tchudi and Joanne Yates, *Teaching Writing in the Content Areas: Senior High School* (Washington, D.C.: National Education Association, 1983). The NEA has published similar titles for teachers in elementary and middle schools.

56. Arthur N. Applebee et al., *Writing in the Secondary School: English and the Content Areas* (Urbana, Ill.: National Council of Teachers of English, 1981), p. 101.

57. Carol Bland and Irene Koppel, "Writing as a Thinking Tool," *Educational Leadership* 45 (April 1988): 58–60.

58. *ASCD Update*, 32, no. 9 (November 1990): 4.

59. Many of these ideas appear in a paper by Alphonse Buccino, "Curriculum and Technology," in *Education and Technology: A Profession at the Crossroads*, ed. Richard C. Steinacher, unpublished volume issued by IBM, Academic Information Systems, 1986, pp. 6–41.

60. Pamela Dronka, "Computer Integration into Instruction Is Stuck: Experts Blame Unclear Optimal Uses and Three Implementation Problems," *ASCD Update* 27 (Summer 1985): 1, 6–8.

61. Mortimer Smith, "Fundamental Differences Do Exist," in *American Education Today,* ed. Paul Woodring and John Scanlon (New York: McGraw-Hill, 1964), p. 29.

What Is Life in Schools Like?

CHAPTER PREVIEW

This chapter attempts to describe the school environment and classroom life as reported by a number of social scientists. It examines some of the characteristics of the school as a social system, the nature of student life, and relationships among students.

This chapter emphasizes that:

● The relationship between environment and conditions for learning is important. For learning to occur, learners must interact with their environment.

● The school is a social system, and the nature of that system is extremely influential in students' experiences of school.

● Studies of life in elementary classrooms reveal that students spend time waiting, experience frequent interruptions, are continually distracted, and frequently experience delayed gratification and denied desire.

● Studies of life in secondary classrooms reveal that different students experience varying commitments of time and resources, according to their "specialness," within schools attempting to meet the needs and desires of increasingly diverse populations.

● A review of instructional practices in high school classrooms from 1890 to 1980 indicates that life in high school classrooms hasn't changed much since the turn of the century.

● Peer groups and the teen-age subculture are extremely influential in affecting the attitudes and behaviors of adolescents in schools.

● Teachers' expectations and their consequent behaviors toward students foster student behaviors that result in achievement levels consistent with those expectations, thus tacitly justifying them and fulfilling an unspoken prophecy.

● Within the social system of a school and particular classroom environments can be found the "winners" and "losers" in the educational marketplace.

E ach of us perceives reality differently. As you read this chapter, you will undoubtedly react to particular passages by thinking, "That's just what life in my school was like!" or "It wasn't like that at all." Someone who attended the same school as you did but whose background and experiences were different from yours may remember the school in an entirely different light from the way you remember it. There is no standard version of reality. Moreover, different socioeconomic groups, different communities, and different sections of the country may produce schools that are dissimilar in certain respects. Even two schools in contiguous neighborhoods may be markedly different, and a single school can change radically in a few years' time. But despite these important qualifications, the authors—and other observers—believe that certain conditions are more typical of schools than they are idiosyncratic and that some observations are authentically generalizable. Let's look at life in the schools and see what we can find out about the school as an environment for learning and as a social system.

THE SCHOOL AS AN ENVIRONMENT

The relative importance of heredity and environment is an old issue, and one that seems unlikely to be resolved in the near future. Perhaps it's insoluble. But one thing seems clear: both heredity and the environment deeply influence an individual's capacity to learn. We all feel intuitively, although we'd probably have trouble proving it, the crucial importance of our environment in shaping who we are. John Dewey, the American philosopher and educator contended that the environment

> leads an individual to see and feel one thing rather than another; . . . it strengthens some beliefs and weakens others . . . it gradually produces in him a certain system of behavior. . . . In brief, the environment consists of those conditions that promote or hinder, stimulate or inhibit, the characteristic activities of a living being.[1]

Interaction essential

If school represents a major aspect of the environment of every child, how important is the school environment in facilitating or impeding learning? For the environment to affect learning, interaction must occur; mere physical proximity to a stimulating environment does not guarantee stimulation. This is why taking a group of children from an inner-city ghetto to an art museum to expose them to cultural riches usually has little or no impact on their lives. As George Leonard, an educational innovator, states:

> No environment can strongly affect a person unless it is strongly interactive. To be interactive, the environment must be responsive, that is, must provide relevant feedback to the learner. For the feedback to be relevant, it must meet the learner *where he is,* then program (that is, change in appropriate steps at appropriate times) as he changes. The learner changes (that is, is educated) through his responses to the environment.
> Within these constraints, the human organism is incredibly flexible. If there are limits on the human ability to respond to learning environ-

ments, we are so far away from the limits as to make them inconsequential. Throughout human history to date, it has been the environments, not the human beings, that have run up against limitations.[2]

An environment must, then, be interactive to exert a strong influence.

Competition with other environments

The school environment also tends to suffer in comparison with other learning environments that are a part of children's lives. At one time in history, school was the child's major source of learning about the world. Just the fact that schools possessed books about the world made them a rich source of information. But today the schools are competing with other learning environments, such as those provided by television, movies, radio, compact disks, and video- and audiocassettes. As a result of interacting with these other environments, children are far more sophisticated and knowledgeable. Schools that ignore this fact and do not provide a stimulating, interactive environment for children will continue to produce discontented students.

THE SCHOOL AS AN AGENT OF SOCIALIZATION

Socialization can be defined as the general process of social learning whereby the child learns the many things he or she must know to become an acceptable member of society. The major socializing agencies in the life of a child are the family, the school, the peer group, religious institutions, youth organizations, political and economic institutions, the mass media, and, in some cases, work environments. Some of these agencies, such as the school, are formally created and organized, and some, such as the peer group, are informally created and organized.

Formal and informal curricula

What students learn in the environment of the school extends beyond the planned curriculum of courses or subjects they will take. The planned content and objectives of language arts, mathematics, science, and all the other subject areas available to students constitute this formal or *explicit curriculum,* to use Elliot Eisner's term.[3] In Chapter 8 we looked at the trends in what schools intend for students to learn from this curriculum. But classroom observers have observed that the schools also teach an *informal* or *implicit* (or *hidden*) *curriculum* through which the classroom and school, as learning environments, socialize children to the values that are acceptable to the institution (and to society at large).

Culture of a school

Each school has its own *culture*—a set of beliefs, values, traditions, and ways of thinking and behaving—that distinguishes it from other social institutions and from other schools. Every school attempts to socialize children by getting them to value those things the school teaches both explicitly and implicitly. The more successful students tend to accept these values, whereas many of the less successful students reject the ways of thinking and behaving that the school tries to teach.

What are these values, and how are they communicated to students? Eisner suggests several ways of thinking and behaving valued by many schools. One of them is compliant behavior as opposed to personal initiative. Students soon learn to provide the teacher with what the teacher wants or expects. Eisner maintains that reward systems used by schools teach students to "read" the teacher and the system to determine just what is expected to get the grade, the teacher's attention, or the sticker with the smiling face. Similarly, competitiveness is learned through the example of athletics, grading systems that compare students to each other, and ability grouping to separate students into classes according to their achievement. The many ways in which students learn what a school values include how the school allocates time to subjects of study, the rules established for the school, and even the architecture of the school. Too often, schools and classrooms are furnished for efficiency and economy, and pay less attention to arrangements that could provide privacy or space for small groups of students to work. Eisner writes, "The implicit curriculum of the school is what it teaches because of the kind of place it is."[4]

In this chapter, we have included several descriptions of the kinds of places schools are. As you read the descriptions, look for their interpretations of what these schools teach because of the kinds of places they are. What rules of behavior, rituals and ceremonies, and accepted patterns of teacher and student interaction are communicated to students at these schools? Does the "climate" of

QUESTIONS ABOUT THE SCHOOL ENVIRONMENT

Believing that schools, not merely classrooms, have enduring effects on the children who attend them, Douglas Heath suggests these questions as a guide for those who wish to understand the environment of a school:

1. Is this school so big I'd feel lost in it?
2. How proud are faculty and students about the school?
3. What are the bathrooms like?
4. Do the corridors remind me of state mental hospitals?
5. Are students I see in the hall aloof, sullen, cheerful, effervescent?
6. Do any spontaneously greet me?
7. Does the principal call students by name; do any stop us to ask him or her a question?
8. Do faculty greet me warmly in the teachers' room, or do they ignore me?
9. Would the noise in the cafeteria give me indigestion?
10. Where are the "warm" areas of the school—where faculty and students go when they're down?

11. Where do I feel chilled?
12. How flexibly, imaginatively, even colorfully, have teachers created their work spaces?
13. Would I want to teach in this school?
14. How do I feel when I walk into the classroom I am to observe?
15. Is this teacher's space any different from that of other teachers?
16. What do the arrangement of desks, the presence of plants, the orderliness of the room, the comments on the blackboard tell me about this teacher's assumptions about how students are to behave and learn in this classroom?
17. What does the room tell me about the teacher?

These questions may help you observe a school's tone and spirit as you continue to visit schools in your teacher-preparation program.

Douglas H. Heath, "Developing Teachers, Not Just Techniques," in *Improving Teaching*, ed. Karen K. Zumwalt (Alexandria, Va.: ASCD, 1986), 1–2. Reprinted with permission of the Association for Supervision and Curriculum Development and Douglas H. Heath. Copyright © 1986 by the Association for Supervision and Curriculum Development. All rights reserved.

the classroom and the school suggest warmth, support, and nurturing of individuals, or do observers describe a mood of disinterest, regimentation, and antipathy among staff and students? With these questions in mind, let's first examine life in elementary school classrooms.

STUDIES OF LIFE IN ELEMENTARY SCHOOLS

All of us have remembrances and images of the days we spent in elementary school. For some of us the memories are good ones; for others they are not. One thing is for certain: we have forgotten much of what life in elementary school was like as we experienced it. The next few pages will probably rekindle thoughts and feelings and stir memories. Compare your remembrances with the studies of life in elementary schools reported here.

The Significance of Routine

Jackson's study

Many descriptions of life in elementary schools have been written. Each presents a view of reality as seen through the eyes of the writer. One of the best perspectives on how time is typically spent in the elementary classroom is provided by Philip W. Jackson's classic study, *Life in Classrooms*.[5] Anthropologists have taught us that the humdrum aspects of human existence have cultural significance, and Jackson asserts that we must look at the most routine events in an elementary classroom if we are to understand what happens there. Are certain trivial acts repeated innumerable times? How frequently do they occur? What is their cumulative effect on the child? What do they teach the child? Jackson's observations of elementary school classrooms demonstrate how revealing the answers to these questions can be.

Have you ever figured out how many hours a child spends in school? In most states the school year is 180 days. The day typically begins at eight-thirty and ends at three, a total of six and one-half hours. Thus, if a child doesn't miss a day of school, he or she spends over a thousand hours in school each year. Including kindergarten, the average child will spend over seven thousand hours in elementary school. How are those hours typically spent?

You may think first of the curriculum—so many hours of reading and language arts, so many hours of mathematics, science, play, social studies, music, art, and so on. But what do students really *do* when they are studying these subjects? They talk individually, to the teacher and to one another. They read silently and aloud. They yawn. They look out the window. They raise their hands. They line up. They stand up. They sit down. In short, they do a number of different things, many of them commonplace and trivial. To understand why some of this happens, we first need to look at what the teacher does.

THE TEACHER'S ROLE   Jackson has observed that the elementary teacher engages in as many as a thousand interpersonal interchanges each day. What is the nature of these interchanges? The teaching-learning process consists, for the most part, of talking, and the teacher controls and directs discussion. The teacher acts as a gatekeeper, deciding who shall and who shall not speak. (One may

Controlling discussions . . .

The teacher must keep alive the spark of wonder, to prevent it from becoming blasé from over-excitement, wooden from routine, fossilized through dogmatic instruction, or dissipated through random exercise upon trivial things.

— JOHN DEWEY —

Waiting and delayed gratification are frequent occurrences in elementary school classrooms.

(Elizabeth Crews)

debate whether or not this *should* be the teacher's role, but clearly most teachers function this way.)

. . . supplies, privileges

The teacher also acts as a dispenser of supplies. Since both space and resources are limited and the number of students wishing to use them at any one time is likely to be greater than the supply, the teacher must dole them out. A related function is the granting of special privileges to deserving students—passing out the milk, sharpening pencils, taking the roll, or operating the videocassette player or movie projector. Although little teacher time is involved in awarding these special jobs, they are important because they help structure the classroom socially as a system of rewards and punishments.

. . . time

Timekeeping is another teacher responsibility. It is the teacher who decides when a certain activity ends and another begins, when it is time to stop science and begin spelling, and when to go outside for recess. In some schools the teacher is assisted in timekeeping by bells and buzzers that signal when a "period" is over. As Jackson observes, things happen because it is time for them to occur and not because students want them to.

Result of crowded conditions

These teacher functions can all be seen as responses to the crowded conditions in the classroom. If the teacher were dealing with one student at a time in a tutorial situation, gatekeeping, granting special privileges, dispensing

9 / What Is Life in Schools Like?

317

supplies, and timekeeping would become superfluous. But since a tutorial setting is not feasible, much time and energy are spent keeping order. The resulting atmosphere has unavoidable effects on the students. What are some of the consequences for students in crowded classroom conditions?

WHAT STUDENTS EXPERIENCE One inevitable outcome for the students that results from what Jackson calls the teacher's "traffic-management" functions is delay. Since students' actions are limited by space, material resources, and the amount of teacher attention they can command, there are definite limits on their freedom in the class. In addition, since the class ordinarily moves toward a goal as a group rather than as individuals, its slowest members often determine the pace of progress.

Waiting

Waiting is therefore a familiar activity for elementary school children— waiting in line to get a drink of water, waiting with arm propped at the elbow to be called on to answer a question, waiting to use the paper cutter, waiting until others have finished their work to go on to the next activity, waiting until four other students have finished reading aloud for a chance to do so.

CLASS SIZE AND STUDENT LEARNING

For many years teachers and their professional organizations have argued strongly for the need to reduce class sizes if education for children is to improve. Controversy continued for years on the effects of class size reduction. Now one of the most recent analyses of the effects of class size reduction gives us some insights on this issue. After examining over one hundred studies, Glen E. Robinson reached the following conclusions:

- The most positive effects of small classes on pupil learning occur in grades K–3 in reading and mathematics, particularly in classes of twenty-two or fewer students. However, there is some question of whether the first year's positive effects are sustained in subsequent years.

- Smaller classes can positively affect the academic achievement of economically disadvantaged and ethnic minority students.

- The most favorable effects of smaller classes on positive student attitudes and behaviors are found in the primary grades.

- Within the range of twenty-three to thirty pupils, class size has little impact on the academic achievement of most pupils in most subjects above the primary grades.

- Little if any increase in pupil achievement can be expected from reducing class size if teachers continue to use the same instructional methods and procedures in the smaller classes that they used in the larger ones.

On this last point it appears that many teachers whose class sizes have been substantially reduced in fact do not change their teaching techniques to take advantage of the smaller classes. They do not provide more small-group and individualized instruction. This finding may explain why stronger effects of class size reduction are not found.

Comparing class size reduction with several other instructional strategies, several researchers have concluded that the most effective instructional strategy we have is providing low achievers with one-to-one tutors, including peer tutors, for some portion of their school day.

Glen E. Robinson, "Synthesis of Research on the Effects of Class Size," *Educational Leadership* 47 (April 1990), pp. 80, 82–88, 90. Reprinted with permission.

Denial of desire
Denial of desire is another common experience for the elementary student. A question goes unanswered, a raised hand is ignored, talking out of turn is not permitted, relief of bodily functions is allowed only at specified times. Some denial is necessary, and some is probably beneficial, but one thing is certain: delayed gratification and denied desire are learned in school. Though you as a teacher will invariably be kept busy, this is not the case for your students, and a certain amount of student frustration is bound to develop as a result of delay and denial.

Interruptions
Students also experience frequent interruptions and social distraction. Interruptions are of many sorts—interruptions of seatwork by the teacher to give additional instructions or to clarify one student's question, mechanical interruptions when the motion picture film starts to flicker, interruptions when messages from the principal's office are read aloud to the class, interruptions for fire drills, interruptions when the teacher is working with one student and another student misbehaves, and so on. Students are expected either to ignore these intrusions or to quickly resume their activities. The emphasis on an inflexible schedule contributes to the sense of interruption by making students frequently begin activities before their interest has been aroused and stop at the height of their interest when the schedule dictates that they must begin another task.

Social distraction
A related phenomenon is social distraction. Students are often asked to behave as if they were in solitude, when in fact they are surrounded by thirty or so other people. At certain times during the day, students are assigned seatwork and required to work on their own. At such times communication among students is often discouraged, if not forbidden. To be surrounded by friends, sometimes seated across from each other at a table, and not be allowed to talk is a difficult and tempting situation. As Jackson remarks, "These young people, if they are to become successful students, must learn how to be alone in a crowd."[6]

Delay, denial, interruption, and *social distraction,* then, are characteristic of life in elementary classrooms. How are children affected by these classroom facts of life? It is difficult to measure their effect because they are present to a greater or lesser degree in every classroom. Also, different students have different levels of tolerance for these phenomena. It would seem, however, that the student who either possesses or quickly develops patience will find school more tolerable than the student who lacks it. The ability to control desires, delay rewards, and stifle impulses seems to be necessary to the "mature" student. Jackson explains:

Patience a necessity
> Thus, the personal quality commonly described as patience—an essential quality when responding to the demands of the classroom—represents a balance, and sometimes a precarious one, between two opposed tendencies. On the one hand is the impulse to act on desire, to blurt out the answer, to push to the front of the line, or to express anger when interrupted. On the other hand is the impulse to give up the desire itself, to stop participating in the discussion, to go without a drink when the line is long, or to abandon an interrupted activity.[7]

The necessary balance is achieved by the majority of students. Others may respond in either of the two ways just described, or in still another manner. If you as a teacher are to understand why children act as they do, an understanding of the dynamics of the classroom is a necessity. Jackson's book offers considerable insight into life in elementary classrooms.

More About Life in Elementary Schools
While public attention during the early eighties was directed toward perceived problems in high schools, some educators were calling for a closer look at what happens in elementary classrooms. With the increased focus on students at risk of dropping out of school, preschool and elementary school practices came under much scrutiny.

EDUCATION: A WORLD VIEW

• •

LIFE IN JAPANESE ELEMENTARY SCHOOLS

Nancy Sato, a doctoral student at Stanford University who speaks fluent Japanese, spent three years in Japan observing fifth- and sixth-grade Tokyo classrooms. The following are some of her observations.

Much of Japanese elementary education is designed to help children assume responsibility. For example, they are responsible for fetching lunches, serving them, and cleaning up afterwards. They are also responsible for classroom discipline. Teachers start class whether kids are sitting down or not, or whether the children are misbehaving or making lots of noise. When asked about this, teachers said that it was the children's responsibility to quiet their peers and to find out what they had missed. As Sato discovered, "Surprisingly, without teacher reprimand, kids would quiet down within minutes. But it never got so quiet that there was not someone talking or someone looking at someone else's notebook. It's orderly and well mannered *in its own way*."

Teamwork and community ownership are other values that are emphasized. Students and teachers spend a portion of each day cleaning the whole school. No job is considered beneath any child or adult. If a student or teacher sees something out of order in the classroom, he or she puts it back *naturally*. If a child spills something, another child *naturally* helps clean it up.

The Japanese never group elementary school children by ability, because then different children would re-

ceive different educational and social treatment. All children begin in the same class, and the cohort advances together from grade to grade. No matter how poorly a student may be doing, he or she is never retained a grade. Conversely, no child skips a grade because there is no concept of the "gifted." Each student is considered gifted in some way. By not grouping or labeling kids, Sato observes, all students learn teamwork, friendship, and taking responsibility for one another.

"Every minute of the school day is time to be used educationally," says Sato. The Japanese define education much more broadly than we do. Sports, art, music, health and hygiene, work habits, and even calligraphy are considered "basic." As a result, even a child who is not doing well in an academic subject has the opportunity to feel positive about school. The student whose answers are laughed at in mathematics might, a short time later, draw a picture that the other children envy.

One of the most significant aspects of the teacher-student relationship is the importance of caring. Japanese teachers feel they must establish the best positive relationship with each student.

How does this description of life in Japanese elementary schools compare with life in American elementary schools with which you are familiar?

Cynthia Patrick, "A Fresh Look at Japanese Education," *Stanford Observer*, January 1990. Used with permission.

Some educators maintain that schools do not put into practice what is known about the stages of children's intellectual development. Classrooms in an elementary school are usually organized according to the ages of students. But, as the psychologist Jean Piaget has shown, not all students of the same age may function at the same level of intellectual development.* Some classroom observers note that in any elementary grade, one-half to one-third of the children may not be developmentally ready for the academic and social demands placed on that age group. It has been estimated that in a chronologically grouped classroom, the developmental ages of the students may span a two-and-a-half-year range.[8] Placing children in grades by their birth year, employing standardized curricula and teaching materials, and using single styles of instruction may be inconsistent with Jean Piaget's findings about children's stages of development.

Different rates of development

In addition, critics of the organization of elementary classrooms observe a trend among schools and parents to require more academic content at younger ages. What students once learned in middle school grades may now be taught in the primary grades. The desire to increase academic achievement has sometimes put pressure on children that may be inconsistent with their developmental stages. On the other hand, children in elementary schools in other countries are often studying subjects that American children don't encounter until much later in their schooling.

More pressure today

Others, who have described the "sameness" of elementary education, report that a nearly standardized curriculum pervades elementary schools across the nation. Teachers have little power to select textbooks, materials, or standards of evaluation; the flexibility to gear programs to individual needs does not exist. Standardized testing programs rule the content of a curriculum set up in a lock-step progression. And, increasingly, the tendency is to specify the time spent on each subject to forestall unequal treatment by teachers who do not like a subject or who feel unprepared to teach it.

Lack of flexibility

This lack of individual spirit has been noted by Dennis Gray, former deputy director of the Council of Basic Education, who has described in an interview the values that children learn in the implicit curriculum of elementary schools. According to Gray, students learn that correctness is valued more than curiosity, that group is more important than the individual, and that the school places more value on the final product than on the process of getting to it.[9]

Values learned

As more attention falls on the strengths and weaknesses of elementary education, we should be able to learn more about elementary schools as an environment for learning and socialization.

---

* Jean Piaget's research led him to conclude that all human beings passed through predictable stages of mental development. Individuals at each stage have a predictable way of thinking about things. Further, the development of each stage is a necessity for advancement to the next stage. These four main stages are the sensorimotor stage (birth to two years), the preoperational stage (two to six years), the period of concrete observations (seven to eleven years), and the period of formal operations (eleven through adulthood).

STUDIES OF LIFE IN MIDDLE AND JUNIOR HIGH SCHOOLS

Little descriptive information

We know much less about the routines and roles of students and teachers in the middle grades than we do about those in elementary grades. One reason for this is that concern with students in the middle grades has only recently become a focus of educators' attention. In the late 1980s, several reports emerged specifically identifying the needs of early adolescents and recommending some educational remedies for students in the middle grades.* They do not, however, provide comprehensive descriptions of what actually goes on in the middle grades. Perhaps another reason that much less descriptive information exists about middle schools is that public school in the middle grades is not very homogeneous, so it is even more difficult to talk about typical schools and experiences. Let's begin our examination of middle schools by taking a look at some

---

* For example, *Turning Points: Preparing American Youth for the 21st Century,* Report of the Task Force on Education of Young Adolescents, Carnegie Council on Adolescent Development (New York: Carnegie Corporation of New York, 1989).

BEGINNING TEACHER EVALUATION STUDY

A study sponsored by the National Institute of Education, the Beginning Teacher Evaluation Study (BTES) was developed to identify teaching activities and classroom conditions that foster student learning in elementary schools. The study focused on instruction in reading and mathematics at grades 2 and 5. From this study we have obtained additional quantitative data on how elementary school children spend their time.

1. *Time allocations.* About 58 percent of the school day was allocated to academic activities, about 23 percent to nonacademic activities (music, art, physical education), and about 19 percent to noninstructional activities such as transitions between activities and class business.
2. *Engaged time.* On the average, students spent one hour and 30 minutes (second grade) and one hour and 55 minutes (fifth grade) actively engaged in reading and math activities. In the highest classrooms the engaged time was about 30 minutes longer, and in the lowest classrooms it was about 30 minutes less than the average.
3. On the average, students were engaged about 73 percent of the allocated time in reading and math.

4. During allocated time for academics, students were unengaged for about 16 minutes per hour, on the average. Half of this unengaged time was taken up with interim activities (such as passing out and collecting papers) or waiting for help, and during the other 8 minutes students were clearly off task.
5. *Seatwork.* Overall, students spent about two-thirds of the allocated academic time in seatwork (or self-paced activities) and about one-third of their time working with an adult. Engagement was higher in teacher-led settings (about 84 percent) than in seatwork settings (about 70 percent). An inevitable fact of classroom life is that if a teacher working alone divides a class into three groups, students will be working alone two-thirds of the time.
6. Student engagement during seatwork increased when there was substantive interaction between teacher and student during seatwork. Such substantive interaction consisted of a teacher (or aide) monitoring seatwork and holding students accountable by asking questions. Such substantive interaction was most effective when it occurred 11 percent or more of the seatwork time.

Barak V. Rosenshine, "How Time Is Spent in Elementary Classrooms," *The Journal of Classroom Interaction* 17 (Winter 1981): 23–24.

of the different ways that public schools in the middle grades are structured and consider some educational implications of these differences.

Most obviously, education in the middle grades differs by grade configurations. In a national survey of middle-grade practices and trends, researchers at Johns Hopkins University found that schools around the country enrolled seventh-grade students in about thirty different grade spans. For example, some schools were structured to educate all students in grades K–12; others served primarily elementary and middle grades, such as K–8; and yet other schools served middle to high school students such as grades 7–12. Some schools were structured just for students in the middle grades, but even within this group there was great variety. "Middle schools" mainly contained students in grades 6–8, but also in 5–8, 5–7, and 6–7. Other schools were strictly "7–8" schools. And another grade configuration of "junior high" schools structured students in grades 7–9, 6–9, or 5–9.[10]

What difference does it make where students in the middle grades are educated? The researchers at Johns Hopkins found that there were direct relationships between grade configuration and such important educational characteristics as school goals, report card entries, course offerings, instructional practices, relationships between students and staff, and other trends in middle-grade practices.[11]

One factor the researchers identified as related to the organization of middle grades was size. In the various schools that were examined, enrollment in grade 7 ranged from 5 students to more than 2,250! Consider for a moment the very different educational experiences these students will have in their middle school years, in regard to familiarity with peers, class size, teacher contact, and so forth.

School goals were also examined across different grade configurations. Regardless of the grade span of their schools, most principals identified mastery of subject matter and basic skills as the most important goals at their institutions. However, secondary goals of educational importance varied by the school organization. As might be expected, principals of K–12 schools assigned more importance to higher-level skills such as reasoning, problem solving, and creative thinking. Principals of K–8 schools put less emphasis on personal growth and developmental issues, such as self-esteem and self-knowledge, than principals of middle schools.[12] Though students in the middle grades are being educated in each of these types of settings, it becomes clear that the educational goals and expectations of students in the middle grades are greatly influenced by the organization or grade configuration of the school.

The goals that schools set for students influence middle school education in other ways as well, including the curriculum offered and the instructional methods used. This same study found that schools serving younger students (K–8, for example) typically offered fewer elective courses, such as home economics or typing, for students in the middle grades. Seventh- and eighth-grade teachers used drill practices more frequently and made less use of higher-order thinking activities such as writing essays, using computers, and discussing

Many grade configurations

Varying school sizes

Varying school goals

Although middle schools vary as to class size and organization, they all share the goals of subject matter mastery and basic skills knowledge.

(*Elizabeth Crews*)

controversial issues. These schools, however, also reported greater use of such methods as peer- or cross-grade tutoring.[13]

Staffing patterns

Another distinction between schools of different grade configurations was seen in staffing patterns. Classroom structure for students in the middle grades varied from completely self-contained classrooms, in which one teacher taught one group of students all major subject areas, to completely departmentalized schools in which each teacher specialized in a single subject area and taught several different classes of students. As you might expect, schools serving younger students (K+) had a larger percentage of self-contained classrooms, whereas middle schools showed a greater percentage of departmentalized staffing.[14]

Certification patterns

Teachers also differed by type of certification held. Teachers with secondary certification were more likely to be "subject matter–oriented," and middle-grade students who were taught by subject-matter "experts" showed higher levels of achievement. On the other hand, teachers who were certified in elementary education were more likely to be more "student-centered" and tended to focus on both the academic and personal development of individual students. The research indicated that relationships between students and teachers in self-contained classrooms tended to be more positive.[15]

So we see a variety of educational experiences occurring along a number of dimensions in the middle grades. Is one means of educating students in the middle grades best? No, probably not. The many aspects of diversity we have just examined—from grade configuration to school goals to teacher orientation—appear to present a series of tradeoffs in educating students in the middle grades. What is consistently being identified as important for educating students in the middle grades, however, is that the developmental needs of early adolescents must be acknowledged and considered in this decision-making process.

STUDIES OF LIFE IN HIGH SCHOOLS

No aspect of our public educational system has received more study than our high schools. During the excellence reform movement of the 1980s, the American public high school became the primary object of reform in our educational system. Several studies described the problems of high schools and addressed ways in which life in high schools could be improved. Let's turn now to some of these studies.

Some Common Characteristics

In 1983 the Carnegie Foundation for the Advancement of Teaching released a study intended to guide discussion about needed reforms in American secondary education. Their report, *High School: A Report on Secondary Education in America,* provides insights about life in high schools.[16]

High School

Although each high school has unique characteristics, Ernest Boyer and his team of investigators found many similarities among the fifteen high schools they visited. Typically, a school day is divided into six or seven 50-minute periods. Hall passes, dress codes, and rules against smoking are often part of life in a high school. From most principals' points of view, absenteeism, class cutting, and parents' disinterest are moderately serious problems; fights, thefts, and vandalism are less serious problems.[17] High school is a place where young people experiment with growing up, find the support that may not be available at home, and attempt to accomplish a variety of goals ranging from marking time to finding social acceptance to preparing for intellectual challenges.

Multiple goals

Tracing the history of the high school, Boyer concludes that "high schools have accumulated purposes like barnacles on a weathered ship."[18] Americans seem to want high schools to accomplish everything. The resulting confusion of goals is evident in the variety of goal statements adopted by the states for their schools, in the written goals found in teachers' manuals or school district curriculum guides, and in the responses given when these researchers asked teachers and students about school goals. Students voiced desires to get out, to be with their friends, to go to a good college, to pass competency exams, and to get a job. Teachers often emphasized preparing students for college or helping students get good grades; vocational teachers expressed their goal as helping students get jobs. What should the schools be expected to accomplish? And how might life in schools be different if they had a clear sense of purpose that was larger than a single class on a single day? Boyer concludes that the vision "must go beyond keeping students in school and out of trouble, and be more significant than adding up the Carnegie units the student has completed."[19]

In an attempt to provide something for everyone, high schools have developed a comprehensive curriculum with many elective courses. How do students decide what to take and what not to take among dozens or, in some cases, hundreds of courses? Students report that their choices are guided more by parents and peers than by guidance counselors or teachers.[20] Boyer and his colleagues conclude that students' academic programs may be shaped most decisively by the "tracks" in which they are enrolled. Academic tracks stress the traditional subjects—English, mathematics, science, and foreign language—as preparation for college. A general track usually allows a greater number of elective courses and less rigorous versions of the traditional subjects. Vocational programs of study may include a combination of academic and job-related courses; students in this track are preparing for a job after graduation. Because of the variations in courses required for these tracks and the differences in standards for student achievement among the tracks, a high school education can take on myriad meanings. Boyer asserts that "putting students into boxes can no longer be defended."[21] Students categorized as "nonacademic" may lose teachers' esteem and forfeit their own place in a world that requires academic and work skills.

Influence of tracking

What happens in classrooms during those six- or seven-period days? These classroom observers found a standardized use of space: rooms equipped with rows of desks for thirty or more students, a teacher's desk at the front of the rows, and the traditional black or green board. The use of time is also routine, consumed by procedural tasks like taking attendance and keeping records, although relentlessly interrupted by announcements on the intercom, pep assemblies, photo sessions, and many other distractions.[22]

Boyer also describes teachers' powerlessness over the factors that influence the quality of instruction they can deliver: the numbers of students in a class, the lengths of school days and periods, the formats of report cards, which courses will be taught, and even what textbooks will be used. Pressures of time and heavy student loads invite traditional, teacher-centered instruction: lecturing, question-and-answer sessions, and routine homework assignments. Too often, students play passive roles in classrooms dominated by regimentation and conformity. Many teachers enter into unspoken compacts with their students: in return for students who will cooperate in preserving an orderly class, the teacher will ask for little in the way of achievement.

Pressures on teachers

These pictures of life in high school classrooms contrast with glimpses of teachers who challenge their students to think, to express themselves creatively, and to struggle with unanswerable questions. Students in such classes are pushed to perform as individuals; their teachers share a vision for them that includes high expectations of success. Which picture is more characteristic of high school life? Did the reform movements of the 1980s create conditions in schools that will encourage teachers to teach well in the 1990s? At the time they finished their study, Boyer and his team felt that the time was ripe for a true renewal of high school education. By the early 1990s, however, this renewal has yet to take place in most high schools.

Instruction in the High School Classroom

In a review of instructional practices in American classrooms from 1890 to 1980, Larry Cuban concludes that the high school of today is remarkably similar to the high school at the turn of the century.[23] While gathering descriptions of over 1,200 classrooms, Cuban examined how classroom space was arranged, the ratio of teacher talk to student talk, the manner of grouping that the teacher used for instruction (whole class, small group, or individual), the presence of learning or interest centers used by students as part of a normal school day, and how much physical movement students were allowed within the classroom. The overall picture showed that there is a striking uniformity between today's high schools and those of the 1890s. Even during the 1965–1975 period, when informal education in the form of student-centered instruction and open classroom practices influenced some elementary classrooms, teacher-centered instruction persisted in most high schools. Whole-class instruction, teachers talking most of the time while students listened, little student mobility, and a narrow range of activities completed by the entire class at one time continued to characterize high school instruction.

Same as in 1890

A National Science Foundation (NSF) study, conducted in 1977 and reviewed by Cuban, surveyed a sample of more than five thousand U.S. teachers on their teaching methods.[24] In high school, regardless of subject, over half the

Dominant teaching methods

How Students Spend Classroom Time

An eight-year study in which over one thousand classrooms were observed has yielded interesting data on how teachers teach and how time in classrooms is used. The amount of classroom time actually spent on instruction was about 70 percent at the elementary school level and 75 percent at the senior high level. At the typical high school, about 70 percent of the time spent on instruction involved verbal interaction or "talk," with the typical teacher "out-talking" his or her class of students by a ratio of three to one. Of the approximately 150 minutes of talk each day, only 7 minutes involved teachers' responses to individual students.

The way in which students spent most of their classroom hours varied from level to level. At the elementary school level, about 60 percent of students' time during a day was spent preparing for and cleaning up after assignments. At the junior high school level, approximately 59 percent of the students' time was spent listening to teachers explain or lecture. Students at the senior high school level spent 54 percent of their time fulfilling written assignments.

The study found that there was very little instructional variability. The major activities of the classroom were lectures, written assignments, and quizzes, particularly in the academic subject areas. In the arts, physical education, and vocational education, there were more demonstrations, discussions, various types of physical performing, and production of products other than written ones, although the differences between these subjects and the academic ones were less than the researchers expected.

Teachers were very much in control. Students were rarely involved in planning or evaluating activities. Instruction usually involved the total class; small-group activity was rare. Overall, there was minimal student movement in the classroom, minimal student-to-student or student-to-teacher interaction, and low, nonintimate affect (either positive or negative).

The researchers conclude that the formal and informal experiences of teachers and the messages they receive from the internal and external context of schooling all reinforce the status quo.

Source: John I. Goodlad, *A Place Called School: Prospects for the Future* (New York: McGraw-Hill, 1984).

time was spent in whole-group instruction. Lecture, discussion, tests, and quizzes were favored methods. Student-centered practices, like student reports and projects or use of lab materials, either decreased from the elementary to secondary grades (except in science classrooms) or failed to constitute more than a reported 25 percent of classroom time.

The apparent invulnerability of high school classrooms to substantial instructional change leads Cuban to conclude that such change is not likely to occur. He notes many structural givens, some of which echo Boyer's observations: teachers generally do not control the number and type of students in their classes, the extra instructional help available to students, the length of the school day or class period, the format or content of the report card, the choice of standardized tests, or the grades or subjects to be taught. Cuban thus suggests the following reasons for the stability of teacher-centered instruction:

> For public schools, chairs in rows, recitations, whole group instruction, worksheets, and textbook assignments need to be viewed as a series of successful solutions invented by teachers to solve daily problems of managing a score or more of students while they also acquired information and values. Coping with these structures, teachers constructed workable pedagogical solutions that proved useful in personally maintaining control while carrying out instruction.[25]

Noting that the margin for change may be slim at the high school level as compared with the elementary level, Cuban recommends reforms that concentrate on teacher-centered approaches to improve instruction; such reforms are more likely to succeed than attempts to shift toward more student-centered approaches that give students more responsibility for controlling their own learning. In addition, the commitment of teachers must be secured and help from outside the classroom must be offered when reforms increase the demands on teachers' time and energy.

Peer Groups and Teen Subcultures

Operating both inside and outside of school is an influential socializing agent—the peer group. Children are members of two social worlds: the world of adults and the world of their peers. As members of the adult world, children are always in a position of subordinate status; adults have privileges and rights that children don't. In the peer world, children have equal status and learn from one another. As members of the adult world, children are expected to show deference and respect for authority. As members of the peer world, they can express their own attitudes, explore personal relationships, and test themselves against others.

Sociologist James Coleman's classic studies of peer relationships among adolescents have resulted in some very interesting observations.* Coleman be-

---

* James S. Coleman, "The Adolescent Subculture and Academic Achievement," in *Society and Education,* ed. R. Havighurst, B. Neugarten, and J. Falk (Boston: Allyn and Bacon, 1967), pp. 109–115. Coleman's findings were first reported in 1960. Do you think his observations are still valid today?

High school social life, with its emphasis on peer groups and subcultures, can exert a strong influence on student values.

(*Susan Lapides 1990*)

lieves that industrial society, by shifting much of the responsibility for a child's training from parents to the school and by extending the necessary period of training, has made the high school into a social system of adolescents. The values and activities of this adolescent subculture are quite different from those of adult society, and its members' most important associations are with one another rather than with adults. Society has created for adolescents a separate institution of their own; home is merely a dormitory, whereas "real" living consists of activities unique to the peer group.

How can teen subcultures be identified? Observers in high schools find several categories of students. In *High School: A Report on Secondary Education in America* (1983) Ernest Boyer reported that visitors to a midwestern high school heard student groups referred to as "burnouts," "jocks," or "socies."[26] Another researcher, Penelope Eckert, spent four years studying teen-age subcultures in schools in the Detroit, Michigan, area.[27] Like Boyer, she also identified the "jocks" and the "burnouts" as the two major opposing categories of

Jocks and burnouts

dents.* Although the majority of high school students are not members of either category, Eckert found that an important part of most adolescents' social identity is dominated by the opposition between these two categories of students. Even the "in-betweens" tend to describe their social identity in terms of traits shared with each of the two categories. The jocks and burnouts are the teen-age embodiments of the middle and working class, respectively, and each defines itself very consciously as what the other is not. As such, they do not constitute clear groups or cliques; they are cultural categories, which define and unify collections of groups and cliques.

The jocks are the "leading crowd," who enthusiastically participate in, and receive the endorsement of, the school. The term *jock* originated in sports, which are so central to the high school culture, but it is broadened to include those nonathletic students whose "clean" lifestyle embraces acceptance of the school and the social institutions within it. The burnouts accept the necessity of high school graduation for entrance into the working class, but they have an adversarial, rather than cooperative, relationship with the high school. Burnouts' alienation with school comes from the sense that it is not serving their needs well. Burnouts focus on the more immediate development of adult status as defined in the working-class world by developing egalitarian social networks to transcend the school context. They disdain the jocks' absorption in the limited context of the high school and their "playing" like adults in that environment. Eckert observes that the resulting jock-burnout split is a function of competition among adolescents for control over the norms and values of their cohorts.

> Responding to different, yet specifically adolescent, needs, each category provides a cultural milieu within which its members can negotiate their way through the difficult period of adolescence, and into their adult social statuses. Participation in either of these cultures represents a very particular way of being an adolescent and serves as training for corresponding adult roles.[28]

The jock and burnout categories emerge upon entrance to junior high school. To differentiate themselves, the two categories begin to separate their worlds by developing opposing territories, appearances, demeanors, and activities. Although the jocks and burnouts know little about each other, everyone knows of their differences in clothing, ways of speaking, hangouts, and habits.

Symbols of membership

Clothing and adornment are probably the most powerful symbolic indicator of category membership. Whereas jocks wear polo shirts, button-down shirts, and crew-neck sweaters, burnouts tend toward rock concert T-shirts and

---

* *Jocks* and *Burnouts* may not be the terms used in the schools in your area, but you are likely to find groupings of students with similar characteristics.

jackets. Jocks wear pastel colors, whereas Burnouts wear dark colors. Their preferences in music are also distinct.

Within the physical environment of the school, jocks and burnouts tend to stake out certain territories as their own, and very little cross-occupation of these spaces occurs. Jocks accept the facilities provided by the school and use them as they were intended: they store their books in their lockers, eat in the cafeteria, and use the bathrooms for their intended purpose. Burnouts, on the other hand, express their counterculture orientation by transforming the school facilities to suit their needs. One of the best examples of this space transformation centers around cigarette smoking: as burnouts' smoking leads them to hang out in parking lots, bathrooms, loading docks, and courtyards. Burnouts also tend to avoid the cafeteria as an eating place, preferring to bring packaged food or to avoid eating altogether.

In another study examining social groupings of students, researchers for John Goodlad's *A Place Called School: Prospects for the Future* asked junior and senior high school students to indicate which of six types of students they thought of as most popular.[29] Junior high students listed athletes and students with good looks as the most popular. At the senior high level these two categories accounted for 79 percent of the choices. Smart student types received only 14 percent of the junior high choices and 7 percent of senior high votes for most popular type. Goodlad concludes that there is more to school for adolescents than "school work." When asked to select one response from twelve available to the question "What is the *one* best thing about this school?" students at both

PROBLEMS OF YOUTH EMPLOYMENT

Another aspect of teen-age culture that affects schooling is youth employment. Prior to 1970, students from the middle class seldom had to combine school with substantial commitments to the work force. Today more than 70 percent of all sixteen-year-olds who are in school now work, and they are spending much more time on the job. Although the jobs that students have are not usually full-time, they may require as many as thirty hours a week, often in the evenings. And although jobs may provide alternative sources of self-esteem or gratification for students who don't do well academically or who don't excel in other school-sponsored activities, for most students they tend to interfere with school. The immediate finan-

cial reward of wages and what they will purchase often overrides the deferred gratification promised for successful performance in school. Prospective secondary school teachers should be aware that they will likely encounter students who have little time to read books or do projects, and who may fall asleep in their classes because they worked late the night before. And many of these students refuse to let schoolwork interfere with their jobs. The problem is compounded when teachers, in response to students who work, reduce the number and complexity of assignments, lower their aspirations for students, and teach less. If you are planning to teach high school, then you will most likely confront this issue.

Kathleen P. Bennett and Margaret D. LeCompte, *How Schools Work: A Sociological Analysis of Education* (New York: Longman, 1990), p. 85.

levels most frequently answered "my friends." At the low end of the spectrum of choices were "nothing," "classes I'm taking," and "teachers." Social aspects of schooling seem to contribute forcefully to students' perceptions of school.

When subcultures begin and fade

Membership in teen-age subcultures begins to form in the junior high schools as cliques develop around particular interests such as athletics, academics, student government, cars, or drugs. These groups strengthen as the teenagers begin to move away from their families, and peer membership becomes a type of new family where youngsters find comfort and support. By the sophomore year of high school, the subcultures have stabilized so much that it is difficult for individuals to move from one group to another. By senior year, however, the hold of the subcultures on students begins to weaken. The students are developing more self-confidence, and they start seeking greater freedom. At this point the friendship group becomes a drag on their autonomy.

Until that happens, however, the teen subcultures exert a strong influence on the values of their members. Conflict between the subcultures often occurs, especially between the jocks and the burnouts, each of which views with contempt the values dominant in the other group. Jocks disdain the burnouts' resistance to authority and achievement. Burnouts are equally contemptuous of the jocks' interest in student government and athletics.

Schools fail with burnouts

Most high schools have done a reasonably good job of making academically-and socially-oriented students an integral part of school life. The schools have not been very successful in doing the same thing with subcultures like the

Don't Be a "Brain/Nerd": Underachieve!

Do American high school students avoid outstanding academic achievement for fear of being labeled as "nerds"? The answer is, "yes," according to two researchers at the National Center for Effective Secondary Schools, once located at the University of Wisconsin-Madison. Drawing on a sample of eight thousand high school students in Wisconsin and California, the researchers discovered that teen-agers often express resentment of high achievers by making these students, often called "brains," look like losers by associating them with "nerds," the losers in the peer social system. This connection between brains and nerds is often reinforced in movies and other mass media.

Many high school students avoid this loser connec-

tion by *underachieving*. To avoid being rejected by their peers as nerds, these high achievers decide it is easier to drop their achievement levels below the criterion level for the brain crowd. It's O.K. to be a good student, but not *too* good a one.

If we are to help students achieve at their maximum level, educators must break this brain-nerd connection. To do this, educators must recognize that there is a tension between academic achievement and social acceptance, and help students structure a social system in which excelling academically doesn't mark a student for social isolation.

B. Bradford Brown and Laurence Steinberg, "Academic Achievement and Social Acceptance," *The Education Digest* 55 (March 1990): 57–60. Condensed from *National Center on Effective Secondary Schools Newsletter*, 4 (Fall 1989): 2–4.

burnouts. In fact, because burnouts reject the schools' values, the schools may in turn be reinforcing the alienation felt by this group. Trying to find ways to bring members of alienated subcultures into participation in their schools, to bring the loners or outsiders into greater contact with their peers, and to channel peer influence as a positive force are major challenges for high school and junior high school educators.

The Shopping Mall High School

You may recall from your reading of Chapter 4, "What Is the History of American Education?" that during the nineteenth century American high schools underwent a fundamental shift in their missions and curricula. In the late eighteenth century, there were two main forms of secondary education in the United States: grammar schools, which prepared individuals, primarily men, for college, and academies, which prepared individuals for vocations in business and trade. By the late nineteenth century, public high schools had replaced both grammar schools and academies as the predominant form of secondary education, but there was considerable debate as to what their mission should be. Should the high school continue the functions of the grammar school by focusing primarily on the preparation of students for college, a mission that would demand a strong curricular emphasis on such subjects as classical and European languages and literature? Or should it instead, like the academy, focus on a more practical curriculum that would enable graduates to participate in the full range of industrial occupations?

Comprehensive high schools

In typically American fashion, a compromise evolved that resulted in the comprehensive high school. Why make a choice when the high schools could serve both missions? By World War II a common pattern in American high school education was a large number of parallel curricula—such as English, college preparatory, manual training, science, and so forth—all offered in a single high school.

Examining how this pattern might have changed by the 1980s, a group of researchers investigated fifteen high schools, searching for recurring patterns or an image that could typify American high schools. Their published study, *The Shopping Mall High School: Winners and Losers in the Educational Marketplace*,[30] suggests that the high schools' characteristics resemble those of a shopping mall, with an emphasis on variety and choice for the consumer.

Emphasis on variety and choice

The authors of this study focus on a reality with which high schools must cope: a diverse student body. In response to this reality, schools have offered an increasingly diverse curriculum in an attempt to provide something for everybody. At the same time that variety characterizes school offerings, the principles of choice and neutrality are equally important. Students are expected to make their own course selections; the schools maintain neutrality in regard to students' or parents' choices among the many alternatives offered. The customer has the final word.

Staying with the shopping mall metaphor, the study found that some customers (students) are serious about buying, others are just browsing and looking for ideas on what to buy, and still others are at the mall to meet their friends and "cruise." Faced with customers with such different levels of commitment, teachers reach accommodations or "treaties" that promote mutual goals or keep the peace. For example, some teachers make their deals crystal clear when they advise students, "Don't get into my class if you don't want to work." If students don't want to play by these rules, they don't have to take the course.

Most classroom treaties are not this formal or public, however, but are *tacit* arrangements made to accommodate students and teachers in a manner satisfactory to all. These classroom bargains combine the opposite impulses to both engage in and avoid learning. If teachers preach or push too hard, some students resist. To avoid this resistance, individual teachers find the appropriate balance in their classrooms between requiring academic rigor and allowing students to opt out of learning engagement entirely. As one teacher commented, "I think I get along fairly well with most of the kids, but to be perfectly truthful I think I get along because I don't put a lot of pressure on them."[31]

Within the shopping mall high school can be found "specialty shops," the niches for students and families wanting more learning and school engagement. These can include top-track programs, special education programs, vocational and technical education programs, and extracurricular programs like band or football. Because the students in these programs have been designated as special, they tend to receive special attention. In contrast, the average or unspecial students are generally ignored by the specialty shops; they do not receive the additional commitment of time, personal relationships, and intensity of learning generally given to specialty-shop students.

Although school personnel were not precise about who the middle students were—using terms such as *average, general, normal,* and *regular*—the researchers concluded that "few characteristics of the shopping mall high school are more significant than the existence of unspecial students in the middle who are ignored and poorly served."[32] These students have no important allies or advocates. Their treaties are characterized by avoidance of learning, not engagement. Schools may attempt to nurture these students' self-esteem but do not make academic demands on them. As a result, parents of these students occasionally demand a specialty program for their children or transfer them to private schools where purposes are more focused and attention is more personal. Without these opportunities to experience the purpose, push, and personalization of a specialty shop, the unspecial students become the losers in the educational marketplace.

As Laurence D. Brown notes in a review of this study,[33] the researchers have offered evidence to support generalizations made by previous high school observers. Among them is the conclusion that although students may have equal access to a high school education, enormous differences may exist in the opportunities available to them within their schools. "Effective" schooling is marked by a consensus of purpose, high expectations for students, and a supportive climate, and the "treaties" notion of this study emphasizes the power that teachers and students have to negotiate the quality of education. But what can schools and teachers do to help all students be winners? The suggestions are many, but

Teachers' expectations and their resultant behavior towards students can greatly affect student learning.

(Elizabeth Crews)

reading this study may provide a beginning place for your thinking about the problem.

OTHER ASPECTS OF CLASSROOM LIFE

Those who study classroom life often observe that not all students succeed; clearly, some fail in their classroom environments. As students progress through the grades, fewer and fewer excel. Some students do not visibly participate in the life of the classroom at all. At the senior high level, many drop out of school, and others "drop out" but remain in the classroom. Explanations for this phenomenon abound. Some blame overly stringent academic requirements; others attribute it to the differences in students' home environments or socioeconomic status. Still others call for a variety of teaching strategies to reach students with diverse backgrounds and differing abilities. In this section of the chapter we'll look at some of the research that reveals the teacher's part in communicating expectations that some students will excel and others will fail.

Teachers do form expectations about a student's performance, and these expectations seem to relate to the student's achievement. The source of a teacher's expectations may vary: a student's social class, race, or sex; information from previous teachers; test scores; or family background information. Teachers may communicate their expectations by the quantity and quality of their interactions with students, including the use of praise or criticism to guide a student's performance.[34]

How Do Teachers Treat High or Low Achievers?

Researchers have not definitely established the causes of some teachers' different treatments of students they perceive as high and low achievers. But observations of many classroom teachers reveal that they often differentiate their behavior toward these two groups of students. Brophy and Good have summarized these differences:

1. Teachers wait less time for lows to answer a question.
2. Teachers give lows answers or call on someone else for the answer instead of giving clues or providing additional opportunities to respond.
3. Teachers reward lows for inappropriate behaviors or incorrect answers.
4. Lows are more often criticized for failure.
5. Lows are praised less frequently for success than highs are.
6. Lows may not receive feedback for public responses.
7. Generally, teachers interact less often with lows, paying less attention to them.
8. Teachers call on lows less often for answers to questions.
9. Teachers seat lows further from the teacher.

10. Less is demanded from lows.
11. Lows receive more private than public interactions; their activities are more closely monitored and structured.
12. When teachers grade tests and assignments, they give highs but not lows the benefit of the doubt in borderline cases.
13. Lows experience fewer friendly interactions, including less smiling and other nonverbal signs of support.
14. Lows receive shorter and less informative feedback to their questions.
15. Teachers make less eye contact and respond less attentively to lows.
16. Less use of effective but time-consuming instructional methods with lows when time is limited.
17. Less acceptance and use of lows' ideas.
18. Lows exposed to an impoverished curriculum.

These varied patterns of behavior may speak forcefully to students about their teachers' expectations for their learning.

Adapted from list on pages 122–123 from *Looking in Classrooms*, 5th ed., by Thomas L. Good and Jere E. Brophy. Copyright © 1991 by Harper Collins, Publishers, Inc. Reprinted by permission of Harper Collins, Publishers, Inc.

Relevant student characteristics

Jerome Dusek and Gail Joseph have reviewed the many studies that attempt to determine the types of student characteristics that teachers use to form their expectations about a student's potential to achieve.[35] Those that seem significant are: (1) attractiveness, (2) classroom conduct, (3) cumulative folder information, (4) race, and (5) social class. Dusek and Joseph concluded that gender and a one-parent family situation were not related to teachers' expectations. Although differences exist in teachers' interactions with students of different gender, the two researchers observed that such differences in treatment do not necessarily reflect different expectations of academic or social achievement. The relationship between teachers' interactions with boys as compared with girls and the observed differences in performance, especially in mathematics and science, is not clear. Many more researchers have documented the relationship between teachers' expectations of performance by members of socioeconomic or racial groups and corresponding levels of achievement.[36]

Self-fulfilling prophecies

Thomas Good and Jere Brophy have suggested a process by which teachers' expectations may foster student behaviors that result in achievement levels consistent with those expectations, thus tacitly justifying them and fulfilling an unspoken prophecy.[37] First the teacher forms expectations of specific behavior and achievement for individual students. Then the teacher's behavior toward these students differs according to the expectations. From this differential treatment students perceive the teacher's expectations for them, which affects their self-concepts, motivation to achieve, and aspiration to excel. To the extent that differential treatment is consistent over time and a student does not resist it, the treatment will influence the student's behavior and achievement. Over time, students of whom much is expected will conform to that expectation, and students of whom little is expected will match that expectation. The process is not automatic; teachers' expectations are not always fulfilled. But research has indicated that teachers can influence which children do or do not achieve in the classroom.

The O.K. Classroom

In a three-year study of classroom interactions in more than one hundred classrooms, David and Myra Sadker investigated the way teachers call on students and their manner of responding to student comments.[38] The classrooms they studied could be described as urban or rural and all white, all minority, or integrated; teachers studied were African-American and white, male and female. Almost half of the classrooms were for language arts and English; the remaining half were for science or mathematics.

The Sadkers first intended to categorize teacher reactions to students' comments as praise or criticism; in initial observations they were unable to categorize anything. "There was no praising or criticizing going on."[39] They found an unexpected flatness in teachers' responses. In later observations, they used an instrument that included four categories of response:

1. praise: explicit and positive comments on student performance
2. acceptance: comments indicating correct or appropriate student performance ("O.K." or "uh-huh")

"I was trying so hard to look as if I were paying attention that I didn't hear what you said."

© Joe Buresch. First published in *Today's Education.*

3. remediation: probing questions or comments cueing a more acceptable response
4. criticism: explicit negative comments regarding performance or behavior

Classrooms are affective deserts

Several patterns emerged from the observed classroom interactions. First, compared with the other responses, criticism occurred with the least frequency and in the fewest classrooms. In two-thirds of the classrooms observed, teachers never explicitly indicated that a student's answer was incorrect. In those classrooms in which criticism did occur, it accounted for only 5 percent of the teacher-student interactions. Also, praise responses constituted 11 percent of classroom interactions; in more than 25 percent of the classrooms observed, teachers never praised student responses. The most frequent teacher response was acceptance; reactions of this type constituted more than half of all teacher remarks. The second most frequent response was remediation, accounting for about one-third of teacher interactions with students. The Sadkers were particularly surprised by the number of acceptance responses, which led them to coin the term *O.K. classroom.* Do these accepting responses provide the kind of specific feedback necessary for students to correct their responses or remediate their behavior? These authors expressed concern about the bland and uninformative nature of many teacher responses to students' performance and behavior.

In general, classroom interactions seemed to decrease in frequency as the grade level of the classroom rose and as the school year progressed. Also, in about half of the classrooms observed, a few students received a disproportionate share of teacher responses whereas some students (almost 25 percent) did not interact with the teacher at all.

Females neglected

Finally, the Sadkers investigated the nature of students who participated in classroom interactions compared with those who did not participate. In all four categories of teacher responses, female students received less attention than male students, although acceptance responses were more even across the sexes than the other three. Males were more likely to receive precise teacher reactions in the form of praise, criticism, or remediation.

Why this difference in teacher behavior toward girls and boys? The Sadkers observed that boys were more likely to call out in class and, unlike girls, were not squelched for such behavior. As a result, boys received more attention simply by demanding it. "Boys are being trained to be assertive; girls are being trained to be passive—spectators relegated to the sidelines of classroom discussion."[40] Also, seating arrangements and group work arrangements were characterized by segregation of the sexes in half of the fourth-, sixth-, and

THE COMMUNICATIONS GAME

The "language game" of the classroom, as Arno Bellack first called it, has rules known by teachers and students alike. Generally, the teacher asks questions and prescribes the order in which students may take a chance to respond. Pupils vie for turns by raising their hands. Penalties for failing to raise a hand, responding incorrectly, or talking out of turn are often part of the game. In a sense, the teacher both plays the game and referees.

In her analysis of this communications game, Greta Morine-Dershimer describes some of the many winning possibilities available to teachers and students. She maintains that this competitive interactive venture, unlike other classroom games, can have many winners. Teachers only win if substantial numbers of their students also win. Her study of language in elementary classrooms reveals some winning ways for those who choose to play.

How can teachers win the communications game by providing opportunities for students to win?

1. by giving students opportunities to practice academic skills, communication skills, and social skills in the same lesson
2. by emphasizing the processing of information and the accumulating of information in the same lesson
3. by giving students opportunities to learn that they are valuable sources of information and experience

These "winning combinations" help students believe that they play an important part in the communications game. In Morine-Dershimer's words, "The most important winning combination was the combination of teacher and pupil, helping each other to win, for neither one could ever win all alone."

Greta Morine-Dershimer, *Talking, Listening, and Learning in Elementary Classrooms* (New York: Longman, 1985). (The quotation is from p. 207.)

eighth-grade classrooms observed. Teachers tended to spend more time in the boys' section of the room; boys received more of their time and attention. As a result of their observations, the Sadkers conclude that "classroom interactions between teachers and students are short on both quality and equality."[41]

A FINAL WORD

Having read about many educational researchers' observations in schools and classrooms, you may want to compare what they have observed with your own observations. The Appendix, which begins on page A-1 (at the end of the book), describes several different techniques that will enable you to learn something about life in schools by direct, firsthand observation. It includes guidelines about how to get the most out of your school and classroom observations, as well as specific details on how to gather information by note taking, observation systems, analysis of classroom materials, and interviews. If you are planning to observe in schools and find out what life there is like, this Appendix should be most useful to you.

Discussion Questions

1. How would you describe the importance of the environment in contributing to a child's learning?
2. Did any of Jackson's, Boyer's, Goodlad's, or Cuban's findings surprise you? If so, which ones and why?
3. What characteristics of Japanese elementary schools did you find appealing? Which ones bothered you?
4. Which characteristics of schools, as identified by *The Shopping Mall High School* study, seemed to fit the high school you attended? Which characteristics were definitely absent?
5. Did your high school harbor student subcultures, like the jocks and the burnouts? With which category did you most closely identify? Were you aware of the effects of peer pressure on your behavior?
6. What changes would you make in either elementary schools or secondary schools so that more students could be classroom winners?
7. Have you personally experienced or observed any of the classroom interactions described by the Sadkers? If so, which ones? How did you feel?

For Further Reading

Bennett, Kathleen P., and Margaret D. LeCompte. *How Schools Work: A Sociological Analysis of Education.* New York: Longman, 1990.

A sociology of education text that analyzes the process of elementary and secondary schooling. The book treats such topics as the social organization of schooling, youth culture, social class, and its relationship to education, ethnic minorities, and gender issues.

Eckert, Penelope. *Jocks and Burnouts: Social Categories and Identity in the High School.* New York: Teachers College Press, 1989.

An ethnographic, easy-to-read description of high school youth categories. Drawing on four years of field study in suburban Detroit schools, the author describes the importance of the jock and burnout student categories in helping teen-agers define themselves, particularly in relationship to the larger society and to each other.

Goodlad, John I. *A Place Called School: Prospects for the Future*. New York: McGraw-Hill, 1984.

> The result of an eight-year study on schooling, this book gives insights into how teachers teach and how classroom time is used.

Jackson, Philip W. *Life in Classrooms*. New York: Teachers College Press, 1990.

> A classic anthropological analysis and categorization of everyday occurrences in classrooms. To understand life in elementary school classrooms, Jackson believes we have to appreciate the cultural significance of its humdrum elements, such as repetition, waiting, interruptions, frustration, and constant rapid-fire interchanges between teacher and students.

Kohl, Herbert. *36 Children*. New York: New American Library, 1968.

> A popular account of a Harvard graduate teacher's first year in a ghetto school in Harlem. Kohl describes the students' initial hostility and the ways he overcame it. The book also describes vividly the difficult conditions under which teaching is practiced in some sections of New York City.

McNeil, Linda. *Contradictions of Control*. New York: Routledge, 1986.

> An examination of four middle-class high schools that focuses on the relationship between internal organizational processes and the curriculum. McNeil asserts that in these schools, and by extrapolation in others like them, education is trivialized as control wins out over serious educational purposes.

Mehan, Hugh. *Learning Lessons: Social Organization in the Classroom*. Cambridge, Mass.: Harvard University Press, 1979.

> A detailed analysis of the tacit rules that organize the social interactions of the classroom, based upon a year of videotaped observations of an inner-city elementary school class.

Powell, Arthur G., Eleanor Farrar, and David K. Cohen. *The Shopping Mall High School: Winners and Losers in the Educational Marketplace*. Boston: Houghton Mifflin, 1985.

> A very readable study that compares high schools to shopping malls in terms of the variety of programs available for a diverse clientele.

Sarason, Seymour B. *The Culture of the School and the Problem of Change*. 2d ed. Boston: Allyn and Bacon, 1982.

> An examination of school cultures and the problems inherent in attempting to bring about change. The author highlights the importance of the role of the principal in any change process.

Notes   1. John Dewey, *Democracy and Education* (New York: Macmillan, 1916), p. 13.

2. Excerpted from the book *Education and Ecstasy* by George B. Leonard, pp. 39–40. Copyright © 1968 by George B. Leonard. Reprinted by permission of Delacorte Press. Reprinted by permission of The Sterling Lord Agency, Inc. Copyright © 1968 by George B. Leonard.

3. Elliot Eisner, *The Educational Imagination: On the Design and Evaluation of School Programs,* 2d ed. (New York: Macmillan, 1985), p. 88.

4. Ibid., p. 97.

5. Philip W. Jackson, *Life in Classrooms* (New York: Teachers College Press, 1990).

6. Ibid., p. 16.

7. Ibid., p. 18.

8. M. Sandra Reeves, "With Little Fanfare, the Spotlight Shifts," *Education Week,* April 16, 1986: pp. 17–18.

9. "Roundtable: The Issues—School: 'Bits and Pieces' for Children Who Are 'Full of Big Questions,'" *Education Week,* April 16, 1986, p. 25.

10. Joyce Epstein, "What Matters in the Middle Grades—Grade Span or Practices?" *Phi Delta Kappan,* 71 (February 1990): 438–444.

11. Ibid., p. 438.

12. Ibid.

13. Henry J. Becker, "Curriculum and Instruction in Middle-Grade Schools," *Phi Delta Kappan* 71 (February 1990): 450–457.

14. James McPartland, "Staffing Decisions in the Middle Grades: Balancing Quality Instruction and Teacher/Student Relations," 71 *Phi Delta Kappan* (February 1990): 466.

15. Ibid., p. 468.

16. Ernest L. Boyer, *High School: A Report on Secondary Education in America* (New York: Harper & Row, 1983).

17. Ibid., pp. 21–22.

18. Ibid., p. 57.

19. Ibid., p. 66.

20. Ibid., p. 79.

21. Ibid., p. 126.

22. Ibid., pp. 141–142.

23. Larry Cuban, *How Teachers Taught: Constancy and Change in American Classrooms 1890–1980* (New York: Longman, 1984).

24. Ibid., pp. 225–228.

25. Ibid., p. 250.

26. Boyer, *High School,* pp. 14, 15, 206.

27. Penelope Eckert, *Jocks and Burnouts: Social Categories and Identity in the High School* (New York: Teachers College Press, 1989).

28. Ibid., p. 23.

29. John Goodlad, *A Place Called School: Prospects for the Future* (New York: McGraw-Hill, 1984), pp. 76–78.

30. Arthur G. Powell, Eleanor Farrar, and David K. Cohen, *The Shopping Mall High School: Winners and Losers in the Educational Marketplace* (Boston: Houghton Mifflin, 1985).

31. Ibid., p. 76.

32. Ibid., p. 173.

33. Laurence D. Brown, "A New Metaphor for U.S. High Schools Provides Fresh and Powerful Insights," *Phi Delta Kappan* 67 (May 1986): 685.

34. Jerome B. Dusek, "Introduction to Teacher Expectancy Research," in *Teacher Expectancies,* ed. Jerome B. Dusek et al. (Hillsdale, N.J.: Lawrence Erlbaum, 1985), pp. 1–8.

35. Jerome B. Dusek and Gail Joseph, "The Bases of Teacher Expectancies," in Dusek, *Teacher Expectancies,* pp. 229–250.

36. As examples, see chapters by Reuben M. Baron, David Y. H. Tom, and Harris M. Cooper, and by Thomas L. Good and Maureen Findley in Dusek, *Teacher Expectancies*.

37. Thomas L. Good and Jere E. Brophy, *Looking in Classrooms*, 4th ed. (New York: Harper-Collins, 1991), p. 115.

38. David Sadker and Myra Sadker, "Is the O.K. Classroom O.K.?" *Phi Delta Kappan* 66 (January 1985): 358–361.

39. Ibid., p. 359.

40. Myra Sadker and David Sadker, "Sexism in the Classroom: From Grade School to Graduate School," *Phi Delta Kappan* 67 (March 1986): 513.

41. Sadker and Sadker, "O.K. Classroom," p. 361.

IV

STUDENTS AND THEIR SOCIAL CONTEXT

The makeup of children in America's schools is changing dramatically. Our culture is becoming increasingly diverse, especially in its ethnic and racial composition. Over 30 percent of the children enrolled in our schools are minorities, and the percentage increases each year. Children are also innocent victims of many of society's ills—poverty, drug abuse, disintegrating families, to name a few—that greatly affect schools' abilities to teach youngsters effectively.

As a new teacher, you must understand these social factors and how they may affect students and your ability to respond to their intellectual, physical, and emotional needs. All of these variables make the task of teaching much more challenging.

CHAPTER PREVIEW

In some ways children never change. In our classic literature we see characteristics of children encapsulated and preserved that are as true today as when they were first written. Look at the conniving, mischievous Tom Sawyer or the overly curious Alice in Wonderland or the tenacious Mafatu in *Call it Courage*. These characters are endearing to us in part because we have all known children like them. Some characteristics of childhood are perpetual and seem to endure unchanged. And yet, we are also products of our society. The world around us shapes our daily experiences and influences our understanding of ourselves. As our society changes, so does the context, the social milieu, in which our children are raised and brought up to understand and form expectations of the world. Children have been called barometers of change. More than any other segment of society, children are affected and shaped by emerging social conditions.

This chapter emphasizes that:

● Studies of the demographic make-up of the country indicate shifts in ethnic composition and family patterns.

● All children have basic needs. Being aware of and understanding these commonalities provides a foundation for sound insight into the diverse needs of students.

● Students have many strengths and abilities that extend beyond the traditional emphasis in our schools on linguistic and analytic abilities. Approaches that recognize multiple views of intelligence and differing learning styles are ways of considering diversity in student learning and ability.

● Schools address the individual needs of students through multicultural, bilingual, special education, and gifted and talented programs.

● There is increasing intercooperation between the school and various support agencies, such as community health, child care, and social services.

● In order to cope in today's classroom, teachers must be aware of many dimensions of student diversity.

T he children of today are very much like the children of yesterday or the children of tomorrow. Certain stages of cognitive, social, emotional, and physical development have been identified, and a similar progression through these stages occurs for everyone. We all have basic human needs for our psychological comfort and physical well-being. These needs are fundamental to the quality of our existence and cut across cultural, age, and gender boundaries. Understanding these stages of development and areas of common needs gives the classroom teacher insight into student behavior and consequently helps the teacher develop appropriate classroom experiences. You will be learning a great deal about these subjects in your courses on child development and educational psychology.

However, it is also important to be sensitive to the great differences among students and of factors in our society that are directly affecting the lives of our students. Through the information presented and discussed in this chapter, we wish to make you more fully aware of the increasing diversity of our society and of our classrooms, of the changing nature of American family patterns, of the range of abilities in your students, and of the school's attempts to address all this diversity. We also wish to make you more deeply sensitive to the sorts of issues, potential problems, and benefits related to this diversity.

DIVERSITY IN THE CLASSROOM

Children in schools are a mirror of society. In public institutions, therefore, many types of diversity will be represented in varying degrees. This diversity will be found in your students along a number of dimensions.

Cultural and ethnic diversity

One dimension will be the increasingly varied *cultural and ethnic backgrounds* of your students. With the development of a richer, more varied society, differences in *values and family expectations* for achievement in school may become more and more evident. Some families may place a premium on school and higher education, whereas other families may emphasize early entry into the work place. But even though you will encounter a range of familial expectations, all children deserve the best educational experience they can attain while in school. Recognition of differences can be best used to provide the understanding and insight needed for more effective instruction.

Parental involvement

Parental involvement may be another dimension of diversity in your classroom. Years of research have shown that there is a positive relationship between parental involvement in education and student achievement.[1] Some parents may be willing and able to participate in their child's education, but other parents may be dealing with a variety of issues, such as lack of time or conflicting work schedules, and may not be able to get involved as much as needed. Parents who speak limited English or who have never completed school may feel extremely uncomfortable in a school setting. It is important that teachers find ways to reach out to these parents and not assume a lack of interest in their children's performance in school. Harold Stevenson conducted a study indicating that, despite economic and social barriers, African-American and Hispanic mothers of low-income families were keenly interested in their children's education and wanted to be involved.[2]

Some of your students may speak a *primary language other than English.*
Though estimates vary, one source estimated that as many as 15 percent of students in American schools do not speak English as their native or home language. Indeed, it has also been estimated that in 1987 approximately 6 percent of the school population were recent immigrants to the United States.[3] As these children and youth enter schools, most will need to make sense of a new language, a new culture, and possibly a new way of behaving. An important function of teachers and schools is to provide an anchor or a source or stability for students experiencing rapid change in their lives. In part, this can be accomplished by becoming more sensitive to the extent of change and possible disorientation these students may be experiencing. Teacher aides who speak the child's language have been used by some school systems to help provide a link between the child and the school. The use of bilingual peer tutors may also help provide a greater sense of stability.

Non-English-speaking students

Psychologists and educators have identified a number of basic needs that are experienced by all individuals, including needs for belonging, safety, and self-esteem. However, students in your classroom develop and mature at different rates and will probably display a range of *diverse needs.* Students also bring their own individual histories, various backgrounds and conditions that have influenced how and whether certain needs have been satisfied. For example, a child from a stable, secure home life may display different needs than a child who has not had this kind of security. Recognizing diverse needs will help you better understand some student behaviors and perhaps increase your insight into how to respond.

Diverse needs

Another dimension of diversity will be seen in the academic *abilities, achievements, and learning styles* of your students. Some students will be able to enter the school environment and excel in their learning. Other students will not appear to respond to the education you are providing them. Remember, children learn in different ways. One of your biggest challenges as a teacher will be to provide a variety of experiences and learning encounters to accommodate the learning styles and abilities of your diverse class of students.

Academic diversity

As we delve into the topic of "today's students," it becomes apparent that there are many sources of diversity in the classroom that you need to be aware of in order to address the educational needs of your students. Let's examine each of these in more detail and consider how they will influence your ability to provide a good education in today's classroom.

OUR CHANGING SOCIETY

American society is undergoing many changes. Though we have always been composed of various cultures, today we are experiencing a time of exceptional cultural diversity. At the same time, social, economic, and political forces are influencing many aspects of our daily lives, including family structures and relationships. Some of these trends are likely to be reflected in your classroom.

The Increasing Cultural Diversity

We live in an increasingly pluralistic society, one with many different cultures. At one time, the United States was considered a "melting pot" of many different kinds of people. Immigrants were expected to give up the language and customs

Modern education is competitive, nationalistic, and separative. It has trained the child to regard material values as of major importance, to believe that his nation is also of major importance and superior to other nations and peoples. The general level of world information is high but usually biased, influenced by national prejudices, serving to make us citizens of our nation but not of the world.
— ALBERT EINSTEIN —

Diversity in the classroom means that your students will come from a wide range of cultural backgrounds, may speak a first language other than English, and have a variety of learning abilities and learning styles.
(Elizabeth Crews/Stock, Boston)

of their old countries and to adopt the language and customs of their new country. During the nineteenth and early twentieth centuries, schools contributed to the concept of the melting pot by socializing and acculturating immigrant children to American ways while discouraging them from maintaining the ways of their homelands. Many states even passed laws forbidding instruction in any language but English. The basic idea was to produce a society with one dominant culture.

Cultural pluralism

During the late twentieth century, the concept of the melting pot has generally been replaced by the concept of *cultural pluralism.* Cultural pluralism calls for an understanding and appreciation of the cultural differences that exist among the nation's citizens. The goal is to create a sense of society's wholeness based on the unique strengths of each of its parts. Cultural pluralism rejects both assimilation and separatism. Instead, it seeks a healthy interaction among the diverse groups constituting our society; each subculture maintains its own individuality while also contributing to our society as a whole. Cultural pluralism is an increasingly important concept in our society as we continue to emerge as a country of diverse people.

Demographic studies indicate that the cultural composition of public school classrooms in the United States is changing and will change even more in future years. Today, 14 percent of all adults in the United States, and about 20 percent of children under seventeen, are minorities, including

African-Americans, Hispanic-Americans, Native Americans, and Asian-Americans. By the year 2000, over one-third of all school-age children, and by 2020, nearly half, will fall into this category.[4]

A breakdown of these statistics by individual minority groups reveals some interesting trends and projections. Hispanic-Americans are a rapidly growing

WHO YOU WILL TEACH

- Number of K–12 students in public schools: **40,896,000**
- K–8: **29,366,000** 9–12: **11,530,000**
- In private and parochial schools, K–12: **4,955,771**
- Proportion of children who come from a family living in poverty: **1 in 4**
- Percentage of the poor population who are children: **40**
- Proportion of children who live with a single parent—usually a working mother: **1 in 3**
- Percentage of black children who come from single-parent families: **50**
- Of Hispanic children: **25** Of white children: **16**
- Percentage of children born to teenage mothers: **14**
- Percentage of students who will become teenage parents themselves: **15**
- Percentage of children born to unmarried mothers: **23**
- Percentage who will be born to parents who divorce before the child is 18: **40**
- Percentage who will be born to parents of whom one will die before the child reaches 18: **2**
- Number of children who live with neither parent: **1.9 million**
- Percentage who have a physical or mental handicap: **16**
- Percentage of students whose native language is not English: **15**
- Percentage who have poorly educated, even illiterate, parents: **10**
- Percentage who are latch-key children with no one to greet them when they come home from school: **30**
- Percentage of student enrollment that will be minority by 2010: **38**

- By 2020: **48**
- Number of the 25-largest school districts with non-white majorities: **25**
- Proportion of states with public school enrollments that are more than 25 percent nonwhite: **Half**
- Percentage of public school students who are minority in:
- Hawaii: **77** New Mexico: **57** Mississippi: **50**
- Texas: **49** California: **46** South Carolina: **45**
- Louisiana: **43** Maryland: **40** Alabama: **38**
- Arizona: **38** Florida: **38** Delaware: **32**
- New York: **32** New Jersey: **31**
- Percentage of American children who live in California, Florida, Illinois, Michigan, New Jersey, New York, Ohio, Pennsylvania, and Texas: **50**
- Number of children who have no health-insurance coverage: **12 million**
- Daily number of teenage girls who give birth to their *third* child: 40
- Proportion of students who will probably not finish school: **1 in 4**
- Of whites: **1 in 10** Of blacks: **3 in 10**
- Of Hispanics: **4 in 10** Of Native Americans: **5 in 10**
- Percentage of high school seniors who have used illegal drugs: **54**
- Proportion of seniors who drink alcohol *daily:* **1 in 20**
- Percentage of seniors who began using alcohol prior to high school: **56**
- Number of boys who carried handguns to school at least once in 1987: **270,000**
- Who did so each day: **135,000**
- Who have access to handguns: **8.7 million**

Source: *Teacher Magazine* April, 1990, p. 39.

minority group, most of whom are of Mexican origin. Other countries of origin include Puerto Rico, Cuba, and various countries of Central and South America. The Hispanic population under eighteen years of age will more than triple by the year 2020, growing from 5.9 million in 1982 to 18.6 million. The increased numbers of Hispanic individuals will account for most of the population growth expected in our schools in this time period. During the same period it is anticipated that the African-American population under eighteen will increase 22 percent, from 9.3 million in 1982 to 11.9 million. White children will constitute a declining segment of the U.S. population: in 1982, white children accounted for 73 percent of our school-age population; in 2020, they are projected to decline to 54.5 percent. An additional 2.9 percent of schoolchildren in 1982 were identified as belonging to some other racial group, typically Asian or Pacific Islander.[5] Asian-Americans are the fastest-growing group of minorities, increasing from 891,000 to more than 5 million in the past two decades. The Asian-American population is expected to double in the next twenty years. By 2050, it is projected that there will be 6 million Asian-Americans living in California, 1.7 million in New York, and 1.2 million in Illinois.[6]

National averages disguise the fact that minority groups are not equally distributed across the country. Seventy-three percent of our nation's Hispanic children are enrolled in schools in five states: California, Texas, New York, Illinois, and Florida. The largest numbers of African-American schoolchildren are found in New York, Texas, Illinois, and California.[7] Nearly 40 percent of all Southeast Asian refugees live in California.[8] The forty-seven urban school districts that constitute the "Great City Schools," including such school systems as New York City and Chicago, also have a large proportion of minority students, including one out of three African-American children, one out of four Hispanic children, and one out of five Asian-Americans.[9] As might be expected with increasing cultural diversity, teachers will encounter more students whose native language is not English and whose cultural backgrounds reflect a Hispanic or Asian heritage.

New American Family Patterns

In addition to increasing cultural diversity, our society is also undergoing dramatic changes in how our families are structured. This relatively new source of diversity among our students has a pervasive influence on children in school. The comic poet Ogden Nash once wrote, "A family is a unit composed not only of children but of men, women, an occasional animal and the common cold." What has been troubling the American family for the last twenty-five years is much more serious than a common cold. As a society we have undergone an enormous number of changes, from how we work to where we live, from what we do with our free time to how we get ideas. One of the major changes has been in the structure of the family. The once common image of the "breadwinner" father, a housewife mother, and two children of public school age now accurately describes only 6 percent of households in the United States.[10] So what is the typical family of our students like today? Actually, there is no longer one "typical" family pattern. Rather, a number of economic and societal trends have resulted in families that come in many forms.

FAMILY COMPOSITION   An increasing number of children are being raised by single parents. A major influence in the composition of our families has been the rate of divorce, particularly among couples who have children. Over half of today's new marriages will end in divorce. In 1989, 15.3 million children were living with one parent, the mother in 90 percent of the cases.[11]

Single-parent households

Being a child in a family where the parents' marriage is conflict ridden and unhappy may be less preferable in some ways than living in a single-parent family, but single-parent families have one major disadvantage: in 1989 the median income for single-mother households was $11,299; for married-couple households, the median income was $36,206.[12] Single-mother families have been called "the new poor." It is not just the absence of one parent but the loss of a two-parent income that puts a special burden on these families. More difficult to pin down is the effect of only one parent bearing the daily chores of monitoring, supporting, and guiding the school-age children.

In addition to divorce, numerous other factors, such as being born out of wedlock, being born to parents who separate, and being born to parents of whom one will die, contribute to the number of children living in single-parent households or possibly with grandparents or aunts and uncles. It is predicted that this figure will increase by 30 percent, growing from 16.2 million in 1984 to 21.1 million in 2020.[13] A breakdown of the figures by racial group reveals that 50 percent of white children are with a mother who is divorced, and 54 percent of African-American children and 33 percent of Hispanic children are with a never-married mother.[14]

Another result of high rates of divorce is the increasing number of children living in blended families with stepparents, stepsiblings, and/or half-siblings. In some cases, parents who have divorced share physical custody of the children, with the result that the children must split their time between parental households.

Teaching implications

Changes in American family patterns will likely influence your interactions with students and their parents in a number of ways. As the classroom teacher, these changes may affect the way you communicate to parents. For example, in divorce situations it may be difficult to keep both parents informed of their child's progress. Or a single parent may have an exceptionally heavy workload and be unable to attend parent-teacher conferences at traditional times. Varied family patterns will also require increased sensitivity in numerous daily interactions, such as when asking students to bring a note from "your mother." It would perhaps be better to say "your parent" or "the person who takes care of you."

Smaller families

There are various other changes taking place in families. One involves family size. The Baby Boomers have made their impact by marrying at a later age and having fewer children. Today, 50 percent of children born are first, and probably last, children, whereas in the 1950s only 25 percent of infants were first-born children. Our society is also aging. Between 1980 and 1987, members of our population over the age of 65 increased by 4.3 million. During the same time period, children under the age of five increased by only 1.9 million.[15]

Of the 91,066,000 households in the United States in 1988, only 27 percent consisted of married couples with children. Twenty-eight percent were non-

"We certainly should—especially since so few kids learn it at home anymore"

Courtesy, Houston Chronicle

The family is a much more periled institution than the school.
— ERNEST BOYER —

family households consisting of single parents and persons living with unrelated others.[16] So as we have seen, the composition of the American family is certainly changing. The typical family structure in our society no longer refers to one set image, but may consist of many alternative forms.

FAMILY RELATIONSHIPS   The changing composition of our families influences the way family members are able to relate to one another. Parents are increasingly being pulled in a number of directions. Two-career families must balance the needs of childrearing and family life with the demands of two work environments. Single-parent families must meet these same needs with the increased pressure of only one adult income. These changes affect the amount of time

Working parents

children and their parents have to spend with each other and potentially affect the quality of that time. Work demands reduce the actual time parents spend with their children. After work, the necessities of maintaining a family, such as cooking, cleaning, and grocery shopping, are relentless and do not allow for a great deal of leisure time to spend supervising and enjoying the children.

Mothers are now going to work or returning to work when their children are much younger. In 1970, 30 percent of all mothers held jobs. By 1980, the figure had increased to 50 percent. By 1995, it is projected that 66 percent of all preschool children and 80 percent of all school-age students will have mothers in the labor force.[17] A result of the mother's changing status is that she is not so involved as she traditionally has been in raising her children—that is, in attending daily to her children's social, intellectual, and moral development. Neither Mom nor Dad is as available as he or she used to be. Sixty percent of today's students live in families where both parents or the only parent work.[18] Now when many children return home from school, rather than talk with their mothers, they watch "General Hospital." Coming home to an empty house or apartment after

Latch-key children

EDUCATION: A WORLD VIEW

• •

A LOOK AT EUROPEAN CHILD CARE AND EARLY EDUCATION

In recent decades, as an increasing number of women have entered the work force, issues of appropriate child care and early education have become topics of debate in the United States. In much of Eastern and Western Europe, child care is approached much differently than it is here. Nursery school, prekindergarten, and kindergarten are typically viewed as public responsibility and are heavily subsidized. Most early education is under the auspices of the public school system and may be located in special facilities or in elementary school buildings. Services stress developmentally appropriate curricula and are free and voluntary for children two to five years old. Programs are typically filled to capacity. Preschool in these countries is seen as essential to both social and cognitive development and is heavily attended. About 95 percent of three- to five-year-olds in France and Belgium attend a preschool.

The French *école maternelle* is one such preschool model that operates as part of the education system. All children from two to five years of age are eligible for free

services; however, when there is a shortage of spaces, children of working mothers receive preference. Programs stress cognitive development and extend through the normal school day, generally from 8:30 A.M. to 4:30 P.M. In contrast to American standards, however, there are often as many as 25 to 30 four-year-olds with a single teacher.

In Sweden and Finland child care is delivered through the social welfare system. Services are available for most children until the age of seven, when compulsory schooling begins. Swedish programs offer some of the highest-quality programs available. Class size, teacher-child ratios, and the qualifications of caregivers are rigorously set and enforced. Again, programs are heavily subsidized by the government. Since demand for services exceeds supply, priority is given to the children of working parents, especially single mothers and immigrants. About 70 percent of three- to seven-year-olds are enrolled in these programs. Beginning in 1991, all children who are eighteen months of age or older are to be guaranteed a place in a preschool or child care center.

Sheila Kamerman, "An International Overview of Preschool Programs," *Phi Delta Kappan* 70 (October 1989), pp. 135–137. Adapted by permission.

school is standard for an estimated 4 million "latch-key" children in our country. In a 1989 Metropolitan Life survey of American teachers, it was reported that three out of four teachers indicated that they worried about the number of latch-key children in their classrooms; one in three teachers rated the lack of supervision as a very serious problem.[19]

Child care issues

For younger children not yet in school, working parents raise issues of adequate child care. If both parents or the only parent is working full-time, who is taking care of the children? Grandparents and extended family used to pitch in and help, but our society is becoming increasingly mobile. It is less and less common for a family to settle in one location for extended periods of time. Reliance on outside help raises the numerous issues of child care facing working families today, including the need for safe, stimulating environments for our children. But parents who have to work can easily be caught in a bind and often must settle for whatever child care they can find.

Teaching implications

As can be seen, trends toward the two-career family and the single-parent family limit the amount of time children spend in close contact with their parents. They also have a direct impact on the schools. Whereas in the past young people were actively involved outside of school in family and community, today the school is being urged to play a larger role in expanding and guiding the limited experiences of children. Schools are being asked to deal with the new problems being brought to them by the new facts of family life and our changed economy. In the past, teachers could count on sure support from families; now teachers often find it difficult to even get in contact with many parents.

DIVERSE NEEDS

In addition to the diversity of cultural backgrounds and family patterns in our society we have discussed so far, another element of diversity occurs within each individual. We all have basic physical and psychological needs that may vary in their prominence and expression because of individual circumstances. One way of understanding the diverse needs of students is to examine how psychologists and educators have conceptualized the basic needs of all individuals. In the following section, we will look at two different theories of individual development and needs and how these vantage points can help you to better understand your students' needs and behavior in the classroom.

A Hierarchy of Needs

Abraham Maslow, an eminent humanistic psychologist, described human needs as occurring in a hierarchy beginning with our most basic biological needs and ascending to our highest-order need for self-actualization.[20] According to Maslow's theory, we must meet our lower-order needs at least to some extent before we can attend to higher levels of human potential. Much of our behavior is the result of attempts to satisfy these needs. The prominence of different needs will vary depending on the individual's life situation: That is, some needs may remain relatively unimportant and unnoticed until other needs have been addressed.

Physiological needs

At the most basic level are our physiological needs consisting of such biological requirements as sufficient amounts of food, water, rest, and oxygen. These are necessary for immediate physical survival. An individual struggling to meet these most basic needs will be unlikely to focus attention on higher levels of attainment. For example, think of the last time you missed a night's sleep. That groggy feeling the next day seemed to overshadow all your activities and your mind kept prompting you to take a short nap. Then consider, perhaps, the student in your classroom who is hungry and unsure where his next meal will come from and how this may be reflected in his lack of concern about his achievement in mathematics.

Safety needs

As physiological needs are satisfied, our motivations for behavior increasingly reflect the next level in the hierarchy. Safety needs lead to behaviors such as the avoidance of danger, pain, or injury. They reflect the desire for a stable, predictable environment that is relatively free from anxiety and chaos. As the home lives of today's students become more complicated by such trends as the increasing incidence of divorce or the raging social problems of poverty, homelessness, or drug abuse, it becomes even more important for schools and teachers to attend to this need and provide safe, structured environments for students.

Love and belonging needs

As physiological requirements and needs for safety are satisfied to some extent, love and belonging needs become more prominent motivators of behavior. These consist of our needs for positive relationships with others over time, the formation of friendships, and the giving and receiving of affection. Some students may come from homes where needs for love and belonging are not acknowledged. These students may cling to or continually seek attention from you. Understanding this behavior as driven by a basic need for love and belonging may help you understand it and develop more patience with it.

Esteem needs

Maslow places considerable importance on esteem needs. Everyone needs feelings of confidence and self-respect, which are often fostered by recognition and appreciation from others. Esteem needs begin to increasingly emerge as the three lower levels of motivators are satisfied. An important source of esteem for children is tied to their success in school. The considerable body of research that has been done on effective schools has revealed that these institutions are places where students are experiencing success. Activities and lessons are structured to insure that students will succeed in school. Such success has shown time and again to bolster the self-esteem of students.

Self-actualization needs

Maslow defines these first four levels of needs in the hierarchy as *deficiency motives:* That is, they are deficits within us that must be fulfilled. The more they are satisfied, the less prominent they become as motivators for behavior. In contrast, the final level in the hierarchy, self-actualization, is deemed a *growth motive.* Growth motives, such as becoming self-directed and discovering one's own potential, actually gain in intensity as they are gratified. For example, the mastery of a skill such as playing a musical instrument well or the fulfillment of an ambition such as becoming a doctor are rewarding and perpetuating behaviors in themselves. The better we become at them, the more we want to do them. Thus schools and teachers can provide support for student needs at all levels in a variety of ways. Certainly, being aware of the diversity your students will bring to the classroom will help you deal more effectively with their individual needs.

Needs for Personal Empowerment

Control theory

William Glasser, a noted psychiatrist, provides a different conceptualization of human needs and behavior based on control theory.[21] *Control theory* is grounded in the premise that each of us is born with fundamental needs for survival, love and belonging, power, freedom, and fun. Throughout our lives, our motivations, actions, and behaviors are attempts to satisfy these needs. According to control theory, if we understand and identify these needs within ourselves, we can make conscious choices about how to best meet them. This recognition of our ability to make choices results in personal empowerment: We have control of how we choose to react to external events and information.

An essential function of teachers, according to Glasser, is to facilitate this personal empowerment in their students through the use of control theory. Glasser states that an effective teacher, whether he or she is aware of it or not, will combine the needs of students with what he or she is asking them to do. By understanding and incorporating basic human needs into the classroom structure, then, the teacher is providing an educational opportunity for students that fulfills their needs at the same time. The more students are convinced that their schoolwork satisfies their needs, the harder they will try and the better quality work they will produce. For example, when asked what is the best part of school, many students respond, "My friends." According to Glasser, this expresses the students' built-in need for friendship, love, and belonging. Rather than structure classroom settings to suppress this need, such as by emphasizing independent seatwork or teacher lectures, teachers should find ways to let students associate with others in class as a planned part of learning. Glasser refers to this cooperative grouping as the use of *learning teams*.

Learning teams, power needs

Teaching students in cooperative learning teams also meets students' needs for power. Glasser uses the term *power* synonymously with *self-esteem* or *sense of importance* and explains that to fulfill this need students must have the sense that someone whom they respect listens to them. Unfulfilled needs for power often result in a number of undesirable attention-getting behaviors. Glasser explains that these inappropriate behaviors are often misguided efforts to achieve power and are the source of 95 percent of discipline problems in school. In accordance with control theory, he suggests that teachers structure opportunities for students to appropriately fulfill needs for power during the school day, such as by providing a forum for students to be heard. In addition to learning teams, where students interact and listen to one another in the learning process, Glasser also suggests that teachers provide opportunities for student input and self-evaluation of homework, classwork, and tests. He posits that students need to be encouraged to set their own standards for quality work and to evaluate whether they are meeting those standards. This helps to satisfy the need for power and instills an internal standard for quality education and work.

Freedom and fun needs

Glasser proposes that student needs for freedom and fun, though important, are not at the core of problems in schools. He explains that students generally understand the need for some structure in dealing with large groups of people and the resulting rules and regulations that must govern behavior in school. Though fun is an essential need, students who have a sense of belonging in school and a forum for personal power are already likely to be experiencing fun.

Glasser explains that motivation to achieve in school comes from within and is based on student needs. It cannot be coerced from outside through either rewards or punishment. In using control theory, teachers help students see that what they're doing in school is important and is fulfilling their own needs. Students become personally empowered through understanding their own needs, making good choices in how to meet those needs, and forming an internal standard for quality work and performance.

Both Maslow's hierarchy of needs and Glasser's theory of personal empowerment provide ways of viewing and identifying a wide variety of student needs. Another dimension of diversity students will bring into the classroom is the range and extent of abilities they possess in a variety of areas.

DIVERSE ABILITIES

In some ways, many of our schools today are not structured to address students' diverse abilities. The majority of our schools tend to emphasize a curriculum that specifically targets the predominantly linguistic and analytic abilities needed to do well on commonly used standardized tests. This constricted focus on a limited range of abilities results in an education system that teaches and reinforces only certain types of achievement. Children who are strong in linguistic and analytic tasks are likely to be successful in school and feel a great sense of achievement. Other children, however, who may be very competent or even gifted in nontraditional school tasks may experience frustration or failure in school. Children do not enter schools as failures. Rather, they acquire this debilitating label from a system that is strongly oriented toward a limited range of student abilities.

As a teacher, it is important to be aware of and help nurture a broad spectrum of abilities and strengths in your students. In the following section, we will look at the theory that students may have many abilities and talents not tapped by traditional schooling. We will also explore learning styles to see how different students learn and to perhaps broaden your views on approaches to teaching. And we will briefly examine characteristics of students along a range of disabilities and talents to provide a broad perspective of the diverse abilities students bring to the classroom.

Multiple Intelligences

Howard Gardner, a leading psychologist, proposes that rather than emphasize only a limited range of abilities in our schoolchildren, we should move toward a theory of multiple intelligences of which linguistic and analytic abilities are only two facets. In Gardner's book, *Frames of Mind*[22] he explains that we all have different cognitive profiles. Strengths, weaknesses, and unique combinations of each compose our individual cognitive abilities. Gardner proposes that Seven different abilities people have at least seven distinct intellectual capacities that they use to approach problems and create products: linguistic, musical, logical-mathematical, spatial, bodily-kinesthetic, interpersonal, and intrapersonal. Traditionally, schools have tended to reinforce a learning profile emphasizing linguistic and logical-

Students can display intelligence in areas outside the traditional categories of linguistic and logical-mathematical abilities.

(*Peter Vandermark/Stock, Boston*)

mathematical abilities to the exclusion or detriment of other possible intelligences.

In Gardner's theory, abilities in diverse areas would be valued as indicators of intelligence and deemed worthy of further nurturance and development in school. To address these varied intelligences, Gardner places emphasis on learning in context, particularly through apprenticeships. Student development in an area like music should be fostered through hands-on practice and experiences.

Even traditional subjects should be taught in a variety of ways to address the varied intelligences of both students and teachers. For example, the history of an era might be conveyed through a number of media and methods, ranging from art and architecture to biographies and dramatic reenactments of events. Assessments should also be tailored to different abilities and should take place as much as possible in the learning context.

Fostering individual abilities

The theory of multiple intelligences emphasizes the highly individualized ways in which people learn and recognizes that each of us has unique intellectual potential. Acknowledging and fostering individual abilities in a variety of areas is a way that schools can help students. This is an emerging idea in education. Though we haven't yet established definite techniques for applying and utilizing the theory on a day-to-day basis in the classroom, pilot efforts are being conducted and will contribute to our knowledge and skills in this new area.

Differing Learning Styles

Another approach to individual abilities and differences is the theory of learning styles. A learning styles approach to teaching and learning is based on the idea that all students have strengths and abilities but that each student may learn in a different way. James Keefe, an expert on learning styles at the National Association of Secondary School Principals, has described learning styles as "characteristic cognitive, affective, and physiological behaviors that serve as relatively stable indicators of how learners perceive, interact, and respond to the learning environment."[23] In other words, with a learning styles approach, the teacher draws on the learning strengths and preferences of each individual student.

Examples

For example, some students learn best through visual means. If they see directions written down, they are more likely to understand and follow them correctly. Other students may have auditory strengths and perform better when something is presented to them orally. Yet other students may prefer kinesthetic approaches to learning and perform best when they have hands-on practice in a learning activity, as when building a model or conducting an experiment. Some students may prefer and learn best in a cooperative environment, whereas others may thrive under competition with their peers. Some learning styles theorists have even identified environmental factors, such as the amount of lighting or the temperature in a room, that influence how students learn best. As a result of these different learning preferences, students respond differently to the classroom environment and instruction. Some students can learn adequately from traditional methods such as lectures, where movement and interaction are somewhat restricted. Other students use their strengths and perform more effectively if they are allowed to learn through alternative means, such as varied instructional strategies, different-sized groupings, and individual response activities.

Disagreements over implementation

Though key advocates and researchers of a learning styles approach to education agree that individual strengths and abilities should be emphasized, they disagree on how to put these theories into practice. Some educators call for a formal assessment of each student's learning style and then a prescription of appropriate teaching methods for that individual. Others feel that students should be assessed and matched with teachers of similar learning styles. Still others warn that current tests are not yet technically adequate and that using these tests may actually harm students because they may result in improper and incorrect labeling of individuals and their so-called learning styles. These educators propose that rather than label students as having a particular learning style, curriculum and instruction should offer varied lessons that appeal to a range of strengths, abilities, and learning preferences over time. In one such approach, Bernice McCarthy has developed a teaching strategy entitled 4MAT that is designed to help teachers plan lessons that encompass a variety of learning styles.[24] If a range of activities are provided, students with different learning styles can benefit from their own instruction and also be exposed to other styles of learning.

A learning styles approach to teaching is currently receiving a great deal of attention in education. Though few schools are strictly adhering to any one "model," learning styles are being applied in varying form and intensity in many schools. Critics of learning styles theory state that greater acceptance of any one model will require more research into the reliability and validity of assessment instruments and more extensive evaluation of programs using learning theory.[25]

Students with Disabilities   Within the range of diversity your students will display in areas of ability and the different profiles they bring of learning styles and preferences, some students in your classroom will have disabilities. PL 94–142 is the public law established to assure these students an appropriate public education. Components of this law will be discussed in more detail in our examination of special education later in

Table 10.1 Children served in federally supported programs for the handicapped, by type of handicap: 1977–1988

	1977	1979	1981	1983	1985	1987	1988
*Type of handicap**	*Percentage distribution*						
Learning disabled	21.6	29.1	35.3	40.9	42.4	43.8	43.4
Speech impaired	35.3	31.2	28.2	26.6	26.1	26.0	21.4
Mentally retarded	26.0	23.2	20.0	17.8	16.1	14.7	13.1
Seriously emotionally disturbed	7.7	7.7	8.4	8.3	8.6	8.8	8.4
Type of handicap	*Number of children served as a percent of total enrollment*						
All conditions	8.3	9.1	10.1	10.7	10.9	10.9	11.1
Learning disabled	1.8	2.6	3.5	4.3	4.6	4.8	4.8
Speech impaired	2.9	2.8	2.8	2.8	2.8	2.8	2.3
Mentally retarded	2.1	2.1	2.0	1.9	1.7	1.6	1.4
Seriously emotionally disturbed	0.6	0.7	0.9	0.9	1.0	1.0	0.9

*Not all handicapping categories are displayed; thus details do not add to 100. See Table 1:12–1 for additional detail.
Note: Figures include children served under Chapter 1 and Education of the Handicapped Act.
Source: U.S. Department of Education, Office of Education and Rehabilitative Services. *Annual Report to Congress on the Implementation of the Handicapped Act,* various years; National Center for Education Statistics, Common Core of Data survey; and unpublished data.

Many students with mild handicaps, like this student with learning disabilities, can take an active part in the regular classroom.

(*Alan Carey/The Image Works*)

this chapter. But for now, let's look at what types of disabilities are included under this law.

Definition of disabilities

PL 94–142 defines children with disabilities as those with mental retardation, emotional disturbance, learning disabilities, speech or language impairments, multiple handicaps, orthopedic impairments, other health impairments, visual impairments, hardness of hearing and deafness, and both deafness and blindness. As of 1989, students with learning disabilities were the largest group, representing 47 percent of all students between six and twenty-one years of age served under PL 94–142 and Chapter 1 of the Education Consolidation and Improvement Act (legislation that provides support for students with disabilities in programs operated or supported by state agencies). Students with speech or language impairment composed 23 percent of students receiving services, and students with mental retardation accounted for 14.6 percent. Emotional disturbance (9.1 percent), multiple handicaps (1.9 percent), and hardness of hearing or deafness (1.4 percent) were less frequent disability categories.[26]

Teaching implications

Students with disabilities will likely be in your classroom for varying amounts of the school day, depending on the types and amount of support services they are receiving. How will you deal with the different needs of these children? Most importantly, remember not to stereotype them. Certainly, different handicapping conditions will have different implications for student learning. For example, a student who is mentally retarded may require repetition and practice to master simple concepts, whereas a student in a wheelchair may learn even the most difficult material rapidly. Even within the different parameters of each type of disability, however, you will probably encounter a wide range of differences. Consider, for example, two students identified as having learning disabilities. One may display a low average IQ and have extreme difficulty in mathematics. The other may have an extremely high IQ and have difficulty in reading. Both of these students have a learning disability, but you would not provide the same instruction and expectations for each of them.

The point is, you should approach instruction for these children similarly as with other students in the classroom: Expect diversity, expect a range of abilities, and look for the particular strengths and learning profiles of each student. A helpful resource for recognizing student abilities and for suggesting instructional strategies will be the special education teacher in your school. The more you and the special education teacher(s) coordinate instruction and services for your students with disabilities, the better the students' educational experiences are likely to be.

DIFFERENCES IN ACCESS TO KNOWLEDGE

One of the questions investigated in John Goodlad's study *A Place Called School* is "whether students as a consequence of the schools they happen to attend and the classes to which they are assigned, have equal of access to knowledge." In general, the researchers found the answer to this question to be "no."

At the elementary school level the investigators found great variability from school to school in the time allocated for instruction in particular subjects. For example, in one school, teachers estimated that 1.1 hours per week were given to science instruction, on the average. In another school, teachers estimated 5.3 hours per week for the same subject. Thus, students' access to school knowledge may vary from school to school.

Starting in the elementary grades and continuing into high school, Goodlad observes, students are soon separated into two groups: those who are good with their heads and those who are good with their hands. The school's emphasis on cultivating the head, or mind, labels the first group as winners. The difference continues in the form of two curricula at the high school level. A program of rigorous academic subjects emphasizes learning by lis-

tening and telling; learning by doing is emphasized only in the areas of the arts, physical education, and vocational education.

Within the academic curriculum common to the secondary schools, divisions occur. Tracking students by their achievement and performance in English, mathematics, social studies, and science is customary at the junior and senior high levels. Entire classes are organized as low, middle, or high achievers. Goodlad notes the studies indicating lower-track students' lower self-esteem, higher dropout rates, and higher delinquency rates. He also describes the disproportionate representation of minority students and those from the lowest socioeconomic groups in the lowest-track classes. Higher-track teachers emphasize higher-level cognitive processes and are perceived as being more concerned about their students and less punitive than teachers in the lower tracks. Goodlad concludes, "there appear to be in our data, then, clear evidence of tracking's differentiating students in regard to their access to knowledge and further, doing so disproportionately for minority students, especially poor minority students, as compared with white students."

John Goodlad, *A Place Called School: Prospects for the Future* (New York: McGraw-Hill, 1984), pp. 131–157.

Gifted and Talented Students   One of the most challenging types of student a teacher can have in the classroom are gifted or talented children. The gifted child is extremely bright, quickly grasping ideas and concepts you are teaching, and making interpretations or extrapolations that you may not even have considered. Gifted children may also display a creativity that manifests itself in original thinking or artistic creations.

Students who are gifted and/or talented are sometimes overlooked when educators talk about students with special needs. However, as Kathi Kearney, founder of the Hollingworth Center for Gifted Children says, "Highly gifted children are as far from the norm in the direction of giftedness as the severely retarded are in the other direction."[27] Therefore they do have special needs.

In 1978 the United States Office of Education (USOE) adopted this definition of gifted and talented:

> The term "gifted and talented children" means children and, whenever applicable, youth who are identified at the preschool, elementary, or secondary level as possessing demonstrated or potential abilities that give evidence of high performance responsibility in areas such as intellectual, creative, specific academic, or leadership ability, or in the performing and visual arts and who by reason thereof require services or activities not ordinarily provided by the school.[28]

Definitions   A survey of definitions used by the education departments in each state reveals wide variations; only four states use the 1978 USOE definition; one uses the

DIALOGUE

Jim: The issue of tracking students by ability grouping is often debated in school districts.

Kevin: I know what you mean. The notion of ability grouping is appealing because it seems logical that teachers can teach more efficiently when differences in student ability are minimal.

Jim: But this is one of those cases where the research doesn't support logic. There is pretty clear evidence that ability grouping per se is unlikely to have a positive effect on student achievement.

Kevin: Right. For students in high-ability classes, such grouping has either no effect or only a minor positive effect on their achievement. The one exception seems to be for honors classes in high school, where especially positive results have been found.

Jim: The real problem, though, is the effects on students who are grouped in low-ability classes. We have lots of research that indicates clearly negative effects on the achievement and attitudes of these students, primarily because these classes receive a poorer quality of instruction.

Kevin: What do you mean by "poorer quality of instruction"?

Jim: There seem to be several factors. First, teachers seem to stereotype the students because of the label "low ability," and consequently they expect less of them. Also, teachers generally don't like to teach low-ability sections, and they often admit they don't prepare as conscientiously for low groups as for their high groups.

Kevin: Another reason is that without some high-achieving students in the class, the low-ability kids don't have good models to emulate and they might become discouraged and alienated from learning. So what's the answer?

Jim: I think the answer is heterogeneous grouping, but with more use of differential assignments, within-class grouping based on specific tasks, and the use of peer tutoring.

Kevin: In other words, more individualization.

earlier (1972) version. The areas in which states identify gifted and talented students can range from intellectual to psychomotor to artistic, with many variations.[29] But the term *talented* most often refers to an ability or skill (musical or artistic talent, for example) that may not be matched by the child's more general abilities, whereas the term *gifted* usually includes intellectual ability. Gifted and talented children are sufficiently different from most other children in intellectual and creative abilities that adaptations and adjustments in the usual curricula are required if they are to attain maximum personal development. Although special educational care and services for students with disabilities have long been recognized and accepted, American education has been very slow to accept the notion that gifted children require special adaptations in both curricula and teaching methods. Because the idea of giftedness implies an elitism to many Americans, it seems undemocratic to provide special services to children who already enjoy an intellectual advantage.

Though exact numbers of gifted and talented students are impossible to obtain, educators who study and work with this population estimate that there are six to ten times as many such children as was previously thought.[30] As a result of neglected needs, many gifted and talented students drop out of school at rates far exceeding the rates of dropouts for their non-gifted peers. Many of those who stay in school feel unchallenged and become bored and apathetic. The result is that many of our brightest and most talented minds are being turned off or underdeveloped. Only recently have school districts begun to make serious efforts to identify gifted children and to develop special programs for them. The problem of identification is especially acute for bilingual children and children adjusting to a new culture, as well as for children in other minority groups.

THE SCHOOL'S RESPONSE TO DIVERSITY

You may be getting concerned about whether you can handle the range of diversities you may face in your classroom. Be assured, however, that you are not in this alone. Besides other teachers and administrators to help you, most schools have specialists who often can give you valuable advice or direct help to your students. At one time the only business of schools was to educate students. But now, because of the increasing complexity and diversity of our students' lives, other needs are being addressed and incorporated into the way schools are approaching "education."

Help for teachers

Various assistance systems have been devised to help the teacher respond to the range of needs of students. Some of this assistance is in the form of support personnel such as nurses, school psychologists, counselors, and administrators. A growing number of parent councils are emerging that are being used to involve parents in giving advice and helping to deal with problems. Teacher aides may be community members who speak the language of substantial minorities in the schools. Interns or students from the local college may help provide another adult in the classroom.

In addition to support personnel, schools have attempted to provide special programs to address some dimensions of student diversity. Multicultural and bilingual education, special education, and programs for gifted and talented students have all evolved out of concern that certain types and degrees of student diversity require different educational strategies to insure an equal opportunity for intellectual stimulation and growth.

Multicultural Education

Multicultural education represents one approach to meeting the educational needs of an increasingly diverse student population. *Multicultural education* is education that values cultural pluralism and that seeks the cultural enrichment of all young people through programs dedicated to the preservation and extension

Definition of cultural alternatives. "A reaction against assimilation and the melting pot myth, cultural pluralism not only assumes that minorities and ethnic groups have rights, but that their life-styles are legitimate and desirable ways of participating in society."[31] Education for cultural pluralism includes four major thrusts: the teaching of values that support cultural diversity and individual uniqueness; the encouragement of the qualitative expansion of existing ethnic cultures and their incorporation into the mainstream of American socioeconomic and political life; the support of explorations in alternative and emerging lifestyles; and the encouragement of multiculturalism, multilingualism, and multiple dialects.[32]

Many school districts are attempting to permeate their curricula with a multicultural emphasis, believing that an emphasis on cultural pluralism is our society's best way to combat the prejudice and divisiveness that exist among the different subcultures of our nation. By developing mutual respect and appreciation of different lifestyles, languages, religious beliefs, and family structures, students may help shape a better future society for all its members.

Some concerns Some educators, however, are concerned about what they believe are potential dangers of cultural pluralism in the schools. They fear that it may destroy any sense of common traditions, values, purposes, and obligations; that it may divert the schools' attention from their basic purpose of educating for civic, economic, and personal effectiveness; and that it may undermine the sense of morality because no universal moral positions are considered acceptable to all elements of our society. These critics do not argue against the need to preserve and value the achievements of the diverse ethnic and racial groups of our country, but they reject the position that everything is of equal value, that the schools have a responsibility to teach every possible belief and value, and that behavior is moral if it is believed to be so by any group.[33] These critics assert that there are limits to pluralism and that those limits must be articulated by schools and school leaders.

The major thrusts of multicultural education are not without controversy. Multicultural education has often been cast as a reform movement, designed to address inequity and discrimination resulting from the race, religion, socioeconomic status, sex, age, exceptionality, or language of students.[34] As with any attempt to redress social ills, excesses and overexuberance can occur. Nevertheless, schools will need to accommodate larger minority populations in such a way that while barriers are removed, the basic purposes of schooling are preserved.

Bilingual Education

Students whose native language is not English constitute one of the most conspicuous failure groups in the American educational system. Because of their difficulty in speaking, writing, and understanding English, many of these students fall further and further behind in school, and overwhelming numbers drop out before finishing high school.

To cope with this problem, Congress passed the Bilingual Education Act in 1968 and amended it in 1974 to make it more explicit in intent and design. The 1974 act provided a definition of what constitutes a bilingual education program:

Definition

> It is instruction given in, and study of, English and to the extent necessary to allow a child to progress effectively through the educational system, the native language of the children of limited English-speaking ability, and such instruction is given with appreciation for the cultural heritage of such children, and, with respect to elementary school instruction, such instruction shall, to the extent necessary be in all courses or subjects of study which will allow a child to progress effectively through the educational system.

Much of the expansion of bilingual programs in the 1970s can be attributed to a series of court cases, the most notable of which was the 1974 U.S. Supreme Court case of *Lau* v. *Nichols.* The case involved a class action suit on behalf of Chinese-speaking students in San Francisco, but it has implications for all the nation's non-English-speaking children. The Court found "that there is no equality of treatment merely by providing students with the same facilities, textbooks, teachers, and curriculum; for students who do not understand English are effectively foreclosed from any meaningful education." Basing its ruling on the Civil Rights Act of 1964, the Court held that the San Francisco school system unlawfully discriminated on the basis of national origin when it failed to cope with the children's language problems. Although the Lau case did not mandate bilingual education as the means by which to solve the problem, subsequent state cases did order bilingual programs. With the advice of an expert panel, the U.S. Office of Civil Rights suggested guidelines for school districts to follow, the so-called Lau Remedies. The guidelines "specified that language minority students should be taught academics in their primary home language until they could effectively benefit from English language instruction."[35]

Lau v. *Nichols*

There are several types or models of bilingual education programs. The *transitional model* uses the child's native tongue only as an interim medium of instruction until the child develops fluency in English. Students move on to regular all-English classes as quickly as possible. The *immersion model* requires students to learn English by being in a classroom where the teacher understands their first language but speaks only in English. In *submersion model* classes, students attend all-English classes; they must "sink or swim" until they learn English. Two other models—*maintenance* and *English as a second language (ESL)*—involve some combination of instruction in the native language and English. Maintenance instruction, sometimes called bilingual education, preserves the student's native language; ESL instruction is generally a tutorial that supplements instruction in an all-English classroom.[36]

Different models

Considerable controversy surrounds the whole issue of bilingual education. Whereas ethnic groups lobby strongly for expanded support for bilingual

Controversy remains

programs, others charge that bilingual programs deliberately impede the acquisition of English skills among minority groups. A four-year study conducted by the Department of Education examined the efficacy of bilingual education by comparing the academic performance of Spanish-speaking students in three general types of bilingual programs: immersion programs, programs gradually phasing in English instruction over four years, and programs introducing English instruction over six years. The researchers found that students in all three types of bilingual education kept pace with the general student body and outperformed other students considered at risk for failure. In comparing the three types of programs, however, they found that students in the immersion programs and four-year exit programs tended to stay in bilingual education for a much longer period of time than originally projected by program models. Less than 26 percent of students in these groups were mainstreamed by the originally expected grade levels. Students in the six-year or "late-exit" programs were found at the end of sixth grade to be gaining in mathematics, English-language, and English-reading skills faster than the general student population. In contrast, the immersion program students appeared to be losing early gains in these areas compared with the general student population. And finally, students in late-exit programs were found to have more homework assignments and greater parental support in completing these assignments. All three types of bilingual education were noted as particularly lacking in the instruction of higher-order thinking skills. Though these research findings are not conclusive, early research appears to support the U.S. Department of Education's current policy, which holds that a variety of programs for bilingual education can be effective, and that specific means for implementation should be chosen at the local level.[37]

Need for bilingual teachers

Many school districts are in desperate need of bilingual teachers, particularly those who speak Spanish and, to an increasing extent, Asian languages. If you speak a second language or still have time to include learning a language in your college program, you could help meet a serious educational need and at the same time greatly enhance your employment opportunities.

Special Education

Students with disabilities are another group of individuals in our schools who have received special attention to insure equal educational opportunities. The Education for All Handicapped Children Act of 1975 (PL 94–142), now referred to as the Individuals with Disabilities Education Act (IDEA), is the culmination of standards and policies of federal commitment to this group of students. PL 94–142 establishes minimal standards for state and local compliance in educating children with disabilities from three through twenty-one years of age.

Basic provisions of law

The basic provisions of IDEA insure that students with disabilities receive a *free, appropriate education.* Because of the wide variety of handicapping conditions and the infinite degrees of severity in which these conditions may be found in individual students, an "appropriate education" must be defined on an individual basis. A written *individualized education program (IEP)* is a mandated management tool that states the child's current levels of educational performance, short-term objectives and annual goals, services to be provided, and criteria and schedules for evaluation of progress. The IEP helps to insure that the educational goals designed for the child are appropriate to individual learning needs and that these plans are actually delivered and monitored. Provisions must be reviewed and revised as needed and at least annually. Teachers, parents or guardians, special educators, other professionals, and (whenever appropriate) the child are all involved in the development and approval of the IEP.

IDEA also stipulates that services for students with disabilities be provided in the *least restrictive environment,* meaning that students with disabilities should participate in regular education programs to the greatest extent appropriate. Determination of what constitutes an appropriate environment has been subject to great debate. Social benefits of the regular classroom must be weighed **Regular education** against educational needs and individual circumstances. Within the field of spe- **initiative** cial education, heated debate has arisen concerning the *regular education initiative (REI),* a proposal to adjust regular classroom teaching in such a manner that most students with disabilities may be integrated full-time into regular classrooms.[38] Proponents of the REI feel that the least restrictive environment and the most appropriate education for individuals with disabilities would take place in the regular classroom. Because of various educational issues and economic realities, a single coordinated education system for all students would be more effective and efficient. Opponents of the REI strongly argue that such an integration of services would result in an unequal education for students with disabilities who have special needs. Further research on the feasibility of REI instructional models is needed before conclusive decisions can be reached.

If there is a failure to agree on any one aspect of what constitutes an appropriate education for an individual child—from matters of identification to evaluation to educational placement—nevertheless parents or guardians and their children are entitled to *due process of law.* Several procedural safeguards have been established, including the right of parents to examine all relevant records, the requirement for written notice and consent before any special education action is opposed, and the opportunity for parents to submit formal complaints and appeal decisions.

In 1986, President Reagan signed the Education of the Handicapped Act **Early intervention** Amendments (PL 99–457). This law provided for early intervention for children from birth to age two who are developmentally delayed. For states that choose to participate, programs must include such services as the provision of a multidisciplinary assessment of the child's needs, a written *individualized family services plan (IFSP),* and case management. Services may draw from a variety of areas, such as special education, speech and language pathology, occupational or physical therapy, or family training and counseling, depending on the developmental needs of the child.

PL 99–457 also stated that by school year 1990–91 a "free appropriate public education" had to be extended to children with disabilities age three to five years old. Although state and local education agencies administer these programs, they may contract with other programs, agencies, or providers to provide a range of services, such as programs that are home based for part of the day. Families are recognized as playing a particularly important role in preschool education, and instruction for parents is to be included in the IFSP whenever that is appropriate and the parents desire it.

Programs for the
Gifted and Talented

Current educational programs for gifted and talented students are quite varied. Some programs establish special schools that are designed only for gifted or talented students and that have special admission requirements. In such schools, stimulating courses can be devised and taught without concern for students who might be unable to keep pace, and teachers as well as students can be recruited on the basis of their talents.

Various approaches

Other programs adapt and enrich the regular school curriculum for gifted and talented children by grouping these students together for all or part of their instruction. This option is normally more flexible and practical than special schools. Classes can be established on a continuing or short-term basis, in any subject area, with the intention of either enriching or accelerating the student. Since 1972 Johns Hopkins University in Baltimore, Maryland, has been operating with great success special classes for mathematically gifted children. In literature and the humanities, special classes have been used to permit deeper exploration of issues not normally covered in regular classes. The "Great Books" program, for example, has been used as a supplementary curriculum for gifted children at the secondary level.

Still other programs are designed as out-of-school programs for gifted and talented youngsters who may have exhausted the resources of their particular school. Internship or work experiences with such professionals as physicians, engineers, and lawyers can provide valuable insights and learning experiences not available in regular secondary schools. Museums, theaters, ballet performances, art shows, nature excursions, and other cultural experiences can also supplement the regular school offerings for gifted and talented students.

Identifying students

Special programs and services for gifted and talented children raise the problem of how to identify children who might qualify. Experts have recommended the following tools, in descending order of preference:

1. individual intelligence test scores
2. earlier achievements, including academic record
3. teacher nomination based on observations
4. standardized achievement test scores
5. scores on creativity tests
6. scores on group intelligence tests[39]

A cautionary note: there is a danger of letting the tools used to locate the children become synonymous with the *definition* of gifted and talented. To avoid this potential danger, teachers and administrators must study and interpret what data the tools provide rather than take the data at face value and use them for hard and fast cutoff points. Whether or not a child is to be recommended for a special program is a decision that should be made by the responsible teacher and other professional educators on the basis of their objective and subjective appraisals of the student, the nature of the gifted program or activity, and the atmosphere in which the student lives and goes to school. Parents should be a significant part of these discussions. The point is that the complexity of the variables involved requires that individual decisions be made by professionals using their best judgments, rather than according to arbitrary, predetermined cutoff points on tests.

*If 2 + 3 is always going
to be 5, why do they
keep teaching it to us?*
— A GIFTED FIRST-GRADE
STUDENT —

If your school or school district does have special programs and activities for gifted and talented students, you may be expected to work with resource teachers to help prepare individualized educational plans for these students. It is more likely that you will discover certain students in your class to be gifted or talented and, lacking any special program, you will be responsible for teaching these students as part of your regular class. What do you need to know?

1. Recognize that gifted pupils generally learn the standard curricular skills and content quickly and easily. They need teaching that does not tie them to a limited range, that is not preoccupied with filling them with facts and information, but that allows them to use the regular class as a forum for research, inquiry, and projects that are meaningful to them.
2. Realize that these students are persistently curious. They need teachers who encourage them to maintain confidence in their own ideas, even when those ideas differ from the norm.
3. Teach these pupils to be efficient and effective at independent study so that they can develop the skills required for self-directed learning and for analyzing and solving problems independently.
4. Help students to apply complex cognitive processes such as creative thinking, critiques, and pro and con analyses.
5. Expand your ideas concerning what instructional materials are available. Consider businesses, religious groups, national parks, and resource people as potential instructional materials, in addition to the textbooks and reference books available in the school.

*Nontraditional
Programs*

All the types of school programs discussed so far in this section address student diversity in a somewhat "traditional" way: that is, they have evolved from the notion that the role of the school is to address issues that arise for children in a standard school setting during the course of the school day. Many of these programs have proven beneficial to a number of students. However, a number of social conditions may complicate the issue of diversity. Social problems such as poverty, homelessness, or inadequate health care are such pervasive influences in some students' lives that we will discuss them in more detail in the next chapter. The more we examine "today's children," the more we realize that societal conditions and problems affecting our students cut across traditional lines of services delivery.

Interagency cooperation

In acknowledgement of the complexity and pervasiveness of these conditions and problems in the lives of children, programs are emerging that emphasize interagency cooperation in meeting the needs of individuals. Edward Zigler, director of the Bush Center in Child Development and Social Policy at Yale University started an initiative called "Schools for the 21st Century" in Independence, Missouri, that has spread to five states. In this initiative, schools function as community centers providing common ground for social and family support services. Home visitation, assistance for parents with infants, day care for three- to five-year-olds, and after-school care for schoolchildren are provided. Teen-age pregnancy prevention programs and adult literacy classes are available.

A host of services are centralized to help children and their families overcome social, psychological, and health problems.[40]

James Comer, a public health physician and psychiatrist, developed an initiative in New Haven, Connecticut, that emphasized structuring the environment to facilitate learning and development rather than placing blame and trying to change children. The "Comer model" attempts to change the climate of demoralized schools and to create a sense of community and direction by bringing together the principal, teachers, aides, and parents to form a school planning and management team. Services of the school social worker, the psychologist, special education teachers, and counselors are coordinated to provide a consultation team to support individual students and teachers as well as the school planning and management team. Comer notes, "Kids don't learn in pieces. That's why it is essential to address the entire social system of the school because of the way the many variables interact and because attitudes, morale, and hope all affect school performance."[41]

Diversity: A Complex Phenomenon

The school programs described in this section have been designed to address student diversity and to create a more equal educational opportunity for children in our school systems. An inherent danger in these approaches to addressing diversity, however, is the tendency to label children and to form stereotypic

JAMES P. COMER
(1934–)

James Comer is a public health physician and psychiatrist who, through his work with low-income New Haven, Connecticut, schools, has shown that it is possible for low-income African-American children to achieve at high academic and social levels.

James Comer received his M.D. from Howard University in 1960, and he then entered the Public Health Service. He became interested in the study of how policies and institutions interact with families and children, and he began to see the school as the place to improve the life chances for children from difficult home situations. He decided that a career in psychiatry would enable him to address the social problems that plagued the people with whom he worked, and in 1964 he began his psychiatric training at Yale University.

At Yale, Comer worked with the inner-city New Haven schools to find out why they were not helping African-American children and how they could be made to do so. He wanted to give low-income African-American children the same opportunities in life that education had afforded him. The more he worked with children, the more he came to believe that schools were the only places where children who were stuck in poverty and failure could receive the support their families could not give them.

With the help of a Ford Foundation grant, Dr. Comer became the director of the School Development Program with the New Haven Public Schools. A team of educational and mental health professionals, consisting of Dr. Comer, school administrators and teachers, a social worker, a psychologist, a special education teacher, and other support staff, worked to involve the parents in the development of a social skills curriculum that integrated academic disciplines. The curriculum included four major areas: politics and government, business and economics, health and nutrition, and spiritual and leisure time, all areas in which the students would need proficiency to suc-

images of who these children are. Placement of children in each of these types of programs is typically based on the best educational indicators currently available and usually with the best of intentions, but student performance in school is affected by many factors, including the social and cultural trends we have been discussing in this chapter. Ability may be depressed or disguised by many layers of disadvantage, such as lack of exposure to mainstream culture, poorly educated parents who are not able to help their children find and nurture their talents, or a tendency not to do well on standardized tests.

Differences, not deficits

As a teacher, we encourage you to remember that we are talking about *differences* in students, not necessarily deficits. The educational groupings we have been discussing are an administrative convenience, not a naturally occurring segmentation of children. Within each of these groups each child will vary along a number of dimensions and have very different learning profiles of strengths and weaknesses.

THE TEACHER'S RESPONSE TO DIVERSITY

So far in this chapter we have presented you with a great deal of information about societal trends shaping and influencing the children you will be teaching. The numbers and statistics may at times have seemed overwhelming. However, as a teacher, you need to be aware of the many influences that affect children

ceed in school and to lead productive lives. Through the curriculum the students became more aware of their community and of how their involvement in it could make a difference.

By adopting child development and behavioral science research, the team concentrated on problem solving, not blame fixing, and made decisions based on consensus. This consensus process gave each team member a sense of participation and ownership of decisions. The project was a great success: students' standardized test scores rose dramatically, project schools had higher attendance rates than other New Haven schools, and students graduated to become school leaders in their later schooling.

The "Comer model" emphasizes the social context of teaching and learning. No academic learning is possible, Comer asserts, unless there is a positive environment at the school where teachers, students, parents, and administrators like each other and work together for the good of all children. Built around three elements—a school governance team, a mental health team, and parental participation—Comer's model seeks to create schools that of-

fer children stable support and positive role models. With the school and parents working successfully together, there is no conflict between home and school. The students acquire desirable values, disruptions at school are reduced, and both teachers and students have more time and energy to focus on academic and social skills learning.

Some thirty-five schools in New Haven and more than seventy in other school districts across the nation have now adopted the "Comer model," and many of them report equally impressive results. Dr. Comer's approach is likely to have even greater national impact. Because of his success, the Rockefeller Foundation has committed $3 million a year for five years to encourage the adoption of his ideas across the country. As Comer says, "We've got to make it possible for all of the children to succeed so they can meet the expectations of school and the expectations of society. If we don't do that, our country is on a downhill course in twenty or thirty years. So we've got to make a difference, and we've got to make a difference very quickly."

Teachers can respond to classroom diversity by encouraging interaction between home and school and by providing opportunities for parents to come in for conferences and meetings.

(*Kathy Sloane/Photo Researchers, Inc.*)

and their learning, because ultimately how these children are educated will come down to you and your daily interactions with them in your classroom. How will you deal with this diversity?

The typical teacher

Consider what we know about the typical teacher today. Women and whites predominate in the teacher force; 69 percent of all public school teachers are women, and 91 percent of those teaching in public schools are white.[42] Profiles of beginning teachers show similar patterns among the newest professionals to the field. In 1989, 75 percent of beginning teachers were female; 93 percent were white, 4 percent were black, and 2 percent were Hispanic.[43] Most of these teachers come from relatively stable family backgrounds. The majority of teachers and future teachers in our classrooms, then, come from very different backgrounds than many of the students they teach. Though diversity can certainly be an asset, it will require increased awareness on your part, as a teacher, of the many implications of this diversity for student learning.

Teacher-student disparity

The match of social and cultural characteristics of students and teachers will directly influence communication and understanding in the classroom. The more alike students and teachers are in social and cultural characteristics, the greater will be the tacit expectations for behavior and academic performance. As social and cultural characteristics become increasingly disparate, the more teachers will need to rely on solid pedagogical training to traverse these differences. The discrepancy between today's typical teacher, the profile of the teacher education student of the 1990s and the increasingly diverse students of the future, emphasizes the growing importance of pedagogical training in sensitizing incoming teachers to the commonalities and differences among students, as well as in providing specific methods and techniques for addressing the plurality of culture and learning styles.

Nor is this cultural disparity between teachers and students likely to lessen in the near future. A 1989 study conducted by the American Association of Colleges for Teacher Education (AACTE) examined characteristics of teachers in training and reported that 81 percent of teacher trainees are female and 92 percent are white. Less than 3 percent of teacher trainees reported they would be able to instruct in any language other than English. Only 9 percent were considering teaching in an urban or multicultural context.[44]

Given this profile, and despite efforts to increase the number of minority teachers discussed in Chapter 2, it appears very likely that a cultural discrepancy will continue to grow in the near future between students and teachers. How can prospective teachers best prepare for this disparity? One way will be for teachers to seek out experiences that will broaden their understanding of societal and cultural commonalities and differences. For example, while traveling abroad or spending extended time in another culture many people experience periods of feeling out of synch with their surroundings or times of confusion in the most basic daily activities. Such experiences increase awareness of the many language barriers some children face every day in school. Many cultural customs and habits that we assume are common to all cultures may be practices typical of only white middle-class Americans. Travel and diverse cultural experiences also increase appreciation for the strategies and ingenuity that are required to perform in such constant dissonance. Through such experiences prospective teachers can increase recognition of and develop empathy for the many potentially confusing or stressful circumstances of students from culturally diverse backgrounds.

Preparing for student diversity

The implications of taking account of the diverse backgrounds, needs, and abilities of your students are far-reaching and will affect everything, from how you organize your classroom and instruct students to the curricula you choose to how you interact with other professionals and parents. A central factor in these decisions will be your attitudes and expectations for your various students. Will you tap the highest educational potential of each of your students, or will you let preconceived ideas interfere with your expectations for the achievement of some of your students? We urge you to take time to learn about and appreciate the values and backgrounds of your students. Not only will this broaden your own cultural awareness, but it will also enhance instruction and facilitate communication with parents. The student whose home values are very different from the predominant values and expectations of school may need your help in understanding differences and meeting the school's expectations. In Chapter 13, "What Makes a Teacher Effective?" we will discuss in more detail the attitudes of effective teachers and how to facilitate attitude change.

Your effectiveness as a teacher dealing with student diversity will also depend on how you organize your classroom and instruct your students. It is always important to teach to strengths rather than to make a child feel incapable or deficient. Recall Howard Gardner's ideas about multiple intelligences and the warning against rewarding and nurturing only a narrow range of abilities. Look for the unique strengths each of your students brings to your class. Allow for teaching and learning to be dynamic. Provide a variety of educational experiences, and find ways for all your students to achieve recognition from you and from peers for being capable or good at something.

One final note: A major goal of this chapter has been to make you increasingly aware of the complexity of issues that directly affect many children's lives and their ability to get an adequate education. With the growing complexity of our society, it is no longer feasible for the teacher to try to attend to all students' needs alone. You will need to use all the resources available to you, including parents and other professionals. Some teachers may initially feel threatened by this involvement or have a sense that the classroom is their "turf." But, as we have seen in our discussion of emerging trends in our society, our students need the coordinated expertise and support of all school professionals and the crucial link with parents to be given a fair shot at acquiring the good education that is their due.

Discussion Questions

1. How do you compare to the profile of the typical teacher described in this chapter?
2. How can you help prepare yourself for the diversity you are likely to encounter in the classroom? What experiences with diversity will you bring to the classroom?
3. What are the pros and cons of living in a pluralistic society? In your opinion, is this preferable to a "melting pot" approach to diversity?
4. What are the general characteristics of your learning style? How can you capitalize on this in your teaching? How will you account for various learning styles in your students?
5. Have you had any contact with individuals with disabilities (for example, a relative or neighbor)? What did you learn from this relationship that might be helpful in your teaching?
6. What other elements of diversity will you find in your students that have not been discussed in this chapter? How will you be sensitive to these differences?

For Further Reading

Comer, James P. *Maggie's American Dream.* New York: New American Library, 1988.

> This is the story of Maggie Comer's climb from extreme poverty to becoming the mother of five outstanding children. The account is written by her son, child psychiatrist and educator James Comer.

Daniels, Harvey A. (Ed.) *Not Only English: Affirming America's Multilingual Heritage.* Illinois: National Council of Teachers of English, 1990.

> A series of chapters written by experts and educators in the field discuss the historical roots and possible implications of the English-Only movement in the United States. Potential responses by educators are discussed.

Education That Works: An Action Plan for the Education of Minorities. Cambridge, Mass.: Quality Education for Minorities Project, Massachusetts Institute of Technology, 1990.

> A blueprint of goals, research, and action steps that focuses on the educational needs and interests of Alaskan Native, Native American, African-American, Mexican-American, and Puerto Rican people in the United States.

Gardner, Howard. *Frames of Mind*. New York: Basic Books, 1985.

> A detailed account of Gardner's theory of multiple intelligences.

Glasser, W. *The Quality School*. New York: Harper & Row, 1990.

> This book proposes an alternative way of managing schools based on Glasser's control theory.

Featherstone, Helen. *A Difference in the Family: Living with a Disabled Child*. New York: Penguin Books, 1981.

> A personal account of life with a child with severe disabilities, including insights and suggestions on how professionals, including teachers, can be most helpful and supportive.

McKay, Sandra Lee and Wong, Sau-Ling Cynthia, (Eds.) *Language Diversity: Problem or Resource?* New York: Newbury House Publishers, 1988.

> Numerous articles written by experts in the field address historical, social, and educational perspectives on language minorities in the United States.

Notes

1. Lisa Jennings, "Studies Link Parental Involvement, Higher Student Achievement," *Education Week,* April 4, 1990, pp. 20–21.
2. Sally Reed and R. Craig Sautter, "Children of Poverty: The Status of 12 Million Young Americans," *Phi Delta Kappan* 71 (June 1990): K-9.
3. John Kellogg, "Forces of Change," *Phi Delta Kappan* 69 (November 1988): 204.
4. *One-Third of a Nation* (Commission on Minority Participation in Education and American Life, n.d.), p. 3.
5. Aaron M. Pallas, Gary Natriello, and Edward L. McDill, "The Changing Nature of the Disadvantaged Population: Current Dimensions and Future Trends," *Educational Researcher* (June–July 1989): 19.
6. Diane Divoky, "The Model Minority Goes to School," *Phi Delta Kappan* 69 (November 1988): 220.
7. Pallas, et al., "The Changing Nature of the Disadvantaged Population," pp. 10–11.
8. Divoky, "The Model Minority Goes to School," p. 220.
9. "For Urban Schools: A Statistical Portent," *Education Week,* June 22, 1988, p. 28.
10. Harold L. Hodgkinson, *The Same Client: The Demographics of Education and Service Delivery Systems* (Washington, D.C.: Institute for Educational Leadership, 1989), p. 3.
11. Ibid.
12. Ibid.
13. Pallas, et al., "The Changing Nature of the Disadvantaged Population," p. 19.
14. Hodgkinson, *The Same Client*, p. 3.
15. Hodgkinson, *The Same Client*, pp. 3–4.
16. Ibid.
17. Lynn Olson, "Parents as Partners," *Education Week,* April 4, 1990, p. 19.
18. Ibid.

19. As cited in "Teachers Find Worsening Social Problems," *Harvard Education Letter* 6 (May–June 1990): 8.
20. Abraham H. Maslow, *Toward a Psychology of Being* (New York: Van Nostrand Reinhold, 1968).
21. William Glasser, *The Quality School* (New York: Harper & Row, 1990).
22. Howard Gardner, *Frames of Mind* (New York: Basic Books, 1985).
23. As cited in John O'Neil, "Making Sense of Style," *Educational Leadership* 48 (October 1990): 5.
24. Bernice McCarthy, "Using the 4MAT System to Bring Learning Styles to Schools," *Educational Leadership* 48 (October 1990): 31–37.
25. Lynn Curry, "A Critique of the Research on Learning Styles," *Educational Leadership* 48 (October 1990): 50–56.
26. *Eleventh Annual Report to Congress on the Implementation of the Education of the Handicapped Act* (Washington, D.C.: U.S. Department of Education, 1989), p. 15.
27. Sarah Wernick, "Hard Times for Educating the Highly Gifted Child," *New York Times,* May 30, 1990, p. B8.
28. Frances A. Karnes and Susan F. Koch, "State Definitions of the Gifted and Talented: An Update and Analysis," *Journal for the Education of the Gifted* 8 (Summer 1985): 285.
29. Ibid., pp. 302–303.
30. Wernick, "Hard Times," p. B8.
31. Theresa E. McCormick, "Multiculturalism: Some Principles and Issues," *Theory into Practice* 23 (Spring 1984): 94.
32. "No One Model American" (a statement on multicultural education issued by the AACTE Commission on Multicultural-Education), *Journal of Teacher Education* 24 (Winter 1973): 264.
33. M. Donald Thomas, "The Limits of Pluralism," *Phi Delta Kappan* 62 (April 1981): 589, 591–592.
34. McCormick, "Multiculturalism," p. 94.
35. Russell Gersten and John Woodward, "A Case for Structured Immersion," *Educational Leadership* 43 (September 1985): 75.
36. "When Children Speak Little English: How Effective is Bilingual Education?" *Harvard Education Letter* 2 (November 1986): 1–4.
37. Peter Schmidt, "Three Types of Bilingual Education Effective, E.D. Study Concludes," *Education Week,* February 20, 1991, pp. 1, 23.
38. Teacher Education Division, Council for Exceptional Children, "The Regular Education Initiative," *Journal of Learning Disabilities* 20 (May 1987): 289–293.
39. Maynard C. Reynolds and Jack W. Birch, *Teaching Exceptional Children in All America's Schools* (Reston, Va.: Council for Exceptional Children, 1977), p. 220.
40. Reed and Sautter, "Children of Poverty," K-10.
41. As cited in Lisbeth Schorr, *Within Our Reach* (New York: Doubleday, 1988), p. 235.
42. C. Emily Feistritzer, *Profile of Teachers in the U.S.* (Washington, D.C.: National Center for Education Information, 1986), pp. 3–4.
43. "You and the System," *Teacher Magazine* April, 1990, p. 38.
44. Nancy Zimpher and Antoine Garibaldi, "RATE Data About Students and Perceptions About Programs," paper prepared for the annual conference of the AACTE, Chicago, February 1990, pp. 4–5.

CHAPTER PREVIEW

Rarely does a day go by on which educational issues fail to make headlines in newspapers across the country. Violence in schools, random testing for drug use, inequality of educational opportunity, competency tests for teachers, and youth suicides are only a few of the issues that we read about daily. Underlying these issues are problems that complicate young people's efforts to get an education, problems such as crippling poverty and child abuse and neglect. This chapter explores some of the most sensitive and controversial issues in American education. Naturally, in such a short space we are able to treat each topic only briefly. However, we urge you to pursue additional reading on each of the issues.

This chapter emphasizes that:

● Some critical problems affect many school-age children, very directly influencing the lives of the children involved and frequently spilling over into the classroom. Among these problems are severe poverty, homelessness, teen-age pregnancy, child abuse, alcohol and drug abuse, and adolescent suicide.

● The subject of public school desegregation and integration continues to raise controversy in American education. Much of the controversy involves issues such as de jure and de facto segregation, busing, the meaning of "equality of educational opportunity," compensatory education, and magnet school programs.

● Access to equal educational opportunity, in addition to being denied African-Americans, has, in some schools, been denied to females. Sexism and gender stereotyping remain an issue in our schools.

● Violence and vandalism, which are not confined to urban schools, continue to be major problems in the schools.

● School dropout rates, although still regrettably high, declined during the 1980s after rising during the 1970s. Good progress was made with African-American males, but dropout rates for Hispanics and Native Americans remain high.

● The American public's concern over declining student performance in the 1970s has led to an emphasis on making the school more accountable, which has spawned the competency testing and accountability movements.

T eaching is said to be a middle-class occupation that recruits middle-class people or people who want to become middle class. More to the point, most teachers come from relatively stable backgrounds. Although this situation is a potential source of strength, it also means that the worlds that children inhabit are often at variance with that of their teachers. Many teachers may have difficulty recognizing and adapting to the differences between their backgrounds and those of their students, especially those differences that contribute to the problems that some children bring with them into the classroom. Under these circumstances, teachers may assume that a child behaves in a particular way solely in response to a particular class or teacher. For instance, a teacher may see a child acting very withdrawn and, after attempting to involve the child, may discover a set of negative attitudes toward school, fellow classmates, and the teacher. At this point, the teacher might tend to personalize the situation, seeing the student's behavior and attitudes as a rejection of his or her efforts and of the classroom. The problem, however, could well lie somewhere else.

The children that stream into a teacher's classroom each September bring with them their own personal histories. Although they may wish to start afresh with the beginning of the new school year, much of who they are is wrapped up in their past and their current out-of-school lives. It is likely that some of these students bear deep scars from their past experiences and that some are currently caught up in desperate problems. Painful pasts, of course, are common; problems, too, are a part of life. Few of us get through life without encountering some pain or misfortune: an alcoholic parent, a serious accident, a long sickness, a disability. That issue is not what we are addressing here. We wish to direct your attention to larger problems, widespread social problems. Our intention is not to suggest that you should be a Mr. or Ms. Fix-It, taking in troubled children and, with a few quick adjustments to their psyches, sending them out into the world cured. Rather, we wish to make you more fully aware and more deeply sensitive to the sorts of problems that will come into your classroom with your students.

SOCIAL PROBLEMS AFFECTING THE YOUNG

In Chapter 10 we talked about changes in our society resulting in increased diversity among today's students. These conditions will affect many students' lives, but they do not necessarily impede their efforts to get an education. Some changes or trends in society pose a more direct threat to the performance of students in school. In our discussion we deal with several difficult conditions and problems in society, including poverty, homelessness, child abuse, alcohol and drug use, teen-age pregnancy, and adolescent suicide. As you will see in the following discussion, these pervasive societal problems do not occur in isolation, but actually tend to cluster or overlap. In real life, it is difficult to separate out discrete sources of social problems. The compounding of risk factors contributes to the incredible scope of these problems and places a number of students "at risk." For such students, the chances are great that they will have difficulty acquiring an adequate education.

"The rich are getting richer and the poor are getting poorer." This well-known phrase aptly describes our society today. In the decade of the 1980s the number of U.S. billionaires quintupled, while the number of children living in poverty increased by 23 percent. The poorest 20 percent of American citizens received less than 5 percent of the national income, while the wealthiest 20 percent

amassed 44 percent.[1] This increase in people earning extremely high or extremely low incomes has resulted in the shrinking of America's middle class. The Select Committee on Children, Youth, and Families of the U.S. House of Representatives reported that the income gap between families with the highest incomes and those with the lowest incomes was wider in 1988 than in any year since 1947.[2]

A profile of this increasing number of families with incomes below the

poverty line may surprise you:

- Less than 9 percent of America's poor people live in inner cities.
- Roughly 17 percent live in rural areas, where poverty rates may reach 50 percent and families have been poor for generations.
- Twenty-eight percent live in suburban America surrounded by wealth and affluence.
- Most (46 percent) live in semi-isolated towns across the country.[3]

Though two-thirds of poor Americans are white, the rate of poverty is higher among minorities: 14 percent of white children are poor, whereas 44 percent of African-American children and 38 percent of Hispanic children are in poverty.[4] (See Figure 11.1.)

The problem of poverty is growing worse, and the prospects for breaking its grip on children are particularly bleak. Former Commissioner of Education Harold Howe II offers this description of child poverty in America:

- Thirteen million children in American are poor.
- More than one in every five children is poor.
- Nearly one out of every four children under age six is poor.
- Almost two out of every three poor children are white.
- Nearly two out of every five Hispanic children are poor.
- More than half of the children in families headed by females are poor.[5]

Harold Hodgkinson echoes these figures, pointing out that many children are "at risk" from birth because they are born into households headed by a single teen-age mother or into a poor household headed by a female. (See Figure 11.2.) Poverty is more common among children than in any other age group.[6]

What does this mean for schools? For one thing, children born to teen-age mothers are often premature and therefore have greater chances for health problems and possible learning difficulties. Howe argues that "greater child poverty means worse nutrition, less health care, more homelessness, less education, and greater despair as opportunities and options are foreclosed."[7] The growing

Figure 11.1 Percent of Children Under Eighteen in Poverty, by Race/Ethnicity: 1960–1987

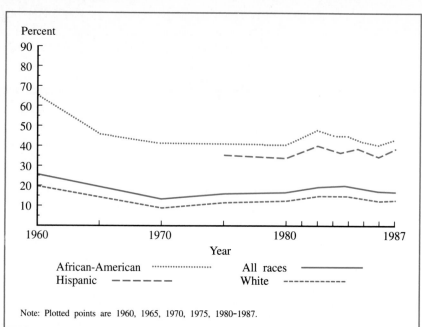

Figure 11.2 Percent of All Children in Female-Headed Households in Poverty, by Race/Ethnicity: 1960–1987

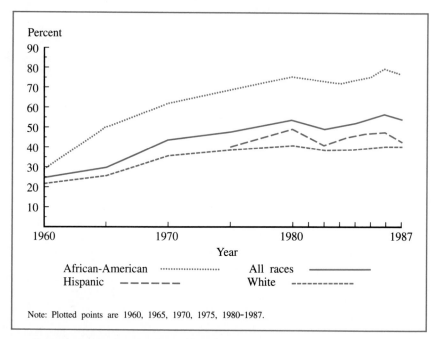

Note: Plotted points are 1960, 1965, 1970, 1975, 1980–1987
Source: U.S. Department of Commerce, Bureau of the Census, *Current Population Reports,* series P-60, "Poverty in the United States: . . . ," various years.

STUDENTS AND THEIR SOCIAL CONTEXT

numbers of single-parent families signal a cycle of poverty from which the families can rarely escape. If, in addition to being poor, children are also members of a minority group, the obstacles to a successful school career may be monumental. Hodgkinson predicts that "what is coming toward the educational system is a group of children who will be poorer, more ethnically and linguistically diverse, and who will have more handicaps that will affect their learning."[8]

Worse for minorities

The increasing numbers of minority children who are poor are in part a result of the widening gap in the standard of living between minorities and whites. In 1986, the African-American family median income equaled only 57 percent of that earned by white families: a median annual income of $17,604 as opposed to $30,809. The Hispanic family median income was $19,995.[9] Between 1973 and 1986 the average annual income for African-American males aged twenty to twenty-four, adjusted for inflation, fell by 50 percent, from $9,818 to $5,299 in 1985 dollars.[10]

In the past it was assumed that poverty was the result of unemployment. After World War II, many high school graduates could get manufacturing jobs that required minimal education and that paid quite well. A high school graduate could support a family of four, buy a house, own two cars, and live comfortably. But the American job market has changed. Well-paying manufacturing jobs can now be done more efficiently and effectively by machines. The job market for unskilled workers today is found mostly in fast food establishments and service

The employed poor

jobs that typically pay minimum wage and offer no benefits. Full-time employment at the current minimum wage is not enough to support a family above the

A FRIEND TO THE POOR AND DISADVANTAGED

Eugene Lang—son of a poor immigrant, graduate of P.S. 121 in East Harlem, and multimillionaire—returned to his school in 1981 to speak before the graduating sixth grade class. Lang's fortunes had taken a turn for the better in the years since his graduation, but P.S. 121 and schools like it in East Harlem had not met with equal success. Students attending these schools, mostly African-American and Hispanic, often dropped out before completing high school; in some years, the dropout rate had climbed to 90 percent of the students.

As Lang stood before the group prepared to deliver the traditional commencement address, he realized that his remarks were irrelevant for those in his audience. He panicked. But he remembered Martin Luther King, Jr.'s "I Have a Dream" speech and decided to act on the dreams

of his students. Leaning forward, he offered a full college scholarship to each student of that graduating class who would complete high school. He also offered individual guidance sessions to all students willing to meet with him.

Since that time, the dropout rate for P.S. 121 has been reduced to 2 percent of the student body. In New York City, five hundred students are funded by Lang and other philanthropists. And the "I Have a Dream" Foundation has spread to twenty-five other cities. For these students, the dream of educational opportunity is not dead.

Why did Lang's offer make a difference? Surely, many of the minority students who completed school would have been eligible for scholarships anyway. However, what Lang did was to provide a guarantee, not just a hope, of college funding and, equally important, he provided a system of support and full-time advocates for the children. This is what made the difference.

David Nimmons, "The Santa Claus Awards," *Ladies Home Journal* 103 (December 1986): 173–174.

poverty line ($12,092 for a family of four in 1989). The U.S. Census Bureau reports that 50 percent of heads of poor households are employed.[11] Obviously, unemployment is not the only problem.

With poverty on the rise, schools have an ever-increasing problem partly because they are not designed to serve poor children. Sociologists point out to us that the schools in this country were created and continue to be supported by the middle class to perpetuate middle-class values. There is nothing particularly startling about this. Middle-class people want their children to be like themselves, or possibly somewhat better. Therefore, they have built and continue to pay for a school system that reflects their values and supports the way of life with which they feel comfortable.

Two views of schooling Many people in our society have thought that we could eliminate poverty through education and that, through schooling, it would be relatively easy to free people from the chains of impoverishment. The efforts have been well intentioned but often too little, too late, and in retrospect, sometimes naive. On the other hand, some critics see our schools as part of an enslavement system. They claim that the schools not only do not help develop the individual talents and strengths of poor children, but also make these children believe themselves to be losers. After eight to ten or eleven years of schooling, these young people see themselves as unable to fit into the middle class and as people who, at best, will do society's menial work. Although some of these critics see this system as a conscious plan of our society, we do not. Such a cynical view suggests that the teachers who are toiling in the urban and rural slums are either people of evil intentions or simply dupes. In our view, many of the teachers who are most heroic and alive are struggling valiantly to aid people oppressed by poverty.

Our past and present inadequacies and failures at educating the children of the poor tempt some to turn away and devote their energies to more solvable problems. We cannot do this. Ours is an evolving society. As a people, we are not finished with our own development. Eradicating the ravages of poverty and its withering effect on children should be at the top of our agenda as citizens of this nation and as educators. Although there are many important and solvable problems to work on, we cannot afford—in justice—to ignore this one.

Homelessness For families close to poverty, the threat of homelessness is very real. Consider the fact that 45 percent of all families in poverty pay more than 70 percent of their annual incomes in rent.[12] With such a large percentage of income consumed by rent payments, one incident or emergency in the family can disrupt the tenuous equilibrium and exceed the family's ability to maintain a home. Imagine, for example, the domino effect that could occur from mechanical difficulties with the one family car. Even minor repairs costing $25 to $50 may be beyond the family's budget. Without a car, the family breadwinner may not be able to get to work. The children may not be able to reach day care. It does not take long in such a situation to lose a job or a long-awaited slot in a day care center. It is easy to see why housing, which consumes so much of annual income, is a particularly vulnerable area for families in poverty.

The U.S. Department of Education estimates that 220,000 school-age children are homeless: 15,600 live in publicly operated shelters; 90,700 live in privately operated shelters; 55,700 live with relatives or friends; and 63,170 live "elsewhere." Sixty-five thousand of these homeless children do not attend school.[13] Imagine the obstacles for a homeless child trying to get an education. Uprooted from their homes, many live in shelters or other locations in other parts of town. To continue attending the child's original school may require extensive transportation, which parents are not likely to be able to afford. Enrolling the child in a new school near the shelter may be a difficult and intimidating process for parents struggling with daily survival. Many parents, believing they will only be homeless for a short time, may not even attempt to transfer their child's enrollment. As days turn into weeks and months, the child may miss a great deal of school. If the child is fortunate enough to attend school, other difficulties arise, such as perhaps having to explain why he has no shoes, why he can't invite friends over to play, or why his family has moved again.[14]

You may have homeless children in your classroom; if so, they are likely to require a sense of stability and understanding from you. Some may be physically dirty because they lack access to shower or tub facilities. They may show emotional needs. Other children may make fun of them. Your support and caring could be crucial in improving their chances for success.

Teen-age Pregnancy

Single-parent households

Each year one million American teen-agers get pregnant. Two-thirds of these teen-agers are not black, are not poor, and are not from the inner city.[15] Many of these teenage ($12,092 for a family of four in 1989) girls are not married, and single parent families are particularly vulnerable to poverty. When we combine the difficulties of single parenthood with the likely occurrence that a

Some schools provide day care services so teenage mothers can stay in school.
(Bill Paxson/Des Moines Public Schools)

teen-ager will have poor work skills, will have limited employment experience, and will receive low wages in the American work force, we gain some understanding of the finding that three out of four children from households headed by a mother under the age of twenty-five are below the poverty level. Even when the teen-age pregnancy results in marriage, these families are three times as likely to be poor as two-parent families over the age of twenty-five.[16]

Short-cycle families

Sometimes teen-age pregnancies are a recurrent pattern within generations of a family. Harold Hodgkinson has termed this phenomenon the "short-cycle family." In such families, a new generation of children is produced every fourteen years or so, resulting in families with a fourteen-year-old mother, a twenty-eight-year-old grandmother, and a forty-two-year-old great-grandmother! Fathers may or may not be present in any of the generations.[17] Considering the short-cycle family in light of what we know about single parenthood and teen-age mothers, it is not surprising that the resulting poverty in these families is often pervasive.

Teen-age parents are faced not only with the enormous task of juggling childrearing and employment but often with premature babies, which are more likely to have health problems and possible learning difficulties. Poverty often correlates with worse nutrition, less health care, more homelessness, and less education.

Schools' responses

To lessen this problem, many schools are working with local health officials to insure that pregnant teen-agers receive prenatal care and parenting advice. They are also encouraging these young women to stay in school and graduate. In many cases the schools are permitting young mothers to bring their babies with them to school. To prevent teen-age pregnancies, some schools have established clinics where birth control devices can be obtained. One thing seems certain: this problem is not going to be solved soon.

Abused and Neglected Children

One of the authors, as an undergraduate in a social psychology class, was assigned to work four hours each week in a settlement house for boys. He had the following experience.

"The first day the director assigned me to work with Pauly. I was told to try to get him to read, to solve simple arithmetic problems, and in general to keep him out of trouble. The director then took me to the playground and separated Pauly out from a crowd of young boys. I was shocked when I first saw him. Although Pauly was only seven, he was large and strong, and his hooded eyes told me instantly that he didn't like what he knew was in store for him. I can remember thinking that Pauly had taken an instant dislike to me. I took Pauly to a small room, where I discovered that he not only acted disagreeably but also smelled disagreeable. It was almost impossible to talk with Pauly. One minute he would be hyperactive, trying to get out of the room or throwing the books around. The next minute he would be withdrawn to the point of not responding to questions. In the three hours or so we were together, he read a few sentences and, through trial and error, solved a few simple addition problems. At the end I was exhausted and convinced that I had failed completely.

STUDENTS AND THEIR SOCIAL CONTEXT

"The next two weekly sessions were pretty much a repeat of my first encounter with Pauly. So, before the fourth session I asked to talk with the director. I told him that I felt I was getting nowhere, but he disagreed. He told me that Pauly talked about me all the time. Although it didn't show in Pauly's behavior, I was buoyed by that slim compliment. Then I noticed that Pauly would be waiting at an upper window when I came on Tuesdays, and he complained bitterly if I was three or four minutes late. Things became easier in the sessions. Somewhere midway in the term I caught the director just as I was leaving and asked him something I had been wondering about. "How come Pauly has those little cut marks on his face and head and those seven or eight odd scars on his arms and legs?"

"Oh, that was a little present from his parents. The face and head marks are from blows, but the burn marks are from cigarettes."

I was stunned."

The education of the young brings us into contact with humanity's best impulses. Occasionally, however, we see the wreckage of its darkest and most vicious urges. For many years, the phenomenon of child abuse, often called the battered-child syndrome, was one of society's dirty little secrets, a truth known only to a small percentage of social workers and law enforcement people. But even though it is still difficult for many to comprehend it fully, we have become more aware of the magnitude of this problem and the variety of forms that abuse can take. In recent years, amid efforts to create stiffer laws and more effective Definition prevention, the problem of child abuse has received national attention. In 1974 Congress enacted a Child Abuse Prevention and Treatment Act; this act defines child abuse and neglect as follows:

> The physical or mental injury, sexual abuse, negligent treatment, or mal-
> treatment of a child under the age of eighteen by a person who is re-
> sponsible for the child's welfare under circumstances which indicate that
> the child's health or welfare is harmed or threatened thereby.[18]

Because of the hidden nature of child abuse and neglect, reliable figures on it are somewhat difficult to obtain. Most professionals in the field acknowledge that a majority of cases are unreported. Figures gathered by the National Committee for the Prevention of Child Abuse indicate that more than 2.4 million incidents of child abuse or neglect were reported to child-service agencies in 1989, a 10 percent increase from 1988 reports. Over 1,200 child deaths were attributed to parental abuse and neglect in 1989, a 38 percent increase from 1988. Survey respondents attributed the sharp increase primarily to substance abuse. They also identified poverty, lack of medical and child care, homelessness, and domestic violence as causes.[19]

Effects of abuse The toll that abuse and neglect take on children's physical, emotional, and psychological development is difficult to assess. Children subjected to violent treatment also sustain injuries that cause physical and mental malfunction. Abuse frequently causes serious learning problems in school. Children may be withdrawn or have trouble concentrating. They suffer enormous stress, and their self-esteem is low. They sometimes have excessive needs for control because they have experienced such helplessness.[20]

One of the particularly unfortunate aspects of child abuse is that people who were themselves abused as children are much more likely than other people to abuse their own children. Experts say that although the cause of child abuse is unclear, a culture, such as ours, that condones the use of force with children contributes to the climate that would let abuse happen.

The teacher's responsibility

The classroom teacher will not directly encounter the problem of abuse very often. However, teachers are legally responsible in all fifty states for reporting suspected cases of child abuse. Teachers must be aware of potential signs of abuse (see Table 11.1) and know school policy and procedures for reporting suspected abuse. (See Chapter 5 for a discussion of teachers' legal obligations as related to suspected child abuse.)

The abused-child syndrome is not a problem that we can always do something about directly. Teachers need to realize that even after an abusive situation has been reported and perhaps disclosed these children's problems in school will not suddenly end. Children who have been abused have a continuing need for emotional safety and stability. They need capable adult role models who can provide varied but predictable activities and measurable classroom achievement. They need trustworthy praise, concrete rewards, and constructive ways to control their classroom environment.[21]

Alcohol and Drug Abuse

Many of the trends we have talked about so far in this chapter can severely stress the functioning of families. As a result, some families get caught up in self-

Table 11.1 Potential Signs of Abuse

> The National Committee for Prevention of Child Abuse has compiled the following list of signs of abuse. Abuse is more likely when more than one symptom is apparent.
>
> —Repeated injuries such as bruises, welts, and burns. When questioned, parents may give unlikely explanations or deny that anything is wrong.
>
> —Neglected appearance. The child seems poorly nourished or inadequately clothed, is repeatedly left alone or wanders at all hours.
>
> —Disruptive behavior. The child constantly repeats negative behavior and is very aggressive.
>
> —Passive, withdrawn behavior. The child is overly shy and friendless.
>
> —"Supercritical" parents. Parents are harshly critical of their children or remain extremely isolated from the school and community. Attempts at friendly contact may be resented and distrusted.

Source: "Abused Responsibility," *Teacher Magazine* (November 1989): 69. Reprinted with permission from *Teacher Magazine.*

destructive patterns of behavior and interaction. Substance abuse is a particularly destructive response. It may entail the use of alcohol or a variety of other drugs. It may be the act of parents or children. But when one family member gets entangled in substance abuse, the entire family is typically a victim.

Alcohol, a major problem

Alcohol, which acts as a depressant, is a major problem in American society. It is used more frequently than other drugs, and the first use of alcohol may occur at a young age, sometimes in elementary school. Historically, the greatest number of alcoholic teen-agers have been male students, especially those with low grades, but the gap between males and females seems to be closing. The problem of alcohol abuse among high school students is widespread. The proportion of high school seniors who drink daily has been reported as 1 in 20.[22] The U.S. Department of Health and Human Services reports that alcohol use among high school seniors has remained stable since 1977 at around 90 to 93 percent. Ninety-one percent of the class of 1989 indicated they had used alcohol.[23] Alcohol-related accidents were the leading cause of death among teen-agers in 1989.[24]

Illegal drugs since 1960s

Marijuana and other illegal drugs have taken a strong hold among Americans since the late 1960s. In one study among high school seniors of the class of 1989, 30 percent reported using marijuana in the previous year; an additional 17 percent acknowledged using it in the previous month.[25] Although marijuana causes some damage to lung and throat tissue, its primary danger comes from the fact that it alters perception and impedes motor coordination, and there is growing evidence that marijuana "interferes with short term memory, reading comprehension, problem-solving ability, and general mental functioning."[26]

A cultural shift?

From 1975 to 1981 the percentage of high school seniors who had ever used illegal drugs increased from 55 percent to 66 percent. However, since 1981, this figure has shown a gradual decline. In 1989, 51 percent of high school seniors reported having used illegal drugs.[27] A survey conducted by the Partnership for a Drug-Free America displayed similar findings, concluding that perhaps a profound "cultural shift" is taking place as parents and teachers are increasingly discussing and educating youth about drug problems.[28]

Despite indications of hope, however, drug and alcohol abuse remain massive problems. Substance abuse by parents has increased, with devastating results for children. Between 1985 and 1988 the number of children born with fetal drug exposure increased fourfold, reaching 375,000 in 1988. Known incidents of child abuse and neglect increased 82 percent between 1981 and 1988.[29] In the early 1980s child protective agencies reported that 30 to 40 percent of child abuse and neglect cases involved substance abuse, often alcohol. In 1990, child protective agencies reported that 50 to 90 percent of child abuse cases involved substance abuse, and much of it involving crack cocaine.[30]

Advent of crack

Crack, a comparatively cheap but extremely addictive form of cocaine, hit our streets in 1985. Since then, in a relatively short time, 1.9 million men and 1 million women, almost all of childbearing age, have begun using crack.[31] Crack produces a feeling of extreme euphoria and can cause addiction within a few days, sometimes after the first encounter. A particularly disturbing finding is that a crack addiction can overwhelm one of the strongest forces in nature, the parental instinct. The emerging picture we are seeing of crack addicts is that they are incapable of caring about themselves or their children.[32]

Physical and emotional damage

The impact of crack on students can be devastating. In addition to having difficult family surroundings, crack babies are likely to be born with birth defects, such as deformed hearts, lungs, digestive systems, or limbs. Many apparently have permanent neurological damage.

At this writing, we don't know all of the learning and behavior problems these kids will bring with them to school. But the evidence is mounting that fetal exposed crack babies will not have an easy time in school. The oldest cocaine-exposed children being systematically studied are now in primary grades. The same types of behavior are being observed in these children as were seen in infants. They typically fail to develop attachments to anyone and often appear emotionally flat. They have a low tolerance for frustration and have difficulty structuring information. They are easily overwhelmed by incoming stimulation. Marilee Rist describes them in this way: "In the typical classroom environment— where noises, voices, instructions, questions, interactions, and distractions crowd one upon the other—cocaine exposed children tend to react in one of two ways. They withdraw completely, or they become wild and difficult to control."[33]

Programs to help

Doctors and educators are only beginning to design the programs needed to help crack kids. One three-year pilot program with fifty drug-exposed kids,

© Scott Santis
Courtesy Commercial Appeal

aged three to five, recommends several elements of a successful school program: small classes (eight pupils to one teacher), fixed seat assignments and a rigid routine, and protection from loud noises and other disturbing stimulation. Activities are emphasized over paper-and-pencil exercises. Generous warmth and praise also help youngsters to achieve an emotional equilibrium. When these procedures have been followed, more than one-half of the drug-exposed children have been able to transfer to regular school classes, with special tutoring and counseling.[34]

Adolescent Suicide

Depending on the source, suicide is believed to be either the first, second, or third leading cause of adolescent death in the United States. Each year more than five thousand people in the fifteen- to twenty-four-year-old age group take their own lives. Estimates indicate that approximately fifty to one hundred youths attempt suicide every day, and things seem to be getting worse. Since 1960 the suicide rate among fifteen- to nineteen-year-olds has increased 142 percent: 143 percent for white males, 112 percent for nonwhite males, 138 percent for white females, and 47 percent for nonwhite females.[35]

Teen-age suicides increase

Studies of young people who have attempted suicide and those who have succeeded reveal several patterns. Among those who attempt suicide, the vast majority are female. Girls attempt suicide about nine times more often than boys, but boys complete suicide about five times more often than girls.[36] White youth kill themselves five times as often as black youth; Native Americans kill themselves at a rate ten times that of white youth. And rural youth kill themselves at a higher rate than urban youth.[37]

Who is at risk?

What kinds of young people are at risk of attempting suicide? Research indicates several social correlates of suicidal behavior in youth. These include family breakdown, unemployment, and decreasing religious observance among the young.[38] Risk factors associated with family life appear to be a history of alcohol and drug abuse, placement outside the family, and symptoms of delinquency, aggression, or depression.

Though such profiles are not foolproof, Barry Garfinkel, director of the Division of Child and Adolescent Psychiatry at the University of Minnesota Hospital and Clinic, has described four behavior patterns of youth who participate in self-destructive behaviors.

- Profile 1 The youths are isolated and passive. Their academic performance may deteriorate, they may have trouble following home and school rules, and they may avoid their peers.
- Profile 2 These youths are highly irritable and so push peers and adults away. Whether intentionally or not, the individuals end up becoming isolated from support systems.
- Profile 3 The youths exhibit aggressive behaviors. They may engage in petty crime or vandalism, but they are more troublesome than truly dangerous.
- Profile 4 These youths may engage in a number of maladaptive coping strategies, such as drug and alcohol abuse. Rather than resolve difficulties, they try thrill-seeking behaviors.[39]

Those who teach often have the opportunity to recognize children and youths who are suicide risks and to help them get the advice and support they need. Although suicidal behaviors are complex and the warning signs can be ambiguous or misleading, it is important to realize that most young people who commit suicide give warning first to signal their need for help. The American Academy of Child Psychiatry recommends that parents, teachers, and counselors watch for these signs:

Warning signs

- changes in eating and sleeping habits
- withdrawal from friends, family, and regular activities
- violent or rebellious behavior
- running away
- drug or alcohol abuse
- unusual neglect of personal appearance
- radical change in personality
- persistent boredom, difficulty concentrating, or a decline in the quality of schoolwork
- frequent complaints about physical symptoms that are often related to emotions, such as stomachaches, headaches, or fatigue
- loss of interest in previously pleasurable activities
- inability to tolerate praise or rewards[40]

WHERE DO YOU STAND?

Before you launch into this section of the chapter, take a few moments to assess your own position by answering the following questions about controversial topics in American education. You may wish to compare your responses with those of your classmates.

- What are the advantages of having desegregated schools? The disadvantages? Do you believe all schools should be desegregated? Why or why not?
- Do schools treat boys and girls equally? What evidence can you provide to support your position?
- Are violence and vandalism problems in the schools with which you are acquainted? In schools where they are problems, how do you think they should be handled?

- Why do so many students drop out of high school before graduating? Who are the students most likely to drop out?
- Why are politicians so concerned about holding educators accountable for students' progress? Should teachers be held accountable for poor student learning if the students don't try to learn? Why or why not?

Opinions on these issues are extremely diverse. Whatever your views, however, you and your classmates probably have limited data on which to base your opinions. This is not unusual, since even people who feel strongly about these topics have often not really investigated the arguments for the other side and weighed the issues to arrive at a reasoned, logical position. Because these topics touch on our religious, political, or philosophical convictions, we often respond to them emotionally rather than rationally.

Cluster syndrome

To add to the tragedy of teen-age suicide, young people sometimes engage in copycat suicides. In this "cluster" syndrome, a wave of adolescent suicides plague an area. In response, hundreds of school districts now offer programs in suicide prevention.[41] Teachers play a particularly important role in recognizing symptoms of adolescent depression and potential suicide. If you observe behaviors that may indicate suicidal tendencies, do not try to handle the burden alone. Seek a support network of the guidance counselor, the school social worker, and/ or the school psychologist. Recognizing symptoms and getting professional help for students who exhibit these behaviors may prevent their suicides and help them develop coping behaviors to deal with their problems.

TENSION POINTS IN AMERICAN EDUCATION

The goal of this section of the chapter is simple: to explore opposing positions on some of the most controversial topics in American education today in order to equip you, as a teacher, with understanding of and sensitivity to the exposed nerve endings of American education. Keep in mind the significance of these tension points; they are the result of an attempt to educate children in a pluralistic society. That is, our society is made up of diverse individuals and groups, each with different axes to grind and different ideas about what a school should be, what it should teach, and what life in school should be like. Tension points are inevitable when diverse groups and individuals, with different objectives for the schools, attempt to achieve those objectives. As a teacher, you will certainly be involved. Since teachers have a deep responsibility to the schools, it is important that they provide leadership in seeking enlightened solutions to the problems arising from these complex and touchy issues.

One warning: our coverage of these tension points will acquaint you with some of the key aspects surrounding these issues, but it is not very deep. You should not be satisfied to stop here. It is your responsibility to dig below the surface if you want to find out what these issues really involve.

Inequality of Educational Opportunity

America is a multiracial, multiethnic, and multiclass society. It is considered by many people to be one of the most successful mixed societies the world has ever seen. However, it is far from perfect, and many children born into poor or minority-group families face severe disadvantages in their attempts to live decent lives and to climb the ladder of success. Schooling is intended to help individuals in this process. Whether or not the schools have been helping or hindering the progress of these children has been a source of raging debate for decades.

One fact seems clear: Large numbers of poor and minority-group students are leaving school without the verbal and occupational skills necessary to function effectively in American society. Who, if anyone, is to blame for this situation? The schools? Teachers and administrators? Or is the responsibility that of society as a whole, and are the schools merely being made a scapegoat? Talk to five different people and you will probably hear five different opinions about where blame should be fixed. But assessing blame is not our function here. One can ask better questions: What is meant by equality of educational opportunity? How is it measured? What are the responsibilities of the school system for providing equal educational opportunity? How can the achievement of poor and minority-group students be improved? It is simple enough to ask these questions, but their answers are guaranteed to be controversial.

Historical definition

Equality of educational opportunity is hardly a new concept in American education, but its components have changed dramatically in recent decades. For a long period in history, the idea of equal educational opportunity involved the following elements:

1. providing a free education up to the age when the majority of students entered the labor force
2. providing a common curriculum for all children, regardless of background
3. providing that children from diverse backgrounds attend the same school
4. providing equality of school conditions within a given locality, since local taxes supported the school system[42]

Brown v. *Board of Education*

The 1954 Supreme Court decision *Brown* v. *Board of Education* held that segregated schools are inherently unequal because the effects of such schools are likely to be different. Thus a new component was introduced into the concept of educational opportunity: that equality of educational opportunity is defined in terms of the effects, rather than the provision, of schooling. In the *Brown* deci-

MARIA MONTESSORI

(1870–1952)

Maria Montessori became a proponent of preschool education, an urban educational reformer, and a believer in equal opportunities for women sixty years before any of these issues were matters of widespread concern.

As a child, Maria Montessori excelled in mathematics and thought of becoming an engineer. Later she developed an interest in medicine, and she overcame tremendous criticism to become the first woman to enroll in the University of Rome's medical school. After graduating, she lectured on anthropology at the university and became associated with the psychiatric clinic. She developed an interest in retarded children and, suspecting that they were far more capable of learning than was commonly believed, founded and headed the Orthophrenic School, where she achieved remarkable results with mentally deficient children.

But it was not until she was thirty-six years old that Montessori found her life work. Believing her methods could be even more effective with normal children, she opened her first school, the Casa del Bambini (Children's House), to the preschool-age street urchins of Rome. Montessori's school was run on the principle of allowing children freedom within a carefully designed environment and under the sensitive guidance of a trained director. The materials and toys available in the school were prescribed, but the children were allowed freedom to handle or ignore them as they wished. Self-learning and individualization were stressed, but there were definite limits on freedom: students were required to come to school clean, and even their free play was structured. However, a child was never forced either to play or to learn. The teachers were instructed simply to wait until the child became interested in a particular game or project. A child who was concentrating deeply on a ritual with a toy was not aided or corrected by a teacher unless she or he asked for help.

Montessori discovered that certain simple and precise educational materials evoked sustained interest and attention in the young child. Children under five years old would concentrate on a single task, oblivious to distraction, for periods of from fifteen minutes to an hour, and afterward seemed refreshed rather than tired. Montessori's close observations of children led her to conclude that,

sion, the Supreme Court found that, even when the facilities and teacher salaries provided were identical, "equality of educational opportunity" did not exist in segregated schools.

Prior to *Brown,* the community and educational institutions were expected only to provide equal resources (teachers, facilities, materials), and responsibility for the advantageous use of those resources lay with the child and the child's family. Today many people have come to consider it the responsibility of the educational institution, not the child, to create achievement.

Others do not accept this assertion, arguing that the school should do its best to provide equal educational resources for all its students, but that it cannot be held accountable for differences in student learning. Although it is agreed that many poor minority children in our schools are not learning at a rate comparable to white middle-class children, opinions vary considerably as to the locus and cause of the problem. At one extreme are those who think that the problem resides in the deficiencies of minority children. Their impoverished home life, their particular cultural milieu, or even their mental capacities are cited as the sources of unequal results in school. At the other extreme are those who claim that the problem is in the schools, which neither stimulate nor instruct the minority child with the intensity that is needed. Teachers expect minority children

from birth to age six, all children possess "absorbent minds," which equip them to learn more quickly and easily than at any subsequent period in their lives. Throughout these years, she found, children experience periods of specialized sensitivity, during which their interest and mental capacity are especially suited to the acquisition of particular knowledge, such as colors, language, and textures. Montessori recognized that small children learn through their senses, and she developed methods of stimulating the child's senses in ways that would enhance learning. For instance, children were taught the alphabet with sandpaper letters that they could manipulate with their fingers. Montessori was the first to use flashcards as a sensory stimulus, and she even introduced the hula hoop, which became a fad in the United States in the 1950s. She was severely criticized for ignoring discipline; she replied that in the conventional schools she had visited, children were "not disciplined, but annihilated."

Montessori's teaching methods have aroused considerable interest in the United States as a result of recent psychological research verifying many of her theories. Psychologists and educators have come to agree with her that the period of early childhood is critical in determining a person's intellectual potential.

Before her death, Montessori traveled widely, establishing schools, teaching teachers, and promoting her still-unconventional ideas. A typical Montessori classroom today is a beehive of activity, each child pursuing an independent task at his or her own speed. A two-and-a-half-year-old carries a tray holding a jug of water and two glasses across the room. On reaching the other side he begins to fill the glasses with dry grains of rice. He is joined by a little girl who sweeps the spilled rice into a pile. A third child appears with a brush and dustpan to collect the deposit. A group of children use colored pencils to shade designs they have made themselves with metal geometric forms. The teacher dictates words to some boys, who compose them on a mat with large movable letters.

New Montessori schools have recently sprung up in this country in response to parents' demands. Teachers of underprivileged or minority children, in particular, claim great success with Montessori techniques. The day care center movement, day care programs, and the early childhood movement, in general, have been significantly influenced by Maria Montessori's views.

to do poorly, and this becomes a self-fulfilling prophecy. This position assumes that it is the school's obligation to diagnose the learner's needs, concerns, and cognitive and affective style and to adjust its program accordingly. As with most controversies, the answer probably lies somewhere in between: The students do have certain deficiencies, but the schools need to learn how to overcome them.

Let's take a look now at three widely advocated approaches to creating more equal educational opportunities for American children: compensatory education, desegregation, and magnet school programs.

COMPENSATORY EDUCATION   *Compensatory education* attempts to overcome deficiencies in the learner by incorporating extra education into the regular school program, or to avert potential learning problems through preschool programs like Project Head Start and Follow-Through. Programs developed in the 1960s, such as the Ford Foundation–supported Great Cities School Improvement Programs, Title I of the Elementary and Secondary Education Act (ESEA), New York City's early Higher Horizons Program, and the More Effective Schools Program, were aimed at remedying specific learner deficiencies—verbal retardation, lack of motivation, experiential and sensory deprivation—that prevent the student from participating effectively in the learning process.

Compensatory programs to address these needs come in many forms. Some programs emphasize early intervention and target children who are "at risk" for later school failure. Readiness skills are typically emphasized to help these children start school on an even footing with children from more advantaged backgrounds. Some programs help teach parents how to interact more effectively in the areas of cognitive and psychosocial development with their babies and young children. Other compensatory programs target older children and focus on basic skill instruction, tutoring, or remediation in a variety of academic areas. Dropout prevention programs, job training, and adult literacy instruction are all attempts to help older individuals improve the quality of their lives through education and to help prevent the cycle of educational disadvantage from being passed down through generations.

A tremendous amount of money and energy has been spent in the attempt to develop special programs to improve the academic achievement of disadvantaged children. Since it was launched in 1965 as part of President Johnson's War on Poverty, the Head Start program has served more than 11 million children and families. For fiscal year 1990, Head Start was funded at $1.4 billion and served approximately 450,000 three- to five-year-olds, roughly 20 percent of the eligible population.[43] For fiscal year 1991 the figure rose to $2.05 billion, and for 1992 President Bush requested approximately the same amount.

The annual budget for Title I of the ESEA (designed to supplement and improve the education of economically disadvantaged children) grew from $1.06 million in 1965–66 to $2.9 billion for the 1980–81 school year.[44] Yet, even in those years, while many students, teachers, and school districts were involved in compensatory education programs, many others were not. Estimates indicate that in 1981–82 only 45 percent of eligible children were served by such programs.[45]

In 1981 President Reagan recommended to Congress that Title I be dismantled and replaced with a consolidated, noncategorical block grant program

Kinds of programs

Head Start programs

giving more discretion to state and local governments. Instead, Congress passed the Education Consolidation and Improvement Act (ECIA); as a result of this legislation, Title I of the ESEA became Chapter 1 of the ECIA. Federal funds for compensatory education programs to serve students from low-income families were preserved as categorical aid, meaning that the funds must be spent for a specific category of students. But as with Title I, the funding for Chapter 1 has not kept pace with students' needs; the program has provided services to only 50 percent of all eligible children in recent years.

The budget for the 1991 fiscal year, however, increased appropriations for Chapter 1 spending to $6.21 billion, up $856 million over the 1990 spending levels.[46] Education of the disadvantaged is likely to be in the news in the years to come because more and more students will come from low-income homes.

Evaluations mixed

Evaluations of Chapter 1 programs have been mixed. Studies indicating that gains have been made in some programs are often contradicted by other studies. The earliest hopes—that compensatory education would increase student IQ scores and scholastic achievement—have not been rewarded with significant results. But long-range studies that have followed students from preschool to age nineteen, like the study of students in the Perry Preschool Program in Ypsilanti, Michigan, provide other indicators of program success. Effective early childhood programs may result in fewer special education placements, more high

SUCCESS FOR ALL

One compensatory education program that is achieving considerable success is the Success for All program developed by the Center for Research on Effective Schooling for Disadvantaged Students at Johns Hopkins University. The Success for All program restructures the elementary school with one goal in mind: to insure that all students perform at grade level in reading, writing, and mathematics by the end of third grade.

Success for All schools provide a half-day of preschool and a full day of kindergarten, both focused on providing a developmentally appropriate learning experience for children. The curriculum emphasizes the development and use of language and balances academic readiness with music, art, and movement activities. The program also implements the Center's research findings on one-to-one tutoring, regrouping for reading, family support teams, frequent assessments of learning with immediate help on problems, and the use of an effective reading program. Two social workers and one parent-liaison work full-time in the schools to provide parenting

education and to encourage parents to support their children's efforts.

The program also includes tutors for children in grades K–3. Each tutor is a certified, experienced teacher who works one-on-one with eleven students per day. First-graders get priority for tutoring.

Evaluation results have been outstanding, much higher than for any other intervention strategy ever tried. The only drawback appears to be the program's expense: $400,000 per school each year. However, as Robert Slavin, the program's director, argues, "The additional per-pupil cost in the 'Cadillac' schools is less than the $865 difference in state and local per-pupil costs between Baltimore City schools and schools in the rest of Maryland. By simply bringing funding for Baltimore City schools up to the state average, not only could every elementary school in the city have *Success for All*, but secondary schools would have millions of dollars to improve themselves as well. . . . The alternative to success for all is failure for many. Can we really afford to continue to write off so many of our children at the very beginning of their school careers?"

Joe Schneider, "The Cadillac Approach to School Improvement," *R&D Preview* 3 (June 1990): 2–4.

school graduations, lower teen pregnancy rates, increased employment, and reduced welfare assistance to those served by the programs.[47] Early intervention may provide the key to the success of compensatory education programs.

Some observers of compensatory education programs criticize them, however, for not showing evidence of improved IQ scores and scholastic achievement for participating students—the original goals of the programs. They see little point in strengthening programs that they feel have failed in the past. Proponents of compensatory education programs argue that, considering the enormity of the problem, expenditures thus far are a mere drop in the bucket. They also argue that a simultaneous attack must be made on external factors that contribute to low achievement, such as poor housing, family instability, and low income.

As a follow-up to President Bush's Education Summit in Charlottesville, Virginia, the National Governors' Association, in concert with the White House, issued a set of national goals for education. (See Chapter 8, page 273 for a listing of these goals.) As part of Goal 1 ("By the year 2000, all children in America will start school ready to learn"), they declared:

National goal #1

> The federal government should work with the states to develop and fully fund early intervention strategies for children. All eligible children should have access to Head Start, Chapter 1, or some other successful preschool program with strong parental involvement. Our first priority must be to provide at least one year of preschool for all disadvantaged children.[48]

The need for early intervention programs for all disadvantaged children was thus officially recognized by both the president and the governors. Toward this end, President Bush and the Congress increased the Head Start program funding by more than $600 million in the 1991 fiscal year budget.

DESEGREGATION AND INTEGRATION   In 1954, in *Brown* v. *Board of Education,* the Supreme Court ruled that laws requiring white and nonwhite students to go to different schools were illegal. The Court concluded that *de jure school segregation,* or segregation by law, violated the Fourteenth Amendment of the Constitution. Early desegregation efforts were aimed at eliminating de jure segregation.

De facto segregation

Throughout the 1960s and into the 1970s, many school systems, often in response to specific court orders, also attempted to reduce or eliminate *de facto school segregation,* that is, segregation resulting primarily from residential patterns. As a result, many school districts in the North and West underwent desegregation efforts.

Desegregation results

What have been the results of these desegregation efforts? Directors at the Center for Social Organization of Schools at Johns Hopkins University have concluded that desegregated schools have accomplished more than an educational reform; for those who have attended integrated schools, they have led to desegregation in several aspects of adult life.[49] Long-term studies indicate these interracial patterns in adult life:

1. Minority students educated in desegregated elementary and secondary schools are more likely to attend predominantly white colleges and universities than their counterparts who attended segregated schools.

STUDENTS AND THEIR SOCIAL CONTEXT

2. Both African-Americans and whites who attended desegregated schools are more likely to later work in desegregated settings than those who attended segregated schools.

3. African-Americans educated in desegregated schools are more likely to have white social contacts and to live in integrated neighborhoods than African-Americans educated in segregated schools.

4. African-Americans who attended desegregated schools are more likely to have cross-racial friendships than African-Americans who attended segregated schools.[50]

Although these long-range findings are quite positive, there have been some negative results of desegregation efforts. One of the major problems has concerned busing. Busing students to desegregate schools was one of the most controversial and inflammatory issues in education in the 1970s and 1980s. Emotions on the topic often ran very high—so high, in fact, that white parents sometimes slashed bus tires, burned buses, and physically prevented buses from running in order to avoid having their children bused to other schools.[51]

Court-ordered busing

The federal court system was the prime mover in ordering school districts to employ busing in the desegregation process. For example, the U.S. Supreme Court, in *Swan* v. *Charlotte-Mecklenburg* (1971), concluded that the need to hasten desegregation was great, and busing was deemed an appropriate measure, provided the distance of travel was not so great as to either risk the health of the children or impinge significantly on the educational process.

Busing to achieve desegregation has had mixed success. One of the most successful busing plans was that initiated in Berkeley, California, in 1968. Berkeley desegregated its elementary schools by two-way, cross-town busing. A later survey found that the whites did not leave the community, that there was no high teacher turnover rate, and that SAT reading scores indicated that white, African-American, and Asian-American students all made better progress after desegregation.[52] On the other hand, in many other communities, attempts to desegregate the schools by busing met with tremendous community resistance, for example, in Boston in the fall of 1974.

White flight

A major obstacle to desegregating big-city public schools is that the minority percentage of inner-city populations has increased dramatically during the past several decades. In part this has been due to "white flight": an exodus of white students whose parents have chosen to move to the suburbs or place their children in private schools. Independent of this population shift, the number of minority students in big-city school systems has also increased. Today, cities such as New York, Baltimore, Chicago, Detroit, Atlanta, Houston, and Dallas have school minority enrollments of 80 percent or more.[53] How can schools in major cities be desegregated when the percentage of racial minority students is growing and the percentage of white students is decreasing?

Big-city desegregation

One solution would be to take the emerging residential segregation as given—minority cities and white suburbs—and to attempt to overcome its effects on school segregation with metropolitan-area-wide school desegregation. This approach uses the strategy of busing children to bring about racial balance over the entire metropolitan area. When this solution was attempted in the Detroit area, the U.S. Supreme Court, in a five-to-four verdict, rejected the plan. The Court seemed to say that the metro solution would be acceptable only if it could be proved that state officials had committed acts leading to big-city segregation. Since this was not proved in the Detroit instance, the suburban school districts could not be forced to integrate with the Detroit city school system. In the case of Wilmington, Delaware, and Louisville, Kentucky, however, the metro solution was upheld by the Supreme Court.

Whether forced metropolitan-area-wide school desegregation plans are judged to be legal seems, then, to depend on the circumstances and history of the participating school districts. If racially discriminating acts of either state or local officials are judged to have occurred in the creation of either predominantly white or African-American school districts, then metropolitan solutions to end school segregation are legally justified. The fact remains that desegregated schools are the law, and where communities operate racially identifiable schools, they violate the law. Metropolitan school desegregation plans certainly offer a viable solution to this problem.

Decline of busing

During the 1980s court-ordered busing lost center stage as the preferred method for integrating the schools. Busing, of course, was never an end in itself. It was only one means of integrating society, and polls indicate that even those who are opposed to involuntary busing agree that our society needs to be integrated. The real problem is that existing housing patterns function to segregate our society and our schools. As long as these patterns continue, desegregation of the schools will continue to be problematic. As of 1989, approximately five hundred school districts in the United States remained under desegregation orders.[54]

In response to the problem of "white flight" to the suburbs, some school districts—Norfolk, Virginia, and Oklahoma City, for example—have adopted plans to end cross-town busing and to implement neighborhood school policies.[55] Norfolk's plan ends forced cross-town busing for elementary students but offers free transportation to students who volunteer to be bused outside their neighborhoods. Court decisions in the Norfolk and Oklahoma City cases suggest a reduction in the federal government's role in actively desegregating the public schools.

Another way to try to stop white flight is to make inner-city schools so attractive and of such high quality that white parents will want their children to attend them. The magnet school programs (discussed in the next section) are examples of this attempt.

Desegregation ≠integration

Another point needs to be made before closing this discussion: desegregation does not necessarily lead to integration. True integration is a very human process that can occur only after desegregation has gone into effect. It happens when people from different racial and ethnic backgrounds learn to be comfortable with one another and to get along together. It means ending racial prejudice and respecting ethnic differences. Anyone who has spent time in racially mixed schools, especially high schools, knows that African-American and white students who attend the same school can still be extremely distant from one another. African-Americans may sit in one part of the cafeteria, whites in another; and similar scenes unfold in many social situations, such as assemblies and athletic events. Just bringing together students from different racial groups, social classes, and neighborhood backgrounds will not automatically lead to friendship, understanding, and appreciation of one another. As long as our society remains segregated, efforts to integrate our schools are likely to produce tension, at least in the short run. How and whether the schools can be used successfully to integrate individuals with increasingly diverse racial, cultural, and linguistic backgrounds remains one of the great challenges to schools and society.

MAGNET SCHOOL PROGRAMS   One alternative to forced busing that has become popular in urban school districts is the magnet school program. *Magnet schools* are alternative schools that provide high-quality instruction in specified areas as well as in the basic skills. They are designed to attract (like a magnet) students of all racial and ethnic groups from all areas of the school district; thus they offer quality education in integrated classrooms.

Magnet schools have been established with considerable success in many areas of the country. Once limited to a few large cities, by 1984 magnet schools numbered more than one thousand elementary and secondary schools in more than 130 urban school districts.[56] In these urban districts, magnet schools enrolled up to 31 percent of each district's youth.[57] In many cases magnet schools have been established as a method of voluntary desegregation, offering quality education to students who meet admission criteria, regardless of the neighborhoods in which they reside.

Diversity

Magnet school programs are diverse. Some emphasize academics: science, social studies, foreign languages, college preparation, and so on. Others stress fine arts or performing arts. Some magnet schools address students with special needs, such as the gifted and the talented. And magnet schools may take a career or vocation, such as engineering or the health professions, as their focus. Elementary magnet schools are often identified with a particular teaching style: emphasis on basic skills, Montessori methods, or open classrooms. Besides diversity, most magnet school programs also offer quality.

Effectiveness

How successful are these schools? Four research studies dealing with student achievement in 139 magnet schools located in eleven cities and suburban areas across the country have revealed the following:

- Student achievement gains in magnet schools exceed those of students in assigned schools.
- Students' attitudes toward school tend to be more positive than those of students in assigned schools, and the longer the students remain in magnet schools, the more positive their attitudes toward the program become.
- Positive student attitudes prevail even among less successful students.
- Despite travel distances to magnet schools, parent involvement is high.
- Teachers express positive attitudes toward magnet schools, and the teacher turnover rate is low.[58]

Although originally designed to achieve voluntary desegregation, magnet programs have also been found to help stem enrollment declines, raise achievement levels, and allay community doubts over the general quality of education. These programs offer parents an opportunity for educational choice within the public school system and have been linked with reduced school violence and vandalism, improved pupil attendance, and more positive student attitudes toward school.[59]

How do mandatory desegregation plans compare with voluntary efforts to integrate schools? Early research studies concluded that voluntary plans did not work.[60] However, a more recent review of seven school districts that dismantled mandatory desegregation plans and replaced them with voluntary plans, including magnet schools, concluded that "when asked to choose between their neighborhood school and a superior magnet school, sufficient numbers will choose the latter, so that plans based primarily on choice will produce more interracial exposure than those based primarily on mandatory reassignment."[61]

School districts that are under mandatory desegregation, even those with magnet schools, experience greater white flight than school districts with voluntary plans (including magnet schools). Another reason is that many whites view mandatory plans as an illegitimate use of government power to force social equality. For these and other reasons, half of the whites reassigned to African-American schools under mandatory plans will not comply. On the other hand, a substantial portion of whites will enroll their children in integrated schools when they view those schools as having superior resources and innovative curricula, as in the case of magnet schools.[62]

Magnet schools are likely to continue and flourish in the future. Their successes have been numerous. Reports indicate that teachers and students in magnet schools are highly motivated. The schools experience few behavior problems. Students achieve well. Costs are reasonable. And the schools contribute to racial integration. The secret of their success seems to be the positive climate for learning created by the mutual and voluntary commitment of students and staff to the school's mission.[63] Providing quality education to students of all types, magnet schools offer a promising step in the direction of equal educational opportunity.

Sexism and Sex-Role Stereotyping

In the preceding section of this chapter, we made the point that racial and ethnic groups have been denied equal educational opportunities throughout our country's history. Another social group also has suffered discrimination and denial of equal educational opportunities: women. Many women assert, and rightfully so, that societal values and mores have discriminated against them as a class and have significantly limited the development of their human potential. Indeed, strong evidence supports the contention that women in our society have been denied educational and employment opportunities that have been extended to men.

A major part of this issue is that women and men experience very different socialization in our society. Constantina Safilios-Rothschild, who has reviewed studies of parents' socialization of boys and girls, has written the following:

> Mothers maintain physically close and affectionate relationships with girls for a longer period of time. Mothers expect girls to be more dependent and give them more physical attention. On the other hand, boys are given more independence training, more punishment and are encouraged more in intellectual curiosity. Mothers place a greater degree of pressure for achievement and punish dependency more in boys than in girls of

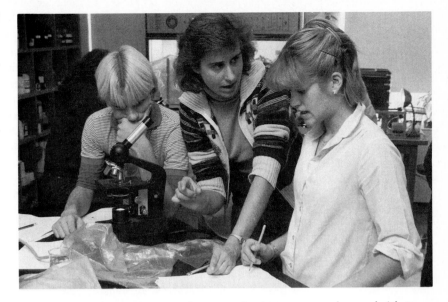

One way schools can counter sex role stereotyping is to encourage boys and girls to pursue all types of studies and careers.

(Paul Conklin)

pre-school age. In addition, boys' aggression is rewarded as appropriate masculine behavior while girls' aggression is never rewarded, though indirect expressions are tolerated. Mothers place pressures on girls for "feminine" neatness, obedience and conformity, while pressure on boys is for independence and achievement.[64]

This situation is not confined to the home, however. Many of us were educated in classrooms where teachers, as a matter of course, pitted the boys against the girls in spelling bees and other academic contests. These same teachers would frown at a girl who was seriously interested in competing in sports such as basketball or hockey. Deeper frowns, still, would be reserved for the young man who took home economics. Such imposition of rigid and stereotypic roles on children is a form of sexism. *Sexism* has been defined as "all attitudes and actions which relegate women to a secondary or inferior status in society."[65] Of course, attitudes that relegate any member of our society to a secondary or inferior status because of sex, race, age, or any condition of birth or upbringing are detrimental to our society as a whole.

Prevalence of sexism

Several researchers have leveled the charge that sexism abounds in the schools and is even taught informally in the curriculum. They argue that, along with the home environment, the schools are where girls and boys learn that a certain set of interests and behaviors are expected of them and that very little deviance is encouraged or even tolerated. That schools actively encourage sex-role stereotyping has many objectionable implications. For one thing, although sex-role stereotyping is damaging to both sexes, it is particularly so for females, since the occupational roles assigned to them are less prestigious and less lucrative than those assigned to males.

How do schools contribute to and perpetuate sex-role stereotyping? Certainly one way is through the textbooks and other reading materials that are used in instruction. Policy analyst Charol Shakeshaft describes the forms that bias can take: "invisibility of female characters, blatant or subtle stereotyping, selectivity, unreality, fragmentation, and male exclusive language."[66] The novels and short stories read by students often center on boys' growing-up experiences. Stories, biographies, or histories that focus on the female experience only rarely appear in the public school curriculum. Even the occasional unit on women in history or women in science delivers the subtle message that women have been somehow peripheral to the mainstream of history, science, literature, and so on. And studies of language indicate that students interpret *he* to mean males only, even if the teacher intends the pronoun to be inclusive. The materials used in instruction often mirror the stereotypes that we described earlier in television programming.

Analysts are concerned not only with how the curricular materials transmit sex-role stereotypes but also with the fact that many teachers and counselors do the same thing in their conversations with students. For example, female high school students are often advised that certain professions are "appropriate" for men, whereas others are "appropriate" for women. One woman reports, "Women have frequently told me that their high school counselors had advised them to become legal secretaries when they wanted to become lawyers, nurses when they wanted to become doctors."[67] Studies of teachers' interactions with students in math and science classes in particular indicate lower expectations for girls. The fact that high school girls generally perform better in reading and writing than in math and science may relate to teachers' expectations for their performance.[68]

> Dear god,
>   Are boys better than girls? I know you are one but please try to be fair.   Love Silvia

Reprinted by permission of Sterling Lord Literistic, Inc. Copyright © 1966 by Eric Marshall/Stuart Hample.

Teachers often communicate their different expectations for boys and girls to their students. Boys generally receive much more attention from teachers and are given more opportunities to talk in the classroom.[69] Teachers are generally unaware of the bias that leads them to favor the boys in their classes.

TITLE IX   In 1972, Congress passed Title IX of the Educational Amendment Act, which states, "No person in the United States shall, on the basis of sex, be excluded from participation in, be denied the benefits of, or be subjected to discrimination under any education program or activity receiving Federal financial assistance." A great deal of confusion arose over which circumstances Title IX applied to and which ones it did not. Although the fine print required interpretation, the large print was at least clear: sex discrimination in educational programs receiving federal financing is against the law.

Forbids sex
discrimination

In 1975, the regulations regarding Title IX took effect. For ten years it was interpreted to forbid sex discrimination in any educational institution receiving federal financial assistance; that covers slightly over 15,000 public school systems and some 3,300 postsecondary institutions. The law has been interpreted to ban sex discrimination in physical education, athletics, vocational education, financial aid, pension benefits, employment and compensation of staff, facilities, and counseling. Included under Title IX have been regulations that require equal opportunity to be provided in all facets of physical education and athletics, such as facilities, game and practice schedules, coaching, travel and per diem allowances, equipment, and supplies. Separate teams have been permissible in contact sports, such as boxing, football, and ice hockey. Whenever a school has had a team in a given noncontact sport for one sex only and athletic opportunities for the other sex have been limited, members of the other sex must be allowed to try out for the team. Title IX regulations have greatly helped to correct inequities resulting from sex discrimination.

But in 1984, the U.S. Supreme Court ruled that Title IX applied only to programs receiving federal aid, not to entire institutions.[70] As a result, the threat of an entire institution losing money was removed if only a program—athletics, for example—was not in compliance with Title IX. After several attempts, in 1987 Congress reacted by passing the Civil Rights Restoration Act, which clarified that entire institutions are subject to civil rights mandates if any program within the institutions receives federal aid. President Reagan vetoed the act, but Congress overrode his veto. Four civil rights laws, barring discrimination based on race, handicaps, age, and gender, were covered by this piece of legislation.[71]

Women's Educational
Equity Act

The Women's Educational Equity Act of 1974 has also promoted more equitable practices in the educational system for females, including programs to improve career opportunities, to reduce sex stereotyping in curriculum materials, and to encourage greater participation by females in athletics.

Teacher's role

It is still clear, however, that the elimination of sexism and sex-role stereotyping in schools will be a complex procedure that will require the cooperation of teachers, administrators, school boards, counselors, educational publishers, teacher educators, and parents. Your role as a teacher will be especially important. As you interact with your pupils and as you select and use instructional materials, your sensitivity to this problem will help determine the attitudes of our future generations. It is to be hoped that educators will lead in efforts to evaluate school policies, curricula, and practices with regard to sex bias and will work to eliminate sex discrimination (along with racial and ethnic discrimination) in our schools. Much remains to be done. For example, women still make up the majority of school teachers, whereas the large majority of principals and superintendents are men. Specifically, as of 1990, 69 percent of teachers, 41 percent of elementary principals, 19 percent of junior high/middle school principals, 10 percent of high school principals, and 5 percent of superintendents were women.[72] Remember, as with all the issues we have addressed in this chapter, if you're not part of the solution, you're part of the problem.

School Violence and Vandalism

Public attention in recent years has been drawn to the issue of crime and violence in schools. Parents, teachers, administrators, and politicians have all expressed concern. How serious a problem is school violence and crime? Where is it most likely to occur? What are the damage costs to repair school vandalism? How can school crime be prevented? The statistics gathered by the National Institute of Education (NIE) in 1976 provide some indication of the problem. Unfortunately, this documentation of school crime has not been reliably updated since the NIE study was published in 1978.

1976 study

- Of all schools surveyed, 8 percent indicated that vandalism, personal attacks, and thefts were serious problems. This figure represents approximately 6,700 schools in the nation.
- During an average month, 282,000 secondary students are attacked and 112,000 are robbed, and 5,200 teachers are attacked and 6,000 are robbed.
- Estimates for the yearly replacement and repair costs due to school crime are around $200 million.[73]

Although educators disagree about the severity of school crime, the fact remains that the level of violent crimes committed by juveniles has tripled since 1960. And the level of crime in the schools reflects criminal activity in surrounding communities, regardless of the racial and ethnic composition of the school.[74] When the U.S. Bureau of the Census undertook its 1987 National Crime Survey, it found that nearly 184,000 people were injured as a result of school crime in one year. This figure includes staff, students, and visitors. In New York City alone, 678 teachers and other staff members were attacked and injured at school in 1988.[75]

Gang problems

Violence and vandalism are hardly confined to big-city schools, but they are more pronounced in urban centers. Severe violence is often associated with gangs. Once confined to inner-city areas, street gangs are now present in smaller urban areas and suburbs. A federal study indicates that one-third of the cities reporting gang problems have populations below 250,000. The character of gang activity has become more violent, too, because increasingly gangs are involved in drug dealing and other criminal activities. The easy accessibility and spread of guns, and the greater tendency to use extreme violence to settle disputes or to revenge even the smallest acts of "disrespect," have also contributed to increased violence. In metropolitan Detroit and Los Angeles, some gang members are children of middle-class, suburban families. Reportedly, they commit acts of vandalism, robbery, and drug dealing out of boredom or feelings of alienation from family and friends.[76]

Costs resulting from incidents of vandalism or violence are difficult to measure. They include the costs of building repairs, skyrocketing premiums for liability insurance, and human costs in terms of injuries to students and teachers, and in extreme cases even deaths, often involving gang violence.

Psychological effects

Speaking about violence and vandalism in the urban schools, Manford Byrd, an experienced Chicago school administrator, stated the problem as follows:

> The losses . . . cannot be measured in terms of dollars. No one has measured the immediate and long-term effects on the education of children resulting from the climate of fear generated by the conditions. Many hours of education are lost because of false alarms and bomb threats. Much harm is done to educational programs when classroom windows are shattered, teaching materials destroyed or stolen, and schools damaged by fire and other acts of vandalism. When students and teachers are fearful of going to school . . . a healthy environment for learning is lost.[77]

With the epidemic of teen-age violence and the drug trade, many teachers are injured attempting either to break up student fights or to halt robberies. Student-teacher disagreements also provoke attacks. Still other teachers are injured not by students but by intruders who may be dealing drugs or who see the elementary schools as buildings with little security and populated by women and children. Some schools have installed metal detectors to deter students and others from carrying weapons into the buildings.

Contributing factors

Some of the other factors associated with school violence are impersonality and alienation, discipline structures, and school governance. Larger schools, and schools with larger classes, tend to experience more violence and vandalism. When teachers and administrators can establish personal relationships with students, thus reducing feelings of impersonality, the risks of violence decrease.

How to reduce violence

Several studies indicate that students, regardless of whether their schools are characterized as being safe or disruptive, are less likely to commit acts of violence or crime if they enjoy positive interactions with faculty and staff, are academically successful, or participate productively in school activities.[78] The climate of a school, especially as established by the principal, can support cooperation among the individuals in the school or hinder it. Principals who can establish common goals for the school and can elicit loyalty and commitment to the goals—from students, staff, and parents—foster self-discipline that minimizes disruptive behavior. A firm, fair, and consistent system for running the school seems to be a critical factor in reducing violence. The rules need to be known and firmly and fairly enforced. Good coordination between faculty and administration also promotes a healthier school climate. If teachers have hostile and authoritarian attitudes toward students, more vandalism can result.

In 1984, the National School Safety Center (NSSC) began operating with a two-year grant from the Office of Juvenile Justice and Delinquency Prevention and continues to operate on federal funds. In Director George Nicholson's words, "the NSSC seeks to create positive school climates that foster feelings of pride and ownership rather than fear and alienation."[79] Nicholson and his colleagues offer recommendations on several components of school climate; we'll take a look at their suggestions in the areas of leadership, discipline, security, and curriculum.[80]

In terms of leadership, Nicholson and his colleagues reiterate the importance of the principal, emphasizing that the principal must be highly visible. High expectations for the behavior and performance of students and staff and the adoption of well-publicized and fair disciplinary standards characterize effective leadership. Constructive discipline encourages students to accept responsibility for their own behavior. Regarding security, a combination of techniques may be required to keep intruders and weapons off school grounds. But equally important are measures that establish the school as neutral territory for all students and staff members, that control rumors, and that monitor students' movement in the building to squelch loitering and tardiness. And the school curriculum can directly affect school safety when it is structured to insure students' feelings of success. When students experience success, they are less likely to become frustrated, disruptive, and violent. Creating a curriculum that supports the values of honesty, integrity, and respect for others may also support a positive school climate and a safe school.

The encouraging news is that although school violence and vandalism are a serious problem, they still affect a relatively small percentage of teachers and students in the public schools, and there are some indications that the levels of violence within schools have reached a plateau. The problem probably reflects as much on societal malaise as on the schools. Boredom, frustration, alienation, despair, and low self-concept are characteristics that teen-agers may experience in their homes and in society in general, as well as in school. High crime and vandalism rates prevail in society; why would we expect anything different in our schools?

Teachers and administrators need not be helpless in dealing with this problem. In addition to those actions already cited, educators can take other steps.

Preventive programs

For example, learning how to defuse a conflict is an important skill for teachers. For over a decade the New York City school system has offered staff members a course called "Peacemaking: The Management of Confrontation." Course participants learn three hundred physical and psychological "survival tricks" on how to defuse a conflict without ending up either in a hospital or in court. For instance, participants are taught to look at the bridge of an angry student's nose rather than directly into the eyes to keep the student from feeling "dared," and to use nonprovoking language to tell kids to do something (instead of telling a student to pick up a milk carton that she tossed at a garbage can and missed, a statement like "You just missed a three-pointer—try again for two" is less challenging and more likely to get results).[81]

Intensive training in classroom management can also increase a teacher's skills and effectiveness in preventing and handling violence. By increasing the number of teachers, communities and school districts can reduce violence in those schools that have serious problems with crime and disruption. One pilot

Vandalism is a serious problem in today's schools.
(*AP Wide World Photos*)

program designed to reduce school crime discovered the following approaches to be successful: the use of peer counseling; the development of alternative programs for disruptive students; conferences among school officials, parents, and probation officers; increased student decision making in policy areas such as finding methods to handle offenders; and training school faculty and students in problem solving and communications.

As a teacher, you will have to be aware that this problem does exist and that it may affect you personally. And you will have to work as hard as you can to alleviate the factors that contribute to its existence.

School Dropouts The National Center for Educational Statistics reports that in 1989, 12.6 percent of students between the ages of sixteen and twenty-four had dropped out of school. Looking at racial makeup, we see that 12.4 percent were white, 13.8 percent were African-American, and 33 percent were Hispanic.[82] Recent dropout data for Native Americans are not available but are estimated to be in the 30 to 35 percent range. Figure 11.3 displays some dropout data on the high school class of 1982.

African-Americans make progress
If we look at an older age group, those twenty-four to twenty-five years old, the picture for African-Americans improves dramatically. In 1989, 90 percent of the white, 85 percent of the African-American, but only 59 percent of the Hispanic students received high school diplomas or their equivalent. For African-Americans, the rate rose 11 percentage points from 1974 to 1989. For

Hispanics, the rate improved only slightly, less than 3 percentage points during the same time period.[83] Comparable data for Native Americans are not available.

Though these numbers are regrettably large, national dropout rates do not appear, on the whole, to be getting worse. In the 1960s the dropout rate was approximately 20 percent. In the following decades the school leaving rate declined and has remained fairly consistent at 13 to 14 percent. However, many of our major cities are experiencing much higher dropout rates. Boston, Los Angeles, Chicago, and Detroit, for example, are reporting dropout rates of such crisis proportions as 40 to 60 percent.[84]

Poverty a major factor

As researchers begin to examine these disproportionately high dropout rates, findings are converging on the fact that disadvantaged students are at especially great risk of dropping out of school. The High School and Beyond study examined indicators of hardship such as low income and limited educational background and found that students disadvantaged in these areas were three times more likely to drop out of school than their more advantaged peers.[85] Other

Figure 11.3 Percentages of Various Groups of 1980 High School Sophomores Who Dropped Out Before Graduation

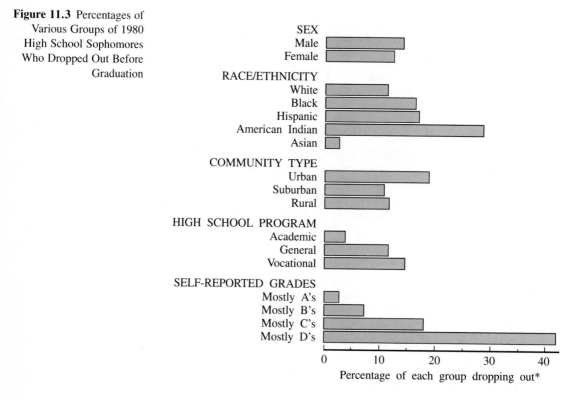

*1980 sophomores who, by 1982, had dropped out of high school.

Source: Dealing with Dropouts: The Urban Superintendents' Call to Action, U.S. Department of Education, Office of Educational Research and Improvement (Washington, D.C.: U.S. Government Printing Office, 1987), p. 4.

studies have found that dropout rates are highest in schools with a larger proportion of students from low-income families. For example, city schools in which less than 20 percent of the student body were poor had approximately a 13 percent dropout rate. Schools in which more than 50 percent of students were classified as poor displayed dropout rates of at least 30 percent.[86]

What is contributing to these high dropout rates? A review of the reasons given by the dropouts themselves indicates that there is no single essential factor causing these students to leave school. Consider the following excerpts obtained through interviewing teen-age dropouts:

- "Education is really important to me. My mother has stressed that my whole life. . . . I just didn't want to be in a classroom. There's a lot to learn, but you can't learn in the classroom."
- "All this year I was getting harassed by the vice principals and the principal. Everybody treated me like a criminal."
- "I didn't like doing schoolwork, even though I had the brainpower to do it. School was boring. And the schoolwork I was learning was boring. Boring, boring, boring. That's it. I feel right now like I know more than I was going to learn this year in my classes."[87]

Reasons for dropping out

Students report poor grades, dislike for school, alienation from peers, marriage or pregnancy, and employment as common causes for leaving school. The most frequently reported factor, indicated by 42 percent of those surveyed in the High School and Beyond study, was poor academic performance. Table 11.2 lists ten factors that may indicate a student is at risk of dropping out.

One cause of dropping out is unrealistic expectations about the world of work. Many with high hopes for the imagined luxury of a regular income fail to realize that wages in the service sector of employment have deteriorated. Other teen-agers may envision starting at the bottom of the work hierarchy and through hard work eventually climbing the ladder of success. However, many of them lack job search skills and typically end up in entry-level jobs with limited

Table 11.2 Common Factors Found in Research on Students Who Drop Out

1. The student is often behind in grade level and older than classmates.
2. The student has a history of poor academic performance.
3. Pregnancy is the most common reason females leave school.
4. The student frequently dislikes school.
5. The student may have experienced recurrent detention and suspension.
6. Work may appear more attractive than school.
7. The student often comes from welfare recipient and single-parent households.
8. The student may prefer to enlist for military service.
9. The student may have undiagnosed learning disabilities or emotional problems.
10. Some students may have language barriers.

Source: Andrew Hahn, "Reaching Out to America's Dropouts: What to Do?" *Phi Delta Kappan* 69 (December 1987): 258–260. Used with permission.

potential for advancement. Despite this reality, the strong motivation to work often proves too powerful an incentive and results in a student leaving school. The immediate rewards of the work place lure some students away from the more remote incentives for attaining an education and staying in school.

Link achievement with work

Albert Shanker, president of the American Federation of Teachers, proposes that a major cause of student failure may be found in the way our society reinforces students' educational attainment.[88] Currently, all students with high school diplomas have roughly equal chances for employment regardless of coursework taken, grades achieved, or attendance patterns displayed during high school. Shanker explains that the message we are communicating to students is that what they do in high school does not count in society. He feels that students must be able to see the connection between effort put forth in school and future attainments in the world of work and life in general. If clear rewards are provided for educational attainment, students will be more motivated to achieve in school. For example, businesses should be encouraged to go beyond traditional criteria of merely requiring a high school diploma and look at the high school transcripts of their job applicants. Better students should be provided with better job opportunities: They might be given priority in getting a job offer, better pay, or a better chance for promotion. This would clearly send the message to students that schoolwork pays off and that society values educational accomplishment. In turn, schools would feel more incentive to challenge their work-bound students to attain these tangible goals.

The Accountability Movement

Americans have always placed a high value on education. We have championed universal education and built a vast network of elementary and secondary schools and community colleges and universities. As a people, we believe in the power of an education. In the 1970s, however, our citizens' faith in public education began to erode. Across the country, local communities turned down bond issues and other methods of taxation for financing schools. Since the mid-1960s newspapers had been announcing regular drops in the scores of high school students' achievement tests, such as the Scholastic Aptitude Test (SAT) and the American College Testing Program (ACT). When asked to grade the public schools in a Gallup poll published in 1982, only 8 percent of the public gave the schools an A.

Public demand since 1970s

Since the 1970s a movement has developed to hold the schools accountable for their perceived failures. During the 1970s and 1980s, as schools became increasingly expensive to operate, as inflation eroded the buying power of the dollar, and as property taxes, which support much of public education, reached their tolerable limits, the public began demanding that the schools demonstrate what they were accomplishing. The public was no longer willing to vote for increased taxes until it could see what it was getting for its money.

Emphasis on student outcomes

The *accountability movement* has insisted that the public schools can no longer measure success in terms of the number of dollars spent on each child's education, the teacher-pupil ratio, or the educational level of teachers. Advocates of accountability argue that these measures are at best indirect, and that the only real test of a school is how well its students learn the knowledge, skills, and

Some students may drop out of school due to the lure of an immediate, tangible reward—in this case a paycheck.

(Sarah Putnam/The Picture Cube)

attitudes it is attempting to teach. Only by looking at the results of students' schooling, they argue, can we ascertain the worth of the schools.

MINIMUM COMPETENCY TESTING   The declining test scores of the 1970s convinced many that the schools were certifying incompetents as competent by passing them from grade to grade, graduating them, and giving them diplomas. The demand that students be required to pass certain competency tests before being graduated has come from disappointed employers, parents, students, and legislators. As of 1990, twenty states required minimum competency testing for graduation from high school.[89] Evaluation expert George F. Madaus explains the origin of the movement:

> Widespread disillusionment with the laissez-faire educational policies of the 1960s led to public perceptions that basic skills in the U.S. were declining, that social promotion was the rule, and that the high school diploma no longer meant anything. These perceptions were based in part on complaints from business, colleges, and the military that disturbing numbers of high school graduates were deficient in both literacy and numeracy skills, that they could not correctly complete applications, read directions, write letters, or perform basic calculations.[90]

Questions about testing

A number of basic questions must be answered within each state. What competencies should be measured? Should the competency areas be limited to the basic skills, or should they include school subjects like biology, Spanish, and history? How are the competencies to be measured? Will the tests be limited to paper-and-pencil measures, or will on-the-job performances and school products such as paintings, experiments, and speeches be permitted? Still another issue is when to measure. Should students be tested during the year or at the end? And an important question is what the minimum level should be and whether it will be the same for all students. If the same level is expected of all students, is a statewide testing program implied? What about levels for students with handicaps or those with limited proficiency in English? Can tests be developed that are not culturally biased in favor of middle-class experiences and values? And finally, what should the schools do with students who fail the competency tests? Give them several more chances? Provide remedial help? Refuse to promote and graduate them until they do pass? Few of these questions have been answered at this point.

Educators are divided regarding the wisdom of competency testing. Some, like Robert L. Ebel, former president of the American Educational Research Association, have argued that the movement will do much to restore concern for cognitive development as the first mission of the school, thus motivating teachers to teach more purposefully and students to work harder.[91] Other educators believe that competency testing will lead to an emphasis on the minimum and that lower standards will result for all children. On the other hand, if standards are rigid and little remediation is offered, socially and academically disadvantaged children may become frustrated by the barriers to success and the dropout problem may increase.[92]

Throughout this book we have referred to research that describes effective schools, effective principals, or effective teachers. The word *effective* is usually defined in terms of students' performance on standardized tests, and this is the problem. A legitimate question to ask is whether several series of multiple-choice questions provide the information needed to assess the quality of a school's programs, a teacher's ability, or a student's knowledge.

Limitations of standardized tests

Take a look again at the list of typical school goals at the beginning of Chapter 8, "What Is Taught?" How many of those goals can be measured by a standardized test? Such tests fail, for example, to assess a student's moral or

Reprinted with special permission of King Features Syndicate, Inc.

ethical growth or the ability to think critically or creatively or to work coopera-
tively with others. Measuring school excellence by standardized tests poses the
danger arising from the limited and simplistic nature of the tests. Evaluation
experts warn that tests external to the schools can limit the curriculum if schools
pattern what they teach to conform to the content of the tests. Schools may fail
to teach what is important or difficult to test. In some instances, the content and
actual form of a test have become the curriculum itself, and weeks of classroom
drill have centered on previous versions of tests. (See the section on standardized
testing in Chapter 6.) Others worry that standardized tests overemphasize technical information and underemphasize educators' professional judgments about
the worthiness of a school's programs.

Instances of cheating

Another problem is that those who equate performance on tests with the
quality of education may be deceived by the techniques already used to boost
standardized test scores. Administrators have been known to switch to easier
tests, eliminate certain populations from testing, use coaching techniques, and
teach test-wiseness to their students.[93] Nevertheless, the pressure to produce acceptable test results as measures of students' learning and the excellence of a

"LAKE WOBEGON" EFFECT: HOW CAN MOST STUDENTS BE ABOVE AVERAGE?

Lake Wobegon is radio humorist Garrison Keillor's myth-
ical town in Minnesota where "all the women are strong,
all the men are good looking, and all the children are
above average." John Jacob Cannell, M.D., borrowed the
name to describe the practice of local school districts using norm-referenced, elementary achievement tests to deceive the general public into believing that their students
are achieving above the national average because they test
above the publisher's national norm on a "standardized"
test. Puzzled by the fact that school districts across the
country were reporting their students as scoring above national norms and yet American children were still doing
poorly on international tests of achievement, Dr. Cannell
investigated further. He discovered that more than 90 percent of the fifteen thousand elementary school districts
and 80 percent of the secondary school districts in the nation were scoring "above the national norm" on "standardized achievement tests," instead of the expected 50
percent. How could this be? Dr. Cannell has several
explanations.

First, it is important to realize that norm-referenced
achievement tests compare current student achievement to
the achievement of a norm group tested in the past. Current national averages are not computed. The norm groups
are supposed to represent an average group of students
tested under conditions similar to conditions used in current testing programs. Dr. Cannell points out, however,
that unlike currently tested students, norm groups are
"tested cold" without any prepping on exact test questions and without having their curriculum "aligned" with
the test questions. The result is that the high scores reported by many school districts, although higher than the
norm group scores, are not necessarily higher than the average of all students taking the tests.

Dr. Cannell further charges that because educators
are under such tremendous pressure to raise test scores,
they sometimes resort to such practices as changing student answers, allowing more time to complete the test,
distributing advance copies of the test, and excluding special education and bilingual students from testing. By excluding "at-risk" students from achievement testing,
some school districts artificially inflate achievement tests.

Dr. Cannell's charges have led to serious examination of practices in the use of norm-referenced achievement tests.

John Jacob Cannell, *How Public Educators Cheat on Standardized
Achievement Tests* (Albuquerque, N.Mex.: Friends of Education,
1989).

school's programs continues; there is no question that standardized test scores have become the nation's report card for its schools.

ADDITIONAL ISSUES RAISED BY ACCOUNTABILITY   Few would deny that the schools should be held accountable for their performance, but the definition and nature of accountability are matters of controversy. The notion of accountability is appealing to many people, but several fundamental questions must be answered before it can be put into practice:

Who should be accountable?

- Who is to be held accountable for any given child's progress? The superintendent? The principal? The teacher? To what extent? How reasonable is it, for example, to hold a given teacher accountable for the progress of students if he or she is teaching in a dilapidated building, using books that are fifteen years out of date, and trying to cope with 50 percent more children than should be there? How fair is it to allow teachers no say in setting the standards to which they are expected to perform?

- If school personnel are to be held accountable, to whom should they answer? The school board? The community? And how are results to be defined and measured?

- How will each educator's contribution to a child's learning be determined and distinguished from that of other educators?

- Should the schools be held accountable only for improvement in reading and arithmetic, skills that are easily measured? Or are the schools also responsible for the personal and humane outcomes of education, which are not so easily measured? If school personnel are held accountable only for improving easily measurable skills, might they not neglect other equally important educational outcomes? In any given year, is the student's improvement in reading more important than the strengthening of his or her self-concept, moral development, and ability to work and play with other children?

Clearly, there are no pat answers to these questions. Many public school personnel who support accountability in theory are concerned about how it might work in practice.

Tensions exist   Recently, much of the struggle in accountability has focused on a tension between political accountability, on the one hand, which requires schools to be answerable for results, and the professionalism of educators, on the other hand, which implies that they possess the knowledge and skills necessary to make judgments and decisions about curriculum and instructional strategies and to match these strategies with particular students.[94] The first wave of educational reform (discussed in Chapter 6, "How Are Schools Governed, Controlled, and Financed?) emphasized political accountability by requiring higher standards for students and teachers. The second wave of reform emphasized the need for professional teachers who are permitted more involvement in important decisions affecting curriculum and instruction. Educational policy makers are increasingly convinced that for real change to occur in the schools, teachers must have a greater say in decisions that affect teaching and learning. But many of these same policy makers are reluctant to back away from mandating to educators what kinds of changes they want to see in the schools. The direction we seem to be going in is toward less regulation *if* performance indicators demonstrate positive outcomes. However, tension is likely to continue.

The issue of accountability is one of the most complicated problems facing education. One thing appears certain: The debate over its merits and drawbacks is bound to help school personnel think more precisely about their goals, methods, and measures of student performance.

A FINAL WORD

Given the range of social problems that we have discussed in this and the preceding chapter, it is not surprising to find the schools bearing an ever-growing burden to guide young people's decision making. How well equipped are the schools to handle this task? Too often, public education has merely reflected the inequities of our society in its treatment of women, racial minorities, individuals with disabilities or disadvantages, the culturally different, and so on. Many of the tension points in American education touch on questions of values: Can equity and excellence coexist? If not, which is more important? Can the rights of the majority and minority receive equal protection? The problems implied by these questions are not easily solved, and these tension points will likely be with us for a long time to come.

Discussion Questions

1. How does poverty affect the lives of students from poor families? What is the teacher's responsibility to children burdened with poverty?
2. What aspects of our culture contribute to the high incidence of child abuse in the United States?
3. Should schools assume responsibility for educating children about alcohol, drugs, sex, and suicide? Why or why not? If so, what aspects of the current curriculum should be dropped to make room for these topics?
4. Do you agree that equality of educational opportunity should be defined by its effects rather than by its provisions? Can you think of an analogy to support your case for or against this position?
5. Do you agree with our prognosis that magnet schools are likely to continue and flourish? Have you ever attended or visited a magnet school? If so, what is your evaluation?
6. Can you recall any sexist behavior that you have observed in schools? Do you think that sexism and sex-role stereotyping are problems in our schools?
7. Were you aware of the problem of school violence and vandalism before you read this chapter? Will it be a major factor in your decision regarding whether or not to teach?
8. One of the six national goals calls for a 90 percent graduation rate from high school by the year 2000. In your judgment, what steps need to be taken to achieve that goal?
9. What are your reactions to the increased use of competency tests? How is the accountability movement related to these tests?

For Further Reading   Cannell, John Jacob. *How Public Educators Cheat on Standardized Achievement Tests*. Albuquerque, N.Mex.: Friends for Education, 1989.

> A book describing the "Lake Wobegon" effect, where all students are above average. The author asserts that professional educators are cheating on the use of standardized achievement tests to deceive the general public in believing that students are learning more than they actually are.

Goodlad, John I., and Pamela Keating (Eds.). *Access to Knowledge*. New York: College Entrance Examination Board, 1990.

> A collection of papers offering a new agenda for a national reform movement for our nation's schools. The book reconceptualizes the problem of failure in our schools and urges classroom changes that respond to diverse student needs.

Havighurst, Robert, and Daniel Levine. *Society and Education*. 8th ed. Boston: Allyn and Bacon, 1992.

> An examination of many of the social issues touched on in this chapter. The authors summarize recent research.

Kirst, Michael W., *Policy Perspectives, Accountability: Implications for State and Local Policymakers*. U.S. Department of Education, Office of Educational Research and Improvement. Washington, D.C.: U.S. Government Printing Office, 1990.

> A short booklet that captures the major accountability issues facing educational policy makers. The booklet examines six broad approaches to accountability.

National Board of Inquiry into Schools. *Barriers to Excellence: Our Children at Risk*. Boston: National Coalition of Advocates for Students, 1985.

> An investigation into topics such as racial, class, cultural, and sex discrimination. The study identifies 104 strategies to achieve fair and excellent schools.

Rossell, Christine H. *The Carrot or the Stick for School Desegregation Policy*. Philadelphia, Pa.: Temple University Press, 1990.

> An examination of the effectiveness of forced busing or magnet schools as tools for desegregating schools.

Schorr, Lisbeth. *Within Our Reach*. New York: Anchor Books, Doubleday, 1988.

> A book that reviews effective and successful programs that significantly change the odds for "at-risk" youngsters to grow up healthy and well educated. Schorr calls for comprehensive and intensive coordination of health, mental health, social service, and education systems to respond flexibly to a wide variety of needs for at-risk youngsters and their families. A book that offers hope for breaking the cycle of the disadvantaged.

Theory Into Practice 25 (Autumn 1986).

> A theme issue on sex equity and education.

Notes

1. Sally Reed and R. Craig Sautter, "Children of Poverty. The Status of 12 Million Young Americans," *Phi Delta Kappan* 71 (June 1990): K-4.
2. Ibid.
3. Ibid.
4. Ibid.
5. Harold Howe II, "The Prospect for Children in the United States," *Phi Delta Kappan* 68 (November 1986): 195.
6. Harold L. Hodgkinson, *All One System: Demographics of Education—Kindergarten Through Graduate School* (Washington, D.C.: Institute for Educational Leadership, 1985), p. 3.
7. Howe, "Prospect for Children," p. 195.
8. Hodgkinson, *All One System*, p. 7.
9. *One-Third of a Nation* (Commission on Minority Participation in Education and American Life, n.d.), p. 4.
10. Ibid., p. 10.
11. As cited in Reed and Sautter, "Children of Poverty," p. K-5.
12. Harold L. Hodgkinson, *The Same Client: The Demographics of Education and Service Delivery Systems* (Washington, D.C.: Institute for Educational Leadership, 1989), p. 7.
13. Reed and Sautter, "Children of Poverty," p. K-5.
14. Deborah Berger, "When School is a Haven," *Parade Magazine*, January 7, 1990, pp. 4–5.
15. Marian W. Edelman, "Defending America's Children," *Educational Leadership* (May 1989): 78–79.
16. Edelman, "Defending America's Children," p. 79.
17. Hodgkinson, *The Same Client*, p. 4.
18. As quoted in Bruce Beezer, "Reporting Child Abuse and Neglect: Your Responsibility and Your Protections," *Phi Delta Kappan* 66 (February 1985): 435.
19. Lisa Jennings, "Child-Abuse Reports in 1989 Up 10 Percent over '88 State-by-State Survey Finds," *Education Week,* April 11, 1990, p. 8.
20. Lois Distad, "A Personal Legacy," *Phi Delta Kappan* 68 (June 1987), p. 744.
21. Ibid., p. 745.
22. "Who You Will Teach," *Teacher Magazine* (April 1990): 39.
23. Laurence T. Ogle (Ed.), *The Condition of Education 1990,* vol. 1 (Washington, D.C.: U.S. Department of Education, National Center for Education Statistics, 1990), p. 72.
24. Deborah Mesce, "Panel: Teens Caught in Destructive Spiral," *The Daily Progress*, June 9, 1990, p. A1.
25. Thomas D. Snyder, *Digest of Education Statistics 1990* (Washington, D.C.: U.S. Department of Education, OERI, 1990), p. 136.
26. Grace J. Craig, *Human Development* (Englewood Cliffs, N.J.: Prentice-Hall, 1980), p. 85.
27. Ogle, *The Condition of Education*, p. 72.
28. "Profound Cultural Shift Detected in Survey Finding Drugs Unacceptable," *Richmond Times-Dispatch*, September 5, 1990, p. A1.
29. Reed and Sautter, "Children of Poverty," p. K-5.
30. Michael Hinds, "Crack Epidemic Splinters Families," *The Daily Progress*, March 17, 1990, p. A5.
31. Ibid.
32. Douglas Besharov, "Crack Babies: The Worst Threat Is Mom Herself," *The Washington Post*, August 6, 1989 p. 8; Hinds, "Crack Epidemic Splinters Families," p. A5: Marilee Rist, "The Shadow Children," *American School Board Journal* 177 (January 1990): 23.
33. Rist, "The Shadow Children," p. 19.
34. Anastasia Toufexis, "Innocent Victims," *Time*, May 13, 1991, p. 60.
35. Walter R. Allberg and Lily Chu, "Understanding Adolescent Suicide: Correlates in a Developmental Perspective," *The School Counselor* 37 (May 1990): 343.
36. John Kalafat, "Adolescent Suicide and the Implications for School Response Programs," *The School Counselor* 37 (May 1990): 360.

37. Jack Frymier, "Understanding and Preventing Teen Suicide: An Interview with Barry Garfinkel," *Phi Delta Kappan* 70 (December 1988): 290.

38. Ibid.

39. Ibid., pp. 290–291.

40. From Deborah Burnett Strother, "Suicide Among the Young," *Phi Delta Kappan* 67 (June 1986): 759. Used by permission of the publisher.

41. "Suicide's Grim Toll," *Teacher* (November 1989): 21.

42. James Coleman, "The Concept of Equality of Educational Opportunity," *Harvard Educational Review* 38 (Winter 1968): 11.

43. Deborah L. Cohen, " 'Silver-Ribbon Panel' Calls for Upgrading 25-Year-Old Head Start," *Education Week,* May 23, 1990, p. 17.

44. Virginia R. L. Plunkett, "From Title I to Chapter 1: The Evolution of Compensatory Education," *Phi Delta Kappan* 66 (April 1985): 536.

45. Ibid.

46. Mary Jean LeTendre, "Improving Chapter 1 Programs: We Can Do Better," *Phi Delta Kappan* 72 (April 1991): 578.

47. Lawrence J. Schweinhart et al., "The Promise of Early Childhood Education," *Phi Delta Kappan* 66 (April 1985): 548–553.

48. "National Goals for Education," a press release from the White House, February 26, 1990.

49. Jomills Henry Braddock II, Robert L. Crain, and James M. McPartland, "A Long-Term View of School Desegregation: Some Recent Studies of Graduates as Adults," *Phi Delta Kappan* 66 (December 1984): 259–264.

50. Ibid., pp. 260–262.

51. See J. Anthony Lukas, *Common Ground* (New York: Knopf, 1985), for a Pulitzer-Prize-winning description of desegregation efforts in Boston, Massachusetts.

52. Howard Ozmon and Sam Craver, *Busing: A Moral Issue* (Bloomington, Ind.: Phi Delta Kappa Educational Foundation, 1972), pp. 33–34.

53. Snyder, *Digest of Education Statistics* 1990, pp. 98–102.

54. Mary Anne Raywid, *The Case for Public Schools of Choice*, Fastback 283 (Bloomington, Ind.: Phi Delta Kappa Foundation, 1989), p. 20.

55. Thomas J. Flygare, "A Return to Neighborhood Schools as a Way of Stemming 'White Flight,' " *Phi Delta Kappan* 67 (May 1986): 679–680.

56. Rolf K. Blank, "The Effects of Magnet Schools on the Quality of Education in Urban School Districts," *Phi Delta Kappan* 66 (December 1984): 270.

57. Mary Anne Raywid, "Synthesis of Research on Schools of Choice," *Educational Leadership* 41 (April 1984): 71.

58. Raywid, *The Case for Public Schools of Choice*, pp. 27–30.

59. "Developing Magnet Programs," *Education Digest* 54 (February 1989): 22–24. Condensed from *Research in Brief*, September 1988, published by U.S. Department of Education Office of Educational Research and Improvement, Washington, D.C.

60. Christine H. Rossell, *The Carrot or the Stick for School Desegregation Policy* (Philadelphia, Pa.: Temple University Press, 1990), p. 21.

61. Ibid., p. 108.

62. Ibid., pp. 187–188.

63. Denis P. Doyle and Marsha Levine, "Magnet Schools: Choice and Quality in Public Education," *Phi Delta Kappan* 66 (December 1984): 268.

64. Advisory Committee on the Rights and Responsibilities of Women, *The Vocational Preparation of Women* (Washington, D.C.: U.S. Department of Health, Education and Welfare, 1975), p. 34.

65. *Guidelines for Improving the Image of Women in Textbooks* (Glenview, Ill.: Scott, Foresman, 1972).

66. Charol Shakeshaft, "A Gender at Risk," *Phi Delta Kappan* 67 (March 1986): 501.

67. Nancy Frazier and Myra Sadker, *Sexism in School and Society* (New York: Harper & Row, 1973), p. 138.

68. Patricia B. Campbell, "What's a Nice Girl Like You Doing In a Math Class?" *Phi Delta Kappan* 67 (March 1986): 516–520.

69. Myra Sadker and David Sadker, "Sexism in the Classroom: From Grade School to Graduate School," *Phi Delta Kappan* 67 (March 1986): 512.

70. Martha M. McCarthy, "The Civil Rights Restoration Act: Culmination or New Beginning?" *Educational Horizons* 66, no. 4 (1988): 141.

71. Ibid.

72. *Education Vital Signs*, 6th ed., (Alexandria, Va.: National School Boards Association, December 1990), p. A13.

73. National Institute of Education, *Violent Schools—Safe Schools. The Safe School Study Report to the Congress,* Executive Summary (Washington, D.C., 1978).

74. George Nicholson, Ronald Stephens, Rory Elker, and Vicky Leavitt, "Safe Schools: You Can't Do It Alone," *Phi Delta Kappan* 66 (March 1985): 496.

75. Denise Foley, "Danger: School Zone," *Teacher Magazine* (May 1990): 58.

76. Del Stover, "A New Breed of Youth Gang Is on the Prowl and a Bigger Threat Than Ever," *American School Board Journal* 173 (August 1986): 19–35.

77. U.S. Senate Subcommittee to Investigate Juvenile Delinquency, *Challenge for the Third Century: Education in a Safe Environment—Final Report on the Prevention of School Violence and Vandalism* (Washington, D.C.: U.S. Government Printing Office, 1977), p. 17.

78. William W. Wayson, "The Politics of Violence in School: Doublespeak and Disruptions in Public Confidence," *Phi Delta Kappan* 67 (October 1985): 129.

79. "An Introduction to the National Safety Center," *Phi Delta Kappan* 66 (March 1985): 492.

80. Nicholson et al., "Safe Schools," pp. 492–494.

81. Foley, "Danger: School Zone," pp. 59–60.

82. Snyder, *Digest of Education Statistics 1990*, p. 110.

83. Laurence T. Ogle et al., (eds.) *The Condition of Education 1991*, vol I (Washington D.C.: U.S. Department of Education National Center for Education Statistics, 1991), p. 28.

84. As cited in Andrew Hahn, "Reaching Out to America's Dropouts: What to Do?" *Phi Delta Kappan* 69 (December 1987): 257.

85. Ibid.

86. Ibid., p. 258.

87. Anne Sheffield and Bruce Frankel (Ed.), *When I Was Young I Loved School: Dropping Out and Hanging In* (New York: Children's Express, 1989).

88. Albert Shanker, "The End of the Traditional Model of Schooling—and a Proposal for Using Incentives to Restructure Our Public Schools," *Phi Delta Kappan* 71 (January 1990): 353.

89. Richard J. Coley and Margaret E. Goertz, *Educational Standards in the 50 States: 1990*, Research Report (Princeton, N.J.: Educational Testing Service, 1990), p. 4.

90. George F. Madaus, "Test Scores as Administrative Mechanisms in Educational Policy," *Phi Delta Kappan* 66 (May 1985): 614.

91. Robert L. Ebel, "The Case for Minimum Competency Testing," *Phi Delta Kappan* 59 (April 1978): 546–549.

92. One article that reflects some of these concerns is Susan K. Peterson, "Minimum Competency Testing: Issues to Consider," *American Secondary Education* 15 (1986): 17–19.

93. "Improving Test Scores—Teaching Test-Wiseness," *Phi Delta Kappa Research Bulletin* 5 (November 1986); John Jacob Cannell, *How Public Educators Cheat on Standardized Achievement Tests* (Albuquerque, N.Mex.: Friends for Education, 1989).

94. Michael W. Kirst, *Accountability: Implications for State and Local Policymakers*, U.S. Department of Education, OERI, Policy Perspectives (Washington, D.C.: U.S. Government Printing Office, 1990), p. 15.

V

TEACHERS

T eachers have always held an ambivalent position in our society. On the one hand, they
have traditionally received low salaries and frequent
criticism for their perceived deficiencies. On the
other hand, virtually every American thanks one or
more teachers who made a difference in his or her
life. Americans seem to revile teachers as a group
but revere teachers as individuals. Keeping focused
in light of such conflicting messages is not easy, but
the chapters in this section seek to provide you with
a useful perspective.

These three chapters examine what problems
you as a beginning teacher can expect to encounter
in your first year of teaching; what attitudes, knowledge, and skills effective teachers possess; and in
what ways teaching does and does not qualify as a
profession.

12 *What Can the New Teacher Expect?*

CHAPTER PREVIEW

Although they have spent an enormous amount of time in schools, many new teachers are shocked and surprised by the actual experience of being a teacher. In this chapter we try to help prospective teachers anticipate some of the problems that lie ahead. Much of the material comes directly from the experience of beginning teachers.

This chapter emphasizes that:

● Although prospective teachers may feel that schools will have few surprises for them, being on the other side of the desk is a very different experience and can cause a sense of culture shock.

● Administrators play an important role in the life of the new teacher, but it is a role with many facets that can be very confusing to the beginning teacher.

● Although fellow teachers are an enormous source of learning and support, they can also be a source of difficulty.

● New teachers learn much about the job in which they are supposed to be experts: instruction.

● Although the teacher's main purpose is to give service to children, students are also a source of both satisfaction and dissatisfaction.

● Working with parents can be surprisingly complex and is rarely what the new teacher has anticipated.

T he first year of teaching has been described as an emotional roller coaster, filled with peaks of exhilaration and dips of discouragement. The first year is a year of great intensity for the beginning teacher. It is intense because of the unexpected demands and because of the surprises that reside in what was thought to be a familiar world—the classroom. In a recent book about his first year of teaching, Garret Keizer reflects on his coming to a rural Vermont community as a new and inexperienced teacher and begins his story:

> I never cared less about whether I lived or died than I did my first year
> of teaching. I never worked harder, I never learned more than I did then.
> I never went anywhere that was more important for me to go than to
> these remote counties, though I did not know that then.[1]

Some of the intensity of the first year of teaching comes from the problems confronted by the teacher; some comes from the satisfaction in solving those problems and in succeeding as a professional.

New teachers often report their surprise at this or that experience or event. These surprises often come to them wrapped in everyday boxes—some contain sweet treasures and others hold booby traps. We have categorized these surprises in the following way:

- the school milieu: the shock of the familiar
- administrators: mixed bag and many hats and many pressures
- peers: a mixed blessing
- instruction: so much to learn
- students: friends or fiends?
- parents: natural allies with different agendas

In this chapter we will look at each of these features of the initial year of teaching. Our aim is not to take the surprise out of the first year. We hope, instead, to achieve three purposes. First, we want to alert you to certain problem areas in teaching. Although we run the risk of unduly frightening some readers, we are convinced that each year many new teachers walk into their own classrooms with energy, high hopes, and rose-colored glasses firmly set on the bridge of their noses. Since these problems can be so troublesome (and to some so devastating!), we are ready to run the risk of painting too bleak a picture.

On the other hand, the intention of each prospective teacher should be to identify areas of potential difficulty and to use his or her teacher education program to find solutions and strategies for what lies ahead.

Second, we wish to make you aware of certain aspects of teaching that may hold special, unexpected satisfactions and deep joys.

THE SCHOOL MILIEU: THE SHOCK OF THE FAMILIAR

One of the oddest phenomena related to becoming a teacher is the new teacher's sense of strangeness in what is, after all, a very familiar setting. People who become insurance sales representatives, astronauts, or psychiatric social workers know they are moving into a strange environment, and they expect these new work worlds to present them with very different experiences from those they had as students. New teachers, however, are re-entering a familiar setting, even if it is not the same school in which they were taught. The school routine of classes, periods, bells, tests, homework, and report cards is in their blood. The hierarchical system of principals, teachers, and students is taken for granted. The rituals and pageants—assemblies, Thanksgiving class presentations, honor society induction, sports rivalries with other schools—are all instantly recognizable. The existence of cliques, in-groups, and out-groups among both students and faculty is no secret either. But despite all their experience and sophistication, beginning teachers are often overwhelmed by their initial exposures to school. The very familiarity of it all lulls many into a false sense of understanding what is going on, and, thus, a false sense of security.

False sense of security

WHAT WOULD YOU DO?

1. You are a woman, a beginning teacher in a ninth-grade English course. As the first semester proceeds, you realize that one of your students, Fred, has a crush on you. He is constantly volunteering to help you pass out papers, and he lingers after class each day to talk to you. He found out your home address and came to visit you one Saturday morning. His actions are becoming obvious to the other students, who are starting to kid him about his infatuation.
What would you do?

2. You are generally recognized as one of the most popular teachers in your school. The students look upon you as a friend who can be trusted, and you have told them that if they ever have problems, school-related or personal, they should feel free to come to you. One day Maryanne, a junior in one of your classes, seeks you out. She is close to hysteria, and tells you that she is ten weeks pregnant. You are the first person she has told. She begs you for advice, but insists you do not tell her parents.
What would you do?

3. You are a third-grade teacher. Until recently, you have been quite comfortable in your class of twenty-seven children. About three weeks ago, you had to speak to Debbie. Although she is the brightest student and the natural leader in your class, she was continually talking when you were trying to address the class. Since then she has been as cool

as ice to you. But, more worrisome, she has turned the class against you. They seem hostile, and there are continued signs of lack of cooperation. The principal wants to talk with you because she has heard many complaints recently.
What would you do?

4. You are a white teacher in a somewhat racially tense school. There are seven African-American students in one of your classes. Because you fear alienating the African-Americans and being accused of prejudice, you make special efforts to treat them fairly. One day three of your white students come to see you and accuse you of coddling the African-Americans and discriminating against whites.
What would you do?

5. You teach in a school that uses a letter grading system. You have assigned your students a term paper. You know that one of your students has spent hours and hours on his report, but its quality is quite poor. The student has already expressed his hope that you will take effort into account when grading the reports.
What would you do?

6. You are the same teacher described in case number 5. When you assigned the term paper, you distributed a sheet containing all the necessary information about the assignment, including the due date. All the reports but two were handed in on time, and those two were both a week late. Adequate time was allowed for the completion of the paper.
What would you do?

The beginning teacher's shock that the familiar is not secure is sometimes manifested in visible signs of mental and physical stress. In the early months of the school year it is not uncommon for the new teacher to experience depression and self-doubt, outbursts of crying, physical exhaustion, insomnia, crankiness, inability to control temper, and even fits of vomiting before going to school in the morning. The anthropologist Estelle Fuchs has studied the world of the beginning teacher. In her words,

> Most of us are aware of the tensions and strains accompanying unfamiliar routines or activities. However, the symptoms expressed by beginning teachers . . . go far beyond the ordinary fatigue associated with a new mode of employment. They are surprisingly similar to the phenomenon described by anthropologists as "culture shock."[2]

Culture shock is the feeling of dislocation people experience when they initially encounter a foreign culture. Peace Corps volunteers, foreign students, tourists, and newly arrived immigrants frequently report that when first thrust into the strange life patterns of a foreign culture, they feel numbingly disoriented, forced to assimilate too much too soon, and afraid they have made a drastic mistake by going to a strange country. It is easy to explain culture shock among Peace Corps volunteers and immigrants, but why teachers? Haven't we just said that teachers, as ex-students, are accustomed to the culture of school?

The familiar now complex

It appears that the new teacher's very familiarity with life in schools is a problem in itself: The teacher expects the old, simple ways and suddenly finds they don't apply. "School" is a very complicated series of structures, people, and interactions, and knowing part of it does not imply knowledge of the whole. Being one of twenty-five students sitting and listening to a teacher is very different from standing in front of twenty-five strange children and taking charge of their learning. People learn a great deal about teaching through years of teacher watching, but there is much that they do not learn. Also, new teachers

Reprinted by permission: Tribune Company Syndicate, Inc.

have to learn not only a new set of school routines for their particular school, but also how to administer them. They have to learn their way around a new building and find out how to requisition the supplies they need. They have to get acquainted with their administration, their fellow teachers, and especially their students. And on top of all this, first-year teachers have to develop lesson plans from scratch. They must build complete units, design bulletin boards, devise an evaluation system, and make up tests. The sheer volume of "newness" puts pressure and strain on the beginners.

The following account by a new second-grade teacher speaks to the kinds of culture shock problems experienced by teachers in many situations.*

JOAN CHEFFERS/SECOND GRADE "The next time I hear someone say, 'Teaching is an easy job,' I think I'm going to slap their face . . . or cry! I can't believe how tired I am. I've been teaching for five weeks, and it seems as if it has been five months. I never realized that life on the teacher's side of the desk could be so different, so tiring. I remember seeing the old movie *Up the Down Staircase* and thinking it was exaggerated. My kids are younger and don't have the kinds of problems those high school kids in the movie had, but

Feeling overwhelmed they still have problems, and they are so demanding. They all want my attention, and they all seem to want it at the same time. 'Miss Cheffers, someone took my pencil! Did you do it?' 'Miss Cheffers, Ralph and Maxine put gum in my hair.' 'Miss Cheffers, my father doesn't think we're doing enough arithmetic in this class and says I can tell the kids to shut up if you won't.' 'Miss Cheffers, I need to go to the nurse. I have a terrible nosebleed coming on!' And on and on.

"And the forms! They never end. Forms for shots. For lockers. For parent volunteers. For books. And we have an attendance procedure here that must have been designed by a sadist! It consumes hours of time. The principal's office continually wants information. I keep filling out forms and sending them in, only to be greeted with more forms. I can't imagine what they do with all the information.

"On top of all this, I'm supposed to teach! I leave school in the afternoon—always the last one out of the building—and I'm numb from the hairline down. On some nights I can hardly unwrap a TV dinner. And I spend what little free time I do have staring at the TV set and having imaginary arguments with Sandra's know-it-all father (whom I have yet to meet) about why we actually are doing just the right amount of arithmetic. What is most discouraging is that Sandra's father wins the arguments.

"Clearly, this has been the most frustrating five weeks of my life. I feel as if I've been swimming in molasses. Student teaching was a breeze compared to this!"

* All the cases in this chapter that are not accompanied by specific citations are slightly altered or fictionalized accounts of situations and problems experienced by the authors or by beginning teachers with whom the authors have worked. The names have been changed to save us all from embarrassment.

Beginning teachers see familiar school experiences from a fresh perspective.
(Elizabeth Crews)

Pleasant surprises

But many of the surprises of school life are very pleasant ones. There is much love and human warmth in the classroom. Some of the aspects of school life that one has dreaded never materialize. The content that one felt unsure of turns out to be one's strength. Also, within the four walls of the classroom, some people find a new self who they didn't know existed.

JOAN GEE/OFFICE MANAGEMENT "All through elementary and high school I was bashful. In my high school graduating class I won the 'Most Shy' award. I dreaded being called on, even when I knew I had the right answer! Part of it is that I blush so easily. So my approach was to be like the furniture or the wallpaper and hope that the teacher wouldn't see me. Still, I liked school and always liked my teachers, even the ones that had fun with my blushing. When I decided to become a teacher, I knew my shyness was going to be a problem, but I figured that I could pass my blushing off as a permanent sunburn.

"Something happened, though, when I became a teacher. I began to notice a change when I was student-teaching, and once I had my own class, it was quite clear: I'm a different person in my class. I feel very outgoing, almost to the point of being aggressive. Also, I've discovered that I'm a ham actor. And what a stage my classroom is! I love it. My students seem to love it, too. It seems so odd that after all these years of trying to be invisible, now I'm discovering a whole new side of myself."

WHAT WORRIES BEGINNING TEACHERS?

One hundred new teachers were surveyed, and included in the survey was the following question:

Every profession has potential problems, and teaching is no exception. Considering the potential problems we have listed below, could you tell us if, during your first year of teaching, you expect them to be (1) definitely major problems, (2) somewhat major, (3) somewhat minor, or (4) definitely minor?

The responses were as shown in the table below.

How would you answer the question asked of the one hundred teachers?

	1	2	3	4	N/A
Class size too large	16	48	32	4	—
Lack of good texts and materials	21	42	31	6	—
Too much paperwork and record-keeping	16	37	40	7	—
Insufficient student skill for the grade level	13	37	40	8	2
Isolation from other teachers	7	22	45	25	1
Lack of administrative support	30	30	27	11	2
Lack of professional autonomy	13	36	35	11	5
Student behavior problems	22	42	31	4	1
Lack of parental support	27	43	24	5	1
Parental interference	15	37	39	8	1
Lack of esteem in the community	11	31	40	16	2
Inadequate preparation to teach certain curriculum areas	13	26	37	22	2

Source: From "Beginning Teacher Survey," *The Instructor* (1985), p. 38. Reprinted from *Instructor,* September 1985. Copyright © 1985 by The Instructor Publications, Inc. Used by permission.

ADMINISTRATORS: MIXED BAG AND MANY HATS

As elementary and secondary school students, most of us had pretty simplistic notions of administrators. The superintendent was a vague presence we occasionally glimpsed in the hall talking to one of the staff or in front of a microphone on ceremonial occasions. The principal was much more a part of our school lives as someone beloved or feared, and occasionally both. Even though the principal was near at hand, our student's-eye view was rather one-dimensional. The principal represented AUTHORITY. In all but the rarest instances the principal stood directly beyond the teacher, supporting the teacher and the system. When, as students, we went to the principal's office, it usually meant we were in trouble.

New teachers' relationships with their principals are not so simple, however. School principals loom quite large in the lives of beginning teachers, and the teacher-principal relationship (and relationships with vice principals, department heads, and master teachers) is many-faceted. The principal is, first of all, *Principals as colleagues* a colleague, a fellow educator* joined with you in the common task of bringing civilization to the young. You are both professionals. You are part of a common tradition. You automatically share common goals (such as improving the educational opportunities of children) and attitudes (for example, that people engaged in the important work of educating the young need more support from the public than they receive).

As leaders Principals are the official leaders. They make decisions, or act as the funnel for the decisions of higher authorities. Decisions made by teachers or students are normally checked with principals. Principals speak for the school community to the superintendent, the press, and the local citizens. Although they are not necessarily the de facto leaders, the most influential people in school communities, they frequently are. Nothing is ever quite "official" unless the principal has been involved. Recent research on effective schools points to the importance of the principal's leadership.

As helpers Principals are helpers. They can dispense information and materials, and, as experienced teachers, they are sources of tips, short cuts, and helpful suggestions. Teachers can directly request their help. Principals also visit classrooms and, ordinarily, hold conferences with teachers. They are there to aid beginning teachers who are encountering difficulties and confusion.

As initiators Principals are initiators. A school system is a bureaucracy whose long arm extends from the state commissioner of education to the local district superintendent of schools to the individual school principal. Principals, in effect, act on behalf of the bureaucracy by introducing teachers into the bureaucratic life of the school and teaching them how to function in it.

As crisis managers Principals are crisis managers. When something happens that a teacher cannot handle, the principal's office is where he or she naturally turns for help.

---

* One of the little curiosities of educationese, the official language of schools, is that administrators refer to themselves as educators—as in "leading educator" and "innovative educator"—and teachers are simply called teachers. Occasionally, when the principal attempts to rally the teacher-troops, she or he broadens it to "we educators." Some few, guilty for having left the classroom (or uneasy with their authority), insist that they are still "just teachers." One thing you can count on, though: "educators" invariably make more money than teachers.

If he or she is to be truly helpful, a principal needs to know about crises in the school to try to deal with them effectively.

As facilitators

Principals are facilitators. Schools run on things—pencils, books, paper, heat, hot lunches, sanitary toilets, lights, construction paper, petty cash, and keys. It is the principal's job to keep teachers supplied so that teachers, in turn, can carry out the aims of the school.

As dispensers of rewards

Principals are reward dispensers. Although the school board actually hires teachers, the board typically acts on the recommendation of principals. Later, principals can give or withhold compliments on teacher performance and give or withhold extracurricular duty assignments. Principals assign classes to teachers, deciding what kind of children they will teach and whether the children will be at the level or in the subject for which particular teachers are prepared.

As judges

Principals are judges. Theirs is the official view of a teacher's performance. First-year teachers are neither permanent members of the faculty nor permanently certified members of the teaching profession. Principals make decisions about a teacher's qualifications that can have a profound effect on his or her future in education. They can enhance or destroy people's reputations as teachers. They can write recommendations for or against teachers. They can insure that teachers are not rehired. They can block licensure. And, of course, they can judge teachers positively and be very positive influences on teachers' entire careers. Obviously, principals derive a great deal of power from their roles as reward dispensers and judges.

As buffers

Principals act as buffers between teachers and angry parents (or, occasionally, angry students). Teachers can be quite vulnerable to public attack. Parents hear tales from their children or from other parents and, if they have a question or a complaint to make against a teacher, go directly either to the principal or to the teacher. If they start with the teacher and do not get satisfaction, they then go to the principal. The principal is thus the official "complaint department." This is a delicate position, requiring the principal to be open and responsive to complaints and at the same time to support the position of the teacher involved. Such situations call for the skills of high diplomacy.

As sacrificial lambs

Principals are the sacrificial lambs. If the community, the teachers, or the school board become dissatisfied with what is going on in a particular school, the school's principal, who usually does not have tenure in that position, is vulnerable. No one suggests replacing the students. The tenured staff cannot be dismissed (except under very special circumstances). The community members are not going to move away en masse. Thus the principal, who may or may not be responsible for the reported problem, is likely to be chosen to pay the penalty. The ease with which the principal can be dismissed is, incidentally, a characteristic shared with beginning teachers.

Having to wear all these hats and to perform all these roles makes for a complicated existence. The principal of a school today has a most difficult job, and to do the job well requires the strengths of a field general, a philosopher, a psychiatrist, and a saint. In light of the general shortage of these strengths, it is not surprising that new teachers sometimes find themselves in conflict with their

Double roles principals. Principals have to make many quick and difficult decisions, frequently with insufficient information or time, and they are sometimes wrong. A factor that contributes to conflict between administrators and beginning teachers is that administrators are often playing several roles at once. When they appear in teachers' classrooms to observe, they are both helpers and judges. They may say that they are there only as sources of aid, but sometime in the future they must make recommendations about teachers to their superiors, and they obviously are influenced by what they have seen during their "helping" observations.

Different priorities Another potential source of difficulty is that administrators must be like ships' captains, concerned with keeping the ship afloat, running, and moving in a particular direction. Teachers, who are there to stimulate learning and creativity, have a somewhat different set of concerns. Bizarre or random activity, questioning, and occasional chaos frequently play an important part in learning. And it is at this juncture that administrators who put too great a value on order most often collide with teachers.

Therefore, it is to be expected that there may be confusion and the potential for conflict between the administrator and the new teacher who is being initiated into the system. For one thing, beginning teachers often do not know how to **Problems with bureaucracy** work in a bureaucracy (that is, make it work for their ends) and sometimes are antibureaucratic, or overly critical and complaining. This can lead them into direct conflict with their administrators, whose job it is to train beginners in bureaucratic procedures but whose primary responsibility is to make sure that the school, as a totality, runs smoothly. Amidst these many roles and different hats worn by the administrator, there can be slippage and breakdown. The following account illustrates such a case.

STEVE MELLONWOOD/JUNIOR HIGH SOCIAL STUDIES   "During the special orientation meeting for new teachers, the principal told us all that whenever we have a problem we should come and see him. He didn't expect us to be perfect and he felt his major job was to help new teachers. Later that week he stopped me in the hall and warmly repeated his offer of help. I really took him at his word. So in early October when I started having trouble planning and finding materials, I just went to see the principal. He was very cordial and, although **Using discretion** he talked a lot about himself, he did give me some fairly helpful advice. I went to see him for three short visits. Just talking the problems out seemed to help. I started finding good materials and my classes really improved. I felt I was really doing well and I couldn't wait to get to school in the morning.

"Then in early December I started getting treated in an odd way by some of the senior teachers. They were always asking me whether or not they could help. Sort of like I had some incurable disease, and could they get me a glass of water. It was weird. Finally, I asked two of them in the lunchroom, 'Why all the concern?' Well, it came out that the principal had told them that I was having big trouble, and he had told a number of the senior teachers to do what they could for me. He had not been in to observe me once. Later in the year he came in for two brief observations (to conform to minimum standards in our district), and he never had time for a conference. He did, however, write up supervisor conference reports. They were lukewarmish and had no specifics. He did mention in both reports that I was improving and overcoming early problems. What improvement? What problems? All he had to go by was what I told him. I got so mad that I wrote him a note to the effect that my self-reported problems had cleared up some time ago and that I felt my teaching was better than his report had indicated. I could see the handwriting on the wall, though. I started looking for another position, and got one without too much trouble. I liked the kids in my first school and many of the teachers. Somehow, though, I put myself in a box for the principal and he wasn't going to let me out."

An error of first impressions can also work the other way; the administrator who seems severe and distant can turn out to be warm and supportive.

VICTORIA KLARFELD/FOURTH GRADE   "Quite honestly, I was afraid of Mrs. Kelly when I first went for interviews. She seemed so businesslike and talked so much about high standards that I was sure that even if I got the job, I'd end up disappointing her. And after a few weeks with my fourth-grade wigglers, I was afraid I'd never get them settled down and working on tasks. I was wrong on both counts. The kids settled down—some too much, so that now my biggest problem is getting them excited and alive. And, boy, was I *really* way off on Mrs. Kelly. She is a jewel! She has so many ideas and gives them to me in the nicest way. I never feel I have to use her suggestions, but in fact, I think I've used every one.

Professional support

"But what has meant the most is that she has treated me like an adult, a professional. Here I am, right out of college and she is asking my advice about assembly programs and what to do about the cliques in our school. She has also made sure that the other teachers don't leave me out of things. I'm the only new teacher in the building this year, and they sometimes forget me. Mrs. Kelly has a great way of weaving me into things.

"I got very overtired and generally strung out after the Christmas vacation. I was depressed about my teaching and how little time or energy I had for any kind of social life. One day Mrs. Kelly intercepted me on my way to the lunchroom and took me around the corner to a sandwich shop. She knew exactly what was wrong with me and got right to the point, giving me super tips on how to organize my time and plan more efficiently. She even started me on a vitamin program that seems to give me much more energy. She has been terrific to me. She's made the year for me."

As the case above indicates, principals (and others who have supervisor responsibility over the beginning teachers, such as department- and grade-level chairpersons) can be a crucial source of professional expertise and moral support. In addition, research shows that supportive administrators actually help teachers become reflective and solve their own problems.[3]

PEERS: A MIXED BLESSING

New teachers are vulnerable to many outside forces and also to their own insecurities. If a supportive administrator can turn a potentially disastrous year into a year of growth, a beginning teacher's professional peers can be even more influential in the process of learning how to teach and how to survive in the classroom. The following example is a case in point.

ANNMARIE LANEY/SIXTH GRADE   "I had a hard time finding a teaching job. I had hoped to teach in my hometown, but there were just no jobs at the level I wanted to teach. The best job was on the other side of the state, and when it became clear that there were no jobs on the local horizon, I took it. I was very excited about teaching; I really felt that I was starting out on an adventure. I was, however, also moving away from my parents. Being so far away from home meant that there were lots of things that were going to be new to me. I had to get a car, an apartment, establish a bank account and lots of other things, and all at once. It was literally like a crash course in being an adult. And that's what I felt like right from the beginning—an adult. It was so different from college and even student teaching. At my school people treated me like an adult, and they expected me to act like one. For the first months I felt as if I was play-acting at being an adult. Well, now I guess the role is comfortable. Or maybe I just have my act down pat.

Emotional support   "Although I made friends with a few people in my apartment building, I was really very lonely at first. I don't think I would have made it without Joan Silver. Joan Silver teaches in the classroom next to mine. She's been, as she says, 'in the trenches' for eighteen years, but she's got more ideas and energy and dedication than any of us fresh troops. Joan was a lifesaver for me. She

YOU KNOW YOU'RE IN TROUBLE WHEN

- You have threatened that if there is one more sound in the classroom you will personally call every parent to complain—and there is a sound.

- The principal asks you what you plan to be doing next year.

- You have your students correct their own tests and the lowest mark in the class is 96 percent.

- It is 10:15 and the class has ripped through three-quarters of the work you have prepared for the day.

- You return after being sick for three days and the students chant, "We want the substitute!"

- It feels like February and it's only late September.

- The teacher across the hall comes in and offers to show your kids how to behave.

- The parents of eleven of your students ask to see the principal and you are not invited.

- Unsolicited, your principal offers to write a recommendation for your placement file.

- You are convinced you have finally come up with challenging and interesting work for your class, and when you present it they chorus, "We did that last year."

- After sitting in your class for five minutes, your supervisor starts to look at the clock.

- You walk into your usually noisy classroom and immediately all the students get in their seats and smile at you.

Some of the beginning teacher's most significant learnings come from his or her fellow teachers.

(Miriam Reinhart/Photo Researchers, Inc.)

took me under her wing even before school started. She has been a source of ideas and a source of great materials and a source of inspiration. And she has never made me feel like a taker or a leech. And actually, I taught her some things. That's one of the reasons I admired her so much. She really wanted to know about the new ideas I had learned in my education courses, and she put a lot of them to work in her class.

"I guess we talked every day after school. A lot of the time we just spent the hour after school laughing. A couple of times the janitor came in thinking there was something wrong, but what he found was the two of us broken up with laughter. And about once a month she would drag me home for dinner. Joan always seemed to know when I was a little low, and that's when she'd insist that I come home with her for dinner.

"There's so much to learn in the first year and not just about subject matter. Important things—like how to get information from the school secretary and how to stay on the right side of the janitor—that you can never learn in education courses. Joan was my guide on everything from how to fill out my planbook to which memos from the front office I had to pay attention to and which I could put in what she called 'the circular file.'

"It seems funny to say this, given the fact that Joan is twenty years older than I am, but I really think she's my best friend. She certainly has made this year a terrific one for me."

Although there are trends toward increasing cooperation among teachers, for the most part teachers work independently, in their own classrooms and with their own students. When they are engaged in their professional work, they are isolated from one another. However, although administrators are the official source of support and help for beginners, fellow teachers are a much more accessible and less threatening source of support. As the preceding case illustrates, a teacher's colleagues can be a powerful influence, especially in the beginning of a career. They can be an ever-ready source of ideas and teaching tips and can initiate the newcomer into the customs of the school. As Joan Silver was, a peer can be an inspiration to the new teacher seeking to gain mastery of a new role. A peer can demonstrate by example what the phrase *teacher as professional* means.

More accessible than principals

On the other hand, other teachers can have a negative influence, undermining a beginning teacher's idealism, lowering his or her standards, and offering no help at all. The teacher's lounge is sometimes the venue for serious disillusionment. Many teachers use the lounge to "unwind." Unwinding often involves harsh criticism of students, mockery of administrators, and negative comments about teaching. Although not especially different from similar "off-camera" remarks in hospitals and businesses, such comments in the teacher's lounge can blunt the new teacher's idealism and enthusiasm. The lounge is a source of much learning for the beginner. But in some cases the private side of his or her colleagues can be a rude awakening for the new teacher. Perhaps some capsule portraits will clarify and illustrate this sad phenomenon. All organizations have people like the following. They are living witnesses to humanity's fall from the sublime.

Possible negative influences

Miss Pyrotechnics: She is a special-effects expert. She and her students spend most of their time decorating her classroom. The displays are beautiful and ever-changing. The desks and chairs are always just right! Even while the class is decorating, the room is spotless. The principal loves to bring visitors to her classroom. She has four special lessons (or routines) she can perform for these occasions.

Some common types

The Mouth: His hobby is gossip. His arena is the teachers' lounge. He thrives on the trade of secrets, and no morsel is too small to be shared with his colleagues. Nothing is too personal to be passed on. He is very interested in hearing all about you and your impressions of your new colleagues and supervisors.

Mrs. Coaster: She has had twelve years of teaching experience. Or, to be more precise, she has had one year of teaching experience, which she has repeated twelve times. She still uses lesson plans from her first year of teaching. She knows not the words *outside preparations.* Her favorite advice is, "Relax! You're gonna burn yourself out!" She puts in time and nothing else. She has eighteen more years to go before retirement.

The Hoarder: His desk and cabinets are a veritable goldmine of goodies. He has chalk and paper enough to make it to the year 2000. He has materials that make the other teachers drool with envy. He is like a squirrel preparing for the long winter. Nothing is safe from his acquisitive hands. He is exceptionally nice to the office secretary, and it pays off. He does not share.

The Big Planner: He is at his best in faculty meetings. He can create out of thin air the most exciting projects and is a champion for all innovative plans. When volunteers are requested, he always seems to be taking a course or has some mysterious but very important obligations somewhere else.

The Sex Bomb: Appropriately, the Sex Bomb comes in two varieties. SHE: In the lunchroom with the women she is rather quiet, even dull. But when he— any "he"—comes within range, she is transformed. Her clothes suddenly look too tight. Her conversation becomes animated, to say nothing of her flashing eyes. As the situation dictates, she is in desperate need of help or the font of all succor. It seems that he and she need to meet after school for some more private discussion. HE: He begins to stop by a new woman teacher's classroom after school to check on "how things are goin'." He's helpful at first. He has a tendency to stand too close. His breath is hot, his hands moist. He knows a great deal about the proximity of intimate little cocktail bars where the two of them could talk about school in a more relaxing atmosphere. (Everyone on the faculty hopes that SHE and HE find each other soon.)

Mr. Up, Up, and Away: He dresses nicely. Carefully, that is. His shoes are shined. He volunteers for all committees. It is difficult to tell whether he is bright or dull. He is beautiful to watch. He never makes a false move. He never tells a joke. He never makes a wave—unless the tide is running in his favor. There is never any noise from his class. His students are always busy doing seatwork, but they seem a little glassy-eyed. He, obviously, is going someplace, but his students aren't.

The Ally Seeker: She courts new teachers. Shortly after you have met, she tells you about The Great Injustice that was done her. She is telling you for your own good, she says. Although it happened to her seven (or was it eight?) years ago, it could be happening to you now. It seems it will be better for everyone if you approach the injustice doer and slap him or her in the face before he or she does anything to you. Also, you will be proving that you are on the side of Justice. Avoid her. She bites.

Although we strongly believe that the teaching profession has a larger percentage of dedicated, selfless people than any other profession (except, perhaps, the ministry), it also has its share of rogues and fools. Beginners should pick their way carefully among this field of new colleagues.

INSTRUCTION: SO MUCH TO LEARN

Success most important

Ultimately, a teacher's only real problem is his or her students' failure to learn and to develop. All other conflicts, triumphs, and defeats pale in significance if the children are learning and developing their human potential. The degree of the children's success as learners is the best measure of a teacher's success or failure. Although the closeness of the relationship between a teacher's instruction and a student's learning is frequently overstated, this relationship is crucial. As we said earlier, teacher effectiveness is an area in which there are few naturals. New teachers generally have much to learn in this area of instruction.

One major difficulty is the sheer newness of the role of teacher. There is no such thing as a gradual immersion into that role. After a little student teaching, you suddenly find yourself in charge of your own class and responsible for taking it from the first day of school to the last. One of the particularly vexing problems for the beginning teacher is the search for effective curricular materials.

BETTY DEWEY/THIRD GRADE   "The overriding question of this year has been 'What works?' I'm in a constant search for materials. It is never-ending. My kids aren't that bright, but they devour material and look at me as if to say, 'Well, what's next?' Our school has a curriculum guide that is only five years old, but it is terribly dated. The students know a lot of the stuff already. They learned it in lower grades or just picked it up. They are bored by a good bit of the rest, too. I'm constantly squeezing ideas and tips from the other third-grade teachers. They are helpful, but they are in the same box I am. Then there is the problem of getting a big buildup on a particular workbook or special unit by a teacher who had fabulous success with it. I try it and I fall on my face with it. Then there are the kids. They are so fickle. A couple of times I took their suggestion on things they wanted to study and work on. After much work and many late hours, I'd get these classes prepared and the very same kids who were so anxious to make the suggestions couldn't have cared less.

"My school district has curriculum specialists. Some of them are very good, too. Particularly the math specialist. He would give me *too* much material. I'd spend hours deciding about which approach to use to teach ten minutes' worth of material. The language arts specialist was a sweet lady, but very rarely available and most of her ideas were really out to lunch. I was on my own there. When you get right down to it, you have to make the curriculum and the materials *yours* before they are any good to you. Someone else's brilliant materials are nothing until you have made them your own. This is hard to do the first year."

"Owning" your own
materials

The actual skills and strategies of instruction can be another problem area. Knowing the terms for different kinds of instruction, such as *cooperative learning* or *higher-order questioning,* and even being able to recognize these methods when you see them does not mean that one *can actually perform them.*

MIRIAM SERECEK/ENGLISH   "I'm living proof that teaching is harder than it looks. I've always been a good student. I did very well in my education courses. In fact, I got an A in methods! However, I just about flunked once I had my own class. I really liked working with the children independently and in small groups, but when I had to be up in front, before the entire class, I'd have trouble. Little things that I had taken for granted became quite difficult to do well. I'd always admired teachers who could ask a lot of good questions and keep things really moving without having to step in and monopolize.

Admiring is not doing, believe me! I discovered that asking questions is a tricky business. First, it isn't that easy to come up with good questions. Then, you want to call on someone you think can answer or explore the question in an interesting way. Now, the really tricky part: listening carefully to what the student is saying and at the same time evaluating what he or she is saying and thinking of an appropriate response to those remarks *and,* on top of that, trying to figure out what the next move should be. Should I ask him or her another question? Should I call on Lois, who is falling asleep in the back? Should I try Charlie, who is so eager with that waving hand and always so painfully wrong with his answers? Where should I go? Should I correct what the first student said or get a student to . . . , meanwhile losing the train of thought I was trying to develop? It's very complex, this teaching game."

But whereas the instructional aspect of teaching can be a thicket of difficulty for many beginners, for others it is very exciting and inspiring.

TOM FASTY/MIDDLE SCHOOL SOCIAL STUDIES   "School has always been hard for me. But then again, if the truth be known, I've always worked hard. In high school I really got turned on to history and I think it was then that I decided to become a teacher. In college I took every history course I could. I was way over the required number of history courses for certification. And I was lucky and taught at a very academic high school as a student teacher. I think I did well, too. At least, that's what everyone said. I was really disappointed when I couldn't find any openings as a history teacher. I was getting very discouraged until I was finally offered a middle school job in the same school district where I had student-taught. My first thought was to let it go and wait for a "real" history job. What they wanted me to teach was social studies. There was some history involved, but there was also a lot of other social science material to teach. What I really wanted to teach were the intricacies of the British parliamentary system and the rise and fall of Oliver Cromwell, and what they wanted was what seemed to me pretty low-level stuff. I was ready to hang it up. I could possibly work for the company my dad works for, or I could go back to school. Well, anyway, I decided I'd give middle school teaching a chance.

DIALOGUE

Kevin: Are we in danger of giving the impression that all teachers struggle through an unhappy survival?
Jim: Come to think of it, we probably are.
Kevin: Then we ought to correct it. Many teachers are quite skillful when they begin their careers. They have

enough ability and training to perform at quite a high level of competence.
Jim: As a matter of fact, I have known a few.
Kevin: Yes, so have I. The only problem for the ones I have known was that some of the older teachers become jealous.
Jim: Yes, teachers share human nature, too.

"The great surprise of teaching for me was not the kids or anything like that. It was, on the other hand, how little I knew about my strength, history, and how intellectually exciting teaching in general can be. I had taken dozens of history courses and considered myself a super buff, but I had missed the essential meaning of history. That's what I have been learning these first two years, and it has been as stimulating as anything in my life. Now I feel I'm just beginning to understand the purpose of history and what should be taught. I came to teach and probably ended up learning more than my students.

"Incidentally, I was offered the position I thought I really wanted, a position on the high school history faculty. I turned it down. I couldn't be happier than I am here."

Relearning one's subject

STUDENTS: FRIENDS OR FIENDS?

Becoming comfortable and sensing that one is effective with children is a major concern for a new teacher. And well it should be. Students are the main event! They make the good days good and usually make the bad days bad. The relationship between teacher and students is multifaceted. An important aspect of the relationship is based on how well the students are achieving.

EDWINA BELLATRE/FIFTH GRADE "I have enjoyed my students this year, probably more than I should have. It was a tremendous kick to have my own class. I was very worried about discipline. I think I jumped on the students so much in the first three weeks that they were shell-shocked until Thanksgiving. But I loosened up, and so did they. I've really liked the whole experience of being a teacher. And I've worked hard. It seems that my whole life this first year has been school.

"The one real down moment I had came right toward the end of the year. Something one of the sixth-grade teachers said really shook my confidence. She made some comment at lunch about how much fun and games was going on in my class. All of a sudden I began thinking that while I was having a great time—and maybe the kids were having a great time—they really weren't learning anything. I tried to think what I had taught them that was really important, and my mind was blank. I tried to think of particular students who I thought had really shown a lot of progress, and I couldn't think of anyone specific. I went around that way for a couple of days and I got sort of panicky. Finally, almost by accident, I came across one of the student's notebooks, which had all of his work from September, even his diagnostic tests. It was really enlightening. I could almost see the change from week to week in what he knew. The problems became more difficult, but he could master them. His compositions became more interesting, and the mechanics became sounder. His handwriting looked so much more mature. I figured, though, that maybe that was just one student. I asked to look at a few other students' notebooks, and there it was. They had changed. They were different. Not just different, but *better*. And I was an important part of that change."

Student progress crucial

There can be little doubt, however, that although students are the primary source of a teacher's success, they are also a source of his or her failure. There are three areas, in particular, that cause problems: discipline, social distance, and sex. Behind each of these areas of difficulty is an inaccurate set of expectations held by the teacher about children.

One indication of these out-of-line expectations is seen in the sharp change in attitudes experienced by people as they go through teacher education and into their first years of classroom teaching. Studies have shown that the longer college students stay in teacher-education programs, the more positive and warm their attitudes toward students become. But among beginning teachers there is a sharp drop in positive attitudes toward students. In fact, beginning teachers score significantly lower on attitude inventories than students just entering teacher education.

Why does this happen? How can this phenomenon be explained? As we do at a number of other points throughout this book, we ask that you stop reading for a moment here and jot down some hypotheses about why beginning teachers' attitudes change in this way.

Teacher-education view
of children

_____

_____

_____

• • • • • • • • • • • • •

The love of nurturing and observing growth in others is essential to sustaining a life of teaching. This implies that no matter what you teach or how you present yourself to your students, you have to be on the learners' side and to believe that they can and will grow during the time that you are together.

— HERBERT KOHL —

What happens between the time one is a college student preparing to teach and the time one actually becomes a teacher is undoubtedly a complicated series of events. We would like to offer our own thoughts on the issue. College students alternate between being highly idealistic and extremely realistic in outlook. However, when they enter teacher training, most become very idealistic about children and education. They believe that as teachers they should have warm relations with students, and they want to make the classroom more relaxed and more responsive to the needs of students than it normally is. As college students take more education courses and observe in classrooms, their views of children become more idealistic and, as a result, more positive. By graduation, the rose-colored glasses are firmly affixed.* Also, college students have managed to completely shut out memories of many of the realities of their own childhood and adolescence. They forget things like the time they joined with the other seventh-graders to put four tacks on Miss Derriere's chair. They blot out all the juicy stories, most of which they knew were untrue, about the young home economics

* This analysis does not, we fear, account for the Lundquist Effect, named after our good friend Ernie Lundquist. Ernie deviated (as is his habit) from the normal. As Ernie progressed through teacher training, he began to dislike children more and more. By the time he graduated he had a well-developed distaste for, as he called them, "the little creeps." So Ernie decided not to become a teacher. He became an administrator. However, Ernie found sitting in his office quite lonely. The only people who came to see him were the children. As Ernie talked to the children about what his school was really like, he gradually came to like, and eventually to love, children. But as for the teachers. . . .

teacher. They forget about how they enjoyed reading (writing?) obscenities about their math teacher on the lavatory wall. They all forget how cruel kids can be to kids.

"Alice, we've decided that from now on we're going to call you Blubber Butt . . . you know . . . because you're so fat. Hey, why are you crying, Blubber Butt?"

"We started this club, Roger, and it's called the Red Devils. But you can't be part of it because you smell real bad, Roger."

"*Zits! Zits! Earl has lots of zits.* . . . Boy, look at old Earl run. And he's crying, too. What a wimp."

"My mother's a *what?!!*"

KEVIN AND JIM'S GUIDE TO THE FIRST DAY OF SCHOOL

1. *Teach your very best lesson.* Often, teachers use the first day for filling out forms, assigning lockers, and essential—but boring—administrivia. Such a day can set a tone for the students that this is just going to be like all the other years, like all the other classes. On the other hand, students will be fresh from the summer, carrying renewed expectations that "This year may be different!" Capitalizing on this attitude with a really interesting lesson will create important momentum for your class. You can catch up on the forms and other items later in the week.

2. *Establish class rules and procedures.* Although a good lesson is most important, getting classroom management under control cannot be stressed too much. On the first day, at least, let your students know you plan to have an orderly classroom with rules that foster respect and a healthy work environment. This suggestion is not to imply that you lay down the law, but that you let your students know that any group needs to have clear rules and that you are open to their suggestions or even co-determination of the rules.

3. *Start learning and using students' names.* As soon as you receive your class lists or rosters, start familiarizing yourself with the students' names. Once you meet them, start matching names with faces, and, whenever possible, use their names. Nothing signals your being interested in them and on top of the situation quite like using their names on Day 1.

4. *Be friendly, but businesslike.* Often the insecurities of new teachers get the best of them. They vacillate between being Mr. or Ms. Nice Guy and Attila the Disciplinarian. The beginning teacher's early commitment to a friendly but task-oriented atmosphere is the key to its realization.

5. *Tell them good news about the year ahead.* Students want to succeed. Even the ones with a history of difficulty with other teachers want the new school year to be better. Don't tell them how hard they are going to work. Tell them how much they are going to know at the end of the year and what they can do with this new knowledge. Share with them your vision for the year ahead.

6. *Begin to establish connections with the other faculty.* Teaching can easily become a lonely, scary profession. Constant communication with your colleagues keeps good ideas flowing.

7. *Establish procedures for communicating with parents.* You need parental support, and students want to know whether you'll contact parents about both good and bad events.

Need we say more? Just think back over your experiences with, and as, children, in and out of schools. Children are a mixed bag. So is the behavior of an individual child. One day the child is eligible for canonization and the next day could be shot by cannons. Somehow, though, the dark side of human nature

Adjusted view recedes from view during teacher education. Fear not. It reappears. Beginning teachers rediscover human fallibility, in their children and in themselves, and the result is that their positive attitudes toward children plummet. Normally positive attitudes make a comeback, although they rarely regain the heights they reached during the latter stages of teacher training.

Nevertheless, it is the beginner's unrealistic expectations that are a great source of his or her problems. And although there are many problems, as we said, we are going to look at just three areas: discipline, social distance, and sex.

Discipline Classroom control, classroom management, or discipline (pick your euphemism) is one of those problems that shouldn't exist. After all, school is an opportunity for children. The teacher works hard to help them. It's simple: the teacher is there to teach, and students are there to learn. Unfortunately, though, things do not work out that way.

The great majority of schools—whether kindergartens or high schools— are organized with the expectation that the teacher will be "in charge" of the class. You may not like this, and there are things you can do about it.[4] But it is

Students expect discipline still what is generally expected of a teacher by the children, the administration, and peers. (We will return to this matter of expectations in the section on social distance.) Few (and lucky) are the teachers who do not have to come to grips with their role as disciplinarian.

A discipline problem occurs when the expected pattern of classroom behavior is violated. Normally, a breach of discipline is an overt act by one or more students that distracts attention from or interrupts the performance of the task at hand. Discipline problems are endemic to the first-year teacher. The basic explanation for this phenomenon is simply that first-year teachers have had little

Ingredients for trouble practice in being "in charge." Few college students have had much opportunity to give orders, coordinate the activities of a group of people, or say such things as "Quiet down," or "Stay in your seat!" In particular, many young women are still somewhat unaccustomed to leadership roles (although this has been changing in recent years). Students, on the other hand, are accustomed to being taught by experienced teachers who know how to control them, usually rather effortlessly.

Further, students can sense inexperience and hesitancy in a new teacher. Finally, school is not fun and games for children, and they can get restless and bored. (Remember when you were in elementary and secondary school. Remember how long the school day was, how long you had to sit still at a stretch, and how much you had to do that didn't interest you.) These conditions, plus the potential for friction in any group of so many people, make it almost inevitable that first-year teachers will have some trouble establishing the kind of productive relationship with students that they seek.

As we have implied, many new teachers start out with quite an idealized picture of children. In this view, misbehavior is a result of some condition external to the child, such as a poor home life or poverty. Often, there is the suggestion that something in the teacher's class provokes or brings forth the problem. If only the teacher would "establish the right environment" or "reach out to the child in just the right way," the problem would be solved. This view is a subset of a larger view that people are not capable of evil, that only social arrangements are capable of evil, an idea that had many adherents in education at one time and still has advocates. The idea that children are innately good, plus the first-year teacher's insecurities and search for approval, makes it difficult for many to deal confidently with their role as disciplinarian.

CAROLE GREEN/FOURTH GRADE   "I was convinced that a good class was a happy class and that I wasn't going to be like those grouchy teachers I remember from my own elementary school. So, in the first part of the year I let a lot of small infractions go unnoticed: talking during silent reading period, lateness on assignments, yelling out the window to students on the playground, and the like. It was a little hard on my nerves, but I thought I was establishing an open and creative environment. It soon became clear that it was open, but not particularly creative. In fact, I first discovered reality when a friendly parent suggested that the room was too noisy and disorderly for the children to get their work done. I tried to 'tighten up,' but the students were already used to my

Mistaken assumptions

TEACHERS BLAMED FOR ROWDY STUDENTS

Ann Landers

Dear Ann: I'll bet you are swamped with letters from teachers complaining about uncooperative, destructive, lazy, rotten students. I hope you will print just one letter from a student. Here's mine:

I'm 15, a freshman in high school (male) who usually makes the honor roll. I'm not an angel but I have never used foul language in class, hit a teacher, stolen or destroyed school property, drunk beer, wine or liquor on school premises or come to school stoned. There are plenty more like me.

I can cite two reasons students "act like animals." First, they learn fast if the teacher is afraid of the students. If the teacher is gutless and can't stand up to a loudmouth

or a bully, the kids get the message. A teacher who has lost control of them can't teach. This is very unfair to those of us who are in school to learn.

The second reason for poor behavior is boredom. Some teachers are incompetent and lazy, plus they really don't like kids very much. Their classes are dull as dishwater—so the bored ones make trouble just to create excitement.

I have had some terrific teachers in my life, and I will never forget them. Most kids want to learn. I say give us more gutsy and competent teachers and there will be a lot less violence and goofing off in the classroom.—THE OTHER SIDE

Dear O.S.: Amen. You wrapped it up beautifully.

From *The Columbus Dispatch.* By Ann Landers, Los Angeles Times Syndicate. Used by permission of Ann Landers.

'open and creative' environment. I just couldn't get them to settle down. Finally, the straw that broke the camel's back—and almost mine—was when the principal came in to observe. The kids behaved horribly. I felt as if they were trying to make me look bad. Whatever their intentions, the situation was not lost on the principal. During the follow-up conference, he was very frank with me, telling me that if I couldn't maintain better discipline, he might have to 'relieve me.' One thing I particularly remember him saying was 'Carole, if you can't *keep* school, you can't *teach* school.' Then he gave me some very specific suggestions. Even with those good suggestions, though, I had a very difficult time working my way back in charge and establishing a more civil and orderly classroom.''

Social Distance   Establishing an appropriate social distance from students occupies a good deal of a beginning teacher's attention and energy. Like disciplinary techniques, a correct social distance does not come with a teaching certificate or one's first job. Beginning teachers frequently take refuge in the two extremes of behavior. Many hide their insecurities by acting strict and businesslike, sometimes bordering on being hostile. Others attempt to be completely "natural." They reject the stiff "teacherish" image and seek to break down all barriers between themselves and their students. The first extreme, the overly strict teacher, can give rise to long-term difficulties, whereas the "natural" teacher usually has short-term problems.

Overly strict behavior   The problem with playing the role of the overly strict, aloof teacher is that it may become a permanent habit. Acting like a Prussian officer may appeal to a hidden need to make others submissive. Also, one may begin to believe that "a quiet class is a good class."

Overly "natural" behavior   The problem confronting overly "natural" teachers is that their view of "natural behavior" is frequently not the same as the children's. The students expect their teacher to interact with them in certain recognizable ways—that is, they expect a certain degree of social distance. They are confused or put off when the teacher acts like "one of the gang." The crux of the problem, then, is that the beginning teacher often wants to be a friend or a pal, whereas the students expect and want the teacher to be an adult. Students, because they are uncertain and striving to be adults themselves, seek to find strength and maturity in their teachers. Often they interpret the beginning teacher's efforts at naturalness and informality as weakness.

JUDITH PLAYER/SEVENTH GRADE   "Most of my year was spent alternating between being Wanda the Witch and sweet little Miss Muffet. I started out determined to be different from all those cold teachers I had had. I was going to be everyone's sweet Big Sister. I really was surprised when this didn't work. The children didn't respond. If anything, they seemed to be confused. Some of them started treating me like their big sister, and I found myself getting annoyed. They became very familiar and started asking me all sorts of embarrassing questions—both in and out of class. The final straw came when one of

To the new teacher, students are frequently a source of both unexpected frustrations and surprising satisfactions.

(*Robert Kalman/The Image Works*)

my boys—one of my favorites, too—came up to me in the hall while I was talking to a senior teacher. Smiling, he patted me on the back and said, 'How's it goin', Miss Player?' I was mortified.

"After that little incident, I became tough. I was all business. If anyone got close to being familiar, I cut them off at the knees. I really said some nasty things. I was just so uptight that I overreacted. I guess I was hurt that my Big Sister routine didn't work. Later I realized that one reason behind my wanting to be Big Sister was simply that I wanted to be loved . . . at any cost. I guess my insecurities led me to seek love from my students. Anyway, I spent most of the year going back and forth on this issue. One week Wanda and the next Miss Muffet. It was really a strain, for me and the kids. Finally, toward the end of the year things began to straighten out and I stopped playing a role. It was much more fun that way. I think everyone was relieved."

First-year insecurities

Sex Sex is one of the great unacknowledged issues in the American school. Sexual attraction and romance between students, and even, believe it or not, between teachers, is recognized. But the idea that there might be sexual attraction or romance between a teacher and a student is taboo. It simply is not talked about. This doesn't mean it doesn't exist. Beginning teachers are more likely than others to be faced with this problem. For one thing, they are nearer in age to the students. Another factor that makes beginning teachers more vulnerable than experienced teachers is that they are often single, new to the community, and lonely. The strain of the new job may increase their need for affection, and this need may find expression in their relationships with students. In the same way, students often become attracted to their teachers. They sometimes get what is best described as a "crush" on their teachers, becoming emotionally attached to them, greeting them in the morning and walking them to their cars after school. This, too, can be a very awkward situation, in that the student wants to be treated as special and to feel that the affection is reciprocated. If the teacher rejects or embarrasses the student, the student can be hurt deeply.

Besides the platonic attachments teachers can have to young children, it is quite conceivable that a twenty-two-year-old teacher will find a sixteen-year-old student sexually attractive. Thus, as the following account indicates, high school teachers are particularly vulnerable to sexual attraction or manipulation. Our only advice in this area is *don't*.

GARY CORNOG/ENGLISH "In one class there dwelt a fair young creature who found me to be an easily flustered appreciator of her many charms. She was a coquette and, to my way of thinking, a dangerous one. She had me at a great disadvantage. While she could liltingly ask special favors of me (such as my continued toleration of her misbehavior in class), I could not cope with her in anything like a spontaneous way. Unless I was in a phenomenally commanding mood, I could expect to hear such daily entreaties as 'Oh, Mr. Cornog! Mr. Cornog! Could you come here and help me?' 'Mr. Cornog, I just don't understand!' (All this spoken in a voice of tender urgency.) She would have her left arm raised, her right arm aiding it, and would be leaning forward and upward from her desk so that (I thought) I would not fail to notice her finer endowments (I didn't).

"'What is it, Julie?' I would reply, hoping the fear in my heart would not be evident in my voice. It nearly always was.

"'Mr. Cornog, there's something here I don't understand. Could you come here and look at it?'

"*Don't,* I tell myself. *Don't.*

"'Read it to me and I'll explain it.' (*From here,* I almost added, but that would be too obvious.) No. She's getting up.

"'I'll bring it up there.'

"She approaches. She arrives at my left side. I note a scent of lemony perfume; an attempt at make-up about the eyes. She leans over to place the book in front of me, and some of her long dark hair grazes my shoulder. By this time I feel thoroughly unwilling to answer any question regarding syntax. *What about private tutoring?* I hear my lecherous innards suggesting. Heaven

Flirtation

forbid! My frustration causes me to blurt a response to her query, hoping that she'll return to her seat. The class by this time has observed me melting into a limpid pool behind the desk. She must be smiling triumphantly above me, her glory reflected in my devastation. If only she had been as innocent of malice in her manipulations as I had been tender in my innocence, then all would have been well. Alas, she was not. She thought it great sport to exercise her arts for the benefit of her friends, and I could think of no way to break the spell. I could not ignore her, because then the class would notice my attempt and think that she had really gotten to me. I could not allow her to continue to dominate me, for then the respect I sought would never appear. Who could respect a hen-pecked English teacher? The befuddled teacher doing battle with the temptress every day—what a tableau! What a cliché. It pained me to see myself in such a humiliating posture. It was so absurd."[5]

Some first-year teachers become terribly discouraged by their relationships with students. Most of us teach because we like young people and want to work with them. When we are rejected or make fools of ourselves, it is painful. Most problems with students are a result of inexperience, and the majority of second-year teachers find that most of their previous problems disappear and they feel very much at ease with their students. Developing satisfying relations with students usually involves some initial uncertainty. However, previous experience with children as a camp counselor, settlement house worker, or tutor can ease the transition. Contacts with children and adolescents before beginning teaching help you learn about how you relate best to children.

Previous experience as authority figure helps

PARENTS: NATURAL ALLIES WITH DIFFERENT AGENDAS

The parent and the teacher are natural allies. Both are concerned about the child. They are both working to help the child become a more fully developed person, and both want the child to be happy, sensitive, intelligent, and well balanced. Frequently, though, the relationship between teacher and parent runs amok and natural allies become antagonists. Instead of devoting their energies toward understanding and aiding the child, they waste them on conflict with one another.

For most prospective teachers, the parents of future students seem very remote. They do not seem particularly important in the light of all the more obvious issues and sources of difficulty. If you try to picture them, what probably comes to mind is a huge, undifferentiated mass of faces. Once you begin to teach, however, certain personalities and types come quite vividly to life. In an effort to speed the process of differentiation, we offer the following capsule portraits of some of the more troublesome types.

Some common types

Mrs. Mysonthegenius: She has a nice boy. He seems to have average intelligence and he's rather nervous. After meeting her, you know why. If he doesn't make it to Harvard, she will be shattered. When she is not busy telling

him to work harder, she is trying to convince you how lucky you are to have a future Supreme Court justice in your class.

Mrs. Putdown: The first thing she tells you is that she was once a teacher. She then finds innumerable opportunities to indicate how much she knows and how good she was . . . and still is. She questions you about your "rationale" for teaching this content or using that procedure. When you answer her, she informs you that she prefers the old ways, the tried and true ways. She has dozens of ways of reminding you that this is only your first year of teaching. You wish she would go back to teaching.

Mrs. Latecomer: Her daughter has really been a problem. The girl is obviously unhappy and seems to have made little progress all year. You have looked for the mother at PTA meetings and open house nights, but she has never shown up. You have written notes home, but they haven't been answered. You have called to make appointments, but she has missed them, having forgotten that she had to go to her garden club those days. You send home a failing report card. She complains to the principal that you don't like her daughter.

Mr. Heavyhands: You are at your wits' end with one student and you need help from his parents. He's picked three fights this week and his work is dropping off badly. Other teachers have been complaining about him. You call his father, who roars that he will be right over to school. He arrives breathing fire. You explain your concern, and he keeps socking his fist into the palm of his hand and describing what will happen when he gets his hands on "that bum!" He is embarrassed and hurt by his son's behavior and he has a very old and simple solution. You are sorry you called him.

Mrs. Youthinkyouvegotproblems: She attends all the school functions. However, she never wants to talk about her daughter. She wants to share her own trials and tribulations with you. She heard you took a psychology course and has chosen you as her therapist. She goes on and on and on about things that have no connection to her daughter, to the school, to you, or anything you know anything about. You get a tight feeling in the pit of your stomach.

Mrs. Specialhelp: Her son is doing very well in your class. She doesn't think so. He is always happy and carefree. She reports that he feels schoolwork is no challenge. She is convinced that he needs special attention. How about after-school tutoring? Maybe Saturday morning? All his other teachers gave him special attention. Aren't you "dedicated"?

Hidden dynamics

The sources of teacher-parent problems are the same as those involved in any human relationship, but encounters are more highly charged than in most relationships. This is to be expected because a child and his or her future are at issue. The following account of Brenda's mother and a new teacher illustrates some of the dynamics that are usually hidden from view.

RUTH BILLSBURY/SIXTH GRADE "It happened in late March. Ten days earlier Brenda's mother called me. She said she wanted to talk to me and asked if there was any day that I stayed late at school. She didn't get off work until 4:30 and couldn't make it to school until 5:15. I often worked late at school, and so I made an appointment for ten days later.

"I was curious about why she wanted to see me and I began to worry. Brenda had something of a reputation in the school. In September during the teachers' workshop before the opening day, two teachers 'sympathized' with me when they heard I had Brenda Carson. They didn't go into great detail why, and I didn't want to ask. However, I was watching Brenda out of the corner of my eye during those first months, and I guess I paid particular attention to her. However, in recent months I hadn't thought much about her. Until her mother called.

"Brenda's mother showed up right on time, and after a few pleasantries she said, 'Well, I know you're busy, so I'll come right to the point. Three weeks after Brenda started kindergarten, Brenda's father and I separated. After a terrible on-again, off-again year, we decided to get a divorce. It was hard on both of us, but it was crushing for Brenda. She's an only child. Maybe she

Effects of divorce blamed herself for the breakup. I don't know. In any event she went into a kind of tailspin. She was trouble at home and she's been a trouble in school almost from the moment of the breakup. She's no genius, but she's bright enough to do better than she's done. She just dug in her little heels and wouldn't try. She wouldn't bring books home. She wouldn't do assignments. Every time I asked her about school, her standard answer was "I hate school." Once I got working and my life started to settle down, we were able to make a life together. But the school situation was still rotten. None of the other girls played with her. She was never invited to any parties. I even suggested that she invite one of her classmates to stay overnight one Friday night and the kid refused. We were both heartbroken.

" 'Then you came along. I don't know what you did to her, but you certainly have turned her around. I sensed it the first day of school. She came home with a funny look in her eye and said, "This year is going to be different. I can just tell." She wouldn't say why, but after a few days I guessed. She was continually talking about you. From what you said to her to what kind of a car you drive. Honestly, one weekend when we were out grocery shopping she made me drive by your apartment, she was so curious to find out what it looked like.

"'And, I guess you know how she's doing in school. I don't think she's missed her homework once. I'm sure she's not your best student, but I know she's doing pretty well, particularly considering the hole she was digging for herself. You look surprised at all this. I figured you might be. Brenda can really keep her feelings to herself when she wants to. But honestly, you have touched that girl in a special place. The difference in her is like night and day. You can't imagine what all this has meant to me. Her pain was my pain and now it's gone away. Brenda even has friends now.

"'Anyway, I just wanted you to know. I just wanted to see you and to thank you.'

"Brenda's mother was out the door before I could respond. It was so unexpected, I don't know what I could have said anyway. That one event has given me a great, great deal to think about."

A parent and a teacher are quite likely to perceive the same phenomenon in very different ways. The nerve-frazzled teacher perceives a child as a wild, undisciplined, raucous menace. The parents perceive their child as energetic, spontaneous, and sociable. Differences in perception are enhanced by the different circumstances under which parents and teachers see the child. An apparently quiet, shy child may turn out to be a chatterbox in the security of home.

Evaluation is another area of difficulty. It is part of the teacher's job to make judgments about a child's performance, a process that can touch on some deep insecurities. It can wound the parents' hopes and aspirations. That this is the Age of Anxiety becomes very apparent to the teacher in his or her contacts with those parents who look to the school as the royal road to success for their children. In our competitive society, being average is taken by some as failure. If a child is average, something must be wrong with the child. Or with you, her teacher. "How can she get over being 'average'?" The thought that their child could be *below* average is more than some parents can bear. For these reasons, the teacher needs to be especially sensitive when dealing with issues of evaluation, and would do well to stay away from what are, after all, meaningless terms like *above average* or *below average*.

Social distance can be a source of difficulty in relations with parents as well as with students. Issues of social distance have been at the nub of much parent-teacher antagonism in recent years. Since most teachers are middle class or aspiring to the middle class, they normally have little trouble communicating with middle-class people. But when they deal with parents from a lower or higher socioeconomic class or a different ethnic group, or both, the potential for communication difficulties is heightened. Upper-class parents can look down on public schools and treat teachers condescendingly. Poor parents often have had unfortunate and unpleasant experiences with schools and, as a result, regard them with suspicion. Often these parents speak a different language or dialect than the teacher. They are put off by educational jargon. What the teacher sees as a humble classroom is to them part of a huge impersonal bureaucracy. In many urban areas this impression of the school as a cold, unfriendly, and impersonal institution is supported by the evidence: The school doors are locked, and parents have to pass by police officers and assorted hall guards before they are given a pass to see the head secretary in order to see the teacher. That many lower-class parents have, as children, encountered prejudice in schools and found attendance at school more discouraging than helpful makes communication even more difficult. Since they have neither wealth nor connections, these same parents are

An Instructor's Guide to Murphy's Law

Murphy's law says, "If anything can go wrong, it will." There are many corollaries and related regularities. Among them:

1. Good students move away.
2. New students come from schools that do not teach anything.
3. The teachers' lounge will be in the worst room of the school. It will contain dusty furniture and one noisy mimeograph machine.
4. The shorter the working time, the more the mimeograph will malfunction.
5. The clock in the instructor's room will be wrong.
6. The school board will make a better pay offer *before* the teachers union negotiates.
7. When the instructor is late, he will meet the principal in the hall. If the instructor is late and does not meet the principal, the instructor is late to the faculty meeting.
8. Children who touch the instructor will have scabies or bubonic plague.
9. When speaking to the school psychologist, the teacher will say "weirdo" rather than "emotionally disturbed."
10. Disaster will occur when visitors are in the room.
11. The time a teacher takes in explaining is inversely proportional to the information retained by students.

12. Students who are blind, deaf, and/or behavioral problems will sit at the back of the room.
13. Extra-duty nights will occur when the best shows are on TV.
14. The problem child will be a school board member's son.
15. The instructor's study hall will be the largest in several years. The administration will view the study hall as the teacher's preparation time.
16. Students who are doing better are credited with working harder. If children start to do poorly, the teacher will be blamed.
17. Extracurricular duties will take more preparation time than classes.
18. Clocks will run more quickly during free time. (This is also known as the Law of Varying Time.)
19. A meeting's length will be directly proportional to the boredom the speaker produces.
20. On a test day, at least 15% of the class will be absent.
21. If the instructor teaches art, the principal will be an ex-coach and will dislike art. If the instructor is a coach, the principal will be an ex-coach who took a winning team to the state finals.
22. A subject interesting to the teacher will bore students.
23. Murphy's Law will go into effect at the beginning of an evaluation.

Duncan Long, "An Instructor's Guide to Murphy's Law," *Phi Delta Kappan* (January 1980): vol. 61. n. 5: 336. Reprinted by permission.

forced to rely heavily on the schools to provide their children with a way out of the deprivation and futility that characterize so much of their own lives.

Mothers in work force

Another factor is the changing American family. Increasingly mothers—who in an earlier era stayed home, kept house, and guided their children through school—are in the work force. Currently, the great majority of women with school-age children work outside the home. The Labor Department projects that by the year 2005, 80 percent of married women with children will be in the work force. Many mothers, too, are single parents bearing their economic and parenting responsibilities alone. It is very difficult, usually, for working mothers to get off work to meet with their children's teachers; many do not have the free time or the energy to attend PTA meetings and after-school functions that would put them in closer contact with teachers. Often, a meeting with a teacher is an unwelcome chore in an already burdened life.

Students' independence from parents

Finally, going to school changes children. School exists to help children change in specified ways: to read, to speak a foreign language, to solve problems. And students do change. They master things. They acquire confidence. And they become increasingly independent of their parents. Some parents rejoice at the child's growing freedom from them. For others, this process of independence is painful. Hearing her little girl talk about how much she loves her teacher may arouse jealousy in a mother and cause her to act hostile when she meets the teacher. When a high school student comes home from school with political or social or religious views that conflict with those of his parents, it can cause resentment and confusion. Thus it is not uncommon for a parent to approach a conference with the teacher with a sincere mixture of appreciation and hostility.

The great majority of parent-teacher conferences are cordial, constructive, and characterized by mutual respect. Although there may be initial problems of perception or communication, the parents' and teacher's shared interest in the child is enough to overcome these minor blocks. However, problems do develop—and they are not always the fault of the parents.

JUSTIN THOMAS/HISTORY "In the late winter we had our annual parents' night. It was a big public relations show, timed about three weeks before the bond issue was to be voted on. All the teachers were to work with students on displays and projects. And, of course, we had to get lots of student work up on the board. The drab old school building looked like the Rose Bowl Parade by the big night. We met the parents in our rooms and gave them an overview of what we were doing for the year. I thought I would be nervous, but somehow I wasn't. I was so distracted and fascinated by their faces. I never suspected that they would look so much like their kids! Or vice versa. And the way some features from one parent and some from the other found their way into their child's face was so absorbing! In the midst of my opening soliloquy in bounced the principal with his flash camera to take a picture of all the fancy decorating I had done. Well, he just looked around the room, decided to save a flash bulb, and headed for the door. My classroom had all the carnival atmosphere of a men's locker room. (We 'chatted' about this a few days later.)

"When I finished my talk, I handed out folders of the children's work and told the parents I would be happy to talk with them individually. Most of my students had been doing fairly well, so most of the evening went well. The parents of my two prize ding-a-lings didn't show, an event I greeted with mixed emotions. Although I had been quite apprehensive about talking to these strangers, things were going well. I had been trying to be as direct and honest as possible. Looking back on it, I think I was especially intent on being honest because I felt the whole showboat atmosphere and intention of the parents' night was dishonest. My overreaction got me in trouble, though. One set of parents hung back. I hadn't met them yet, but I knew immediately who they were. They were Ted Sharp's parents. He, poor kid, had gotten the worst features of both parents. Ted is a great big happy kid. He is not bright and he is

Overreacting

KEVIN AND JIM'S TEN RULES FOR SURVIVING THE FIRST YEAR OF TEACHING*

1. *Find a mentor.* Find an experienced, skillful teacher in your building who can act as a friendly advisor and coach for you.
2. *Don't look for love in the classroom.* Maybe respect, but not love.
3. *Deal with your authority problems before entering the classroom.* Come to terms with the fact that you will be responsible for maintaining an orderly and civil environment, and think about how you will accomplish this feat.
4. *Get plenty of rest and recreation.* The first year of teaching can be tiring and stressful. Therefore it is important that you not ignore those activities that will replenish your emotional and physical energy.
5. *If you are not organized, get organized.* Coping with the planbooks, student papers, office memos, attendance records, grades and report cards, and on and on requires much more organization than many beginners are used to or have practiced.
6. *When in doubt, think.* Instead of simply fretting about problems or panicking, use your best tool: your mind. Problem-solve. Try to identify the problem, possible solutions, what seems best, and then act and judge whether or not that option helped the situation.

7. *Love thy school secretary and custodians.* Many beginners fail to realize how important the school secretary and custodians are in enabling teachers to do an effective job, and how important they are in the "informal communication network" of the school.
8. *Focus on learning.* Many beginners fail to concentrate on making sure their students really learn something and thus have feelings of accomplishment. Students will put up with a great deal of "beginning teacheritis" if they sense that they are learning.
9. *Decide to teach a second year before the beginning of your first year.* Although many beginners have satisfying first years, many also have trying years and have to learn a great deal the hard way. Most people agree that the first year is not a good basis on which to make a career choice.
10. *Don't—we repeat—don't get married two weeks before the start of your first teaching job.* For reasons unknown to the authors, each year thousands of new college graduates decide to jump *at the same time* into two of life's most difficult undertakings: beginning a career and starting what they hope will be a lifelong relationship.

*The authors promise that if you follow these ten rules faithfully and carefully, you will survive the first year of teaching. You may even like it! On the other hand, if you do not survive the year, return the unused portion of the book to your instructor for a refund.

quite lazy. All he likes to do is play his guitar, which he is pretty good with. The only time I have gotten any work from him was during a unit on the Civil War. I got him to look up the folk songs and marching chants of the Civil War. He gave a 'singing and strumming' report to the class. But, after that . . . nothing! I'm an easy grader and he was carrying about a C– at that time. Well, the Sharps asked a lot of questions and I stayed with my straight-facts approach and avoided generalizations. Then Mr. Sharp glanced anxiously at his wife, looked over his shoulder to see that none of the other parents was within earshot, and said, 'Tell me, Mr. Thomas. We're both college men. My son, Ted. Is he . . . you know . . . college material?'

"I didn't know what to say, so I said, 'What do you mean?'

" 'We just want to know if we should be saving to send him to college. Does he have it for college?'

"All I thought of was that here was a guy who really wanted a straight answer, so I said, 'No.' Then I looked at Mrs. Sharp. I should have looked at her before answering. After the tears came the hostility. 'How dare you prejudge my boy! Admit it, you don't like Teddy. You are trying to ruin his chances. We work hard to raise our only son and then some young know-it-all teacher ruins everything!' Underneath the hysteria, which subsided in about

Making quick judgments

five long minutes, she was right. I had no right to make that judgment. Also, I didn't have enough data. Well, I made another appointment with them. During this I saw that frightening intensity behind their desire to get my class's number-one guitar player into college. Some good things came out of this conference, though. Ted's work picked up. I learned a good lesson, too. Somewhere T. S. Eliot says that human nature can stand just so much reality. I believe him."

A FINAL WORD

Most new teachers are very proud of themselves at the end of their first year. They have learned an enormous amount in nine or ten months. This sense of personal growth has been captured well by one young teacher we know. She had an extremely difficult first year but went on to become an outstanding teacher. A week or so after the end of her initial year of teaching, she made the following statement:

> I could see myself as a teacher now. Before I was somebody pretending to be a teacher. I just couldn't believe that I was responsible for these children. I now realize that we can spend a whole period talking and things don't have to be so organized all the time. I now realize that I have the power to call a parent or send a note home or tell a child to stay in from recess. Now I know I should do what's best for me and not be afraid or fearful. I've liked giving of myself—it's something I've needed to do. I've learned to be more mature. I think I'm becoming
>
> *Achieving confidence*
>
> grown up. The kids have helped me. At first I was trying to be what everyone at the school wanted me to be. Now I know that to make it as a teacher I need to be myself and accept myself for what I am. It took a whole year but now I am confident and relaxed. I am strong and tough when I need to be. I think I've made it.[6]

Along with the trials captured so well in "An Instructor's Guide to Murphy's Law," teaching has its pleasures and bright moments, too, often making it a rewarding and fulfilling occupation. English novelist Joyce Carey has written that human joy comes not from the great events but from the little everyday things, like a good cup of tea. Much joy can be found in the events it is easy for us to overlook. The joys and satisfactions of teaching can lie in everyday happenings and small surprises. As a teacher you may find joy in:

- experiencing those electric moments when you can *feel* the children thinking and *see* them making new connections
- watching two lonely kids whom you brought together walking down the hall together, now friends
- getting your planbook back from the supervisor with the comment "These appear to be excellent lessons"
- finding, in your box on a rainy Friday afternoon, a note written in a childish scrawl, "You are my most favorite teacher. Guess who?"

Dear Mrs. Shulman,

Hooray! It's the last day of school. You are as happy as we are, we bet. Being a teacher, you can't say so, can you??

You probably hate us all. We were a bunch of rats a lot of this year. If you never teach again, we'll understand. We were not very nice. We would feal real bad if you decide that. You are the nicest teacher we ever had. You really tried and were always fair. Even when we weren't. Specially, the boys. We did lots of interesting things in class this year but the most interesting thing was you. Nice and interesting.

We will all miss you. Have a nice summer. You deserve it. Keep teaching.

The Room 208 Gang

- shopping downtown and meeting one of your students, who proudly introduces you to her mother as "my teacher," and being able to tell by the way the mother responds that you are respected in their household
- having a former student call to tell you that he has a problem and needs to get your advice
- turning in a plan for a new curriculum that you and five other teachers labored over and knowing that you did a good job and that it will make a major improvement
- chaperoning a dance and having your most hostile student smilingly introduce his girl to you
- hearing in the teachers' lunchroom that your supervisor called you "a real professional"
- dragging yourself back to school at the end of Christmas vacation and being greeted enthusiastically by your students as you enter your classroom
- agonizing in advance over a conference with your most troublesome child's parents, only to have them back you up all the way
- being observed by the principal and having your students make you look terrific
- seeing the look of pride in a child's eyes as she brings her artwork for you to see
- feeling the excitement as you move toward your classroom with what you know is going to be a knockout lesson
- surviving until June, being bone tired but proud of what you and your kids have been able to do
- cleaning out your desk on the last day of school after the kids have been dismissed and finding a box of candy with a card signed by the whole class
- realizing—be it daily, weekly, or monthly—that what you are doing with your life *really does make a difference*

Discussion Questions

1. Think of an occasion when you have experienced "culture shock"—when traveling abroad or in another part of this country, in an unfamiliar social milieu, or perhaps, on first entering college. Try to remember in as much detail as possible how it made you feel. Did you eventually overcome it? How? Can you trace the progression of your feelings and behavior from the first encounter to the final adjustment? What, if anything, does this suggest to you about ways to minimize the possible effects of culture shock when you begin teaching?

2. Can you remember or imagine any common types of teachers, like Mrs. Coaster or The Big Planner, whom we have not included in our descriptions? Try writing a short description of one or two.

3. How do you explain the different attitudes toward students of prospective and first-year teachers?

4. Where do you stand on the issues of discipline and social distance? Do you believe the school should be concerned with discipline? What is your concept of an effective degree and method of discipline? How much social distance do you feel is appropriate for you? Is there anything about these topics that frightens you? What can you do to prepare yourself?

5. In your school experience did it seem that the administrators were a help or a hindrance to new teachers?

6. What do you believe is the primary reason many beginning teachers have rocky relationships with students' parents?

7. If you were to begin teaching tomorrow and were free to evaluate your students in any way you chose, or not to evaluate at all, what would you do? Be prepared to defend your position.

8. What do you expect to be the major problems you will encounter as a beginning teacher? What can you do now to begin solving them? What can you do after you begin teaching? What do you envision as the joys and satisfactions of a career in teaching?

For Further Reading   Bullough, Robert V. *First-Year Teacher.* New York: Teachers College Press, 1989.

    An in-depth case study of the first year- and-a-half of a seventh-grade teacher's experience. The problems encountered by Kerrie are typical of those encountered by all new teachers.

Greenstein, Jack. *What the Children Have Taught Me.* Chicago: University of Chicago Press, 1983.

    An autobiographical reminiscence of a former teacher and principal. Jack Greenstein's reflections on his years as an educator working with the urban poor is both moving and insightful. It is also filled with good advice.

Howey, Kenneth R., and Richard H. Bents (Eds.). *Toward Meeting the Needs of the Beginning Teachers.* Minneapolis: Midwest Teachers Corps Network, 1979.

    An incisive book of essays that summarizes what is known about the induction into teaching. The authors look at the issues from the vantage point of the teacher, the administrator, and several others.

Keizer, Garret. *No Place but Here: A Teacher's Vocation in a Rural Community.* New York: Penguin Books, 1988.

    An autobiographical account of a teacher's first year as a high school teacher. The story is funny, rich in detail, and filled with wisdom.

Kohl, Herbert. *Growing Minds: On Becoming a Teacher.* New York: Harper and Row, 1984.

    Herbert Kohl is one of the most prolific and sensible modern writers in education. This book is filled with practical suggestions and provocative ideas for the beginning teacher.

Ryan, Kevin (Ed.). *The Roller Coaster Year: The Stories of First Year Teachers.* New York: HarperCollins, 1991.

> This collection of twelve accounts of beginning teachers gives an honest account of the events and feelings that fill the lives of people as they begin their new careers. The twelve teach at a variety of levels and subjects and in a variety of settings.

Notes

1. Garret Keiser, *No Sense of Place* (New York: Penguin, 1988), p. 1.
2. Estelle Fuchs, *Teachers Talk: Views from Inside City Schools* (Garden City, N.Y.: Doubleday, 1969), p. 21.
3. T. M. Wildman and J. A. Niles, "Reflective Teachers: Tensions Between Abstractions and Realities," *Journal of Teacher Education* 38, no. 10 (1987): 25–31.
4. Carl Rinne, *Fundamentals of Classroom Control* (Columbus, Ohio: Merrill, 1984).
5. Kevin Ryan (Ed.), *Don't Smile Until Christmas: Accounts of the First Year of Teaching* (Chicago: University of Chicago Press, 1970), pp. 18–19. Copyright © 1970. Reprinted by permission.
6. Kevin Ryan et al., *Biting the Apple: Accounts of First Year Teachers* (New York: Longman, 1980).

What Makes a Teacher Effective?

CHAPTER PREVIEW

This chapter explores what we believe to be the essential attributes that distinguish teachers from other educated people. More specifically, the chapter examines what knowledge, skills, and attitudes are demonstrated by the effective teacher. Effective teaching is much more than an intuitive process. A teacher must continually make decisions and act on those decisions. To do this effectively, the teacher must have both theoretical knowledge about learning and human behavior and knowledge about the subject matter to be taught. A teacher also must demonstrate a repertoire of teaching skills that are believed to facilitate student learning and must display attitudes that foster learning and genuine human relationships.

This chapter emphasizes that:

● Teachers are required to make many decisions, both preactive and interactive, as they make plans for instruction, implement teaching strategies, and evaluate outcomes of their planning and strategy.

● Four major types of teacher attitudes affect teaching behavior: (1) attitude toward self; (2) attitude toward children; (3) attitude toward peers and parents; and (4) attitude toward the subject matter.

● A teacher should have an intimate knowledge of the subject matter being taught, both the instructional content and the discipline from which it derives.

● To be able to recognize and interpret classroom events appropriately, a teacher should be familiar with theoretical knowledge and research about learning and human behavior.

● Effective teachers demonstrate a repertoire of teaching skills that enable them to meet the different needs of their students.

● Research has identified a number of these skills in, to name a few areas, classroom management, effective questioning, and planning techniques.

Before we get to the main issues of this chapter, we would like you to consider the case of Carol Landis. Carol is beginning her first year of teaching. She prepared to be a high school social studies teacher, graduated, and accepted a job in her own community, a small city in the Northwest. The school is lower middle class. The bulk of the children come from solidly blue-collar, working-class backgrounds.

Carol has been assigned three periods of world geography and two periods of American history. We'll join her in thought as she prepares the first lesson of a new unit in world geography.

Carol plans to require her ninth-graders to work in groups to prepare panel discussions about a country of their choice. Since she believes that students should see relationships among the geography, political history, and culture of a country, she wants her working groups to research these relationships and share what they find in panel discussions with the rest of the class. When Carol started planning this class during the summer, she also set these goals for her students: that they could work together in groups and that they could make effective oral presentations of their research. This assignment is designed to help her students accomplish those goals.

But now that Carol is planning how to present the assignment to her classes so they will meet the specific objectives of researching their countries and presenting informative and interesting panel discussions, she has many

questions. Do these students know how to use the library? If not, will she need to provide directions for using reference materials? Maybe the librarian has already done this, and they'll just need a review. Do these students know what *culture* means or understand general concepts that will help them look for relationships among culture, history, and geography? What background do they need before they start researching a specific country? And do these students know how to work in groups? Have they ever participated in a panel discussion? In planning how to help her students complete this assignment, Carol bases her decisions on what she thinks she knows about them as learners.

Although Carol has already planned this assignment to fit into the social studies curriculum, she is concerned about whether the books she has in her room and the library will provide the information her students need. What other resources are available? She knows that other teachers have back issues of *National Geographic,* for example. Maybe she could make those available to her students. If information is too limited, she may have to guide students as they choose a country to research.

Carol also considered having each student submit a written report; she believes her students should learn to communicate in writing, too. But for this first research assignment, she decides that an oral presentation by the group is appropriate. Later, she'll work with the classes on report writing. In the beginning, she wants her students to enjoy her classes, to feel a part of a group, and to get to know each other. She hopes this assignment will accomplish that. And Carol prefers listening to her students to grading written reports anyway, so this assignment fits her style of teaching.

After the first day of library research, Carol reflects on her second-period class and wonders what went wrong. One group argued the whole period and never did select a country. Maybe she should have assigned groups and not let students choose their own partners? She tried to ignore the group, believing they should work out their own differences and come to a group decision. But what if they never work together? She noticed that another group was completely dominated by one of the top students. He decided what country they would research, he assigned the topics, and he told them where to look to get information. When Carol urged the other members to share equally in the group decisions, they asserted, "Tom always gets A's. We don't mind if he tells us what to do." Carol didn't know what to say; she didn't know how to respond to their concern for grades without insulting Tom. So she said nothing.

Incident with Tom

Later in the period, Tom asked her what religion predominated in Indonesia. Carol wasn't sure but was afraid to admit her lack of information, so she told him, "Just look it up." Tom responded, "So you don't know either?" At the time Carol exploded and informed Tom that she was not his personal encyclopedia, that if he was so smart, he shouldn't have to ask. Now she wonders if she overreacted. Maybe she should have admitted she didn't know; was Tom challenging her authority when he responded, or was he just reacting to the sharp tone in her order to look it up? Did she succeed in turning Tom and his group against her?

Carol's frustrations

Carol also wonders whether the other groups worked productively. She spent so much time watching the arguing group and Tom's group that she didn't even have time to notice whether all the chatter from the other groups was work or play. Maybe it didn't hurt to let the other groups have some fun today, anyway. She could always direct her attention to them tomorrow. There was so much to watch and monitor when students worked in groups. And so many questions: "Where do I find this?" "Mr. Shaw won't lend me his magazines; he says he doesn't trust me. What do I do now?" "This library stinks. Why do we have to do this assignment anyway?" "Miss Landis, what did you do this weekend?" Carol wonders if she will ever learn to field all her students' questions and comments and discern the words on the surface from the real messages. And what to do about Ron, who started reading a novel about life in Siberian concentration camps? Carol thinks it is the only book she has ever seen him read. But it won't help his group do their panel discussion on Zaire. Maybe this assignment wasn't such a good idea in the first place, Carol thinks. Or maybe she just wasn't up to working with her classes in groups. The stares from the librarian and the study hall teacher certainly indicated that they didn't think she could handle her classes. And Carol hasn't even thought about how she will grade her students' panel discussions. Just thinking about it all exhausts her; how will she ever get through another day with that second-period class?

We present Carol's case to you not to exhaust you or to overwhelm you with the number of decisions that a teacher has to make. But it is true that the teacher's role can be accurately portrayed as one of decision maker. Indeed, skill in decision making has been identified by some educational researchers as the most important teaching skill. Some decisions are made as teachers quietly deliberate curricular and instructional goals; many more must be made almost instantaneously as teachers and students interact. Teachers make *preactive decisions* as they select goals and objectives for their classes and locate the necessary resources and materials. Information about the characteristics of the learners, the curriculum, the teacher's preferences—all inform planning decisions. Teachers also make *interactive decisions* dealing with monitoring students' work, managing the classroom, and responding to students' questions. Carol's story illustrates some typical decisions faced by any teacher. Let's look at some of the particular decisions that Carol made or will make.

Carol as decision maker

Carol wants her students to understand the relationships among geography, history, and culture. What exactly does she want them to know about the relationships? What do her decisions to let students choose their own country, to work in groups, and to report their research orally indicate about Carol's goals for her students' learning?

Carol decides that a panel discussion will provide evidence of her students' learning. But what characteristics of the panel presentation will indicate whether students have learned the intended concepts? Carol's decision to use this method of evaluation reflects her personal preferences, her goals for her students' learning, and also her skills in methods of evaluating students' learning.

Carol's strategies for fostering her students' learning are based on a series of judgments about their ability to do research, to work in groups, and to present panel discussions, as well as on judgments about how long they will need to work together and what resources they will require. From several teaching techniques, Carol chooses independent group work. As she implements the planned assignment, she is faced with decisions about what help she will provide to groups that don't work well together or to individuals who don't work with their group.

As Carol teaches this lesson or series of lessons, she has to make decisions about when and how to intervene with some of her groups, whether to allow Ron to continue reading a novel, and what response to make to students' questions. After the first day's library work, Carol examines her interactions with the students, facing decisions about what adjustments to make in her strategies for the next day. As the groups continue to search, she will also face decisions about how to evaluate the impact of her planning and instruction on her students' learning.

In each of these planning, implementing, and evaluating stages of instructional decision making, Carol chooses among alternative concepts her students could learn, approaches to help them learn the concepts, ways to manage the classroom to facilitate their learning, and ways to measure their learning. Could her planning, implementing, and evaluating decisions improve with more adequate knowledge, skills, and attitudes?

In this chapter we will explore the areas of competence that help teachers make more effective decisions. We, along with many other educators, believe that to be effective decision makers, elementary and secondary teachers require attitudes, knowledge, and skills unique to the teaching profession. Teachers must ask themselves not only "What am I going to teach?" but also "What should my students be learning?" "How can I help them learn it?" and "Why is it important?" To answer these questions, teachers must be familiar with children and their developmental stages. They must know something about events occurring outside the classroom and about what society needs and requires from the young. They must have enough command of the subject they teach to be able to distinguish what is peripheral from what is central. They must have a philosophy of education that guides them in their role as teacher. They must know something about how human beings learn and about how to create environments that facilitate learning.

Areas of teaching competence

What are the specialized skills and attributes of the effective instructional decision maker? The four areas of competence that we consider essential for a teacher are:

1. attitudes that foster learning and genuine human relationships
2. knowledge in the subject matter to be taught
3. theoretical knowledge about learning and human behavior
4. skills of teaching that facilitate student learning

Teachers draw on their competence in these four areas to inform the many decisions they make as they plan instruction and as they spontaneously interact with the students in their classes. Figure 13.1 indicates the relationship of these areas of competence to the process of instructional decision making. In the rest of this chapter, we'll examine these areas of competence, occasionally referring to the instructional decisions that Carol made and the attitudes, knowledge, and skills influencing her decisions.

WHAT ATTITUDES DOES THE EFFECTIVE TEACHER POSSESS?

Many people believe that the teacher's personality is the most critical factor in successful teaching. If teachers have warmth, empathy, sensitivity, enthusiasm, and humor, they are much more likely to be successful than if they lack these characteristics. In fact, many people argue that without these attributes an individual is unlikely to be a good teacher.

For years, educational researchers sought to isolate the characteristics essential to good teachers. In a comprehensive study, David Ryans concluded that effective teachers are fair, democratic, responsive, understanding, kindly, stimulating, original, alert, attractive, responsible, steady, poised, and confident. Ineffective teachers were described as partial, autocratic, aloof, restricted, harsh, dull, stereotyped, apathetic, unimpressive, evasive, erratic, excitable, and uncertain.[1]

But this information is not very useful. After all, what human interaction wouldn't be improved if the participants possessed only positive traits? Getzels and Jackson, summarizing fifty years of research on teachers' personalities and characteristics, conclude, "Despite the critical importance of the problem and a half-century of prodigious research effort, very little is known for certain about

Figure 13.1 Relationship of Teacher-Competence Areas to Process of Instructional Decision Making

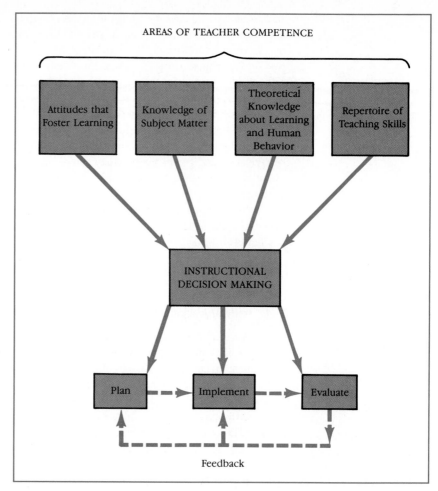

AREAS OF TEACHER COMPETENCE

| Attitudes that Foster Learning | Knowledge of Subject Matter | Theoretical Knowledge about Learning and Human Behavior | Repertoire of Teaching Skills |

INSTRUCTIONAL DECISION MAKING

Plan → Implement → Evaluate

Feedback

Source: From James M. Cooper, "The Teacher as a Decision Maker," in *Classroom Teaching Skills, 4th ed.*, ed. James M. Cooper (Lexington, MA: Heath, 1990), p. 9. Used by permission.

the nature and measurement of teacher personality, about the relation between teacher personality and teaching effectiveness."[2]

Definition of attitudes

A person's *attitudes,* or predispositions to act in a positive or negative way toward persons, ideas, and events, are a fundamental dimension of that person's personality. Almost all educators are convinced of the importance of teacher attitudes in the teaching process. Attitudes have a direct, though frequently unrecognized, effect on our behavior in that they determine the ways we view ourselves and interact with others.

The Teacher's Attitude Toward Self: Self-understanding

We believe that there are four major categories of attitudes that affect teaching behavior: (1) the teacher's attitude toward self, (2) the teacher's attitudes toward children and the relationship between self and children, (3) the teacher's attitudes toward peers and pupils' parents, and (4) the teacher's attitude toward the subject matter.

If teachers are to help students have meaningful experiences, develop their aptitudes and abilities, face their inner difficulties, and accept themselves as people, they need to know and understand those students. But before teachers can do that, they must work at knowing and understanding themselves. Empirical evidence from psychology indicates that people who deny or are unable to cope with their own emotions are unlikely to be capable of respecting and dealing with others' feelings. A person who never admits to feelings of anger and hostility, for example, may overreact to, ignore, or deny the legitimacy of another person's anger, or may consider it "bad" to feel anger. The same is true of fear, feelings of inadequacy, and most other natural human emotions.

Thus if teachers are to understand and sympathize with students who are hostile, they must face hostile tendencies in themselves and recognize the implications of these tendencies for their students and others with whom they deal. Unless teachers recognize their own anxieties, they will be unlikely to understand and empathize with their students' expressions of anxiety. They may not recognize that students' inabilities to learn, inattentiveness, impudence, or irritability may be the result of anxiety. Teachers also need to recognize that their own anxieties may make them irritable, causing the students in turn to feel anxious and to display similar symptoms. As Arthur Jersild has said, "A teacher's understanding of others can be only as deep as the wisdom he possesses when he looks inward upon himself. The more genuinely he seeks to face the problems of his own life, the more he will be able to realize his kinship with others."[3]

The question remains, "How can one achieve understanding of self and, after achieving it, accept it?" Jersild suggests that "to gain knowledge of self, one must have the courage to seek it and the humility to accept what one may find."[4] There are a number of potential sources of increased self-understanding. Jersild suggests that books by sensitive and compassionate people who have made progress in their own struggles to know themselves can be a valuable aid in self-examination. For prospective teachers, such books might include Sylvia Ashton-Warner's *Teacher,* an account of her teaching experience in a Maori infant school in New Zealand, Tracy Kidder's *Among Schoolchildren,* and Herbert Kohl's *36 Children.* Another method Jersild suggests is *participant observation,* the process of observing a class and recording what you hear, see, and feel as you observe. Your record is then compared with the records of other observers. This experience may demonstrate to you that what you notice in any given situation is determined in large part by habits of thought that you take for granted. It may also illustrate that your "objective" perceptions are often projections of your own subjective state, and thus may tell you more about yourself than about the people you have observed.

Self-examination can also grow out of day-to-day relationships with others. The procedures by which you gain self-understanding are less important than the courage and desire to do so. We constantly find ourselves in new situations with new people who challenge us in new ways, and as a result, self-understanding is a continuous process. Because teachers interact with and influence so many young children, they must work particularly hard to understand themselves and their actions in order to understand the children in their charge.

A teacher's positive attitude toward self and students can help create an environment conducive to learning.

(*Bill Paxson/Des Moines Public Schools*)

College and self-examination

Your college years are likely to be a time of protracted self-examination. As you gain new independence from your family, examine values you may have taken for granted, test yourself against rigorous academic standards, encounter new ideas, and live in close quarters with others your own age, you will probably find yourself experiencing new feelings and recognizing unfamiliar things about yourself. College is also likely to offer you more leisure than any future period of your life (believe it or not!) to explore and learn about yourself. Some colleges offer sessions run by trained leaders, as well as personal counseling sessions, to help you face and cope with feelings of limitation, insecurity, inferiority, or confusion, the need to be liked and approved of, lack of direction, and other problems. We urge you to regard self-examination as a serious commitment, and to undertake it, *as a prospective teacher,* in an effort to make a good decision about whether to teach and to become the best teacher you are capable of becoming.

Consider for a moment a need basic to most people—the need to be liked. Teachers, too, especially beginners, need to be liked by their pupils and their peers. Many teachers do not realize how strong their need for approval is; they may approve particular student actions not because the actions are in the students' best interests but for fear that if they disapprove they might lose the students' affection. Unfortunately, teachers rarely recognize their own motivations when such incidents occur. Unless they are aware of the strength of their own need, they will be in no position to examine and judge their actions correctly.

Carol's self-concept

Remember Carol's attitude toward Tom when he asked for information she didn't have. And recall her seeming "live and let live" attitude toward the argumentative group and the student reading a novel. What may these attitudes about student behaviors indicate about Carol's self-concept? Is she afraid to admit limitations in her knowledge? If Carol sets rigid standards for her own performance, how will she react to students' shortcomings? Does she hesitate to discipline off-task behavior because she thinks her students will no longer like her? Maybe Carol overreacts to Tom's request for information because she is insecure with the role of teacher and feels threatened by his authority among his peers. Although Carol's case does not provide enough information to verify these speculations, we can say with confidence that her self-esteem will influence her behavior toward her students. As Carol develops a realistic self-concept—recognizing behavior patterns that may be in conflict with the personable, supportive image she wishes to communicate—she will be on the road to changing her attitudes toward her students and improving her relationship with them.

The Teacher's Attitude Toward Children

Children are sensitive observers of adult behavior, and they frequently recognize, and become preoccupied with, aspects of the teacher's attitude toward them of which the teacher may be unaware. Consider how a teacher's effectiveness might be reduced by these feelings or attitudes toward students:

- strong dislike for particular pupils and obvious fondness for others
- biases toward or against particular ethnic groups
- a bias toward certain kinds of student behavior, such as docility or inquisitiveness

Few teachers are entirely free of negative attitudes at the outset, and self-awareness can be the crucial factor distinguishing a teacher who is able to control these attitudes and adopt attitudes that students interpret as fair rather than biased. Thus it is important that prospective teachers confront their own attitudes early, perhaps through group discussions, role playing, or simulated and real experiences. It is necessary to acknowledge one's attitudes in order to change them, but even then, change is neither easy nor automatic.

Feelings and cognition

Any attempt to change attitudes must take into account both of their components: feelings and cognition. Attitudes may be based almost entirely on feelings, as when dislike for a particular student causes a teacher to refuse to let the student participate in a particular activity. Or a teacher who feels strong rapport with a certain child may tend to let the child "get away with" more than other students. An example of cognition as the primary component of an attitude is the assessment of a student's needs that causes a teacher to require the student to participate in particular activities, even those the child might dislike.

Recall again how Carol's attitudes toward Tom and Ron differ. While communicating disapproval for Tom's behavior in dominating his group, Carol indulges Ron's not working with his group. What is the basis of this different treatment of the two students? If Carol's attitude toward Tom is based on a negative feeling about students showing strong leadership, for example, it may be amenable to change through counseling or role-playing techniques. If Carol could attempt to suspend her feelings about his behavior and portray in a role-playing session the behavior and feelings of a student in Tom's situation, she might be able to project herself imaginatively into his identity. Role playing as a technique is based on the belief that one of the most effective ways to change attitudes is to participate in experiences in which one can observe the effect on others of attitudinal behavior: The process creates the content.

If, on the other hand, Carol's attitude is based on cognition, perhaps an incorrect assessment of Ron's ability to do the work, new information may be effective in producing attitude changes. In Chapter 9 we talked about the importance of teachers' expectations for their students' success. If a teacher expects a student or group of students to behave in a certain way, the teacher's attitude may serve as a *self-fulfilling prophecy:* That is, the students may behave in the predicted manner in response to the teacher's attitude and not as a result of the other factors on which the teacher's expectations are based. Does Carol have different expectations for Ron's performance than for Tom's, and does she as a result demand less from Ron? Teachers' expectations that all students can suc-

Self-fulfilling prophecies

EXCERPTS FROM THE DIARY OF A STUDENT TEACHER

The following excerpts are from a teaching journal of an English student teacher, Kate Davis. As you read these excerpts, try to identify what attitudes the teacher is manifesting toward self, children, peers, and subject matter.

September 11   I am lax in beginning this journal because I haven't had time to put a pen to paper. That's not to say I'm not thinking of teaching all the time. Driving down the highway, watching TV, swimming laps, in the shower—my mind is always thinking of my students, my teaching, my lesson plans—what worked, what didn't. Certain moments of "something working"—a connection with a student—have me on a high for the rest of the day. Unfortunately, the opposite is true too: days of hell. . . .

September 16   Fourth period disintegrated into chaos today. After the test my intention was to talk about elements of drama. In their minds, a test is enough for one day. The situation was not helped by my inability to keep from laughing at their silly remarks. It's hard to teach and repress laughter at the same time. It's very clear to the students that I'm trying not to crack up. All the wisdom I've gathered about being an authority figure flies out the window, and I am left feeling more like one of the guys than

the teacher. Still I enjoy myself so much in that class despite their misbehavior. I don't think they have ever had a teacher before who cannot control her laughter over a Moby Dick joke.

September 21   Period 6's classwork presents another challenge. The planned lesson demands that I be clear and make fine distinctions. The difference between archetype and metaphor is both immediately apparent and easily confused, especially because both can act symbolically. . . . I am feeling the limits of my knowledge and my inexperience with handling concepts. In college, knowledge of such terms was assumed both by professors and by me. As a teacher, I am forced to articulate what I know: a distressing and revealing activity!

October 16   I know more than the students do but not enough to feel authoritative about it. I'm teaching things I haven't read since high school or at all. So in a sense I'm learning along with my students. Such a circumstance sounds good, but it doesn't make for assertive teaching. . . . My one strength is that I attempt. I come to school every morning with some sort of plan. However, my plans reflect a lack of a sense of direction—an ignorance about what I feel these kids need to know, and more importantly, why. . . . A conflict that rages inside me while I am actually teaching is *why* am I teaching this and for whom? For the system? For society at large? For the student? I'm just not clear why.

ceed has been identified as an important characteristic of schools that seem to make a difference in students' achievement. Such positive attitudes can be cultivated by teachers who have been shown that the abilities of certain groups of students—boys, girls, the poor, and so on—are not inherently inferior to those of other children. Teachers' attitudes toward these youngsters are likely to change somewhat as a result of raised expectations.

Carl Rogers's views

At this point let us consider the position—most eloquently expressed by Carl Rogers, a noted counselor, psychologist, and therapist—that significant learning depends on certain attitudinal qualities that exist in the personal relationships between the facilitator and the learners. Note that Rogers used the term *facilitator,* rather than *teacher,* because he believed it emphasizes what happens to the learners rather than the performance of the teacher. The term *facilitator* also implies significantly different functions than does the term *teacher.*

October 21   No school today. What a boon. The past couple of days have gone fairly smoothly.

October 27   I need to *act* like a teacher. I need to think about all those teachers I've seen on TV or in film and imitate them. Then maybe authority in the classroom will not be such a sticking point. . . . I laugh too much in fourth period. . . . At this point, authority and my personality are like acid and water—they just don't mix. How to overcome this problem? . . . Should I be teaching? Do I need five more years out in the world before I create my own in the classroom? Is the classroom an ideal world or a mirror of the world? Should it be one or the other? Where are the answers? Am I being dense? Are they all around? Where does "vision" or "philosophy" merge with practice or inform practice?

October 30   Martha's [her supervising teacher] mid-term evaluation reflects her clear mind and healthy perspective. She does not gush—she just reflects thoughtfully on what she sees happening. She is definitely more optimistic than I am, and if someone like Martha has faith in my abilities, there must be something there.

November 3   I see myself as too wrapped up in how well or not so well I'm doing. I enter each class with a sense of foreboding—worried that something will happen that I can't handle. It's also being afraid that someone will find you out. . . . Once again I need a balance between seri-

ousness and humor. Teaching is filled with balances: authority and looseness, quiet and noise, order and chaos, too much work and too little work. The ideal job for a Libra, you might say.

November 30   I have three weeks left and then I'm no longer a student teacher. The next time I walk into a class, I'll be the teacher simply. . . . I've got the blues—can't write when I am so dazed and confused. Gonna catch a freight train—take me down the line—better mornings and cheap wine—teacher, preacher, creepy creature feature.

December 8   Yesterday I was asked if my teaching experience was a success. I danced around the issue. . . . No, I don't think my teaching was a success. . . . I don't think I even did any teaching in my fourth-period class. I was too traumatized. . . .

But now I have to put this in perspective. I am new at this. For my teaching to be anything more than bad would be an extraordinary achievement, primarily because my criteria for what is a good teacher are very high. So, from the students' point of view, this was not a success. From mine, I learned a lot. Period.

Kate Davis, "Reflections on Learning the Craft of Teaching," *The Teacher's Journal* 1 (Spring 1988), Brown University, Education Department: 5–8. Used by permission.

Realness

According to Rogers, *realness,* or genuineness, is the attitude most basic to the learning relationship. The facilitator must be a real person, one who "is *being* himself" and who is free to be enthusiastic, bored, interested, angry, sensitive, and sympathetic. Instead of presenting a front or playing a role, the facilitator enters into a relationship with each learner.

Valuing

Another essential attitude Rogers described is *valuing* the learners—their feelings, their opinions, and their persons—as they are and as worthy in their own right, and accepting both their imperfections and their potentialities. The facilitator who possesses this attitude can accept students' occasional apathy, fear of failure, or hatred of authority as well as their more positive characteristics. In short, this attitude is an expression of the facilitator's confidence and trust in each learner's capacity as a human being.

Empathic understanding

A third attitude that Rogers considered essential to the establishment of a climate for learning is *empathic understanding.* "When the teacher has the ability to understand the student's reactions from the inside, has a sensitive awareness of the way the process of education and learning seems to the student, then again the likelihood of significant learning is increased."[5] Empathic understanding implies that the facilitator understands the learner but does not judge or evaluate the learner. Recall the student who said to Carol Landis, "This library stinks. Why do we have to do this assignment anyway?" An empathic, nonevaluative response by Carol might be "You don't care for the library, and you don't understand why you have to do the assignment. What do you find the most troublesome about the assignment?" Rogers urges that a teacher initially set the goal of making one nonevaluative, accepting, empathic response per day to a student's demonstrated or verbalized feelings. By doing so, he believed, the teacher will discover the potency of this approach.

Facilitator-learner relationship

Rogers's approach is intended to create a classroom environment conducive to self-initiated learning. He maintained that the teacher's skills, knowledge of the field, curricular planning, lectures, and selection of books and other learning aids are all peripheral; the crux of the learning situation is the relationship between the facilitator and the learner, which should be characterized by *realness, valuing,* and *empathy.* Unless the learning environment is characterized by the three attitudinal predispositions described, according to Rogers, it is sterile and cannot produce significant learning.

There is little question that if you have empathy for your students, value them as unique individuals, and are secure enough to be yourself without playing

a role, you will be a more successful teacher. In addition, the atmosphere in your classroom will make possible for you and your students a joy, excitement, and closeness absent from many classrooms.

The Teacher's Attitude Toward Peers and Parents

The teacher is not isolated in the classroom. He or she interacts daily with teachers, administrators, and other school personnel and must often have very sensitive dealings with parents. It can happen that a teacher who is very gifted in work with children has a disastrous professional life because of uncontrolled attitudes toward the adults he or she encounters. However, most teachers do not have significantly different attitudes toward adults than they would have toward children possessing the same characteristics. Therefore, much of what we have already said about teachers' attitudes toward themselves and toward children also applies to their attitudes toward peers and parents. Some attitudes enhance a teacher's effectiveness, and others detract from it.

AUTHORITY/COLLABORATION   One source of conflict may be the teacher's attitude toward those who represent authority (ordinarily administrators, but for prospective teachers, the university supervisor or the cooperating teacher).

Resentment toward authority

Teachers may find it hard to be themselves while dealing with people who outrank them in position or prestige. Sometimes teachers find that they yield too readily to demands from those in authority, and as a result they feel guilty about complying rather than standing on their own convictions. When this occurs, the result is often a continuing undercurrent of resentment toward the person in authority.

If teachers can assume a role of collaboration with those in authority, seeing themselves as part of a valuable partnership in the enterprise of education, they may be able to overcome any predispositions to hostility or any anxiety unwarranted by reality. Resentment of those in authority only impedes communication and understanding.

COMPETITION/COOPERATION   Some teachers develop a strong drive to compete with other teachers for recognition from both authority figures and students. They strive to have the best lesson plans, to be the "most popular teacher," or

Need for recognition

to maintain the friendliest relationship with the administration. Such persons are striving to be recognized and rewarded. As a result of this attitude, they sometimes cut themselves off from much-needed help and severely limit their ability to be of help to others. Carol Landis has taken an important first step by enlisting the help of other teachers to procure the necessary resources for her students. For the benefit of staff and students, teachers need to cooperate and share ideas.

SUPERIORITY AND PREJUDICE/ACCEPTANCE   One attitude that never fails to cause trouble for teachers is a feeling of superiority to other teachers and parents of students. They may feel intellectually superior to colleagues or socially superior to students' parents, or both. Some teachers simply have little tolerance for people who differ from them in values, cultural background, or economic status, and, as a result, they treat others with disdain and contempt rather than patience and respect. Again, effective teachers—those who work well with colleagues and parents to empower children to achieve—show attitudes of acceptance. In their dealings with other teachers and parents, teachers can again benefit from Carol Rogers's advice: be real or genuine, value other persons as worthy in their own right, and show empathy.

Lack of tolerance

*The Teacher's
Attitude Toward the
Subject Matter*

Must feel enthusiasm

This section is short because our message is simple: It is most important that whatever subject matter you teach, you feel *enthusiasm* for it. Just as students can usually discern the teacher's attitude toward them, they are also very sensitive to the teacher's attitude toward the subject matter. One of the most striking characteristics of the excellent teacher is enthusiasm for what she or he is teaching, or facilitating. The bored teacher conveys boredom to the students—and who can blame them for failing to get excited if the teacher, who knows more about the subject than they do, doesn't find it engaging?

Some teachers find it difficult to feel enthusiasm for a curriculum they haven't constructed themselves, or don't identify with, or don't want to teach. The surest way to guarantee that teachers are enthusiastic about what they are teaching is to allow them to teach what they are enthusiastic about. And we do not mean this as a mere play on words. We would rather see an enthusiastic teacher teaching Turkish military history or macramé than an uninspired teacher teaching Shakespeare. As one student put it, "There is nothing worse than sitting in a lesson knowing full well that the teacher is dying to get rid of you and rush back to the staff-room to have her cup of tea."[6]

Try not to allow yourself to be pressured into teaching something you care little about. Make sure you have a positive attitude toward the subject you teach. Enthusiasm—if the teacher has it, life in the classroom can be exciting; if it is missing, there is little hope that the students will learn much of significance.

**WHAT SUBJECT-
MATTER
KNOWLEDGE DOES
THE EFFECTIVE
TEACHER NEED?**

The prospective teacher's subject-matter preparation can be seen as having two facets: study of the content of the discipline itself, and familiarity with the knowledge derived from it that can be taught to the pupil.[7] In some fields, such as biology, the discipline is the same as the subject to be taught; other teaching fields, such as social studies, draw on many subject-area disciplines. In all fields, though, the knowledge to be taught is less extensive and advanced than the content of college disciplinary courses; the content of the school curriculum is selected from the available knowledge on the basis of the students' prior learning and the limitations of time. This is one reason that expertise in a discipline is not a guarantee of success at teaching the same subject at the elementary or high school level. Another is that, in addition to the two kinds of subject-matter preparation just described, the teacher must have *knowledge about knowledge,* that is, sufficient perspective on a subject to be able to analyze and convey its elements, logic, possible uses, social biases, and relevance to the needs of the students. When a teacher can assert that a process for solving a particular political problem is correct or incorrect or can identify a certain ethnic bias in a literary passage, the knowledge he or she draws on to make these assertions is what is meant by *knowledge about knowledge.*

Let's turn to the teacher's preparation in the disciplines that will constitute his or her teaching field. Most teacher education programs draw heavily on the disciplines. We consider training in specific disciplines to be as essential to a teacher's general education as it is to that of a doctor or a lawyer. However, we believe that one of the major faults of existing teacher education programs is that the disciplinary approach fails to prepare teachers for the second facet of subject-matter preparation: the knowledge to be taught to the pupil. For instance, teachers who majored in mathematics might find that their college courses, however rigorous, simply didn't prepare them to teach elementary mathematics or algebra. The mathematics courses required of prospective teachers probably differ little from those prescribed for mathematics majors planning on careers in

Knowledge about knowledge

Knowledge taught to pupil

A sound understanding of the subject being taught is an essential ingredient of effective teaching.
(Elizabeth Crews)

industry. As a rule, despite the involvement of many scholars in the curriculum reform movement, university professors are not concerned about preparing teachers to teach the subject matter that elementary and secondary school students are expected to learn. Most college courses are designed to prepare students for more advanced study within the discipline. The methods courses offered in schools of education represent an attempt—not always successful—to remedy this situation. In short, much of what prospective teachers learn from their study of the disciplines is not taught to children, and thus it is not directly applicable to teaching. This is particularly true for elementary school teachers, who are called on to teach content virtually ignored by the academic departments of the universities.

If a teacher's college education should include the study of various disciplines, and if the disciplines in themselves are inadequate preparation for teaching youngsters, what then do we propose? The teacher education program should offer opportunities for prospective teachers to develop curriculum units that are apt to be of interest to students, drawing on concepts and approaches from several disciplines. The mode of study should focus on problem solving, with the prospective teachers working through the units, analyzing the problems, selecting and organizing the materials, and carrying on discussion. Through this process they would learn to think through problems on their own and would acquire the skills necessary to identify and locate relevant materials. By experiencing the same kinds of difficulties that their own students will be likely to encounter, prospective teachers would be better prepared to deal with them effectively.

Pedagogical content knowledge

Knowledge of the curriculum is closely related to another kind of knowledge as well. Lee Shulman of Stanford University coined the term *pedagogical content knowledge* to describe the knowledge that bridges content knowledge and pedagogy and that distinguishes the understanding of a content specialist from that of a teacher of that content. Pedagogical content knowledge represents the "blending of content and pedagogy into an understanding of how particular topics, problems, or issues are organized, represented, and adapted to the diverse interests and abilities of learners, and presented for instruction."[8] The essence of pedagogical content knowledge is in the teacher's capacity to transform the content knowledge he or she possesses into forms that have great teaching power and that are directed at the unique needs and abilities of the students. To do this the skilled teacher draws on the most powerful analogies, illustrations, examples, explanations, and demonstrations to represent and transform the subject so it is comprehensible to the students.

Identifying pedagogical content knowledge in each subject and for students of different ages and abilities can be a difficult undertaking. But we are convinced that if prospective teachers practice organizing materials so as to focus on what makes learning of specific topics easy or difficult for students, they will find teaching much easier. As B. O. Smith noted:

> To be prepared in the subject matter of instruction is to know the content to be taught and how the content can be related to the interest and experience of children and youths. To prepare the teacher in this subject matter will require courses oriented to the teacher's need for knowledge

that can be tied in with the life of children and youths rather than discipline-oriented courses.[9]

We thus urge that prospective teachers know intimately the content they are to teach, and that this content be arranged around human physical and social problems and issues relevant to students' lives. This is not to slight the importance of being well versed in the disciplines from which the instructional subject matter comes. In Smith's words, "The first is necessary for teaching anything at all. The second supplies a depth of knowledge essential to the teacher's feeling of intellectual security and his ability to handle instructional content with greater understanding."[10] Finally, as mentioned, teachers must have knowledge about knowledge as a whole so that they can structure facts, concepts, and principles in any situation, regardless of the subject matter.

Four types of knowledge

These four types of knowledge—of discipline content, of curriculum content, of pedagogical content, and of knowledge about knowledge—are, we believe, essential for effective teachers. Did Carol Landis have such knowledge? We suspect not, at least not to the degree that she could communicate information and concepts to her class with the authority and expertise required for effective teaching. In the next section, we'll examine more closely another area of the effective teacher's knowledge: theoretical knowledge about learning and human behavior.

WHAT THEORETICAL KNOWLEDGE DOES THE EFFECTIVE TEACHER NEED?

Theories-in-Use

Often unexamined ideas

Let's recall for a moment the case of Carol Landis. In the incident described, Carol operated on the basis of certain ideas, or what some call theories-in-use, which are different from pure theories.[11] A *pure theory* is an unproved explanation of why something happens the way it does. In its simplest form, a theory is a hypothesis designed to bring generalizable facts, concepts, or scientific laws into systematic connection. On the other hand, a *theory-in-use* is something people have in their heads and apply in their dealings with people and the world. Theories-in-use are often quite different from the theories people come up with when asked to justify doing this or that. Often they are unexamined. We all have these theories-in-use, and they guide us as we make our way through our daily lives. You support a particular political party because you believe it advances sounder economic policies. You eat certain foods because you have an idea that they have a healthy effect on the body. Or you decide to take a summer job in a public playground, believing that you'll get to know children better and that future prospective employers might be pleased or impressed when they hear you've had that kind of experience.

Carol's theories-in-use

As you may have observed, Carol Landis has several theories-in-use. For example, Carol has the theory-in-use that groups should operate democratically and not be dominated by one student. She also has a theory-in-use that some children will perform better in school than others, and as a result, she expects certain behavior from certain kinds of students. She also has a classroom management theory-in-use that she should give students some leeway before she resorts to firm discipline. Some of Carol's theories-in-use are clearly questionable. A few may have contributed to her problems that day in the library, and some may cause her more problems further down the line. But notice that Carol was not worried about her theories-in-use. She was worried about what she did and what she will do. She didn't question some of her conceptions. Theories-in-use were the last things she had in mind, but they, in fact, caused some of her problems.

Why Study Educational Theory? The fact that Carol did not reflect on the truth or falsity of her theories-in-use or try to recall some theories that she had learned during her teacher education is not uncommon. Indeed, many teachers question the basic usefulness of theory. It is not at all uncommon for beginning teachers to be told by a senior colleague, "Forget all that theory they've been giving you at the university. Here's what works in the real world. . . ." Further, preservice teachers often complain that courses are too theoretical. They want to get out to schools where the action is. This desire (perhaps it is your own desire) for things that work and ways to cope with real situations is important, and we do not want to diminish it. As a teacher you will need practical techniques and solutions to real problems. But to need Theoretical knowledge practical tools does not mean that educational theory is less important. Theoretical knowledge about learning and human behavior equips the teacher to draw on concepts from psychology, anthropology, sociology, and related disciplines in order to interpret the complex reality of the classroom. The teacher who lacks a theoretical background will be obliged to interpret classroom events according

Theoretical knowledge is necessary

TEACHING: ART OR SCIENCE?

One of the pioneering investigators of research on teaching, N. L. Gage, professor emeritus at Stanford University, sees teaching as a blend of both art and science. Gage asserts that teachers, "because of the inevitable complexity of the teaching process, engage in artistic activity." Teaching can be considered an art because teachers must improvise and spontaneously handle a tremendous number of factors that interact in often unpredictable and nonsystematic ways in classroom settings. Teaching cannot be reduced to formulas or recipes for action, in Gage's opinion. Yet, to speak of teaching as a purely spontaneous, intuitive, ineffable, or totally unpredictable activity is not helpful for teachers who hope to improve their teaching artistry.

Although science can't provide absolute guidance for teachers as they plan and implement instructional strategies, research can provide a scientific basis for the art of teaching. Educational research has provided scientifically developed knowledge about the relationships among classroom variables. For example, the research on *academic engaged time* has demonstrated the importance of keeping pupils on task with intellectually challenging, but not too difficult, subject matter. Thus, empirically-derived knowledge of the relationships among teacher behavior, pupil behavior, material to be learned, and desired student learning can provide guidance to teachers as they make artistic decisions about their teaching. As artists, teachers make instrumental use of the research on these relationships, even if they are only weak generalizations, to accomplish the artistry of moving a unique classroom of unique students toward intended learning.

Is teaching an art or a science? The answer is "yes."

N. L. Gage, *Hard Gains in the Soft Sciences: The Case of Pedagogy* (Bloomington, Ind.: Phi Delta Kappa, 1985), pp. 4–11.

*Education must bring
the practice as nearly as
possible to the theory.*
— HORACE MANN —

to commonly held beliefs or common sense, much of which is, unfortunately, based on outmoded notions of human behavior. The case of Carol Landis is an example of how lack of theoretical knowledge of classroom management can lead to inappropriate behavior on the teacher's part.

First, although you, like Carol, may have your own theories-in-use, these need to be challenged and tested. The best way to do this is to pit them against other theories and ideas. Carol probably would not have become involved in such trouble if more of her ideas had been challenged.

Good theories
are practical

Second, we believe that theoretical information *is* practical. The problem is not that theory is wrong or unworkable, but that many teacher education programs offer students few opportunities to apply theory to practical situations; it is usually up to the neophyte teacher to translate theory into practice on the job. But theory is extremely important, even if you occasionally fail to apply it effectively. As the great American educator John Dewey said, "Nothing is so practical as a good theory."*

Third, by giving attention to theoretical knowledge now, we are looking ahead to the future. In other words, even if it doesn't interest you much at this point, we want you to know that at a later stage of your development you will encounter theories that will enlighten and enrich your work with the young.

Every teacher should be familiar with currently respected theoretical knowledge about human behavior and social systems. In addition to such general knowledge, there exists specialized theoretical knowledge, which is the unique province of the effective teacher. Teaching is neither static nor a matter of intuition; it has given rise to a body of theoretical knowledge that is constantly growing. A distinguishing characteristic of professionals is their ability to draw on specialized knowledge to inform their decision making. In the teacher's case, this specialized knowledge must include subject-matter knowledge and theoretical knowledge about how teaching and learning take place.

For these reasons, then, we think it is important for you to give attention to educational theory both now and throughout your training.

*How Does One
Acquire Theoretical
Knowledge?*

Theoretical knowledge relevant to teaching is derived from courses such as educational psychology, educational sociology, educational anthropology, linguistics, foundations of education, tests and measurement, and classroom management. But because the relationship of theoretical knowledge to a given occupation is typically indirect, it is not enough for you simply to take the appropriate courses. Theory develops within a discipline and is formulated in terms suitable to that discipline but usually unsuitable or inadequate for a learning

Must be adapted
to classroom

situation. For teachers, this means that principles derived from psychology must be adapted to a classroom before they become useful. A classroom is always subject to a number of variables that are absent in the experimental situation. In the late afternoon of a school day, for instance, both teacher and students are likely to be tired, and their behavior is likely to differ from their morning

---

* For the moment we will downplay the fact that John Dewey was primarily an educational theorist.

"Hey wait a minute! You're cleaning erasers as a punishment? I'm
cleaning erasers as a reward!"

Courtesy, Phi Delta Kappan

behavior. In contrast, the laboratory experiments from which theory is derived
are controlled to eliminate such variables. Thus, to make the necessary adaptations, a teacher must have a command not only of the theoretical knowledge but
also of the learning situation.

Carol and reinforcement
theory

Perhaps going back to the case of Carol Landis will help clarify this point.
Carol knew from her educational psychology course that any behavior that is
reinforced will be strengthened and any that is not rewarded or is punished will
be weakened. Nevertheless, she adopted a teaching practice in which she allowed some groups to "have some fun" but planned to get them in line the next
day. Her past experiences should have told her that many students enjoy testing
the teacher and "having some fun;" further, she should have realized that these
activities do not contribute positively to learning outcomes or to a constructive
classroom atmosphere. Somehow, though, the theoretical knowledge about reinforcement and punishment did not carry over to her professional practice—to
her teaching. Carol failed to grasp the concept that allowing the students to have
some fun for a day could possibly be reinforcing their behavior. Her failure to
apply mild discipline, stopping the behavior before it could escalate, indicates
that she never quite internalized the theoretical knowledge she "learned" in her
educational psychology course.

How Can Theoretical Knowledge Be Used?	A teacher's theoretical knowledge can be used in two ways: to interpret situations and to solve problems. (Practical knowledge, on the other hand, is more limited in applicability and is used primarily to respond to familiar situations.)[12] For
Interpret and solve problems	example, a teacher may see a child acting like a bully and interpret the child's aggression as a reaction to some frustration the child had experienced. In doing so the teacher would be drawing on theoretical knowledge about frustration and its possible consequences to interpret the child's behavior. To solve the problem, the teacher would avoid shaming the child but would seek the causes of her frustration and try to channel the child's energy in a more constructive direction. Adults lacking theoretical knowledge would be likely to attribute the child's aggression to "bad character" and be unable to deal with the situation.

Problem solving is a primary aspect of the role of the teacher. Teachers are constantly required to make diagnoses and decisions about problems related to learning and to human relations. To do so effectively, teachers must possess a high degree of theoretical understanding. They apply this understanding by formulating hypotheses both about the interpretation of problems and about the

RESEARCHING THE CHARACTERISTICS OF THE EXPERT TEACHER

To gain more information about the teaching behaviors thought to characterize expert teaching, educational researcher David Berliner and his colleagues have attempted to identify expert and experienced teachers and compare them with ordinary or novice teachers. Although experts' teaching performance may not be perfect, their particular approaches to accepted teaching tasks may prove helpful in training novice teachers. By observing expert teachers, researchers may be able to determine what these teachers implicitly know that allows them to "know how."

Berliner compares the expert teacher to the expert chess player. Expert chess players quickly spot trouble areas in any chess board pattern; likewise, expert teachers quickly recognize trouble spots in a classroom setting. Experts in chess or teaching draw on their hours of experience to build a repertoire of recognizable patterns. In one experiment, expert and novice teachers were asked to look at a photograph of a classroom and identify the class activity. Experts were better able to "read" the classroom, making inferences about what was happening in the picture. When expert teachers have been observed in action, they also show greater ability to gather information in a

short time for multiple purposes. For example, an expert teacher may be able to accomplish many tasks in an opening review session: gather attendance information, identify who did or did not do the homework, and locate students needing help with the next lesson.

In comparison, novice teachers described the surface characteristics of the classroom pictures they saw. And when presented with descriptions of student problems, the novices relied again on the literal features of the problems to suggest solutions. Their analyses did not correspond with the higher-order classifications used by expert teachers.

Although their research is not complete, Berliner and his associates suggest that experts in any field demonstrate skill in classifying problems and formulating solutions. This is no less true for teachers; the expert teacher shows problem-solving skills like those of other studied experts, whether it be in chess, bridge, or physics. Berliner also believes that the process of moving from novice to expert teacher takes considerable time because extensive experience is necessary to develop episodic knowledge to interpret information about classrooms.

David C. Berliner, "In Pursuit of the Expert Pedagogue," Presidential Address at the 1986 Annual Meeting of the American Educational Research Association, *Educational Researcher* 15 (August–September 1986): 5–13.

actions they should undertake in response to them. But there should be no air of finality about their proposed solutions. If the actions a teacher has chosen do not solve the problem, the situation should be reinterpreted and alternative responses sought and tested.

"Single-solution rut"

Classroom problems are rarely entirely original, except for the new teacher, to whom nearly all are unprecedented. As a result, once teachers have developed and incorporated a solution to a given problem, they tend to use the same solution, with appropriate modifications, when confronted by similar situations; a solution that worked once in a particular situation is habitually relied on as the "correct" way to handle all related problems. One teacher's way to handle disruptive outbursts might be to separate the offending child from the others. But this solution deals only with the symptom rather than with the problem itself, which might vary from insecurity because of parental neglect to dislike of the school environment. Single-solution behavior is dangerous because it fails to take into account all the variables of individual situations. Teachers must guard against the "single-solution rut."

Because of their insecurity and lack of theoretical knowledge, beginning teachers often seek "recipes" to solve certain categories of problems. "What do I do when one child hits another?" Questions of this type are requests for pat answers. Unfortunately, these plugged-in approaches rarely work. The reasons one child hits another are as numerous as are the possible and appropriate teacher responses.

As a teacher, you should not only refrain from using single solutions but also avoid seeking them; instead, you should acquire knowledge about learning, patterns of behavior, how children from different cultural backgrounds behave, and what values influence them. You should also become familiar with such concepts as motivation, self-concept, feedback, reinforcement, attitude formation, perceptions, and peer approval.

Example of problem solving

Let's consider an example of how theoretical knowledge can help a teacher interpret classroom events and solve the problems arising from them. In psychology, *self-concept* is defined as the sum of a person's beliefs about and evaluations of himself or herself as a person. All people have images of the kind of people they are, derived from previous experiences, and they tend to behave in ways that are consistent with those images. Children's self-concepts are an important factor both in their ability to learn and in their interaction with other children and the environment. For instance, if children view themselves as likable and outgoing, they are apt to respond in a friendly manner when meeting new children. If children are insecure because they view themselves as weak, ugly, or unwanted, they will not respond easily to a group of new children.

Suppose a teacher observes that a particular boy is doing poorly in science. The problem is how to help this child improve his performance in that subject. A number of factors may be influencing his performance: he may possess inadequate or incorrect scientific concepts; he may not be interested in science; he may not be very intelligent; or he may view himself as inept in science and thus not try as hard as he might. Several of these factors may be interrelated in complex ways.[13]

A teacher who functions as a problem solver will hypothesize that the boy's poor performance could result from any of these factors and will proceed to investigate further by collecting information about the child's previous performance in science, his intelligence level, and his self-concept. In this way the teacher can determine whether the child's self-concept is an important determinant in his poor science performance.

If the child's intelligence level is high and his previous experience indicates that he should be doing reasonably well in science, the teacher might hypothesize that one possible reason for the boy's poor performance is his conception of his own abilities. What can the teacher do? Can a teacher help change a child's self-concept? The answer is an unequivocal "maybe." If the teacher is one of the child's major sources of self-information, he or she may be able to encourage a revised self-concept through a guidance program designed to help the child gather reliable information about himself. Sometimes children lack self-understanding to such an extent that they must be referred to specialized professional help before progress can be made. Again, the teacher may have to make that decision on the basis of his or her own observations and knowledge.

If the child's problem does not seem serious enough to require referral to a specialist, the teacher might try any of several approaches to improve the child's self-concept in science. Discussing his abilities with him, helping him view his abilities more realistically, and arranging for successful experiences are among the potential ways to change the child's self-perception. The teacher proceeds throughout as a hypothesis maker, forming tentative ideas about experiences that might improve the child's self-concept, and testing those ideas. The teacher's hypotheses will become more perceptive and accurate as his or her understanding of the variables influencing the child's self-concept increases.

Common sense not enough

A teacher needs much more than a common-sense understanding of human behavior. The capable and effective teacher uses theoretical knowledge drawn from various education-related disciplines to formulate and test hypotheses about human behavior in the classroom. In our opinion, the translation of theory into practice cannot be left to chance; you must constantly take advantage of opportunities that allow you to apply theoretical concepts to classroom situations and to receive guidance and feedback from your instructors about the application of these concepts.

WHAT TEACHING SKILLS ARE REQUIRED OF AN EFFECTIVE TEACHER?

Knowing Versus Doing

Simply knowing something does not guarantee the ability to act on that knowledge. There is a profound difference between *knowing* and *doing*. Teachers may know, for example, that they should provide prompt feedback to their students on written assignments, but they are not always able to act on that knowledge. No teacher education program can afford to focus exclusively on theoretical knowledge at the expense of the practice, or "doing," dimension of teaching, just as no individual teacher can rely solely on knowledge of subject matter. All prospective teachers need to develop a repertoire of teaching skills to use as they see fit in varying classroom situations.

Research has not yet conclusively identified the teaching skills that have the most beneficial impact on student learning, but many educators have independently defined the skills they believe essential to effective teaching. Among them are the following:

- the ability to ask different kinds of questions, each of which requires different types of thought processes from the student
- the ability to reinforce certain kinds of student behavior
- the ability to diagnose student needs and learning difficulties
- the ability to vary the learning situation continually to keep the students involved
- the ability to recognize when students are paying attention and to use this information to vary behavior and, possibly, the direction of the lesson
- the ability to use technological equipment, such as computers

WHAT ARE SOME CHARACTERISTIC BEHAVIORS OF EFFECTIVE TEACHERS?

We have already described some of educational researcher David Berliner's work. In a broad study, he attempted to provide an answer, based on contemporary research on teaching, to the question "What is an effective teacher?" His answer focuses on teacher behaviors that give students the opportunity to spend sufficient time engaged in and succeeding at tasks that help them achieve intended learning. Several behaviors seem to distinguish effective teachers:

- They monitor students' independent work, checking on their progress and providing appropriate feedback, to maintain a high level of student engagement with the task at hand.
- They structure lessons to let students know what is expected of them and what procedures to follow.
- They pace instruction rapidly to deliver a maximum amount of the curriculum to students.
- They ask questions requiring students to analyze, synthesize, or evaluate, demand answers at the same level as the question, and wait at least three seconds for students' answers.

- They communicate high expectations for student success.
- They provide a safe and orderly classroom. Deviant behavior is managed sensibly, and academic achievement is rewarded.
- They foster a convivial atmosphere in their classrooms.
- They capitalize on the instructional and motivational uses of tests and grades.
- They provide feedback to students in the forms of praise, use of student ideas, and corrective forms that allow students to respond appropriately.

This list is not comprehensive; these nine categories of teaching behaviors are only examples of behaviors that distinguish effective teaching. But the relationship of this collection of attitudes, knowledge, and skills to a research base indicates their importance in the repertoire of the professional teacher.

David C. Berliner, "Effective Classroom Teaching: The Necessary but Not Sufficient Condition for Developing Exemplary Schools," in *Research on Exemplary Schools,* ed. Gilbert R. Austin and Herbert Garber (Orlando, Fla.: Academic Press, 1985), pp. 127–154.

- the ability to judge the appropriateness of instructional materials
- the ability to define the objectives of particular lessons and units in terms of student behaviors
- the ability to relate learning to the student's experience[14]

Developing a Repertoire of Teaching Skills

The list of skills just given is far from complete. It does make clear, however, that teachers need a large repertoire of skills to work effectively with students with varying backgrounds and different educational experiences. Varied approaches are necessary to meet the multiple needs of students.

A case for teacher training

We believe strongly that a teacher education program should train candidates in the performance of selected teaching skills. Many teachers and teacher educators, however, take exception to the term *teacher training*. They regard training as something one does with animals, not human beings; human beings, they say, should be educated, not trained. We don't agree. We believe that a teacher's preparation must consist of both education and training. The objection that training teachers makes them robots and prevents the release of their creative energies is contradicted by what we know of training in other occupations. Surgeons and pilots, for example, are trained to perform certain operations proficiently and even automatically. This level of mastery enables them to turn their attention and energy to tasks more worthy of their creativity.

Importance of overlearning

The rapidity with which the classroom teacher must field students' questions, check on their understanding, alter the pace of instruction, or manage disruptive behavior places demands on the teacher's command of certain skills—verbal interaction, monitoring, planning, and classroom management, to name a few. In each instance, the teacher must rely on a range of skills and knowledge so well learned that they are internalized and readily available to inform the teacher's almost instantaneous decisions. Such skills must be overlearned to the point of becoming automatic; otherwise teachers will have difficulty calling up these skills in the classroom's complex and rapidly paced setting.[15] As Figure 13.1 illustrated, effective use of teaching skills, along with appropriate attitudes, knowledge of subject matter, and theoretical knowledge, leads to better instructional decision making.

Classroom Management Skills

No other dimension of teaching causes more concern for beginning teachers than that of managing the classroom and maintaining discipline. "Will I be able to manage and control my class(es) so I can teach effectively?" is a question most beginning teachers ask themselves. Because there is such a great concern about this aspect of teaching, we have chosen to spend considerable time on this skill area first, before turning, somewhat more briefly, to two others: questioning and planning skills.

Classroom management—definition

Let's start by examining what we mean by the term *classroom management*. Wilford Weber argues that teaching consists of two major sets of activities: instruction and management.[16] *Instructional activities* are designed to help the students learn their subjects. Asking questions, evaluating progress, and presenting information are examples of instructional activities. *Managerial activities* are intended to create and maintain conditions in which instruction can take place efficiently and effectively. *Classroom management,* then, is the set of behaviors by which the teacher establishes these conditions. Developing teacher-student rapport, establishing productive group norms, and rewarding promptness are examples of managerial behavior. Managerial behavior also includes housekeeping duties like record keeping and managing time and resources in the classroom. Remember Carol Landis's concern that she spent so much time watching the arguing group of students and Tom's group that she didn't even have time to notice whether the chatter from the other groups was work or play. She is worried about classroom management related to students' on-task behavior (discussed later in this chapter).

Often, a particular teaching behavior may be viewed as serving both instructional and managerial purposes, but it is useful to distinguish between these two types of activities when one is faced with classroom problems. Trying to solve managerial problems by instructional means, and vice versa, will not produce very effective results.

As with most complex teaching skills, classroom management requires a thorough understanding of theoretical knowledge and research findings, as well as practical experience. The knowledge or theory comes primarily from educational, social, and humanistic psychology. As with many other areas of investigation, there is no consensus regarding the one most effective approach to classroom management. Instead, there are different philosophies, theories, and research findings, each tending to address particular dimensions or approaches to classroom management. A brief overview of some of these different approaches will be helpful.[17]

BEHAVIOR MODIFICATION   Of all the approaches, this approach to classroom management has the strongest base in theory and research. Its basis comes from behavioral and experimental psychology, particularly the work of B. F. Skinner, and it views classroom management as the process of modifying student behavior. The teacher's role is to foster desirable student behavior and to eliminate undesirable behavior. This is accomplished primarily by consistently and systematically rewarding (reinforcing) appropriate student behavior and removing rewards for, or punishing, inappropriate student behavior.

B. F. Skinner's contributions

SOCIOEMOTIONAL CLIMATE   The roots of this approach stem from counseling and from clinical psychology, which places great importance on interpersonal relationships. Advocates of this approach believe that effective classroom management is largely a function of positive teacher-student relationships. The teacher's task, then, is to build positive interpersonal relationships and a positive socioemotional climate. Theorists who would be classified as proponents of this approach include Carl Rogers, discussed earlier, who believed that attributes such as realness, accepting, and empathic understanding must be present if the teacher is going to be able to facilitate learning; Haim Ginott, who stressed the importance of effective communication in promoting good teacher-student relationships; and William Glasser, who argues that teachers must help students develop a sense of identity, worthiness, and success.

Positive interpersonal relationships

GROUP PROCESS   Social psychology and group dynamics form the base of this approach to classroom management, particularly in the work of Richard and Patricia Schmuck and of Lois V. Johnson and Mary Bany. The basic assumption is that learning takes place within a group context and, as a result, the nature and behavior of the classroom group affect each individual's learning. The teacher's role is to establish and maintain an effective, productive classroom group. To do so the teacher must help the group achieve unity and cooperation, establish standards and coordinate work procedures, use problem solving to improve conditions, and substitute appropriate goals for inappropriate goals.

Groups affect learning

AUTHORITY   This approach views classroom management as basically a process of controlling student behavior. The role of the teacher is to establish and maintain order in the classroom, primarily through the use of discipline. This approach is not vindictive or mean but can be very caring. There is no doubt, however, as to who has the authority in the classroom. The authoritarian approach advocates establishing and enforcing classroom rules, using soft reprimands and orders to desist, and using commands and directives. One authoritarian system that is currently receiving considerable attention is *assertive discipline,* developed by Lee and Marlene Canter. They argue that the teacher has the right to establish clear limits and expectations, insist on and reward acceptable behavior from the students, and follow through with appropriate consequences that are known in advance to the students when rules are broken.

Assertive discipline

"I'm your teacher, Mrs. Gridley. Learn to read, write, and do arithmetic, and nobody will get hurt."

Courtesy, Phi Delta Kappan

Teachers should not perceive these different approaches as being mutually exclusive. In fact, Weber argues that the most effective classroom manager will be one who uses a pluralistic approach and applies the managerial strategy or strategies that appear to have the best potential to be effective in a particular situation. To do so requires that the teacher ultimately become a decision maker who possesses a repertoire of different approaches.

Research Related to Classroom Management
The last twenty-five years or so have produced significant new knowledge about effective classroom management practices. This section describes some of those findings. One clear message that emerges from this research is that by effectively engaging students in learning tasks where they experience a high success rate, monitoring the students' progress, and nipping potential behavior problems in the bud, teachers can greatly reduce discipline problems.

ACADEMIC ENGAGED TIME During the 1970s, the National Institute of Education (NIE) funded numerous research studies in an attempt to discover the basic skills of teaching. Because of the great concern at the time with declining student achievement in reading and mathematics, most of the research efforts focused on the teaching of these subjects in the elementary grades. The early attempts tried to identify teaching behaviors (such as teacher talk, number of higher-order questions, clarity of presentation) that were related to student

NEVER 'WHY?' NOR 'IF . . . , I'LL . . .'

How to Cut Your Discipline Problems by 50%

Q: "Why are you fighting?"
A: "We're not fighting; we're just playing."
Q: "Why are you chewing gum in class?"
A: "Tastes good."
Q: "Why are you smoking?"
A: "I like to smoke."
Q: "Why didn't you have a pencil?"
A: "I forgot."

As a teacher or school administrator, would you like to decrease discipline problems in your school by 50%?

Teachers who are faced with the responsibility of disciplining students use the "Why?" question as a very natural, almost instinctive response to inappropriate behavior. In tracing the origins of a great number of serious discipline cases over the past five years, I have found that

over half began with a relatively minor misbehavior on the part of the student, followed by a why from the teacher.

Asking why of a student who has misbehaved or performed incorrectly is not sensible. Most often, it invites a flippant response or even overt hostility. Instead of asking why, tell the student what he has done or is doing incorrectly and give the student direction. This can best be done in a calm, polite, serious, and firm manner, as in these examples:

"Tom, you're late. Go to your seat quietly."

"Betty, you're smoking on campus. See me at 3:05 today."

"Dotty and Jane, I have reason to believe you cheated on your exam. Please see me five minutes before the end of the period."

There is no reason to ask why: The student will come and tell you why if he has a good reason for being late, or chewing gum, or fighting, or cheating, or being in the hall. If the student does not have a valid reason, we should not demand to hear it, nor should we place the

High amounts of academic engaged time—a classroom variable examined extensively in studies of effective teaching—is correlated positively with student learning.

(*Paul Conklin/Monkmeyer Press Photo Services*)

student in a situation which demands covering up or being untruthful.

Another point: In many incidents where the why question is used, a threatening "If . . . , I'll" statement often follows the student's answer.

"Why are you late?"

"If you're late again, I'll have to keep you after school."

"Why are you fighting?"

"If I catch you two fighting again, I'll send you to the office."

"Why are you smoking on campus?"

"If I see you smoking again, I'll suspend you for five days."

What about this "If . . . , I'll" threat? Many teachers believe that students have the right to know the consequences for misbehavior beforehand. I agree that every misbehavior must have a consequence. The consequence may be very minor—talking to the teacher after class—or it may be severe—a lengthy suspension or even expulsion. *But it must be given consistently, and it must follow an instance of misbehavior.* And there is no need to threaten if consequences are given consistently. Students soon learn what the consequences are from experience—their own or others.

Consider this: When a teacher says, "If I catch you cheating again, I'll have you stay after school," she is implying that it's O.K. to cheat this time but not the next time. This confuses students. The teacher should say, "You are cheating. Stay after school Tuesday." Here there is no threat. Both the offender and the other students learn the consequences of misbehavior, and a realistic chance to improve his behavior is offered to the misbehaving student.

These two concepts may sound simple, yet the leadership necessary to obtain a large majority of the teaching staff to implement the "Never 'why?' nor 'If . . . , I'll' " philosophy is not at all simple. However, the increase in teacher satisfaction and the improvement in student attitudes and behavior are worth it.

Marvin J. Woodstrup, *Phi Delta Kappan* 58 (April 1977): 609. © 1977, Phi Delta Kappan, Inc. Reprinted by permission.

achievement. For many reasons, this line of research did not prove particularly productive. However, when the focus shifted from teacher behaviors to student behaviors—primarily *academic engaged time* (also known as *academic learning time*)—some interesting and relevant findings emerged.*

Definition

Academic engaged time is the time a student spends being successfully engaged with academically relevant activities or materials. Several research studies indicate that academic engaged time in reading or mathematics is strongly related to achievement in those subjects.[18] Simply put, the more time elementary students spend working on reading or mathematics activities that provide them with highly successful experiences, the more likely they are to achieve in those areas. Although this finding may not seem very startling, observations indicate that tremendous differences exist in the amount of time individual students spend engaged in academic activities, both across classrooms and within the same classroom.

Research findings

The research on academic engaged time clearly indicates that a primary goal of elementary teachers (and probably secondary teachers, although the research has been limited to elementary schools) should be to keep students on task. We know that classes that are poorly managed usually have little academic learning time. A major task of teachers is to learn how to manage their classes so that students are productively engaged.

Numerous studies, including the BTES study mentioned in Chapter 9 (page 322), indicate that the most efficient teachers are able to engage their students about 30 minutes a day longer than the average teacher. If the most efficient teachers are compared with the least efficient, daily differences of an hour in academic engaged time appear. Spread out over 180 days, students of efficient teachers get 90 hours more of academic engaged time than students of average teachers, and 180 hours more than students of inefficient teachers! Differences of this magnitude may help explain why students in some classes learn more than students in other classes.

KOUNIN'S RESEARCH   Jacob Kounin's research on classroom management in the elementary school grades provides us with some insights about which skills can help teachers improve their classroom management and keep pupils on task.[19] Of the concepts Kounin identified to describe teacher classroom management behavior, three seem particularly useful. The first concept he termed *withitness*. Teachers who are "with it" are ones who communicate to pupils, by their behavior, that they know what is going on. Teachers who are "with it" will pick up the first sign of deviancy, will deal with the proper pupil, will ignore a minor misbehavior to stop a major infraction, and so forth.

Withitness

---

* *On-task behavior, time-on-task,* and *academic engaged time* are related concepts. *On-task behavior* refers to students being engaged in activities that are appropriate to the teacher's goals. *Time-on-task* refers to the amount of time students spend engaged in on-task behavior. *Academic engaged time* adds the dimensions of a high success rate and academically relevant activities or materials to the concept of time-on-task.

Smoothness

The second and third concepts are concerned with the problems of lesson flow and time management. *Smoothness* concerns the absence of behaviors initiated by teachers that interfere with the flow of academic events. Examples of teacher behavior that do not reflect smoothness are when a teacher bursts in on children's activities with an order, statement, or question; when a teacher starts, or is in, some activity and then leaves it "hanging," only to resume it after an interval; and when a teacher terminates one activity, starts another, and then initiates a return to the terminated activity.

How to Evaluate and Improve Classroom Management

On the basis of research in over three hundred elementary and secondary classrooms, Carolyn M. Evertson and her former associates at the University of Texas at Austin have developed a checklist that helps teachers know when a change is needed in the organization and management of a classroom. They recommend that teachers consider the effects of their management systems on student behavior, especially in the areas of on-task rates, disruptive behavior, student cooperation, and completion of assignments. We'll reproduce a few of the questions that teachers can ask themselves to determine causes of students' off-task or disruptive behaviors or causes for lack of cooperation or completion of assigned work.

Can you see all students from any place in the room at which you instruct or work?

Are students who frequently need your attention or assistance seated where you can easily monitor and reach them?

Do some students frequently bother others who sit near them?

Are your major class procedures, such as those governing student talk, raising hands, movement around the room, use of equipment and supplies, being followed without constant prompting and reminders?

Are you spending as much time going over directions and procedures now as at the beginning of the year?

Do students sometimes claim that they didn't know an assignment was due or what its requirements were?

Do many of your students fail to complete assignments or not turn them in at all?

Do you reward good student behavior, including effort, in a variety of ways?

Do you find yourself assessing penalties more and more often and rewarding students less than you previously did?

Do you tend to notice misbehavior only after it involves several students?

Do you sometimes have the feeling that some students are misbehaving simply to gain your attention?

Do you often discover that students have not understood your presentations and that they therefore cannot complete assignments correctly?

Are transitions from one activity to another taking a long time?

Are a few of your students so far behind the class that you have just given up on them?

These questions represent a sampling of those that Evertson and her colleagues suggest for diagnosing problems in the classroom. The questions focus attention on important features of effectively managed classrooms in several areas: room arrangement, rules and procedures for student conduct, accountability procedures, consequences for appropriate and inappropriate behavior, detecting misbehavior, and management of instructional activities.

Carolyn M. Evertson et al., *Classroom Management for Elementary Teachers,* 2d ed. (Englewood Cliffs, N.J.: Prentice-Hall, 1989); Edmund T. Emmer et al., *Classroom Management for Secondary Teachers,* 2d ed. (Englewood Cliffs, N.J.: Prentice-Hall, 1989). The questions appear on pp. 189–193 in both books. Adapted by permission.

The third concept, *momentum,* concerns the absence of teacher behaviors that slow down the pace of the lesson. Kounin conceptualized two types of slow-down behaviors: *overdwelling* (when a teacher dwells too much on pupil behavior, on a subpoint rather than the main point, on physical props rather than substance, or on instructions or details to the point of boredom) and *fragmentation* (when a teacher deals with individual pupils one at a time rather than with the group, or unnecessarily breaks a task into smaller parts when the task could have been accomplished in a single step). Momentum is judged by the absence of such slow-down features.

Momentum

Kounin found strong correlations between teachers' use of withitness, smoothness, and momentum and their pupils' work involvement and freedom from deviancy. Educational researcher Jere Brophy describes Kounin's effective teachers: "Effective classroom managers succeed not so much because they are good at handling disruption when it occurs, but because they are good at maximizing the time students spend attending to lessons and engaging in assignments. They are good at preventing disruptions from occurring in the first place."[20] It is our hope that future research will provide us with more answers about how teachers can increase their effectiveness in keeping students productively engaged.

OTHER RESEARCH FINDINGS   Within recent years, many researchers have replicated and extended Kounin's work. Here are a few of the most recent findings about effective classroom management:

1. *Showing and telling students what to do is important.* Teachers must be clear about rules and routines. The ability to explain and, if necessary, demonstrate desired behaviors for students contributes to effective management. Effective managing means teaching "students what to do before the fact rather than applying 'discipline' following misconduct."[21]

Establish clear rules

2. *Ensuring students' compliance with rules and demands is important.* Teachers must be willing to establish procedures that make students accountable for their work and to enforce penalties for late or unacceptable work. Teachers must be willing to punish students for repeated misconduct. While managing their classrooms in these ways, effective managers maintain a positive emphasis, attempting to correct and improve students' conduct and performance. Their attitude is not threatening or punitive.[22]

Enforce rules consistently

3. *Monitoring what is going on in a classroom is important.* Effective managers attend to what is going on in the entire room—*group activity, the conduct or behavior of individual students, and the pace and rhythm of classroom events*—and are able to identify misbehaving or off-task students among the group. They anticipate problems and intervene early. Moreover, such teachers maintain an instructional momentum that maintains order and student involvement.[23]

Monitor the classroom

We are learning more about what constitutes effective classroom management behavior. Understanding the related theories and research, and practicing the skills that this body of knowledge has identified as being effective, will help you to establish and maintain the conditions that promote student learning.

Questioning Skills   The questioning process is a central feature of most classrooms. Studies indicate that teachers may ask hundreds of questions in a day's lessons, but they often fail to ask questions that require students to process and analyze information, and their questions require only a rote response of memorized facts. They also tend to rush students' responses, not allowing them adequate time to provide varied and thoughtful answers. Some teachers do not direct as many questions to certain groups of students—boys, girls, "slower" learners—and thus deprive them of the opportunity to interact actively in classroom learning.[24] Mastery of questioning skills contributes to students' learning, and thus is important for effective teaching.

KEVIN AND JIM'S SUGGESTIONS FOR CLASSROOM DISCIPLINE PROBLEMS

1. *When students misbehave, check your instruction.* Many discipline problems result from problems with instruction. Students are bored or confused and their response is to get off task and into trouble.

2. *Spend the time to make sure that students fully understand your classroom's rules and procedures.* As the old adage has it, "You have to keep school before you can teach school." At the beginning of the year, and again if and when things begin to break down, teachers need to fix in the minds of their students how the class is to be ordered.

3. *Regularly monitor the entire class.* Successful classroom managers frequently scan the class, noticing what each student is doing. Although it is not necessary for the teacher to react to every sign of off-task behavior or deviation from the established procedure, it is nevertheless important for students to know that what they are doing is being noted.

4. *Move in on repeated or flagrant breaches of conduct quickly and directly.* Do not let things drift. Students will think you are afraid to confront them, and they may end up confronting you!

5. *Correct in private.* As much as possible, deal with student misconduct in private. Don't disturb the rest of the students and get them off task simply to get one or two students back to work. Also, public reprimanding may backfire and get you involved in a game of escalating remarks with a student.

6. *Don't make empty threats.* Do not say you are going to "do" something to a student or the class unless you have thought it over carefully and are really ready to do it. For instance, do not threaten to call the parents of every child in the room and tell them what rotten children they have unless you have a good deal of time, a WATS line, and alternative plans for next year.

7. *Don't put a hand on a student in anger or even annoyance.* Do not even think of striking a student, no matter how much you are tempted. When a situation is emotionally charged, even your well-intended gesture can be misinterpreted. On the other hand, if students are fighting, for their own good you may need to restrain them physically.

8. *Think through discipline problems.* When your class or an individual student is not behaving up to your expectations, treat the event as a problem-solving activity. Do not flail around or get panicky or discouraged. Coolly identify exactly what the problem is, consider possible causes, and test some possible solutions.

9. *Get help.* If management problems persist and you cannot solve them on your own, get help from a colleague or one of the administrators. Do not let things fester. Do not be shy about asking for help, particularly about discipline problems, which are so common for so many beginning teachers.

10. *Be sure there is a back-up system.* If you need to remove a youngster from your room, you need to know that there is a system that will back you up.

11. *Be sure that your rules accord with schoolwide expectations.* For example, if the school has decided that chewing gum is tolerable and you crack down on it, you can expect to have more trouble than the issue is probably worth.

Those who have studied the relationship between specific questioning strategies and student achievement have identified these techniques as signs of effective teaching:

1. Phrase questions clearly to insure appropriate responses.
2. Ask questions that are primarily academic.
3. With elementary students of low socioeconomic status, ask many questions that demand recall of information.
4. Ask questions that demand original and evaluative thinking.
5. After asking a question, allow three to five seconds of wait-time before requesting a response.
6. Encourage students to respond in some way to each question asked.
7. Balance responses from volunteering and nonvolunteering students.
8. Encourage a high percentage of correct responses; assist with incorrect responses.
9. To stimulate thinking, probe students' responses or demand support for their answers.
10. Acknowledge students' correct responses; be specific and discriminating in the use of praise.[25]

With knowledge and practice, teachers can learn questioning strategies that engage all students in the verbal interaction that supports learning.

WAIT-TIME

Good questioning behavior requires that the teacher provide students with sufficient time to think about and respond to questions. Mary Budd Rowe, a science educator, determined in a series of studies that the teachers she observed waited less than one second before calling on a student to respond. Furthermore, after calling on a student, they waited only about a second for the student to answer before calling on someone else, rephrasing the question, giving a clue, or answering it themselves.

Rowe followed up these observations with studies designed to train teachers to increase their wait-time from one second to three to five seconds. She reported amazing results, including the following:

1. an increase in the average length of student responses
2. an increase in unsolicited but appropriate student responses
3. an increase in student-initiated questions
4. a decrease in failures to respond
5. an increase in student-to-student interaction
6. an increase in speculative responses

In short, she found that longer wait-times led to more active participation on the part of more students, with an increase in the quality of their participation. Subsequent research by others replicated her findings.

In analyzing these research findings on wait-time, Good and Brophy conclude that "pacing and wait-time should be suited to the questions being asked and ultimately to the objectives their questions are designed to accomplish. A fast pace and short wait-times are appropriate for drill or review activities covering specific facts." On the other hand, they state, "If questions are intended to stimulate students to think about material and formulate original responses rather than merely to retrieve information from memory, it is important to allow time for these effects to occur."

Thomas L. Good and Jere E. Brophy, *Looking in Classrooms*, 5th ed. (New York: HarperCollins, 1991), pp. 482–483.

Planning Skills Another skill related to a teacher's effectiveness is skill in planning. The plans that teachers make for lessons influence the opportunity that students have to learn, because plans determine the content students will experience in a lesson and the focus of the teaching processes.[26] Effective teachers base their plans on a rich store of perceptions of classroom events and of their students' progress toward educational objectives. This store of perceptions—ways of looking at students and classroom activities—also helps the teacher make adjustments during instruction when plans must be adapted to the immediate situation.

EDUCATION: A WORLD VIEW

TEACHER EVALUATION IN THE U.S., GREAT BRITAIN, AND AUSTRALIA

One way of viewing the effectiveness of teachers is through periodic evaluations of teacher performance. You are probably familiar with many of the procedures for evaluating teachers in the United States. Typically, school principals conduct teacher evaluations, though in some school districts this may be the responsibility of assistant principals or perhaps department chairpersons. Most often evaluation is based on direct classroom observation, and performance may be rated in terms of a checklist of instructional and professional behaviors, an assessment of how well the teacher achieves goals and objectives, or possibly of how well the students achieve learning goals. Such procedures are usually established at the local level by persons directly involved in the process of evaluation. Major purposes of evaluation may include improving teacher performance, enforcing minimum competencies, or terminating incompetent teachers.

In Great Britain, teacher evaluation is the responsibility of an inspectorate system. Her Majesty's Inspectors (HMI) are housed in the central Department of Education and Science. They have far-reaching educational responsibilities, including assessing the national quality and standards of teaching and evaluating how local and national policy initiatives are working in practice. HMIs have a great deal of professional independence and have been described as not merely concerned with reporting standards but with providing pressures and incentives to raise them. The findings of the HMI are reported to the secretary of state and are often the basis for future policy making. At the local level, another group of inspectors is employed by the Local Education Authority (LEA). These local inspectors are under direct control of the chief education officer and conduct inspections and evaluations specific to local need.

The inspectorate system of England was introduced into Australia in the mid-1800s. However, since that time teacher evaluation has been modified and the use of an inspectorate system has greatly diminished. Currently, in the state of New South Wales, for example, teachers' "fitness to teach" is evaluated annually. Principals complete a Teacher Assessment Review Schedule and rate teachers as "efficient" or "unsatisfactory." If a teacher is judged "unsatisfactory," further observation and evaluation are conducted by outside inspectors. Inspectors are also used to evaluate teacher candidates for promotions. In the state of Victoria, inspectors are no longer in use for teacher evaluation. Typically, the principal evaluates first-year teachers and assesses whether they are eligible to continue in the teaching profession. To be considered for promotion in teaching, teachers are interviewed and required to provide relevant documentation to a panel of teachers, parents, teacher unionists, principals, and representatives of the Education Department.

R. F. Goodings and J. E. Dunford, "Her Majesty's Inspectorate of Schools, 1839–1989: The Question of Independence," *Journal of Educational Administration and History* 22, (January 1990):1–8; and Andrew Gitlin and John Smyth, *Teacher Evaluation: Educative Alternatives* (New York: Falmer Press, 1989).

Researchers who have examined plans made by teachers find that they often neglect the following topics that are important to effective instruction:

- students' psychological characteristics that may influence their levels of understanding and ability to process information
- the instructional content
- detailed descriptions of particular instructional strategies to accomplish learning outcomes
- allowance for departures from the planned lesson routine
- alternative strategies if the lesson deviates more than allowed for in plans[27]

Effective teachers anticipate situations likely to occur in a classroom and generate appropriate strategies and contingency plans to adapt instruction to students' needs.[28]

We have looked at three skill areas: classroom management, questioning, and planning. Skills in these areas and others have been identified by researchers as competencies demonstrated by effective teachers. What does this mean for those preparing to teach? During the 1980s states like Virginia, Florida, and Georgia, among others, began to assess beginning teachers for their mastery of these competencies. Gaining skills in areas like classroom management, questioning, and planning is likely to become an important concern for those planning to teach.

A FINAL WORD

You may have found this chapter difficult because of its theoretical emphasis. We think it is an important one, however, because it provides you with an overview of what a truly effective teacher needs to know and be able to do. It may have been a frustrating chapter if you concluded that there is no way that you can achieve the ideal that we describe. We share that frustration, since we ourselves have not measured up to this ideal in our own teaching, and we're not certain that we ever will. Nevertheless, we continue to aspire toward being the type of teacher we have detailed in this chapter. If you, too, can fix your sights upon this conceptualization of what makes an effective teacher and can continually work toward this ideal, you are certain to observe positive and rewarding results in your own classroom.

Discussion Questions

1. As we have previously stated, teachers' low expectations of poor children can be changed if the teachers are provided with evidence that the children's abilities are not inherently inferior to those of other children. What do you think might constitute such evidence?
2. Carl Rogers argues for a teacher who "is *being* himself" and shows feelings. Do you agree? Have you known any teachers who did so? Do you think children can cope with any reaction from the teacher as long as it is honestly expressed? Do you think this kind of teaching requires any particular prior training?
3. Do you have negative feelings about any group or type of people? Can you

identify the basis of those feelings? Do you want to change them? How might you try?

4. Do you agree that it is preferable for an enthusiastic teacher to teach an unimportant subject than for an uninspired teacher to teach a crucial subject? What implications do you see in this remark? On what assumptions about teachers, students, and subject matter is it based?

5. Has reading about Carol Landis and her theories-in-use helped you identify any of your own theories-in-use or those of teachers you have known? If so, how?

6. What is the difference between common sense and theoretical knowledge?

7. We have maintained that decision-making skills are important for teachers. What do you think you can do to improve your ability to make good decisions as you plan and deliver instruction?

8. Which of the skills listed on pages 484–485 seem most important to you? What skills would you add to the list? Subtract from it?

9. Do the research findings on academic engaged time surprise you at all? If you think the findings reflect common sense, why do you suppose teachers vary so much in their ability to keep students on task?

10. We have included several researchers' suggestions for managing a classroom. Which seem most useful to you and why?

For Further Reading   Charles, C. M. *Building Classroom Discipline*. 3d ed. New York: Longman, 1989.

A practical, easy-to-use book that examines several different models and approaches to classroom management.

Cooper, James M. (ed). *Classroom Teaching Skills*. 4th ed. Lexington, Mass.: Heath, 1990.

A self-instructional book designed to help teachers acquire basic teaching skills such as writing objectives, evaluation skills, classroom management skills, questioning skills, and interpersonal communication skills.

Emmer, Edmund T., et al. *Classroom Management for Secondary Teachers*. 2d ed. Englewood Cliffs, N.J.: Prentice-Hall, 1989.

A practical guide that emphasizes what teachers can do to manage their classrooms more effectively.

Evertson, Carolyn, et al. *Classroom Management for Elementary Teachers*. 2d ed. Englewood Cliffs, N.J.: Prentice-Hall, 1989.

This book deals, in a chapter-by-chapter treatment, with topics such as room arrangement, rules and procedures for student conduct, how to deal with inappropriate behaviors, and managing instructional activities.

Good, Thomas L., and Jere E. Brophy. *Looking in Classrooms*. 5th ed. New York: HarperCollins, 1991.

An excellent book that provides teachers with concrete skills that enable them to observe and interpret the classroom behavior of both teacher and students.

Joyce, Bruce, and Marsha Weil. *Models of Teaching*. 3d ed. Englewood Cliffs, N.J.: Prentice-Hall, 1986.

> A useful book for both teachers and teacher educators. It describes numerous teaching models that are based on different assumptions about teaching and learning.

Perrone, Vito. *A Letter to Teachers*. San Francisco, CA: Jossey-Bass, Inc., Publishers, 1991.

> Drawing on his conversations with teachers across the country and his own experience working in public schools, Perrone offers insights and practical advice designed to help teachers renew their commitment to their profession and inspire a love of learning in their students. He shows teachers how to restore the intellectual challenge to their work and avoid slipping into routine.

Smith, B. O., et al. *Teachers for the Real World*. Washington, D.C.: American Association of Colleges for Teacher Education, 1969.

> Focuses on the knowledge, skills, and attitudes teachers need.

Notes

1. David Ryans, *Characteristics of Teachers* (Washington, D.C.: American Council on Education, 1960).
2. J. W. Getzels and P. W. Jackson, "The Teacher's Personality and Characteristics," in *Handbook of Research on Teaching,* ed. N. L. Gage (Chicago: Rand McNally, 1963), p. 574.
3. Arthur Jersild, *When Teachers Face Themselves* (New York: Teachers College Press, 1955), p. 83.
4. Ibid.
5. Carl Rogers, *Freedom to Learn* (Columbus, Ohio: Merrill, 1969), p. 10.
6. Edward Blishen (Ed.), *The School That I'd Like* (Hardmondsworth, England: Penguin Books, 1969), pp. 141–143.
7. B. O. Smith, *Teachers for the Real World* (Washington, D.C.: American Association of Colleges for Teacher Education) 1969. The authors are indebted to B. O. Smith, author of *Teachers for the Real World,* for many of the ideas expressed in this section.
8. Lee S. Shulman, "Knowledge and Teaching: Foundations of the New Reform," *Harvard Educational Review* 57 (February 1987): 8.
9. B. O. Smith et al., *Teachers for the Real World,* pp. 121–122. Reprinted by permission of the publisher.
10. Ibid., p. 122.
11. C. Argyris and D. A. Schon, *Theory in Practice: Increasing Professional Effectiveness* (San Francisco: Jossey-Bass, 1974), pp. 3–19.
12. Smith et al., *Teachers for the Real World,* p. 44.
13. The authors are indebted for this example to Frederick J. McDonald, *Educational Psychology* (Belmont, Calif.: Wadsworth, 1965), pp. 439–441.
14. Partially adapted from Smith et al., *Teachers for the Real World,* p. 71.
15. Bruce R. Joyce and Beverly Showers, *Power in Staff Development Through Research on Training* (Alexandria, Va.: ASCD, 1983), p. 25.
16. Wilford A. Weber, "Classroom Management," in *Classroom Teaching Skills,* 4th ed., ed. J. M. Cooper (Lexington, Mass.: Heath, 1990), p. 285.
17. These approaches are identified and described by Weber in "Classroom Management," pp. 247–285.
18. David C. Berliner, "Effective Classroom Teaching: The Necessary but Not Sufficient Condition for Developing Exemplary Schools," in *Research on Exemplary Schools,* ed. Gilbert R. Austin and Herbert Garber (Orlando, Fla.: Academic Press, 1985), pp. 136–138.

19. Jacob S. Kounin, *Discipline and Group Management in Classrooms* (New York: Holt, 1970).

20. Jere Brophy, "Classroom Management as Instruction: Socializing Self-Guidance in Students," *Theory into Practice* 24 (Autumn 1985): 236.

21. Ibid.

22. Ibid.

23. Walter Doyle, "Classroom Organization and Management," in *Handbook of Research on Teaching,* 3d ed., ed. Merlin C. Wittrock (New York: Macmillan, 1986), p. 414.

24. Meredith Gall, "Synthesis of Research on Teachers' Questioning," *Educational Leadership* 42 (November 1984): 40–47.

25. William W. Wilen and Ambrose A. Clegg, Jr., "Effective Questions and Questioning: A Research Review," *Theory and Research in Social Education* (Spring 1986): 153–161.

26. Christopher M. Clark and Penelope L. Peterson, "Teachers' Thought Processes," in *Handbook of Research on Teaching,* pp. 255–296.

27. Philip H. Winne, Wolfgang Rothen, and Ronald W. Marx, *Docent: Artificially Intelligent Courseware for Teachers* (Burnaby, B.C., Canada: Simon Fraser University, 1986), pp. 1–2.

28. David C. Berliner, "In Pursuit of the Expert Pedagogue," Presidential Address at the 1986 Annual Meeting of the American Educational Research Association, *Educational Researcher* 15 (August–September 1986): 5–13.

14

Is Teaching a Profession?

CHAPTER PREVIEW

This chapter focuses on the teacher as a professional, or member of an occupational group. We attempt to show how this rather abstract concept, *professionalism,* affects the daily life of the classroom teacher. In effect, we put the role of the individual teacher in the larger context of the profession.

This chapter emphasizes that:

- Teachers can become involved in different types of situations and conflicts in which they will need counsel or support.

- Teachers have become more powerful in recent years, but they don't have the same kinds of power that members of some other professions have.

- The question of whether teaching is a profession can be judged by reference to specific criteria. Furthermore, there are cases both for and against teaching's being a profession.

- The education of the American teacher has evolved substantially since colonial times.

- Current educational demands require the teacher to be a continuous learner. Teachers can continue their professional growth in various ways.

- The National Board for Professional Teaching Standards and its potential effect on teachers is an emerging issue.

- The National Education Association and the American Federation of Teachers, the most influential teacher organizations, have quite different origins and are competing for the support of classroom teachers.

- The teaching profession is still defining itself, and much depends on its capacity to maintain the public's trust.

he essence of a career in teaching is work and involvement with the young. When people think about becoming teachers, their thoughts and daydreams usually revolve around working with students. Rarely do they bother with hypothetical issues beyond the scope of the classroom. This is both natural and appropriate, since the teacher's success or failure depends on his or her effectiveness with children. Nevertheless, there is more to being a teacher than this. Teachers work within a system that exposes them to pressures from many quarters. Prospective teachers are frequently somewhat naive about the pressures and forces that will impinge on them, and naiveté can be dangerous, in terms of both making a career decision and making a successful career.

Teaching within a system

To help you see this point, we would like you to indulge in a set of daydreams for a few moments. We will offer you a series of brief scenarios, and, after reading each one, you should reflect on how you might react. As you read each one, imagine yourself teaching in that ideal classroom you carry around in your head. Assume that you appear to be doing a fine job. You are really enjoying it. Your students are making nice progress. They seem to be interested in their work. A few parents have indicated that although they were initially worried that their precious child was to have a new (read "untested") teacher, they are thrilled with the child's progress in your class. Okay. Things are going very well, and . . .

1. As happy and totally immersed in your new job as you are, you can't help but be bothered by the negative attitudes of some of the school's teachers. Before school, in the teachers' lounge, at lunch, at meetings, they take every chance to carp about the principal, their salaries, the parents, and especially the kids. The same ones who are always complaining never volunteer for anything, and you are sure they are going to trample one of the first- or second-graders one of these days as they race from the building to see who can be the **Last hired; first fired** first to roar out of the parking lot. It is April, and your principal sits you down and tells you that although you are the best new teacher he has ever had in the building and that everyone is very pleased with your work, he has to let you go. The increased salary and benefits package for next year that the union won from the school board means that the board, which will have the same amount of money for teachers' salaries next year as it does this year, is going to have to economize by releasing a few teachers. According to the contract, the district can't fire the ones felt to be least effective but must let go teachers according to seniority. It's the old rule of "last hired; first fired." You are at the bottom of the totem pole. As the impact of what the principal is saying sinks in, a picture comes to mind of the teachers' lounge next September, with those deadbeat teachers casually slandering their students while you. . . . What will you be doing?

2. Four days in a row representatives of the Yearbook Committee burst into your classroom unannounced and literally take over. They claim they are signing up subscribers for the yearbook, but they take a good 10 minutes each time, most of which is devoted to wisecracking, showing off, and subtly putting you down in various ways. Their attitude is something on the order of "Look, teach. You're new in this school and you've got a lot to learn. We've

501

been here four years and we know our way around. Don't try to pull rank on us." When they finally leave, it takes a long time to get your students back in a mood to do some serious work. You complain to the principal (as it happens, a former yearbook advisor), who says, "Yearbook is one of the biggest things in this school. It is a student-run activity in which everyone takes great pride. Last year the yearbook won honorable mention in the South-Southwestern Regional Yearbook Conference for high schools with over 2,000 and under 2,500 students with a lower-middle-class socioeconomic population. All of us who were here last year were very proud of the kids and what they did for the school. I know once you're here with us a little longer, you'll get into the swing of things. I'll send you a few copies of past yearbooks. I know you're going to help this year's yearbook staff in every way you can. They're really great, live-wire kids and come from some of our best families." You ask around and find out that you should expect visits from the yearbook staff three or four times a week for the next two months. They have pictures to take, workers to enlist, advertisements to sell . . . and new teachers to break in.

Limited support from principal

3. You get a special-delivery letter from a group called PAP (Patriotic American Parents). You have heard that they are very active in your area and are especially interested in schools. Their letter informs you that their lawyer is preparing a case against you for using books that are on their disapproved list. (You didn't know there was such a list but, sure enough, there is, and you have.) They claim they have evidence that you are waging a subtle but nevertheless vicious war against the cause of justice and liberty and have succeeded in temporarily deflecting the minds of some of your students from the truth. Furthermore, they want to know why you display the U.N. flag. Finally, you are said to recite the Pledge of Allegiance in a much too hasty fashion, which is clearly a sign of your disrespect for your country. This is the first you have heard of these charges or even of the Patriots' interest in you. You think of yourself as patriotic and are shocked by the letter. They have requested that you respond in writing by next week or they will begin legal proceedings.

Target of pressure groups

4. In late January, the superintendent—who holds a conference with each new teacher—told you she thought you were doing a fine job and that she wanted you to return next year. In passing, she remarked that she would be getting a contract to you in the spring. Toward the end of April, you got a little nervous and called her. You spoke to her executive secretary, who said not to worry, that you were on the list, and that a contract would be coming before long. You stopped worrying. Today is the last day of school, and you find a very nice personal note from the principal in your school mailbox. He thanks you for your fine work during the year and says he is sorry you will not be back next year. You call the superintendent's office. She is in conference, and her executive secretary says that they are not renewing your contract. She cannot remember speaking to you in April. She knows nothing about the case. She does know, however, that the board of education has put on a lot of pressure for cuts in next year's personnel budget. She ends by telling you, "You must be very disappointed, dear. I know how you feel."

The invisible contract

5. You noticed something peculiar when you sat down at the faculty dining table one lunch hour. Conversations stopped, and you had the distinct impression your colleagues had been talking about you. A few days later, an older teacher stopped you in the hall after school and said, "I don't want to butt in, but you really are upsetting Mrs. Hilary and Mr. Alexandra." Mrs. H. and Mr. A. have the classrooms on either side of yours. Apparently, they claim your class makes so much noise that they can't get anything done. Both are very traditional in their approach to education. You believe in a more activity-oriented approach. Although your class is rather noisy occasionally, it is never chaotic, and its noise is usually a by-product of the students' involvement in the task. Twice Mr. Alexandra has sent messengers with notes asking that your class be more quiet. You have always complied. You hardly know either teacher. You have never really talked to Mr. Alexandra except to say hello. Mrs. Hilary, with whom you've chatted, prides herself on being a disciplinarian. What she means, you have inferred, is that she is able to keep the children quiet. You know Mr. Alexandra is chummy with Mrs. Hilary. You go to the vice principal, who seems to know all about the case, but only from the Hilary-Alexandra angle. Inexplicably, the vice principal gets quite angry and claims that until you came along the faculty got along beautifully. Furthermore, you are being very unprofessional in making complaints against experienced teachers. You feel as if you are trapped in a Kurt Vonnegut novel.

Conflict with colleagues

6. You had been teaching industrial arts for two months when you met another new teacher at a faculty meeting. A few weeks later you both were assigned to chaperon a dance. Then you began going out on "real dates." By Christmas you knew you were over the edge. On New Year's Eve you became engaged. You plan to get married on the first Saturday in June after school ends. On Valentine's Day you both announced the news to your students (none of whom were surprised) and to your faculty colleagues (who didn't have a clue). You have both been doing well and want to stay on at your jobs next year. On April Fools' Day, you get a notice from the personnel director calling your attention to the board ruling against hiring couples. You know that there are no openings in any nearby schools.

Obstacles to marriage

Keep in mind that these little horror stories are not everyday occurrences. Also, it is important for you to know that entrance into any profession has its trials. These accounts were written to help you realize that you can be an effective teacher and still have trouble keeping your job. What is the common theme running through each of these anecdotes? You, the teacher, were succeeding in your work with children, but forces outside the classroom began to impinge on you. Union salary demands meant there was no room in the budget for your teaching position. The Patriots wanted to make a target case of you. When the yearbook wiseacres started playing havoc with your class, the principal failed to back you up. On two occasions the school system bureaucracy was ready to put you on the unemployed rolls. Two of your colleagues damaged your reputation with the faculty and administration. Other than that, it was a super year.

Although you may feel confident that you could handle some of these

Although conflicts can arise between teachers working closely together under a lot of stress, they are also a great resource for sharing insights they've gained through experience over time and in varied teaching situations.

(Alan Carey/The Image Works)

Organizational support

situations, it is doubtful that you could cope with all of them. In some cases you would be powerless to respond effectively to your adversaries, and you might end up a helpless victim of circumstance. Fortunately, a teacher is not alone. Like people in many other occupational groups, teachers have organizations that protect them from such indignities and injustices. These organizations function on several levels, from the local to the national. Their very existence often keeps situations like those described from occurring, and when they do occur, these organizations are there to support the teacher, even though seniority usually rules.

In becoming a teacher, you are not just committing yourself to work with children. You are joining an occupational group comprised of other individuals with similar responsibilities, concerns, and pressures, whose help you may need and who, in turn, will need your help. It is also an occupational group with a long and rich history in American society.

TEACHING IN AMERICA: AN HISTORICAL PERSPECTIVE

The education of teachers for their profession has made extraordinary strides since the colonial period, when the only real criterion was that a teacher had to know more than the students. In the nineteenth century, the expansion of the common schools required larger numbers of teachers, and the development of public high schools required that the quality of elementary teaching be improved.

"What homework? These are hall passes, insurance forms, attendance reports, competency updates, and my grocery list."

Ford Button/Phi Delta Kappan

These demands gradually resulted in increasingly higher standards for teacher education. By the 1900s, new theories about psychology, learning, and the nature of teaching made professional training even more necessary. Normal schools, colleges, and universities began to offer sophisticated programs that, in recent years, have increasingly become subject to public pressure for teacher accountability.

The Colonial Period

Teachers not highly valued

QUALIFICATIONS   Most teachers in the colonial period were not guided by any particular professional or long-term motivation. Teaching was generally viewed as a temporary position that was all right until something better came along. Teachers had to be acceptable, usually in terms of their religious orthodoxy, civil loyalty, and moral standards. For instance, in 1653, the head of Harvard College was fired because, unlike the Puritan authorities, he did not favor infant baptism. Prior to the American Revolution, teachers were required to sign loyalty oaths of allegiance to the crown of England; once the Revolution started, they had to sign loyalty oaths to the various states. Even though rigidly prescribed moral behavior was variously defined, it was a criterion for teaching in virtually every community.

Although much emphasis was placed publicly on the religious, political, and moral worthiness of teachers, the public had very low expectations concerning teachers' professional training. There were no specialized schools to train teachers; the only educational training any teacher had was simply having been a student. Generally, a teacher was expected to know just enough about the subject matter to be able to pass along this knowledge to the pupils. Thus began the teacher's tradition of being only one page ahead of the students. Many contracts with elementary teachers required only that the teacher be able to read, write, and calculate.

No professional preparation

Throughout the colonial period much attention was paid to insuring that teachers lived up to the expectations of the people who controlled education. In New England, teachers were approved by town meetings, selectmen, school committees, and ministers; in the Middle Colonies and the South, teachers were issued certificates by governors and religious groups.

STATUS   The highest salaries and status were granted to college teachers, the next best to secondary school teachers, and the lowest to elementary school teachers. Salaries were often irregular in payment and were frequently supplemented with payment in produce or livestock. The colonial teacher, then, received wages equivalent to those of a farmhand.

Poor pay

Teaching was hardly considered to be a profession in colonial America. Schools were poorly equipped, and students attended irregularly. The school term was short, in many cases making teaching a part-time occupation. Many patrons of education felt that teaching was a fairly undemanding task, and they would add to the duties of the teacher such custodial chores as cleaning out the church, ringing the assembly bell, providing for the baptismal basin, running errands, serving as messenger, digging graves, assisting the pastor in reading the Scriptures, leading the singing at church services, keeping records, issuing invitations, writing letters, visiting the sick, and generally being useful. The teacher was often "boarded round," living with a different family every few weeks to stretch out meager school funds.

Undesirable conditions

As a result of these and other indignities, the turnover rate among teachers was high and contributed to keeping the status and quality of teachers low. In many ways, the idea of teachers being a professional group, with a "calling" to their vocation, did not develop until the 1800s.

The Nineteenth Century

TEACHERS FOR THE COMMON SCHOOLS   The common school movement of the early nineteenth century (described in Chapter 4), with its consequent demand for better-trained elementary school teachers, was one of the most exciting periods in the history of American education. In no other period do we find in speeches and pamphlets greater emotional and intellectual challenges to place education at the center of the endeavor to maintain democracy. In no other period

Call for better teachers

do we find more compelling calls to raise the standards of training, salaries, and professional qualifications for teachers. The vocation of teaching was put forth as an intellectual, religious, and patriotic calling.

Teacher-training academies

In the period between 1820 and 1865, educators began to call for special training for teachers. The academies were, by and large, the teacher-training institutions during this period, but as the name implies, they provided training in academic subject matter only, not in the principles of teaching. Educators called for coupling academic secondary education for teachers with education in the principles of teaching.

WOMEN TEACHERS   As in colonial times, teachers' salaries were quite low. Wages continued to reflect a general attitude that teachers were considered to be people who were unable to hold a regular job, or were a bit eccentric, or had nothing much else to do anyway. Indeed, it was at this time that a shift from men to women teachers began in the elementary schools. The result of that trend is still evident today, over 150 years later. Today, 69 percent of teachers in the public schools are women.[1]

Shift to women teachers

There were several reasons for this change. With the growth of popular democracy and the beginnings of the common school movement, the idea developed that practically anyone, including women, could function as public servants. Another reason, perhaps the major one, was that the increase in the number of schools also increased the number of teaching positions. Each of these positions had to be paid for, and women, quite frankly, could be paid less—in some places only about one-third the salary that men teachers received.

Women teachers cheaper

Other factors also encouraged the greater involvement of women in education in the 1830s. In formerly handcrafted production, such as embroidery, industry was gradually replacing housewives with machines. Seeking a higher standard of living, men began to move either westward or to the industrializing cities. As a result, when the common schools began to require better-quality teachers, the female academies, seminaries, and normal schools began to provide them.

NORMAL SCHOOLS AND COLLEGES   The idea of the normal school originated in Europe. The term *normal* referred to teaching teachers the *norms,* or rules, of teaching. The first two normal schools in the United States were established in 1823, in Vermont, and in 1827, in Massachusetts. The normal schools were essentially private academies that offered additional training in teaching methods and classroom discipline. A decade later, in 1837, Catharine Beecher became a full-time advocate of normal schools to train women for teaching. In addition, Beecher established the National Board of Popular Education, which sent over four hundred Eastern women teachers to the West. By 1860, there were twelve public normal schools in eight states. There were also informal teachers institutes, offered for six-week sessions between teaching schedules, and colleges even began to offer an odd course or two on teaching methods.

Development of teacher education institutions called "normal schools"

GROWING PROFESSIONALIZATION   Following the Civil War, the greater demand for public secondary education carried with it the inherent demand for
more highly trained teachers. In addition to the sheer increase in the number of
available teaching positions, new educational theories and techniques and the
development of the field of child psychology all required that teachers receive
greater training if they were to implement the new strategies in the classroom.
It became less and less tolerable that so many reasons other than educational
criteria were used as qualifications for teaching positions.

BEFORE WORLD WAR I   By the turn of the century, balanced teacher-training
programs had been developed that included instruction in the academic content
the teacher was going to teach, the foundations of educational theory, the administrative aspects of teaching, child psychology, and pedagogical strategies.
Every state had at least one public normal school. Most schools accepted students who had about two years of high school background. Most graduates be-

CATHARINE BEECHER

1800–1878

Catharine Beecher believed strongly that for women to be
properly prepared as teachers, they needed special training
institutions similar to the model of men's colleges and universities already in existence. She spent nearly fifty years
improving the quality of women's education and raising
women's status in the teaching profession.

　　Born in Connecticut, Catharine Beecher received
her first formal education from her father, the well-known
clergyman Lyman Beecher. After the untimely death of
her fiancé, Beecher decided to devote her life to the service of mankind as a teacher. Not long afterward, in 1828,
she founded the Hartford Female Seminary. The establishment of this institution for the education of females set the
pattern for her life's work.

　　At a time when women had to leave the teaching
profession upon marriage, Beecher urged them to become
teachers before fulfilling their calls to be wives and mothers. However, she emphasized that the quality of women's
education needed to be improved, pointing out that the
model of female loveliness that included fainting and
playing the "pretty plaything" was not adequate for the

roles women were expected to assume. Beecher called
upon the leading female schools in the country to establish
a uniform course of education adapted to the character and
circumstances of women to correspond to what was done
in colleges for young men, and she urged the benefactors
of female institutions to provide suitable facilities for instruction, such as libraries and scientific equipment.

　　Beecher advocated a division of labor within the
faculty so that the loss of a teacher would not interrupt the
educational program, and she saw the need for teachers
who were not generalists, but specialists in academic disciplines. Throughout her life Catharine Beecher spoke and
wrote extensively on ways to improve the education of
women, while establishing female seminaries in New
England and across the Midwest. Each of these seminaries
was attached to a model school supported financially by
the children who attended it. The faculties were prepared
to teach at other seminaries to establish a regular and systematic course of education to be implemented throughout
the country. For women who were unable to pay for their
preparation as teachers, she urged that alternative public
institutions be maintained. At a time when it was uncommon to campaign for educational reform and defend the
needs of women, Catharine Beecher spent her life striving
to do both.

came elementary school teachers after two years, although some took a four-year program to become high school teachers and administrators.

College training increases

College-level teacher training grew with impetus from two directions. One was the expansion of normal school course offerings into four-year curricula; the other was the development of university courses and, eventually, departments of education. Both were stimulated by the increasing demand that high school teachers should have some college training. By 1900, there were thus several ways to acquire teacher training: normal schools, teachers colleges, university departments of education, and the less formal teachers institutes.

The Twentieth Century

Four-year colleges

After World War I normal schools continued to become four-year colleges, which quadrupled in number between 1920 and 1940, from about forty-five to more than two hundred. The Great Depression of the 1930s actually helped to raise the standards for teachers, simply as a function of supply and demand. With more people than there were jobs, school districts could require additional training for qualifications.

From training to education

A number of major changes in teacher training can be traced over the first fifty years of the twentieth century. The most important change was the move to *teacher education,* not just teacher training. This change in labels was no empty symbolism. It signaled a change in the substance of what teachers were expected to know. By 1950, most teachers had at least a four-year college degree, with a specific content area of instruction, professional courses in teaching methods and educational psychology, and some period of practice through observation, laboratory experience, and student teaching. It was also recognized that elementary as well as secondary school teachers needed four years of college.

Extending the education period

The four-year time period has been the norm until the present. Today, only a small percentage of states require teachers to have five years of college education before they can be certified. But many teacher educators, believing that adequate teacher preparation cannot be accomplished in four years of college, are calling for extended teacher-preparation programs that combine a baccalaureate degree in a discipline with a master's degree in professional coursework. This is not a totally new idea, since many of the nation's best universities have had master of arts in teaching programs for many decades. These MAT programs are designed typically for liberal arts graduates who are preparing to be high school teachers. The new effort is for making all teacher education extend into the graduate level. In particular, the Holmes Group, an association of approximately one hundred deans of schools of education across the country, is advocating such a change.[2] As a result of its efforts, some research universities have already implemented five-year or fifth-year teacher-preparation programs. Public concern about teacher competency and teacher educators' desire to enhance the professional status of teaching will likely reinforce efforts to lengthen and make more rigorous the preparation required for teachers. Whether or not the current proposals, such as that offered by the Holmes Group, take root, of one thing we are certain: as the importance of schooling becomes more and more clear to greater numbers of Americans, higher and higher standards of teacher competence and preparation will be demanded.

THE TEACHER AND POWER

As a society we are becoming increasingly aware of how our lives are affected by big institutions and power blocs. Policies and activities of the giant corporations, large labor unions, and big government daily affect events and details of our lives and the nation's economic health. Further, we have a new appreciation for how the power of the American Medical Association affects the quality and nature of health service in our country and for how the American Bar Association affects the delivery of legal services. These groups of men and women have power. They can affect the lives of those around them. People who have power can use it for good or for evil. Anyone who wants to effect major change in an institution must first have power.

As we have seen from our whirlwind tour through history, for years teachers wielded little influence in American society, except that which they wielded in their own classrooms. Indeed, until the 1960s teachers were considered a quiet and docile occupational group. Beginning around 1960, teachers became better organized and more vocal. Whether the general public has liked it or not, teachers have gained power.

Increasing political power

Teachers seem to have two great sources of power. First, through their professional organizations (which we will discuss later in this chapter) they have a great deal of political power in federal, state, and local elections. Politicians court the teachers' votes and listen to their views. Also, teachers can strike or participate in a work stoppage (or, as they euphemistically say, "withhold their professional services"). Since so many parents today work and rely upon schools to provide child care as well as education, when teachers strike, not only do schools close, but many parents are forced to stay home from work to take care of their children. Being able to stop a school in its tracks means having power. Second, teachers also have immense power in their own classrooms. Although they are usually assigned a particular curriculum, they decide just how it will be taught. The teacher decides which student will be given special attention, which student will be rewarded, and which student will not be rewarded. As everyone who has ever been a student knows, the teacher has enormous influence on the daily lives of students.

Great power in classroom

Nevertheless, teachers do not seem to have much power in many other ways. They have very little say about the conditions of their daily employment. They don't make decisions about what subjects are taught, which teachers are hired or fired, who the principal and other administrators are, what the school's grading policy is, how long the school day is, and so on and so on. If a new school is to be built, the teachers who will work in the new building are rarely, if ever, consulted about the kind of environment they would consider most suitable and conducive to learning. When a new principal is chosen, the teachers are not asked to participate in the decision-making process. Rarely are they even asked what they think the new principal's qualifications should be. As one Ar-

Little power outside classroom

> *When teachers come to regard themselves as persons of key importance in the society, they will retain much longer than at present something of the respect in which the young should naturally hold them.*
>
> — J. GLENN GRAY —

The use of the strike by teachers has been a source of great controversy among teachers and in the general population.

(Mike Penney/David R. Frazier Photolibrary)

kansas teacher stated, "I've been teaching in this same school and living in this same community for twenty-six years. I've had all sorts of commendations and good teaching awards. But in twenty-six years not once has anyone on the school board or any of the administrators asked my advice on an educational matter. I haven't been asked about one darned thing."*

Discouraging as this picture may seem to some of you, not all teachers are dissatisfied with the existing state of affairs. Some are quite content to simply teach and leave all the squabbling to those they call "the activists." They think that teachers have come a long way in recent years and that they should be satisfied with what they have gained. They would agree with the statement "Education is too important to be left in the hands of the educators." The more activist teachers, however, feel that this attitude is itself the problem, and that this kind of passivity has kept teachers oppressed and the quality of their service low. They assert that teaching will not fully become a profession until their colleagues take a more vigorous, independent position. And this leads us directly to the question "Is teaching a profession?"

The activists' stand

WHAT IS A PROFESSION?

A *profession* is more than a group of individuals all engaged in the same line of work. Professions have a more-or-less recognizable set of characteristics that distinguish them from nonprofessions.[3] As you read the following list of characteristics, check whether or not you think teaching qualifies on each premise.

Does Teaching Qualify?

First, a profession renders a unique, definite, and essential service to society. Only the people in the particular profession render the service. For instance, only lawyers practice law. The service rendered must be considered so important that it is available to all the people in a society.

Yes ☐   No ☐

Second, a profession relies on intellectual skills in the performance of its service. This does not mean that physical actions and skills are not needed, but rather that the emphasis in carrying on the work is on intellectual skills and techniques.

Yes ☐   No ☐

Third, a profession has a long period of specialized training. Because professional work requires special intellectual skills, specialized intellectual training is needed. General education, such as that represented by a bachelor's degree, is valued, but not considered adequate. The specialized training must cover a substantial period and not be obtained in cram courses or correspondence schools.

Yes ☐   No ☐

Fourth, both individual members of the profession and the professional group enjoy a considerable degree of autonomy and decision-making authority. Professional groups regulate their own activities rather than have outsiders set policies and enforce adherence to standards. Whereas factory workers have very

---

* Personal communication. Name withheld upon request (this teacher admits he is powerless, but he's not stupid).

limited decision-making power and are closely supervised in the performance of their work, professionals are expected to make most of their own decisions and be free of close supervision by supervisors.

Yes ☐   No ☐

Fifth, a profession requires its members to accept personal responsibility for their actions and decisions, and in general for their performance. Since the professional's service is usually related to the human welfare of individuals, this responsibility is an especially serious one.

Yes ☐   No ☐

Sixth, a profession emphasizes the services rendered by its practitioners more than their financial rewards. Although the personal motives of any individual professional are not necessarily any higher than any other worker's, the professional group's public emphasis is on service.

Yes ☐   No ☐

Seventh, a profession is self-governing and responsible for policing its own ranks. This means there are professional groups who perform a number of activities aimed at keeping the quality of their services high and looking out for the social and economic well-being of the professional members. Also, these self-governing organizations set standards of admission and exclusion for the profession.

Yes ☐   No ☐

Eighth, a profession has a code of ethics that sets out the acceptable standards of conduct for its members. For a professional group to regulate the quality of service, it needs a code of ethics to aid it in enforcing high standards.

Yes ☐   No ☐

These characteristics, then, are the major requirements of a profession. Few professions satisfy all of them fully. However, the list does serve as a bench mark by which occupational groups can measure themselves and direct their development if they wish to enjoy professional status.

Importance to quality of life

The question "Is teaching a profession?" probably arouses little interest in many of you. Most people thinking about a career in teaching are more interested in whether it will be a personally rewarding way to spend their time than in whether or not it is a profession. Will teaching bring me personal satisfactions? Will it provide an outlet for my talents and energies? Will I be effective with kids? These questions are, we suspect, closer to your skin. Nevertheless, the question of professionalism and the related issues are important to teachers and have an effect on the *quality of education* teachers provide for children. They will also affect the quality of your life as a teacher.

TWO SIDES
OF THE ISSUE

*The Case FOR
Teaching as a
Profession*

Have great responsibility

The very nobility of the teacher's work is evidence in favor of its status as a profession. Society has entrusted teachers with its most important responsibility: the education of its young. Throughout the course of history, many great minds have acknowledged the teacher's worth. Martin Luther asserted that the teacher's vocation was second only to that of the ministry. Thomas Carlyle in *Sartor Resartus* calls teachers "fashioners of souls," who ought to be "world-honored dignitaries" like generals and field marshals. As more and more people recognize how crucial education is to the fulfillment of our personal and national goals, the opportunities and rewards for the teacher will improve, as they have improved rather steadily in this country throughout the last three centuries and particularly in the last sixty years.

Although children learn from many people—from parents to television personalities—teachers are the specialists who pass on to the young the key skills necessary to participate effectively in the culture. They aid the young in acquiring the most difficult, if not the most important, skills: those that involve thinking and manipulating ideas. Neither reading nor geometry is often learned on the street. Although teachers do not undergo a particularly lengthy period of specialized training, they are in a sense continually training. Teachers are expected (and, in some states, required by law) to upgrade their teaching skills continually.

Teach unique skills

The autonomy of the teacher, like that of every professional, is somewhat limited. Unlike lawyers and doctors, who can reject clients, teachers have students assigned to them. They also have a supervisor, their principal or department head. They teach a curriculum that has been chosen or developed largely by others. However, within these limits, teachers have an immense area of personal control. They normally determine the method of instruction. They decide which aspects of the curriculum they will highlight and which they will cover quickly. The limits on their creativity are few or nonexistent. After the initial few years of teaching, they are seldom observed and evaluated. Teachers' classrooms are their castles. If teachers feel that they do not have enough autonomy or do not agree with their administrators, they are free to move to another school. However, a teacher's autonomy is accompanied by a responsibility to teach effectively. Like any professionals, teachers must be able to justify the manner in which they render their social services. They must be able to justify their grading policy and evaluations of student work. Teachers are expected to take responsibility for their actions and to be open to criticisms of their teaching performance.

Have a domain of control

Teachers are represented by organizations, such as the National Education Association and the American Federation of Teachers, whose major function is improving education by improving the teaching profession. They provide information and aid to classroom teachers; they support them against unjust pressures from members of the public or the school board; they set standards and censure teachers who violate these standards; they provide ancillary economic services, such as travel programs, group insurance policies, investment programs, and professional book clubs; and, finally, they attempt to influence the laws and regulations that govern schooling and the teaching profession.

Have professional organizations

Some argue that teaching is not a profession because teachers lack the autonomy of, say, a small-town lawyer, or because they have not achieved the economic status of dentists and doctors. These arguments are superficial and, in many cases, outdated. More and more doctors are employed by health maintenance organizations and are forming unions to protect their rights. A similar situation is facing many dentists. Also questionable is the assertion that teaching is not a profession because many teachers do not act like professionals. Neither do many ministers, architects, or lawyers. Certainly the crucial nature of the teacher's work and the selfless spirit of service of the best teachers raises teaching to the level of a profession.

Nature of work counts

The Case AGAINST
Teaching as a
Profession

The roots of the teaching "profession" go back to ancient Greece, where slaves called *paidagogos,* or pedagogues, taught children to read and write and helped them memorize passages of poetic history. Recently teachers, along with such other occupational groups as barbers, beauticians, taxidermists, athletes, and—according to a TV commercial of a few years ago—even dishwashers, have latched on to the term *professional* in an attempt to raise their incomes and their status. But a careful look at current practices reveals that teaching does not qualify as a profession. If education is a teacher's unique function, the teacher has a great deal of competition. Ignoring for a moment the mounting criticism of compulsory miseducation (such as forcing children to attend school even when education is inferior), let us admit that teachers have no monopoly on education. Children today learn a tremendous amount from the media: "Sesame Street," public affairs specials, *Time,* Peter Jennings, Bart Simpson, MTV, novels, Eddie Murphy, *Seventeen,* and *Popular Mechanics.* Then there are the nonteacher educators: parents, ministers, older friends, neighbors, employers, best friends, coaches, scout leaders, playground and camp counselors, and grandparents. The world is bursting with teachers, and those who hold forth in school buildings have only a small piece of the action.

Hardly a unique service

Although teaching has intellectual and theoretical foundations, it requires a rather short period of specialized training (considerably less than some of the skilled trades), and entrance into the occupation is not especially competitive, particularly on intellectual grounds. If it is a profession, it is one largely composed of college graduates with a wide range of ability and academic achievement and a wide range of motivations for becoming teachers.

Training not rigorous

Although there is a good deal of talk about teachers' autonomy and decision-making power, both exist at a very low level. Teachers are at the second rung from the bottom (superior only to students) of the hierarchy commanded by the board of education. They teach whom they are told, what they are told, and when they are told. If their supervisors do not like the results, teachers are only rarely protected by their professional group from being fired (or, more gently, "not rehired") by the local school board. Most of the important decisions that affect teachers' daily lives, even those that bear directly on the standards of their own profession, are made by nonteachers (administrators and citizen school board members). Teachers do not formally evaluate other teachers. Administrators do that. Teachers, typically, do not have much to do with and very little say in the preservice training of teachers. Although teachers are beginning to get a say in the licensing and certification of teachers, laypeople and bureaucrats wield a great deal of decision making power. Some teachers, like factory workers, even have to punch a time clock (more genteelly, they "sign in and sign out" . . . to the same effect). In sum, they have very little to say about what goes on in their "shop."

Little decision-making power

The same is true of the teacher's responsibility. Teachers rarely lose their jobs because Johnnie can't read or Samantha failed calculus. After a teacher achieves tenure, it takes some form of gross negligence, clear incompetence, or serious sexual offense for him or her to be fired. As for the professional organizations policing their own ranks, there is much rhetoric but next to no action.

Little accountability

The professional organizations for teachers are just like other self-serving organizations, whether composed of teamsters or dentists; their primary energies go to their own survival and growth. Secondarily, they attempt to protect their members, increase their salaries, and expand their welfare benefits. Most teachers, however, just pay dues and are minimally involved and interested in professional organizations and their activities, except when they call a strike—a somewhat odd activity for a "profession."

Most teachers claim they are too busy to take an active role in professional affairs. This lack of real involvement in professional activities might stem from the fact that so many teachers have second jobs, either as homemakers or in the labor market. They are unenthusiastic about working for higher standards because one of the first sacrifices to professionalism would be their second jobs. In actual fact, teachers work in circumstances very different from those of other professionals. They are hired, like other public servants, rather than operating as independent agents. They are on a fixed salary schedule and are protected by tenure laws, rather than independently having to find a market for their services. Teaching is a low-pay, relatively high-security job, rather than a high-pay, low-security profession. Seniority as a teacher may be more important than competence. Talk about professionalism may be personally satisfying to teachers, but it does not conform to the reality of the teacher's occupational life.

A Third Possibility   Like most important questions, "Is teaching a profession?" cannot be answered satisfactorily with simple pro-and-con arguments, such as those just offered. Also, teachers differ so much in the conditions under which they work and possess such varying degrees of knowledge, commitment, and expertise that it is difficult to come up with a definitive answer. In some schools, teachers fulfill many of the criteria of professionals. In other schools, they seem to function as clerks and technicians. Perhaps we could say that teaching is a semiprofession. In certain ways teaching is clearly eligible for professional status, and in certain others it deviates sharply from accepted canons of professionalism. On the one hand, teachers provide an intellectual service to the community. They undergo specialized training to master the theoretical basis of their work. Ethical standards guide their work with students. On the other hand, they function too often like many other lower-level white-collar workers and civil servants. Too often seniority and security are the rule, rather than excellence and independence. Like many other occupational groups that are called professional, teachers, at this moment in history, only partially qualify.

Another way to look at the issue, and one we favor, is to think of teaching as being *in the process of becoming a profession*. As shown by the historical descriptions of the work and living conditions of teachers discussed earlier in this chapter, the life, status, and education of teachers have changed dramatically.

Whether teaching becomes a profession in your career lifetime will depend on some of the following factors. First, teachers must take on a larger role in the governing of their career affairs. Whereas the direction of education and the schools should be in the hands of many groups (parents, community leaders, students, and teachers), control over the teaching profession per se should be in

Few criteria apply

Teaching as a semiprofession

Need more self-determination

the hands of teachers. Up to now, the great majority of teachers has taken the attitude of "Let George do it". As a result, outsiders make the major decisions about who should teach, how teachers should be trained, and under what conditions they should render their services. Although teachers are eating better these days, they still lack self-determination.

Second, teachers must demand better preparation requirements. As long as the public feels that any college graduate with a smattering of education courses can walk in off the street and do a teacher's job, people will not treat teachers as professionals. We do not for a moment mean to imply that teachers should adopt artificial trappings, like a doctor's smock or a general's uniform, to seem more distinctive and impressive. Rather, teachers must appear better because they are better. Like architects and surgeons, teachers must know their work, and it must be imbued with a sense of high purpose. Also, they must know a great deal about what they are teaching and how it can be taught most effectively. When that happens, the public will decide whether or not teachers should be treated as professionals.

Third, we may simply have to recognize that all of the two- and-a-half million people working in the American schools are not interested in and, in some cases, not capable of measuring up to the standards of professionalism. At present, what we are calling (and, incidentally, will continue to call) the *teaching profession* is a mixed bag, with a great many transients "just passing through," a great many rather uncommitted teachers, and a great many truly excellent, dedicated career teachers.

About thirty years ago, Walter Beggs captured what we believe to be the essence of the professional teacher:

> Let us define a career teacher as one who plans to, and actually does, make a life occupation of teaching; one who is philosophically, emotionally, and spiritually committed, that is never satisfied with what he does and how well he's doing it, and who fully intends to keep on growing for the rest of his life.[4]

Beggs goes on to estimate that only about one out of four presently practicing teachers fits his definition. And herein lies the difficulty. Until the great majority of teachers qualifies by Beggs's definition, or until there is a qualitative regrouping of those presently identified as "teachers," teaching will not be called a profession. But, currently, there is a move afoot to recognize and provide greater support to superior teachers, and in the process to strengthen the claim of professionalism for the career of teaching.

THE NATIONAL BOARD FOR PROFESSIONAL TEACHING STANDARDS

The lack of recognizable high standards has discouraged some potentially outstanding people from entering teaching and has lowered the level of aspiration of others. High standards have a way of focusing people's attention and harnessing their energies. For example, in long-distance running the 4-minute mile was long considered the unbreakable barrier. For years and years, sports commentators pontificated that it was beyond the capacities of humans to run a mile in 4 minutes or less. Then, in 1957, Roger Bannister, a relatively obscure medical student, broke the magic barrier. A new standard was set, and runners reset their sights. The following year thirty-seven runners broke that "unbreakable barrier." Today, breaking the 4-minute barrier is commonplace, and the reason is that a new standard has been set and people have risen to it in great numbers. The National Board for Professional Teaching Standards (NBPTS) intends to perform a similar function for the teaching profession.

Formed in 1987 and not yet fully operational, the NBPTS is working to establish standards for teaching practice and to develop a series of board certification assessments based on these standards. In turn, board advocates believe that these standards will allow teachers to gain a highly regarded, professional credential like that available to physicians, accountants, architects and other professionals. Observers have concluded that national boards in these other fields have improved the work of the professionals in them.

As currently envisioned, the National Board for Professional Teaching Standards will have a number of distinguishing characteristics. First, the NBPTS will be for experienced teachers, teachers with a baccalaureate or advanced degree, who have graduated from an accredited college or university and who have at least three years of experience. Second, "taking the boards" will be completely voluntary. It will not be a condition of work, like state licensure, but an achievement testifying to an individual teacher's having attained a high level of professionalism. Third, "taking the boards" will involve submitting oneself to a set of examinations and assessments in particular areas or subject matters, such as early childhood, English language arts, and physical education/health. Fourth, these assessments will not be the typical paper-and-pencil tests. Teaching, by its very nature, is an active mixture of thought and action and is not measured well by traditional "sit-down" testing. Although the final NBPTS assessments are still being developed, it is clear that a mix of techniques will be involved. The mix may well include interviews; several observations of teaching; assessment of the candidate's performance on specially designed, teaching-relevant exercises; and examination of materials submitted as part of the teacher's professional portfolio. Such a portfolio might include examples of students' work, sample lesson plans, and items judged by the teacher to support his or her candidacy. Fifth, the NBPTS, and presumably the board examiners, will be comprised of a majority of practicing teachers. Although administrators, teacher educators, and the general public are represented on the NBPTS, the strong representation of teachers is seen as important and a further step toward achieving professionalism in teaching.

The National Board for Professional Teaching Standards has gained the support of the major teachers associations (NEA and AFT), the National Governors' Association, and a number of other associations and corporations. Its primary function, again, will be to raise standards, thus attracting and maintaining more talented people to our nation's elementary and secondary schools. Advocates believe that Board certification will mean higher salaries for those teachers so designated. And it will mean, in effect, that school boards have a recognizable basis upon which to award merit pay, other than questionable criteria such as, "Her children do well on tests" or "He seems to work long hours and is popular with the brightest students."

Besides raising standards, however, there are a number of other advantages to board certification. Those having achieved board certification may be professionally "more portable," and able to move more freely across state lines. Also, this effort promises to stimulate research on what constitutes superior teaching. And it should trigger more attention to this research-based knowledge within teacher education and throughout the teaching force. Most of all, however, it should contribute to the essential but difficult mission of what is a mass occupation: that is, to create dedicated professionals, who are able to provide quality services without sacrificing equity.

Advantages of the NBPTS

The National Board for Professional Teaching Standards, however, is not without its critics. There are those who claim that there is no solid knowledge base in teaching (as opposed to medicine or architecture) upon which to ground such assessments. Others see the NBPTS as a public relations move to enhance the status and salaries of teachers with artificial trappings ("Brunnehilde is board certified, but we all know she couldn't teach a duck!"). Still others, suspicious that the NBPTS is controlled by its majority of teacher members, see it becoming a vehicle primarily to serve the economic interests of teachers and to insulate them further from their "clients," the students. Some university teacher educators see Board approval as a way for individuals to enter the teaching profession without having graduated from an accredited unit or approved teacher education program. Finally, some caution a wait-and-see attitude, acknowledging the strengths in the *idea* of a board, but waiting to see it in operation before passing judgment. It is anticipated that the NBPTS will be operating its first assessments by 1993 or 1994. Teachers, however, are not without groups concerned with standards or the welfare of teachers. It is to these groups we now turn.

Disadvantages of the NBPTS

THE PROFESSIONAL ASSOCIATIONS

The protection of teachers' rights and the improvement of their working conditions and rewards will not just happen. In the words of the distinguished educational policy analyst Ernie Lundquist, "Nobody gives you nothin' for nothin'."* Whatever advances teachers make will occur largely as a result of their hard work and readiness to stand up for what they believe.

Teacher salaries (which are the major cost of schooling) and other educational expenses come out of the taxpayers' pockets. Tax revenues are used for many purposes and are heavily competed for by groups attempting to fight crime and delinquency, to increase aid to the elderly and the poor, and so on. In the rough-and-tumble of a democracy, teachers need someone or something to look out for their interests and the interests of the recipients of their services—children. This is the function of teachers associations. At present, there are two national organizations, the National Education Association (NEA) and the American Federation of Teachers (AFT), that claim to speak for teachers. In 1990, 65 percent of all public school teachers, nearly two-thirds, reported belonging to the NEA. At the same time, 12 percent claimed membership in the AFT and

Need for an advocate

* Verbal communication. Ernie rarely commits himself to paper, claiming "I don't write so good."

approximately a fourth of all teachers recorded no membership at all.[5] These two large associations, then, represent three out of four teachers and speak for them to the federal, state, and local governments, to educational authorities at the state and local level, and, finally, to the general public. It is important to know something about them, because if you become a teacher, they will claim to be speaking for you.

Before discussing the National Education Association and the American Federation of Teachers, we should point out that there are many different educational organizations besides these two major organizations of teachers.

Nationwide Special-Interest Groups in Education

Schooling and education are a major part of our national life, and millions of people are concerned about our schools. As elsewhere in American life, people with common interests band together to advance the programs and policies in which they believe. In education, the result has been a broad array of organizations, some involving educational professionals and some involving educators and laypeople. Among these are the following:

- The National School Boards Association
- The National Congress of Parents and Teachers
- The American Association of School Administrators
- The Association for Supervision and Curriculum Development
- The American Educational Research Association
- The Council of Chief State School Officers
- The Association of Teacher Educators
- The American Association of Colleges for Teacher Education

Specialized Associations of Teachers

Although teachers are eligible to belong to some of the nationwide organizations, such as the Association for Supervision and Curriculum Development and the Association of Teacher Educators, by and large, teachers tend to affiliate with organizations devoted to promoting their particular areas or special interest within education. There is a great number of these organizations, of which the list below is but a small sample:

- The Council for Exceptional Children
- The Rural Education Association
- The National Science Teachers Association
- The National Council of Teachers of English
- The National Council for the Social Studies
- Music Educators National Conference
- The National Association for the Education of Young Children
- The American Industrial Arts Association
- The American Vocational Association
- The International Reading Association

- The American Council of the Teaching of Foreign Language
- The National Art Education Association

Organizations such as these serve the specialized needs of teachers and students, advocating for issues and their place in the educational landscape. Most of the organizations operate on a multiplicity of levels, with groups at the regional, state, county, and sometimes local levels. Through journals, inservice training or professional development institutes, and conferences and conventions, they play an important part in keeping teachers informed about research and developments in their fields. It is here where much of the teacher's professionalism, the working in groups to bring about curriculum changes and better preparation and inservice education, goes on. We urge you to consider joining the association closest to your interests. Also be aware that many of these organizations offer special membership discounts for students.

In this chapter we will focus our attention on the large teacher umbrella organizations, the NEA and the AFT, since these two have the most immediate and crosscutting effects on the lives of teachers. As you read the following pages, be aware that the NEA and the AFT are concerned about gaining the attention and support of people who are considering becoming teachers. Recently, Keith Geiger, president of the NEA, and Albert Shanker, president of the AFT, each agreed to write a special letter to readers of this book. Their letters appear in this section, along with the letter of a former teacher who found that, for a beginning teacher, the professional associations were more of a threat than a resource.

The National Education Association

Founded in 1857, the National Education Association today is a complex institution that is difficult to describe briefly. It operates on the national, state, and local school district levels and serves a very diverse clientele of rural, suburban, and urban teachers. In 1990, the NEA reached a long-cherished goal and passed the 2 million membership mark. Although the bulk of this membership is made up of classroom teachers, also included are teacher aides, administrators, professors, and retired educators. In addition, the parent organization has over 13,500 local affiliates existing in over 85 percent of the nation's school districts.[6]

SERVICES TO MEMBERS To serve the special needs of members within the association, the NEA has many program-related standing committees (such as Human Relations, Teacher Benefits, Teacher Rights, and Instructional and Professional Development) and several special committees (Minority Affairs, Teacher Retirement, Resolutions Study, and National Public Relations). In addition, the NEA has three types of support services: communication, research, and UniServ.

Three support services

- A number of publications and other communication media are used to disseminate information about the NEA's policies and programs, both internally to the profession and externally to the public.
- NEA research is designed to provide information needed to achieve NEA goals and objectives. Research and information services compile data in

areas such as negotiations, salaries, school finance, teacher retirement systems, and surveys.

- The Uniserv program is a cooperative effort by which local, state, and national associations provide professional staff at the local level to improve the service programs at all levels of the association. Currently, the NEA is devoting 35 million dollars, one-quarter of its yearly budget, to this program and has 1,380 UniServ professionals in the field serving teachers.[7]

WHY JOIN THE NEA?

Keith Geiger

Since the founding of the National Education Association in 1857, we've remained unrelenting in our efforts to adapt to shifting educational climates and shifting social realities. We've never regarded the status quo as sacred. We've always welcomed the challenge of change. We've never wavered in our belief that before America's children can know the blessings of liberty, they must first know the blessings of learning.

For 134 years, we have devoted our energy to mobilizing the national will behind Horace Mann's philosophy, a philosophy he so beautifully expressed when he wrote that "If ever there was a cause, if ever there could be a cause, worthy to be upheld by all the toil or sacrifice that the human heart can endure, it is the cause of public education."

For more than a century, our democratically elected representatives have affirmed and reaffirmed our dedication to this principle. During this entire time, we have been guided by the four single words that conclude the Pledge of Allegiance—the words "and justice for all."

And our efforts, like our perseverance, have paid off. Our efforts proved pivotal in securing passage of:

- the 1946 National School Lunch Program.
- the 1958 National Defense Education Act.
- the 1961 law providing funds to train teachers of the deaf.
- the 1963 Vocational Education Act.
- the 1976 Education for All Handicapped Children Act.

- and the 1979 creation of the U.S. Department of Education.

These few benchmarks testify to the singleness of purpose that characterizes our Association. That singleness of purpose—tempered by Horace Mann's philosophy—is the reason we've been so successful. It's the reason our Association is unrivaled as an advocate for public education—and for public education employees. And it's the reason why everyone who aspires to become part of our noble profession ought to consider membership in our Association a must.

We carry out a myriad of responsibilities on behalf of our members, their families, their students, and their communities.

We are determined to see to it that America's teachers receive the respect, the dignity, the professional status, and the professional compensation they have so long deserved. Our Association focuses on individual members—on their unique needs, their career development goals, their vision, their ideals, their hopes.

Through *NEA Today,* our monthly newspaper, our Association keeps members apprised of the latest developments in the teaching profession.

The NEA Research Department—the nation's leading source of educational research materials—issues papers and special reports dealing with subjects ranging from students' achievement and dropout prevention to education funding and retirement benefits for America's teachers.

Having pioneered initiatives in dropout prevention, school restructuring, site-based decision making, and curricular innovation, we've now gone a few steps further.

In addition to the three types of support services, a number of special services are available to members, such as travel programs, insurance policies, mutual fund programs, and book club programs. Also, the NEA aids teachers (like those in the vignettes that began this chapter) whose legal rights are being violated or who are being treated unethically.

The goals of the NEA, as declared in its charter, are "to elevate the character and advance the interests of the profession of teaching and to promote the cause of education in the United States." In the 1950s and 1960s the NEA was

With our National Center for Innovation, created in January 1990, we will be able to strengthen, expand, and better coordinate the more than 600 school renewal and restructuring programs we've developed over the past five years.

To further help our members, our Association holds a series of regional and national conferences throughout the year. They provide forums that foster professional development and networking. They promote collegiality. They give our members a chance to share ideas—and to share the joys and frustrations that are an inevitable part of the daily life of all who serve in the classroom.

And when it comes to protecting the rights of our two-million members, we do an excellent job. Indeed, we've developed the nation's largest legal defense program for education employees, which provides $1 million of employee liability insurance protection for each member.

Of course, the protection we provide our members doesn't stop there. Through our UniServ staffing program we provide on-site financial support to members for the enhancement of professional skills, help in crises, and for day-to-day monitoring of their rights and benefits.

We also offer our members excellent, low-cost life, homeowner, accident, and hospital insurance, as well as reduced rates on books, car rentals, and prescription drugs.

All of these benefits were established to support our members, to lift some of life's burdens from their shoulders so that they might better concentrate on the job to which they've dedicated their lives; educating our nation's students, educating the future guardians of our democracy.

Of course, our Association knows that the days are

long past when teachers could go it alone. That's way, while counting on the initiative and expertise of our members, we also forge partnerships with various segments of our society, especially policymakers. And we encourage our members to do so also.

Not much encouragement is needed. Our research shows that the majority of newly certified teachers make their decision to enter the teaching profession before they even enter college. And they know that policy decisions—whether they come from local school boards, state legislatures, or even the White House—have a decisive impact on their day-to-day work.

But the vast majority of newly certified teachers also have something else in common: they intend to make a long-term commitment to the teaching profession. That's why they need an Association whose commitment matches their own.

By belonging to NEA, teachers and student teachers have such an organization, an organization that guarantees them a voice in building a sounder American education system.

So as you cross the threshold of our profession, I welcome you. I welcome you and say Godspeed and fare forward, voyager.

You are not the same person you were when you decided to enter our profession . . . and our profession is not the same profession you decided to enter.

New education challenges and new education opportunities are changing our profession—changing it for the betterment of our nation, for the betterment of America's children, and for the betterment of the members of the National Education Association. Two million strong, we're meeting those challenges and taking advantage of those opportunities.

influential in improving the preservice training of teachers and raising the entrance qualifications for teaching. But although the NEA is currently supporting the National Board for Professional Teaching Standards, most of its energies and monies have been expended on service for its membership: practicing teachers. One recent effort to "promote the cause of education" is the recent formation of the National Center for Innovation, the NEA's experimental arm that is concerned with restructuring and renewing public education. The center's aim is "through renewal projects to have every student educated to his or her potential."[8]

POLITICAL ACTIVITIES   Beginning in the 1970s, the association became much more politically oriented. For example, in 1976 the NEA for the first time endorsed and vocally supported a presidential candidate, Jimmy Carter. Carter's campaign manager said at the time, "The massive support from teachers was critical to our winning this very close election. All over the nation we turned to the NEA for assistance. We asked for help and they delivered." In the same election year, the NEA endorsed and assisted 272 successful candidates for election to the House of Representatives, a majority of the House. Teachers had flexed their muscles, and politicians all over the country took notice. The grateful president showed his appreciation by bringing into realization a long-time NEA dream: the establishment of a cabinet-level Department of Education.

The NEA and politics

WHY SHOULD NEW TEACHERS JOIN THE AFT?
Albert Shanker, President, AFT

Every once in a great while, and usually spurred by crisis, a combination of forces and ideas comes together in a way that makes real change possible. In the field of education and in the lives of prospective and current teachers and students, now is such a time. The impending teacher shortage and the current organizational structure of the country's public schools are probably the two biggest problems public education faces today. The American Federation of Teachers (AFT) recognizes the challenges both these issues create and realizes that these same challenges also offer our greatest opportunity to create a self-governing teaching profession and to redesign our public schools.

The AFT vision of transforming teaching into a full profession, unimaginable just a few short years ago, is now at center stage of the national discussion of the condition of public education. Throughout its history the AFT has recognized that unionism and professionalism are inextricably linked and that public schools must be, first and foremost, institutions of teaching and learning. To achieve this goal, we must seek the full professionalization of teaching, restructure our schools and rethink the way we approach education.

Professionalizing teaching means all the things this union has long stood and worked for: higher salaries, smaller class size, a manageable work load, and relief from non-teaching chores. It means working conditions that other professions so take for granted that they often go unmentioned: an office, a desk, a telephone, a quiet place. It means enough textbooks to go around, equipment that doesn't fall apart, school buildings that are clean and safe. It also means time for preparation, new learning, discussion and work with one's colleagues, and an opportunity for advancement without having to leave the classroom.

However, the next three presidential elections told a very different story and dramatically underscored the limitations of the NEA's political strength and strategies. In 1980, Jimmy Carter lost to Ronald Reagan, who campaigned across the nation saying that he would eliminate the Department of Education (a threat he failed to follow through on). Although NEA-endorsed congressional candidates won in 209 of 278 House races, the NEA did not fare so well in the Senate campaign. Of the 31 Senate candidates the NEA supported, 16 lost. In 1984, the NEA supported Walter Mondale, publicly endorsing him a full year before the election. And in 1988 the NEA endorsed Michael Dukakis against George Bush, only to lose again. During the same period, however, the political action arm of the NEA (NEA-PAC) had a rather good record. For instance, in the 1990 elections, 85 percent of the NEA-PAC-endorsed candidates won their campaigns for the House or the Senate, 247 in the House and 19 in the Senate. The NEA believed that the newly elected 102nd Congress would be the most pro-education group in twenty years.[9]

Recent political performance

The verdict is still out on the political potency of teachers. On the one hand, one political commentator referred to teachers as "bright, articulate, and reasonably well informed making them naturals for political activism."[10] Also, teachers have the best record of any occupational group in registering to vote: well over 70 percent.[11] On the other hand, teachers do not have the huge financial coffers from which to pour money into elections as have other political pressure

Teachers' political nature

But the professionalization of teaching requires an even more basic ideal—the need to empower teachers, to give them control over the standards of their profession and the conduct of their work. It is the recognition that professionalization entails new responsibilities as well as new prerogatives that makes the AFT unique.

In discussing the empowerment of teachers, I want to be very clear on two points. First, the AFT is not suggesting that teachers should be the instructional leaders because we are a well-organized, powerful group that demands that position. We are that, but that is not where the legitimacy for teacher authority lies. The call for teachers to be instructional leaders must rest on the demonstration of our professional expertise and integrity.

We have before us the great possibility of forever transforming the lives of teachers and the status of public education in America. Many good people are on our side. For students—especially for those whose life has not been so kind—it will be a new chance. And for teachers, it will mean the opportunity to give them that chance. It will mean a real profession and a real community of learning.

But with this hope comes the fear of change. Is the change going to be in the direction we want? Will things get better or worse? Oftentimes, despite our high hopes, our fears take hold and we ask if it is better to hold on to what we have now and just readjust our dreams to the status quo or what is most familiar.

In this battle between hope and fear, the AFT will be instructed by our experience over the past few years and indeed over the last seventy years. This union and its members have always been good at taking risks. We stood for unionism when no one else believed in it. With only a handful of members—when others said it would be suicidal—we called for collective bargaining elections because we believed that when teachers had sketched before them a vision of what could be if they joined together, they would go with their hopes and not their fears. They did then, and I believe they will now and in the future. I hope you will be part of that future.

Used by permission of the American Federation of Teachers.

sapped its energies. Nevertheless, the federation has taken on a more progressive appearance, owing largely to the efforts of its long-time leader, Albert Shanker. Once seen by many as the champion of raw "teacher power" and as concerned only with the good of teachers, Shanker in recent years has been a strong advocate of educational reform and has lobbied both his organization and the public hard in support of many reform efforts, such as certain kinds of merit pay, minimum standards for teachers, and longer and more intense teacher education (see the Shanker letter on page 524). In contrast, the NEA has appeared to oppose or to support only reluctantly many of these reform efforts, such as providing parents with greater choices of school for their children.

Shanker's influence

For almost twenty years, the leaders of both the NEA and the AFT (along with many members of the press) have been discussing merging into one teacher organization-union that would represent the entire teaching force. The advantages of one giant organization being able to speak authoritatively for all the nation's teachers attracted many people. It was suggested that political strength in national elections and the ability to call a nationwide school shutdown would give teachers enormous power. The leadership of the two organizations, however, has been unable to bring about this amalgamation. Presently the NEA and the AFT remain two organizations competing with each other and at the same time trying to attract the attention and support of the public.

Rumors of merger

PROFESSIONALISM AT THE CROSSROADS

Mixed results

There has been a great deal written and said about teacher power. The basis for this power is said to have two elements: work stoppage and politics. As an occupational group, teachers have made substantial gains in the last thirty years, both in their salaries and in the purchasing power of their salaries. In the school districts where teachers and boards of education have engaged in collective bargaining or teachers have engaged in strikes and other militant activities, teachers have received more money than in districts where they have been less active. On the other hand, this new activism has done little to enhance the role of teachers in determining educational policies, and there has been only marginal improvement in teachers' working conditions.

Although the leaderships of the large teacher organizations have shown great enthusiasm for active participation in the political process in the recent past, that fervor seems to be cooling. Undoubtedly, there will be substantial involvement of teachers in forthcoming local, state, and national elections, but the strategies will no doubt vary. And many still cling to the dream of one professional association of teachers that has over two million dues-paying members who are ready to be a major force on the American political scene and flex their muscles for education.

As we mentioned earlier, the teachers' capacity to close down schools through strikes and work stoppages is another source of their power—power not just to stop education but also to force mothers or fathers to stay home and tend to their children. Besides their impact on education, these actions could have severe economic impact on the states and even on the nation. Therefore, between politics and work stoppages, the teachers organizations wield a great deal of

Potential benefits

power. This new power could be used, of course, to the direct benefit of children. It could be used to improve teacher education, to give teachers a greater say in their own professional affairs, to divert more funds to educational research and innovative projects, and, in general, to improve the educational services available to the public.

Potential abuses

The new power and autonomy of teachers is not necessarily good, however. Nor is professionalism in itself necessarily desirable. Professionalism may, indeed, work against the highest goals of education. When all the rhetoric is pruned away, professional groups—whether they be the American Medical Association, the American Bar Association, or the National Education Association—appear to exist primarily for the benefit of their members. In the interest of protecting and expanding the rights of its members, a professional group may ride roughshod over the needs and rights of the client group. For instance, insisting on tenure rights for all teachers who have taught for three years or more makes it difficult to get rid of those teachers who turn out to be genuine incompetents. In the big cities, basing eligibility for transfer to more congenial schools on seniority may be robbing the most difficult schools of exactly the experienced teacher talent they need. Behind the jargon of professionalism, one often finds naked self-interest. Occasionally, teachers use their "professional status" as a barrier to protect themselves from criticism by children and parents: "How dare

A Dissenting Voice: The Profession as Enemy

The most important concern of a beginning teacher is his or her job, *and* being able to keep it for a second or third year. While, theoretically, the professional associations are advocates for every teacher who joins and pays dues, in reality they serve as a support system only for those teachers with seniority and tenure. Therefore, the "best" teacher becomes the one who has more "years-in" rather than the one with superior skills, abilities and achievement. In a situation where two teachers are hired in the same year, "experience" can mean the difference in the dates and times on their signed contracts. Do our professional associations support this practice? YES. As a beginning teacher, who will support *me*?

Professional growth is not encouraged through this type of hiring and firing. In a capitalistic society, the incentive to do a better job through hard work and self-sacrifice is removed when teachers are evaluated according to their years "in-service" and advanced college hours rather than on criteria such as professional successes and classroom achievements. Yet, through the power of collective bargaining, the poor teacher is rewarded, the average teacher is appeased, and the outstanding teacher is overlooked. Do our professional associations support this practice? YES. As an outstanding, but beginning, teacher, these are not *my* associations.

In cases such as teacher strikes, individual teachers must suffer the consequences if they take an action contrary to an Association vote. When board negotiations have otherwise failed and the Association members have voted to strike, this "unlawful" resistance can lead to personal fine, imprisonment, and loss of job. In this case, individual human rights become secondary to what de Tocqueville referred to as the "tyranny of the majority." Do *our* professional organizations have such little regard for individual preferences among teachers? As a "rookie" who is dedicated to her job, *no* professional organization is there to help *me*!

Debra Hallock Phillips. Copyright © 1991. Used with permission.

Teacher empowerment

you question what I have done? *I am a professional!*" The question of professionalism is a tricky one. It seems that ultimately it reduces to a need for balance. The teacher's right to be rewarded and safeguarded against unfair practices must be carefully balanced against the students' and the taxpayers' right to be served justly and well by the teacher. It is a constant struggle to strike an even balance. Myron Brenton raises the following point:

> Every professional group closes ranks to protect its own; teachers are no exception. But teachers are the exception in that they seem to want—at this juncture, at least—the best of both worlds: the security of the civil servant and the prestige and rewards of the professional. More than that, they want a major say in matters of educational policy while getting tenure protection. In other words, they want power without accountability, which is basically an antidemocratic stance.[17]

At the present time, we are in the midst of a national effort to reform and restructure our educational system. Although much ink has been spilled on reports on the schools, the final report card on what has been called the "excellence movement in education" has not been delivered. The early grades look promising, but long-term, substantial reform of our schools will take the energetic and sustained support of the teaching profession. There is a phrase, however, that is cropping up more and more in discussions and descriptions of educational reforms and restructuring efforts. The phrase is *teacher empowerment*. It is a movement to give teachers greater say in and responsibility for how they prepare and deliver their professional services. Examples of teacher empowerment are seen in the strong representation of teachers on the National Board for Professional Teaching Standards and on professional standards boards, which exist in many states (and which effect certification standards). At the local district and school level, teachers in many places are involved in decision-making roles that previously were considered the arena of administrators. In our view, the issue of teacher professionalism will be strongly affected by how, in fact, the teacher empowerment movement contributes ultimately to the improvement of schools.

PROFESSIONALISM AND CONTINUING EDUCATION

Our economic challenges

Related to the issue of teachers' status and empowerment is their competence: Are they up to the task? Polls over the last decade show that public faith in public education is at a very low level. People are concerned about the performance of schoolchildren and seem to be saying that teachers are not getting the results that the public wants and expects. Part of this concern over the performance of the American student is a result of pressures from abroad. Whereas just a few years ago there was widespread concern about our capacity to meet the potential military challenges from the Russians, now the worry is that American students will not be able to meet the economic challenges provided by their Japanese and German counterparts.

A related aspect of this concern for the level of teacher competence has to do with social change. At one time it was considered adequate for a teacher to have obtained an undergraduate education and a teaching license and then to have no further training; however, forces both inside and outside the teaching profession now have adopted the stance that the teacher must be a continuous learner. Many states have legislated continuing education for teachers. In fact, in more than one-half of the states, it is no longer possible to gain permanent certification.[18] More and more states are requiring teachers to keep up with developments in education.

Need for computer literacy

Central to this drive for the continuing education of teachers is the growth of new knowledge and the demand for new skills. A dramatic example is the rising interest in computer literacy. As American society has become increasingly dependent on mechanized information services, the needs and advantages of being comfortable and competent with computers have become clear. Therefore, elementary and secondary schools and colleges are rushing to provide students with this new competence. In 1983 a number of colleges all but required computer literacy for admission. For example, for almost ten years, Clarkson College has required each incoming student to pay an extra fee for the use of a personal computer.[19] For these college students, the personal computer has become as important as the pen and the library card. Movements such as the computer revolution require teachers, if they are to prepare students for the demands of the world, to think of themselves as—and in fact to be—continuous learners.

In-service workshops are one way teachers can extend their range of skills and knowledge.

(*Robert Kalman/The Image Works*)

One of the aims of education is to develop the ability to engage in independent study. *Independent study* is jargon for being able to go it alone. Although this approach is much discussed by educators, students seem to get little actual practice in choosing their own areas of interest and systematically investigating them. Independent study, though, is one of the most important means for continual self-renewal available to the teacher. Teachers are confronted daily with things they do not understand about children and knowledge and their interaction. "What are children really doing when they yell out answers to homework problems?" "What are the fundamental skills of composition that children should know?" "How can I help my students use history for their own benefit?" Such questions are daily grist for the teacher's independent study mill. Of course, the teacher's study should not be confined to professional problems. His or her own personal interests may lead into such areas as organic gardening, physical fitness, old movies, the politics in colonial America, or the humanizing of the corporate state. Not by professional problems alone doth the teacher live!

Group study is another common form of continuous learning for the teacher. It frequently takes the form of committee work. Problems arise in the school for which there are no apparent solutions, so a group of people take on themselves the task of exploring the problem with a view toward recommending an enlightened course of action. In recent years, to obtain opinions from outside the school, teachers and administrators have begun inviting community residents to these study groups. Typical issues these groups might take on are alternatives to a second-grade reading program, an analysis of the unused educational resources in the community, and the potential benefits and costs of using paraprofessionals in a high school.

A third way to continue to learn is to take courses or to work toward an *advanced degree.* Most colleges and universities offer courses suitable and interesting to teachers. Special and regular courses are offered in the evening and during the summer vacation. These courses and degree programs not only allow teachers to gain a deeper understanding of their work but also make it possible for some teachers to train for other jobs in education, such as guidance counseling, administration, or college teaching.

A fourth way to grow and learn is to attend an *inservice program* or *professional development program* sponsored by the school or school district. Inservice programs are often targeted at school- or districtwide problems or issues. For instance, if students in a particular school are getting unsatisfactory grades on standardized achievement tests, the district may choose to provide special inservice training for the faculty, or it might decide to switch to a new, supposedly better mathematics program. Such a change would require special training for the faculty and would thus become the focus of the inservice program. Inservice training often takes place weekly or monthly, before or after school. Also, special days are sometimes set aside on which school is canceled or the students are dismissed early so the teachers can participate in inservice training.

A fifth form of continuous learning comes through *supervision.* During a teacher's early years in the profession, school districts provide professional advice in what amounts to one-to-one help. For instance, if you are a new high

Table 14.1 Percentages of All Teachers Participating in Professional Growth Activities, 1971–86

Activities	1971	1976	1981	1986
Workshops sponsored by school system during school year	58.6	68.3	67.4	72.7
Workshops sponsored by school system during summer	20.5	21.9	13.4	15.1
College courses in education during school year	40.1	45.4	21.3	21.4
College courses in education during summer	30.4	33.8	13.3	12.4
College courses in fields other than education during school year	26.1	25.9	12.7	9.2
College courses in fields other than education during summer	21.5	16.2	5.7	4.3
University extension courses	32.6	33.8	18.7	15.0
Association-sponsored activities	24.5	23.3	27.1	31.5
Curriculum committee	40.8	44.7	34.2	30.5
Committee other than curriculum	35.3	38.6	32.6	33.9
Educational TV	11.3	12.2	13.4	12.9
Educational travel, not sabbatical	26.4	23.0	14.7	9.6
Sabbatical leave—travel	3.8	7.2	2.4	17.6
Sabbatical leave—full-time college	2.4	3.7	0.6	0.6

Source: "The Status of the American Public School Teacher, 1985–86" (conducted by the National Education Association). Used with permission.

school teacher, your department head will observe your classes regularly and discuss the observations with you. Or if you are an elementary school teacher, your building principal may make regular visits and follow them with feedback sessions. Although supervision can sometimes be quite threatening, particularly to nontenured teachers, it offers an opportunity to obtain valuable information about your teaching techniques and skills. And it is worthwhile for a teacher to try to change it from a threatening situation to a learning situation.

Table 14.1 gives some additional types of continuing education activities and suggests just how widespread this movement toward professional education is. Although the table indicates a drop in the percentages of teachers involving themselves in a number of categories of advanced training over a fifteen-year period, this change may very well be explained by other factors. For instance, the number of new teachers declined sharply between 1975 and 1986. Fewer new teachers meant that fewer teachers would be returning to universities for master's degree programs and coursework for specialized certification areas.

Continuing Education: A Final Word

Great athletes and great musicians do not become great by accident. Nor do they simply turn themselves over to a coach or mentor and soon reach excellence. Individual athletes and musicians work hard for their achievements. They consciously set out to discipline their minds and bodies and to master the needed skills and knowledge. Once they reach a level of mastery, they continuously work to maintain their skills and acquire new ones. To achieve and maintain a degree of excellence, the individual *must* take an active role; in this respect, what is true for tennis and the piano is true for teaching.

Becoming a teacher may be compared to sculpting a work of art from a piece of stone. The difference is that the teacher is both the sculptor and the stone. The teacher begins with a vision of what he or she wants to be and then sets to work transforming the vision into a reality. The process requires an understanding of the material with which one is working—the self—and of the tools one can use. It also requires a vision of what one needs to become. Finally, it takes long hours of chipping away at and smoothing surfaces. To be a teacher, particularly a teacher who is continuously moving forward, is a lifelong commitment.

Discussion Questions

1. How do people react when you tell them you are thinking of becoming a teacher? Why?

2. Do you know of a situation in which a teacher needed protection or in which a teacher's rights were violated?

3. What basic changes have taken place in teacher education in America's history?

4. Do you think that teachers should devote themselves to becoming professionals? If so, what must they do? Are you willing to do it? How do you feel about Walter Beggs's description of the "career teacher" on page 517?

5. Does the idea of a national board for professional teaching standards appeal to you? When you have completed three years or more of teaching, do you see yourself applying for board certification?

6. Do teachers need a professional organization? What are the essential functions performed by such a group?

7. What dangers or weaknesses seem to be endemic in professional organizations? Would you be willing to sacrifice security for professionalism? Will you be a professional? Why?

8. What is your opinion of tenure for teachers? What arguments for or against it can you suggest? Would you be willing to work in a school system that does not offer tenure?

9. For you, right now, what seem the most important issues for teachers to concern themselves with? Increased power? Higher salaries? Better training? Something else? Be prepared to defend your choice. What can you do to work for the changes you consider most important?

10. How do you, personally, react to the idea of the teacher being a continuous learner? Which of the forms of continuing professional education has the most appeal to you? The least appeal?

For Further Reading

Clifford, J., and J. Guthrie. *Ed School.* Chicago: University of Chicago Press, 1988.

This book is a study of the institutionalization of teacher education, providing a detailed history of the field and how schools and departments of education currently function.

Lieberman, Myron. *Education as a Profession.* Englewood Cliffs, N.J.: Prentice-Hall, 1956.

Carefully analyzes the occupation of teaching to determine how it does and does not "fit" the standard qualifications of a profession.

Liebermann, Ann. *Building a Professional Culture in Schools.* New York: Teachers College Press, 1988.

Based on studies of teachers and school districts, this book has a great deal of information and insight on how teachers can reach higher levels of professionalism and make teacher empowerment operational.

Lortie, Dan C. *Schoolteacher: A Sociological Study.* Chicago: University of Chicago Press, 1975.

A sociological view of the ethos of the teaching profession, that pattern of orientations and sentiments that are peculiar to teachers.

National Education Association. *Status of the American Public School Teacher: 1989–90.* Washington, D.C.: National Education Association, 1990.

This report is one in a series of studies conducted every four years. It contains a massive amount of information on who teachers are, what is on their minds, and the conditions of their work.

Ravitch, Diane. *The Troubled Crusade.* New York: Basic Books, 1983.

Essentially a history of attempts to reform schools between 1945 and 1980, this book has valuable insights into the activities and roles of teachers associations.

Waller, Willard. *The Sociology of Teaching.* New York: Wiley, 1965.

Originally written in 1932, this survey of what students and citizens thought of teachers and education over forty years ago still contains much of value. It is classic, rich in incisive analyses of the teacher's role and suggestions for prospective teachers.

Notes

1. T. D. Snyder. *The Digest of Educational Objectives, 1987* Washington, D.C.: U.S. Government Printing Office.
2. The Holmes Group, *Tomorrow's Teachers: A Report of the Holmes Group* (East Lansing, Mich.: Holmes Group, 1986).
3. We have drawn heavily on two excellent books: Myron Lieberman, *Education as a Profession* (Englewood Cliffs, N.J.: Prentice-Hall, 1956), and Robert B. Howsam et al., *Educating a Profession,* Report of the Bicentennial Commission of Education for the Profession of Teaching (Washington, D.C.: American Association of Colleges for Teacher Education, 1976).
4. Quoted at 1963–64 convention of the National Commission on Teacher Education and Professional Standards (NEA), in Myron Brenton, *What's Happened to Teacher?* (New York: Coward-McCann, 1970), p. 242.
5. Emily Feistritzer, *Profile of Teachers in the U.S—1990* (Washington, D.C.: National Center for Education Information, 1990).
6. *NEA Today* 8, no. 6 (February 1990): 3.
7. Ibid., p. 25.
8. Letter and attachments from Jean O'Neil, NEA Staff, February 27, 1991.

9. *1990 Election Results*, NEA Government Relations/National Council of State Education Associations (Washington, D.C.: National Education Association, November 1990), p. 1.

10. Steven Chaffman, "The NEA Seizes Power: The Teachers' Coup," *New Republic*, October 11, 1980, pp. 9–11.

11. Stanley Elam, "The National Education Association: Political Powerhouse or Paper Tiger," *Phi Delta Kappan* 63 (November 1981): 169–174.

12. Chester E. Finn, "Teacher Unions and School Quality: Potential Allies or Inevitable Foes?" *Phi Delta Kappan* (January 1985): vol. 66, no. 5:332.

13. E. Saihoz, M. Lord, and D. H. McDonald, "Teaching About Nuclear War," *Newsweek*, July 18, 1983, p. 78.

14. Elam, "National Education Association," p. 173.

15. American Federation of Teachers, *Goals of the American Federation of Teachers AFL-CIO* (Washington, D.C., American Federation of Teachers, n.d.), p. 3.

16. Letter from Bella Rosenberg, assistant to the president, American Federation of Teachers, January 18, 1991.

17. Brenton, *What's Happened to Teacher?* p. 255.

18. Marge Scherer, "Who's Afraid of Teacher Competency Tests?" *Instructor* (February 1983): 48.

19. *New York Times*, April 5, 1983, p. C1.

Schools of the Future

While preparing for a career in education, it is easy to forget that there is more to education than schools. As we observed in Chapter 7, schools are only part of society's machinery to help people grow and develop. Family, friends, churches and synagogues, civic groups, the mass media, businesses, all have an educative impact on the individual. The impact of formal schooling, however, is special in a number of ways. While the school may not always have the power to mold a person in the way parents and family do, its impact on the intellect and on values is nevertheless enormous. From the age of four or five to seventeen or eighteen children spend a great percentage of their waking hours in school. This time in school is not only long, but also fills a very impressionable period in a human life.

Our schools are imperfect instruments. While some children love school and thrive on everything presented to them there, others seem to shrivel and almost disappear in school. They spend their school days with one eye on the clock (waiting for three o'clock) and the other on the calendar (waiting for the end of the school year). Some students, often the majority, are so bored by the material and by the teaching that they tune out and, either mentally or physically, drop out.

Having come this far in our book, we hope you will conceive of the schools as social creations that are made by people and that reflect the purposes of a society and the ideas and commitments of individuals. Although schools are the responsibility of many individuals and groups, teachers have a special duty: they not only need to be effective in the schools we have now, but also need to possess a vision of what schools can become.

What follows, then, is our vision of what the schools can and ought to be. We have borrowed from many sources, but for good or ill, the mixture of ideas is ours. We don't intend that our vision should become your vision, but that our vision should encourage you to form your own views about what the schools ought to become.

REDESIGN OF THE TEACHING CAREER

There can be little doubt about the centrality of the teacher in a good education. Although good school boards, good administrators, first-rate curricula, and well-equipped buildings all contribute to an excellent education, they will come to little if the school is not staffed by well-prepared, dedicated teachers.

A Remodeled Teacher Education

Need for broad understanding

A LIBERAL EDUCATION　To teach well, teachers should first possess a solid liberal arts education; only a broad understanding of the world's most important thought can provide a foundation for teaching. In our vision of future schools, this liberal education will begin during high school and will be broadened and deepened during the college years. Such serious and extended study should be more than just a smattering of survey courses; it should make the future teacher at home with the social sciences, the natural sciences, and the great works of the humanities, both classical and modern.

Need for a specialty

In addition, each teacher should know one discipline extremely well. In-depth study of one subject will yield an understanding of what scholarship is and an appreciation for the structure of knowledge. The future teacher should become something of an expert in one field of study or, more probably, one aspect of one field. More than being simply personally "liberating," therefore, the liberal education should provide both the content and the direction of the future teacher's professional work.

Rigorous, practical preparation

PROFESSIONAL TRAINING　The teacher's professional preparation will build on this liberal education, in effect enabling him or her to pass on to the next generation what he or she has learned. This professional training will be rigorous and practical, reflecting the high standards of the teacher's chosen field.

Schools as training sites

Teacher preparation will take place, as it does now, in colleges and universities as well as in elementary and secondary schools. However, the relationship between the colleges and the schools will be made closer by networks of demonstration schools associated with each teacher-preparation institution. These will have two functions: to provide outstanding education to future teachers *and* to help them become highly skilled at their work. Master teachers will play a significant role in this new training format. They will move freely between their elementary or secondary schools and the university, where they will lecture and demonstrate frequently. In turn, professors of the arts and sciences and of education will observe and teach classes in the schools, working as colleagues with teachers-in-training.

Demonstration schools will be specially equipped to carry out their teacher education mission. For instance, each will have videotaping facilities so that teachers-in-training can review their performances with their master teachers. The master teachers, too, will be videotaped regularly for analysis by the future teachers.

NATIONAL CERTIFICATION   Although many states have reciprocity* with other states, currently each person seeking to teach in the public schools needs to be licensed by the department of education in the state where he or she intends to teach. An individual who later moves to another state must seek licensure in the new state. National certification would create a set of standards consistent from state to state. The reform we outline here calls for a national certification board similar to the one described as coming into being in Chapter 14. The standards set by the board will be established after careful study by the nation's outstanding teachers. Future teachers will have to pass examinations comparable to law or medical board examinations; these will insure that a *board-certified* teacher not only possesses a great deal of knowledge but can also demonstrate the ability to teach that knowledge. The public will know that a nationally board certified teacher will be able to advance the students' development intellectually, physically, aesthetically, and morally.

Certification on national basis

Differentiated Staffing

Elementary schools are currently organized by what has been called "the egg carton principle," with identical classrooms arranged off a main hall and with one teacher instructing in all subject areas approximately the same number of students. Middle and high schools represent a minor variation of this "egg crate" approach. One effect of this structure is to treat teachers like interchangeable parts and to expect all teachers, old and new, to do all teaching tasks equally well.

The *differentiated teaching staff* concept aims to correct this current situation and rests on the idea that teaching takes in many different skills, from explaining complex material to correcting papers. Further, teachers, like most people, do some things well and other things not so well. We want to maximize the talents of each teacher and minimize each one's areas of weakness. Therefore, we would attempt to fit teachers into roles according to their individual talents. A faculty would be composed of many different kinds of teachers, each doing those teaching tasks he or she does best and teaching those subjects he or she knows best.

Maximizing teachers' talents

* Reciprocity means an agreement between states, so that if you are licensed in one state, you are eligible for licensure in another. If you are interested in teaching in a state other than the one in which you are currently in training, you may wish to check that state's certification requirements. Appendix B has a directory of state teacher certification offices in the United States. Your college placement office might also have this information.

This plan would break up many of the physical and structural rigidities in school life, making the all too familiar picture of one teacher in one classroom with twenty-five or so students fade from view. The plan would allow some gifted teachers to advance through gaining additional degrees *and* through outstanding performance, and to earn a salary double or triple what they presently earn. Not only would it allow some teachers to make an important but limited contribution, but it would help attract and hold excellent teachers who see an opportunity to grow professionally and to express their creative capacities.

Career ladders

At the heart of the differentiated teaching concept is the *career ladder,* an idea reflecting that human differences exist among teachers, that these differences should be taken advantage of to improve the instruction of students, and that the resulting differences in work assignments should be related to the rewards teachers receive. Although there are potentially many different schemes, we propose an approach that has three levels of practitioners: instructors, professional teachers, and career professional teachers.[1]

THE INSTRUCTOR   The instructor's primary role will be to interact with students about the subject or subjects the instructor knows well. Each instructor will work under the direct supervision of a higher-level teacher. In addition to achieving a college degree in an academic area, instructors will have undergone several months of intensive study in education. Further, they will have to pass examinations in any subject they intend to teach, as well as exams in writing, reading, and basic pedagogy. Instructors will have no involvement in curriculum setting and other policy issues. They will not evaluate students or counsel them. Finally, they can be instructors for no more than five years; after that, it will be literally "up or out."

Entry level: basic competence

THE PROFESSIONAL TEACHER   This role is closest to the teacher's current image as most of us perceive it. However, professional teachers will have gone through more rigorous training than is available to most beginners entering classrooms today. They will have earned a master's degree, passed all the examinations and tests at the instructor level, and demonstrated to a review board of peers command of a variety of teaching skills over a range of academic subjects. Professional teachers will work in a variety of ways, depending on their strengths and the needs of their community.

Second level: more training

THE CAREER PROFESSIONAL TEACHER   To reach this highest level, individuals will first have to serve as professional teachers and perform in an outstanding manner. Although many career professional teachers will have earned doctorates or accomplished some equivalent feat, their main qualification will be that they are good at their work. All teachers are expected to be good, but the difference between the career professional teacher and the others is perhaps best captured by the words of the baseball immortal Willie Mays: "It ain't hard to be good once in a while. It's being good all the time that's hard!"

Highest level: consistent quality

A small percentage of the teaching force, somewhere between 15 and 20 percent, will be made up of teachers at this level. Their salaries will be double and triple what teachers with comparable years of service receive today. The exact activities of teachers at this level will depend on their special expertise. Some will devote all their attention to teaching children. Others will teach and be heavily involved in teacher education, often combining work in their schools and in the university. Still others will teach and be involved in curricular reform, classroom-based research projects, and other problems calling for informed leadership.

Advantages of
differentiated staffing

Although there is resistance to this differentiated staff concept, there is much to recommend it. For one thing, it provides a larger professional canvas for the creative energies of the better teachers who enter the field. In addition, in this plan good teachers will affect more students, and so will have greater impact. Instead of the current tight little boxes of twenty-five students to one teacher, this scheme will have truly gifted teachers spreading their skill as widely as possible. For instance, the teacher who is competent in teaching mathematics to elementary students will teach this subject to as many as one hundred students a day, while others will teach the language arts and social studies aspects of the curriculum. Further, the differentiated staff concept will allow for a more structured and careful introduction of beginners into teaching. This plan will have beginning teachers work under the supervision of a senior colleague and gradually take on more instructional responsibilities as they gain more skill.

This concept also breaks the current lock-step salary scale, which is based on years of service and amount of education and pays little attention to competence in teaching. Higher salaries for good teachers will slow down the drain of excellence from the classroom substantially. Although differentiated staffing will have many different benefits for teachers, the ultimate winners will be the children, since the concept promises to improve the quality of the instruction to which they are exposed.

A NEW STRUCTURE FOR SCHOOLING

The new teacher needs a new school. And so do children. Our schools, both physically and intellectually, were designed in the nineteenth century. They are pre-television, pre-computers, and pre–mass higher education. They are also based on the concept of the know-it-all teacher doing the job alone in the classroom with screwed-to-the-floor desks. Over the years, we have unscrewed the desks from the floors (in most schools, anyway) and added a reading specialist here and a teacher's aide there, but we have not fundamentally reordered the way we do schooling. What we propose, then, is a new model for a new time, a school structure for today and for the near future.

A three-tiered structure

In our new school structure, children will begin school on their fourth birthday and graduate the spring after their sixteenth birthday. Having children start school on their fourth birthday (rather than in September of their fourth or fifth year) will catch them at the right developmental moment. The school will be structured around three levels of schooling, each lasting four years. Notice that we did not say "covering four grades." Our plan will dismantle the cherished grade system and replace it with a nongraded structure by which students will be carefully tracked through each of several subject areas, advancing according to their performance. There will be no more cumbersome, yearly decision to pass or hold back students.

A more important change will be that students will not have one or a series of teachers exclusively for a year and then be passed on to the next grade's teachers for another year. Instead students, grouped in the three levels, will be educated in units of approximately one hundred students, called *communities*. Each community will have approximately a fourth of its students at each of the level's four ages. During a particular year, a new group of twenty-five or so will come into the group and twenty-five or so will "graduate" to the next level.

These units will be called communities because establishing a sense of community is at the heart of our proposal. We want students to spend their formative years with a close, interdependent group of students and teachers. Although students' progress will be monitored carefully, there will be no grades, such as first grade or sixth grade. In addition, there will be no special tracks for bright or slow students. In effect, each student will be in his or her own track.

Great attention will be paid to the emotional quality of these communities. We want no "outsiders," no lonely faces in the crowd who are ignored year after year by teachers and students. Our communities of one hundred students and a team of four or five adults (more about the teachers shortly) will be based on sharing—sharing knowledge, skills, hurts and disappointments, and love. They will be extensions of the family at its best.

Three or four communities will typically make up a school. Therefore, there will be approximately three or four hundred students and twelve to twenty teachers per school. Of course, they will all share the same buildings and school grounds. In our plan, the three levels of schooling will all be in the same place, ideally in three different buildings in close proximity, rather than spread out over a community. They might be in different corners of an educational park, sharing sports fields and certain athletic facilities. This plan creates a community-style stability as well as several other benefits. First, it solves a major problem in American education: the fragmentation of the curriculum. The staffs from the three levels will be together to plan, adjust, and work on implementing the curriculum. Teachers at the lower levels can directly report on what their children actually learn and can help the upper-level teachers interpret the performance of individual students who experience problems of various kinds. Second, this educational reform aims to involve young people in helping and sharing activities. Older students will work with teachers on various tasks involving smaller, younger students. One such task is peer tutoring, whereby an older student provides extra, face-to-face instruction for a younger student.[2]

Although some students with very academic orientations are reasonably pleased with the current structure, many others have difficulty developing in the often hostile, regimented, and impersonal world of the American comprehensive high school. The high rates of dropping out, absenteeism, vandalism, and fighting suggest that what we currently have is simply not the answer for late adolescents.

To give students more direction, we propose a two-year "experience" for young people starting right after their graduation from high school (the completion of their twelfth year of schooling) and before they go off to college or job training. The experience will be called *national service* and will combine work, study, and service. National service will be seen, as it is in many countries around the world, as a citizen's contribution to the welfare of the nation's society and as an opportunity to have some rather special experiences. It will be, quite frankly, an effort to wean adolescents away from their preoccupation with themselves and their peer group, from a life that for too many is devoted to self-indulgence and escapism in the form of drugs, hours of television, and irresponsible sex.

The national service will attempt to knit late adolescents into the fabric of the larger culture. Some young men and women will train for military service. Some will do social work, such as helping feed and shelter the poor. Some will work with the increasing numbers of elderly citizens. The work will be real work, demanding responsible behavior. Some training will go with every assignment, so that at the end the young will take something practical away, in addition to the sense of satisfaction from having been of service to others.

Gaining some training

Staffing the New Schools

Staffing considerations are an important part of this plan. What we are proposing will not take additional financial resources to pay for *more* teachers. Nor are we necessarily claiming to have *better* teachers. Rather, we are suggesting a more careful use of teachers' talents. In this system, teachers will have different responsibilities based on their skills, interests, and levels of commitment. We also see each community as having four or possibly five teachers, typically a career professional teacher, two professional teachers, an instructor, and possibly an aide. In addition, schools will be encouraged to use volunteers and sometimes older students. Together this team of professionals and helpers will teach *all* the students. And the professionals, at least, will stay with them for four years. The hundred students and four or five adults will together form a stable, continually learning community.

Importance of parents

An important part of these communities will be the students' parents. They will perform all sorts of tasks, from assisting teachers with instruction to occasionally providing direct instruction in their areas of expertise. Because of the size and enduring qualities of these communities, parents will feel closer to the staff and students than in the current situation. Even though they may have no formal or professional role in this new design, their close and regular involvement will be essential.

A new administrative structure

The three or four career professional teachers in a school will have leadership roles and will head their communities. Each of them will also specialize in a particular area of the curriculum and will act as a specialist in that area (say, science or social studies) to the staffs of the other communities. In effect, then, they will be the leadership team, thus eliminating the need for a principal, at least as the principal tends to function now. Much of what principals do today will be done by the school's administrative assistants, who will take care of logistics like schedules, maintenance, and the many details necessary to support the educational mission of the communities. The administrative assistants for the three levels of schools in a locale will report to a headmaster, who will be the chief administrator and, more importantly, the top educator for the three schools. He or she will be concerned primarily with curriculum and matters of school climate and will work directly with the career professional teachers and other faculty members. Also, the headmaster will be responsible for teacher evaluation, a task to be carried out jointly with the senior teaching staff.

There will be some losses, particularly at the high school level with this plan. Not so much specialization among the faculty; a smaller "talent pool" for sports teams, band, and plays. On the other hand, many more students would play competitive sports and be involved in activities like band and school plays. While the nation's scholastic and intercollegiate sports machine might have to alter its course, we are emphatic that where education and student development are concerned, "smaller is better."

NEW LEARNING FOR NEW SCHOOLS

The reforms we have suggested so far in the staffing and the structure of schools will be limited in their value unless the schools also renew their curriculum. In our discussion of curricular reform we will focus on something old and something new. The old issues are cultural literacy and character education, and the new are learning skills and technology.

Technology and the Schools

Today, America is an information-based society. More than ever before, schools need to help students acquire and retain large amounts of good information, and students need to be able to fully understand and use that information. We believe that computers will be an irresistible force in the improvement of education. Nothing can equal the computer's capacity to deliver information, particularly when it is linked with other technologies, such as video disks, software banks, and satellite communication networks. Here are some of the advantages of the computer-driven learning systems that are currently being tested:

Computerized learning systems

- self-paced interaction between the student and the subject matter to be learned.

- individually customized instruction for students that takes into consideration their past learning, most effective styles of learning, mental capacities, needs, and other characteristics

- infinitely patient and "friendly" presentation of information (no more fear of asking the teacher to explain the equation for the third time!) and tireless management of learning records and routine drill

- multimedia and multisensory learning through integration of video educational materials and interactive computer programs

- capability to communicate with other students and teachers and to access information resources through state, national, and international computer networks

To illustrate, let's compare the teaching of the assassination of President Kennedy by a good high school teacher and by the kind of computer-driven learning system that exists today. First, the teacher must develop a presentation, which means working up a lecture, possibly getting films and slides of old photos and newspaper accounts. Next, the teacher needs to get and hold the attention of twenty-five different learners with different background knowledge of the topic and different learning styles and capabilities, to name but a few variables. Once the teacher presents the material, having to aim for the middle level in the class, he or she must devise a method of evaluating whether or not the students learned the major ideas and must devise some sort of remediation for those who have not learned.

Compare this scenario with that of a student learning about the same historical event using the computer technology we currently have. First, the student goes to a learning station when ready and begins the learning program on the Kennedy assassination. Using video disk technology, the terminal screen presents an excellent documentary on the background and highlights surrounding the event. This is followed by three leading historians giving different interpretations of the assassination and its effect on the country. Although summary notes are available, the student is encouraged to take notes while viewing the video and can stop the presentation at any time, replaying points about which he or she is unclear. Further, the student can type in questions, such as "What do we know about Lee Harvey Oswald's connections with the Russians?" and get detailed answers. The program will begin and end with attempts to connect this event with things already learned, such as past assassinations of presidents, and other themes, such as the social legislation that followed Kennedy's death.

When the presentation is over, the student can check his or her comprehension by taking a test right at the terminal. Concepts or information that the test shows the student did not understand will be presented again, but this time in a manner more appropriate to the student's learning style. A student who wants to follow up with other questions about the Kennedy administration can dial up the information bank at the Kennedy Museum in Boston or the museum at the assassination site at the Dallas Book Depository. And, if answers are not readily available, the student can speak directly to the information specialists and researchers at the museums. Then, if the student wants to investigate the event further, he or she can consult with the teacher about next steps, steps to deepen understanding of the assassination and its effect on the course of American history. The student and teacher may decide to discuss it themselves, or the student may choose to organize a discussion among students within the community, or may initiate or join a network of other students *around the country* who have scheduled a video conference discussion on an assassination-related topic. In effect, a student will be able to simply type into a *nationwide network* a question ("Who wants to talk about the possibility of Oswald being directed by the Mafia?"), a time, and a suggestion of how many people should be in the discussion, and then see if there are any takers. The student will be connected not only with vast information sources and learning tools but also with other

The supreme end of education is expert discernment in all things—the power to tell the good from the bad, the genuine from the counterfeit, and to prefer the good and the genuine to the bad and the counterfeit.
— SAMUEL JOHNSON —

students all over the country with similar interests. In effect, the computer will function for the student as an intellectual assistant.

The kind of computer-assisted education described here will have several benefits. First, it will keep students continually at the frontier of what they are learning, instead of bored or lost. Second, because of the self-pacing, the time involved in learning will be greatly reduced. Students will learn in an hour at the computer what formerly they learned in two days of traditional class time. Third, because instruction will have built-in self-testing and regular reviews, students will be able to use and retain what they have learned more effectively. Fourth, the computer's word processing capability will greatly help students to write well, reducing the mechanical tasks associated with research reports and creative compositions. Fifth, this method of acquiring information will leave students much more time than they currently have to develop skills of discussion and artistic expression (music, dance, painting) and to master various sports and physical skills. The time saved will allow students to become more involved in community service projects, or go on extensive field trips, or maybe even sit quietly under a tree and read a book.

Benefits for teachers

But what about teachers? How will the computer revolution affect them? First, it will free them from a good deal of the tasks related to presenting information—not completely, but in major ways. Also, they will have to do much less testing for comprehension (and thus will be deprived of their age-old weapon, the pop quiz!). Instead, the teacher will be much more involved in higher-level evaluation of performance: observing students' discussions and evaluating their interactive skills, listening to a report by a group of students and giving them feedback, and reading early drafts of student papers and making suggestions for their final drafts. Computers will also enable teachers to do a good deal of what Theodore Sizer refers to as *coaching*,[3] working with students one on one, helping them grapple with troublesome math problems, guiding them as they struggle with new reading skills, or counseling them about difficulties in their community service projects. Finally, like students, teachers will have more time for innovative types of learning and teaching. They will have time to collaborate with students, paint murals with them, be in plays with them, and go on archaeological digs with them. The teacher of the future will be a model of what the schools are attempting to develop: people as continuous learners. And much of this new freedom to teach and learn will be a direct benefit of the computer.

Learning to Learn

Somewhere in the third or fourth grade in the American schools the content to be learned shifts from learning skills, like reading and penmanship and numbers, to knowledge. The focus of learning becomes state capitals, the history of the country, the metric system, short stories, the solar system, plant life, the musical scale, and so on. Certainly skills in reading and measuring are being taught and practiced along the way, skills like speaking, analyzing, and observing. There are, however, a whole group of skills that many students pick up in the process of learning content knowledge and that other students do not. We call these *academic learning skills*.

Academic learning skills

SCHOOLS OF THE FUTURE

The human brain is a glorious instrument capable of enormous feats of creativity, from writing symphonies to making scientific breakthroughs. The average brain can store and manipulate more information, by several hundred times, than our largest computers. But the brain has its drawbacks. For one thing, it loses or "misfiles" information. Lots of ideas and facts and assorted messages enter it through the eyes, ears, and other senses and somehow get lost.

Brain needs training When we want to remember an idea, it often is simply "not there." Or somehow the facts get "modified," so that when we take the exam, we are sure that there are 2 quarts in a gallon and 4 pints in a quart. So although the brain is humankind's treasure, it is not perfect, and it needs to be trained to work well.

By *trained,* we mean we have to teach people how to use their brains. In the same way that reading extends the power of the brain by giving access to vast amounts of important information, so too other tools can make the brain more efficient. By *more efficient,* we mean able to better take in, store, retrieve, **Needed skills** and process information. Here is a list of some of the skills that can and ought to be taught to *all* students:

- *A variety of methods of remembering important information.* A large part of this is teaching people how not to forget, how to move information from the fleeting and slippery short-term memory to the long-term memory.

- *Two or three methods of taking notes and "saving" important information.* There are definite skills associated with capturing what another person is saying, and students should systematically learn these skills.

- *What we call "study reading."* One practices *study reading* when the material is not simple and contains information one wants to remember later.

- *How to prepare for different kinds of tests.* Show students how to study for different tests, such as objective and essay tests, and how to deal with test anxiety in different situations.

- *How to do research.* Show students how to get answers to questions, how to use libraries and librarians, experts, and data sources of all kinds.

- *How to think through a problem in a systematic way.* Instead of jumping to conclusions or relying on how they "feel" about an issue, students should learn how to think critically.

- *How to "get the academic job done."* Students need to know how to set goals, monitor their own behavior, and gradually become more successful at academic learning.

In athletic programs all over the country, young men and women are learning sophisticated, revolutionary techniques to improve their performance in various sports. Athletes have been taught new "tools for learning," from imaging to biofeedback to new methods of weight control to goal setting. A like focus on learning academic skills can and ought to occur in our schools. Of course, we must attend to the three R's, but in addition there are the new basics: advanced reading, remembering, recording, analyzing, listening, and problem solving. These are the tools that students should be taking out of high school into college and into the work place.

Character Education

Pros and cons

Character education is the effort to help the young acquire a sense of right and wrong and the habit of behaving in a way that advances the common good. It involves both knowing what is good and doing what is good. Some argue that the public school has no role in character development and moral education because values and morals are rooted in deeply held religious world views. As such, they are out of bounds to the public school, which should concentrate on cognitive skills exclusively.[4] These people claim that if parents want attention to morals and values, they ought to put their children in private schools. We believe, on the contrary, that most educators know that it is impossible to educate the young in a moral vacuum and that the process of schooling necessarily affects the way children think about issues of right and wrong. Every teacher, knowingly or unknowingly, signals to children what he or she considers good behavior and poor behavior, what is admired and not admired. In addition, to have children in school as long as our society does means that inevitably the children's values and moral thinking will be affected.

Core American values

Further, certain values are supported by the overwhelming majority of Americans, regardless of religion, class, region, or ethical posture. Some of these are respect for law and individual rights, the need for honesty and responsibility in our dealings with one another, the need to show consideration and care toward those in distress, and the importance of persistence and courage in the face of adversity. Few would not wholeheartedly support the school's vigorous advocacy of these values and the character traits that go with them.

Schools, public and private, must reassume the responsibility, shared with the family and religion, to vigorously pass on to the young the best of our culture's values. One major approach is simply to teach more directly the positive moral values that are embedded in our culture. Our history and literature are **Using the curriculum** permeated with value issues and lessons from the past. Instead of simply having students study the facts of a historical period or read a story to build vocabulary or appreciate style, the teacher can confront them with ethical dilemmas and moral lessons that are integral to the subject matter. Instead of simply teaching scientific methodologies and findings, the teacher can have students examine the implications of applied science, such as genetic manipulation. They will see that the use of science and technologies—such as nuclear energy, fossil fuels, and high-speed computers—is not neutral, but has ethical implications.

To have meaning, values must be practiced; they must overflow into deeds. A major reason for organizing schools into the small communities we described earlier is to give students opportunities to learn the value of cooperation and mutual support. Service to others will be a major theme of school life. As stu- **Using service programs** dents get older, they will be given more and more responsibility for working with and caring for younger students. In the later stages of high school, groups of students will take on projects in the larger community, such as assisting a parent with a mildly retarded child or helping with an exercise class at a senior citizens' center. Individual students will provide companionship to elderly shut-ins or peer counseling to troubled youngsters. The emphasis will be not merely on the study of values, but also on values in action.

The older generation has always worried about the behavior of the young. Such concern is quite valid, since a lack of strong values in the new generation can impede or even destroy a society's progress. We believe that children need values and a sense of what is right and what is wrong if they *and* their society are to survive and flourish. Clearly schools can and should play a major role in passing on society's best values to the young.

A FINAL WORD

This epilogue is our attempt to state where we believe education should be going. The schools of the future, we hope, will have a restructured teaching force, in which outstanding teachers spread wide their influence, but do it in a smaller and more community-like structure. And the schools of the future will have a revitalized curriculum, one that promotes excellence not only in intellectual development and the acquisition of important knowledge, but also in character. Whether or not the specifics of the plan we have put forth in this chapter will achieve those goals is yet to be tested fully. It is important, though, for all teachers to have a vision of what education ought to be. Long ago, Socrates said that the purpose of education is not just to make people smart, but to make people good. Whatever education plans or reforms our society adopts must contribute to making that old ideal a reality.

Notes

1. See the Holmes Group, *Tomorrow's Teachers: A Report of the Holmes Group* (East Lansing, Mich.: Holmes Group, 1986), pp. 10–13.
2. See P. Cohen, J. Kulik, and C. Kulik, "Educational Outcomes of Tutoring: A Meta-Analysis of Findings," *American Educational Research Journal* 19 (1982): 237–248.
3. Theodore Sizer, *Horace's Compromise* (Boston: Houghton Mifflin, 1985), pp. 99–108.
4. See Chapter 6 ("Against Moral Education") in Barry Chasan, *Contemporary Approaches to Moral Education* (New York: Teachers College Press, 1985).

This appendix is designed to help you develop skills in observing classrooms and schools. You will probably benefit most by reading the rest of this section rather quickly now and rereading it carefully before you observe schools and classrooms. The material on the following pages is somewhat technical, and you can probably assimilate it best when you know that you will be making use of it soon.

Issues Related to Observation

Virtually all teacher education programs provide opportunities for the prospective teacher to observe experienced teachers. Observation may take place "live," or it may involve viewing videotape recordings of classroom sessions. Either alternative can be extremely valuable if it offers an opportunity for insight into how a classroom is organized, how the teacher relates to different students, or how different forms of instruction can be used. On the other hand, observation of a classroom can be boring, tedious, and educationally irrelevant. What is it that makes observation valuable or worthless? The difference is a matter of knowing specifically what you are attempting to observe and why, being able to gather information accurately, and interpreting your information in order to learn from it. Thus, to really benefit from observing an actual classroom, you must have some training in observational techniques.

Need for training

It is physically and mechanically impossible to record *everything* that occurs in a classroom, let alone in an entire school. Thus any technique used to gather data about the classroom environment must of necessity be selective. This is a built-in and unavoidable limitation of all recording instruments and techniques of observation.

Be selective

Furthermore, the background and training of the observer influence the classroom phenomena he or she chooses to focus on and the ways in which he or she interprets them. If the variable in question is aggressive behavior among students, for example, an educational psychologist may interpret a classroom outbreak as a result of the teacher's inconsistent reward pattern. An anthropologist might view it as a normal event within the youth subculture. A student teacher, because of personal needs and anxieties, might assume that the students are misbehaving because they don't really like him or her. For this reason, objective interpretation is as impossible as comprehensive observation. But knowing the limitations of observational techniques will help observers interpret the data better, and being aware of their own particular perceptual habits will help them exert caution in interpretation.

Observer bias

Another problem is that anytime someone or something new and different enters a classroom, that person or thing affects the dynamics of the group in some way. Your presence may cause the teacher to be somewhat more nervous, thus affecting his or her behavior. The students, aware of your presence, may turn their heads to see what you are doing. If you are collecting data using some mechanical equipment, such as a videotape recorder, the teacher's and students' behavior will be affected. Therefore, you can never observe or collect information completely free from the effects of your presence. What you can do, however, is to become a frequent enough visitor to the classroom that your presence will not produce unusual or severe reactions from the regular participants in the

Observer's impact on classroom

classroom. You can also locate yourself physically in the room to reduce your obtrusiveness and to stay out of the students' direct line of sight.

Behave professionally

As an observer in someone else's classroom, you are a guest and, as such, need to behave accordingly. This means that your dress and appearance should be consistent with what the school expects its teachers to wear. If you are uncertain about this, ask your college instructor. You should also refrain from judging the school or teachers too quickly if you see things happening with which you disagree. Remember, you probably don't have all the information you need to make such judgments, and you need to accord the teachers some respect for their judgments and decisions. As the old Native American proverb states, "Don't judge another until you've walked a mile in his moccasins." Keep in mind also that you should not assume that what you see one day is typical of what occurs often. That may or may not be the case. Frequent observations are necessary before one can speak with confidence about patterns or typical behavior.

Confidentiality

Another aspect of behaving professionally is maintaining confidentiality. Although you may need to report your observations in some format to your college instructor, it is unprofessional to tattle or gossip to your peers about a particular teacher or classroom. If you feel the need to discuss some incident or events that occurred in a particular school or classroom, try to maintain confidentiality regarding the identities of the particular persons involved. The classroom participants should not suffer embarrassment or harm as a result of your field experience.

Data-Gathering Techniques

The observational methods used in education were developed by the behavioral and social sciences to gather data about and interpret complex environments; they were later found to be appropriate for use in schools as well. This section will introduce you to some of these tools and approaches and to the kinds of preliminary decisions and subsequent interpretation that give meaning to observation. The scrupulous observer must ask certain questions: What specifically will be observed? Which method of gathering data will be most effective? What do these data mean? To learn from observation, then, the observer needs (1) objectives, (2) a way to record observations, and (3) a way to interpret observations with respect to objectives.

Purposeful observation

Observation should not be aimless. If you are to find out what life in the classroom is like, you must decide which aspects you wish to focus on. Your objective may be very broad, such as "What does the teacher do and say during a class period?" Or it may be as narrow as "How many times does a particular student speak to another student?"

Form hypotheses

From the data that you collect you can form a hypothesis about why certain things occur, and you can test this hypothesis by making predictions about what should happen if it is correct. If your prediction is not validated, you can reexamine your data and try to develop another explanation. If your prediction is validated repeatedly, you will know that you are moving in the direction of understanding what is happening in the classroom and, possibly, why. For example, suppose your objective is to examine the teacher's verbal interaction with each individual student. After performing frequency counts—recording how many times the teacher calls on each student, or how many times each student volunteers information or asks the teacher a question—over a period of a week, you might hypothesize about the frequency distribution for the following week. If your predictions are validated, you should then try to interpret your findings. Was the teacher displaying a bias against certain students? Did the teacher systematically ignore the students seated in a particular part of the room? Were certain groups of students—for example, girls or certain socioeconomic groups—treated in particular ways? Caution must be exercised in drawing conclusions, however, because rival hypotheses may explain the same phenomena.

The point to be emphasized is that to understand the happenings in a classroom, you must select objectives that provide you with a focus. Since you can't see, hear, and interpret everything, you must be selective. To be selective, you must establish the purpose of your observation.

You may find one of the following techniques of data gathering particularly appropriate, given your objectives, the equipment available, and the degree of access you have to a school. All have been used profitably by classroom observers.

NOTE TAKING   Probably the most common means of gathering data in the school is note taking. The method is borrowed from cultural anthropologists, who take copious notes of their observations while living with the natives of an unfamiliar culture. You can use the same approach to accumulate information about the interpersonal relationships, values, or social status of individuals in a class.

Preliminary decisions

If you choose the note-taking approach, certain preliminary decisions will have to be made. First, how comprehensive should your notes be? You will be attempting to record everything you see that relates to your objective. Thus the broader your objective, the more you will have to record. In many instances it will be difficult for you to decide quickly on the relevance of a specific event. A handy rule of thumb: When in doubt, write it down. Too much information is better than not enough, for insufficient data can lead to frustration and to erroneous conclusions.

Second, should you write a description of what you see and hear, or should you simply record what is said verbatim? Should you write down your impressions of incidents, or should you be as objective as possible? We recommend that, whenever possible, data be recorded verbatim. In trying to summarize or describe what takes place, you are likely to substitute your own perceptions for what was actually happening. If you wish also to record your impressions, insights, inferences, and comments, keep them in the margin or draw brackets around them to distinguish them from the raw data. This distinction is crucial because of the tendency to make inferences based on selected perceptions or personal biases. If we are happy, we tend to see happy people; if tired, we see the teacher's and students' behavior through the filter of fatigue and interpret it accordingly. We may see relationships that don't actually exist and miss ones that do. Therefore, recognizing that complete objectivity is impossible, we should still aim to achieve it rather than rely on our own interpretations of events.

You will find that recording nonverbal behavior tends to be much more impressionistic than recording verbal behavior. If we observe a student fidgeting in her seat, picking her nose, and looking out the window, it is tempting to assert that she is bored; yet that is an inference. Keep checking on yourself to make sure you are distinguishing between actual behavior and inferences drawn from behavior.

It is much easier to be comprehensive in your note taking if you establish a standard format and abbreviations. For example, indenting student comments will help you distinguish them from teacher comments and will save you from repeatedly having to indicate who is talking. Abbreviating words by omitting vowels, employing homonyms, and using phonetic representations will also allow you to record more efficiently and quickly.

Advantages and disadvantages

Note taking has a number of advantages as a means of gathering data about classroom actions. It is relatively simple and very economical. You can flip back and forth in your notes easily when you begin to interpret the data. The notes can be cut up and juxtaposed in whatever fashion you want to help you discern patterns or repeated themes. You can assimilate ideas and events rapidly by scanning written notes. And notes constitute a permanent record, which you can keep to compare with other observations and to develop, support, or reject hypotheses.

A major disadvantage of note taking is the difficulty of recording everything you can see and hear. Even though you have selected limited objectives to guide your observations, action often develops so fast that you fall behind and miss some of what is said or done. Taking notes forces you keep your eyes on the paper in front of you and prevents you from observing the class uninterruptedly. In other words, your observation system tends to become overloaded with stimuli. Nevertheless, note taking is probably the most frequently used method of gathering data in the classroom.

SYSTEMATIC OBSERVATION SYSTEMS   Systematic observation systems make use of lists of categories—as minuscule as sneezes or smiles or as broad as teacher-student rapport—to record verbal or nonverbal interaction in the classroom according to predefined rules and definitions. Prior to the observation, decisions are made concerning what is to be observed, the method of observation and recording data, and how the data will be analyzed and used.

Although many observation systems have been developed, only a few are in general use. Probably the best-known category system for observing teachers and pupils is Flanders's Interaction Analysis (see Figure A-1). Flanders identified ten different categories of verbal behavior; the first seven apply to teacher talk, the next two to student talk, and the final category records silence or confusion. The categories are: (1) accepting student feelings; (2) giving praise; (3) accepting, clarifying, or making use of a student's ideas; (4) asking a question; (5) lecturing, giving facts or opinions; (6) giving directions; (7) giving criticism; (8) student response; (9) student initiation; and (10) confusion or silence. Categories 1–4 represent indirect teacher influence, and categories 5–7 represent direct teacher influence. An observer using Flanders's system records every three seconds the category of verbal behavior occurring at that instant; then an analysis

Figure A.1 Categories for Interaction Analysis, 1959

TEACHER TALK

Indirect Influence

1* ACCEPTS FEELING: accepts and clarifies the tone of feeling of the students in an unthreatening manner. Feelings may be positive or negative. Predicting or recalling feelings are included.

2* PRAISES OR ENCOURAGES: praises or encourages student action or behavior. Jokes that release tension, but not at the expense of another individual, nodding head or saying "um hm?" or "go on" are included.

3* ACCEPTS OR USES IDEAS OF STUDENT: clarifying, building, or developing ideas suggested by a student. As teacher brings more of his own ideas into play, shift to category 5.

4* ASKS QUESTIONS: asking a question about content or procedure with the intent that a student answer.

Direct Influence

5* LECTURING: giving facts or opinions about content or procedure; expressing his own ideas, asking rhetorical questions.

6* GIVING DIRECTIONS: directions, commands, or orders which students are expected to comply with.

7* CRITICIZING OR JUSTIFYING AUTHORITY: statements intended to change student behavior from unacceptable to acceptable pattern; bawling someone out; stating why the teacher is doing what he is doing; extreme self-reference.

STUDENT TALK

8* STUDENT TALK—RESPONSE: talk by students in response to teacher. Teacher initiates the contact or solicits student statement.

9* STUDENT TALK—INITIATION: talk initiated by student. If "calling on" student is only to indicate who may talk next, observer must decide whether student wanted to talk.

SILENCE

10* SILENCE OR CONFUSION: pauses, short periods of silence, and periods of confusion in which communication cannot be understood by the observer.

*There is NO scale implied by these numbers. Each number is classificatory, designating a particular kind of communication event. To write these numbers down during observation is merely to identify and enumerate communication events, not to judge them.

is made of verbal interaction during the entire class period. Thus a profile of the teacher's direct or indirect influence can be obtained.

Flanders's system has limitations, but it can be a helpful and informative tool in analyzing a certain kind of verbal behavior in the classroom. It has been used extensively, and considerable research data have been collected. Instructional booklets and audiotapes are available to students interested in learning to use the system and to interpret data. Many universities and colleges, as well as public schools, have used Interaction Analysis to help teachers analyze their teaching.

Using seating charts as an observational tool provides a familiar way of looking at classrooms. Seating charts are useful for collecting important aspects of classroom behavior, such as pupil attentiveness, and they are easy to use. Figure A-2 illustrates how a seating chart can be used to collect data on student on-task and off-task behavior. Each box represents a student, and the boxes are located on the paper to reflect each student's physical location in the classroom. Within each box is a sequence of numbers, each representing one observation of the student. Depending on the length of the observation time period, there may be fewer or more than the eleven observations represented in this instrument. A list of categories with their code symbols, a legend, is also given. The on-task and off-task behaviors are symbolized by letters that represent shorthand reminders of the behavior categories. (Figure A-2 has the coded observations already recorded.) This instrument and others like it are flexible and can be adapted to fit the observer's and the teacher's needs. Many of the on-task and off-task behaviors can be anticipated in advance of the actual observation, but should one occur that was not anticipated, just add it to the legend.

When you are ready to begin the observation, identify the time you begin and then observe the first student. What is he or she doing? Code the behavior appropriately and place the code in the box next to the number 1. Then move quickly to the next student and repeat the process, again placing the code next to the number 1. Continue until you have observed all the students (or at least the ones that you are observing), and then start your second round of observations with the first student and repeat the sequence. Each time you get ready to begin a new observation cycle, record the time you start. The times that you see listed on the instrument in Figure A-2 are not placed there in advance of the actual observation. They are there simply to remind you to record the time so you will know how much time was required for each observation cycle.

With some practice and familiarity with the instrument, you will soon be able to move quickly from student to student while coding their behavior. Remember, you are sampling the students' behavior. The more observations you make, the greater the confidence you can have that your sample validly and reliably represents the full set of behaviors the students demonstrated.

Whereas you can analyze each student's pattern of behavior by looking at each box, it is much more difficult to grasp the broader picture of the total class's on-task and off-task behavior. However, you can do this by developing a matrix with the types of behavior listed along one dimension and the time intervals

Figure A.2 Pupil On-Task/Off-Task Behavior

Purpose: To determine which students are on or off task during a lesson, and what specific behaviors they are engaged in.
Lesson Type: Teacher-led discussion in eighth-grade social studies.

Note:

On Task	Off Task
L = listening	R− = reading (non class related)
TN = taking notes	T− = talking (non class related)
H = hand raised	WS = working on another subject
T+ = talking (discussion	OS = out of seat
related)	O = other

Time	1 9:15	2 9:17	3 9:20	4 9:22	5 9:25	6 9:27	7 9:29	8 9:32	9 9:34	10 9:37	11 9:40
Corrine	L	L	TN	TN	H	T+	L	L	TN	TN	OS
Mike	T−	T−	WS	WS	WS	WS	OS	T−	H	OS	OS
Jim	T−	T−	L	L	L	TN	H	TN	T+	T+	O
Nancy	R−	R−	R−	L	L	L	TN	T+	OS	OS	OS
Jo	WS	WS	L	L	TN	TN	L	L	H	T+	T+
Mary Kay	L	L	TN	TN	TN	T+	T−	L	L	H	H
Will	OS	O	O	O	T−	R−	R−	R−	R−	H	OS
Mildred	L	L	L	TN	T+	T+	H	L	L	L	H
Carlos	L	L	L	L	L	TN	TN	TN	TN	TN	TN
James	OS	T−	T−	T−	L	L	L	TN	TN	TN	L
Frank	H	H	TN	TN	TN	L	L	L	L	L	T+
Betty	L	L	L	L	L	TN	L	L	L	L	L
Marilyn	R−	R−	R−	WS	WS	WS	WS	WS	WS	H	H
Fran	H	L	L	T+	T+	L	H	TN	TN	TN	TN
Howie	OS	L	L	TN	TN	T+	T−	T−	T−	OS	OS
Jack	T+	TN	TN	TN	L	L	L	WS	WS	WS	WS
Bob	T+	TN	L	L	L	TN	H	H	O	O	O
Maria	L	L	L	L	H	L	L	L	L	L	L
Vince	T−	T−	T−	L	L	L	H	T+	OS	OS	OS
Chet	R−	R−	R−	R−	L	TN	TN	TN	TN	R−	R−

Source: Adapted from James M. Cooper, "Observation Skills," in *Developing Skills for Instructional Supervision*, ed. James M. Cooper (New York: Longman, 1984), p. 96.

along the other dimension; in this way you can obtain an overall view of the class (Figure A-3). To interpret these data with some accuracy, it is necessary to know what activities are supposed to be occurring throughout the lesson. Don't try to interpret too much from data unless you know what happened in the class.

There are several things worth noting about the data presented in Figure A-3. First, note the percentage of pupils on task throughout the lesson. At the beginning of the lesson the figure is 50 percent, and it climbs to 85 percent after 10 minutes. Is there some explanation for why it took 10 minutes to reach an 85 percent on-task rate? Similarly, why was there a sharp decline in the on-task percentage rate during the last 6 minutes?

Second, during the beginning of the lesson there were as many as four students engaged in non-class-related talking. Why?

Third, why were so many students out of their seats during the last 6 minutes of the class? Was the teacher aware of them? The data do not provide us with answers to these questions, but they do provoke us to ask the questions.

If you are interested in learning more about other observation systems, the following books and articles will be helpful:

Sources of observation instruments

- Acheson, Keith A., and Meredith Damien Gall. *Techniques in the Clinical Supervision of Teachers.* 2d ed. New York: Longman, 1987.

Figure A.3 On-Task/Off-Task Matrix

	BEHAVIOR CATEGORIES										
	1	*2*	*3*	*4*	*5*	*6*	*7*	*8*	*9*	*10*	*11*
	9:15	*9:17*	*9:20*	*9:22*	*9:25*	*9:27*	*9:29*	*9:32*	*9:34*	*9:37*	*9:40*
On Task											
Listening	6	8	9	8	9	7	7	7	5	4	3
Taking notes	0	2	4	6	4	6	3	5	5	4	2
Hand raised	2	1	0	0	2	0	5	1	2	3	3
Talking (discussion related)	2	0	0	0	2	4	0	2	1	2	2
Off Task											
Reading (non class related)	3	3	3	1	0	1	1	1	1	1	1
Talking (non class related)	3	4	2	2	1	0	2	2	1	0	0
Working on another subject	1	1	1	2	2	2	1	2	2	1	1
Out of seat	3	0	0	0	0	0	1	0	2	4	6
Other	0	1	1	1	0	0	0	0	1	1	2
Percentage of students on task	50	55	65	70	85	85	75	75	65	65	50

- Cooper, James M. "Observation Skills" and "Analysis Skills." In *Developing Skills for Instructional Supervision,* ed. J. M. Cooper. New York: Longman, 1984. Chapters 4 and 5.
- Good, Thomas L., and Jere E. Brophy. *Looking in Classrooms.* 5th ed. New York: HarperCollins, 1991.

ANALYSIS OF ARTIFACTS   Much can be learned about life in the classroom without directly observing teachers and students. The textbooks and supplementary materials in use can reveal a lot to the careful observer. Similarly, the tests given, the placement of chairs and desks, the materials displayed on the bulletin board, and the audiovisual equipment used (or neglected) are clues about what activities take place and what kind of learning is valued. What kinds of questions are on the examinations? Do they emphasize the acquisition of facts to the exclusion of solving problems, analyzing or synthesizing ideas, making evaluations, comparing or contrasting different points of view, drawing inferences from limited data, or forming generalizations? Do the chairs and desks always face the teacher, the dominant person in the classroom? Or are they frequently grouped in small circles, indicating opportunities for pupil-pupil interaction? Is a multimedia approach used so that students may learn from a variety of sources?

You probably have the idea by now: clues about what a teacher thinks is important, whether students are involved in instruction as well as learning, and how the teacher views his or her role can be garnered by a careful analysis of materials used and produced in the classroom. Valuable inferences may be made from data available to the naked eye, but it is crucial to remember that such inferences are only hypotheses and that additional data must be gathered to confirm or invalidate them.

INTERVIEWS   Interviewing teachers, students, administrators, counselors, librarians, and other school personnel is an excellent way to gather data about life in school. People who play different roles in the school, and thus see it from different vantage points, often have highly disparate views of it. The cook in the school kitchen may have a very different opinion of the food's quality than the students or the teachers, and the administrator's view of detention hall is probably very unlike the students'. Questioning the students about what occupies most of their time in the classroom, what they think the school's purpose is, why they go to school, or how their good teachers differ from the poor ones can produce fascinating and highly valuable data. Some sample questions, the answers to which should help you better understand life in a particular school, follow:

1. Where is the school located in the community?
2. How old is the school?
3. Is it a parent-, teacher-, administration-, or student-centered school? What evidence leads you to your conclusion?
4. Does the school have an adjoining playground or recreational area? When is it used most: before, after, or during school?

5. Is there a school library? Where is it? How does a student gain access to it? What are the library procedures?

6. Where is the nurse's office? What are the major concerns of the health administrator in this school? What are the major complaints (types of illnesses)? What are the procedures for being sent home or remaining in the health office?

7. Where does physical education take place? What is the usual activity? Who participates? What do students do if they are not participating?

8. What is the procedure for tardy students?

9. Who administers this procedure?

10. Do students move from one classroom to another during the school day? How is this accomplished?

11. Is there a dress code? Who decided on its standards? How are infractions handled?

12. What are some frequent causes of disciplinary action against students?

13. What is the system for reinstating a student who has been suspended or expelled?

14. Is there a teachers' lounge? What is the function of this lounge?

15. Are teachers allowed to make educational decisions? If so, what kind?

16. How does a student make an appointment to see the principal or a counselor? What is the usual waiting period?

17. Does the student council have any real power to promote change in the school? If the answer is "yes," ask for some examples.

18. Does the student council represent the entire student body, or is it a select group?

19. Do parents come to the school? If so, when and for what reasons?

20. Is there a lunchroom in the school? Describe the facility. Do students congregate in identifiable patterns during lunch?

21. Are there extracurricular activities? Music, sports, clubs, meetings?

22. Does the school empty faster at the end of the day, or during a fire drill?

23. If you are investigating a secondary school, does it have a newspaper? Ask the editor or a staffer what its function is and how much freedom students have to print what they wish.

24. Is there an auditorium? How often is it used? Why?

25. Are students bused to school? Ride a school bus one day to see what it's like. Is it different in the morning than in the afternoon?

26. Listen to the students' language, in class and out. Any difference?

27. Ask an administrator, secretary, custodian, teacher, librarian, and nurse to describe the student population.

28. Are students trusted? What evidence can you find one way or the other?

29. Are teachers trusted? Must they sign in and out? In what areas of school life do they have decision-making power?

30. What is unusual about this school?

31. Which students are most popular with their peers? Which are most respected? If there is a difference, why?

32. Which teachers are most popular with students? Which are most respected? If there is a difference, why?

33. What do the school's administrators do? What are their major areas of responsibility? What are the major pressures on them?*

VIDEO- AND AUDIOTAPES   Public schools and colleges are making increasing use of mechanical recording devices as analytical and training tools. Audiotape recorders have been available for quite a while, but portable videotape recorders are a relatively recent innovation. Both devices, particularly videotape recorders, have enabled teachers and researchers to analyze what happens in the classroom more completely and objectively. Videotape recorders can register both the image and the sound of classroom interaction, and the resulting record is more accurate and comprehensive than either notes or an observation schedule. Videotapes have many other advantages: The tapes can be replayed without limit, they are reusable after erasing, the fast forward and rewind components make it possible to locate or repeat a particular passage quickly, and the data can be stored almost indefinitely.

Many advantages

The same criteria or objectives may be applied to taped data as to live observation. The advantage, of course, is that something that is missed in the first viewing can be repeated until the viewer has absorbed it, a luxury unavailable in live observation. You might wish to analyze verbal interactions using Flanders's Interaction Analysis, or to watch the behavior of a particular child, or to count the number of encouraging gestures the teacher makes toward students. The possibilities are endless.

Many teacher education programs are collecting videotapes to demonstrate particular classroom phenomena to prospective teachers; some show only a single "critical incident." The tape can be stopped to allow speculation about how the teacher will or should respond, started again to view the teacher's actual actions, and stopped for further discussion.

We have not attempted to train you in the techniques, methods, and tools of classroom observation, believing that to be better and more appropriately accomplished as part of your teacher education program. Instead, we have tried to acquaint you with methods that have been and are currently being used by educators to better understand school environments.

---

* The authors are indebted to Professor Emma Cappelluzzo of the University of Massachusetts for many of these questions. Used by permission.

APPENDIX B
DIRECTORY OF STATE
TEACHER CERTIFICATION
OFFICES IN THE U.S.

Alabama
Division of Professional Services
Department of Education
404 State Office Building
Montgomery 36130-3901, 205/261-5290

Alaska
Department of Education
Teacher Education and Certification
P.O. Box F
Goldbelt Building
Juneau 99811-0500, 907/465-2810

Arizona
Teacher Certification Unit
Department of Education
1535 West Jefferson
P.O. Box 85002
Phoenix 85007, 602/542-4368

Arkansas
Department of Education
Teacher Certification and Education
#4 Capitol Mall, Rooms 106B/107B
Little Rock 72201, 501/682-4342

California
Commission on Teacher Credentialing
1812 9th Street
Sacramento 94244-2700, 916/445-7254

Colorado
Teacher Certification
Colorado Department of Education
201 East Colfax Avenue
Denver 80203, 303/866-6628

Connecticut
State Department of Education
Division of Curriculum and Professional
Development
P.O. Box 2219
Hartford 06115, 203/566-4561

Delaware
Department of Public Instruction
Supervisor of Certification and Personnel
Townsend Building
P.O. Box 1402
Dover 19903, 302/736-4688

District of Columbia
Division of Teacher Services
District of Columbia Public Schools
415 12th Street, N.W., Room 1013
Washington 20004-1994, 202/724-4250

Florida
Department of Education
Division of Human Resource Development
Teacher Certification Offices
325 West Gaines Street
Tallahassee 32399-0400, 904/488-5724

Georgia
Department of Education
Division of Teacher Certification
1452 Twin Towers
East Atlanta 30334, 404/656-2604

Hawaii
State Department of Education
Office of Personnel Services
P.O. Box 2360
Honolulu 96804, 808/548-5802

Idaho
State Department of Education
Teacher Education and Certification
Len B. Jordan Office Building
Boise 83720, 208/334-3475

Illinois
State Board of Education
100 North 1st Street
Springfield 62777, 217/782-2805

Indiana
Department of Education
Center for Professional Development
Room 229, State House
Indianapolis 46204, 317/232-9010

Iowa
Board of Education Examiners State of Iowa
Grimes State Office Building
Des Moines 50319-0146, 515/281-3245

Kansas
State Department of Education
Certification, Teacher Education and
Accreditation
120 East 10th Street
Topeka 66612, 913/296-2288

Kentucky
State Department of Education
Teacher Education and Certification
18th Floor, Capital Plaza Tower
Frankfort 40601, 502/564-4606

Louisiana
State Department of Education
Bureau of Higher Education and Teacher
Certification
P.O. Box 94064
Baton Rouge 70804-9064, 504/342-3490

Maine
Department of Education and Cultural
Services
Teacher Education and Higher Education
State House Station 23
Augusta 04333, 207/289-5992

Maryland
State Department of Education
Division of Certification and Accreditation
200 West Baltimore Street
Baltimore 21201-2595, 301/333-2142

Massachusetts
Division of Educational Personnel
Department of Education
Quincy Center Plaza
1385 Hancock Street
Quincy 02169, 617/770-7517

Michigan
Department of Education
Teachers/Preparation and Certification
Services
P.O. Box 30008
Lansing 48909, 517/373-3310

Minnesota
State Department of Education
Capitol Square Building
550 Cedar Street
St. Paul 55101, 612/296-2046

Mississippi
Department of Education
Office of Teacher Certification
P.O. Box 771
Jackson 39205, 601/359-3483

Missouri
Teacher Education
Missouri Teacher Certification Office
Department of Elementary and Secondary
Education
P.O. Box 480
Jefferson City 65102, 314/751-3486

Montana
Certification Services
Office of Public Instruction
State Capitol
Helena 59620, 406/444-3150

Nebraska
Department of Education
Teacher Certification/Education
310 Centennial Mall South
Box 94987
Lincoln 68509, 402/471-2496

Nevada
State Department of Education
1850 Sahara, Suite 200
State Mail Room
Las Vegas 89158, 702/486-6457

New Hampshire
State Department of Education
Bureau of Teacher Education and Professional
Standards
State Office Park
South 101 Pleasant Street
Concord 03301-3860, 603/271-2407

New Jersey
State Department of Education
Teacher Certification and Academic
Credentials
3535 Quakerbridge Road, CN 503
Trenton 08625-0503, 609/588-3100

New Mexico
State Department of Education
Educator Preparation and Licensure
Education Building
Santa Fe 87503, 505/827-6587

New York
Office of Teacher Certification
Cultural Education Center, Room 5A 11
Nelson A. Rockefeller Empire State Plaza
Albany 12230, 518/474-3901

North Carolina
State Department of Public Instruction
Division of Certification
114 West Edenton Street
Raleigh 27603-1712, 919/733-4125

North Dakota
State Department of Public Instruction
Teacher Certification
State Capitol, 9th Floor
Bismarck 58505, 701/224-2264

Ohio
Department of Education
Teacher Certification
65 South Front Street, Room 1012
Columbus 43266-0308, 614/466-3593

Oklahoma
Department of Education
Hodge Education Building
2500 North Lincoln Boulevard, Room 211
Oklahoma City 73105-4599, 405/521-3337

Oregon
Teacher Standards and Practices Commission
630 Center Street, N.E. Suite 200
Salem 97310, 503/378-3586

Pennsylvania
Department of Education
Bureau of Teacher Preparation and
Certification
333 Market Street, 3rd Floor
Harrisburg 17126-0333, 717/787-2967

Puerto Rico
Teacher Certification Division
Department of Education
Box 759
Hato Rey 00919, 809/758-4949

Rhode Island
Department of Education
School and Teacher Accreditation,
Certification and Placement
Roger Williams Building
22 Hayes Street
Providence 02908, 401/277-2675

South Carolina
State Department of Education
Teacher Education and Certification
1015 Rutledge
1429 Senate Street
Columbia 29201, 803/734-8466

South Dakota
Division of Education and Cultural Affairs
Office of Certification
Kneip Office Building
700 Governor's Drive
Pierre 57501, 605/773-3553

Tennessee
Department of Education
Office of Teacher Licensing
6th Floor, North Wing, Cordell Hull Building
Nashville 37243-0377, 615/741-1644

Texas
Division of Teacher Certification
William B. Travis State Office Building
1701 North Congress Avenue
Austin 78701, 512/463-8976

Utah
State Office of Education
Certification and Personnel Development
250 East 500 South
Salt Lake City 84111, 801/533-5965

Vermont
State Department of Education
Certification Division
Montpelier 05602, 802/828-3124

Virginia
Department of Education
Division of Teacher Education and
Certification
Box 6Q, James Monroe Building
Richmond 23216, 804/225-2094

Washington
Office of the Superintendent of Public
Instruction
Director of Professional Certification
Old Capitol Building
Mail Stop FG-11
Olympia 98504-3211, 206/753-6775

West Virginia
Department of Education
Office of Professional Education
Capitol Complex, Room B-337, Building 6
Charleston 25305, 304/348-2703

Wisconsin
Bureau of Teacher Education, Licensing and
Placement Teacher Certification
State Department of Public Instruction
125 South Webster Street
P.O. Box 7841
Madison 53707-7841, 608/266-1027

Wyoming
State Department of Education
Certification and Licensing Unit
Hathaway Building
Cheyenne 82002-0050, 307/777-6261

St. Croix District
Department of Education
Educational Personnel Services
#21, 22, & 23 Hospital Street
St. Croix, Virgin Islands 00820, 809/773-1095

St. Thomas/St. John District
Department of Education
Educational Personnel Services
44-46 Kongens Gad
St. Thomas, Virgin Islands 00802, 809/774-0100

United States Department of Defense
Overseas Dependent Section
Recruitment and Assignment Section
2461 Eisenhower Avenue
Alexandria, Virginia 22331-1100, 202/325-0885

GLOSSARY

academic engaged time The time a student spends on academically relevant activities or materials while experiencing a high rate of success.

academic freedom The freedom of teachers to teach about an issue or to use a source in teaching without fear of penalty, reprisal, or harassment; a subcategory of freedom of expression.

academy A type of secondary school during the early national period that tried to combine the best of the Latin and English grammar schools. During the nineteenth century it took on a college-orientation.

accountability movement A movement in education in which schools and educators are required to demonstrate what they are accomplishing and are held responsible for student achievement and learning.

aesthetics A branch of philosophy that examines the perception of beauty and distinguishes beauty from that which is moral or useful.

alternative certification A procedure offered by many states to license teachers who have not graduated from a state-approved teacher education program.

American Federation of Teachers (AFT) The nation's second-largest teachers association or union; founded in 1916 and affiliated with the AFL-CIO, the nation's largest union.

assertive discipline Classroom management approach based on establishing clear limits and expectations, insisting on acceptable student behavior, delivering appropriate consequences when rules are broken.

attitude A person's predisposition to act in a positive or negative way toward persons, ideas, or events.

axiology The philosophical study of values, especially how they are formed ethically, aesthetically, and religiously.

back-to-basics movement A theme in education reform during the 1970s and early 1980s that called for more emphasis on traditional subject matter such as reading, writing, arithmetic, and history.

bilingual education A variety of approaches to educating students who speak a primary language other than English, including transitional, immersion, and submersion models of instruction.

busing The controversial practice of transporting children to different schools in an attempt to achieve racial desegregation.

categorical grants Federal aid to education that must be spent for purposes that are specified in the legislation and by the federal agency administering the funds.

certification As normally used, the procedure of becoming licensed to teach in a particular state. Technically, licensure is a state responsibility, and certification is a professional designation.

classroom management The set of teacher behaviors that create and maintain conditions in the classroom permitting instruction to take place efficiently and effectively.

collective bargaining A procedure for reaching agreements and resolving conflicts between employers and employees; in education, it covers the teacher's contract and work conditions.

common school Public elementary schools that are open to children of all classes. During the nineteenth century the common school became the embodiment of universal education.

compensatory education Educational support to provide a more equal opportunity for disadvantaged students to attain an education through such activities as remedial instruction, special activities, or early learning.

competency testing The practice of requiring students or teachers to show mastery of minimal levels of achievement.

computer-assisted instruction (CAI) The use of microcomputers in providing individual instruction to students.

computer-based instruction (CBI) An umbrella term that consists of two major functions: computer-assisted instruction (CAI) and computer-managed instruction (CMI).

computer literacy The ability to use computers in one's work at some reasonable level of competence.

computer-managed instruction (CMI) The use of microcomputers in facilitating teacher planning, record keeping, and monitoring of student performance.

contract A legal agreement between two or more parties resulting in an exchange of some kind.

cooperative learning An instructional approach in which students work together in groups to achieve learning goals.

core curriculum A common course of study for all students, often called for by essentialist reforms in the 1980s.

corporal punishment Punishment inflicted directly on the student's body; administered for disciplinary reasons (e.g., paddling or whipping).

critical thinking A general instructional approach intended to help students evaluate the worth of ideas, opinions, or evidence before making a decision or judgment.

cultural pluralism An approach to diversity of individuals that calls for understanding and appreciation of cultural differences.

culture A set of beliefs, values, traditions, and ways of thinking and behaving that distinguishes groups of people from one another.

curriculum All the organized and intended experiences of the student for which the school accepts responsibility.

dame school A school run by a housewife during early colonial days.

deduction A type of reasoning from the general to the particular; reasoning in which the conclusion follows from the premise stated.

de facto segregation Segregation in the schools resulting primarily from residential patterns.

de jure segregation Segregation in the schools that occurs by law.

district school The school that succeeded the town school and moving school in New England. Each township was divided into districts having its own school, taught by its own master and funded by the town treasury.

due process The deliberative process that protects a person's constitutional right to receive fair and equal process of the law.

education The process by which humans develop their minds, their skills, and/or their character. It is a lifelong process marked by continual development and change.

Education for All Handicapped Children Act (P.L. 94–142) 1975 federal legislation providing certain stipulations for the education of students with disabilities including such types of exceptionality as hearing impairment, vision impairment, mental retardation, emotional disturbance, and learning disabilities.

Education for all Handicapped Children Act Amendment Federal legislation passed in 1986 providing for early educational intervention for children with disabilities from birth to age two.

English as a second language (ESL) A method of teaching English to non-English speakers.

English grammar school A form of secondary education in the latter half of the colonial period that provided a practical alternative education for students who were not interested in college.

epistemology A branch of philosophy that examines the study of the nature of knowledge, its origins, its foundations, its limits, and its validity.

essentialism An educational philosophy that asserts there is a core body of knowledge and skills that an educated person must have and that all children should be taught.

ethics A branch of philosophy that examines the right and wrong of human conduct. Can also refer to a particular moral code or system.

excellence in education movement A phrase used to describe the major emphasis of the education reforms of the mid-1980s in which greater academic rigor and higher standards were required.

existentialism A philosophical doctrine that a person is not part of an ordered universe but that individuals must create their own meaning and purpose in life. In education, an existentialist believes that each student must ultimately make meaning through individual learning, not group learning.

expulsion The act of dismissing or sending away, usually as a penalty for misconduct. In school, an expulsion means a student is permanently barred from attending the school because of gross misconduct.

formal (explicit) curriculum Those subjects that are taught in school and the instructional approaches used to transmit this knowledge.

gifted children   Children who demonstrate or give evidence of potential for high achievement or performance in creative, academic, artistic, or leadership areas, typically including high intellectual ability.

Head Start   A federally funded compensatory education program, in existence since the mid-1960s, that provides additional educational services to young children suffering the effects of poverty.

hornbook   An instructional material during early colonial days that consisted of a page of ABCs, numerals, and so forth, that was laminated with a transparent material from boiled down cows' horns and then attached to a flat piece of wood.

idealism   The belief in ideals, or models of perfection, and the attempt to realize those ideals. Also, the idea that thought is concerned with representation rather than with material objects, and that therefore the mind is an essential tool in understanding reality.

immersion model   A form of bilingual education in which the teacher understands the student's first language but instruction is given entirely in English.

in loco parentis   The responsibility of the teacher to function "in the place of the parents" when students are in school.

individualized education program (IEP)   A management tool required by P.L. 94–142 that contains current levels of performance, short- and long-term instructional objectives, services to be provided, and criteria and schedules for evaluation of progress for each student with a disability receiving services under P.L. 94–142.

induction   A type of reasoning from the particular to the general; reasoning in which one can make a general conclusion based on a number of facts.

informal curriculum   The teaching and learning that occur in school but are not part of the explicit, or formal, curriculum; also called the hidden curriculum.

instrumentalism   A philosophical theory that the truth or authority of any idea rests in its usefulness.

kindergarten   A division of school for children below the first grade, usually for children between the ages of four and six, imported from Germany during the nineteenth century; a "children's garden," where pleasant children's activities were used to lay a foundation before formal education began.

Latin grammar school   First type of secondary school in the colonies, whose main purpose was to prepare students for college.

learning disability   A disability classification identifying individuals who have a disorder in basic psychological processing that affects the individual's ability to listen, think, speak, read, write, spell, or do mathematical calculations. A learning disability is not primarily the result of visual, hearing, or motor disabilities, of mental retardation, of emotional disturbance, or environmental, cultural, or economic disadvantage.

learning style   Characteristic way a student learns, including such factors as the way an individual processes information, preferences for competition or cooperation, and environmental conditions such as lighting or noise level.

least restrictive environment   A requirement stipulated in P.L. 94–142 that students with disabilities should participate in regular education programs to the greatest extent appropriate.

logic   A branch of philosophy that involves the study of reasoning or of sound argument. In a more specific sense, logic is the study of deductive inference.

magnet school   Alternative school that provides instruction in specified areas such as the fine arts, for specific groups such as the gifted and talented, or using specific teaching styles such as open classrooms. In many cases, magnet schools are established as a method of promoting voluntary desegregation in schools.

Maslow's hierarchy of needs   A model of human development proposed by Abraham Maslow that identifies an ascending hierarchy of human needs, beginning with our most basic biological needs and progressing to our highest-order need for self-actualization.

mastery learning   An approach developed by Benjamin Bloom in which the form of instruction and the time available for learning are based on the individual needs of the student. Instructional objectives are defined and taught directly. Immediate feedback is provided to the student.

melting pot   A response to diversity in the schools during the late 1800s and early 1900s in which immigrant children were acculturated to dominant American ways and discouraged from maintaining the ways of their old country.

metaphysics   A branch of philosophy devoted to exploring the nature of existence or reality as a whole, rather than the study of particular parts, as the natural sciences do. Metaphysicians try to answer questions about reality without referring to religion or revelation.

Morrill Act Federal legislation passed in 1862 that granted each state federal land to establish colleges for the study of agriculture and mechanical arts. A second Morrill Act, passed in 1890, provided similar federal support to create "separate but equal" colleges for African-Americans.

multicultural education An approach to education that recognizes cultural diversity and fosters cultural enrichment of all children and youth.

multidisciplinary assessment Examination of needs and abilities of an individual student from several professional perspectives, including such areas as special education, speech and language pathology, physical therapy, and family counseling.

multiple intelligences A theory of intelligence put forth by Howard Gardner that identifies at least seven dimensions of intellectual capacities that people use to approach problems and create products.

A Nation at Risk: The Imperative for Educational Reform A 1983 national commission report calling for extensive education reform, including more academic course requirements, more stringent college entrance requirements, upgraded and updated textbooks, and longer school days and years.

National Education Association (NEA) The nation's largest teachers association; founded in 1857 and having a membership of over two million educators.

National Teachers' Examination (NTE) Standardized tests developed by the Educational Testing Service (ETS) to measure teachers' knowledge in three core areas—general knowledge, professional knowledge, and communication skills—and specific subject-matter areas. The NTE tests are used in many states as screening tests for beginning teachers.

new federalism A term arising in President Reagan's term of office referring to a less intrusive role of the federal government in state and local affairs and a return to local autonomy in school policies.

"new math" A term used to describe the elementary and secondary mathematics curricula of the 1960s that stressed structure and conceptual understanding rather than drill and computational skills.

normal school A two- or four-year teacher education institution that gained great popularity in the nineteenth century and faded out in the twentieth century.

NTE

on-task behavior Student engagement in activities that are appropriate to the teacher's goals.

perennialism A particular view of philosophy that sees human nature as constant, changing little over time. Perennialism in education promotes the advancement of the intellect as the central purpose of schools. The educational process stresses academic rigor and discipline.

philosophy The love or search for wisdom; the quest for basic principles to understand the meaning of life. Western philosophy traditionally contains five branches of philosophy: metaphysics, ethics, aesthetics, epistemology, and logic.

Plessy v. Ferguson A Supreme Court decision in 1896 that upheld the constitutionality of separate but equal accommodations for African-Americans. The ruling was quickly applied to schools.

pluralistic society A society composed of people of many different cultures and heritages.

pragmatism Belief that one tests truth by its practical consequences. Truth, therefore, is relative.

profession An occupation or occupational group that fulfills certain criteria; among other things, it must require training and knowledge, must perform a social service, must have a code of ethics, and must have a sense of autonomy and personal responsibility.

progressivism A form of educational philosophy that sees nature as ever-changing. Because the world is always changing and new situations require solutions to problems, learners must develop as problem solvers.

public comprehensive high school The predominant form of secondary education in America in the twentieth century. It provides both a preparation for college and a vocational education for students not going on to college.

realism The philosophical doctrine that ideas or universals have an absolute existence outside the mind. An attitude that is based on facts and reality rather than on emotions or imaginings.

reduction in force (RIF) The elimination of teaching positions in a school system because of declining student population or funding.

schooling Formal instruction typically conducted in an institution, adhering to standardized practices.

site-based management A theme in educational reform that calls for increasing parental involvement and individual school control and decision-making.

social reconstructionism The theory of education that schools and teachers need to engage in the restructuring and reforming of the present society to eradicate its present ills and shortcomings.

socialization   The general process of social learning whereby the child learns the many things he or she must know to become an acceptable member of society.

special education   Educational programming provided by schools to meet the needs of students with disabilities.

staff development   The efforts by a school or school district to improve the professional skills and competencies of its professional staff. Also called "in service" training in education.

state board of education   The state's primary education policy-making body for elementary and secondary education.

state department of education   State bureaucracy, operating under the direction of the state board of education, whose responsibilities typically include administering and distributing state and federal funds, licensing teachers and other educational personnel, providing educational data and analyses, and approving college and university educational licensure programs.

submersion model   A method of learning English in which students receive instruction in all-English speaking classes.

superintendent of schools   A professional educator selected by the local school board to act as its executive officer and as the educational leader and chief administrator of the local school district.

suspension   The exclusion of a student from classes for a specified period of time as a penalty for misconduct.

teacher empowerment   The process of giving teachers (or of teachers taking) greater control over their professional lives and how they deliver their educational services.

tenure   A legal right that confers permanent employment on teachers, protecting them from dismissal without adequate cause.

"time on task"   The amount of time students are engaged in academic work during a given class period or a given day.

town school   A New England elementary school during the early colonial period, required in every town of fifty or more families.

tracking   The homogeneous grouping of students for learning tasks on the basis of some measure(s) of their abilities.

transitional model   A form of bilingual education in which native language instruction is used until the student develops fluency in English.

withitness   A term coined by Jacob Kounin to convey monitoring or teacher awareness of what is occurring in the classroom, and communicating that awareness to students.

whole-language curriculum   An approach emphasizing the integration of language arts skills and knowledge across the curriculum. It stresses the provision of a literate environment and functional uses of language.

writing across the curriculum   An instructional approach using writing as a tool for learning in all subject areas.

INDEX

Dallas Book Depository, 545

Dame schools, 103

Data-gathering techniques (in classroom observation), 551–560

Davis, Kate, 470–471

Day care centers, career opportunities in, 63

Dead Poets Society, 15

Decision making, instructional: characteristics of effective, 465, 466 (fig.); preactive vs. interactive, 464;

Defense, U.S. Department of, 42

Deficiency motives, 356

Delderfield, R. F., 15

Democracy and Education (Dewey), 86

Demographics, 36–39, 345–346, 349–355, 381

Demonstration schools, 538–539

Desegregation, *see* Segregation, school

Descartes, René, 73

Developing Skills for Instructional Supervision (Cooper), 558

Dewey, John, 73, 86–87, 313, 479, 526; concept of citizenship, 29–30; and Progressive Education Association, 116; and progressivism, 83

Diary of Anne Frank, 280

Disadvantaged children, 117, 410

Discipline (behavior): assertive, 487; and classroom monitoring, 492; in colonial schools, 105; and Mann, 110; in nineteenth-century schools, 106; problems, 493; and rules, 492; student, 259, 444–446; and student compliance, 492; "Why?" approach to, 488–489

Discipline (subject matter): and microcomputers, 301–302; defined, 285; teacher attitude toward, 474; and writing across the curriculum, 300

Discovery (or inquiry) method, 269

Dismissal, teacher, 161–162

District school, 104, 115–116

Doll, Russell C., 251–253

Donne, John, 147

Douglas, Justice William O., 182

Dropouts, 136, 137, 379, 409–412

Drug use, 180–182, 389–391

DuBois, W. E. B., 133

Due process, 157–160, 177, 369

Dukakis, Michael, 524

Durkheim, Émile, 245–246

Dusek, Jerome, 337

Early childhood education, *see* Pre-elementary education

Eastman Kodak, 212

Eckert, Penelope, 329–330

Eclecticism, 93–96

Economic conditions: depressions/recessions, 38–39; effect on, teaching field, 38–39, 46

Economic Opportunity Act, 142 (tab.)

Edgewood v. *Kirby,* 225

Educating Americans for the 21st Century (National Science Foundation), 271, 275, 276 (tab.)

Education; "back to basics" movement in, 117, 270 (tab.), 271–273, 280; bilingual, 137, 366–368; careers in (teaching and nonteaching), 35–67; in colonial period, 101, 117–120; control of, *see* Governance and control of schools; double-track, 120; employment in, 35–67; European influence on, 110–112; "excellence in," 272–273; goals of, 266; history of (American), 100–145; of minorities, 131–143; multicultural, 137, 366; nineteenth-century, 102, 107–112; philosophy of (American), 71–99; and psychology, 113; vs. schooling, 236–238; tension points in, 393–417; themes in (American), 101–103; twentieth-century, 102, 110, 113–117, 124–131. *See also* Common schools; Elementary education; Secondary education

Education, Office of, *see* Education, U.S. Department of. *See also* State boards/departments of education

Education, teacher: and classroom observation, 550–560; in colonial period, 505–506; differentiated staffing and, 116, 539–541; drawbacks of, 475–476; in the future, 538–539; graduation rates, 39; nineteenth-century, 506–509; and Pestalozzi, 113; philosophy of, 97; and salaries, *see* Salaries, teacher; vs. training, 509; twentieth-century, 509–510. *See also* Certification

Education, U.S. Department of, 47, 63, 135, 214, 216–217, 287, 364, 384; and the NEA, 522, 524; study by, of bilingual education, 368

Educational opportunity; for gifted/talented students, 364–365; inequality of, 379, 393–402; for minorities, 120, 131–143; for students with disabilities, 361–363; for women and girls, 103, 120–121

Education Amendments Act, Title IX, 142 (tab.), 290, 405–406

Education and Science, British Department of, 495

Education Consolidation and Improvement Act (ECIA), Chapter 1, 142 (tab.), 226, 362, 397

Education for all Handicapped Children Act (PL 94–142), 142 (tab.), 179, 270 (tab.), 361–362, 368, 522

Education of the Handicapped Act Amendments (PL 99–457), 369

Education in other countries; Belgium, 354; China, 198–199; England, 129, 292–293; Finland, 354; France, 128–129, 354; GAO study of, 292–293; Germany, 293; Japan, 256–257, 293, 320; New Zealand, 278; Sweden, 290, 293, 354; Turkey, 16–17

Education Reform Act, 129

Education summit, 273, 398

"Educator's Oath, The" (Lanier and Cusick), 156

Edwards v. *Aguillard,* 175, 176 (tab.)

U.S. Departments/Offices (cont.)
407–408; Labor, 47, 454; Public
Health Service, 372; Select
Committee on Children, Youth,
and Families (House of
Representatives), 381.

Values, 76–77; and character
education, 548–549;
communication of, 313–314;
Rogerian approach to, 472;
"Values Clarification," 90, 93.
See also Ethics; Existentialism
Videotapes: and audiotapes, in
classroom observation, 560; and
copyright, 170–171
Vietnamese Parents Association, 143
Violence: and child abuse, 171–
172, 386–388; gang, 406–307;
and teacher self-defense, 164–
165; and vandalism, 406–409.
See also Discipline (behavior)

Vocational education: business
training, 63; criticism of, 291
Vocational Education Act, 522

Wait-time, 494
War on Poverty, 396
Washington, Booker T., 133
Weber, Wilford, 485, 488
Webster, Noah, 108, 141 (tab.)
Whittle Communications, 214
Whole-word method, 277
"Why Join the NEA?" (Geiger),
522–523
"Why Should New Teachers Join
the AFT?" (Shanker), 524–525
"Why Teach? A Turkish View"
(Kaya, 16–17)
Willard, Emma, 121, 141 (tab.)
Williams, Emlyn, 15
Wilson, Pres. Woodrow, 157
Wingate, John, 108
"Withitness" of teacher, 490

Women/girls: changing status of,
354; colonial education for, 103–
105; educational opportunity for,
111; secondary education for,
120–121; and sex-role
stereotyping, 402–406; teachers,
nineteenth-century, 507; teacher
response to, 339–340; working,
454
Women's Educational Equity Act,
405
Workforce 2000 (Hudson Institute),
213
Writing across the curriculum, 300
Wynne, Ed, 258–260

Xerox, 212

Zend, Robert, 74
Zigler, Edward, 371

An Invitation to Respond

In the previous editions of *Those Who Can, Teach,* we included a form with which students evaluated the book and provided us with feedback. Many of the changes made in this edition were based on these student evaluations. Please help us respond to the interests and needs of future readers by completing the questionnaire below and returning it to College Marketing, Houghton Mifflin Company, One Beacon Street, Boston, MA 02108.

Kevin and Jim

Please tell us your overall impression of the text.

	Excellent	Good	Adequate	Poor	Very poor
1. Was it written in a clear and understandable style?	———	———	———	———	———
2. Were difficult concepts explained?	———	———	———	———	———
3. How would you rate the cartoons and illustrations?	———	———	———	———	———
4. How does this text compare with texts you are using in other education courses?	———	———	———	———	———
5. Did the book's informality help your reading?	———	———	———	———	———

Can you cite examples that illustrate any of your above ratings?

_____

_____

Were there any chapters or features that you particularly liked or disliked? If so, why?

_____

_____

Were there any topics that were not covered that you believe *should* have been covered?

_____

_____

Do you think this book has influenced your career choice? Which way? And how?

_____

_____

Which chapters did you read because they were required by your instructor?

_____

Which chapters did you read on your own?

_____

We would appreciate any other comments or reactions you are willing to share with us:

_____

_____

_____